THEO-DRAMA
Volume V

THEO-DRAMA

Volumes of the Complete Work:

HANS URS VON BALTHASAR

THEO-DRAMA

THEOLOGICAL DRAMATIC THEORY

VOLUME V
THE LAST ACT

Translated by Graham Harrison

IGNATIUS PRESS   SAN FRANCISCO

Title of the German original:
Theodramatik: Vierter Band: Die Endspiel
© 1983 Johannes Verlag, Einsiedeln
With ecclesiastical approval

Cover by Roxanne Mei Lum

CONTENTS

II. ASPECTS OF THE FINAL ACT

CONTENTS

The Hegelian babble about the real being the true is therefore the same kind of confusion as when people assume that the words and actions of a poet's dramatic characters are the poet's own. We *must*, however, hold fast to the belief that when God—so to speak—decides to write a play, he does not do it simply in order to pass the time, as the pagans thought. No, no: indeed, the utterly serious point here is that loving and being loved is God's *passion*. It is almost—infinite love!—as if he is bound to this passion, almost as if it were a weakness on his part; whereas in fact it is his strength, his almighty love: and in that respect his love is subject to no alteration of any kind.

There is a staggering perversity in all the human categories that are applied to the God-man; for if we could speak in a completely human way about Christ we would have to say that the words "My God, my God, why have you forsaken me?" show a want of patience and a want of truth. Only if God says it, can it be true, i.e., even if the God-man says it. And since it is true, it is also truly the climax of pain.

The relationship to God is evidently such a tremendous weight of blessedness that, once I have laid hold of it, it is absolute in the most absolute sense; by contrast, the worldly notion that my enemies are to be excluded from it would actually diminish this blessedness.

The Journals of Søren Kierkegaard

NOTE

After the first volume of this work (*Prolegomena*), the second volume was anthropological, the third christological, and the fourth soteriological; this concluding volume is trinitarian.

Here many passages from the works of Adrienne von Speyr are reproduced and referred to in footnotes; title abbreviations of these works are given below. These quotations are not intended to give a full picture of her theology: that would require far more space; I quote her to show the fundamental consonance between her views and mine on many of the eschatological topics discussed here.

Karl Rahner has dubbed our theology "gnostic"; in all probability he will find his verdict even more strongly confirmed when he reads the chapter on "the pain of God". We find his verdict unacceptable, however, for reasons that will be made clear in the final chapter of this book, which once again treats of God's immutability, an immutability that persists in all aspects of the economy of salvation.

Elsewhere the same critic has called our theology "Neo-Chalcedonianism", which he personally wishes to avoid, preferring to call a halt at the classical Chalcedonian view that the divine and human natures of Christ are "unconfused". It is a fact, however, that the formula "One of the Trinity has suffered", which no doubt upsets him, was held to be orthodox (DS 401, 432); I cannot see how the *pro nobis* of Christ's Cross and Resurrection can avail for us if the one who was crucified and risen is not "one of the Trinity". Otherwise people might be quite right to say, "God (or Jesus) may be having a hard time, but so what? That doesn't help me when I'm having a hard time."

As this final volume of *Theo-Drama* comes to an end, it broadens out into what Karl Rahner rightly and emphatically refers to as the "mystery of God". Anything we say, by way of a conclusion, regarding the "last act" of the play that involves earth and heaven is nothing more than an astonished stammering as we circle around this mystery on the basis of particular luminous words and suggestions of Holy Scripture. We have tried to go as far as revelation permits—some may feel we have gone one step too far—resolutely stopping at the point where pseudo-logical speculations have been shown to lead only into an abstract void or to superfluous lists of what is forbidden. There is nothing "scientific"—and this applies equally to theology—about speaking with "exact" precision about things that are unknowable (for example, the "intermediate state"). Following Aquinas, we have tried to erect theology on the articles of faith (and not vice versa): on the Trinity, the Incarnation of the Son, his Cross and Resurrection on our behalf, and his sending of the Spirit to us in the apostolic Church and in the *communio sanctorum*. It is only on the basis of such a theology, today and in the future, that men can give witness in their lives and in their deaths to that "highest gift of God" which is "irreversible and unsurpassable".

ABBREVIATIONS

Abbreviations of the titles of books by Adrienne von Speyr (all published by Johannes Verlag, Einsiedeln). Where translations have been published by Ignatius Press, page numbers refer to that edition, but where this translator has referred back to the original German, somewhat altering the translation of particular passages to fit the present context, "GT" appears in parentheses after the abbreviation.

A	*Das Angesicht des Vaters* [*The Countenance of the Father* (San Francisco: Ignatius Press, 1997)]
Ap	*Apokalypse* (Johannis)
B	*Bergpredigt*
Be	*Die Beichte* [*Confession*, (San Francisco: Ignatius Press, 1985)]
Bi	*Das Licht und die Bilder*
C	*1 Korinther*
E	*Elija* [*Elijah*, Ignatius Press 1990]
Ep	*Epheser (Kinder des Lichtes)* [*The Letter to the Ephesians* (San Francisco: Ignatius Press, 1996)]
3F	*Drei Frauen und der Herr* [*Three Women and the Lord* (San Francisco: Ignatius Press, 1986)]
F	*Sie folgten seinem Ruf* [*They Followed His Call* (San Francisco: Ignatius Press, 1986)]
G	*Der grenzenlose Gott*
GE	*Gebetserfahrung*
Gh	*Das Buch vom Gehorsam*
Gl	*Gleichnisse des Herrn*
H	*Die heilige Messe*
Hj	*Job*
Hl	*Das Hohelied*

Is	*Isaias*
1–4 Jo	*Johannes* vols. 1–4 [vol. 1: *The Word Becomes Flesh*; vol. 2: *The Discourses of Controversy*; vol. 3: *The Farewell Discourses*; vol. 4: *The Birth of the Church* (San Francisco: Ignatius Press, 1987–1994)]
K	*Kolosser* [*The Letter to the Colossians* (San Francisco: Ignatius Press, 1998)]
Ka I–II	*Kath. Briefe*, vols. 1–2
KW	*Kreuzeswort und Sakrament* [*The Cross: Word and Sacrament* (San Francisco: Ignatius Press, 1983)]
L	*Über die Liebe*
M	*Der Mensch vor Gott*
MH	*Magd des Herrn* [*The Handmaid of the Lord* (San Francisco: Ignatius Press, 1985)]
Mt	*Passion nach Matthäus*
OM	*Objektive Mystik*
P	*Die Sendung des Propheten* [*The Mission of the Prophets* (San Francisco: Ignatius Press, 1996)]
Pa	*Passion von innen* [*The Passion from Within* (San Francisco: Ignatius Press, 1998)]
Pf	*Die Pforten des ewigen Lebens* [*The Gates of Eternal Life* (San Francisco: Ignatius Press, 1983)]
Ph	*Philipper (Dienst der Freude)*
Ps	*Achtzehn Psalmen*
Sc	*Die Schöpfung*
SL	*Sieg der Liebe* (Romans 8) [*The Victory of Love* (San Francisco: Ignatius Press, 1990)]
St	*Christlicher Stand* [*The Christian State of Life* (San Francisco: Ignatius Press, 1986)]
T	*Das Geheimnis des Todes* [*The Mystery of Death* (San Francisco: Ignatius Press, 1988)]
W	*Die Welt des Gebetes* [*The World of Prayer* (San Francisco: Ignatius Press, 1985)]

INTRODUCTION

A. THE IDEA OF A
CHRISTIAN ESCHATOLOGY

1. Christ the Governing Center

If, in the context of theology, we speak of the "final act" in the world drama of creation and redemption, we automatically think first of the particular internal events expected at the conclusion of the history of the world. There are many indications in the New Testament that these events will be of a qualitatively special kind: they will be characterized by a heightening of the antagonism between the kingdom of Christ (cf. 1 Cor 15:24) and the kingdom of the prince of this world, who, once he has cast away all disguise, will appear as the "Antichrist" (2 Th 2:3–12). However, Christ, at his Second Coming, will destroy him "with the breath of his mouth", whereupon the "last things"—resurrection, judgment, including purgatory, eternal salvation or condemnation—will take place. It is largely in the framework of such ideas that traditional dogmatics has set forth the concept and the treatise "of the last things", or eschatology.

In more recent times, however, roughly since the work of Johannes Weiß and his followers, exegetes have introduced a different concept of eschatology. This concept, while it is not totally clear and self-evident, nonetheless addresses the view of the world found in the realm of the New Testament events. It proceeds in one of three ways: either (1) it addresses the general, late Jewish "apocalyptic" expectation of an imminent end of the world, which seems to provide a context for the expectation of this end as seen by Jesus and the primitive Church, or (2) it concentrates on Jesus' own expectation of the end. While many writers acknowledge that Jesus' own view differs from that predominant in the Jewish world of his time, they assert that it too must ultimately be described as "eschatological" in its own way. Or finally, (3) it addresses primarily the primitive Church's expectation of the imminent end of the world and the return of Christ. Again, this ecclesial expectation can be interpreted in various ways. It can be regarded as the continuation of Jesus' own—allegedly "apocalyptic"—expectation of the end of the world, whereby both he and the Church are seen to have been mistaken. Or it can be regarded as at least a partial misunderstanding of what, in fact, Jesus' personal expectation was, in which case the Church had quietly fallen back into Jewish apocalyptic expectations. We have already discussed these problems on several occasions earlier in the present work and have given a clear account of our own attitude toward them;[1] we shall not go into them again here. On the basis of what we have already discovered, it is possible to reconcile the two divergent concepts of eschatology—the "dogmatic" and the "exegetical"—albeit in a way that may astonish us and call for some serious rethinking and a new way of seeing.

If we respect the fundamental thrust of the New Testament, we find that there are two main accents in it, namely, the consciousness of Jesus and the consciousness of the primitive Church that believes in him.

To Jesus, his own destiny—which is inseparably bound up with the coming of the "kingdom of God"—is something close, imminent. His mission to the world will be "accomplished" through his personal death in that mysterious "hour", and through his subsequent "resurrection" or "glorification" or "coming again". Thus, in a new and original sense, he arrives at the "end of the world", whether or not our world-time pursues its chronological succession. His eschatology embraces all continuing chronological time and qualitatively determines it. His eschatology is primary: of itself it qualifies the secondary eschatology of those who continue to live on earth, whether or not they believe in him. Naturally Jesus' own expectation of the imminent end bears some relation to the current late Jewish expectation; but we must not imagine it to be dependent on the latter. In fact, in the perspective of salvation history we must say rather that the atmosphere of Jewish apocalyptic is providential, preparing the Chosen People for the one saving event that is truly final and conclusive—however many misunderstandings this actual, historical apocalyptic puts in the way of a grasp of the person of Jesus. If Jesus was the Messiah of Israel—and he knew that he was, even if, for good reasons, he rejected the title

---

[1] *Theo-Drama* III, 130–34, 138f.; *Theo-Drama* IV, 231–40.

—it meant that the end-time for which Israel had looked with such passionate longing had actually arrived; the nation found it all the harder to see this because of the fantastic imagery with which it (the nation) had colored its expectation of the end.[2] What sealed Israel's fate was not this, however, but the theological decision about whether Jesus was the Messiah and the Son of God. Henceforth Israel's destiny is inextricably woven into the personal eschatology of Jesus Christ. Thus Paul's view is that ultimately "all Israel shall be saved", namely, when it cries out "Blessed is he who comes in the name of the Lord!" (Lk 13:35). If this is true of Israel, it applies all the more to those who believe in Jesus, his Church: the Church's whole destiny proclaims that she belongs to him and that her destiny is shaped by his.

This second fundamental affirmation of the New Testament is of special relevance to the status of the (Christian) Church as the "Israel of God" (Gal 6:16). It is true that there are elements of Jewish apocalyptic in many New Testament writings, but after Paul—the first great interpreter of the events that have taken place in Christ—the main emphasis is not on these but on the fact that Christians are affected and defined by the eschatological destiny of Jesus: they have died with him and are risen with him (in however hidden a manner: Col 3:3). It is a mistake to try to "spiritualize away" this assertion by saying that the Christian is risen "in spirit" but not in his earthly existence. For Paul already bears "on [his] body the marks of Jesus" (Gal 6:17), is "always being given up to death for Jesus' sake, so that the [risen] life of Jesus may be manifested in our mortal flesh" (2 Cor 4:11). And, according to the Apostle, what is particularly visible in Christians, the fact that their existence is governed by the eschatology of Jesus Christ, which is primary, is true of all men. For if "one has died for all; therefore all have died. And he died for all, that those who live might live no longer for themselves but

[2] The Synoptics endeavor to bring in all this imagery at the death of the crucified Jesus: the darkness over the face of the earth testifies to the eschatological shaking of the cosmic powers. Matthew goes beyond this to describe the earthquake, the eschatological opening of the graves and—after Jesus' Resurrection—how those who lay in the graves were resurrected with him. This corresponds to the ultimate imagery of Jewish, and, in particular, Pharisaic, expectation of the end.

for him who for their sake died and was raised" (2 Cor 5:14–15).[3] Christological eschatology is therefore a primary law, of universal application, even if some do not realize it and perhaps continue to maintain what is an anachronistic stance, expecting a *dénouement* in the Jewish apocalyptic manner.

At this point, however, we discern within the New Testament a certain "interference" effect between the two modes of thought. On the one hand, we have the fact that, after Christ, mankind (and the Church in particular) is fundamentally defined by the Christ-eschatology with all its nuances and distinctions: the "already" and the "not yet", the "hidden" and the "open", or the primacy of "faith and hope" over "seeing and possessing". On the other hand, as a way of articulating and illustrating these specifically New Testament polarities, we still have the Jewish apocalyptic expectation at our disposal, and the latter is all the more suggestive since it too speaks of the unveiling (*apokalypsis*) of saving realities that are already present (though in hidden form) in heaven. This "interference" can be observed, not only at a time when the primitive Church lives in chronological expectation of the imminent end—an expectation that is almost inevitable, given Jesus' own words regarding it and the general apocalyptic atmosphere—but also in the wider context, in many images and categories of Jewish apocalyptic, now projected into the future.

Here too, however, we need to draw distinctions. In *Theo-Drama* IV we drew attention to a basic christological law regarding the (horizontal) history of the Church and the world. This law states that there is an ever-intensifying No to the Yes uttered by God in Christ. We saw in the structure of the Book of Revelation that the decisive "No" (on the part of the anti-Christian pseudo-"trinity") only surfaces after the birth of the Messiah-child. Clearly it was felt necessary to clothe this specifically christological theologoumenon in the imagery of Jewish apocalyptic, according to which the manifestation of the Messiah must be preceded by the time of distress, of the "birth pangs of the Messiah". The use of this Jewish language to express some-

---

[3] On the tension between the Christian's "having died" and "being risen", and the inner unity of the two, cf. *Theo-Drama* IV, 383–88.

thing Christian is clear in the so-called "little apocalypses" of
the Synoptics (and it remains an open question how far existing Jewish themes were adopted and adapted and how far the
Christian writer made use of Jewish images). Once one has acknowledged the priority of christological eschatology, with its
power to put its imprint on all the residue of history (including
the law of the reciprocal intensification of Yes and No), it is
not difficult to give a correct assessment of the purely futurist
Jewish imagery that is used in the New Testament to express
christological eschatology.

We must add a special consideration here. No one who reflects upon the matter will deny that Jesus foresaw and predicted
the fall of Jerusalem. But if we are to realize the full significance
this event had for him, we must try to enter into his personal
eschatology. This is, as it were, the negative side of his positive certainty that, in his divine mission, he is to deal once and
for all with the world. He knows that he must and will reach
the world's "inner end". The Johannine "I have overcome the
world" is formulated from the vantage point of successful con-
quest. Jesus does not doubt that, through failure and suffering, he
will attain the goal appointed for him. He will be baptized with
the baptism that awaits him, and the fire he will cast upon the
earth will truly burn. He lives for this *eschaton*, yet this "hour"
involves and includes a negative decision on the part of Israel-
Jerusalem, an eschatological decision that—as John will portray
it—constitutes the "Jews'" judgment upon themselves, the negative end of that history of "salvation" that leads from the most
grievous breaches of the covenant, divine punishment and exile
right up to Jesus. The great catastrophe in the time of Jeremiah
and Ezekiel was a final illustration and warning: it showed that, as
a result of the rejection of the last of the prophets—the Messiah
—God's progressive salvific revelation within history had come
to an irrevocable end. Thus it is entirely in accordance with Jesus'
eschatological perspective when the end of Jerusalem is equated
with the end of the world, whatever one may think of the apocalyptic additions in Mark 13 (parr.). No longer, henceforth, can
there be a specific Jewish salvation history; the Chosen People,
insofar as it holds on to faith and hope, clearly comes under the
law of christological and ecclesiological eschatology: Jews may

continue to await their Messiah, but only by looking forward, together with Christians, to the return of Christ (Acts 3:17–26). One cannot contradict this by quoting Romans 11—which seems to base salvation-history entirely on the root and stem of Abraham's faith, regarding Christians as only alien branches grafted on to this stem—because, as far as Paul is concerned, Abraham's faith in God's promises looks unequivocally toward his "offspring", toward Christ, who is the sole apex and fulfillment of this faith (Gal 3:18; cf. Rom 4:23f.). On the other hand, the time of the promises (the time of Abrahamic faith) moves into the phase of fulfillment (faith in Christ) not only negatively, by being brought to an end, but also positively, insofar as the old faith was itself wholly fashioned with a view to its goal (Heb 11; Gal 3:24). Thus the time of Jesus also embraces and contains the time of the Old Testament—and in a way beyond all we can imagine—since the ultimate purpose of this time is "not the world's judgment, but its salvation" (Jn 3:17); although faithless Israel has passed judgment upon itself according to its own obsolete concepts of justice, its salvation becomes possible because of the overarching meaning and purpose of the time of fulfillment.

2. The Johannine Emphasis

It is clear from the foregoing that the so-called "realized eschatology" of the Gospel of John does not represent anything new as against the Pauline and other New Testament writings: it is simply a development and clarification of them. Furthermore we must note that the One speaking here is not—solely and one-sidedly—the pre-Easter Jesus, but the Redeemer who is able to integrate his entire destiny, a destiny that includes his "exaltation" (death and Resurrection). Martha's Jewish hope for the end-time, "I know that he will rise again in the resurrection at the last day", is sharply countered by the here-and-now assertion, "I am the resurrection and the life" (Jn 11:24–25), which leaves it an open question whether Jesus, in his present experience of the Last Day and of his Resurrection, includes or excludes Jewish faith.

One way or another Jesus' assertion constitutes a "corrective" not only to the Jewish expectation of the end as such but also to those vestiges of Jewish expectation that persist within the primitive Church and her documents, just as John, at many a point, quietly "corrects" the Synoptics.[4] For John, the Christ-event, which is always seen in its totality, is the vertical irruption of the fulfillment into horizontal time; such irruption does not leave this time—with its present, past and future—unchanged, but draws it into itself and thereby gives it a new character.

By adopting the great "I am" utterances of Yahweh (in Ezekiel and Deutero-Isaiah and dependent texts, including liturgical ones), Jesus presented "the most audacious self-utterance";[5] thus it is clear from the outset that John, too, considers the Old Covenant to be positively fulfilled by Jesus. The apparent opposition between the "Law" that was given "through Moses" and the "grace and truth" that "came" with Jesus (1:17) is explained by saying that Moses wrote of Jesus and that anyone who believes the writings of Moses must also believe in Jesus (5:45–47); moreover, Abraham rejoiced to see the day of Jesus; "he saw it and was glad" (8:56). Thus if the past is drawn into Christ's eschatological presence, those few elements in John that point to a futurist *eschaton* can equally be referred to the same "realized" presence of the *eschaton*. "All judgment" has been given to Jesus by the Father (5:22), and there can be no doubt that he exercises this judgment now by being manifested in the world: "The hour

----

[4] "The Fourth Evangelist corrects the Synoptics on the basis of a claim to be an eye-witness who knows Jesus and his history better than the older evangelists, who had to get their material second-hand. He corrects tiny details, . . . he corrects the Synoptics' whole chronology. . . . Thus he also corrects the Synoptics' messianic eschatology, and quite evidently this task of correction is extremely serious to him. There can be no doubt that *in christologicis* the Fourth Evangelist is better instructed than the Synoptics. *A priori*, then, we must reckon with the possibility that, *in eschatologicis* too, John has portrayed the figure and message of Jesus more correctly than his predecessors": E. Stauffer, "Agnostos Christos" in *The Background of the New Testament and Its Eschatology*, ed. W. Davies and D. Daube (Cambridge: University Press, 1956), 286.

[5] "I AM: this means, where I am, God is; where I am, God lives, speaks, calls, asks, acts, decides, loves, chooses, forgives, rejects, hardens hearts, suffers, dies. There can be no more daring utterance or idea": E. Stauffer, *Jesus, Gestalt und Geschichte* (Berne: Francke, 1957), 145.

is coming, and now is, when the dead will hear the voice of the Son of God, and those who hear will live" (5:25). At whatever time the dead may have lived, in a world alienated from God, the voice that wakes them is the voice of the Word of God who has come into the world; if they follow what this voice says to them, they escape judgment; but if they resist it, they thereby pronounce judgment upon themselves. This is the consistent Johannine teaching. Ultimately it matters little whether 5:27–28 is regarded as an interpolation by an "ecclesiastical redactor" (Bultmann) or as applying what has been said to the intramundane eschatological situation (J. Blank); it is in any case "no more than an extension of the train of thought and of secondary importance":[6] "for the hour is coming when all who are in the tombs will hear his voice and come forth, those who have done good, to the resurrection of life, and those who have done evil to the resurrection of judgment (5:28–29)." The same thing applies to his teaching on the "bread of life" in chapter 6: here too the central fact is that the reality is present: "He who believes [in me] has eternal life" (6:47); the four times repeated "and I will raise him up at the last day" (6:39, 40, 44, 54) may be a clarification for the benefit of those who think in linear, Jewish terms, or it may signify that linear time is incorporated into christological-eschatological time by Jesus himself. The crucial point here is that John's "realized eschatology" is not directed against futurist eschatology but draws the latter into that central eschatology that flows from Christology.[7] In any case, wherever

---

[6] R. Schnackenburg, *The Gospel according to St. John* II (London: Burns & Oates, 1980), 106.

[7] *Ibid.*, 114–19; 426–37. "The suspicion cannot but arise that these passages are insertions by another hand" (116).

C. Schütz, "Christologischer Grund der Eschatologie" in *Mysterium Salutis* V, 649ff., says: "The decisive eschatological impulse comes from an eschatology that is experienced and realized, not from an unveiling of future events" (654, cf. 660, 673). Here futurist eschatology is wholly based on the christological here-and-now. W. Breuning, "Neutestamentliche Eschatologie" in *Myst. Sal.* V, 783, says: "Never was eschatology in all its dimensions more transparently centered on Jesus Christ than in recent studies." We are basically in agreement with these views. However, *W. Kreck*, in his *Die Zukunft des Gekommenen: Grundprobleme der Eschatologie* (Munich: Kaiser, 1966), is absolutely right to take issue with the oversimplified and purely present "realized eschatology" put forward by Bultmann,

and whenever eternal life is given, it comes from the Son who was sent into the world and from his self-sacrifice.[8] It is thoroughly Johannine when the seven churches of the Apocalypse are seen standing before the judgment of the glorified Son of Man, a judgment that is all the more implacable because it is a judgment of love. The fact that the light—which, as such, is life and love—"shines in the darkness" (1:5) is already the final and utter judgment upon this darkness. And there is an inner heightening of polarity here, for while the light "convicts/convinces"[9]

Althaus (in the early editions of his *Die letzten Dinge*), the young Barth, Gogarten and Tillich. Guided by Barth's *Church Dogmatics*, Kreck lays great emphasis on the future dimension that is inherent in, and develops out of, a christological, realized eschatology (cf. 120–98: "Gegenwart und Zukunft Jesu Christi"). "We must bear in mind that only on the 'Last Day' shall we fully realize the radical and uncompromising nature, manifested in Christ's death, of God's No to sin" (129). Even in John "the accent on the present" does not obliterate the future that lies within it (170). True, "we cannot talk about this present reality and its future 'coming' by using an abstract concept of time but only by speaking christologically" (187). Following Barth, Kreck refers to Christ's own, special time frame: "Jesus lived within a circumscribed time span in one place and at one time, but since this 'time' of the man Jesus was simultaneously God's 'time', it spills over, as it were, backward and forward. Thus its circumscribed nature is not a barrier but a door" (111) opening into a divine eternity that is not simply timelessness but a present that always was and is always coming. Cf. also George Eldon Ladd, *The Presence of the Future* (London: SPCK, 1974): Jesus fulfills the Old Testament future expectation but, arising out of his own person and the arrival of the kingdom in this world, issues further promises (307).

When Paul has to campaign against a confined, gnostic "realized eschatology" (1 Tim 4:1ff., 2 Tim 2:18; 3:1ff.), his orientation to the future remains anchored in the Resurrection of Jesus, even if, in his late writings, he makes more use of Jewish categories (cf. H. Vorgrimler, *Hoffnung auf Vollendung: Aufriß der Eschatologie*, QD 90, 66).

[8] This fundamental insight is found in F. Mußner's study of the word "life" in the Fourth Gospel, ZOH (Munich: Zink, 1952): "The Johannine view of the present reality of *zōē aiōnios* in the believer . . . arises out of Johannine Christology. It is not that a 'radicalized' Johannine eschatology is the basis of the teaching of the present reality of salvation: this eschatology is itself a consequence of the Christology" (147). This view is shared by J. Blank in his article "Die Gegenwartseschatologie des Johannesevangeliums" in K. Schubert, *Vom Messias zum Christus* (Vienna: Herder, 1964), 279–313; cf. also his *Krisis: Untersuchungen zur johanneischen Christologie und Eschatologie* (Freiburg: Lambertus, 1964).

[9] On the concept of "*elenchein*", cf. *ThW* II, 470–74 (Büchsel). The word occurs at John 3:20, 8:46, 16:8.

darkness of its negation, it does not simply uncover the fact of
a static negativity: under the influence of the light, the negation
actually hides itself. Thus this "conviction" leads to a movement
of concealment and flight; benighted man "hates the light, and
does not come to the light, lest his deeds should be exposed"
(3:20). In this sense, light intensifies the darkness, which we saw
to be the fundamental dramatic theme in *Theo-Drama* IV. The
light reveals the innermost nature of the darkness that shies away
from it (cf. 9:41); but where it is accepted, where it "comes to
its own", it produces the eschatological miracle of "resurrection
from the dead" (5:21, 24–25). In each case this resurrection applies to the whole person, which "makes it difficult . . . to draw
a distinction between the 'spiritual' and the 'physical' resurrection of the dead".[10] As in the Synoptics, the presence of Jesus in
the world means that man is faced with an ultimate alternative:
his decision now determines the eternal decision of the "last
judgment" (Mk 8:38 par.). "Now is" (*nun estin*) both salvation
and judgment: "The *nun* is . . . christological, and hence eschatological."[11] Wherever the event becomes present in temporal

---

[10] Blank, *Krisis*, 126. From this point it would be possible to look back at the
doctrine of freedom we set forth in *Theo-Drama* II. There we were concerned
with the creature's "natural", constituent freedom, which can only be fulfilled
within absolute (divine) freedom—and hence must transcend itself. Here this
sphere of self-transcendence is seen to be the kingdom of light, life and truth that
is bestowed, freely and supernaturally, by God; man's part is to surrender to it in
faith. He is able to refuse, in which case he sins against the light (which he himself
claims to be: Jn 9:40) and so remains in his darkness.

[11] *Ibid.*, 136. Cf. also E. Hoskyns, *The Fourth Gospel*, ed. F. N. Davey, 2d ed.
(London: Faber and Faber, 1956), 268: "In Jesus the world is confronted by the
End. This does not mean that the eschatology of the earlier tradition has been
transmuted into an inner, present, spiritual mysticism: it means that the Evangelist
judges the heart of Christian eschatology to lie less in the expectation of a second
coming on the clouds of heaven than in the historical fact of Jesus, in His words
and actions; there the final distinction is made between life and death." Cf. on John
5:24–25: Hearing the word of Jesus, understood as passing from death to life, "is
no mere stage in an evolutionary process: it is the eschatological occurrence. . . .
The place of life and of judgment, the place where the final eschatological decision
is made, is no transcendental, mystical, supernatural activity of the Son or Word of
God. The place of decision is the flesh of Jesus, His audible words and His visible
death." Jesus adopts the role of the symbolic Son of Man, Daniel, while keeping the eschatological significance of the latter. Jesus executes judgment. "Thus
the Evangelist holds his readers to the theme laid down in the prologue (1:14), and

history, this *nun* applies; we shall see that this "now", ultimately, does not pass away: "I will come again" (Jn 14:3) in order to "dwell" with you (14:23); "lo, I am with you always, to the end of the age" (Mt 28:20). If this "end" is a reality to be taken seriously, it must show an inner relationship with the central *eschaton* of the Christ-event; in this case we shall not be surprised at the references to the "last day" in John 5:28–29 and the four places mentioned in chapter 6. Both natural, intramundane eschatology and Jewish eschatology are shown in their relation to their new and determining center.

In the face of this situation we must establish the following principle: What appeared (in the fourth volume) to be a *predominantly horizontal* theo-drama must now give place, *when the final act begins*, to the primacy of the *vertical theo-drama*; or rather, the

---

also to the eschatology of the early Christian tradition" (270–71). So Hoskyns can accept verses 5:28–29 as authentic: "The Evangelist has not, in emphasizing a present judgment, discarded altogether the expectation of a last day" (as mentioned four times in chapter 6). The prospect of the return of Jesus and the "last day" is dependent on the eschatological event that is present here and now.

Karl M. Woschitz, in his *Elpis/Hoffnung* (Vienna: Herder, 1979), 669–709, gives a good overall presentation of the Fourth Evangelist's "dialectical movement of thought". He draws attention to the negative factors (the disobedient "shall not see life", 3:36), whereas faith of itself implies hope (*ibid.*). "Doing the truth" likewise involves the hope of "coming to the light" (3:21). In the "hour" that "is coming, and now is" (5:25) "we encounter a twofold eschatology: it is both of the future and realized in the present" (Woschitz, *Elpis*, 683). The evidence that Jesus, present here and now, is the one who raises from the dead "is set forth and ratified both now and in the future" (685). The raising of Lazarus in present chronological time is a pledge that Jesus is the resurrection and the life not only now but also ultimately ("at the last day") (690). And in the future tense he says: "He who believes in me, though he die, yet shall he live" (Jn 11:26). In 12:48 ("He who rejects me and does not receive my sayings has a judge; the word that I have spoken will be his judge on the last day") the future dimension can hardly be excluded from the whole sense of the passage. And in 11:23 "it is impossible to deny that the Evangelist is emphasizing the last day" (708). In the Farewell Discourses the references to the future (the return, the sending of the Spirit, which does not come at the end of the world) are constitutive, as they are in the farewell prayer to the Father. Even if one were to assume that some "ecclesial redactor" had imported futurist eschatology into the text, is it conceivable "that the disciples would have contradicted their master by reintroducing the traditional eschatology, or that they would not have maintained one of his essential concerns —if it was one?": Schnackenburg, *St. John* II, 434.

horizontal must be integrated into the vertical since the latter *gives it both meaning and form*. This is basically self-evident in a *theo*-dramatic context, that is, where God, independent of world-time, is the primary actor. In such a context it is essential that God's action should not shrink to a single, instant, immutable point in time that is constitutive of every moment of earth-time; God's "abiding forever" must not be seen as a "non-time" but as a super-time that is unique to him; and this is illustrated in the fact that Christ's time mediates between God's "time" and world-time. Christ's time recapitulates and comprehends world-time, while it also reveals God's super-time. Jesus' time, particularly in John, has a kind of inner periodicity that, while of course colored by the human time in which Jesus shares, has its own intrinsic validity as a result of his relationship with the Father; in other words, it has a trinitarian significance. The essential division between the life of Jesus and his "hour" (which embraces death and Resurrection in a single unity)[12] divides his "glorification" into two phases. The first began with the manifestation of his glory at his first miracle, a glory that was intrinsically a glorifying of the Father and to which Jesus looks back in 13:31, while at the same time he looks forward to the second phase, the imminent ("at once") "glorification" through his exaltation on the Cross and his Resurrection (13:32–34). The voice from heaven in 12:28 has already confirmed these two phases: "I have glorified it, and I will glorify it again." This future event, to which the whole of Jesus' life looks forward, cannot be precipitated; it can only be prayed for: "Father, the hour has come; glorify thy Son that the Son may glorify thee" (17:1; cf. 4–5). The disciples, too, are affected by these phases: in the Farewell Discourses Jesus' "time" enters the phase characterized by his death and Resurrection, his going away and coming again; the emphatic caesura between this and the former phase creates a hiatus for the disciples: accordingly, as he can no longer look after them himself, Jesus entrusts them to the Father for the duration of the hiatus (17:11). Jesus seeks to console them by speaking of a "little while" (16:17–19), yet for the disciples it will be long enough for "weeping and

---

[12] *Theo-Drama* IV, 231–40.

THE IDEA OF A CHRISTIAN ESCHATOLOGY

lamenting", while the world rejoices; indeed, Jesus compares it
with the pains of a woman in childbirth, a reference that, at least
remotely, recalls the Jewish expectation of a time of the "birth
pangs of the Messiah". In the terms of Jesus' own "time", this
caesura is the duration (which cannot be measured chronologically) of his Cross, of his God-forsakenness, of his dwelling in
the realm of the dead. As far as the disciples are concerned, it is
an open question whether it represents the time up to his Resurrection or up to his coming again; in a Johannine perspective
one would be inclined to assume the former, but such a view is
contradicted by the prophetic utterances concerning the persecution of Christians as they seek to follow their Lord (15:20–16:4)
—utterances that refer to the whole of the Church's "time".

Words that announce the sending of the Spirit point even more
strongly to the "in-breaking" into world-time, in and through
the Christ-event, not only of eternity but of a divine super-time.
Of necessity the Spirit can be sent only after the Son's departure
(16:4). According to John, the sending of the Spirit is clearly
linked to the crucified Son's surrendering to his Father of the
Spirit of his mission; it is also linked to the incident of the piercing, and to the Risen One's breathing of the Spirit upon the
Church. The details of the Spirit's task speak even more plainly:
as the "time" of the Church unfolds, he will interpret the entire
work of Jesus more profoundly and plumb its depths (16:13); as
yet, it hardly exists at all. It is very characteristic that, on the one
hand, Jesus seems to have said everything, so that the Spirit will
need only to "remind" the disciples (14:26), and, on the other
hand, he can say: "I have yet many things to say to you, but you
cannot bear them now. When the Spirit of truth comes, he will
guide you into all the truth" (16:12–13). Nonetheless the Spirit
does not speak on his own account but draws everything from
the treasures of Christ, which are those of the Father (16:13–
15). This means that everything not yet uttered, every apparently
new interpretation and understanding, was always there in the
"utterance" that Jesus is—and here we must think first and foremost of his whole existence as Word of the Father rather than as
the word uttered in human terms. What he "is" always implies a
"coming", a future, that "ever-greater" which is inherent in the

Word of God made man.[13] Thus the "now" (*nun*) encompasses a "soon" (*euthus*, Jn 13:32; *en tachei*, Rev 1:1, and so on): "Now is the judgment" (Jn 12:31), a judgment that takes place on the "last day" (6:39ff.). This extension into the future characterizes the "time" of discipleship and of the Church, a "time" that is immanent in the central Christ-event; here the Christ-event attains its own special space, its breadth. But it is nonetheless the effect of a superordinate divine "super-time" of the economic Trinity (sending the Son and, after his mission is complete—Jn 17:4—the Holy Spirit), which in turn is subordinate to the "super-time" of the immanent Trinity with its order of processions.

John's particular emphasis, therefore, means that everything in the horizontal dramatic dimension is seen in the context of the vertical; thus it acts as a corrective to Jewish eschatology. But this vertical is the locus of a dramatic tension in which the action taking place between God and mankind, centered in Jesus Christ, differs fundamentally from any pagan and mythological epic, whether it be of fallen aeons or descending divinities. Here the drama of Christ remains the direct fulfillment of Yahweh's covenant drama with Israel, which has been going on throughout the whole of history.

John's emphasis corresponds in all essentials with the fundamental assertions of the rest of the New Testament. We can give no more than a brief summary here. The view that, in Jesus, the light from above has broken through to the "darkness and shadow of death" of a sinful world was already demonstrated by Matthew (4:16) on the basis of Isaiah 9:1f.; we do not need to invoke some special Johannine dualism to account for it. That man's acceptance or rejection of this light even now determines his destiny is a view familiar to the Synoptics (Mk 8:38; Lk 12:9), who see it as an eschatological decision between heaven

---

[13] "The Spirit proclaims to the community what is coming as what is coming to it, so that its members will act accordingly": Schnackenburg, *St. John* III, 136. "But when he proclaims what is to come, it will be less a matter of individual future events than of the future quality of truth itself. . . . He mediates at all times between the firm structure of what perdures and the varying requirements of the present": 3 Jo 246–47.

and hell (Mt 25). The descent and subsequent ascent of the Savior is found in Ephesians 4 (following Phil 2), and the concept of "exaltation" is found several times in both Old and New Testaments.[14] The assertion that, prior to the coming of the Savior, this world lay under the power of the devil is the substance of the parable in Matthew 12:28 (par.) and many of Paul's utterances (1 Cor 2:6; 2 Cor 4:4; Eph 6:12, and so on). Faced with Christ, however, man freely decides, and he is free if he opens himself in simplicity to God's light, if "his eye is single" (Mt 6:22 AV). Anyone becoming a disciple of Christ must leave behind everything, including his own self, or, as Paul puts it more precisely, together with Christ he must die to the world and be raised to the kingdom of God, he must share in changing the polarity from the "first" to the "second" Adam (1 Cor 15:21ff.); but it is with a view to the Second Adam, Christ, for him and through him, that all things in the world are created (Col 1:16ff.; 1 Cor 8:6), since it is by him that they are to be redeemed. That Jesus is the principle of the resurrection is known to Matthew (27:51–53) just as much as to Paul (1 Cor 15:22–23). And the conviction that, finally, the entire work of redemption springs from the love of God the Father is found in the Synoptics in all Jesus' references to his Father's utter goodness, perfection and mercy; this is as explicit in Paul as in John (Rom 8:32). The only remaining question is whether John's strong emphasis on the "already" of redemption and judgment does not actually mask the "not yet" that is stressed by the other writers, in such a way as to obscure man's situation, a situation in which he always has to decide. For it cannot be disputed that the standpoint of Johannine theology is primarily christological; it is anthropological only within the overarching Christology. At the same time we must not forget the constant Johannine exhortation to "abide", which is parallel to the Synoptics' command to "watch". As far as the believer is concerned, everything depends on the "if" here: You cannot bear fruit "*if* you do not abide in me" (15:4); "*If* you abide in me, and *if* my words abide in you, ask whatever you will, and it shall be done for you" (15:7); "Abide in my love. *If* you keep my commandments, you will abide in my love" (15:10); "You

---

[14] Blank, *Krisis*, 83.

are my friends *if* you do what I command you" (15:14). There are many other conditional sentences of this kind: "*If* you continue in my word, you are truly my disciples" (8:31). "*If* you were Abraham's children, you would do what Abraham did" (8:39). "*If* God were your Father, you would love me" (8:42). "*If* I tell the truth, why do you not believe me?" (8:46). "*If* you were blind, you would have no guilt" (9:41). Words such as these leave man his anthropological freedom to make a decision, which is what the Lord requires of him; this is in complete contrast to the notions of predestination found in Gnosticism.

3. The Synoptic Discourses on the "End" and the Johannine Emphasis

It is a commonly held view that the Synoptic "little apocalypse", burdened as it is with many Jewish apocalyptic images and ideas, differs sharply from the "realized eschatology" of John.[1] This view calls for some examination. Here we shall stick quite straightforwardly to the text (Mt 24; Mk 13; Lk 17 and 21), mostly following the Matthean version, without going into the question of how far the specifically "apocalyptic" expressions can be traced back to Jesus himself or to what extent they have been interpolated by the evangelists (in this case, chiefly Mark) on the basis of possibly Jewish sources.

If we examine these texts with an open mind, we shall be astonished how many of them—leaving aside those involved in prophesying the fall of Jerusalem—are concerned with the direct effect of Jesus' presence in the world. In *Theo-Drama* IV we saw that Jesus' presence has certain unavoidable consequences for that world history which continues after him (the "end-time"): these consequences are developed on a broad canvas in the Synoptic texts, largely without any specifically apocalyptic

---

[1] "The eschatological language shows . . . that New Testament eschatology and apocalyptic depend to a high degree on tradition stemming from the Old Testament and early Judaism": K. H. Schelkle, *Theologie des Neuen Testaments* IV, pt. 1: *Vollendung von Schöpfung und Erlösung* (Düsseldorf: Patmos, 1974), 18. "The New Testament follows the linguistic usage of Jewish apocalyptic" (e.g., with regard to the "Day of Judgment", the "two aeons", etc.): *ibid.*, 16.

garb. Where such garb is employed, one must ask whether it is really left in its original Jewish context of understanding or whether it is not rather incorporated into the new, christological, context. If we concentrate on this clear central thrust of the Synoptic apocalypses, we can say that, in formal terms, they do not differ from the Johannine view: statements and warnings attributed to Jesus regarding the historical future all focus on the fact that he is and has been here in historical reality. Thus his "word" (which signifies his entire existence, his life, death and Resurrection) embraces the whole of world history; accordingly it is present in, and governs, all temporal futures: "Heaven and earth will pass away, but my words will not pass away" (Mt 24:35; Mk 13:31; Lk 21:33).

a. The discourse on the fall of the Holy City forms the prelude to the "little apocalypse" and can be taken as read here. We have already mentioned the cardinal point: In Jesus' own self-consciousness this collapse is—quite legitimately—bound up with the fact that he himself has reached the end of this world of history and transience. Just as he himself is the capstone of God's revelation in the form of history (for in him the triune God gives himself for the world in a way that surpasses all human comprehension), and all subsequent temporal process is only the vast unfolding of this concluding event, so too the fall of Jerusalem (because it rejected the Messiah) is eschatological. (Moreover, the "salvation of all Israel" cannot be an event within history but belongs to the "mystery" of the transcendent Judgment.)[2] The prediction of the city's fall is identical in all three Gospels (Mt 24:1–2; Mk 13:1–2; Lk 21:5–6); Luke alone clearly refers the Mark 13:14–20 passage, which urges people to flee to the mountains and not to return home, proclaims woe to the mothers with child and with suckling infants, and bids readers pray that this distress should not overtake them in winter, to the imminent destruction of the city (Lk 21:20–24; cf. 17:31). In doing so, he suppresses certain elements of Jewish apocalyptic, for example, the Danielic "desolating sacrilege" in the holy places (Mk 13:14a) and the shortening of "those days"

---

[2] *Theo-Drama* III, 389f.; *Theo-Drama* IV, 449.

for the sake of the elect (Mk 13:30), replacing them with the concrete trials that take place when the city is surrounded and taken. Here Luke gives us the first significant example of "de-apocalypticizing" in favor of a christocentric eschatology; and it can remain an open question whether, and how far, Mark and Matthew too apply the relevant exhortations to flee, to make haste, and the woes regarding the mothers, and so on, to the destruction of Jerusalem (the most terrible events of all history: Mk 13:19).

b. When the disciples express their curiosity about the "when" of this catastrophe, which they automatically equate with the end of the world and (Mt 24:3) the return of Christ, Jesus does not simply say that this time is hidden from men (Mk 13:32; Mt 24:36); in fact this particular dictum comes at the end. First he gives a great many instructions that flow from the fact that he is and has been present in the world.[3] Here world history is interpreted theologically as consequences of the Incarnation of the Word of God, consequences that signal both a forward movement and universality. Initially we have the warning against other putative Messiahs who will lead many astray (Mt 24:4-5), throwing doubt on Christ's uniqueness and trying to go beyond him. This warning is repeated in 24:11: Many false prophets will prove to be successful in deceiving others. Verse 23: "Then if any one says to you, 'Lo, here is the Christ!' or 'There he is!' do not believe it." The false prophets will be many, working great miracles and misleading "even the

---

[3] Cf. K. Rahner, "The Hermeneutics of Eschatological Assertions" in *Theological Investigations* vol. 4 (London and Baltimore, 1966, 1974), 323-46. In this important article, after lengthy evaluation of the possibilities and limitations of prediction of the future in revelation and human faith, Rahner addresses our topic thus: "Christ himself is the hermeneutic principle of all eschatological assertions. Anything that cannot be read and understood as a Christological assertion is not a genuine eschatological assertion. It is soothsaying and apocalyptic, or a form of speech which misses and misunderstands the Christological element, because couched in a style and an imagery borrowed from other sources. It is therefore read in the light of the *terminus a quo* of its origin and not of the *terminus ad quem*, which is Christ. . . . We can derive from our experience of Christ all that can and may be said objectively in the Catholic theology of eschatology" (342-43).

elect" (24:24). If they say he is in the wilderness, or in particular rooms, "do not believe it" (24:26). "Lo, I have told you beforehand" (24:25). Christ's absolute uniqueness is announced three times, followed by a related topic: the unavoidable discernment/separation [*Scheidung*] of spirits. Matthew had set forth the essential issue in his account of the sending out of the disciples (10:17–22), whereas Mark and Luke only mention it at this stage: "And brother will deliver up brother to death, and the father his child, and children will rise against parents and have them put to death" (Mk 13:12). This second topic emphasizes two things: first, the forward movement implied by this situation of *krisis* and the resultant increase in apostasy (13:10), "because wickedness is multiplied, most men's love will grow cold" (Mt 24:12), cf. Luke 18:8: "Nevertheless, when the Son of man comes, will he find faith on earth?" Secondly, it is foretold that the disciples will encounter persecution in their discipleship of their Lord (Mk 13:9): they will be handed over to be oppressed and killed, "and you will be hated by all for my name's sake" (13:13). Matthew and Luke add that the disciples should not be anxious when they are brought to court; the Spirit (or the Lord himself) will give them the necessary words. Nothing can harm the man who holds fast in faith; he will be saved (Mk 13:13 par.). Thus the Christ-event is shown to be of world-historical dimensions; Mark adds the explicitly universal perspective: before the end comes, "the gospel must first be preached to all nations" (13:10).

c. On the one hand, we have this clearly christological core, and, on the other, we have a small number of passages that come from the realm of Jewish apocalyptic. The latter must be divided into those that can or probably should be provided with a context within Christology and those that must stay at the level of general apocalyptic language. Immediately after Jesus' first warning to the disciples not to be led astray by false Messiahs, we read (Mk 13:7): "When you hear of wars and rumors of wars, do not be alarmed . . . the end is not yet." Such things are still in the midst of history, for "nation will rise against nation, and kingdom against kingdom." These same events, as well as the subsequent catastrophes of hunger, plague and earthquake, are expected by the Jewish apocalyptic writers too.[4] The hostile treatment of the disciples, however, can also be interpreted in terms of society, in terms of those divisions within the family —for the sake of Christ—to which all the Synoptics refer. The other tribulations, hunger, disease and earthquake, come from the same apocalyptic imagery of the "end" as the expression used by Mark and Matthew (but suppressed by Luke): "the beginning of the sufferings". The glorious reign of the Messiah, to which all were looking forward (irrespective of whether it was regarded as the final period of the world or as the penultimate period, before the Judgment), was to be preceded by the period of tribulation, the "birth pangs of the Messiah". These would include the shaking of the foundations not only of the earth but also of the cosmos in its entirety. In the "little apocalypse" these signs are harbingers of the coming Son of Man: "After that tribulation, the sun will be darkened, and the moon will not give its light, and the stars will be falling from heaven, and the powers in the heavens will be shaken" (Mk 13:24–25; Mt 24:29; Luke shortens this but adds the "distress of nations in perplexity at the roaring of the sea and the waves": 21:25). It is only in these passages that clearly alien imagery interposes itself, imagery that has not been christologically assimilated; evidently it serves to provide a fitting introduction to the topic of the parousia: "And then they will see the Son of man coming in clouds with great power and glory" (Mk 13:26; according to Matthew, the sign of the Son of Man appears in the heavens prior to his appearance in person; Luke, more modest, speaks of "a cloud"). This logion, in terms of origin and status, is quite different from those that precede it, for it is either a quotation (Mt 24:30) or a recasting (Mk 8:38) of Daniel 7:13–14, a text that Jesus applies to the Son of Man who comes in judgment, in other words, to himself in his exaltation (Mt 10:32). (Cf. Jesus' testimony before the Sanhedrin, Mt 26:64; Mk 14:62; Luke adds, "seated at the right hand of the power of God", and leaves out the cloud, 22:69.) So even the few passages that

---

[4] Cf. Paul Volz, *Die Eschatologie der jüdischen Gemeinde im neutestamentlichen Zeitalter* (Tübingen: Mohr, 1934), sec. 31.

originate in the realm of apocalyptic, read in the context of this particular word of Jesus, actually acquire something like a christological function.

At this point a new question presents itself for our attention. The idea that the Son of Man—who now takes the place of God in judgment—is to come to judge the world at the end of time, even if it is not a purely apocalyptic notion, is surely a central Old Testament theme, familiar at least since the first prophets; and is not this futuristic notion the very thing to which John opposed his "realized" eschatology: "Now is the judgment" (Jn 12:31); "the hour is coming, and now is, when the dead will hear the voice of the Son of God" (5:25)?

Before proceeding, however, we must highlight a tension that is to be found in the words that conclude this discourse. For, on the one hand, "this generation will not pass away before all these things take place" (Matthew, Mark, Luke), and, on the other hand, "no one knows the hour, not even the angels in heaven, nor the Son, but only the Father" (Matthew and Mark; Luke leaves this sentence out). It is possible to minimize this tension by referring "this generation" to the disciples, who remain faithful during the great tribulation, or by regarding it as a reworking of the logion in Matthew 16:28 and Luke 9:27, pointing, not to the end of the world as such, but to the Resurrection of Jesus. At all events, the tension remains, kept in place by the constant exhortation to be vigilant, to be ready, to pray. The New Testament's eschatological "soon" is more than the merely chronological "soon" of apocalyptic writing; it implies the primacy of Jesus' "time" and "super-time" over world-time. We have already dealt with this adequately in *Theo-Drama* III, 130ff., 135ff. It is characteristic that these two assertions—the imminence of the events and the fact that no one knows the hour—are simultaneously *separated* and *united* by the peerless saying: "Heaven and earth will pass away, but my words will not pass away" (Mk 13:31 par.).

4. The Day of the Lord and the Judgment

Jewish eschatology looks forward to a salvation that is unequiv-ocally in the future, in linear time.[1] This is true even where the "two aeons" idea in many apocalypses envisages the "coming aeon" as existing already, hidden in God, in vertical relationship to the present; here too, when it actually manifests itself, it will take over from the present, transitory aeon and proceed in a lin-ear manner. The borderline is "the Day of the Lord", on which,

[1] Here we must of course distinguish between the strangely vague, as it were embryonic "eschatology"—if the word can be applied at all—of the classical Old Testament and Jewish eschatology, which is different. Shemaryahu Talmon has shown convincingly, in his "Eschatologie und Geschichte im biblischen Juden-tum" in R. Schnackenburg, ed., *Zukunft, Schriften der Kath. Akad. in Bayern* (Pat-mos, 1980), 13–50, how "unmethodically" the ancient Hebrews thought where time was concerned. "The notion of an 'absolute ultimate', an 'absolute end' seems to be very remote from ancient biblical thought" (21); "time is in eternal flux, and one stage merges into the next without pressing teleologically toward a final goal" (25). So whether man contemplates salvation or disaster, in either case it will come only at the "end of a time span", at "a time set by God" (27); "in practice, the experienced time span embraces about seven to eight generations" (29). These hopes show a marked "restoration tendency": situations from Israel's early period are seen in transfigured, utopian terms and projected into the future. Even when the prophets speak of a "new covenant", it is seen in connection with the original Covenant; and if this Covenant is called "eternal", it must therefore be "renewed from time to time" (38). The future cannot be envisaged "as absolutely 'new'; . . . the image remains an earthly one" (42). And even when there is mention of a watershed in history, "people and nations will continue thereafter in their groupings and states; . . . the relationship of fathers and sons persists." "Ideas of 'redemption', 'resurrection' and 'life after death' play only a subordinate role" (43). "Death" in the classical Old Testament remains "a genuine finale: the individual dies and becomes nothing; the community continues and so has a future" (46). Thus Talmon's analysis sets the Old Testament, which she regards as normative, against the exaggerations of apocalyptic and of Christianity. For apocalyptic, "the center of gravity lies in the earthly" (48). To that extent the classical Old Testament expectation of the future is also "linear"; in Judaism it is radicalized, becoming a predominantly linear eschatology that, despite all the intimations of a "beyond", remains "earthly". On this issue, cf. G. Fohrer, "Die Struktur der altt. Eschatolo-gie" in *ThLZ* 85 (1960), 401–42 (there was no eschatological situation prior to the Exile); H. D. Preuß, ed., *Eschatologie im Alten Testament*, Wege der Forschung, 480 (Darmstadt, 1978), esp. T. C. Vriezen, "Prophetie und Eschatologie", 88–128: Classical prophecy is "pre-eschatological", then "proto-eschatological"; not until Deutero-Isaiah is it an "actualizing eschatology"; it is the later disappoint-ments that lead to a "transcendentalizing" eschatology.

in judgment and in salvation, God will call the past aeon to account; this image persists ever since the time of the Prophets, even if there are great variations in the way the eschatological events are seen (the Messianic age, the woes of the end-time, the collapse of the world, and judgment),[2] and even if "the Day of the Lord" can be expressed in different but equivalent terms.[3]

In the Old Covenant the concept of the "Day of the Lord" (or "the Day", "that day", and so on) goes through three phases. First there is a pre-prophetic phase (which we can only surmise) looking forward to an epiphany on the part of Yahweh, who would deal with Israel's enemies and help his people to final victory. We should observe that, by contrast with the Babylonian and Egyptian prototypes that, no doubt, provided part of this imagery (God's appearance on that "terrible day",[4] bringing sword, hunger, plague, with earthquake, darkness, and signs and wonders in the heavens, and so on), the borrowed imagery itself is only the cosmetic decoration of an event that is envisaged in a temporal future, as is appropriate to the historical nature of Israel's covenant with Yahweh and the promises attached to it.[5]

---

[2] P. Volz, *Die Eschatologie der jüdischen Gemeinde im neutestamentlichen Zeitalter* (Tübingen: Mohr, 1934), 255f., 273, 284–86.

[3] Von Rad/Delling, art. ἡμέρα in *ThW* II (1953), 948f.

[4] Cf. the Babylonian parallels cited by G. Hölscher, *Der Ursprung der jüdischen Eschatologie* (Gießen: Töpelmann, 1912), 13.

[5] A. Jespen correctly points this out in his article "Eschatologie im Alten Testament" in *RGG*, 3d ed. (1958), II, 661 (refs.). This renders obsolete Gunkel's attempts to establish precedents (*Schöpfung und Chaos in Urzeit und Endzeit*, 1895) and also H. Greßmann's more nuanced study (*Der Ursprung der israelitisch-jüdischen Eschatologie*, 1905), as well as the work of E. Meyer, who tried (1906) to find an Egyptian origin for Jewish eschatology. Images of the world that are essentially mythical and cyclical cannot explain Israel's linear world view. The same applies to S. Mowinckel's attempt to trace Old Testament and Jewish eschatology back to the cult, or rather to its ossification (that is, since there was no longer a vivid experience of God's ever-new "coming" at his annual enthronement festival [*Das Thronbesteigungsfest Jahwes und der Ursprung der Eschatologie*, 1922]. The most convincing is G. von Rad's cautious attempt to identify the original core of the ideas of the "Day of Yahweh" in the ancient images and concepts of the holy war, in which God appeared present, fighting with Israel and employing "sacral panic" to help them to victory. See his "The Origin of the Concept of the Day of Yahweh" in *Journal of Semitic Studies* 4 (1959), 97–108; cf. his *Old Testament Theology* II (SCM, 1965), 119–25. Instead of starting with the brief reference in

Even though this expected intervention of God long remains purely intrahistorical, and can therefore be termed "eschatological" only in a qualified sense, it does contain the nucleus that will eventually be developed into the doctrine of the end-time.

There is of course a second phase, which first comes to light in Amos (5:18−20): here the expected "Day of the Lord" is not a bright day of victory for Israel but a dark day of judgment on the people. These images are gradually intensified, right up to the terrifying portrayals of Zephaniah.[6] But this does not alter the formal structure of the Day of Judgment; it only means that now Israel is subjected to the hardest and most humiliating judgment.

In the final, post-Exilic phase, after the great trial of Israel's banishment, the prophecy of salvation dominates once again: judgment and its attendant catastrophes are restricted to the heathen nations, the enemies of Israel, and the godless in Israel, whereas the Judgment becomes a day of redemption for the Chosen People.[7] This represents a decline as compared with

---

Amos 5:18−20, which, while it is the earliest prophetic utterance concerning the Day of the Lord, does not use the relevant images, von Rad adduces texts such as Isaiah 34, Ezekiel 30, Ezekiel 7, Joel 2, Zephaniah 1, where the battle of Yahweh is described in the same or very similar terms. Von Rad's theories are rejected by Meir Weiß, "The Origin of the 'Day of the Lord' Reconsidered" in *Hebrew Union College Annual* 37 (Cincinnati, 1966), 29−73: The imagery of the Day of Yahweh ("epiphany") does not come from the ancient battles of Yahweh, nor can it be shown that the term "Day of Yahweh" was used prior to the advent of prophecy (Amos). So the question of origins remains open.

[6] Zeph 1:14−18: "The great day of the Lord is near, near and hastening fast; the sound of the day of the Lord is bitter, the mighty man cries aloud there. A day of wrath is that day, a day of distress and anguish, a day of ruin and devastation, a day of darkness and gloom, a day of clouds and thick darkness, a day of trumpet blast and battle cry against the fortified cities and against the lofty battlements. I will bring distress on men, so that they shall walk like the blind, because they have sinned against the Lord; their blood shall be poured out like dust, and their flesh like dung. Neither their silver nor their gold shall be able to deliver them on the day of the wrath of the Lord. In the fire of his jealous wrath all the earth shall be consumed; for a full, yea, sudden end he will make of all the inhabitants of the earth."

[7] Greßmann, *Der Ursprung*, 157; v. Rad, ἡμέρα 948: "The prophecy becomes a prophecy of salvation, and the Day of Yahweh of which it speaks means rescue, re-instatement and ultimate salvation for the deeply humiliated people." Collapse

classical prophecy, which had succeeded in keeping alive the great tension implied in the Day of Yahweh: judgment is at its most severe when applied to the elect, but it does not signify rejection. Much of the New Testament's concept of judgment finds its preliminary adumbration here.

The picture becomes threatening again in apocalyptic. The "Day of the Lord", "that day", "that great day", is above all a day of "judgment", of "wrath and anger", "the great and terrible day of God's reckoning with the world", the day of "vengeance and cursing", of "violence", of "punishment", of "fear", of "tribulation", but also "the day of the elect" of the Son of Man, of the rescue of the righteous, a day of "mercy" and "consolation".[8] Judgment is always preceded by the "terrible last times" involving anguish not known since the beginning of the world; the end will come when distress is at its height. The nations unite for the attack on Jerusalem; all the wild animals fight against the Lamb (the Messiah) (*Test. Jos.* 19); mankind is overcome by many plagues and led astray by false predictions (*Apoc. Bar.* 48:34); the very constellations are out of kilter (*En.* 80:6f.; 2 Esdras 5:4; *Sib.* III, 80f.); the righteous are guarded by angels throughout the period of tribulation (*Ethiop. En.* 100:5). But the end comes soon; "the 'soon' is part and parcel of the nature of eschatological faith."[9] God will "suddenly" destroy the nations attacking Jerusalem.[10] "Judgment comes suddenly and thereby takes the godless, in particular, by surprise."[11] The Judge is almost always God himself. In *Ethiopic Enoch* 62 the visionary sees God and the Son of Man together in judgment: "Here it is the Son of Man who judges, whereas God pronounces the final sentence."[12] God often appears in judgment accompanied by his heavenly host (*En.* 1:4).

All this—and many other features could be adduced—is in-

---

is prophesied for the heathen nations, but "for Jerusalem defense (Zech 12:2ff.), refining (Malachi 3:2), cleansing (Zech 13:1), the giving of the spirit (Joel 2:28; Zech 12:10), paradisal rains and waters (Joel 3:18; Zech 14:8)."

[8] For references (all from Jewish apocalyptic) cf. Volz, *Eschatologie*, 163–64.

[9] *Ibid.*, 135.

[10] *Ibid.*, 161.

[11] *Ibid.*, 274.

[12] *Ibid.*, 275.

tended to illustrate the pressure exerted on the New Testament concepts by Old Testament Jewish eschatology with its expectation of God's Day of Judgment in the end-time. Jesus' largely "christological" discourse regarding the future was occasioned by the disciples' characteristic question: "Tell us, when will this be, and what will be the sign when these things are all to be accomplished?" (Mk 13:4). The Pauline and other letters consistently look forward to "the Day" (1 Cor 3:13; 1 Th 5:4; Heb 10:25) as "the day of wrath" (Rom 2:5) and of judgment (Rom 2:16; 2 Pet 2:9; 1 Jn 4:17; Jude 6). It is "the day of the Lord" (which in Old Testament terms can mean "the day of God": Acts 2:17–20; 2 Pet 3:12; in the New Testament it is the day of Christ: 1 Th 5:2; 2 Th 2:2; 1 Cor 1:8; "the day of Jesus Christ": Phil 1:6; cf. 2:16). The language of the Gospels corresponds to that of the Letters: the Gospels point forward to "the day of judgment" (Mt 11:22; 12:36), to "that day" (Mt 7:22; Lk 6:23). Luke explicitly says that the "day" will dawn when least expected (17:26ff.); the day comes "like a snare" (21:34), "like a thief in the night" (Mt 24:43; 1 Th 5:2, 4; 2 Pet 3:10; Rev 3:3; 16:15). We have already seen that the idea of a disaster-laden end-time (including social and cosmic catastrophes) migrates into New Testament concepts; it is defined with particular clarity in the early Paul's notion of the Antichrist: on his return, Christ will slay his opponent "with the breath of his mouth and destroy him by his appearing and his coming" (2 Th 2:8; cf. Isa 11:4; Ps 33:6).

Here the primitive Church seems to have missed the true meaning of Jesus' own "expectation of the imminent end" and to have directly adopted the Jewish perspective of an end to earthly history, in particular by assuming that a period of the "birth pangs of the Messiah" would precede the end (since for the Jews, in one way or another, this "end" signalled the arrival of the Messianic age). Furthermore, certain words of Jesus (or of the evangelists) seem to indicate a final act *within* world history, for example, the appearance of "the sign of the Son of man in heaven", after which "all the tribes of the earth will mourn" (Mt 24:30), or the sending forth of the angels to gather the elect from the four winds (Mt 24:31) and to separate the evil from the righteous (Mt 13:49).

There are, however, important *contrary* indications. Thus the appearing of the Son of Man "in his day" is likened to lightning that "flashes and lights up the sky from one side to the other" (Lk 17:24; "from east to west": Mt 24:27). The context is significant: in Luke it had been preceded by Jesus' teaching that the kingdom of God is not here or there, that earthly means cannot observe its coming, and that the kingdom is "in the midst of you"; this was in reply to the question of *when* the kingdom of God would come (17:20 par.). Immediately after this comes the warning to the disciples: They will be urged to "look here!" and "look there!" for some purely historical Messiah, but they must not allow themselves to be led astray, because Jesus will return like a flash of lightning. Similarly in Matthew: If people point to a Messiah in the desert (where so many Jewish leaders assembled their troops) or hidden in houses (as indicated by many legends), "do not believe them." This is followed by the metaphor of the lightning.

In 1 Thessalonians (5:1ff.) Paul dispels his readers' anxieties with regard to the coming of the Lord by pointing out that this coming cannot be predicted and that only those who are lulled into a false sense of security will be taken by surprise; accordingly the letter ends with an exhortation to vigilance, readiness and the practice of every Christian virtue. Second Thessalonians equally warns its recipients against being knocked off balance by those who say "that the day of the Lord has come", but it goes on to give reasons for the delay: the "son of perdition", the Antichrist, has not yet appeared; for the present something is hindering him from stepping forth openly, although "the mystery of lawlessness" is already at work. Here, no doubt, we see the influence of an element of Jewish apocalyptic[13] that has its origin in Daniel 7–8, to which the Letter clearly refers. Here, indisputably, Jewish linear expectation of the end is transposed into Christian terms; but the expected Antichrist is not a Jewish (false) prophet: he is a figure confronting Christ directly, even if his appearance is accompanied by Danielic motifs.[14] As in the

---

[13] *Ibid.*, 282.

[14] On the indebtedness of 1 Thessalonians to Jewish apocalyptic, cf. B. Rigaux's summary, "Les Épîtres aux Thessaloniciens" in *Études bibliques*, 1956, esp. 247–80.

Gospels, the "signs" of the end (a Jewish theme) indicate the zenith of evil, as at the time prior to the Flood (cf. Lk 17:26ff.; 2 Tim 3:1–3); what "restrains" the Antichrist from appearing openly—namely, the linear extension of world history—is also, initially, a Jewish theme. As in the rest of the New Testament, however, these elements of Paul's Jewish education are outshone and, as it were, reabsorbed by the central christological theme. If the "mystery of godlessness" is even now at work—and for Paul this godlessness can be nothing other than the negation of the Christian reality—it follows that the Antichrist is already present and putting forth his influence, exactly as 1 John asserts: Anyone who denies the Incarnation of Christ "is not of God. This is the spirit of antichrist, of which you heard that it was coming, and now it is in the world already" (1 Jn 4:2–3). "Children, it is the last hour; and as you have heard that antichrist is coming, so now many antichrists have come; therefore we know that it is the last hour" (1 Jn 2:18). What, in the Jewish milieu, was the expectation of the "evil time" of the Messiah's birth-pangs, becomes, in the New Testament, a consciousness of living in the "end-time", or "the last hour", or "at the end of the aeons" (Heb 9:26), in the wake of the death and Resurrection of Christ. Within this end-time it is superfluous to make qualitative distinctions between periods: the only feature that will ultimately persist and establish itself, whether visibly or invisibly, is the "*krisis*", the decision, the scission, that Christ has introduced into the world.

At this point we must mention an important topic to which we shall have to return in more detail later.

If we examine what the New Testament has to say about judgment, we find a peculiar discrepancy. At the formal level there is a holding fast to the Old Testament idea that the world will be judged at the end of the ages and also that the dead will rise. At

---

The theme of the great "fall" must be linked "à ses parallèles dans l'apocalyptique juive" (253). There are also Jewish precedents for the "delayer" (*katechōn*, 277–78), which means that it can hardly represent a definable historical entity, and certainly not the Roman Empire (274–79).

the same time, however, judgment is depicted as an individual, not a universal, event. Accordingly, the individual's death and his judgment are brought close together, as Hebrews 9:27 explicitly says: "It is appointed for men to die once, and after that comes judgment." The old "Day of the Lord" was primarily a judgment on the "nations", then (in the Prophets) on the "people" of Israel too; later, after the Exile, it was once more understood as a judgment on the nations and the godless in general. But under the influence of Ezekiel's teaching (the sinner will be punished for his own sin) and also, no doubt, of the growth of Hellenistic thought, which envisaged the individual being rewarded and punished according to his deeds, the old concept of judgment was filled with a new content: individual responsibility. According to Paul, at the Judgment everyone must account for his own deeds (Rom 2:6; 14:12; 1 Cor 3:13, 15; 4:4; 2 Cor 5:10; Gal 6:7, 9), and since judgment belongs to God alone, everyone should refrain from judging his brother. Similarly James 4:11 (cf. 1 Pet 1:17); the Gospels are no different (Mt 7:1f.; Lk 6:37). Most striking here is the great judgment scene that in Matthew concludes Jesus' public ministry: it is clearly an end-time setting, following Daniel's depiction, and the separation of the good from the evil (sheep and goats) follows Ezekiel 34:17; the core of the entire scene is the announcement of the criterion to be used in judgment, namely, the presence or absence of works of mercy. This criterion was well known to the Jews, but what is new here—and has "no prior analogy"[15]—is that these works are regarded as being done to the Judge, who equates himself with the poor and hungry, and so on. It is this very personal relationship with the judging Lord that will decide the individual's eternal salvation or perdition "on that day" (Mt 8:22). Although, in accordance with the ancient concept of the "Day of the Lord", "all the nations" (Mt 25:32; cf. Rev 1:7) are assembled in this scene, it is not nations that are judged but only individual persons.

It is well known that, in contrast to the apocryphal writings, the New Testament engages in practically no speculation about

---

[15] W. Grundmann, *Das Evangelium nach Matthaus* (Berlin: Evangelische Verlagsanstalt, 1968), 525.

a supposed intermediate state between the individual's death and the (final) Judgment. While a majority of the apocryphal writings assume that death is immediately followed by blessedness or its forfeiture, and that this state is not determined by a "particular" Judgment,[16] the New Testament makes very few references to it (Lk 16:22ff.; 23:43; Phil 1:23; 2 Cor 5:1ff.; Jude 6: the fallen angels are held in chains until the Judgment); evidently the New Testament is not interested in this theoretical hiatus. The ideas of individual death and final judgment are so loosely connected that Paul has no difficulty in saying that he is certain of being with Christ immediately upon dying (Phil 1:23), while shortly afterward (3:11) he can say that he would like to imitate Christ in his death, "that if possible I may attain the resurrection from the dead". On the one hand, he hopes that, after death, he will not be found naked, but "clothed with a heavenly dwelling"; on the other, he speaks of having to appear before the "judgment seat of Christ" (2 Cor 5:2, 10)—undoubtedly the Christ of the end-time. Why does the New Testament differ from the apocryphal speculations here? It can only be that the New Testament reflects from within the Christ-event, where this hiatus has been radically overcome. Thus the New Testament writers are thinking neither in the linear time of Jewish eschatology nor in the terms of that anthropology which is latent in Christology.

Ultimately, however, it is the Johannine, purely christological eschatology that retains its validity. As we have shown, it can include occasional references to the "Last Day", but treats them as belonging to the sphere of the Christ-event in its power to judge and save. This means that, apart from unimportant and incidental vestiges of Jewish eschatology, *the New Testament no longer entertains the idea of a self-unfolding horizontal theo-drama; there is only a vertical theo-drama in which every moment of time, insofar as it has christological significance, is directly related to the exalted Lord, who has taken the entire content of all history—life, death and resurrection —with him into the supra-temporal realm.*

[16] Volz, *Eschatologie*, sec. 38, "Die Lehre von der Vergeltung im Zwischenzustand und die endgültige Entscheidung über den Einzelnen gleich beim Tod", 256–72. This heading is somewhat misleading insofar as there is no mention of a particular judgment, except in the Greek "Life of Adam" (263). The "judgment" is always a single act at the chronological end of history.

5. Jewish and Pagan Ideas of the "End" Are Fulfilled and Transcended

For Christians, the end for which Jews continue to wait is already at hand. From a theological point of view, nothing more is possible and nothing more is to be expected in world history over and above the fact of the Christ-event, apart from its interpretation and its continuing effects, both of which, henceforth, more and more provoke and stimulate the dramatic action within history. For Christians, accordingly, from the outset, it is not simply that individual prophetic passages of the (Old Testament) Scriptures are fulfilled: "the scriptures" in their entirety are fulfilled (1 Cor 15:3, 4; Lk 24:45; Jn 5:39).[1] At the same time the Jewish expectation of the end is raised to a new plane in that, as a result of Jesus' Cross, descent to hell, Resurrection and return to the Father, the linear scheme has been interrupted and abrogated (for the "new aeon" is not the continuation of the doomed "old aeon"). From now on world history comes under the authority of the exalted Lord; since he is both earthly and ascended, he controls—"from above"—everything that is theologically relevant in this earthly history (cf. Eph 4:10ff.).

As we see in Peter's address in the Temple, if Jewish hopes still have any substance in terms of salvation history, it is within the Christian, not the Jewish, dispensation. God will "send the Messiah appointed for you" at the end of world-time, but this Messiah is the "Jesus" whom the Jews refused to recognize and "whom heaven must receive until the time for establishing all that God spoke" (Acts 3:21). But he for whom the Jews should hope is no longer a merely future Messiah, and accordingly Peter urges them to repent immediately (v. 19), because God has already "fulfilled" (v. 18) what they are still regarding as a promise for the future. This both fulfills and transcends the apocalyptic idea of a preexistent Messiah or Son of Man

[1] On the special meaning of this plural in 1 Corinthians 15, cf. Karl Lehmann's important remarks in *Auferweckt am dritten Tag nach der Schrift*, QD 38 (Herder, 1968), esp. 262–90. But since the watershed of the new reality actually occurs in the *triduum mortis*, it is boldly asserted that "the scriptures" in their entirety refer to these same events of the "end", e.g., "by the mouth of all the prophets" (Acts 3:18; cf. Lk 24:46).

dwelling with God in heaven: he is no longer purely a figure of the other world but also a figure of *this* world; it is because of his earthly history that God has elevated him to be the norm of all history.

Since what is *final*, "of the end", is now *present*, a further element of (late) Jewish eschatology is rendered obsolete, namely, the attempt to calculate the time of the Messiah's advent and (theologically) to discern periods within world history.[2] Apocalyptic prophecy was largely this kind of prediction of future historical events according to a divine plan revealed to a seer.[3] As we have already shown (*Theo-Drama* IV, 26ff.), it would be a mistake to assume that the Johannine Apocalypse, in setting forth its visions in sequence and furnishing them with numerical details, is adopting this division of history into periods; it is concerned solely with the law that characterizes a Christian theology of history, namely, the law of the "ever-more", the law of continual heightening within the same fundamental structure. No: according to the Gospel of John in particular, the Messiah who is supposedly "hidden" in heaven is the same who has been hidden, misunderstood and rejected on earth. True, he *is* described as hidden from the Jews, and even from Christians themselves (Col 3:3), but the latter remain in touch with him in an entirely different way: in fact, he is visible to them in a spiritual manner (Jn 14:19) in faith, hope and love, and he is in relationship with them through the sacraments and through the way they live by his word; and none of this is possible to the Jew who is waiting for the Messiah to be manifested.

Pagan eschatology, if we can consider it such, seems to have a certain prima facie affinity with Christian eschatology because of its essentially vertical structure, at least in the mystery cults that, in different ways, share a special interest in dying and rising divinities. This affinity is also seen, later, in the gnostic systems that speak of a redeemer who comes down from heaven and, having completed his saving work, returns thither. First of all

---

[2] On these calculations and schemes, cf. P. Volz, *Die Eschatologie der jüdischen Gemeinde* (Tübingen: Mohr, 1934), sec. 36, 135–37.

[3] Cf. *Ethiopic Enoch*, the "Book of History", chaps. 83–90, and the "Ten Week Apocalypse", chaps. 93, 91.

we must focus on these elements, particularly as the "history of religions" school at the beginning of the century, and subsequently Bultmann, attempted to show that these forms of religion had influenced the shape of the message about Christ. We are less concerned with other ideas, such as the notion that a cosmic primal man has been fragmented and will be reintegrated at the time of the end—a notion that, some allege, is behind certain of Paul's theologoumena (the "first" and "second" Adam, the ecclesial-cosmic "body of Christ").

Late New Testament writings are at pains to distance themselves from what they call "myths", which are no more substantial than "fables" (1 Tim 1:4; 4:7; 2 Tim 4:4; Titus 1:14; 2 Pet 1:16). Of course this does not refer to the "mysteries" or gnostic teachings on redemption we have just mentioned: it refers to futile, inquisitive theories within the Christian community, propagated by "arrogant" "babblers" on the basis of late Jewish (Titus 1:14) speculation on Scripture; such things are a danger to faith. Yet these too—though we have so little knowledge of the individual teachings—represent an early form of Gnosticism and are surely not uninfluenced by the attempts to revamp the old (Homeric) myths. Such attempts, no doubt involving much "deception" (*goētēs*: 2 Tim 3:13) and worse (the rank growth of magic at the time), were made in Ephesus and Crete, and it is to these communities that the Pastoral Epistles are addressed.[4]

Even at this early stage in the dispute with the phenomenon of myth—which, in the great gnostic systems, will deliberately develop its vertical structure contrary to Christianity—the Christian is given a clear view of the fundamental opposition between it and Christian teaching. On the one hand, there is inconsistent, futile and confusing speculation, "disputing about words" (2 Tim 2:14); on the other, "God's firm foundation", "sound teaching" as taught by the Church, the "pillar and bulwark of the truth": namely, the mystery of Christ, "manifested in the flesh" (1 Tim 3:15-16). Right from Paul and John up to Ignatius, Irenaeus and Tertullian, this "in the

---

[4] On the "myths" mentioned in the Pastorals, cf. C. Spicq, *Les Épîtres Pastorales*, 4th ed. (Paris: Gabalda, 1969), I, 85-119.

flesh" is the central argument against all the mythical teachings on redemption, however similar they may seem to Christianity, and whether they are pre-Christian or copies of the Christian teaching. The vertical systems of non-Christian Gnosticism may have arisen from a dramatization of philosophical speculations (for example, the worldly multiplicity having fallen from the divine unity)[5] and so call for a reintegration. But such systems, even when dramatized in this way, are necessarily anti-material. That the unifying principle itself should actually enter into a body (and an individual body at that) is something that must contradict them. All Christian teaching proceeds from the experience of the bodily Resurrection of Christ, which is by no means mythical and speculative but sober and historical; and this Resurrection illuminates the truth and the meaning of his Cross and, behind it, of his entire Incarnation. "Christ's Resurrection from the dead, as proclaimed by the oldest kerygma, is not a myth."[6] Sometimes it is suggested that, in John for instance, the pattern of the Redeemer's descent from God and ascent to God is gnostic: this is contradicted by the fact, first, that John is quite clearly interpreting historical events and, second, that he lays very heavy stress on the Incarnation, right up to the final scene with Thomas, right up to the Epistle that says that "we have seen with our eyes, . . . we have looked upon and touched with our hands" (1 Jn 1:1). Anyone who attempts to "dissolve" this Incarnation is an Antichrist.[7]

In the face of this basic datum, all the vestiges of mythical ideas, of mythical thinking and speaking in the New Testament shrink to purely formal ways of expressing something that is completely new and unique.[8] Without the images, archetypes

[5] Esp. Festugière, *La Révélation d'Hermès Trismégiste* I–IV (Paris: Gabalda, 1950–1954).

[6] H. Schlier, "Das Neue Testament und der Mythus" in *Besinnung auf das Neue Testament* (Herder, 1964), 83–96, esp. 88.

[7] In his *Krisis, Untersuchungen zur johanneischen Christologie und Eschatologie* (Freiburg: Lambertus, 1964), passim J. Blank establishes (against Bultmann) this opposition between John and Gnosticism.

[8] What once were myths have now faded to mere "conventional symbols that have finally come to be used as the formal tools for understanding and illustrating the processes of salvation": H. Schlier, "Das Neue Testament", 86–87.

and concepts necessary for human pictorial language, even God's word cannot make itself intelligible to man; furthermore, man's (even sinful man's) relation to God necessarily gives him a certain "pre-understanding" of what God's "redemption" might be, even if the (mythical) images man draws up are subsequently transcended and completely refashioned by what God actually does. Of necessity, a Redeemer must come from God (and hence "from above") and break down the wall that separates the sinner from God. "But it is Jesus Christ who, in his Incarnation, has breached the world's wall and has completed the entire work of salvation that the myth so dreamed of and longed for. He accomplished this, not mythically, but in real historical terms 'through his Cross'; it was through his Cross that he set out for heaven."[9] "From this vantage point there can be no 'demythologizing' of the New Testament."[10]

The text of 2 Peter 1:16 is very characteristic: "For we did not follow cleverly devised myths when we made known to you the power and coming of our Lord Jesus Christ, but we were eye-witnesses of his majesty." There follows a description of the Transfiguration on Tabor. In other words, knowledge of the *dynamis*, that is, of the divine power that the exalted Christ now has, and of his *parousia*, his coming in glory, rests on a historical experience on the part of Peter when "we were with him on the holy mountain": there they saw his earthly flesh irradiated with divinity. Here, even Christ's return in glory is anticipated in a historical event that provides us with some "pre-understanding" of it. And this pre-understanding, the passage goes on to say, thus confirms all prophecy; for prophecy is a lamp shining for us in the darkness of this life, "until the day dawns" (v. 19). In Johannine terms, we have already "seen his glory" in the Incarnation of the Word; and on the Cross we have seen the full extent of his "glorification", which—going beyond the distinction between "this world" and "the other world"—is the beginning of the vision of that "glory" that the Word of God "had . . . before the world was made" (Jn 17:5).

---

[9] *Ibid.*, 93–94.
[10] *Ibid.*, 95.

So the eschatology oriented to Christ is seen to be something qualitatively new vis-à-vis both Jewish and pagan teaching on the "end", even if occasionally it is formulated in inherited images and concepts.

B. THE SUBJECT MATTER
OF THIS VOLUME

The brief critical survey of what is customarily regarded as Christian eschatology has shown us what we may and may not expect of this concluding volume of *Theo-Drama*. But is this volume really necessary?

We have already set forth the theodramatic "action", so why do we need to elaborate on the "final act"? The question seems justified, since the action itself could not have been described without revealing its *ultimate* theme, namely, the world's "ever-greater" (that is, ever-increasing) resistance to the "ever-greater" divine, incarnate love. This theme, however, was not static, for it governed the dynamic course of the drama; accordingly the *dénouement* had to come to light, at least to some extent; it lay, fundamentally, in the Cross, which is the acceptance of this "ever-greater", (ever-increasing) resistance to God.

This leaves us, however, with a whole series of open questions, crystallizing around the central question: Can divine freedom, even if it is the freedom of love, simply "overpower" created freedom? On the other hand, if, as Irenaeus and the Fathers used to maintain, the divine freedom operates "by persuasion, not by force",[1] can it be sure of attaining its goals? In the latter case, surely, may we not have to envisage a final refusal, resulting in a final rejection?

Is there a way forward here for a *theologia viatorum*? Or must it not quite legitimately call a halt when faced with the ultimate, the *eschaton*? Furthermore, if we are to speak, in earthly theology, of "eschatology", what do we mean by it?

Leaving aside for the moment the question of the fate of finite freedom, we shall find that the path we have so far described in dramatic terms will help us toward an answer. Our starting point was the interplay of infinite and finite freedom (vol. II), where

---

[1] Irenaeus, *Adv. Haer.* V, 11: "Non cum vi, sed secundum suadelem". Epistle to Diognetus: "[God] has sent [his Son] as was proper: as a rescuer, a persuader, not as an enforcer. For there is no violence in God" (7, 4 Marrou, SC 33, 68). "Neminem enim invitum vicit Christus, sed suasione (peithōn), cum sit Verbum Dei": Origen, *Sel. in Ps.* (PG 12, 1133 B).

God only came within sight as the One. Then (vol. III) we
discerned the figure of the God-man, making possible and embracing all that is creaturely; this revealed (in "Christology")
an initial glimpse of the divine Trinity. Confronted with the
world's alienation from God (in vol. IV), Christology changed
into "soteriology". Further insight was granted here into the
trinitarian depths of God, but the topic was not yet discussed
as such. All the same it is clear that the Trinity, and not Christology, is the last horizon of the revelation of God in himself
and in his dramatic relationship with the world. This is the true
eschaton as seen from the theocentric, not the anthropocentric,
perspective. In any case, the latter is out of place in a science
of revelation; we may only discuss the anthropological *eschata*—
traditionally man's death, judgment and final destiny—within
the framework of a theocentric eschatology. This rule will be
adopted here, in the concluding volume, as in the others.

Not only must we begin once more (and in a new way) with
the question of the *imago trinitatis* in the creature and seek a new
understanding of the dramatic interplay between God and man
on the basis of the justness (*rectitudo*: Augustine, Anselm) or the
perversion of this image; we must also give God's "time" primacy over the "time" of the creature, whose future, past and
present must be measured by and orientated according to God's
mode of duration. In concrete terms this would mean that God's
presence for man, which is the presence of the "ever-greater",
is always something coming toward him (*avenir*) of which he is
not the master; this it *could not be* if it were merely "what has not
yet happened" (that is, the unknown, *futur*) and not at the same
time "what has always been". It is right, therefore, that human
faith (in what has taken place historically in Jesus Christ) should
exhibit an inner dimension of hope[2] and that God's *mysterium*
that has come—and this is not only the Old Testament view but
definitively that of the New—is always the expected *mysterium*,
"that which is to come": indeed, it cannot be the *present mysterium* in any other way. It must not be envisaged, however, (and

---

[2] F. Kerstiens, *Die Hoffnungsstruktur des Glaubens* (Mainz, 1968). For an assess-
ment of Kerstiens: R. Schaeffler, *Was dürfen wir hoffen? Die katholische Theologie der
Hoffnung zwischen Blochs utopischem Denken und der reformierten Rechtfertigungslehre*
(Darmstadt, 1979), 179–99.

this is fundamental) according to extensions of anthropological time—for in this case Christian hope would extend toward a worldly *futurum*—but primarily according to divine or, rather, christological "time", in which anthropological time is assumed into the divine form of duration. Of course, "assumed" does not mean "annihilated", as if human time is rendered meaningless; but it does mean that this human time and all that takes place in it, and everything of Christian significance that is yet to take place, becomes dependent on Christ's "time" and its unique mode of duration. This must be particularly borne in mind in a "theology of hope".

Clearly, the Johannine eschatology we have already described will be of central importance in this volume. We have seen that it can be called "realized" eschatology only with certain reservations; the term can be misleading unless it is used to refer, not to anthropological, but to christological time (with, behind it, the trinitarian mode of duration). Everything that is understood anthropologically as the doctrine of the "last things" must be integrated in and subordinated to this trinitarian "time".

The real "last thing" is the triune life of God disclosed in Jesus Christ. Naturally this Omega also implies the Alpha; it is what is present, first and last, in every "now". And what is this but Being itself? For apart from Being there is "only nothing", while within it there is that mysterious vitality disclosed through christological revelation, so that everything that comes from absolute Being must bear its seal, with revelation giving us access to the fount of God's life. Theo-drama, in its final act, in its final aspect, can only be trinitarian.

I. THE WORLD IS FROM GOD

A. THE WORLD IS FROM THE TRINITY

1. The Scholastic Axiom

For High Scholasticism, creation is embraced within the Trinity, which is its inalienable precondition. "The possibility of creation rests in the reality of the Trinity. A non-trinitarian God could not be the Creator."[1]

Thomas makes this lucidly clear in the celebrated prologue to the *Sentences*. In creation, the Son, the Wisdom of God, "has caused streams to flow from him". "Flumina ista intelligo fluxus aeternae processionis, qua Filius a Patre et Spiritus Sanctus ab utroque ineffabili modo procedit." Initially these streams remained hidden within the creature's "likeness" role and in the riddles of the Old Covenant Scripture; in becoming man, the Son brings them to light. But this incarnate Son is from all eternity "the image of the (triune) God and (to that extent) the firstborn of all creation, for in him all things hold together."

> So it is rightly said of the Son's Person, "I am an arm (*trames*) of the river's infinite waters"—which indicates the *order* and *manner* of creation. The *order*, since, just as the arm is part of the river, so the temporal procession of creatures comes from the eternal procession of the Persons. . . . For the source is always the cause of what comes afterward; thus the first procession is the cause and ground of all subsequent processions. As to the *manner*, it is indicated in two ways. First, from the standpoint of the one who creates, who, while he fills everything, is not an attribute of anything (which shows us the meaning of the word "infinite"); and, second, from the standpoint of that which is created: for, just as the arm of the river is an extension of the riverbed, so the creature comes forth from the unity of the Divine Being, which, like the river bed, contains the flowings-forth of the Persons.

So when the Son becomes man, he "comes forth from paradise like an aqueduct", and "though he does not lose the paradise of the Father's glory, he conceals it"; he directs into creation those streams of grace—the Church, the sacraments, the vari-

[1] A. Gerken, *Theologie des Wortes* (Düsseldorf: Patmos, 1963), 81.

ous orders of saints—that ultimately "flow from the wound in his side".[2]

Thomas continually repeats this teaching. For him, naturally, the entire triune God is active in creation, in the wisdom and goodness of his being, but also, and in particular, according to the order of Persons within the Godhead: "Thus God the Father effects creation by his Word, who is the Son, and by his love, who is the Holy Spirit. Thus it is the processions of the Persons that cause the generation of creatures, to the extent that they include attributes of being, namely, of knowing and willing."[3] The power of the Creator belongs primarily to the Father by a certain order, "*ordine quodam*".[4] The birth of the Son from the Father "is the foundation of every birth out of what is other than itself, for it alone, quite naturally, seizes the entire nature of the One who generates; other births only do this in an imperfect manner. . . . All subsequent births, consequently, are deduced from this primal birth by way of a certain imitation. . . . The same is true of the Holy Spirit."[5] If we consider "the substance, as it were, of this ability" (to generate), the processions within the Godhead and the creative processions are "not only to be viewed together: they are actually one. The fact that we call them 'analogous' arises from the direction of the act."[6] "For the procession of Persons in unity of essence is the cause of the procession of creatures in diversity of essence."[7]

Since Thomas always regards world process as a procession (a "going-out") from God and a "return to him", what we have said here must apply to both aspects. With regard to the procession of creatures from God,

> two things must be borne in mind: first, the *nature*, from whose fullness and perfection every creaturely perfection is produced and in which it has its blueprint; and, second, the will, whose *generosity*

[2] *1 Sent.* prol. (Moos I, 1-5); "Ex processione personarum divinarum distinctarum causatur omnis creaturarum processio et multiplicatio": I, d 26, q 2, a 2 ad 2.

[3] Ia, 45, 6 c.

[4] *Ibid.*, ad 2.

[5] *In Boeth. de Trin.* prol. (*Opusc. theol.* II, Marietti 314).

[6] *De Pot.*, q 2, a 6 ad 3.

[7] I, d 2, div. text.

(not necessity) communicates all this to creatures. If, according to our faith, we assume the procession of the Divine Persons, . . . this perfect procession must be the cause and ground of the procession of creatures. However, just as we trace the procession of creatures, representing the perfection of the divine nature in an imperfect manner, back to the perfect prototype, the Son—who is the principle, prototype and ground of creatures' quasi-natural procession from God—this same procession of creatures, since it results from the generosity of the divine will, must be traced back to a principle that, as it were, provides the foundation for this whole, freely given communication. This is nothing other than love, which causes everything to be given willingly; so there must be in God a Person whose procession is in the manner of love, and this is the Holy Spirit. This is why certain philosophers have asserted that love is the principle of the whole created world.[8]

Nor is this enough. For just as God, in generating the Son, expresses not only himself but also his whole power as Creator (and thus, everything that God can create), "so the Father's love, which goes out toward the Son, is the basis of all the effects of love that God imparts to creatures; so too the Holy Spirit, who is the love of the Father for the Son, is also his love for the creature, since he imparts his perfection to it. So the procession of love can be regarded in two ways: insofar as it goes out to an eternal Beloved (and thus it is an eternal procession), and insofar as it is love for a created beloved . . . , and so it is termed a temporal procession, since, because of the new effect, the creature acquires a new relation to God."[9] It is clear from this that, once we presuppose the creation, *processio* within the Godhead and *missio* outside it are one and the same as far as the Divine Persons are concerned, even at the point where the Son and the Spirit enter the visible realm of creation: "sicut processio temporalis non est alia quam processio aeterna essentialiter, sed addit aliquem respectum ad effectum temporalem, ita etiam missio visibilis non

---

[8] I, d 10, q 1, a 1 sol. No doubt Thomas is thinking initially of Boethius ("amor quo coelum regitur", *Consol.* II, cant. 8). On the background and origins of the formula, cf. Cornelia J. De Vogel: "Amor quo coelum regitur. Quel amor et quel Dieu?" in *Atti del Congresso Internazionale di Studi Boeziani* (Rome, 1981), 193–200.

[9] I, d 14, q 1, a 1 sol.

est alia essentialiter ab invisibili missione."[10] With regard to the Son's and the Spirit's mission to the world, "utraque processio dicitur missio".[11]

As for the creature's return to God, it is effected, in our world order, by these same missions to the world on the part of the Son and the Spirit. This *missio* on the part of the Holy Spirit can be carried out both invisibly, by creating in man's spirit the knowledge and love of God, and visibly, as in the human form of the Son and the visible symbols of the Spirit (dove, tongues of fire, and so on). Both missions lead back to the Father, "to whom we return at last. And since, by being receptive to these two (the Son and the Spirit), we acquire an inner likeness to the specific qualities of the Persons, we may say that the Divine Persons are in us in a new mode of being, just as the prototype (*res*) is in its copy (*similitudo*); thus we are assimilated to them in a new way."[12]

We find the same teaching in Bonaventure: "God could not have brought forth the creation on the basis of his will if he had not already brought forth the Son on the basis of his nature."[13] Here again, "the Word" means both God the Father's self-expression within the Godhead *and* the expression of everything God can create *ad extra*: "In the same Word God utters both himself and creatures", since "the Word points to what is expressed by it; that is, it points not only to the Father but to what is created"[14] or can be created. Thus the same Word is "*similitudo Patris imitativa* and *similitudo rerum exemplativa et . . . operativa*."[15] The Seraphic Master goes farther than Thomas in asserting that in the Word the entire series of trinitarian processions is expressed, including the processions of the Holy Spirit. Otherwise the divine Word could not be the image of the three-personal God in creation: "Verbum et Patrem et Seipsum Sanctum exprimit—et omnia

[10] I, d 16, q 1, a 1 sol.

[11] I, d 15, q 4, a 1 sol.

[12] *Ibid.*

[13] Bonaventure, I, d 7, dub 2 (Quar. I, 144b).

[14] I, d 27, p 2, q 2 fund 4 (I, 484b).

[15] *Ibid.* c (I, 485b). Thus God's creative activity already has a "prius in eodem genere" in himself: 3, d 1, a 2, q 3 c (III, 30).

alia.''[16] At the same time the Spirit (as in Thomas) retains his own function: he is the "gift" given within the Trinity, and as such he is also God's "communicability" (*donabilitas*)[17] on the basis of his "generosity" (*liberalitas*)[18]. But this essential quality of God is—like everything—"expressed" "in the Word", so that *expressio* becomes a central category in Bonaventure, primarily expressing God's inner, personal fruitfulness.[19] This means that, first and foremost, it is this inner vitality of God that creatures will reflect more or less obscurely or brightly; what are called God's "general attributes" will only come to light as the consequence and the expression of this inner-trinitarian vitality. This is what is referred to by the axiom—which only the Christian believer can find intelligible: "De necessitate si est productio dissimilis praeintelligitur productio similis. . . . Inaequalitates oriuntur ex aequalitate."[20]

This Scholastic teaching shows that the mystery of Being is not something closed but a mystery that utters and manifests itself; at the same time it shows that this self-utterance is not a natural process subject to necessity but something freely given and freely giving. If creaturely thought is to contemplate both of these at the same time without contradiction, the inner-divine mystery must freely reveal itself. For, though essentially different from the creature, this mystery emerges as the *sine qua non* of the creature's knowledge of Being (and hence of its own self). Creaturely logic can only have a correct estimate of itself if it sees itself as participating analogously in an absolute Logos that traces its origin backward to the Father and forward to the Spirit of freely given love who pours forth from him and from him who is his Source. Formal creaturely logic, too, is grounded in the Trinity and molded by it.

---

[16] *Hexaem.* IX, 2 (V, 373).

[17] I, d 18 (I, 322ff.).

[18] I, d 6, q 3 c (I, 129b): "est donum in quo omnia dona donantur".

[19] Cf. *Hexaem.* III, 7 (V, 344).

[20] *Hexaem.* XI, 9 (V, 381).

2. Implications

a. Being—Event—Becoming

The *aequalitas* that characterizes the Divine Persons does not mean identity, unless by that we mean their identity in the one divine essence (*essentia*) or absolute Being (*esse*), in whose concreteness they are identical at every point "except where the distinct relationships [between the Persons] requires otherwise". But since each Person, existing as one element in the stream of processions, is per se identical with God's essence or being, there is no question of the latter being regarded as a fourth thing, aloof from the busy to-and-fro of what passes between the Persons: no, it must be identical with it. If we take this seriously, it will be impossible to engage in the kind of reflection upon the "divine attributes" that, starting only from the divine essence or absolute Being, excludes from consideration the internal processions within the Godhead (as commonly happens in treatises *De Deo Uno*). For example, with regard to the creation of the universe, it is quite possible to speak of God's almighty power, but at the same time, on the basis of the trinitarian events, one must ponder the way in which the triune God wishes to be almighty. He wishes to be almighty not solely by creating: by begetting and breathing forth, and allowing himself to be begotten and breathed forth, he hands over his power to the Other—whoever that Other may be—without ever seeking to take it back. If one wanted to see this "limitation" of the divine power that pertains to each of the Persons as a "necessary" limitation within the trinitarian process, that is, as a kind of "powerlessness", it would be possible to reconcile these two sides of the divine power (genuine omnipotence and the genuine handing over of power) in the higher concept of absolute love, which ultimately can be spoken of only in *De Deo Trino*. The same procedure would have to be carried out with regard to all the other attributes that are exclusively predicated of the divine essence. The fact that certain of these attributes become visible in the Old Covenant—for example, the divine mercy that averts a strictly speaking just sentence (cf. Hos 11:8-9)—at a time when the triune process is not as yet perceived, shows how Old Covenant theology is moving along a path; unless it is fulfilled in the theology of the New Covenant, it is always in danger of slipping into a gnostic theosophy. (This is what happened in the initial stage, when God was split into Yahweh and his *shekinah*, which was "banished" in the world; later the split became explicit in the Cabala.) Accordingly, Christian theology has to hold on unswervingly to the fact that the God who manifests himself in Jesus Christ exists in himself as an eternal essence (or Being), which is an equally eternal (that is, not temporal) "happening"; when we ponder God's being, we must not forget this fact for an instant.[1] Indeed, from the perspective of the New Covenant we must say that the revelation of God that takes place in Jesus Christ is primarily a trinitarian one: Jesus does not speak about God in general but shows us the Father and gives us the Holy Spirit. Thus it is on the basis of Jesus' trinitarian relationship with God that we should construct a picture of the divine "essence" and "being"; for the latter manifests itself, in the historical "happening" of Jesus himself, as an eternal "happening".

What happens in the Trinity is, however, far more than a motionless order or sequence, for expressions such as "beget", "give birth", "proceed" and "breathe forth" refer to eternal acts in which God genuinely "takes place". We must resolve to see these two apparently contradictory concepts as a unity: eternal or absolute Being—and "happening". This "happening" is not a becoming in the earthly sense: it is the coming-to-be, not of something that once was not (that would be Arianism), but, evidently, of something that grounds the idea, the inner possibility and reality of a becoming. All earthly becoming is a reflection of the eternal "happening" in God, which, we repeat, is per se identical with the eternal Being or essence.

Let us examine this "reflection" in more detail. Within the confines of the world there is an all-pervasive distinction, the most mysterious distinction with which philosophy has to deal: the distinction between the unity of all existing beings that

[1] At best, the distinction between the treatises *De Deo Uno* and *De Deo Trino* has an apologetic usefulness, insofar as it is addressed to people who believe in God and who are to be confirmed in the faith they have before coming to embrace the trinitarian mystery. In New Testament theology, however, the distinction cannot be maintained.

share in being and the unity of each individual being in the
uniqueness and incommunicability of its particular being. We
cannot dissolve this distinction by taking the first member of
the unity as the highest of the genera (*ens commune*) that unites
all genera, species and individual beings by subordinating them
to itself; for, in the first place, the second member, being-as-an-
individual, belongs to the same concept of being; moreover, the
"concept" of reality is not exhausted by the uncountable multitude of things that exist more or less by accident. (Countless
others could become a reality, coming forth, as it were, from the
abyss of unity between the actual that grounds the potential and
the potential that brings things into actuality—while not being
self-subsistent.) Every limited being (*essentia*) participates in real
being (in the *actus essendi*), but none of them is identical with it,
nor can the totality of limited beings exhaust it.[2] From Thomas
onward this mystery is called the "real distinction". Evidently,
this specifically creaturely constitution of being has something
to do with the distinction in God between that being which is
common to the Persons and the qualities that distinguish them,
although the "real distinction" is a characteristic of the creature
in its irreducible otherness vis-à-vis God. Modern thinkers have
tried in various ways, on the basis of the fundamentally developmental process of the world and illuminated by the light of faith,
to discern the primal trinitarian mystery behind this process.

It must suffice here to indicate three attempts at a trinitarian
interpretation of the world's being. The first is the "sketch of
a trinitarian ontology" (*Entwurf einer trinitarischen Ontologie*) by
Clemens Kaliba, a pupil of Heidegger.[3] For him (as for Gustav
Siewerth, whom he follows) non-subsistent being, which is the

---

[2] "Quia (intellectus noster) in ipsum (Deum) devenire non potest nisi ex effec-
tus similitudine, neque in creatura invenit aliquod perfectum quod omnino imper-
fectione careat, ideo ex diversis perfectionibus in creaturis repertis ipsum nititur
designare, ita tamen quod quidquid alicui istarum perfectionum imperfectionis
adjungitur, totum a Deo amoveatur. Verbi gratia esse significat aliquid *completum
et simplex, sed non subsistens*, substantia autem aliquid subsistens significat, sed alii
subjectum. Ponimus ergo in Deo substantiam et esse, sed substantiam ratione sub-
sistentiae non ratione substandi, esse vero ratione simplicitatis et complementi,
non ratione inhaerentiae, qua alteri inhaeret" *De pot.* q 1, a 1 c.

[3] *Die Welt als Gleichnis des dreieinigen Gottes* (Salzburg: O. Müller, 1952).

creative ground from which all self-being proceeds, in direct contact with God, who is pure being, is God's first image and likeness. This is because, transcending all finitude[4] but receiving from God that world-idea [*Weltidee*] which is the epitome of all finite essences,[5] it posits itself as real in the degrees of self-being [*Selbstsein*]. These degrees are approximations, in the terms of this world, to absolute Being, and as such are a preliminary representation of the latter's trinitarian nature: first of all the sphere of existence, then that of consciousness that is based upon it, and finally—based on both these spheres and transcending them[6]—the "I" that is the "root of all knowing". (With regard to consciousness, the two aspects must be seen as inseparable, namely, the world's objective illumination and penetration by the light of reflection, and man's subjective involvement, through his senses, in such penetration.) The finite "I", in turn, can be seen to possess "volition, cognition and conation, whereby it masters being (which it needs for its fulfillment) and becomes master of itself".[7] At this point Kaliba is giving his own version of the Augustinian *imago trinitatis in anima*. The way he describes the relationship of these distinct faculties governs the view of the trinitarian mystery that follows. On the one hand, the will, freely positing itself, is the primal substratum of the person, determining everything else—albeit in a finitude that can never fully grasp its self-posited existence; this will locates rationality in the grasp of self and of being, albeit (again) in a finitude within which all being must be "let be". Then, from this twofold grasp (of self and of being) emerges the feeling of self [*Selbst-Gefühl*], its fundamental faculty, its self-affirmation as "good", its complete circle of interiority—which again, since it is finite, is absolutely open to the infinite Good. This is what Augustine calls the insatiable *desiderium*. From the three faculties, and "from the same origin", arises freedom,[8] which can be considered to be "self-possession" only insofar as it stretches out toward the "divine idea", the freest possible model of fulfillment for this freedom.[9] It must be noted, however, that the will could

---

[4] *Ibid.*, 165.
[6] *Ibid.*, 49.
[8] *Ibid.*, 92.

[5] *Ibid.*, 33f.
[7] *Ibid.*, 51.
[9] *Ibid.*, 121.

not "posit itself as free and active" without the "rational will
that grasps itself as free and rational"; the two form "an inner
unity" and emerge "at the same moment";[10] nor could will and
rationality posit themselves without the "I's" concomitant sense
of itself. Thus there exists between the faculties a genuine order
and at the same time a genuine *circum-incessio*.

When he turns to contemplate the nature of the Trinity (which
is only possible because of the Christian revelation), Kaliba does
so with great caution. For in the first place it can be objected
against a directly analogous application of the above results that
the triadic structure of the finite "I" owes its inner distinctions
to its finitude; accordingly, in *infinite* being, which is as such a
subsistent self, the differences disappear, initially at least. It cannot be denied "that the distinction of spiritual powers in the
infinite reality of pure Being ceases to be a real distinction and
survives only as a virtual distinction; consequently it cannot directly provide the basis for a real distinction between the three
Divine Persons."[11] Nonetheless God's "I" [*Ichsein*], by contrast
with the creature's "I", has "complete control of his existence"
[*Dasein*] "in the identity of existence and will".[12] This will is a
rational will that posits itself with equal spontaneity and autonomy as an "I"; this is only possible if, with like spontaneity, the
Spirit, that is, the conjunction of will and reason in the blissful
awareness of being a self in all its dimensions, forms this identical self as a third "I" [*Ichsein*].

So we arrive at the following structure. The Godhead: "Pure
Being posits itself, knows itself and is aware of itself. God the
Father: the self-positing 'I' that knows itself and is aware of itself
as such. God the Son: the self-knowing 'I' that posits itself and is
aware of itself. God the Holy Spirit: the self-aware 'I' that posits
and knows itself".[13] This brings us to Kaliba's central thesis,
namely, "that no spontaneous origin [*Ursprung*] can exist apart
from the other spontaneous origins. Since there is no process
of development in the Godhead, all origins are interrelated by
way of anticipation or consequence."[14] "What is original, what

[10] *Ibid.*, 58–59.   [11] *Ibid.*, 129.
[12] *Ibid.*, 130.   [13] *Ibid.*, 134.
[14] *Ibid.*, 141.

springs forth, is already, in its own way, the originator of other things, causing them to spring forth; from its very origin it facilitates their springing-forth. . . . No relationship springs forth that has not already sprung forth in the original, playing its part in grounding its own origin."[15] "The Father's self-knowledge is grounded in the act of generation and is at the same time the basis on which generation is possible. . . . If a particular origin were to condition the other origins without being similarly conditioned by them (retroactively and in advance), such origins would not be origins of pure Being. An origin cannot be an origin in isolation: it must be so together with other origins."[16] "The divine Logos and the Holy Spirit are the common a priori origin of the Father as a self-positing holy Person, just as Father and Son are the common genetic origin of the Holy Spirit."[17]

It is not necessary here to repeat our survey of the created world, in which we uncovered the trinitarian structure that informs it, or our portrayal of the supernatural elevation whereby the "likeness" of the Trinity is enabled to participate in the life of the Trinity of which it is a copy. We simply need to ask one question: Does this equation of the genetic processions with the *circumincessio* of the Persons (on the basis of an identical Self or essence) give us a true picture of that clear relationship between the processions that is familiar to us from the texts of revelation? Or does the attempt to exclude from God, not only all development, but even anything analogous to development actually cause us to lose an essential aspect of Jesus' self-disclosure? In the present volume we shall try to give an answer to this question.

First, however, we shall outline a further attempt, this time on the part of a scientist, to uncover an analogy between the triune God and the triune constitution of the world's being: *Wilhelm Moock*, in his *Briefen über die Heilige Dreifaltigkeit* (*Letters on the Holy Trinity*),[18] adduces astonishing examples. Although he does not speak in terms of "real distinctions", the question

---

[15] *Ibid.*, 142.

[16] *Ibid.*, 151. The consequence is also what grounds such consequence: 150; as applied to the Holy Spirit: 154, 160 ("The Holy Spirit not only proceeds from the other two Persons: he is the a priori basis of their fellowship as loving Persons").

[17] *Ibid.*, 163.

[18] Dülmen: Laumann, 1940.

between *esse subsistens* (God) and *non subsistens* (the basis of creaturely reality) does exist for him too, in the form: "What is the
relationship between the unity of created nature, which is the
precondition for everything, and the uncreated unity of God?"[19]
The unity of all world-being exists in a "fatherly"[20] relation to
individual forms; itself seemingly formless, it brings forth individual forms (thereby showing itself to be "true").[21] At the same
time we must note that no form can stand in isolation but only
in a context;[22] moreover, form shows itself to be "reality" (and
hence as "good") only when there is reciprocal communication
between it and the unity that has produced it. It must exist in
vital rhythm with this unity; it must keep returning to it in an
"ordered movement."[23] Being is a "giving and taking" between
the unity and the form;[24] so is the beauty of the real, a "game"
that, in world process, is a dialogue between periodic movement
and progression (although these two ultimately coincide.)[25]

This ontology confirms once again the course we are taking
in our entire endeavor. *The Glory of the Lord* (*Herrlichkeit*) took
as its starting point that "form" (of the incarnate Word, Jesus
Christ) which was true and radiant ("glorious") only insofar as
it proclaimed its origin in the unity of the Father and returned
thither in the Holy Spirit. But this "proclamation" and this "return" take place in a *Theo-Drama* (*Theodramatik*) that, both in
inner-worldly terms and in the economy of redemption, reveals
an eternal Trinity in intense motion and interaction. Moock's
work points in the same direction. He emphasizes the unfathomable depth of the paternal unity that, in God, is able to express its own fullness in a *single* Word,[26] whereas the depths of
created nature—"created by God according to the image of his
infinite abyss"[27]—already contains that unity of existing things
that continues to bring forth the latter through infinite spaces
and millions of years. (N.B.: The process of evolution does not
show gradual transitions[28] but rather the sudden emergence—
on the basis of inchoate forms [Dollo's law]—of new approxi-

[19] *Ibid.*, 132f.   [20] *Ibid.*, 20.
[21] *Ibid.*, 27ff.   [22] *Ibid.*, 140.
[23] *Ibid.*, 59, 63, 70f., 207.   [24] *Ibid.*, 64.
[25] *Ibid.*, 197.   [26] *Ibid.*, 12.
[27] *Ibid.*, 137f.   [28] *Ibid.*, 97.

mations to the form ultimately intended.)[29] What is essential for us is, first, the fundamental trinitarian constitution of all finite being ("the interplay between unity and form")[30] and, second, the event character of everything (including absolute Being) that comes forth from its fruitful depths to be manifested as *true* in its form and *good* in its origin and in its return to it. In God, however, this return means "not that the event character is at an end . . . but that it is, as it were, held fast and rendered eternal *in statu nascendi*, as the chemists say. It is eternally new, there is no time between beginning and end, and yet it is eternally unchangeable, not an ossified movement, but the origin of all movement; not movement itself, but the mother of movement."[31] Thus an ontology can speak of unity, form and rhythm: "The trinitarian reality also sets the pattern for creatures."[32]

Before moving on we refer briefly to the highly concentrated and aphoristic *Thesen zu einer trinitarischen Ontologie* (Theses on a trinitarian ontology), by the philosopher of religion *Klaus Hemmerle*.[33] If mankind is to understand God's Word that is uttered to the world, philosophy is presupposed; conversely, this means that man's finite reason must exhibit an openness beyond itself if it is to be receptive to the divine speech.[34] On the basis of this twofold, reciprocal a priori of philosophy and theology, Hemmerle asserts that, while Christian theology's adoption and adaptation of secular (Greek) philosophy did make significant advances toward a new understanding of Being in its totality,[35] nonetheless there remained a certain "historical deficit of Christian ontology": "What is distinctively Christian did not . . . ultimately refashion the anticipatory understanding of the sense of being."[36] The foundation of this ontology remained the question, "What remains?" (—substance in its identity), and "What changes?" (—what is accidental and in motion). If, within the horizon of Christology and hence of God's self-revelation, the New Testament answer had been given: "What abides is love", this would surely have resulted in the expansion of philosophy's world-bound ontology. For love "abides" only by giving itself,

---

[29] *Ibid.*, 156f.

[30] *Ibid.*, 79, 204.

[31] *Ibid.*, 215.

[32] *Ibid.*, 219.

[33] Einsiedeln: Johannes Verlag, 1976.

[34] *Ibid.*, 16–18.

[35] *Ibid.*, 36, 53f.

[36] *Ibid.*, 21–22.

right from its very first source, just as Jesus' self-giving for the
world shows that he is given up by the Father. So we see that
what is primary is not the substantial *noun* (substantive) but the
transitive *verb*; we begin "with happening, action, consummation".[37] But "to give oneself" is not to lose oneself; it is the essential realization of oneself. *Ekstasis* and *enstasis* are one, simply
the two sides of the same thing. "If it is by going out of ourselves
that we come to ourselves, if self-emptying is the dawn of authentic being", it follows that "analysis and synthesis, being and
happening, state and event, freedom and necessity" imply each
other.[38] "Giving does not retain what it has but contains what
it gives."[39] In bolder terms it can be said that "self-giving preserves its identity by giving itself away. By relinquishing itself,
it preserves itself. Through innovation (freedom, synthesis) it
remains identical (necessity, analysis). . . . And this identity has
its origin in the event, in the innovation of self-giving."[40] Of
course this does not mean that everything needs to dissolve in
functionalism or dialectic, least of all at the end of the modern
period! To counter this we have the philosophical interpretation
of being that, in the form of the theological a priori, attains its
full sphere of influence in the Christian reality: the economic
Trinity, which has become understandable in Jesus Christ and
which points back to the immanent, absolute Trinity. It is this
ultimate self-giving, self-emptying (in the Word of God) and
self-reacquisition (in the Holy Spirit) that ground the various
trinitarian world-structures of being, thinking and speaking in
their "plurality of origins".[41] The intelligibility of the "form"
(*Gestalt*) comes from the way in which, of itself, it points to a
manifold context of relationships.[42] And as we indicated at the
beginning of this section, absolute self-giving is beyond "power"
and "powerlessness": its ability to "let be" embraces both. In
this context, "substance" is there for the purpose of "transubstantiation", for "communion".[43] In this way it is quite possible

[37] *Ibid.*, 39.   [38] *Ibid.*, 61.
[39] *Ibid.*, 47.   [40] *Ibid.*, 62.
[41] *Ibid.*, 42.   [42] *Ibid.*, 51.
[43] *Ibid.*, 48.

to reconcile "God's unchangeability and God's involvement in history".[44]

Several conclusions can be drawn from this. The first concerns the structure exhibited by the ideas put forward by inhabitants of the world and points back to Bonaventure. If these ideas are in the Logos by way of essence, because God's work of creation flows from the generation of the Logos in God, it follows that they are always transcending themselves, since the Logos only exists together with Father and Spirit; he is the divine "effulgence" and as such expresses the entire life of the Trinity. Every idea or *essentia* is transcendent toward its ground (the Father); its inner destiny is to surrender itself (in the Spirit). This is because it is grounded in the Father, which implies not only the power of self-expression but also the power of self-surrender; just as, in trinitarian terms, the Son, in receiving himself from the Father, also receives the (natural) will to breathe forth the Spirit, to attune himself to that self-surrender which characterizes generation by the Father.

This clarifies what we said in *Theo-Drama* II (209ff., 238), namely, that in the finite being *reflexio completa* coincides with "letting be" everything that shares in being. This now appears as *imago trinitatis*, since in God each Hypostasis can only be itself insofar as it "lets" the others "be" in equal concreteness. Indeed, as we shall see, it can only be itself insofar as it endlessly affirms and gives thanks for its own existence and all that shares existence. This also sheds light on that "real distinction" in the world which is regarded as the structural reflection of triune Being. While it is true that no individual created being can be identical with its participation in Being, and cannot be deduced from the latter, but has its unity in and of itself ("essentia habet esse per seipsam, non propter esse suum": *De Ver.* 21, q 5, a 8), it remains the case that Being cannot be attributed to it from outside, since outside Being there is simply nothing (*De Pot.* 7, q 2, a 9). In the first place both aspects characterize the creature's non-divinity: neither can its particularity (*essentia*)

---

[44] *Ibid.*, 64.

give itself reality (*esse*), nor can its participation in reality (*esse*), which is universal, guarantee its essential particularity (*essentia*). Nonetheless this fundamental quality of creaturehood (its unlikeness to God) must have some basis in God himself if it is to be posited at all. Of course it cannot be said that the substance possessed in common by the Divine Hypostases is like that being in which all finite beings share; after all, these finite beings are precisely *not* identical with their real (posited) being, whereas each of the Divine Hypostases *is* identical with the divine essence, otherwise there would be three gods. Nonetheless, just as the divine essence is not a blank, homogeneous block of identity but a giving (in the Father), a receiving (in the Son), a gift given to the Spirit by Father and Son together, and a cause of thanksgiving by Son and Spirit, so the kind of being that is given to finite creatures also possesses a fluidity and a transitional quality that is "fixed" only in such creatures. They, in their individuality, owe their existence to that divine kindness which posits them "in connection with the pouring forth of all being from God" (*S. Th.* I, 45, 4 ad 1). Thus it is only through and in them that being can have its unity (a unity that transcends them all); only thus can the variety of beings reflect the complementarity of Hypostases within the Godhead ("ipsa enim differentia quoddam ens est": *De Pot.* 3, a 16 ad 3). Again, just as the Divine Persons are *themselves* only insofar as they go out to the Others (who are always Other), the created essences too are *themselves* only insofar as they go beyond themselves and indicate their primal ground (whence being in its totality shines forth) and their vocation of self-surrender. They are to surrender themselves for their neighbor (whoever he may be); thus, concretely, they offer their self-surrender through every particular instance to Being in its totality. So the totality of created being, just like Divine Being, is both non-finite and particular, albeit in a different manner. And while created being owes both aspects to the entire Divine Being (since the three-personal God performs all his works in concert), it owes its essential particularity in the first place to the Logos, its participation in non-finite being to the Father (to whom the creation is dedicated), and its vocation of self-surrender to the Spirit, who is the embodiment, in God, of love's generosity.

A second conclusion refers to the dynamic relationship between creature and Creator, or the way in which *becoming* is
rooted in absolute *Being*. We cannot avoid using the concept
"process", "procession" in the context of the life of the Trinity
to denote its constant vitality; this concept is the link between
creature and Creator, between being and becoming. The eternal
life that God is, and that remains "ineffable", cannot be described
as a becoming, for it is unacquainted with that "poverty which is
the ground" of our "striving", of our "restlessness". "The divine
life", precisely because it is "the fullness of life . . . [is] perfect
peace"[45]. Yet this peace, or rest, is not inert, but "eternal movement",[46] since the divine processions that give rise to the fellow-

---

[45] 1 Jo 42–43. "God is subject to no development", but "his immutability is
not inert, it is eternal life": C 413.

[46] "All must . . . participate in the dynamic movement of the Trinity": 1 Jo 275;
St 69. "And through Son and Spirit the world is in motion toward the eternal
motion of God": OM 93. The question of how to reconcile rest (*stasis*) and motion (*kinēsis*) in being begins with Plato's *Sophist*, where the visitor from Elea asks
how contradictory things such as rest and motion can be predicated of the same
thing, namely, being; he wonders whether being should not be regarded as transcending both of them. On the other hand, he points out that this is impossible,
since we cannot deny that the genuine existing being "lives and thinks"; nor does
the latter "stand immobile, deprived of lofty, holy reason"—and such reason is
inconceivable without inner motion (248e).

At this point Plotinus joins in the debate: In speaking, albeit not of the One,
but of the *nous*, he says that it is simultaneously rest and motion (*hestēke gar kai
kineitai, Enn.* II, 2, 3), i.e., circling in itself.

As so often happens, Gregory of Nyssa transposes Plotinus' teaching into Christian terms. He identifies rest and motion in the soul that God has invited into
his infinity: "Know, says God to her, that there is so much space in me that no
one hurtling through this space will ever come to a stop. From a different angle,
however, this headlong flight is rest: 'I shall set thee upon the rock.' Here, surely,
is the zenith of paradox: rest and motion are identical (*to auto kai stasis esti kai
kinēsis*) . . . and the more a man becomes established in the good and becomes
immovable, the more speedy his flight will be; rest itself becomes his pinion"
(*Vita Moysis*, PG 44, 405BD). It is the same in the commentary on the Song of
Songs: the bridegroom guides the bride like an arrow "to the blessed goal", she
is "hurled through the rooms", yet "rests between the hands of the Lord" (PG
44, 852D–854A).

Maximus the Confessor understands the concept of motion (*kinēsis*) in the
manner of Aristotle, as teleological movement toward a goal (which is *stasis*);
accordingly he cannot adopt Gregory's paradox in all its implications. He too,
however, considers that we can never "arrive" at God, since God's "infiniteness"

ship of Persons are not subject to temporal limitation but are eternally operative. "Eternal" here also means infinite, which cannot be expressed by an ultimate superlative (like "highest good") but only by a comparative that is open to the "ever-greater".[47] It is true that God is "ever-greater" than man can grasp, even when the latter has reached eternal bliss; yet, though God himself is perfectly "light", he is also "ever-greater" even to himself:[48] he is that "exuberance" which is most vividly expressed in personal terms by the Holy Spirit: "He is the eternal superabundance, that which is ever more, ever greater—the fountain of life. That is why everything living is three, . . . and must be taken up and plunged into the trinitarian life if it is to live."[49] Man will always be seeking God, even when he has found him—and particularly then;[50] this is not only because of the weakness of man's finite

---

leaves infinite room for the motion (*kinēsis*) of the Spirit (*Mystag.*, PG 91, 677A; in 696BD, he speaks of the "motionless eternal movement surrounding God", or of "rest that is eternally in motion and constant motion that is at rest": *Quae. ad Thal.*, PG 90, 760A).

Similarly John Scotus Erigena, on the basis of our spirit, draws conclusions about God: "Intima corda penetrat . . . et cum hoc peragat, semper in seipso manet; et dum movetur, stat; et dum stat, movetur; est enim status mobilis, et motus stabilis" (*De Div. Nat.* 1, III, 4; PL 122, 633CD).

[47] "I have a testimony that is greater." "He does not use a superlative but uses a comparative, which, however, is infinite, and so the true superlative": 1 Jo 308.

[48] OM 575; cf. "The ever-greater Lord": L 39–42; 4 Jo 291, 298; faith "is a giving of consent which includes the greater reality that always eludes it": F 68, cf. 80: "Those in heaven are engaged in a contemplation that is constantly striving to see more . . . but no ambition is involved: it is a forward movement that is not composed of steps": OM 569.

[49] 1 Jo 26.

[50] "One has never found God in such a manner that one would not need to keep on looking for him": 2 Jo 393; for "the mystery must not, cannot and should not lose its character as mystery through the fact of revelation": 2 Jo 201. All the same, God certainly "remains mysterious and beyond our grasp . . . , yet not like an opaque mystery that one cannot get behind, but rather through the very infinity and openness of his mystery itself": 3 Jo 364. Every item of understanding on the part of believers contains "the infinite overflow that overwhelms" that understanding (3 Jo 342). Thus "we will always have to seek him because he is the Ever-Greater; but our seeking will never be hopeless, because all true seeking takes place in his presence and the Lord will unfailingly grant it a finding—which, in turn, will at once be supplanted by a new, urgent seeking": 4 Jo 189–90. "The community would not seek God if it did not already have the Lord, and it would

cognitive powers but also because of the superabundant vitality of infinite life itself. It is characteristic of "genuine love" that it "cannot tire of looking at the beloved. . . . Thus the Son, in the Father's presence, is for ever beholding him in a new way", and although "he knows that, from whatever side he sees him, he attains the whole Father, he is not slow to see him from new sides and, by eternally finding him, to be continually seeking him."[51] There is no contradiction involved in saying that God's eternal here-and-now allows him to bestow his infinite riches as he will, displaying aspects that are ever new; otherwise, in his essence, he would not be absolute *freedom*. This freedom is equally operative in the relationship between the Persons. Thus "the Son is both the primal expectation of the Father and his primal fulfillment; for all eternity he remains what he was and is: expectation and fulfillment. This unsurpassable expectation is being continually surpassed in its fulfillment, even though the expectation itself was unsurpassable. . . . This same exuberance is at work in the procession of the Holy Spirit: Father and Son see their reciprocal love surpassed as it proceeds from them as a Third Person."[52]

So we can say that, if human love is enlivened by the element of surprise, something analogous to it cannot be excluded from divine love. It is as if the Son born of the Father "from the outset surpasses the Father's wildest expectations".[53] "God loves despite his omniscience, constantly allowing himself to be surpassed and surprised by the Beloved."[54] The vitality and freedom of eternal love in the realm of Divine Being constitutes the

---

not have the Lord if it did not seek God": 4 Jo 285, cf. 2 Jo 126–27.

[51] W 226.

[52] W 23.

[53] W 22.

[54] W 42, cf. W 240: The communion of the Three Persons is always "a communion of surprise". "God himself wishes to be surprised by God, by a fulfillment that overflows expectation": GE 10. "Although God knows everything, he again and again allows himself to be surprised": Ka I, 141. In the case of Christ: "The Son knows exactly what he is doing when he performs a miracle, yet he leaves the overall perspective to the Father. . . . In the miracle the Son, too, experiences surprise": OM 75. Cf. A 21; "All love contains an element of surprise and of wanting to be surprised": K 52. "So the truth of Father and Son in the Holy Spirit is absolute unity, a unity that surpasses the expectation of each Person, a

prototype for what love can be, at its best, in the realm of creaturely existence and development.

Thus it is that all creaturely being and becoming is oriented
to the eternal, incarnate Son; everything is on its way to him,
as Scripture expressly says (Eph 1:10; Col 1:16), and if we are
to understand it, we must see it in relation to its goal.[55] "All
things are created with a view to the Son, including man and
his consent. By saying Yes, man acknowledges that he is destined for the Son; . . . by giving his consent, he allows God to
fashion this world in such a way that man's heavenward orientation predominates."[56] "The entire creation bears the mark of
the Son, all things stretch out toward him, and all things are
held together by him in his kingdom, not by the compulsion
of external chains, but freely, from within, in an obedience that
stems from the Son's obedience."[57] The world's becoming has
its origin in the sublime transactions between the Persons of the
Trinity.

Finally this brings us back to the fact that the Son's eternal
processio, which carries out God's plan for the world, is identical
with the Son's *missio*. "The word by which God brings about
the creation is contained within that Word which he utters from
before all time and which, from before all time, appears before
him as his Son. . . . What is created is not foreign to what is begotten. And since, in the Person of the incarnate Son, his being

---

living unity that infinitely transcends itself. . . . Father and Son, each allowing
the other to surpass him by their truth, give each other all the credit (for without
this love cannot exist), although they do not forfeit reciprocal knowledge. But
since they have the Holy Spirit between them (who is the Spirit of love), their
very knowledge of each other takes on the forms and laws of love": Ka II, 301–
2. Cf. the detailed treatment in Ka II, 307–8.

[55] "That all things are oriented to the Son . . . is the very foundation stone
of worldly existence. . . . However, man has become accustomed to look at the
things of the world with the eyes of his memory, comparing them with what they
have been, instead of looking ahead creatively and considering them with a view
to what they are to be": M 59.

[56] F 72–73; SL 84; Bi 14f.; A 124–25; Sc 11; M 58; "Thus the Son is everywhere
present in the world as its goal": GW 111.

[57] C 506, where the "Son's final submission (to the Father, 1 Cor 15:28) is the
ultimate reason for the world's eternal subjection to God".

begotten and his being created form a unity, so too the created
world is, as it were, drawn into the begetting."[58] By giving man
speech, God puts into him "a reflection of his Son's character as
Word",[59] thus showing him the direction his existence should
take. "As a result of our very creation we are in essence already
on our way to the Son",[60] since, according to God's gracious
plan for the world, the *processio*, which includes the *creatio*, is to
be fulfilled in the Son's *missio*. "I proceeded and came", says
Jesus (Jn 8:42). "The will of the Father to beget him and to
send him into the world forms together only one single will. To
come forth and to come are thus one single action and movement for the Son: the internal mission and the external mission
are one. . . . Since this will is also to be fulfilled and expressed
in the Christian people and in the world, these too are included
in the birth and mission of the Son."[61] "Love and eternal life are
. . . immanent movement. Mission, by contrast, is transcendental movement. And yet ultimately both movements are one."[62]
"The first mission was the sending of the Son. By begetting
the Son from all eternity, the Father laid the foundation for his
mission. This embraces the mission of all the prophets, of all
the martyrs and of all the saints." Indeed, the whole world is
created by the Father "after the pattern of the Son"; "he creates
the world in the Son . . . since everything holds together *in him*"
(Col 1:17).[63]

b. Positivity of the "Other"

The foregoing implies a second truth about God, substantiated
by the revelation in Christ. It is a truth that, by analogy, also applies to creation: the fact that "the Other" exists is *absolutely good*.
This was affirmed as early as the Council of Nicaea, in opposition to Arius. The Other, the Son, is equal in substance, dignity
and eternity to the One, the Father. According to revelation,

[58] Sc 11; cf. A 61–62.
[59] Bi 80.
[60] M 19. The Father gives the world to the Son: 2 Jo 290–91.
[61] 2 Jo 199.
[62] Is 174.
[63] K 32.

this is shown by the fact that God is love; for love, in the words of Gregory the Great, can only be *agape, caritas,* if it reaches out toward the other.[1] This provides the starting point for Richard of Saint-Victor's doctrine of the Trinity, which sees the latter as necessarily interpersonal.[2] He is followed in this interpretation by A. Brunner.[3] In presenting this approach, Richard is rightly at pains to exclude all suspicion of tritheism; four of his six books are devoted to the unity of God's essence, and the Persons of the Trinity are only "modes of procession" within this unity. But if God is love, he must be so not only in an "intransitive" sense[4] but must love the Other "transitively". This means that "in God unity and distance are not opposites"[5] and that God's fruitful love is a further reason why his essence is ever greater.[6]

The ideal of a mere unity without "the Other" (Plotinus' *hen,* but also the *Monos Theos* of Judaism and Islam) cannot do justice to the Christian affirmation that God is love. Such a unity would be self-sufficient and could not be communicated; "otherness" would be a mere declension from it. But where God is defined as love, he must be in essence perfect self-giving, which can only elicit from the Beloved, in return, an equally perfect movement of thanksgiving, service and self-giving. Absolute self-giving of this kind cannot exist in the creaturely realm, since man has no control over his existence and, hence, over his "I", and "we cannot give away that over which we have no control."[7] We must try to grasp the fact that where absolute Being is concerned, Being that has possession of itself, "divine self-possession expresses itself in perfect self-giving and reciprocal surrender; furthermore the creature's own existence, over which it has no con-

---

[1] "Minus quam inter duos caritas haberi non potest. Nemo enim proprie ad semetipsum habere caritatem dicitur, sed dilectio in alterum tendit, ut caritas esse possit": *In Evang.* 17, 1 (PL 76, 1139).

[2] Richard of Saint Victor, *De Trinitate* (PL 196).

[3] *Dreifaltigkeit: Personale Zugänge zum Geheimnis,* Sammlung Kriterien 39 (Einsiedeln: Johannes Verlag, 1976).

[4] Which, of course, he is also. Cf. 1 Jo 26–27.

[5] W 48; OM 108. On the goodness of otherness, cf. A 22–23.

[6] In love God is continually creating the "ever-greater" in himself. This is the constant witness, not only in the Holy Spirit, but equally in Son and Father, of their own "ever-greater": C 412–13.

[7] Brunner, *Dreifaltigkeit,* 24.

trol, is drawn into this movement."[8] This self-giving cannot be
motivated by anything other than itself; hence it is a boundless
love where freedom and necessity coincide and where identity
and otherness are one: identity, since the Lover gives all that
he is and nothing else, and otherness, since otherwise the Lover
would love only himself. Yet, even where it is a case of total reciprocal self-giving, this distinction cannot be ultimate: without
disappearing, it must transcend itself in a new identity of love
given and received, which the lovers themselves are bound to
regard as the miracle, ever new, of their mutual love. Thus in
God there must be "an eternal amazement at, and affirmation
of, this reciprocal otherness that accompanies the oneness"[9] and
"an eternal newness characterizing perfect, supratemporal con-
stancy".[10]

When we speak of God "begetting", we must envisage him
sharing his full divine freedom with the Begotten, and sharing it
ultimately, irrevocably and forever. And since this "begetting"
is timeless, the Son's turning to his Father-Origin in gratitude
is equally eternal. This has consequences for the Son's *missio* to
the world: from the very first moment of his entry into the
world, sent forth from the Father, he is on his way back to the
Father. The same applies to all created reality: it does not exhibit
two phases, the *egressus a Deo* and the *reditus in Deum*. Since God
wishes from the very outset to give freedom to the creature (just
as the Father does in the case of the Son and the Spirit), we can
see the error in all the allegedly Christian mysticism that, on the
basis of an identity between God's ideas and his essence, equates
the return to God with a sacrifice of the creature's own free otherness. Such mysticism ought to recognize, rather, that the only
way forward is to build a bridge between the creature's "abiding
in itself" and its "abiding in God". The miracle that transforms
man's (relative) distance from God (particularly in his sinful existence) into "nearness to God", "bestowing a more than earthly
fullness upon earthly life", is "a life that comes from God and
overflows on to man": "grace".[11] The fact that the creature is

[8] *Ibid.*, 25.
[9] *Ibid.*, 42.
[10] *Ibid.*, 45.
[11] Ph 52.

other than God does not mean that the Creator has abandoned it; it is sin that denies the bond of love between Creator and creature, and it is sin that feels itself alienated.[12] "But the fact that the creation comes from God . . . means that we can look forward to its return to God."[13]

However, we must ponder the Father's primal begetting of the Son—manifesting his will to give himself in such a way that the "wholly other"[14] comes into being—and ask what it implies. In giving himself, the Father does not give something (or even everything) that he *has* but all that he *is*—for in God there is only being, not having. So the Father's being passes over, without remainder, to the begotten Son; and it would be a mistake to suggest that he, the Father, *becomes* or *develops* as a result of this self-giving; this would be a false interpretation of Hemmerle. This total self-giving, to which the Son and the Spirit respond by an equal self-giving, is a kind of "death", a first, radical "kenosis", as one might say. It is a kind of "super-death" that is a component of all love and that forms the basis in creation for all instances of "the good death", from self-forgetfulness in favor of the beloved right up to that highest love by which a man "gives his life for his friends". "Life is only genuinely alive insofar as it . . . grows beyond itself, lets go of itself. It is rich only insofar as it can be poor, insofar as it loves. . . . Death will not allow itself to be pushed to the very end of life; it belongs right at the center, not in mere knowledge, but in action. Death characterizes our breakthrough into a life that is ever greater. It is through this positive death that we amass life."[15] This is based on a trinitarian prototype: "The Father steps forth from

---

[12] K 69; G 9; SL 86–87; A 123–24; Ph 85; Ep 27, 184–85; Ka I, 139, 397; C 285, 419.

[13] Is 137. Since the Son is always the One who returns to the Father, he is also in time "the Son of Man, the son of all men . . . [i.e.,] the one toward whom life in time tends, in whom it reaches its goal, and in whom it is fulfilled. . . . He is the one coming . . . and the one returning to the Father in the (eternal) future": 1 Jo 286.

[14] The Divine Persons are "wholly other" to each other (in the identity of their essence) insofar as, in God, there can be no abstract concept of "person" that applies to all Persons.

[15] Ferdinand Ulrich, *Leben in der Einheit von Leben und Tod* (Frankfurt: Knecht, 1973), 29–30.

himself in his living Word, giving the Son the entire riches, the whole fullness of divine life. God is love, eternally given away to the Son, the absolute unity of riches and poverty . . . life and death."[16] Absolute love is only realized where there is this sur-render of what is one's own, where this *separation* is taken seri-ously (for the "other" must be himself, and not I), where there is this "going under" so that the Other can "rise up" in himself; only this absolute love can guarantee the unity of essence; only in this love, in the sphere of the God-man, can that sacrifice take place which grounds *communio* in Christ; only in this context can true love, and its suffering, prove fruitful.[17]

c. Positivity of Letting Go

If we describe Divinity as *actus purus*, what distinguishes the creature is its *potentiality*. On the other hand, if we ask about the *imago trinitatis* in the creature, it will be obvious that within the trinitarian process one Person is, as it were, passive, while another Person is active. The Father begets; this implies neces-sarily that the Son is begotten.[1] Thus we can say that "there is a passive generative potentiality in the Son predisposing him to be begotten."[2] Accordingly, in the case of both Son and Spirit we can speak of an active and a passive mission.[3] Divine conception has its roots, on the one hand, in the ability to "let be" and, on the other hand, in the ability to allow oneself to be brought to birth, to separate oneself, really and in fact, from what is one's own. Otherwise the Son and the Spirit would never be con-ceived as such by the Father. At the same time we must hold fast to the fact that the Giver (whose act of giving is eternal) does not lose what he gives, that is, himself: "We cannot say that

---

[16] *Ibid.*, 132. On the archetypal death in "the Father separating himself from the Son" and in "the total mutual acquiescence of the three Divine Persons", cf. Hl 91–92.

[17] "In genuine love it is absolutely essential that the partners give freedom to each other. To love truly is to give credit; the lover does not watch the beloved anxiously. The lover gives the beloved room for personal growth, and by doing this the lover must accept the risk of letting the beloved go": Ka II, 198.

[1] Bonaventure, d 9, a un q 2 concl (I, 183a).

[2] *Ibid.*, d 7, dub 7 (I, 145f.).

[3] *Ibid.*, d 15, q 3 (I, 262f.).

the Father, in begetting, gives his substance to his Son by way of a bequest, that is, not retaining it himself; for in this case he would cease to be the divine substance" (Fourth Lateran Synod, DS 805). We need to hold the two things simultaneously and affirm their identity: the genuine, active giving that involves the entire Person who gives, and the eternal Being of the Person that remains constant throughout this act of self-giving.

The counterpart of this in the Son (and in the Spirit vis-à-vis Father and Son) is a letting be that is just as eternal as the act by which he is brought forth; it is implicit in this act. This is the Son's antecedent consent to be begotten and the Spirit's antecedent consent to proceed from Father and Son. This "passive *actio*" is a condition of the "active *actio*" and imparts to the latter a certain quality of "letting go". Thus the Father causes the Son to be, to "go"; but this also means that the Father "lets go" of him, lets him go free. (So too, in the act of begetting, a man causes his seed to go on its way while he himself retires into the background.) Moreover, only by the act of begetting does the Father *conceive* the Son; only by their mutual breathing forth of the Spirit do Father and Son *conceive* the Spirit. It was Kaliba (see above) who best showed how passive *actio* is involved in active *actio*. Where absolute love is concerned, conceiving and letting be are just as essential as giving. In fact, without this receptive letting be and all it involves—gratitude for the gift of oneself and a turning in love toward the Giver—the giving itself is impossible.

"Because the Son is God, the perennial generation of the Son is at the same time the Son's always being in existence already";[4] "right from the outset there is a reciprocal closeness. For the distance—implied by his being begotten—embraces the closeness—implied by his return to the Father; his filial relation to the Father is the constant result of the Father's paternal relation to the Son. There is no hiatus here between question and answer."[5] The joyous unity of mind on the part of the proceeding Persons is so great "that, in a certain respect, the Father cannot cease begetting the Son, and Father and Son cannot cease from

[4] Ep 21.
[5] Ka II, 238.

causing the Spirit to proceed; and in a more passive manner the Son and Spirit cannot but place themselves at the disposal of their generation in a process of becoming which always exhibits all the qualities of being."[6] "In God everything is full of these loving details which contribute essentially to understanding the Trinity, full of these prior ententes built into and fulfilled in reality. The Son even cooperates in his begetting by *letting* himself be begotten, by holding himself in readiness to be begotten. And within the relationship based on nature, everything is repeated on the level of freedom."[7] Within this trinitarian context we can begin to see the origin of the Son's obedience in becoming man: "The Son prefers nothing to doing the Father's will, for even in being begotten he carries it out. . . . On the other hand the Father also gives him the distance inherent in his independence. Yet the Son acts independently within the Father's permission and invitation to be free and independent."[8] "The divine processions occur in eternal simultaneity",[9] so that the Father's very act of begetting "is an act of surrender to the Son, to which the Son replies with his surrender. And gratitude is contained both in surrender and in its acceptance. The Father's act of begetting contains a gratitude to the Son for letting himself be begotten, just as the Son's willingness contains a gratitude to the Father for his wanting to beget him."[10] So, even in the Father's "active *actio*", there is a certain passivity, qualified by the "passive *actio*" of Son and Spirit.[11] Hence there is "no less love in receiving than in giving. Perhaps there is even more, since what is received and conceived is divine."[12] The Son and the Spirit "show that God's love in heaven involves an eternal interplay of active generation

---

[6] W 32–33.
[7] W 65.
[8] W 67.
[9] W 245.
[10] W 213.
[11] "Thus the Father also receives from the Holy Spirit that form of love he has desired, so that he might be the Father of the Son. The Son, by proceeding from the Father, and the Spirit, by proceeding from Father and Son, both cause the Father to be Father. . . . All the Persons define each other reciprocally": OM 104. On the aspect of "letting be" in the Father, cf. Ap 247.
[12] L 114.

and passive being begotten and being breathed forth, of love's imprinting and the loving acceptance of it".[13]

From this standpoint we can already see that certain dualisms become possible within creation, between act and potency, for instance, between action and contemplation and between the sexes.

Before going into this in more detail, however, we must touch on a particular divine mystery that is opened up by the foregoing and lends depth to what we have said. Doubtless, the processions in God are not free in any arbitrary sense, even though God is not subject to external necessity. They arise from a natural or necessary will in God, which, proceeding from Father to Son and from Father and Son to the Spirit, grounds an irreversible order. If we trace this order back to its very origin (if we "recapitulate" it),[14] we find that it is a "hierarchy" that applies even to the absolute freedom of the Persons. This, then, is "freedom's primal shape. In order for a will to be free, it must be part of a hierarchy."[15] And this, if we look back to God's "letting go", has a twofold significance. In the first place, the Son, in being begotten, admits "the fullness of the Father's necessary will . . . in no way intervening with the free will with which he was begotten, as if to contribute toward his own fashioning". On the other hand, however, "the Father has given the Son everything", including his will.[16] So if the Father has a (primary) intention— perhaps with regard to the shape of the creation he has planned —he communicates this intention to the Son in begetting him, giving him "preludes, beginnings taken up by the Son to be realized"; thus he leaves it to the Son to "promote the fatherly purposes".[17] In begetting the Son, the Father, as it were, addresses a request to him, and the Son in turn wishes nothing other than to employ his entire filial freedom in fulfilling the Father's will. So "the Father is the first to ask: and he asks the Son, in order to give him the joy of granting his request. . . . Even before the Son asks him" (for instance, to be entrusted with the task of

[13] Ps 155.
[14] W 58.
[15] W 57f.
[16] W 59.
[17] W 63.

saving the world through his Cross), "the Father wants to make his request, as if to give the Son precedence in the delight of granting." As for the Spirit, whose specific part it is to choose and decide in all freedom (since the Spirit is the absolute, divine will), one might say that he embodies that reciprocal "mode of granting requests" which is an invention of the whole Trinity, so that the decision on the part of the united Trinity (within the order of processions) is completely mutual and common to all the Persons.[18] At the same time each Person surprises and surpasses the Others by coming up with a "divine ever-greater", a divine "heightening" and "exuberance". The unanimity of the decision expresses the unity of a love that is vital and creative.[19] The Father, in sending the Son into the world, "fulfills the Son's will, allowing him to come to us, so that the sending and the allowing arise from the same love".[20] Thus we come to see that it "belongs to his nature to know *consideration*. God is considerate of God. God loves God in the loving responsibility of God."[21] When Paul calls for reciprocal subordination among the faithful, he is following a "law of life that characterizes the Trinity".[22] He is referring to the same law when he says that the Son subordinates himself and all things to the Father, who has given all things to the Son.[23] And when we read in John that "All that is mine is thine, and thine is mine", this means that in God there are things "which belong to the Persons and are peculiar to them; . . . But even that which is the foundation of the Persons as such

[18] W 60–65.

[19] "Perhaps the Father would have had other suggestions, other ideas pertaining to redemption that would not have made the abandonment of the Cross necessary. But he does not express them; he leaves redemption up to the Son. In love, what is best is always what the other wishes. But the Son, too, goes along wholly with the will of the Father inasmuch as he makes ready to embark upon his redemptive course. They love each other so strongly that their wills always coincide, not in the sense of meeting somewhere in the middle and uniting, but within an eternal, absolute unity in which each one forgoes what is his and each is in agreement with the other from eternity, not within a rigid, dead identity but within that eternal life of love from which everything that bears the name of grace flows": 4 Jo 380–81.

[20] Ka II, 161.

[21] St 80–81.

[22] C 569.

[23] C 505.

is common to all of them, and they know this communion in the Holy Spirit."[24] In what Father and Son *are* "there are essential differences . . . but in terms of what they possess, they both possess Fatherhood and Sonship. This mystery becomes more clear to us with the Son than with the Father. . . . In relation to mankind [the Son] possesses the qualities of the Son and the Father at the same time." The Father, however, leaves his Son to accomplish his burdensome task on the world's behalf; "he does not interfere. . . . Stepping back before the Son's autonomy, he sets the Son above himself. Thus, for his part, he adopts the filial qualities of the Son."[25]

In this way the creative vitality welling up from eternal love show us that creation's potentiality can be something utterly positive. Since there is no "development" in the eternal life of God, and yet that there *is* love's "ever greater", love's constant element of surprise, its inexhaustible manifestation of unity (seen from whatever angle), the development that characterizes the creature is the highest possible approximation to such unattainable vitality. The active and passive aspects of potentiality are complementary: indeed, they cannot be clearly separated. Receptivity presupposes an active potentiality for suffering, whereas activity presupposes a locus into which such action can be introduced.

"Activity and passivity", however, together constitute "the original unity of action and contemplation",[26] and this applies both "within the divine nature and in creation": "The distance between the Persons, a distance that is ever greater but ever bridged, is the foundation of contemplation and is in turn founded upon it. Each determines the other. And yet it is equally true that contemplation acquires its shape through the action which lies within it and through the nature of the Persons contemplating one another. God, who contemplates himself within this eternal contemplation, is both subject and object of contemplation and fashions himself for this purpose in such a way that he continually reveals contrasts to promote the triune love."[27] Nonetheless this results in no "development" in God: "God's act

[24] 3 Jo 328–29.
[25] 3 Jo 248–49.
[26] W 43.
[27] W 50–51.

of creation introduces . . . no changes into his vision", whereby he has always beheld the world within his will.[28] It was "purely for the needs of creatures" that God's internal processes were "translated from eternity into time and separated out" in the sequential interplay of work and rest, "so that we may understand something of God and his eternal life, and of the unity of intention and realization which exists there."[29]

Finally, the divine unity of action and consent—which, as we have seen, share equal dignity within love—is expressed in the world in the duality of the sexes. In trinitarian terms, of course, the Father, who begets him who is without origin, appears primarily as (super-) masculine; the Son, in consenting, appears initially as (super-) feminine, but in the act (together with the Father) of breathing forth the Spirit, he is (super-) masculine. As for the Spirit, he is (super-) feminine. There is even something (super-) feminine about the Father too, since, as we have shown, in the action of begetting and breathing forth he allows himself to be determined by the Persons who thus proceed from him; however, this does not affect his primacy in the order of the Trinity. The very fact of the Trinity forbids us to project any secular sexuality into the Godhead (as happens in many religions and in the gnostic *syzygia*). It must be enough for us to regard the ever-new reciprocity of acting and consenting, which in turn is a form of activity and fruitfulness, as the transcendent origin of what we see realized in the world of creation: the form and actualization of love and its fruitfulness in sexuality.[30]

d. Positivity of Time and Space

Our primal ideas of time and space, too, originate in the coming-to-be of the divine processions. Unless we see eternal *being* in terms of eternal *event*, we are condemned to see the form of its duration as a mere *nunc stans*, which deprives it of everything that makes world-time (in all its transience) exciting and delightful. Everything would contract to a single unmoving point, thereby

[28] W 43.

[29] W 44.

[30] H. U. von Balthasar, "Die Würde der Frau" in *Communio: Internat. Kath. Zft.* 11 (1982), 346–52.

abolishing the very space that allows scope to time itself. Thus we see how closely knit time and space are: time "makes room" for existent being, indeed, it creates an acting area in which it can realize itself as event. In turn, space requires time so that it may be mapped, investigated and conquered.

This positive aspect of creaturely existence points to something in God that makes it possible, something that—evidently —cannot be discovered in a mere substance but only in the trinitarian process that is taking place in the eternal now. The best way to approach this is by considering the awareness of existence enjoyed by the God-man, which is not exclusively creaturely but as such always expresses something of the Trinity as well. "The Son can do nothing of his own accord," says Jesus, "but only what he sees the Father doing; for whatever he does, that the Son does likewise. For the Father loves the Son, and shows him all that he himself is doing" (Jn 5:19–20). We can get even closer if we listen to the passages in which Jesus *hears* from the Father the Word that he himself *is*, where he is, as it were, "uttered to himself" (Jn 3:32; 8:40; 8:55; cf. 12:49–50). We begin to see that, in the eternal process of being begotten, the Son eternally receives himself from the Father in a *presence* that includes both his always-having-been and also his eternal future (his eternal "coming") from the Father. His acceptance of himself, of his being, of the absolute fullness of Godhead, is from before all time: it has always been, yet never in isolation from that act whereby the Father begets in love. This act remains his future, that "coming" whereby, receiving the gift of himself, he comes to himself. So his eternal presence as such is not a *stans* in the original meaning of the word; rather, it is an entirely event-filled presence for and in response to the Father. Incidentally, the German word for "present" and "presence" is *Gegenwart*: the suffix *wart* comes from the Latin *vertere* (cf. German *werden*) and suggests a "turning" of oneself "toward" [*gegen*]; thus John 1:18 speaks of the Son "being in (= "into", "toward") the bosom of the Father"—*ōn eis ton kolpon tou Patros*. Insofar as the event is always the coming about of something that has always been, it is also the overfulfillment of an expectation: something transcendent, something "ever more", is immanent in the self-realizing

event.[1] From the perspective of the Father, who has no origin,
the dimensions of "eternal time"[2] are equally clear: the Father,
as Father, is the "essence" of the act of eternal begetting, which
is the eternal *prius* of its result (the Son). The Son is and always
has been ever present to the Father yet is also present to him in
the mode of *coming*, of future being; thus the Son's coming always over fulfills the expectation that lies in the act. "And in the
perpetual immediacy of this sudden moment, without limits of
time, without sequence in their reciprocal vision, both of them
know in perfect simultaneity of their reciprocal love. In their
communion, which was from eternity and yet is created afresh
at every instant, they know of their ineffable, expectant love for
the Spirit, who at this precise moment is proceeding from them
both as the expression of their common purpose and expectation. . . . And the Spirit knows that he is eternally expected by
Father and Son, and in his own being he sees them both as the
perfect fulfillment of what he had eternally expected", yet in
such a way that "he can bring them the complete fulfillment
they were expecting."[3]

With regard to the aspect of *space*, its primal origin in the Trinity lies in the way in which the Persons of the Trinity "make
room" ("space") for one another, granting each other freedom
of being and action. Thus the Giver detaches himself from the
One on whom he bestows this gift, and the latter receives him-

---

[1] "The eternal moment is effective retrospectively and prospectively, including
everything from all eternity and for all eternity. What is 'now' always was, and
it is so full that it is unsurpassable: not in such a way that the present moment
stifles freedom of action, but in such a way that expectation and fulfillment exactly coincide. . . . It is as if, from his prototypical existence, [the Son] had always
lived in his Father's eternal expectation and has now, at the end of this eternal
waiting, *at last* appeared: as if he too, now that *at last* he sees the Father, finds his
expectation satisfied. Though he, the Eternal One, has had no time in which to
wait, he still experiences this fulfillment as the result of an eternal expectation.
Indeed, through this fulfillment, both become aware of the presence of an eternal
expectation and, through it, of the presence of the fulfillment": W 38.

[2] C 418. The valid insights of process theology could—with caution—be
brought in at this point. Cf. W. Pannenberg, *Theology and the Kingdom of God*
(Philadelphia: Westminster Press, 1969), 62.

[3] W 38–39.

self from the Giver in genuine freedom and so distinguishes himself from him. It is a question of "that area of freedom which is necessary for keeping the relationship alive". Of course "in God no spatial separation is possible or necessary. It is replaced by the hierarchical distance of the processions. There is a primal beginning in which the Father is 'alone', even if he was never without the Son, for ultimately it is he, unique and alone, who begets the Son."[4] So too the Father gives the Son "the distance inherent in his independence".[5] "The Father does not beget within himself but out of himself." Nor does this mean that he initially occupies the whole "space" and then (as the Cabala suggests) has to "withdraw" in order to make room for the Son and the Spirit; for he is "Father" only insofar as he is the One who, from before all eternity, begets and bestows freedom. It is an essential aspect of the love of the Persons in God that they mutually grant each other freedom. In love, "some things can be said better near at hand, others at a distance; lovers can put into letters things . . . which did not come out while they were together."[6] Again, we must not see the "distance" in opposition to, or in conflict with, the "closeness" (of *circumincessio* in the one divine nature); at the same time such distance is necessary, for two reasons: first, in order to hold fast to the personal distinctness of each Person both in being and acting; and second, in order to establish the basis within the Trinity for what, in the economic Trinity, will be the possibility of a distance that goes as far as the Son's abandonment on the Cross.

In God, distance and nearness exist in a unity that exhibits their constantly intensifying relationship: "The more the Persons in God differentiate themselves, the greater is their unity."[7] It is like the relationship between the sexes: "The more different the other is, the more worthy of love he appears. There may come a point of interpenetration in their union where neither is aware any longer of where one begins and the other ends; but in this

[4] W 65–66.

[5] W 67; cf. W. Maas, *Gott und die Hölle* (Einsiedeln: Johannes Verlag, 1979), 200f.

[6] W 66. Cf. 210: "Love needs this play of closeness and distance, and both are gifts from God to love."

[7] Ep 100.

very unity the Thou is even more exalted." No doubt this image is only remotely approximate. But in God "each shares himself with the other in such a way that he is not thereby compelled to be any less himself."[8] Accordingly, this is an essential aspect of the reciprocal "presence" of the Persons to one another in God. If there is to be this reciprocal indwelling, however, it follows that what is specific to each Person must not be withheld from the others; not only does "all that is said of one Divine Person also apply to his relationships with the others",[9] not only is "that which is the foundation of the Persons as such . . . common to all of them",[10] but—as we have already said—one of the Persons can, by way of the divine "economy", embody and represent the qualities of the others.[11]

e. The Absolute Quality of Prayer

Since each Person of the Trinity enjoys the one divine will in divine freedom, a decision in God can only come about through the mutual integration of the Persons' "points of view". Thus we glimpse "how boundless is the divine love that realizes itself in this eternal conversation, and how boundless, too, is that mystery in God to which we give the name 'obedience': perfect harmony, the perfectly loving agreement of God with God."[1] The Son, with his "divine filial will", has "no greater joy from all eternity than to do the Father's will", so much so that even as man, in the distance of suffering, when the Father's will appears "alien and unintelligible" to him, he will carry it out to perfection.[2]

We already adumbrated a form of this mutual integration when speaking of the unity between the wish and its granting. Indeed this was the only way we could understand, in some fashion, the divine decision to redeem mankind, whereby the Father acts, as it were, as the supplicant, leaving it up to the Son's initiative to

[8] W 73.
[9] Ka II, 206.
[10] 3 Jo 329.
[11] 3 Jo 232.
[1] Gh 111–12.
[2] B 174–75.

offer himself and to obey the Father.[3] But there is a deeper and more comprehensive sense in which the trinitarian conversation is the prototype of all prayer. When God stands before God we can say "that God shows honor to God"[4] "in a reciprocal glorifying",[5] "in an eternal, reciprocal worship".[6] "Worship as we know it is a grace that comes from the triune worship. Nothing is more rooted in God than worship."[7] "All worship has its primary basis in the other's otherness. Where there is mere oneness, worship is not possible. The Son does not worship the Father because the Father is like him; that would mean that the Son found himself worthy of worship and that he worshipped himself. Worship is a relation to a Thou, a relation so strong and pure that only the Thou is of any account. Thus worship does not rest on a need, but in the being (and the 'being-thus') of God for God and for creatures."[8]

Such worship, however, is full of life and vitality. God's prayer-dialogue, where the darkness of the world is its topic, can become a kind of "struggle", it can become "troubled".[9] Yet it can never relativize the absolute quality of divine love: all else must be integrated and subordinated to the latter. "In God there is no dominance of knowledge over love, no possibility of increasing insight to a point where it no longer corresponds to love."[10] "The Father shows the Son less his total knowledge than his total love, which conceals something whose concealment lets love radiate even more brightly."[11] In God there are things that exist "only to provide love with every opportunity for development, to give it the room which it would lack if everything were stale foreknowledge—room which it needs, for it cannot exist without self-surrender, movement and flight."[12] The event-quality

---

[3] W 57–67.

[4] Ka I, 319.

[5] Ph 20: "The three Persons in God live in their eternal heaven; each lives for the honor and praise of the others, in a reciprocal glorification."

[6] OM 82.

[7] W 56.

[8] W 209.

[9] Ka II, 241.

[10] W 55.

[11] W 49–50.

[12] W 34.

of absolute love calls for much that can be traced back to the process of begetting and "breathing" within the Trinity, albeit in a supereminent mode far above the creaturely; nonetheless, the prototype is to be found in God.

Much of what we have already discussed is relevant at this point, for instance the unity of expectation and fulfillment, of willing and letting-it-happen, which all goes to show that "in the scope between the divine and the personal, divine love shows itself in its fruitfulness and wealth of creativity."[13] But in worship there is more: "astonishment and gratitude: astonishment that God is so great and gratitude that he allows himself to be contemplated".[14] There are also the "divine virtues" that take their place next to love: faith and hope.[15] If we consider faith from the bottom up, so to speak, arising from man, then of course it is characterized by a "blind" trust; yet such faith "cannot be defined as a state of loss of vision". In the mystic, the element of fulfillment, of vision, is more pronounced, but "mysticism is always an expression of faith; it can only take place within faith." Of course, "our faith will be transformed when we enter heaven. . . . [It] will be a much more concrete, proven and evident form of faith. But far from destroying faith, this vision will fulfill it."[16] If, however, we consider faith from God's perspective, faith as it exists in God, it is in harmony with "irrefragable knowledge" but is not swallowed up by it, because the love that grants freedom to the other always offers him something "that transcends his capacities of knowing", something that has an utterly unique origin, springing from the "hidden depths of the one and communicated to the hidden depths of the other". "There is an exchange of love in God whereby, in gratitude, each of the three Persons desires to attribute his own inner, hid-

[13] W 41.

[14] W 53.

[15] "And precisely those highest gifts of God which come directly from his inner-divine life, faith, love and hope, are far better adapted to reveal his nature than any power of our creaturely nature as such." Therefore they are to be used "as access to his nature". W 35. On God's "hope", see the chapter below entitled "The Form of Christian Hope".

[16] W 35. On the relationship between faith and vision in Christ, cf. W 78–83. 81: "The Christian faith is by no means an impoverished vision. . . ." On "faith" as it exists in Christ and in God, cf. the introduction to Ka I, 6–26.

den self to the Other, and actually knows that he so owes it."
"From before all time, the barriers are down." In God, however,
the freedom-bestowing self-surrender to the Other (who is God
and therefore worthy of worship) is "an expression, not only
of love, but of 'faith' ". In begetting the Son, the Father does
not determine him; rather, "he endows him with freedom to
explore the infinite realm of his own free sonship, of his own divine sovereignty." Accordingly it is the Father's will to be "outstripped, for all eternity, by the Son's love. Faith is, as it were, the
space that must be opened up so that there is room for infinite
fulfillment, beyond the limits of all expectation." "Faith is constant readiness, the basis of all love."[17] Thus faith becomes also
the "fount of action", of petition, of the surprise that fulfillment
brings. All this refers us back to the element of distance that is
indispensable to love: "In true love the lovers do not cling to
each other: they have the distance which is essential if they are
to see and encounter each other completely."[18] Each leaves the
other "time" and "space" to reflect on and present his wishes
and to "prepare his gifts". Without this personal distance in the
circumincessio of the Persons it would be impossible to understand
either the creature's distance from God or the Son's "economic"
distance from the Father—a distance that goes to the limit of
forsakenness.

Having said this, it is important to insist that there is nothing merely potential, formless and indefinite about these modalities. They are all positive features of the eternal, free, animated
life of the Trinity. This life is eternal: but that does not contradict the fact that God is always "definite"; there is nothing
"vague and indefinite" about him. On the contrary, everything
is "differentiated and decided to the highest degree. But . . . God
differentiates in order continually to reunite; but he unites in order continually to make new decisions."[19] "Each shares himself
with the other in such a way that he is not thereby compelled to
be any less himself. This is part of God's firmness of decision."[20]

[17] Ka I, 138–41.
[18] W 66.
[19] W 72.
[20] W 73.

3. The Idea of the World

At the end of this work we shall confront the question of why God wills there to be a world, why he plans it and brings it about, and what "benefit" to him is this teeming existence of relative, temporal-spatial multiplicity. By way of anticipation, however, we can already assume that *if* God designs and creates a world, it can only be that he wills thereby to communicate his trinitarian life of love, which it must therefore reflect. Furthermore, it must not reflect the trinitarian life in the way a finished, discrete copy reflects its prototype: since God's very essence is communication, the "copy" must continue to be open to the "prototype", there must be a sharing between them. There is a difficulty in this idea in God when one goes into detail: since freedom is of the very essence of love, God cannot and will not withhold such freedom from the chief beings in the world, and this in turn means that, from all eternity, he designs the world in such a way that it includes the eventual misuse of freedom in the form of human (and angelic) sin. This is not exactly the same as saying that God, because of his foreknowledge of the Fall, plans the world with a view to the Son of God, who will become incarnate, will suffer and rise again. For if we cannot say the world's sin compels God to change his plan for the world, neither can we say that, from the outset, he envisages the world as the scene of alienation and redemption. We have to keep things in balance: according to the primary plan, the world is created as purely positive after the pattern of the triune life, yet in such a way that, if negativity does arise from the world itself, it can be effectively countered by the essentially positive features of the life of the Trinity as described above. All we can say is that "there resides in creation from the very beginning an adumbration, a prefiguring, of the Cross that is to come",[1] for instance in the initial horizontal and vertical separations that are described in the creation process. This adumbration acquires definition in the history of creation: "Now the Cross becomes the dominant form of the entire creation."[2] "The Son is ready. . . . Anxiously

[1] Sc 31.
[2] *Ibid.*

he accompanies Adam. The moment sin appears there is a confrontation between sin and the Cross."[3] "In the beginning God utters his Word, and at the end he sees its fulfillment. Every utterance of a word of God is an anticipation of the final sending of the Son. Even the word of creation uttered by the Father is an expression of the Son's perfect readiness to go forth from the Father. . . . And the Father cannot spare him this premonition of the Cross that arises from the unfolding creation. . . . It is almost as if the Father keeps warning him: You see how everything is arranged and what it is pointing to?"[4]

a. Time Is from Eternity and to Eternity

The idea of the world is from God and in God. Accordingly its whole (non-divine) reality cannot be located anywhere else but in him. "For the 'world' is not only this external, temporal world: its being has its foundation in God, and it is oriented toward eternity. It comes from God and goes to God, and, even when it distances itself from him, it is not outside God."[5] The world unfolds as the reflection of the eternal self-realization of the Divine Being; it cannot avoid being orientated to the latter. Thus "the whole of transitory time acquires a meaning once man learns that both its 'ends' are hooked up to eternity: the very duration of transitory time is an analogy of the eternal."[6] "World time is not cut off from heavenly time; although it consists of a succession of moments, it has a meaning in God and for God: it does him service."[7] Just as "the eternal time preceding creation" bears the imprint of the face of the Father, so he, the Creator, lends "any and every time"—including worldtime—"its visage".[8] With time, even space and its fulfillment by a multiplicity that is initially material (and whose meaning is ultimately spiritual) acquires its role as an image, which originates in the positivity of otherness in God. Insofar as it is an

[3] Sc 38.
[4] Sc 50–51.
[5] 2 Jo 151.
[6] Bi 17.
[7] Ps 28.
[8] A 12.

image of God, the temporal/material becomes something vital and living; insofar as it is an image of the Trinity, it becomes generative and fruitful. This living reality, however, since it undergoes finite development, must maintain itself at the cost of other living things, and so we can begin to understand that nature's "surrender to termination" (things eat and are themselves eaten) is first of all a reflection of what, in a trinitarian perspective, we saw as the "good" or "positive" death. It is only sin that changes it into a "negative death", and even then it is made possible and undergirded by the reality of the "positive" death. The same positivity of otherness in God, which, far from being an obstacle to his infinity, actually facilitates it, guarantees that a world whose destiny is God shall retain its necessary "distance" even in God: it will not be swallowed up by his infinity. On the contrary, we can say that everything that is in process of becoming, within the world's total becoming, has a somehow indefinite profile until it attains its definitive shape, ultimately, in full participation in the life of the Trinity. Everything is a particular image of God, and this image of God in things points beyond itself to the primal image, which is why it is impossible to have fixed and final ideas about it: "The true possessor of thought is and remains God himself. It is only in the infinity of God that thought has its final, definitive form. . . . In reality a thing needs infinity if it is to acquire contour and definition."[9] This is because, in its subjection to time, the finite is bound always to measure in finite terms; accordingly, if it is to learn to love, it must "forget the boundaries it has so painstakingly drawn" in the face of God's "boundlessness and immeasurability". "Time, now, is where the eternal desires to find a place; measure, now, is where the immeasurable must find a home." And as far as man is concerned, "everything that comes from the beyond, everything that God offers, is beyond measure."[10] "There is a deep analogy"[11] between time and eternity, so eternity can always be inside time, just as time can participate in eternity. "God has not created us for time, but for his eternity.

---

[9] OM 59.
[10] M 75, 79.
[11] Pf 107.

What is eternal is prior. . . . In this light, our life and death seem
an episode on the way to eternal life. Thus, the more convinced
we are of God's eternal life, the more we bear it within us."[12] So
"the concepts of our daily life are immeasurably expanded."[13]
We must not just use our time as a measuring rod: we must
"use it as an instrument of our obedience to the triune God".
In this way Christians can "make each hour God's hour; if they
do this, they will be living more in eternity than in time. Time
is no longer a closed system: in the very midst of time they can
step over the boundary to eternity."[14] "Again and again the Lord
shows us that he has no time, that heaven will not use our way
of reckoning, . . . and that eternity's encounter with our time
must be just as sudden as the moment when God called the
world into being."[15] "Earth belongs to heaven. And mankind is
created for heaven. The heaven of the triune God, with every
infinity at its disposal, has enough space to accommodate earth
and its inhabitants"[16] without causing them alienation. On the
contrary, time finds its real home there, in its origin. "Our time
will be taken back up into eternal time."[17] In what follows we
shall have to show that this will all take place through the mediation of Christ's time.

b. The Self-Transcendence of Essence and Nature

If each of the Persons in God was himself because of his pure
transcendence to the other two, and therefore, for each Divine
Person, the divine essence had the attribute of the "ever greater",
it follows that a world that is essentially developing can only exist
in self-transcendence, especially since in its developing it is completely dependent on the priority of the Divine Being and can
strive toward and attain this being only in virtue of prior divine
grace and condescension. As we have already indicated,[1] this lies

[12] T 49.
[13] Pf 114.
[14] C 286.
[15] C 542.
[16] Pf 127.
[17] A 127.
[1] See pp. 67–68 above.

at the very heart of the developing system, insofar as no existent essential being enters reality solely by participating in universal being, and universal being can realize itself only by infusing itself into a particular hypostasis. This gives us a preliminary and, as yet, purely formal *imago trinitatis* in the creaturely likeness. We see it also in the still formal (and equally immutable) bifurcation of the absolute unity, in material beings, into two poles: the pole of the species and the pole of individuality, which is again a remote reflection of the mystery of the Trinity, where each of the Persons is identical with the divine essence yet distinct from the other Persons.

Quite apart from its dependence on its fellows, the finite being, thus constituted, is radically self-transcendent in that it can only find meaning (that is, direction and a path to follow) in its process of development provided it can eventually arrive at Being-as-such without becoming annihilated. "All that can be measured and grasped reveals its meaning by pointing beyond itself to the unfathomable reality of God."[2] In itself it cannot do this, it cannot cross this bridge unless it is led by the grace of the Divine Being. "What is transitory is transitory only because it is a reflection of eternity. The form crumbles because it is striving toward the eternal; the borderline is so hard because it faces a world that has no borders." An even deeper mystery lies here, however, namely, "that God has given something of himself to the created image, to accompany him along his path; he has breathed into the transitory form something that will not pass away." Otherwise it would be impossible for "the image to have an inner relationship with the Word" of God.[3] Since nature owes its transcendence to its origin in the sovereign power of Being, the latter is always stronger than nature.[4] By the power of grace we can step over time's "boundary with eternity in

---

[2] Bi 17.

[3] Bi 92–93.

[4] In Christian terms: "Christ is stronger than man. Eternity has triumphed over transitory life. The victory of the Word is assured, even where the one who proclaims this Word has no relationship with it. . . . From the very outset, supernature has triumphed over nature, the Church over the individual believer, the Cross over the world": Ph 30.

the very midst of time".[5] Man, "existing in this world, . . . has been created for a world where he can belong to the Son. By giving his assent, he can let God shape his life in this world in such a way that the fact of his being created for that other world comes to prevail."[6] And this is because what causes the other world to "prevail", namely, heaven and the grace of heaven, cannot be changed into nature: "no matter how much heaven may stretch toward earth and be conferring, promising, and fulfilling of itself, it always remains greater than anything that can be understood from an earthly standpoint."[7] This interplay between self-transcending nature and the grace that alone can fulfill it is, again, an *imago trinitatis*, a likeness of eternal trinitarian Being, translated into the terms of that being which is subject to development. It recalls what we have already said about expectation and the fulfillment that surpasses it; but in particular—since the creature is created preeminently in the Logos—it recalls the fact that the Father, insofar as he is the Origin, is always greater than the Son; for the Son expresses his indebtedness to the Father (by sharing the power to breathe forth the Spirit) in that he attains the Father's (power of) so breathing him forth. This interplay of nature and grace, in which the latter retains its ontological primacy, can be seen illustrated in the highest product of nature, Mary, at the moment of her greatest fulfillment, when she was assumed into heaven: here

> The distance and difference between heaven and earth are as if bridged over and obliterated for the Mother. For she who is now received by the Son into heaven is none other than she who received him on earth from heaven; and as her way expanded more and more, starting with the Son's conception and going all the way to her present reception into heaven by the Son, so this reception also expands to its high point in the Son's conception by her. The two high points intensify one another, and neither direction can be designated as the definitive one: from earth to heaven or from heaven to earth. It is an eternal circuit between God and man, heaven and earth, spiritual world and material world.[8]

[5] C 286.
[6] F 93.
[7] P 63.
[8] MH 146.

In all this, of course, it is clear that grace has the primacy, the grace of the Immaculate Conception, giving nature—albeit a nature created from the outset with a view to receiving this gift—the grace to receive grace in its fullness. Here the divine idea of a world, seen from the creature's perspective, reaches its zenith; and this idea becomes the immediate precondition for the union of God and man in the God-man.

c. Relationship, Reciprocity, Exchange

Thus we have already reached the result envisaged in the idea of the world as *imago trinitatis*. We recall the notion of personal presence [*Gegenwart*] in God, which we saw was a "turning-toward" [*Gegen-Wendung*], a turning of the Other to the One, and since this turning is achieved by the turning of the One to the Other (in begetting the Son), the whole relationship speaks of reciprocity. It is not as if each keeps to his own side; it is not a mere vis-à-vis: since the Other is begotten by the One and responds with total self-surrender, there is a genuine exchange, which is perfected and sealed in their joint breathing forth of the Spirit. If God's idea of the world is to bring heaven and earth together in Jesus Christ in the fullness of time, so that "we may be holy and blameless before him" (*katenōpion autou*, Eph 1:4), it follows that this incorporation of all created beings into the Begotten is, in trinitarian terms, the most intimate manner of union with God. For it implies that the creaturely "other-than-God" is plunged into the uncreated "Other-in-God" *while maintaining* that fundamental "distance" which alone makes love possible.[1] "The exchange of love that takes place within God is now open to the world in the form of an exchange between heaven and earth, God and man"; the creature is not confronted with anything "alien" but "the innermost truth about the being and destiny of things and himself".[2] The Son, since he is the Word of the Father, is given dominion over all things and in particular over mankind; this is because he is the Second Adam and, as God, possesses all that is the Father's in a more perfect manner.

[1] Cf. Jean-Luc Marion, *L'Idole et la distance* (Paris: Grasset, 1977). Cf. M 53: "Distance now signifies fullness."

[2] Bi 17–18.

It is only through him that things and "men acquire their full meaning."[3]

The fact that man, the dependent other, exists *in* the Son, the original Other, implies something else: "The world [as] an expression and an image of God", can only be "rooted in the word"; "its inmost essence rests upon the word." If creatureliness is the question God poses to the world's essence in the form of the Word, so too "there is the creature's answer to God in the word." This answer cannot depend on the whim of the creature: "Prior to the realm of choice and to the sphere of our vacillation and irresolution lies the sphere that does not fall within the orbit of our freedom and which we cannot disturb" namely, the Eternal Word. "It is only above and beyond this foundation that we enter the sphere of hesitation, the sphere in which the word of God may be heard or not heard, received or not received, answered or not answered."[4] This is what is meant by saying that the entire created universe has come into being in, through and for the Word. This is also the meaning of the offer Jesus makes to the Samaritan woman: he will give her living water for eternal life.[5] Man may refuse to speak to God, but "this does not alter the fact that the ground of his being, the unalterable character of the creature, whether he wills it or not, is involved in a dialogue with God."[6] So "the Yes that man utters . . . is not the same as the Yes that God hears"; God hears it "as part of the Word of the Lord", so much so that man "does not even recognize it as his word".[7] Now it has acquired "the dignity of a valid answer to God's own Word".[8] When to "the wretched worm Jacob" God says "Do not fear; I will help you", Jacob understands that "not even his obedience results from his own judgment, his own

[3] Ph 150.

[4] 1 Jo 31–32.

[5] God's "gift is what you yourself are, for you are God's gift to yourself; you are God's promise to yourself, to other people, to God. His gift to you is also what I [Jesus] am: the eternal Son of the Father, his promise, and the gift to the world that fulfills it. Our relationship is not only beginning at this moment; . . . You did not know this until now. Had you known it, you would have long since asked me for water": 1 Jo 223.

[6] 1 Jo 32.

[7] M 52.

[8] M 54.

decision. His obedience is something that finds its expression in
God from before all time: it is as if Jacob is introduced to his
own obedience and shown how to follow it. He must use the
power that is lent to him, but what he thus does is done by this
power. Yet it is not done without him; from before all time he
has been drawn into this power, surrounded by it, watched over
and strengthened by it."[9] This is perfected—in a way that goes
beyond our being created in the Word—by the consummated
work of Christ: "In the Old Covenant everyone was what he
was by his own efforts; in the New Covenant we are what the
Lord is. . . . He has made himself the exemplar of our nature,
a nature that was designed in heaven, and it is in him that we
possess this nature."[10] The person who dies defenseless in the
face of God's love returns to the Word of origin that is prior
to him, in the same way that the child comes forth from him
defenseless. Again, this is only possible "through Christ". The
curve that man describes, coming from God and returning to
him, "is only possible because . . . [it] is enclosed within the
curve of the word made man, which runs its pure course in
God, from the birth of the Lord to his death."[11] The difference
is that when man the sinner returns to God, having estranged
himself from him, he will have to be "through the grace of the
word of God made man, purified, burst open and expanded by
by purgatorial fire to the breadth and the fullness of his word
deposited in God."[12] And if we add to the Lord the perfected
Church to which, in him, we belong, the reality for which we
are bound when we die is "that picture of ourselves that the
Church and the Lord cherish within them. Thus, transcending
ourself, we shall be enabled to find our real 'I' in him."[13]

[9] Is 50. Cf. 197: Although God has experienced his sons' faithlessness, "their
faithfulness is so enveloped by his mercy that it remains greater than their faithlessness. . . . For the Word, which is his Word and hence greater than any deed
on their part, is absolute truth. . . . No human trespass is big enough to give the
lie to the Word of God."

[10] Ka II, 184; cf. 237: "Thus we are in him before he is in us, just as, in a royal
house, blood and kinship form the essential basis upon which the superstructure
of dignity and offices is built."

[11] 1 Jo 34.

[12] 1 Jo 37.

[13] L 93.

Created man initially seems to be free and almost alien vis-à-vis God;[14] here we see that only a trinitarian God can guarantee that man will not forfeit his independent being when united with God.[15] God "does not put us into a uniform of love. He lets his own love, out of which he has created every man, be reflected in the particular way in which each person loves."[16] "Thus the unity bestowed by the Lord not only preserves all that is personal, it actually promotes it where hitherto it was hard to recognize"; just as, in the unity of the Trinity, we become aware of the distinction of Persons, "so, in the unity that the Lord bestows upon us, we always discern both his fundamental imprint and our own personal imprint."[17] This is the basis of that eternal dignity which belongs to every human being.[18]

In the reciprocal relationships within unity there takes place the *exchange*. First it is the exchange of the earthly man for the heavenly: "We can now exchange our life, the finite for the infinite, the perishable for the eternal", life under the "law of death" for life "in the freedom of the Spirit", for "an enlarged life. Enlarged not only as to its length but also to its breadth: its space is the eternal space of the Lord."[19] And therein the second exchange takes place, the exchange between the earth of men and God's heaven, the "reciprocal indwelling: heaven is to find its home on earth, and earth is to have a domicile in heaven; transitory time acquires its significance in eternal time, but eternal time gives meaning to the transitory days."[20] There is an exchange of graces: "God gives me the grace of baptism, and I give him the grace of my return to him. . . . He gives me the grace of sending me out, and I give him the grace of acting as

[14] Is 222–24.

[15] "When God gains the upper hand in us . . . all the potentialities with which God initially endowed his creature blossom forth. He does not destroy his work when he lets it dwell in him but sees that everything in it comes to fulfillment. . . . Estranged from him, it becomes stunted, and its best attribute, its independent being, does not even come to birth": Ka II, 143.

[16] Ka II, 170.

[17] Ka I, 227.

[18] Ka I, 319.

[19] SL 16.

[20] Gl 7.

his representative. . . . For although all grace comes from God",
God still desires my response. "For what God gives, he gives
absolutely and entirely, giving us the right of ownership, though
everything ultimately comes from him."[21]

---

[21] 1 Jo 125–26.

B. EARTH MOVES HEAVENWARD

1. Dimensions of the World

Where the dramatic interplay is primarily vertical, the protagonists being "God above" and "man below", we inevitably come up against the dimensions or poles of the "stage". As we saw in *Theo-Drama* II, 173–88, this stage was inaugurated as an integrating feature of the action itself; here we must again draw attention to its complex and yet utterly indispensable significance. We saw that, without the heaven/earth distinction with which the first account of the creation begins, the action remains unintelligible; both are created (for heaven is not divine), and yet heaven is, initially, the place from which God acts upon man and together with him. But, because of its very close connection with the ineffable God, heaven can no more be pinned down than he can. It is created, and so God is superior to it in the same way that he is exalted over all the earth. But it enjoys a relationship with God insofar as it is, so to speak, the place within the world from which God operates. Thus God is represented as dwelling "in heaven"; there he is less and less alone, surrounded by creaturely beings who are supereminently "with God": the "heavenly host", the now cancelled gods of the other nations, which have become patrons of nations and peoples, angels with their tasks and commissions. Between heaven and earth, however, there is not only a relationship of distance but one of dramatic exchange: Enoch and Elijah are transported alive into heaven, which—increasingly decosmologized—finally comes to mean "being with God". Even the God of Genesis is also a God who "comes down"; Jacob sees angels ascending and descending on the ladder between heaven and earth; and the Lord of the Sinai covenant desires to have a tent in the camp of the people and later to live in the Temple—which, again, is but "his footstool". This mysterious relationship is finally ratified in the destiny of Christ: he is the only one to come down from heaven (Jn 3:13; 8:23), and he is the living Temple of God on earth; at the same time he is visibly on his way back to heaven, taking his earthly body and his entire earthly fate with him. Yet, nullifying the distance between heaven and earth, he remains on earth, invisibly, to the end of time, thus in a more concrete manner than ever before (cf. Is 55:10–11), in order to promote the exchange between heaven and earth; indeed, he *is* this exchange. Christian discipleship thus reveals a paradox: believers have their dwelling place prepared for them in heaven; having mysteriously died with Christ, their real life is already hidden with him in heaven (Col 3:3), and they have come "to the city of the living God, the heavenly Jerusalem" (Heb 12:22); but, on the other hand, they live on earth as "pilgrims and strangers", waiting "in Christ" for that time when they will finally "be with Christ" (Phil 1:23). Thus death, which had been a physical event at the end of their earthly lives, shifts into the center of their existence, not dividing it into two but, on the contrary, uniting the two aspects of their freedom: linking the free decision for God (in a faith that does not see) with the perfect freedom of the creature within the perfect freedom of God.[1] (And no one can share in absolute freedom except through such a decision.) Philosophically speaking, this unity of the two aspects of being cannot be rendered visible on a purely this-worldly basis because it presupposes the primary initiative of the grace-giving Creator. It is the Creator, revealing himself as triune, who first of all shows the creature that the latter's this-worldly, developmental existence will not be swallowed up by an abyss of pure being (or pure nothing) but will be given a home and a genuine scope for freedom within the eternal trinitarian relationships. The possibility and shape of this transition, of course, is completely in the power of God and remains a mystery. It is only within this transitional state that the world has reality; every attempt at self-fulfillment on this side of physical death is contrary to man's being and destructive of it. "The peoples labor for nought, and the nations weary themselves only for fire" (Jer 51:58; cf. Hab 2:13).

Initially we can give a formal outline of the structure of the world's reality, in order to provide the basis of a "vertical eschatology". It can be given content, however, only in the next two steps: first it must be shown that the formal structure is fulfilled

---

[1] Cf. "The radiance of freedom" in *The Glory of the Lord* IV (San Francisco: Ignatius Press, 1989), 267–86.

only in Christ (and his "extension", the Church), since it was for him that it was envisaged in the first place; and then it must be shown that this Christ has gone deeper than the sinful world's alienation and has overthrown it.

We have already given the outline of an idea of the world; now we must go on to describe this world as it is in reality, a world that can only manifest itself in transcendence. All the time we shall have to bear in mind that the basis of its "philosophical" transcendence lies in the "theological" final *prius* of grace over nature's efficient causality.[2] For only "grace can put something of the being of God into our becoming."[3]

As interpreted by many of the Church Fathers, the creation of man "according to our image and likeness" (Gen 1:26) is a description of the finality and transcendence that is inherent in our becoming, our developmental being. Man is created as *imago*, an abiding image, even if obscured by sin, and he is intended to unfold in the direction of *similitudo* by the exercise of freedom of choice.[4] This presupposes that something of abiding being is infused, by *act* or at least by *potentiality*, into man's striving: "Here below, the fact that we are led along a path, the path to life, is itself an expression of life."[5] "While the life we live is human and earthly, it has been offered to the eternal, heavenly life . . . of the triune God."[6] And since God's grace is offered to us to render our striving more effective, "the little span of time that remains in our control on earth is itself embedded in eternal life, over which we have no control whatsoever. This little span of time is given to us so that we may affirm the eternal life that is being offered us",[7] because "our temporal life only has meaning within our eternal life."[8] On earth, man must

---

[2] On the relationship between nature and grace in A. von Speyr, cf. W 273–94, and esp. OM 29–40 ("Natural and Supernatural Knowledge of God", "Can Reason Know God without Faith?", etc.).

[3] OM 107.

[4] Where this distinction is not drawn (e.g., in Gregory of Nyssa), the *imago* itself is regarded as essentially the seat of transcendence and self-transcendence.

[5] B 259.

[6] C 352.

[7] B 215.

[8] B 211.

pursue partial aims, but insofar as they are in accordance with his mission, which expresses his main goal, they strive toward it.[9] The relationship between this world and the world beyond can be expressed in very different ways: "Some live here below and have a relationship to the beyond. Others live already in the beyond and share almost superficially and nonessentially in earthly life."[10] In both cases, however, it is true that "the passing of the earthly day makes room for eternity",[11] for "God has not created the world to abide in itself but so that it shall develop in him. . . . By creating what is good in this world, he has set it apart from himself so that it may return to him."[12] So man, essentially, must always live in a "borderline situation": "His transitory time becomes, for him, a sign of God's eternity, and his limitations become a sign of infinity. . . . For God has made man in his own image, and an image cannot contradict what it shows forth."[13] "Limited existence", as such, is a "demonstration" of eternal life and the "way into" it.[14] For man, in his borderline experience, eternal life is both the presence and the future of the temporal: it is presence, since the eternal is the basis of all temporal movement toward it,[15] so that we have to "live on the basis of eternal life in the very midst of time".[16] "Whenever anything is done in faith, it is no longer done solely for this world but as part of a heavenly commission"; this is what is meant by "building one's house upon a rock".[17] This presupposes, however, that there is already a fountain of eternal life welling up within us, "the living link between life here below

---

[9] C 502.

[10] 1 Jo 281. "The emphasis of some commissions lies so much in the beyond that here below only desperation is visible": 3 Jo 37.

[11] Ka I, 46.

[12] Ka II, 64.

[13] M 10.

[14] Ka II, 247.

[15] Cf. Ep 113–14; Ph 97: From Christ's vantage point, "the meaning of earthly life is completely transformed. Its meaning now has an orientation in the eternal . . . it is a meaning given by God."

[16] Ka II, 218.

[17] B 283. There is in Christian mysticism an impressive argument for this vertical coincidence of temporal and eternal life, the possibility "of the simultaneous existence of a gazing in heaven and on earth": Bi 101.

and life beyond, between God and man".[18] Primarily it is "faith, love and hope" that are "the anticipation, the foundation and the beginning of eternal life", even on earth.[19] "The strength of the faith in which a Christian knows the Lord through his grace is so great that it is no longer from this world: it comes from the heavenly world and itself belongs to that world."[20] The same is true of hope, which carries us from the present aspect of eternal life to its future aspect: "Though we have not seen God, we live by him, because he sees us; we live in hope one day of seeing him as he sees us."[21] So the future quality of eternal life is not something merely absent but in prospect: it is promised to us on the basis of its present reality. Of course it is not something that simply "arrives" but is something addressed to man's freedom, something set before him. Later we shall discuss the shape of Christian hope. It is man's milieu while he is "on his way from earth to heaven";[22] it is a "link between earthly and heavenly things, but this link exists within the earthly insofar as the Christian himself is stilll on this earth. The Christian remains on this earth particularly because of the task he has to fulfill."[23] It is true that "all our paths are trinitarian paths", but "We shall be in the Trinity only after death. . . . Now we are *en route* to the Trinity."[24] What, here below, is "like a bud of eternal life" will "develop to full bloom" in the world beyond. "Nevertheless, there is an unbroken connection between bud and blossom. The initial steps and beginnings of eternal life are inspired in us by the Lord already here below, and no new act of sowing will be necessary in order to bring eternal life to development in us."[25] God can give men the gift of prophecy, but "he can never hand everything over to them; what he reveals are truths of his heaven, whereas men cannot live fully in heaven while they are still on earth"; they only receive the truth "piecemeal". This is connected with our earthly finitude: "The time boundary has been withdrawn from our sight: we can shape events within our transitory time, but it is God who shapes our eternal time."[26]

[18] 1 Jo 225.
[20] 2 Jo 274.
[22] Ka I, 422.
[24] 2 Jo 210.
[26] C 416.

[19] 1 Jo 235.
[21] C 21.
[23] 1 Jo 196; cf. 2 Jo 46.
[25] 2 Jo 289.

Nonetheless, since it is "faith" that "mediates between heaven and earth",[27] and we "live in faith and possess death" (where "death is no longer a breaking-off" but the "fashioning anew of our existence in God"), both "present and future reality are given to the believer here and now." "Where death belongs to man and not man to death, the temporal world has been shattered and invaded by the eternal world. Even eternity—God's time—belongs to the believer; his earthly time is fixed within eternity and cannot fall out of it."[28] But "everything that does not lead from nature to supernature is blind, self-enclosed and hence barren and"—in a bad sense—"dead". It "lives in the past of its former sins" and thus has turned away from the promised future. "If a man truly recollected his past, he would be open to his future", he would be on the way "to the free, limitless life of eternity", where God makes it easy for the one who strives "to step over the threshold. This step is not only something to which God invites us, it is something we rehearse throughout our whole life in this world."[29]

This leads us back again to the priority of heaven. Not only has heaven given earth the ability to transcend itself and move toward heaven, it is always supporting it in its journey toward fulfillment. "Heaven suffuses the earth" with an "atmosphere" that comes from it.[30] "When God reveals himself to the world, there is always a kind of rent in time, a suspension of its limitations."[31] In this way even God's joy can become part and parcel of this world,[32] and all the things of the senses can become transparent, allowing us to discern God's joy through and behind them.[33] "The answer to every question in the world lies hidden in the Father. There is no question that was not first of all an answer. All questions come from the answer and return to the answer."[34] "Everything eternal taking place in time is it-

---

[27] 4 Jo 185.
[28] C 112–13.
[29] Ka I, 423–25.
[30] OM 70–71.
[31] Ps 136, cf. 96.
[32] "God's joy becomes this-worldly": L 133–36.
[33] 1 Jo 237–38, 239, 241.
[34] 1 Jo 124.

self beyond time and before all time. The greater and deeper something is, the more timeless it is. . . . Everything heavenly precedes the earthly. What is timeless is the real. . . . The true meaning of time is eternity."[35]

This does not mean that people should abandon the earth and dream their way into heaven. The saints had such a share in the grace of heaven here below, but "their mission puts them on earth, and only with great discretion do they make use of their heavenly life. They themselves give earth the preponderance. For the mission wills it so."[36] All the same they are constantly aware "that heaven is always open toward the earth and that the things of earth have a mode of existence in heaven".[37] But it is the saints and the real believers who possess the good death, "which is willed and created by God" and which is "the seal of God's power over the life of his creature" and "permeates the whole course of earthly life". "Without the ferment of death, finite life would not be life."[38] Similarly, in an emphatically Christian perspective, life, suffering and death are wedded together in that whole movement of transcendence whereby earthly life goes toward the coming kingdom of God: "The love that suffers the pangs of childbirth for the sake of the kingdom is both heavenly and earthly. . . . All its renunciations and sacrifices are part and parcel of its forward movement. . . . Everything that belongs to the old world reminds us of the coming of the new; but both have come so close that it is all like a feast, a celebration of pain and joy, of dying and living, of earth and heaven."[39]

This may seem to be the product of an inflamed imagination or abstract wishful thinking, but in fact it—and not the self-enclosed cosmological and anthropological world views that have banished heaven—is the real world. Of course this can only be grasped by faith, which finds its dimensions ratified in Jesus Christ, the Mediator between the creation and the Trinity. Properly speaking, after what we have said here and before going on to describe the Mediator, we should have added a description of

[35] 1 Jo 145.
[36] MH 92.
[37] P 86.
[38] 1 Jo 42.
[39] OM 562–63.

the world in its sinfulness and alienation from God (the world that is usually regarded as the "real" world); for the present, however, we will presuppose what can be found in *Theo-Drama* IV (95ff., 137ff.) on the subject of sin and death. We shall take up the topic again in the second part of the present volume.

2. Fulfillment in Christ and the Church

a. Christ the Trinitarian Meaning of the World

So far we have described heaven's movement toward earth and earth's movement toward heaven. These movements converge on a coming: "The new heaven and the new earth come about through the Son's Incarnation." Both, united in the Son, are to "become creation's definitive form. This form can never be dissolved or surpassed." It is eschatological. "Time will no longer be characterized by separation, as formerly: it will run on into eternity, just as our transitory earth will pass over into the intransitory heaven, and our humanity will pass over, in the being of the Son, into eternal life."[1] After Adam's preliminary encounters with God in paradise, and even more after the sinner's time has shut itself off, what is required is "the coming of the Son and the founding of his Church in the dimension of time, in order to restore a genuine presence of the eternal within time".[2] And this "eternal" is not only the triune God—represented in the world by the Son—but also creation, already perfect in heaven, with, at its head, the Firstborn, the risen Christ, who has become the head of the heavenly and the earthly Church. "The Church exists on both sides, in heaven and on earth. And its heavenly part is turned toward the earth just as its earthly part is turned toward heaven."[3] This unity is inaugurated by Christ, whose "life on earth is no different from his life in heaven", since "his life in time is inseparable from his life in eternity",[4]

---

[1] Is 248.

[2] Pf 13. "The way of the Lord" is "that whereby he unites heaven and earth, the eternal lowered into our temporality": C 394; cf. 19.

[3] Ap 409; cf. Ep 113.

[4] T 67.

and so "the Son established in himself an uninterrupted union between heaven and earth", the "mirroring of heaven . . . among us", and "precisely thus becomes the center of the world".[5] He can "cause heaven to begin on earth"[6] because, "dwelling in them [on earth], . . . he does not abandon heaven."[7] He does not offer us a "prospect" of eternal life "after this earthly life has run its course, but presents us with it—an eternity that has already begun—in the very midst of earthly life".[8] "He does this by bringing himself and the love of the Father with him from the beyond into this world. . . . He carries this world over into the beyond; he effects the blossoming of the world into his Kingdom."[9] "The Son overcame, and annihilated in himself, the whole of the distance between heaven and earth: as true man, he is at the same time the likeness of the Father in God."[10] This is "the image of redemption brought to completion, indeed, the image of eternity in heaven, which has taken up all the places and times on earth into itself. . . . He is Place; he is Time, in that he is the time of each individual and has pitched his tent, taken up his abode in each one."[11] Through him the redeemed live "under an open heaven, since God has created heaven in the new earth, or the new earth in heaven. The risen Son is earth in heaven; his Eucharist is heaven on earth." And "if we were to try to describe his earthly existence as an expression of his divine, heavenly existence, we could just as well (since he is genuinely man, just as we are, like us in all things but sin) describe his heavenly, God-man's existence as earthly."[12] "The Son comes to the world in order to glorify the Father; so it is clear that this glorification also takes place in heaven, for the Son does nothing else on earth but what he does in heaven: the will of the Father."[13] At this "meeting point between heaven and earth,

[5] Pf 49.
[6] 2 Jo 334 (GT); in more detail: Ka II, 212–14.
[7] Ep 142.
[8] Ka II, 275.
[9] 4 Jo 54.
[10] 4 Jo 82.
[11] K 122. Cf. Ep 48–49, B 110, 284.
[12] Is 217.
[13] B 280.

where they intersect in the Incarnation", Christ also "takes the transitory nature of the Old Covenant"—which knew nothing of an eternal life for creatures—"up into his eternal life";[14] "for the grace of redemption he will earn, as man, on the Cross is something he already possesses, as the eternal God, when he comes into the world." Thus even "before the Cross" he can "dispense" its fruits.[15] Even before the Cross he can describe himself, to Pilate, as the King.[16] However, when he reconciles heaven and earth on the Cross, "in heaven, too, reconciliation takes place—whatever has turned its back on the sinful world makes peace with it." In virtue of the "blood that has been shed, those in heaven acquire an attachment to the world", even "in the face of the evil things that still keep happening on earth". The blood of the Cross flows "back and forth", forever reconciling earth and heaven to one another.[17]

In the first place, however, the union between heaven and earth in Christ presupposes God's triune nature. This is because the Son on earth cannot represent his own divine nature (this would constitute a form of monophysitism): rather, he translates his eternal relationship with the Father into the terms of time and creatureliness. In the second place, accordingly, everything will revolve around the question of how his trinitarian being and action can be translated into something that (by grace) can be imitated by creatures. Such a transposition will be possible only on the basis of the fact, outlined above, that the being of the Trinity and the interplay of the Persons is the prototype, and the developmental being of the creature is a reflection of it.

[14] Ka I, 53.

[15] B 118.

[16] "We see death, which we strive against, as an end. For here below, everything strives toward death. As long as one sees everything from here below, one can only speak of death as a boundary "beyond" which, perhaps, something else begins. The Lord, by contrast, who sees everything from above, discerns in everything the signs of incipient entry into his Kingdom, the first approaches to eternity": 4 Jo 57. "He has brought about unity in himself": Ph 45; but in such a way that the Son is "the beginning and the opening", so that we can gain "access to the divine" through his humanity: Ep 45.

[17] K 41-42. On the Cross as the seal of atonement between heaven and earth: KW 56-57.

The Son is the *revelation of the Trinity*. He "creates on earth an extrapolation of the Trinity: he lives in a fully trinitarian way yet is a man among men."[18] More particularly, "on the one hand, Father and Spirit reveal themselves in the Son in order to demonstrate his divine nature, and, on the other hand, the triune God (with the Son in himself), using the Son's human nature, demonstrates how he can reveal himself in the holiness of a holy man. The humanity of Christ can be employed in both directions for this trinitarian purpose."[19] "His life on earth is an image and an expression of the undivided triune life in heaven. In his individual being he manifests the uniqueness of the Father, and of the Son, and of the Spirit."[20] "He lives in the Holy Spirit, whom he receives, and in the vision of the Father, speaking to him in prayer and doing his will";[21] this applies to the Eucharist also, for it "points beyond the surrendered Son to the surrendering Father and to the Spirit, who is himself this surrender". Eucharist "therefore points to God's manner of being, which is always active love".[22]

Jesus wishes in and through all things to be the revelation of the Father, and so he shows both their eternal unity and their distinction: "There will never, then, be two possibilities of seeing God: one through the Father, and the other through the Son. Rather, the Son is the revelation of God the Father . . . entire openness to the eternal Evermore of the Father."[23] And this takes place, according to his own words, through the Holy Spirit, who is the bond of both.[24] When he prays to the Father, "I have given them your word", he himself, the Word of God, is this gift, but he makes "no sensation about it": he does not give himself away "as a private existence or an autonomous ego, but

---

[18] OM 98.

[19] OM 95. In more detail: Ep 62.

[20] C 240.

[21] OM 106.

[22] OM 101. With regard to the Holy Spirit, "every presence, every work of the Son also demonstrates the presence and work of the Spirit. We cannot say that the Spirit continues what the Son has begun. Beginning and continuation are a single act of them both": C 175.

[23] 3 Jo 101.

[24] 3 Jo 145.

only as the gift of the Father".[25] He bridges the distance between God and man by his perfect "transparency", the "pure openness" whereby "certainly, he remains mysterious and beyond our grasp . . . yet not like an opaque mystery that one cannot get behind, but rather through the very infinity and openness of his mystery itself."[26] He is pure motion from the Father and back to the Father,[27] in such a way that he leaves the Father every opportunity to speak to us,[28] ultimately through the surrender of his Son and Word.[29] Thus God "surrenders what is most intimately his", and does so in a trinitarian manner:[30] he surrenders his love, which is both "transitive", focusing on the other, and "intransitive", since God's entire being "is love".[31] So the Son can say that the kingdom of God is coming through him.[32] "This explains the fundamental importance of a trinitarian contemplation of the Son; in contemplating the Son we must not for a moment abstract from the Trinity."[33] The Trinity will be revealed "fully and centrally on the Cross";[34] while the triune mystery in the incarnate Son is something, "not presented to the senses, but uttered in silence",[35] believers nonetheless receive, "not some vague intimation, but a genuine vision of God".[36]

Here arise more difficult questions concerning the christological *transpositions* of the divine into the human.[37] What is not difficult is the idea that the Son, as man, continues the eternal dialogue of prayer of the Divine Persons in heaven; it is not difficult to think of the eternal Word clothing himself in human words. And since Christ gives us a share in his own prayer,[38] every word of the Lord is a prayer to the Father and a gift and a task for the Church.[39] And just as God's prayer causes each Divine Person to do the will of the Others, so on earth the Father always does

[25] 3 Jo 341; cf. 4 Jo 52.   [26] 3 Jo 363–64.
[27] Ka II, 130.   [28] L 52f.
[29] SL 93–94.   [30] Ka II, 94.
[31] OM 108.   [32] C 172.
[33] OM 115.   [34] Bi 21.
[35] Bi 116.   [36] Bi 18.
[37] Preliminary material in *Theo-Drama* III, 122–48.
[38] B 134. On the Our Father as the Son's prayer: B 168ff.
[39] 4 Jo 327.

the will of the Son, who is obedient to him in all things (Jn 11:42).[40] Anyone who asks in the Spirit of Christ, that is, in a trinitarian context, will infallibly be heard.[41] Such a person has power over God;[42] he has the "key to heaven".[43]

On earth, the Son is obedient to the Father in the Spirit, even to his death on the Cross. This is the intelligible form of his eternal attitude to the Father who begets him, namely, that of primal obedience in willing cooperation and gratitude. True, what we have already termed the "trinitarian inversion" (*Theo-Drama* III, 183–91) applies here: now, instead of breathing forth the Spirit "consubstantially" with the Father, he (as man) receives the Father's will in the Spirit; having the same Spirit within him as the Spirit of obedience. All the same it must be said that this "kenosis of obedience" ("emptying himself of the form of God": Phil 2:7) must be based on the eternal kenosis of the Divine Persons one to another: it must be *one* of the infinite aspects of eternal life. Now, however, divine obedience requires that he surrender to men as well as to God: "In his obedience and exposure before God and men, the Son is not passive; he must perform this action himself. Demands are constantly made of him from both sides; he is plundered from both sides. The final result bears his distinctive stamp."[44] Even the plans he himself makes are made in obedience.[45] Christ will infuse this exact obedience of his into the Church.[46] In obedience lies the unity of Christ's life,[47] a unity that will persist undiminished into the night of the Cross, when every sight and feeling of the Father is taken from him. Christ invites his Church to follow him[48] even into this absolute obedience, "which must be like dying in the very presence of God".[49]

On the Cross, Jesus is deprived of the sight of the Father. This raises the question of how the immediate vision of the Father, which Jesus—as the God-man—must enjoy, is related to the faith that the Christian must have, namely, a trusting self-surrender to God, for the most part unsupported by sight. It is

---

[40] 3 Jo 275.

[41] 3 Jo 107, 109.

[42] B 166.

[43] K 149.

[44] Ka II, 272.

[45] 4 Jo 17.

[46] 4 Jo 292; Gh 103f.

[47] Gh 51.

[48] C 531.

[49] C 516.

an indispensable axiom that the Son, even in his human form, must know that he is the eternal Son of the Father. He must be aware of the unbreakable continuity of his *processio* and his *missio*, or, in other words, he must know of his transcendental obedience, which upholds his entire earthly existence (*Theo-Drama* III, 165ff., 515ff.).[50] This vision "did not prevent him from being perfectly obedient to the Father. In this vision, therefore, he sought nothing other than the Father's will."[51] Nonetheless the Son, insofar as he is man, must be able to experience faith, albeit a faith that is only analogous to what we have described above as the "primal faith within the Trinity". This being so, he would be "the Son who both sees and believes, who expresses the Father", and many of his words could be described as "items of faith, uttered out of the midst of vision; as soon as they are embraced by faith, they lead on to vision." They are vision, understood as an "opening of a sense of the eternal",[52] whereby our faith participates to a certain degree in the Son's vision.[53] In the Lord's Passion his sight is veiled, whereas his obedience remains intact,[54] and to that extent we must also say that Christ has a real "faith".[55] Otherwise "the gift of faith would not really have come from him."[56] He must possess a faith that fulfills and transcends the Old Testament faith yet is "by no means an impoverished vision, a mere 'not-yet', the negative of vision"; he must possess the fullness of faith as found in the genuine believer.[57] Thus he must embody a Christology not only from

---

[50] 1 Jo 176, 2 Jo 99–100, 4 Jo 142; K 155; B 26f., 160; G 18, 33, 37, 51, 54, 56–58; A 54, 60–61, 69, 101, 112; GE 11; Bi 56, 95; Gh 40, 103; Be 47, Pf 35, 68; Ep 30–31; MH 103; W 39, 260; Ka I, 355: Vision comes through mission. Ka I, 321: "The mission epitomizes the Son's life, . . . the Son's relationship with the Father is all of a piece with his relationship to his mission. . . . It is in virtue of his mission that he looks up to the Father." Cf. C 261: "The Son, on earth, has a direct and absolute knowledge of the Father, . . . which corresponds to an absolute mission."

[51] G 84.

[52] Gl 8.

[53] Ka II, 168–69.

[54] Ep 61.

[55] Ka I, 140; "radiant faith": Pa 17.

[56] W 79.

[57] W 81.

above but simultaneously from below: "As man he must attain
to, press forward to, the awareness of his divinity. Thus, from
his human nature, he can make a path for mankind to his divinity, to the whole triune divinity."[58] This presupposes (right
from the Incarnation) a certain veiling of his sight of the Father: he must leave it in abeyance, refrain from using it;[59] this is
possible because of the distance between Father and Son in the
Trinity.[60] Now, however, the divine distance between Father and
Son must be translated into the Christian distance between God
and man. The Son now lives in this distance in such a way that,
in order to "learn it, he has ultimately to *draw it out of himself*".
The divine vision must be transposed into this divine *humanity*,
so that through this imparted vision he becomes the "origin and
harbinger of the vision of many who are to come after him";
it is "based almost more on faith than on the heavenly vision".
Yet his attitude "is all of a piece, like himself". "And in fact it is
in the mission itself, in grasping it and keeping it alive, that the
unity of the Son's adoration is shown and fulfilled, a unity which
strives increasingly to become a unity of the adoring believer—
fully and visibly achieving this in the Cross."[61]

Clearly, we are operating here at the heart of the mystery, as
is evident from the following observations on Christ's "time".
Who, for instance, can bring transparency into the fact that,
"since the Incarnation, what is limitless can now be found within
our limitations",[62] because God's Word to men, "even in this
limitation, has not lost the limitless quality of the eternal",[63]
which guarantees "his abiding significance through all the cen-

---

[58] W 82. "As man, the Son must discover and enter into the fullness of the
Word that he himself is": M 45. "He must get to know his eternal Word, he must
encounter it with the reverence that is appropriate to the Word of God. He is 'I'
as man and as God, and in this 'I' there must be no discrepancy of any kind, since
as man he is not a reflection of his own divine nature but the unequivocal Word
of the Father; he is the incarnate, only begotten Son in the whole profundity and
uniqueness of this Word": M 46.

[59] W 78.

[60] W 83–84.

[61] W 85–86. (These entire pages should be read for the sake of continuity of
thought.)

[62] M 12.

[63] M 23.

turies"[64] and "by grace consumes, as it were, and obliterates all human limitation".[65] For "the believer's spirit obeys now new directions and principles. These are not the law imposed by the limitations of human existence in space and time. . . . Life thus takes on at once the meaning and the fullness of the eternal. The infinite belongs to it."[66] But this mysterious communication between time and eternity—a time that is not destroyed by eternity yet is embedded in it—is something we owe to the *time of the Mediator*, Jesus Christ.

We observed the eternal prototype of maturation at work in the trinitarian process: "While everything takes place in such detailed correspondence and the highest fulfillment, the eternal moment is effective retrospectively and prospectively, including everything from all eternity and for all eternity. What is 'now' always was, and it is so full that it is unsurpassable: not in such a way that the present moment stifles freedom of action, but in such a way that expectation and fulfillment exactly coincide"[67] —and the fulfillment always overfulfills the expectation. Now, once the eternal God determines to create a world-time characterized by *becoming*, his eternal time will be, of necessity, contemporaneous with every moment of transitory time, and this contemporaneity will be the time "which, in his grace, God takes to concern himself with us".[68] However, his time does not simply bridge our time, neutrally, as it were: it gives each moment its content,[69] indeed, its urgency.[70] This is possible because, right from the start, created time bears "the mark of its divine origin" and exhibits an analogy to it; "The temporal or-

[64] M 43.

[65] M 45.

[66] SL 36–37.

[67] W 38.

[68] Ka I, 206.

[69] "There is the time that must be waited for and the time that must be kept. . . . God's will reveals itself according to a temporal plan": Ka I, 208f.

[70] "Revelation's urgency at any given moment is like a reflection of eternity in time": Is 117. The various forms of time in the Book of Revelation are witness to this urgency: they correspond to no earthly time (Ap 16), but with their "soon" (Ap 37) or "near" (Ap 44), as with their simultaneity of Old and New Testament (Ap 464), they express the irruption of eternal time into temporal time; when temporal time is taken up into eternal time, "time is no more" (Ap 348).

der is neither an overflow nor a waste product of eternity"[71] but
a being distinct from it and that looks toward its origin. (Only
when temporal man deliberately turns away from God does "the
time of sin become a time of decay", an evil transience.[72] And
yet even the unbeliever cannot "cobble together a fully satisfying world view from what is purely transitory", for "though
he may not call them by name, what he is seeking are eternal,
divine values.")[73] God intends not only to dominate creaturely
time from above but to embed it, with all its created reality, in his
eternal time. It is to become "a time in God, . . . a time hidden
in God's time".[74] And the believer must concern himself with
eternal time "because eternity is a form of duration in which he
is to participate".[75] Everything in the world is "envisioned for
a time that ultimately belongs to eternal life".[76]

Here, then, Christ's "time" acquires its significance. "The
Lord possesses a *time* that has validity for him alone, because it
belongs to God and cannot be compared to any other time."[77]
As a human being he lives, as all others do, in a time that is successive and segmented, but "his 'time', each individual section
of the commission he has received, lies so much in the hand of
the Father . . . that the Lord has no possibility of disposing over
it and planning it in detail. . . . As his commission comes from
God, so his time comes from God. His time is God's time."
For the sake of obedience, he has renounced his divine foreknowledge and given it into the Father's keeping: "This lack
of knowledge in him is something perfectly serious, not in the
least a game in which he would merely make a pretense of not
knowing. Even his supernatural, human knowledge in God is
made use of by him only to the extent that this is necessary for

[71] Pf 8. "When God created time, he did so without in any way affecting the
substance of eternity. He did not cut time out of eternity. On the one hand there
is transitory time; on the other there is an intact eternity. . . . Through eternity
what is transitory acquires a meaning, and death becomes an element of life,
man's way of going to God": T 34–35.

[72] Pa 73.

[73] G 32.

[74] 2 Jo 93; cf. Ka I, 206–9.

[75] G 27.

[76] Is 248.

[77] 2 Jo 89.

his task. . . . That is where it has its boundary, where it is rather the lack of knowledge that is necessary for him to carry out the commission he has received."[78] "By allowing the hour to come, by remaining aware of it in every context without letting himself be overwhelmed or hindered by it, he shows that he regards time as merely an arrangement designed to accompany him by the Father, that he knows how everything included in time belongs to eternity. . . . By refusing, while he was on earth, to anticipate the hour as a historic one . . . he remained *timeless* in the midst of his temporal life."[79] His final and decisive acceptance of God's time was his death. This death—an expression of his constant obedience—remains, in him and in God, just as timeless as his life. Thus he will be able to exist timelessly in our time in the form of the Eucharist, which contains both his death and his life.[80] "Life and death both bear witness to the Lord. In his death he is life, and in his life he dies. So we begin to comprehend that both conditions are simultaneous in the Lord (who is God) and that everything temporal about him always has an eternal side." "Even in his temporal existence he lives in the here and now of the eternal present, showing this to us in his death and in his life." So "life and death coincide in Holy Mass; they have become one, they have become the sign of concrete eternity."[81] In his Resurrection, Jesus has already taken the whole of transitory time (including life and death) with him into that eternal life which was the source of his constant obedience to the Father's commission. This means that he has also recapitulated the "non-time" of the dead.[82] It also means that the Risen One does not live in some "intermediate time" before the "end of the world".[83]

[78] 2 Jo 89–90.

[79] 4 Jo 435.

[80] 4 Jo 436: mortal, he "enters the transtemporality of the Father, receiving, within his time, participation in eternity; thus his dying into the Father is also the beginning of his eucharistic Incarnation."

[81] H 69.

[82] 4 Jo 345. "In dying, everyone finds that Jesus has already died before him. Everyone's death has its reality in him. Furthermore, he has died everyone's death, so that all the dead have a share in his being": K 29; cf. T 90.

[83] "He rules in eternity. It is not as if, between his Resurrection and the Last Judgment, he lives in a kind of preliminary period. . . . The vanquishing of his

Two questions remain to be discussed: the way in which *Jesus bestows his time upon the Church* and upon believers (who thus come to live in eschatological time or "end-time"), and how we should understand the future (the "coming") or the return (the "coming again") of Christ. There is a specifically "Christian time", which bears fruit in eternal time.[84] "The Son, therefore, puts his time—passing, yet replete with eternity—at our disposal in the Church as the Church's time, the Church's year, the Church's life, so that by living in it we shall share in Christ's own time."[85] The time that Christ "has borrowed" from human time "he gives back to men from *his* time, which is an indivisible, eternal time, . . . so that from now on man, within time, shares in eternal life." Since God's entire, eternal plan is fulfilled in Jesus' death on the Cross, "the Son, in dying, bends the trajectory of time back into the circle of eternity. In ultimate powerlessness and darkness he reverses the whole course of time."[86] This "removes the whole atmosphere of despair and lostness"[87] from our mortal existence; believers find that "paths" are revealed to them "leading to eternal time".[88] Christ's death, we must remember, was the highest expression of life: it was death *as* life.[89] If we participate in Christ's time, it means that, in him, we share in bringing our time into eternal time, insofar as Jesus' past (as a historical person) is the guarantee of his future. In his Epistle, Peter takes the trinitarian experience on Tabor as proof of the return of Christ.[90] And it is this future only because "it is a living presence in our present, bestowing genuine future upon it."[91] But "the time of his return is the

---

enemies refers to the extension of the eternal lordship of Christ in the temporal world": C 503.

[84] F 125.

[85] Pf 25.

[86] OM 69.

[87] C 552.

[88] Ps 67. "If a man is set free to engage in Christian love, he makes his transitory time into something that already belongs to eternal time; thus, by anticipation, even in his human time he participates in God's eternal time": OM 103–4.

[89] 1 Jo 44, 3 Jo 283, 125; C 35.

[90] Ka I, 431–40.

[91] C 497.

ultimate encounter between eternal time and our time"; eternal
time opens in order "to embrace and enfold our time, thereby
putting an end to our time, an end that is rather a beginning. Accordingly, through the Resurrection, space is given a new place
within heavenly space."[92] Until then, Christian time is an "end-
time" because the promised Coming is already here: "The child
about to be born is already there and has its own pulsating life
in the womb";[93] Christ's return to the world has already begun
in the Eucharist.[94] "Each time the Lord goes away, there is the
promise of his return. For he is always going forth and always
returning", he is always going in two opposite directions, and
we have to add that this is something "we can never grasp".[95]
Jesus "speaks the whence and the whither simultaneously: he is
going to the Father *who sent him*. This path is his essence and
his life", and he imparts it to the temporal existence of those
who are his.[96] He has "set our being in motion again, toward
him, on the eternal path of the Son", namely, to the Father in
the Holy Spirit.[97] In this sense, where eternal time and eternal
future are immanent within transitory time, the historical revelation is always maturing, addressing each age and each moment:
"Nothing is concluded, then; everything is becoming and growing, and therefore it is Christian revelation."[98]

Tentatively, we can ask about the mode of creaturely duration once it has been admitted into God's eternity. We have
"no words" to portray it. But we can say that "there is constant
activity but no decay. Everything steps out of the restrictions
of finitude, but not in the way a river oversteps its banks: life
is transposed from our tiny form into the immeasurable form
given by God. The paradigms of our present existence here be-

[92] C 499.

[93] Ka I, 418.

[94] 3 Jo 123–24. The Son's return to the world is trinitarian: bodily, as the Risen
One at Easter, spiritually through the sending of the Spirit at Pentecost, and finally
in the Eucharist, which comes to us from the Father's hand: 3 Jo 123–24. On the
unity of his return to the Father and his coming again to the world: 2 Jo 122–23.
On the Son's dwelling within us together with the Father: 3 Jo 133.

[95] 3 Jo 151.

[96] 3 Jo 225.

[97] C 242.

[98] 3 Jo 377.

low are a compromise. In eternity, however, there is an elasticity
that is unknown to us here; there is also a mysterious encounter
between every "here" and "now" and every *other* "here" and
"now". Space and time meet in an entirely different way from
what we know on earth." Now our creaturely becoming has a
share in the ineffable "becoming" of the Divine Being. "In the
midst of our vision of God" there is "a joyful movement toward
him in which we are always arriving at our goal and yet are
still moving forward".[99] "Eternal duration cannot be measured.
Its sole destination, the worship and glorification of the triune
God, is continually being reached—and only *because* it has already been reached can we reach it anew. Becoming coincides
with being."[100]

b. The Church as Prolongation of Christ

Having spoken of the transposition of vision into faith, and of
Christ's time into our time, we have already said some fundamental things about the way the Church issues from, and is
set on her way by, him who is the Mediator between heaven
and earth. The Church is the prolongation of Christ's mediatorial nature and work and possesses a knowledge that comes
by faith; she lives objectively (in her institution and her sacraments) and subjectively (in her saints and, fundamentally, in all
of her members) in the interchange between heaven and earth.
Her life comes from heaven and extends to earth, and extends
from earth to heaven.

   If, in God, the idea of the world exists as an organism to which
he has given its own freedom, this idea now becomes concrete
in the risen Mediator. "He has made himself the exponent of our
nature as heaven designed it, and we have this nature in him",[1]
insofar as he has borne our personal sin and put us in concrete
touch with God's idea of us. "In this sense we are in him before
he is in us", and by being "in him" we are given a participation
in his being begotten of the Father.[2] Here we have a concrete

[99] OM 74-75.
[100] C 501.
[1] Ka II, 184.
[2] Ka II, 227.

case, expressed in terms of the world, of the primal truth that
the world's "essence and foundations are rooted in the word",
that "its inmost essence rests upon the word", and that "such is
the creature's nature, and it is not in his power to change it", but
"prior to the realm of choice and to the sphere of our vacillation
and irresolution lies the sphere that does not fall within the orbit
of our freedom."[3] There is a part of us that "no longer belongs
to ourselves, . . . because it lies in him, is deposited with him. In
each person who believes, loves and hopes, there is this place in
which [the Lord] speaks openly of the Father", and at this place
"his hour has already come."[4] "Our apparent unprotectedness
in this world is grounded in our protectedness in God."[5] "Ultimately everyone is confronted with his word as deposited in
God", with "God's image of each particular man, present in him
from the beginning";[6] but this idea is always an idea in Christ,
and that is why it is to Christ that the judgment is entrusted.
And at the same time this image and pattern is also implanted
in the community of Christ, the Church, so that we on earth
are bound to try to reflect it: "It is that picture of ourselves that
the Church and the Lord cherish within them, enabling us to
find our real 'I' in them, beyond our selves": it is the "I" of a
"perfect organ of the Lord".[7]

The Church, considered as a unity, is first of all a reality situated in time by heaven: "What is given us from heaven is the
unity of faith, love and hope, the unity of sacramental grace, the
unity of the teaching of the Church. . . . This unity can be given
only from heaven, that is, through the unity of the Trinity."[8]
"The Church is the presence, indeed the living presence of eternity in time, a prospect of heaven from earth's point of view . . .
[providing] access to the heavenly mysteries in such a way that
they with their celestial logic, in their essential being, are not

---

[3] 1 Jo 31; cf. "The Yes that is kept safe in God": M 50–52, and this "Yes" is
"given its distinctive quality by Christ": M 54–57.
[4] 3 Jo 282.
[5] 3 Jo 79.
[6] 1 Jo 36.
[7] L 93.
[8] 1 Jo 208.

disturbed but can remain what they are."[9] Through the Spirit
"the Church lives within eternal life, which she must continually mediate to the earthly lives of believers; and this mediation
is also an adaptation."[10] Thus she lives both in heaven and on
earth and "so bridges the distance between them".[11] It is quite
in order to consider and understand the Church from the point
of view of her heavenly reality;[12] as the prolongation of Christ,
however, she has "two vantage points: one invisible, in heaven,
and one visible, on earth. Yet even the visible one is invisible
insofar as it has links with heaven at all points, and we can never
say that the life of the earthly Church is merely illusory and unreal, whereas her true reality is solely in heaven."[13] Mediation is
always going on, but the vantage points can be different: Peter,
for instance, lives more on the earth, looking toward heaven,
whereas John looks more from heaven to earth.[14] For the Christian saint, heaven is not (as in the Old Testament) in the future.
Rather, "he himself takes part in its fulfillment. He lives in the
certainty of eternity", even though he may be anxious about the

---

[9] K 170; cf. G 72: "The Church, with all her sacraments and ordinances, breathes
the heavenly air of eternity; she cannot help communicating something of this to
her surroundings."

[10] Ka I, 296.

[11] Ka I, 404. As far as the earthly Church is concerned, we can say, therefore,
that what she undergoes on earth as the Bride of Christ "is only a small part of
the totality of heavenly relationships between Father and Son in the Spirit. True,
this totality is open to earth, bends down toward the earth, but in its fullness it
is found only in heaven." And precisely because the earthly portion is just that,
a portion, "it draws us into the eternal, heavenly revelation": I Ka, 382.

[12] As Paul does; but, "when he is sent out in mission and office, Paul suddenly
discovers the whole earthly side of the Church; he brings her back to earth, a
little like Moses brings back the tablets from the mountain, and he sees her now
in her earthly aspect working from earth toward heaven": Ep 134–35.

[13] GE 26. The Church is "quite actually the locus of the beginning of . . . eternity
in the midst of time": A 103. The Christian has "the consolation of knowing that
he is attempting to realize, within the earthly sphere of the Church, something
that succeeds eternally in the heavenly one and that his transient time thereby
has a place in the eternal time of the Father." Christians know "that they should
not interpret their creaturely life, in its transitional movement toward heaven, as
anything but a symbol of what awaits them once they are with the Father." "The
unity between transient and eternal time is assured through this sort of beholding
of the Church": A 106–7.

[14] 4 Jo 301ff.; 401ff.

Judgment. "But he is so aware of eternity's triumph over transience that his truth really lives in heaven; . . . he is privileged
to regard it as his daily bread."[15] In fact the same can be said of
everyone whose faith is alive.[16]

Christians know above all else that the Church's *sacraments*
directly communicate heavenly reality to them by bringing to
them the heavenly Lord, who comes to earth.[17] As a result, in a
way that exceeds their knowledge and experience, parts of their
life of faith are transposed, "through the fullness of sacramental life", into God himself, where "they have their existence
and their fulfillment."[18] The sacraments constitute "a plurality
of modes of access" to eternal life,[19] to its "eternal liturgy".[20]
First and foremost Holy Mass is a union between heaven and
earth; its "sacrificial action embraces everything": the personal
sacrifice of the faithful cannot be separated from that of the
Church, "which in turn can never be divorced from the sacrifice of Christ; and this is founded on the Father's sacrifice for
the world",[21] whereby he gives his Son for it. It is in order
to draw our hesitant sacrifice into his own that Christ "offers
himself in sacrifice anew unnumbered times every day".[22] The
Son, who has received his mission on earth from the Father as
his "food"—something that is familiar to us in our daily lives
—wants to be our nourishment, in the Eucharist, by his flesh
and blood, since this gives us access to the essence of eternal
life; "unlike the Son, we never have eternal life in ourselves but
can only receive it from him."[23] "So we possess him on earth
in a way that is similar to the way the Father possesses him in
heaven."[24] "The Father gives the Church a share in his power to
make the Son present"; thus the Eucharist becomes "a meeting

[15] T 93.

[16] Ph 146–48.

[17] A 110.

[18] A 113. "Considered objectively, this sacrament—like every sacrament—is a
heavenly fruit produced on earth": KW 26.

[19] Ka II, 218; cf. Pf 49ff.

[20] Pf 22.

[21] H 82.

[22] 2 Jo 62.

[23] 2 Jo 72.

[24] C 174.

point, even more, a synthesis, a flowing source of the Son and of belief. Time and eternity come together; temporally, the transformation is one moment among others and definable as such. But the second at which the transformation occurs contains in itself the value of an eternity: the whole of nontemporal and nonspatial eternal life is projected into the small-sized host."[25] And when the Son gives himself in communion, "it is as if he were simultaneously giving heaven and earth. He opens up both perspectives: the view toward the Father through his presence as a man among those who are his own, and that of his abiding with the Father on earth through his offering of bread to them. But inasmuch as he gives them this twofold gift, he gives them a third, namely, that which is his absolutely: the inseparable, everlasting glorification of the Father." By giving what he is, he makes all giving visible: the Father's gift to the world becomes visible in the Son.[26] "The moment we communicate, the two planes, heaven and earth, coincide . . . and the promised heaven becomes its fulfillment."[27] "The Lord bestows in advance what he achieves through Cross and Resurrection, namely, incorruption."[28] "No one who has communicated knows how much he has received. He has received something from the beyond and has remained in the beyond a little while."[29] "Conversely, the Church's unity also enters into the unity of the communicant",[30] since he belongs to the Lord only to the extent that he is given a share in the Lord's unity, which unites heaven and earth in his Church.

This vertical, eschatological unity becomes visible in the representative of ecclesial office, the priest. We see "that the priesthood comes so much from heaven that it already manifests the transition from earthly life to heavenly life", yet at the same time, in the priest's temporal life "what is earthly is not obliterated but transfigured and rendered incorruptible, just as the Lord's humanity does not pass away in eternity."[31]

To mention another sacrament: confession, too, visibly comes

---

[25] 4 Jo 308.
[27] H 82.
[29] 3 Jo 371.
[31] Ka I, 394.

[26] 4 Jo 336.
[28] C 545.
[30] 3 Jo 370.

from heaven and mediates heavenly life. This is clear from its connection with the Cross (seen as a universal confession of sin) and Resurrection (seen as absolution for the sinful world).[32] "In absolution God breathes on man with a breath of his own eternity",[33] so that all who confess properly "participate in advance, through absolution, in heavenly existence".[34] Precisely by attempting to "present *his truth* to God", he is given the grace "to be able to live . . . in God's truth".[35]

While the entire Church's year shows us that "by the standards of eternal life we are all still living in expectation", "her feasts and significant events will be absorbed into God's infinity, without disappearing in it."[36] We are meant, not to "skip over temporality, but to live with [Christ] in time in such a way that it acquires an importance that the Father will not refuse to acknowledge".[37] In bidding us "lay up treasures in heaven, the Lord shows us what a mysterious relationship with heaven we already have. We are to work on earth and do what God requires of us, and this work will bring forth fruit; we have the right to harvest this fruit—but in heaven. Our entire temporal life has its fruit in heaven."[38]

The whole visible Church, founded by the Lord on earth, is built according to this law. "In doing this, the Lord has taken heavenly relationships, formerly existing only in heaven, or at most in a shadowy way on earth, in Old Covenant worship, and has given them a visibility, so to speak, a framework, within which the heavenly reality can make its presence felt with increasing clarity. The visible Church, the Bride of Christ on earth, is fashioned by the Lord in such a way that, by his grace, she is enabled more and more to resemble the Bride of Christ in heaven."[39] By teaching her and us the Our Father, "he bestows his familiar heaven upon us, his Father's house. Nor is this heaven empty either: it comes together with the Father; we are given both the property and its Owner."[40] The Father draws "from the fullness of the Son's self-surrender in order to supply

---

[32] 1 Jo 164–65.
[33] Be 195.
[34] OM 574.
[35] 2 Jo 218.
[36] Pf 32.
[37] Pf 24.
[38] B 192.
[39] B 140.
[40] B 169.

and transform what is lacking in man", and he does this through "heaven's readiness to accept the earth, through an opening in eternity that admits our time into it".[41] And if we are "in this world as he is in heaven, it is not through our own efforts but because he abides in us." This "abiding in us" exhibits the quality of God's unchangeability in heaven; thus "it is not he who changes: he changes us. What he adopts, he fulfills." "His constant being" is, in us, "continual growth. God does not grow in himself: he grows in us."[42]

So it is that all subjective efforts within the Church share in the same life, which is a transition from earth to heaven. Through baptism we are born again from God,[43] we have "passed from death to life in union with Christ" and been "received . . . into heaven" with him;[44] and if we "consider our earthly life to be a constituent part of the eternal life of faith, the Son will continue to give a divine vitality to our faith. Similarly he inspires our hope and nourishes it by his grace, so that this hope confirms our faith in his Resurrection and Ascension to heaven"—events that show this hope to have been already fulfilled.[45] "Faith, which the Father gives us today, has the same concreteness, the same truth, the same being as the Incarnation of the Son had in its day. He takes possession of the human, but in order to refashion it, . . . to guard and cherish it for the salvation that comes from Father, Son and Spirit."[46] "The believer lives entirely by faith. Having died to earthly life, he lives in eternal life, which indwells him by faith. . . . Love and hope come from it."[47] "In faith we are already living in the 'eternal now': now is the Son promised us, now he has become man, now he is crucified, buried, risen; now he comes again as Judge, now he is the eternal Ruler! For this very reason, the 'eternal now' cannot be compressed into temporality, as if something could be made present in time that can

[41] Ph 176.
[42] Ka II, 179.
[43] Cf. the magnificent portrayal of this rebirth in the experience of a saint: 1 Jn 111–16.
[44] Ep 84.
[45] Ka I, 281.
[46] Ka I, 256–57.
[47] Ka I, 261.

only be possessed as present in eternity, that is, in faith." This means that on earth, where genuine faith is concerned, "one of its essential parts is always expressed as hope", and this hope is not forged by faith itself but is "given by the triune God".[48] Faith of this kind lives in everyday life and matures toward its goal; it does not need to be in a hurry, for "every moment has direct contact with eternal life."[49]

We are familiar with the idea that, when we pray to God, we are praying in eternal life. We do not realize to the same extent that genuine prayer is already a sharing in heaven.[50] For "eternity is prayer",[51] trinitarian and ecclesial prayer. In prayer "God allows man to shake off his limitations; turned toward God, he prays in such a way that prayer lifts him above his temporal existence. For God accepts his prayer, he bends down even before answering it and lifts it up to him, giving it a share in eternity."[52]

The Beatitudes show that what seems to be farthest from heaven, things such as poverty and mourning, can be closest to it. "The poor are more apt to understand" what the kingdom of God's triune love is, and the Spirit leads them "into their own inheritance".[53] All believers live "in the condition of a permanent poverty, but one that already bears tokens of the boundless coming fulfillment".[54] The task that they have been given, placed as they are in the rhythm of time, comes from God; they must never forget this eternal origin, which has taken possession of them, soul and body. "If a person believes in the resurrection of the body, this taking possession must seem utterly reasonable: his bodily life on earth fulfills a task that, in its entirety, has its place within eternal life. What God desires

---

[48] Ka I, 263.

[49] OM 100. "Even here below [believers] live the eternal life of faith in their everyday existences": Ka I, 345. "Faith is not only faith in eternal life but also the pledge of it": 1 Jo 200. The believer lets "all the little questions of our earthly life flow into the great answers of heaven. . . . For eternal life does not begin only after death: it begins already now, in faith, love and hope": 2 Jo 59–60.

[50] Cf. GE 21.

[51] GE 104.

[52] L 113–14.

[53] B 12–13.

[54] C 21.

eventually to have with him, entire and complete, in eternity must already be offered to him, entire and complete, in time."[55]

In this portrayal of life in the Church we have spoken more of participation in "eternal life" than explicitly of the trinitarian working-out of this life; we have always presupposed that life in the Church is essentially a sharing in the life of the God-man, who, since he is both God and man, always has an explicitly trinitarian life. He comes from the Father and goes to him, and in both directions he does so in the Holy Spirit. This movement "from and to" accords with his eternal Sonship, and so his "economic" movement is not solely restricted by historical time but stretches beyond it, since his historical return to the Father takes the form of an ever-new (eucharistic) coming to his Church (and through the Church to the world). This transcending of the time boundary is made possible by the fact that it was also his death (and *specifically* his death) that interpreted the mission he had received from eternal life. At the climax of his mission he overcame the evil death of sin by the living death of his love and, by so doing, threw down "the dividing wall" between those going to their doom in the futility of transience and those enjoying eternal life. Thus, in Christ, those who have a living faith find that death has lost its sting and that physical dying can be the transition to an eternal life that was already present. According to Paul, the baptized, believing Christian has already died together with Christ and so entered the new, heavenly life (Col 3:3). "The extent of this new life can be fathomed only through death . . . not in some act of imagination,

---

[55] Bi 39. "Man's work too, justified by God, is enabled to enter into eternity. And if the Christian labors and endeavors to act in an apostolic way, he knows that transience cannot affect his work, no more than the passing nature of the Son's earthly days can affect his work on earth": T 111–12. "It is not as if man on earth performs purely earthly work, and God rewards him in heaven with eternal life as heavenly recompense. The reward is rather the faith and love which God bestows on men and which enable them, according to their abilities, to work for the kingdom of God. Just as the Son, working on earth, *is* the kingdom of heaven shared out for men, so too the kingdom of heaven becomes the inheritance of the man who believes and loves, as he works together with the Son in faith and love." Thus the reward that God gives is "no longer something commensurate with a human accomplishment": K 143.

but in the absolute truth of the Cross. As the Son takes man
with him into the Resurrection, so he takes him into death, so
that he might free him from his sins."[56] True, according to Paul
(Rom 8:10), death remains a punishment for sin: this was seen
most graphically in Christ's Cross and must remain visible in
believers; but it is possible to say that even this punishment was
an act of mercy: "God interposes death to put an end to the
creature that chose sin, lest its state of guilt should persist in-
definitely. The appointed end is both punishment and mercy:
it bears the indelible mark of a measure taken by God, looking ahead to the coming redemptive death of his Son."[57] Once
man is living under the law of this redemptive death, which is
the work of eternal trinitarian love, "death is of no importance"
for believers, "it is no limit to love."[58] For the disciple whom
Jesus loved, "awareness of such limitations can never become
consolidated. . . . He never sees the hindrance as lying before
him, but always as only behind him, as something that the Lord
has already overcome for him."[59] Jesus can call Lazarus' death
a "sleep"; "this death of Lazarus is no genuine death . . . death
is something definitive, a passing away, a conclusion. But here
it is the opposite: a beginning, an opportunity, a promise. The
whole mystery of the Lord's redemption is prefigured in it. In
comparison to the promise of God, which grows out of the death
of the body, this death has no longer any importance at all; it is
simply overlooked."[60] If it was a punishment for sin, "the Son
did not come to put an end to the Father's work, to the measures he has taken, but to show them to be based on the love of
the Trinity. . . . What the Son achieves through death rests on
the foundation of what the Father has done."[61] But death's penal
character is experienced on behalf of sinners, and so it is changed
into the opposite of sin: love. Love for Christ thus becomes a
dying with him. "In reality no one dies his own death, for the

[56] K 109–10.

[57] G 19; cf. C 181. On these various aspects of death, cf. J. A. Fischer, *Studien
zum Todesgedanken in der alten Kirche* (Munich: Huber, 1954).

[58] 4 Jo 414.

[59] 4 Jo 415.

[60] 2 Jo 309.

[61] T 58–59.

death he is to die is swallowed up in the Lord's death." The Lord of life gives everyone "the very death the Church needs at this particular time". For the Church, together with Father, Son and Spirit, "has a role in the administration of death."[62] Since the whole world is involved in the Son's trinitarian movement, in the Spirit, to the Father, "death in its entirety belongs to the past."[63] For it is only "he who does not love" who "remains in death" (1 Jn 3:14); "so he never shared in life. Love, by contrast, is the constant transformation from death into life."[64]

3. The Shape of Christian Hope

a. The Vertical Dimension

What we have said so far has emphasized the presence of faith's content in the Christian act of faith to such an extent that one might wonder whether there is enough room left for hope, which after all presupposes that the beatific vision and ultimate possession are "not yet". Before going into this question in more detail, however, it is essential to distinguish Christian hope—which does certainly rest on the presence of what is believed—from non-Christian hope, partly pagan and partly Jewish.

Paul denies pagans any hope whatsoever (since for him hope involves man's salvation and the resurrection): they have "no hope" (1 Th 4:13; cf. 1 Cor 15:19); "having no hope and without God in the world" (Eph 2:12). The hope he means is that which is grounded on God's promise to the Jews, who possess "the Law" and "the promises" (Rom 9:4). The pagans may exhibit traces of a flawed hope, and the Jews may cherish a futurist hope, but Christians, by contrast, have a "better hope . . . , through which we draw near to God" (Heb 7:19), because they wait for a resurrection from the dead that has already been fulfilled in Christ and that is unknown to pagans.

---

[62] T 61.
[63] Ka II, 123.
[64] Ka II, 124–25.

Genuinely *pagan* hope, such as we find in the ancient world of Greece and Rome,[1] limits itself, as far as mortal existence is concerned, to addressing a problem common to all men, namely, uncertainty about the future,[2] which is why we find the usual mixture of hope and fear, with greater hope among the young than among the old.[3] According to Aristotle and the Stoics, hope was attributed to the emotions and so was to be kept under control and transcended; it should be changed into a mere trust in providence. Seneca regards hope and fear as very close sisters,[4] and he advises us, for the sake of *tranquillitas animae*, to renounce hope and attain impassivity.[5] As far as life after death is concerned, various hopes enter philosophy through the mystery religions. This is clear as early as Pindar, and we find it, finally, in Plato. But such hopes always entail a dualism of (mortal) body and (immortal) soul that tears man asunder. In his *Apologia* Socrates has "great hope" (*pollē elpis*) for the soul; thus death appears not as an evil but as a good, provided that one is oneself striving for the good.[6] The *Phaedo* entertains the possibility of proving immortality and speaks of a "great and beautiful hope",[7] and on this basis the dualistic hope of immortality lives on through the medium of Hellenism; Cicero provides

---

[1] See the detailed analysis in Woschitz, *Elpis/Hoffnung* (Vienna: Herder, 1979), 63–218.

[2] This is clear in Hesiod's Pandora myth: the evils creep forth out of the opened box, but it is shut before Hope can escape. According to Aeschylus, Hope is blind.

[3] *Semonides Fragment* (29, 3ff.); Aristotle says that the old people are *dyselpides*, disillusioned through experience (*Rhetoric* II, 13; 1389, 11). Cicero, *Cato Maior de senectute*, 68.

[4] "Spem metus sequitur" (*Ep Lucil.* V, 7, 9).

[5] *Ep.* V, 7; *Ad Marciam de consolatione*.

[6] *Apol.* 40 ce.

[7] "Kai kalē elpis": *Phaedo* 71a. Cf. the conclusion of Socrates' defense (*Apol.* 41C). He is "hopeful of winning the greatest of prizes in the next world after death" (*Phaedo* 64A). "There is good reason for anyone who reaches the end of this journey which lies before me to hope that there, if anywhere, he will attain the object to which all our efforts have been directed in life gone by. So this journey which is now ordained for me carries a happy prospect for any other man also who believes that his mind has been made ready—and pure" (*Phaedo* 67B–C: in Plato: *The Last Days of Socrates*, trans. H. Tredennick and H. Tarrant [Penguin, 1993]).

a superlative example of it.[8] This whole eschatology is purely vertical (and in predominantly spatial concepts); there is no idea that history, in its temporal succession, might have a *result*.

Jewish hope, on the other hand, is always projected into the temporal future. It is "Messianic", even in the absence of a concrete Messianic figure.[9] This hope rests on the promise made by the God of the Patriarchs and takes the form of a "patient waiting" in trust and confidence and, when calamity arises, in seeking refuge in God. From the very beginning, the idea of the "blessing" (promised to Abraham), which will accompany Israel down through the ages, is an important one. The promise to David and his line gives concrete shape to the general hope for salvation, focusing it on a person who is to appear in the salvific future. It is astonishing that this hope remains purely earthly and horizontal, even in the latest period, eschewing all personal hope of survival (this is even true of Jesus Sirach).[10] This results in the head-on clash between an ethical optimism with regard to the individual in this world and the despair of the sufferer in the Book of Job. The narrowness of this horizontal theology of hope is invaded from two sides: first in the late Book of Wisdom—an Alexandrine work—which introduces the hope of immortality, no doubt partly within a Hellenistic framework, and then by those who interpret the eschatological images of salvation in apocalyptic terms. (Thus Ezekiel's vision of the resurrection of the dead bones in chapter 37 is expanded into a hope of resurrection for the individual in Daniel 12:2.) At this point, however, as we have already mentioned, there is a certain limit in Jewish eschatology: even if, as in Deutero-Isaiah, Israel's calling becomes universal, embracing the salvation of all the nations, there remains the ingrained conviction that God's

[8] "Est enim animus coelestis ex altissimo depressus et quasi demersus in terram, locum divinae naturae aeternitatique contrarium" (*Cato Maior* 77), from whence, particularly if he has won merit for his fatherland, he will ascend to the "certum . . . in coelo definitum locum, ubi beati aevo aeterno fruantur" (*Somn. Scip.* 3, 13).

[9] On forms of Messianism without an "anointed" Messiah, cf. H. Cazelles, *Le Messie de la Bible: Christologie de l'Ancien Testament* (Paris: Desclée, 1978).

[10] V. Hamp, *Zukunft und Jenseits im Buch Jesus Sirach*, BBB1 (Bonn, 1950), 86ff.

righteous judgment will involve a separation in which the pure will be saved and the others will be rejected. This conviction remains unshakeable, even in the eschatological transposition of apocalyptic: some are destined for salvation in God, which means that the others are equally destined, but for perdition. In late Jewish circles (both pre- and post-Christian) it is inconceivable that there could be hope for the whole of mankind.[11]

For Judaism, the salvation still awaited is so much in the future that the fact that God's promises are "now" and "already" can be forgotten. Ultimately the awareness of the promises becomes secularized and endeavors to understand itself as an autonomous, free-standing movement: the "hope principle". In this case Judaism means "a particular Messianic emotional state",[12] "a prophetic movement"[13] that is worldwide (which is why Ernst Bloch is disgusted by Zionism and the "petty", "Arabian" state of Israel). It claims support from the Jewish-born Joachim of Fiore[14] and believes that "the Jew Marx"[15] is the final "witness . . . of the Messianic approach", which "has its destination in socialism".[16] "For Moses Heß, socialism was 'the victory of the Jewish mission in the spirit of the Prophets' ".[17]

Christian hope, accordingly, can describe itself as "better" because it is based on the Resurrection of Christ, which has already occurred, on the realized Jewish *eschaton*, and on something that no pagan doctrine of the end ever dared to envisage, namely, the salvation of the whole man, soul and body. Furthermore, the Resurrection of Christ is not only the object but the efficient cause of this better hope, since what we hope for is already

---

[11] Examples: Dan 12:2; Is 66:24; Judith 16:17; *Syrian Apoc. Bar.*: "There is coming a period that will remain forever and a new world that will not consign to corruption those who are immediately destined for bliss but will have no mercy for those who depart to torment. . . . Fire is the habitation of the multitude of others" (44, 12, 15). *Ps. Sal.* (12, 4; 13, 9–10), 4 Esdras; the dualism of Qumran (1 Q IV, 26), etc.

[12] E. Bloch, *Das Prinzip Hoffnung* (Suhrkamp, 1959), I, 709.

[13] *Ibid.*, 712f.

[14] *Ibid.*, 712.

[15] *Ibid.*, 708.

[16] *Ibid.*, 713.

[17] *Ibid.*, 702.

hid with Christ in God, ultimately to be manifested and handed over to us (Col 3:3–4). First Peter 1:3–5 brings all these elements together: "Blessed be the God and Father of our Lord Jesus Christ! By his great mercy we have been born anew to a living hope through the resurrection of Jesus Christ from the dead, and to an inheritance which is imperishable, . . . kept in heaven for you, who by God's power are guarded through faith for a salvation ready to be revealed in the last time."

Naturally, a hope of this kind, which stakes all on the manifestation of the Lord's Resurrection, demands the greatest sacrifices from man. He must allow the word of the Resurrection preeminence over everything, "even when he does not entirely understand this word. Thus Christ asks of man a greater renunciation than he can naturally make, a stronger faith than he can discover within himself, a more daring hope than he can ever entertain."[18] The required renunciation extends even to the "I" who is so well known to me, for, in following the Risen One, I shall be given this "I" in a form that is as yet undreamed-of. That is why Christian hope is grounded entirely upon the Lord. "It is not simply a vague expectation that things will turn out better; it is something that has been opened up to us at a supernatural level, containing, "right from the start, a kind of surrender". In hoping, we "renounce the right to test and determine what will happen to us in the future"; our hope exhibits "something of the character of faith and love; for between the three reigns a sort of reciprocal inhabitation."[19] Thus "hope is an essential part of faith."[20] Consequently hope can experience the same mode of certainty as the latter, as Bonaventure expressly says.[21] Indeed,

[18] C 493.

[19] Ep 53.

[20] SL 73.

[21] The Master of the Sentences regards it as "certa exspectatio futurae beatitudinis" (3, d 26, 1); then Bonaventure explicitly asks "utrum spes in suo actu sit certitudinalis, an dubia" (III, d 26, a 1, q 5), and initially gives an affirmative answer, while admitting that it is difficult to give a closer definition of this certainty. Of course this applies only to the theological virtue of hope, and not to natural hope, which must be exercised with moderation lest it fall into presumption: "praesumit de misericordia Dei": *ibid.*, q 3 ad 1. But just as faith enables us to affirm primal truth, and love enables us to cling to primal goodness, hope—which is a pure gift of grace—causes us "to expect things that exceed all human assessment". There-

it can be so "boundless", "much too great to be fulfilled, too immense to dare believe in";[22] thus, at the Pharisee's table, the woman who was a sinner receives more than she could have believed possible.[23] However, this entire movement on to a new level would have been impossible without hope's "not yet". As Peter says, our "imperishable inheritance" is "kept in heaven" for us (1 Pet 1:4); this inheritance will be fulfillment, but "as long as we are on the earth we share in this fulfillment in a veiled manner."[24] This veiling is necessary since we have to be purified "through many trials" in view of the manifest glory we are to attain; and this is "something so glorious that man can only cherish the hope of it"; what is laid up for us in God "remains, even when revealed, the proclamation of an overwhelming mystery of God. So much so that the hope for it constitutes a part and a beginning of this glory."[25] The goal for which, since it is "not yet", creation groans, the goal for which, in hope, it longs since it cannot see it, is at the same time the *means* of its salvation (Rom 8:24). So the whole delay in the fulfillment of the beatific vision (since it is "not yet") has, *as such, a divine, trinitarian basis:* in those who exercise hope the Spirit addresses the Father "with sighs too deep for words", that the Son's redemption may be fulfilled in the world. This makes it clear that hope is a theological virtue, a virtue springing from the life of the Trinity. So even in the world that is alienated from God there is this hope, "small

---

fore we should "cling to this immeasurable generosity for its own sake and above everything else" (*ibid.*, q 1 sol). If it be objected that no human will can be sure about itself, the answer is: Indeed, "insofar as the will relies on itself" it is bound to vacillate; "but if it bases itself on God, who is our unshakeable foundation, it has strength and certainty" (*ibid.*, q 5 ad 2). In fact, this very looking away from ourselves and trusting in God "gives us a kind of certainty that we shall attain to salvation". Since the certainty of hope is intimately connected with faith and love, it is not the kind of certainty "manifestae scientiae", but "confidentiae". A living faith includes this confidence (*ibid.*, ad 4). Bonaventure means by this a certainty, not of the reason (which belongs to faith), but of the heart (*affectus*).

[22] 3F 57–58.

[23] She is redeemed "far beyond the measure of her hopes" (3F 75). "In her there is sin; there is no basis for hope. All hope lies in the meeting with the other, the Lord" (3F 77).

[24] Ka I, 254.

[25] K 53.

perhaps, dull and hardly visible, yet hope that is irresistible. . . .
In every No that [the sinner] utters, in every finality he chooses,
he has to experience faintly the Yes and the promise of something quite different. The absolute belongs so fully to God that
man can seek it only there."[26] And although suffering persists in
our temporal life, eternity keeps breaking into it, and one of the
signs of eternity is hope, "which cannot be conquered by all the
continuing suffering".[27] All that the Son has shown us "confirms
our hope but does not show the fulfillment. . . . The content of
hope, even if can be circumscribed with words of faith, remains
hidden and is inaccessible to us. And it belongs again to faith
that we leave an open space for this superabundance in every
fulfillment, and therefore for hope."[28]

From all this it follows that Christian hope is *vertical*, since it
is grounded in the Christ-event, which is now "above". At the
same time it is not vertical in the pagan sense, because it rests on
a historical event that is not, as such, pure past history but is always coming to meet us. This means that we need to reexamine
what is involved in the Jewish expectation of a historical future.
All the same, while the Old and New Covenants may be united
in their "patient waiting", it cannot be said that their "waiting"
has the same structure in each case. For Christian hope is the

---

[26] SL 65. "In reality we will what he wills. In reality, although we are not aware
of it, we will our suffering, our pain, and our loneliness, while imagining that
we will only our joys. We imagine that we fear death and flee from it, whereas
we actually will this death just as he willed his. In exactly the same way that he
sacrifices himself on every altar where Mass is celebrated, he dies again when
every man undergoes his death-throes. We will everything that he wills, only we
do not *know* that we will it; we do not know ourselves, for sin causes us to live
on the surface of ourselves. Only when we die do we return to ourselves, and
there He is waiting for us.

"It is not a question of harmonizing our will with his, for his will *is* ours. All
we succeed in doing, if we resist him, is to wrench our whole inner being, mon-
strously squandering our self. Our will is united with his ever since the foundation of the world. He created the world together with us. . . . What a wondrous
thought that, even when we hurt him, we never entirely cease to long for what
he longs for in the most hidden sanctuary of our soul" (from Agenda 1948, in:
Das Sanfte Erbarmen, Briefe des Dichters [Einsiedeln: Johannes Verlag, 1951], 124–
25).

[27] SL 69.

[28] SL 72–73.

gift whereby we are "reborn by God's mercy" and seized or "apprehended", as Paul describes it: "Not that I have already obtained this or am already perfect: but I press on to make it my own [RV: "that I may apprehend"] because Christ Jesus has made me his own" [RV: "I was apprehended by Christ Jesus"]. And since, for my part, I have been apprehended "from above", it follows that I have been called, not primarily to pursue a horizontal, forward path, but, quite expressly, an "upward" path (anō klēsis, Phil 3:12–14). Hope is not the result of a yearning or a postulate, but a gift that comes from the goal of our hoping. "But it is a greater good that we are held by Christ than that we hold him. For we can hold him only so long as we are held by him."[29] What Paul means by being seized or "apprehended" encompasses the entire economy of salvation that, while prior to us, is applied to us "while we were yet sinners": so God reconciles the world to himself through Christ, making us righteous before God; and this is not something external, for we actually died with him and were raised with him even before we knew anything about it (2 Cor 5:14; Rom 5:10). However, once we have learned of this, come to believe in its truth and have entered into it sacramentally in baptism, we live no longer on the basis of our own center. For "Christ lives in me" at a deeper level than this, and it is by faith in him that we live (Gal 2:20). For us, both to live and to die "is Christ" (Phil 1:21). According to Paul, this life of faith in and from Christ can be expressed in two ways: pneumatologically and christologically. To be "in Christ" (Rom 8:1) means being indwelt by God's Spirit, who is also the Spirit of Christ (v. 9), and insofar as he dwells in us he will "give life to our mortal bodies" as surely as he "has raised Christ Jesus from the dead" (v. 11). This certainty is reinforced by the fact that the Spirit is described as the "seal" of the good things for which we hope (2 Cor 1:22; 5:5; Eph 1:14) —a deliberately realistic expression implying that faith brings with it something of the substance and quality of its object; thus faith itself is a seal of the vision of God: inchoatio visionis.[30] The

[29] Paschasius Radbertus, De Fide, Spe et Caritate, 1 2 c 1 (PL 120, 1437), quoted in J. Pieper, On Hope (San Francisco: Ignatius Press, 1986), 34.
[30] Cf. The Glory of the Lord I, 155–71.

Spirit (or God himself: 1 Jn 5:10) bears witness of these things to our spirit (Rom 8:16) since, in Paul's teaching, the Spirit of God has been inwardly entrusted to us, poured into our spirit (Rom 5:5). Paul's letters from captivity express the same thing in a christological way: the fullness of the mystery of God that has been bestowed on the nations (this is the New Testament emphasis; in other words, not only on Israel) is this: "Christ in you, the hope of glory" (Col 1:27). Here *elpis* is so much a gift that it is almost equivalent to *arrabōn*, "pledge".[31] This is even clearer in Colossians 1:5, which speaks of the "hope laid up for you in heaven": "The hope by which we hope has become the hope for which we hope", because "the temporal dimension is no longer fundamental."[32] The Letter to the Ephesians speaks to the same effect of the "inner man": "that . . . he may grant you to be strengthened with might through his Spirit in the inner man" so that "Christ may dwell in your hearts through faith" (Eph 3:16–17). Here the "inner man" is the place where Christ becomes present in us (cf. Eph 3:16–17; Gal 2:20).[33]

The primary axis of this entire relationship is vertical, as we find expressed in Hebrews 6:19–20: initially we were exhorted to "seize the hope set before us".[34] Now, however, "we have

[31] E. Schweizer, *The Letter to the Colossians* (SPCK, 1982), 109.

[32] *Ibid.* Cf. G. Bornkamm, "Die Hoffnung im Kolosserbrief" in *Studien zum Neuen Testament und zur Patristik*, Festschrift E. Klostermann (TU, 1961), 56–64. For *elpis* as the epitome of salvation, cf. Col 1:23; Titus 2:13; Heb 6:18–20. In this sense "hope" is practically the same as the "victor's wreath" that awaits us (2 Tim 4:8) or our "inheritance" (Heb 9:15). A parallel to Colossians 1:23 is Ephesians 1:18, where "the hope to which he has called you" is expounded as "the riches of his glorious inheritance in the saints" and the "immeasurable greatness of his power in us who believe", in accordance with the divine power by which Christ was raised from the dead. Bornkamm sees Ephesians and Colossians as the transition from the genuinely Pauline eschatology (temporal, futuristic and influenced by apocalyptic) to one that thinks in "realized", spatial and gnostic terms. But why could not Paul himself have sloughed off the apocalyptic husks from his eschatology, which after all is built upon the Resurrection of Christ and not on the end of history?

[33] Cf. M. Barth, *Ephesians*, Anchor Bible (Garden City, N.Y.: Doubleday, 1974), I, 369, cf. 390ff.

[34] On *krathēnai* in the sense of "saisir, s'accrocher, s'emparer de force de l'objet même de l'espérance", cf. C. Spicq, *Hébreux*, Études bibliques (Paris: J. Gabalda, 1963), II, 163.

this as a sure and steadfast anchor of the soul, a hope that enters into the inner shrine behind the curtain, where Jesus has gone as a forerunner on our behalf." Just as the anchor—which has since become the great symbol of Christian hope—reaches down and holds fast to the sea bottom, the anchor of the soul, hope, is hooked to the holy of holies ("behind the curtain") of God himself, which is vertically above the soul. But how can our hope reach the heart of eternity? It must follow the movement of the risen Christ, who has made a path "for us" and gone ahead "to prepare a place" for us. According to Hebrews 6:20, he does this as High Priest of the New Covenant, as the One who has suffered on our account.

This shows us another essential difference between Christian hope and Jewish and pagan hope. In standard Jewish thought, God is most hidden, the Messiah is most absent, in times of calamity and extreme distress. In the pagan idea of God, where it is cleansed of mythical features, suffering cannot be reconciled with divinity. All hope yearns for happiness or, at a deeper level, for salvation or the fulfillment of human wholeness; and as a result it experiences the abyss of the "not yet". Even Paul has to speak of our being "away from the Lord" so long as we live in the body, and "we would rather be away from the body and at home with the Lord" (2 Cor 5:6, 8). In this context "faith" and "sight" are contrasted (v. 7). This kind of language is completely relativized, however, by the Apostle's many statements in which he says that he shares in "the sufferings of Christ": here, at what looks like a considerable distance from the Lord, a greater nearness to him is manifested on the part of both Paul and his community. So, paradoxically, hope grows from a second root: for we know that "suffering produces endurance, and endurance produces character, and character produces hope"—and this hope from below meets the hope that comes from above: "hope does not disappoint us, because God's love has been poured into our hearts through the Holy Spirit who has been given to us" (Rom 5:5).

We would fail fully to grasp the vertical axis of Christian hope if we attended only to the one side of the Johannine "exaltation" and "glorification" and were to neglect the other side, on which the Evangelist so insists: the piercing, on the Cross, of that heart which will be shown to the disciples at Easter and offered to Thomas so that he may touch and verify it. There is nothing gnostic to be read in the Fourth Gospel if one keeps in mind the First Epistle (1 Jn 2:2; 4:10).[35] The ubiquitous allusions[36] show that the presence of the Risen One also comprehends his status as the Exalted One (the "serpent in the desert"). He who really *was* "dead", yet now lives "for evermore" (Rev 1:18), takes his pierced heart with him to heaven; on God's throne he is "the Lamb as it were slain".

How can these two aspects be brought together? It is not enough to point to the logia on persecution in John 15–16, which predict that Christians will be identified with Jesus in their sufferings. What we find in 17:17–19 is far more crucial: the disciples' consecration, their self-sacrifice, is inserted into the Son's consecration and self-sacrifice with a view to his Passion. Here, just as in the image of the Lamb who, in the midst of the heavenly glory, is "slain", we find that the aspect of the Passion's "exaltation" is coextensive with the disciples' suffering (and hence with all world history), which can only be explained by the fact that the Passion is, in its internal dimensions, supratemporal and so can indwell all moments of historical time. We have already mentioned this in the context of Christ's "time". What Pascal said, namely, that Christ's agony will last until the end of the world, expresses the fact that this suffering cannot be encapsulated within time and so become "past". Supratemporal suffering is within the realm of him who has been taken up into the divine super-time ("all-time"), and the two together form the milieu through which Church history and world history proceed. At every moment of time, the *"qui tollit peccatum mundi"* is equally operative and active—particularly since the *peccatum* historically

---

[35] Contrary to the one-sidedly gnostic interpretation of "glory" and "exaltation" found in E. Käsemann's *Jesu letzter Wille nach Johannes 17* (Tübingen: Mohr, 1966), 14–52. "In Christ the end of the world has not only come close: it has become permanently present", and as a result "the distinction between realized and futurist eschatology . . . can be maintained only with difficulty; ultimately it is no longer relevant": 35. "The gospel's 'antidocetism', which is assumed by practically everyone today, is a pure postulate": 51.

[36] Cf. O. Cullmann, "Urchristentum und Gottesdienst" in *AThANT* 3, 1944.

exemplifies the law of the "ever greater".[37] What John brings together in his concept of exaltation and glorification is not so contradictory that it cannot be undergirded by the absolute stance
of trinitarian self-surrender and—albeit in a way that remains
mysterious—thus reconciled. So what is "realized" about this
eschatology is of course primarily christological, but in a way
that illustrates the reciprocal relationship between Christ's act of
redemption and the act of faith and hope that seeks to embrace it.
Is there any reason why, ultimately, we should not also speak of
a reciprocity of hope as such? We have already identified hope's
prototype in the Trinity; so we shall not be surprised, at the end
of this section, to find Charles Péguy portraying God's hope for
the *oikonomia*.

First, however, we must tackle what today is such a burning
question: Does vertical theological hope have a horizontal dimension, and if so, in what sense? This problem is at the heart
of modern eschatology.

b. Horizontal Hope?

A horizontal, forward-looking, theological hope—for here we
are concerned exclusively with *theological* hope—was the genuine
contribution that the Old Testament and later Judaism made to
eschatology. Christian hope changes this one-sided movement
toward the future into a hope for something that is present and
final, although it still waits for its fulfillment. Jewish eschatology, however, particularly in its secularized form, has had a crucial influence on the modern age's doctrine of the end and on
the way it experiences itself. The new priority has been heavily supported by two features of our culture: the discovery of
the cosmos' evolutionist tendency, in particular the discovery of
the ascent of living forms right up to man, and the increasing
spread of technology, whereby what was once regarded as given
by nature is now subject to human manipulation. No thinker
can avoid the problems of this apparently irreversible forward
motion; the question is, has this forward motion—which is not
intelligible in the absence of a hope that sustains it—any relevance within a Christian eschatology?

[37] Cf. *Theo-Drama* IV, 56ff., passim.

First we shall mention two attempts that give an answer that is positive, though cautious. The first is that of Teilhard de Chardin, who sees himself confronted primarily with the "neo-humanist" phenomenon of a "belief in the future" in the form of scientific evolutionism and the worldwide advance of technology and its sociological consequences. The second is that of Jürgen Moltmann, whose main concern is to overcome secularized Jewish eschatology by means of Christian theology and to situate the former within the latter. After setting forth these two views we shall ask, on the basis of the (Johannine) approach of the present work, how the "futurist" element of hope and eschatology can be integrated into the "realized" context.

α. *Teilhard de Chardin*

Teilhard de Chardin[1] is cautious in what he says about Christian hope. His main problem—which must be faced in the modern world—is how to reconcile the forward thrust of humanist mysticism with the upward thrust of Christian mysticism.[2] The latter can no longer ignore the former. Note that the former, the forward thrust, is labelled as "not Christian": it is regarded as a problem for "Christian mysticism", something the latter has in some way to integrate and perhaps even to acknowledge as having a priority. We shall see that Teilhard endeavors to reach the desired synthesis in the depths of a Christology and so believes that he is justified in giving what was originally an extrinsic "neo-humanism" a place in theology. The theological element of his thought was discovered and developed in the war years, at the battle-front; after 1920 he basically reworked the essential insights he had acquired. Accordingly it will suffice to examine his early sketches of a system. Teilhard is fond of taking his own consciousness of the world

[1] *Oeuvres* I–XIII (Paris: Seuil, 1955–1976) (volume no. in Roman numerals, page no. in Arabic), apart from the *Ecrits du temps de guerre* [Writings in time of war] (= vol. XII), which is quoted from the first edition (Grasset, 1965) and designated "ET". *Lettres Intimes*, 2d ed. (Aubier, 1974), is designated "Li", and *Genèse d'une Pensée: Lettres 1914–1919* (Grasset, 1961) is designated "GP".

[2] XIII, 35; V, 343f.; VII, 288f.; X, 87. The forward thrust (already found in ET 45f., cf. 366) is emphasized more and more as time goes on. Adolf Haas' *Chardin-Lexikon* (Herder, 1971) contains surprisingly few texts on the subject of "hope".

as a measure of the modern consciousness in general[3] and analyzes it as
such.[4] One side of his consciousness reflects the modern consciousness
of the world in technology and research; the other side, the Christian
side, manifests the inheritance of a Christology based almost exclusively
on Paul and John (the primacy of the incarnate Logos over all worldly
reality)[5] and, appropriately, on the Greek Fathers.[6]

THE PATH TO A SINGLE GOAL FOR THE WORLD. The crucial theological discovery of his early writings, an insight that is firmly maintained thereafter—coming thirty years before H. de Lubac's *Surnaturel*
(1946)[7]—is that the world that raises its superstructure on the basis of
matter has only *one* ultimate goal—a supernatural goal. For Christians,
according to Teilhard, love for the world and love for God must form
a unity,[8] and this unity is seen primarily as an encounter between the
(ascending) earth and the (descending) heaven.[9] For its part, however,
the world must have within it a principle guiding its development up
to the level of the Spirit. Initially this principle is called the "world
soul".[10] Its goal seems to be reached when man comes on the scene,
since he recapitulates the cosmos in himself.[11] However, if we ask about
man's meaningful goal, we meet a "limitation":[12] there is "no name"

[3] "Que mon cas est significatif, et à ce titre, qu'il mérite d'être enregistré": X,
117.

[4] "Le Coeur de la Matière" (XIII, 19–91) is both autobiography and a confession of faith in the context of the spirit of the age. Cf. also IX, 65ff. This gives
rise to the numerous criticisms of the spirit of the Church of his time, e.g., XI,
21–44.

[5] GP 117; ET 39, 48; IV, 139; VII, 271; IX, 39, 210, 239; X, 107, 210, 222,
etc.

[6] ET 39; IX, 210, 229; X, 76f., 211, where Teilhard says he applies the same
tactics once more, "boldly equating the Jesus of the Gospel with the Alexandrian
Logos"—and interpreting the latter as the "developmental principle of a world in
process of becoming". Ref. to Irenaeus: VI, 208; to Cusanus: VII, 77. Of course
Bergson (XIII, 33) played a great part in Teilhard's development.

[7] Scheeben, following Thomas, had already looked in this direction even be-
fore de Lubac and Teilhard, as Norbert Hoffmann shows in his *Natur und Gnade:
Die Theologie der Gottesschau als vollendeter Vergöttlichung des Geistgeschöpfs bei M. J.
Scheeben*, Anal. Greg. B 51 (Rome, 1967), 40–82.

[8] ET 37, 54; IV, passim. He even sees the evangelical counsels as constitutive
of "love for an evolving world": XI, 116.

[9] ET 67, cf. also 374f.

[10] ET 15, 21, 217.

[11] ET 25, 28.

[12] ET 286, 412.

for this goal.[13] Seen from below, therefore, from the point of view of the "world soul", the world seems to be a "defective construction",[14] and the history of the cosmos lands in a "crisis",[15] a "breach".[16] The idea that the world could have a "natural and ultimate center" is only a dream.[17] It has a "sting" within it[18] that points beyond it. Only the Christian knows the way out of mankind's crisis, for no immanent goal can be envisaged: the Christian knows that the final goal is given from above, by grace, not as the result of world development.[19] This goal has come to earth in the Incarnation of Jesus Christ (whose divinity, in Teilhard, is untouched by the least suggestion of doubt): he alone is the final goal of the natural development,[20] which he "prolongs"[21] and thus also presupposes.[22]

In this phase of Teilhard's thought the world has two centers, which he calls Omicron and Omega.[23] "God must first create a natural soul, which he *subsequently* supernaturalizes."[24] If the ultimate goal is to be reached, an "intermédiaire naturel" is necessary.[25] This, however, is far more than a mere "cooperation of nature and grace",[26] for "Christ and the world soul are not two distinct realities, independent of each other; rather, the one is the milieu within which we are transformed into the other."[27] Later Teilhard calls this "world soul" a merely "inchoate, vague soul".[28] For the present it seems as if the world soul and the cosmic Christ are mutually interdependent: "The world soul, drawing its life from the Logos who has been set at its heart, is at the same time the necessary requirement so that the Incarnation may take place. It provides the material out of which the Mystical Body will be formed."[29] The two sides are "complementary",[30] but in such a way "that natural development is subordinated to the kingdom of God".[31] At this point the conditions are met for the decisive spark to jump: the question was bound to arise as to the relationship between world soul and Incarnation. The breakthrough comes in the essay "Forma Christi" (November 1918). The notion that the cosmos could have and pursue "a definite, natural, final goal" is clearly rejected: the true final goal "comes down" from God. Otherwise the world would be "a flock without a shepherd". Nonetheless man has a certain intimation that there must be an as yet "undefined, impersonal, generic" goal toward which the world is moving, the "precise character of which is inaccessible to reflection until God has spoken". Thus the final goal

[13] ET 73–75.	[14] ET 73.	[15] ET 122f.	[16] ET 77.
[17] ET 160.	[18] ET 288.	[19] GP 207.	[20] ET 49, 59.
[21] ET 125.	[22] ET 324.	[23] ET 274.	[24] GP 91.
[25] ET 226.	[26] ET 46.	[27] ET 227.	[28] ET 422.
[29] ET 228.	[30] ET 272.	[31] ET 275.	

shows itself to be *supernatural*, but because of the Incarnation of the Logos it has a *natural* aspect: the human nature of the Logos will be the truth of what manifests itself initially as the "world soul" but is actually the process of bringing the cosmos into the divine sphere.[32]

From now on Teilhard's thought circles around this "informing" of the world that results from the Incarnation.[33] He speaks of a priority of the Logos-made-man in his role as "natural center" over his function as "supernaturalizer".[34] Logically Teilhard assumes that the Incarnation is "the first event of creation, not only *in ordine intentionis* but also *in ordine naturae*; it forms the basis for all further creation." Life's entire evolution has been anticipated in the "mysterious preexistence"[35] of the Incarnation. Consequently, "in virtue of a mysterious anticipatory effect, Christ has always been risen."[36] "All the preparations" for his historical Incarnation "were cosmically and biologically necessary",[37] which means that "the Incarnation is an act that is coextensive with the duration of the world."[38] The ancient myths contain genuine intimations of the Incarnation.[39] Teilhard cites Blondel's maxim "everything holds together from its apex" as expressing his own fundamental view.[40] Christ—and this too is from Blondel, giving a new interpretation of Leibniz[41]—is the *vinculum substantiale* of the cosmos.[42]

[32] ET 337–42.

[33] ET 350.

[34] ET 480f. Christ as "a kind of world-soul": 409, n; IX, 209f.; X, 88, 147, 168, 183f. In X, 25 he attempts what is certainly a dangerous formulation, saying that Christ's presence "secundum suam naturam humanam" is a "présence antécédente (in ordine naturae) à l'habitation des Personnes divines dans l'âme sanctifiée".

[35] IX, 89.

[36] ET 353.

[37] IX, 90.

[38] IX, 92. Thus he often quotes Paul's "in him all things hold together" (Col 1:17): VI, 88; IX, 78 etc.

[39] ET 341 n.

[40] "Tout tient par en haut" IX, 78; "En Lui tout monte comme vers un foyer d'immanence"—insofar as he has already and always become man. "Mais de Lui aussi tout descend, comme d'un sommet de transcendance": VI, 88. Cf. ET 410, X, 126, 133.

[41] M. Blondel: *Une énigme historique: Le "Vinculum substantiale" d'après Leibniz et l'ébauche d'un réalisme supérieur* (Paris: Beauchesne, 1930). Translation and commentary of his Latin thesis, *De vinculo substantiali et de Substantia composita apud Leibnitium 1893*. Cf. H. de Lubac, Blondel et Teilhard de Chardin, *Correspondance commentée* (Paris: Beauchesne, 1965).

[42] ET 128, 286, etc.; Li 29, 30.

From this vantage point it becomes possible to understand the radicalism of the formula *"milieu divin"*. For if all things are grounded in the hypostatic union of the Logos, and if the latter is coextensive with the world, this "third nature" of Christ—which is not only divine or only human but "cosmic"[43]—is simultaneously natural and supernatural. Accordingly, everything that is evolving in it and through it and toward it already has a share, in some way or other, in the divine, in the sphere of grace.[44] This is the basis for Teilhard's demand that the world's knowing, if it is to be objective, must always think simultaneously from below upward and from above downward.[45] To think solely from below would be to enclose the world in itself with no hope of escape.[46] The world may be "unconscious" of its attraction toward the Christ-Omega,[47] yet in some way this attraction has an effect in the world of experience,[48] as a "postulate" of reason in its attempt to grasp the cosmos as something meaningful.[49] Teilhard has no intention of saying that the cosmos is drawn into the hypostatic union; at the same time the natural world-center, which is the Incarnate Logos,[50] points beyond itself to a presence of the divine, as is expounded in detail in the important work *Le Milieu divin*.[51]

In the later period this vision becomes ever more crucial, as Teilhard finds himself confronted with all forms of humanistic and scientific immanentism. Such immanentism, while it is "religious" to the extent that it discerns the unavoidable "convergence" or "complexion" (that is, involution, convolution) of the noosphere (the totality of humanity's consciousness) yet seeks in vain for a final goal within the natural cosmos. It does not matter whether such interpretations are "pantheist"[52] or "materialist" (merely analyzing down to the lowest level, the

[43] XIII, 107.

[44] "Avec l'Univers christifié (ou, ce qui revient au même, avec le Christ universalisé) un super-milieu évolutif apparaît—je l'ai appelé 'le Milieu Divin'—" and thus there appear "absolutely new psychic dimensions for all men": XIII, 110.

[45] VII, 149ff.

[46] VII, 155, 414, passim.

[47] VI, 56.

[48] VI, 139.

[49] Transcendence is ultimately written into the biological sphere: IX, 280.

[50] IX, 209f.; X, 88, 147, 168, 183f.

[51] Vol. IV. This is preceded by "Le Milieu mystique" ("à la fois divin et cosmique": ET 143: ET 137–69. On the "mysticism" of the "Milieu", cf. ET 166; X, 149; XIII, 105. In X, 86, he rejects the formula that the hypostatic union extends to the entire cosmos.

[52] This view is present as early as ET 19f., 141, 224, 278, 403f.

material),[53] or "idealist"[54] or "neo-humanist":[55] they all miss the essential point, namely, that the world's evolution is proceeding toward a Person and hence (within this Person) also has a personalizing effect. In opposition to the depersonalizing mysticism of the East, Teilhard calls for a personal "mysticism of the West"[56] that will set a standard for all mystical encounter with the *milieu divin*. The noosphere is enclosed in itself, the subjective world-soul is deprived of its opening into the supernatural realm: this, coupled with the unstoppable and ever-growing unification of mankind, produces a terrible "growth crisis"[57] in the latter, a weariness of life, since the collective that is herded together on the narrow planet[58] can discern no "way out".[59] Mankind "is stifled to death"[60] by its own strength,[61] since the increase in complexity of the spirit goes hand in hand with "progress".[62] With all his soul Teilhard affirms this scientific and technological progress,[63] but at the same time he is aware of the rising anxiety and loneliness that threaten to bring despair upon imprisoned mankind.[64] Teilhard's suggestion— that the compression of mankind should lead (even biologically) to an "amorizing" of the globe[65]—is and remains all too utopian in the face of the *apocalyptic* situation toward which evolution is heading. In his eschatology Teilhard will come to a more realistic evaluation.

First, however, we shall set forth the "Incarnation" principle in its various Dimensions, since it is the foundation of everything.

THE DIMENSIONS OF INCARNATION. With respect to the Bible, Teilhard's Christology is based solely on the central affirmations found in Paul and John; he maintains a certain sceptical relativism vis-à-vis the letter of Scripture.[1] Teilhard's norm is the tradition of the Church and

---

[53] VI, 28; IX, 47f.; X, 73f.

[54] ET 30f.

[55] ET 369; X, 138ff., 238f.

[56] VII, 235; X, 109, 134f.; XI, 47–64; for a nuanced presentation of the oriental mystics and their contribution to "evolutionary" occidental mysticism: XI, 149–60.

[57] IV, 199.

[58] The collective outweighs the personal: VII, 70f.

[59] IX, 134, 136.   [60] VII, 257f.   [61] VI, 139.   [62] XIII, 49.

[63] From ET 53 onward.

[64] ET 240, 309ff.

[65] VI, 192: "Love as the historical product of human development".

[1] "Il est urgent que nous ramenions à leur juste proportion les dons que Dieu nous a faits dans l'Écriture": ET 376. For Teilhard, the scientist and psychologist, the miracles reported in the Gospels are more an obstacle to, than evidence for, the credibility of revelation. There are very many examples of this.

the "infallibility" that is at its root;[2] he has no difficulty about practicing devotions such as veneration of the Heart of Jesus but incorporates them into his evolutionary world view. The incarnate Christ who grounds all world reality, who is Alpha and hence also Omega ("*Christ-Évoluteur*"), constitutes the unquestioned center of his view of the world: Christ's dual nature is able to unite his "Christian" (supernatural) and "pagan" (nature-loving) soul.

"The Incarnation is the mystery that epitomizes Christianity."[3] Having voiced his reservations about the traditional doctrine of redemption, he goes on: "Things are quite different when we come to the idea of the Incarnation"; here "the countenance of Jesus, projected onto an evolving universe, unfolds without difficulty."[4] Even though the event "took place two thousand years ago, that does not prevent it from being the axis and apex of a universal process of maturation".[5] Here God has finally entered into the whole process of becoming; he has incorporated the world's entire nature into himself, in the sense of the Greek Fathers, in virtue of his taking flesh. "The body of Christ . . . forms a natural, new world, an ensouled, vibrant organism in which we are all physically, *biologically* united. The only essential world event is the physical incorporation of the faithful into Christ, who is God; this foundational work unfolds with the rigor and harmony of a natural evolution."[6] "In the Christ who is" we can "passionately love the Christ who is becoming",[7] his "cosmic Body, present throughout the universe".[8] Every human body, by definition, has been transferred into this cosmic Body.[9] "Through the Incarnation, man's ignorance [of the goal] has been overcome and the universe has been given back a taste for its single future": it is in the Incarnation that we break through to meaning.[10] For it is only the religion of the Incarnation that can allot an adequate meaning to the world's unfolding.[11] "Through his Incarnation Christ"—and hence God—"becomes internal to the world, rooted in the very heart of the smallest atom."[12]

What is striking in Teilhard's doctrine of the Incarnation is that for him, even more strongly than for the Greek Fathers, the act of becoming man concentrates all subsequent aspects of Christ's existence.[13] The

[2] X, 181.   [3] X, 146.   [4] X, 105.   [5] X, 107.
[6] ET 39f.   [7] ET 42.   [8] ET 47.   [9] IX, 34, 87.
[10] ET 125.   [11] VII, 169.   [12] IX, 62.

[13] This is clear in the section IX, 85–94: as a result of the Incarnation, everything has been "physically 'christified'" (87), Christ is able to gather all human suffering and all joy into his heart (90f.); thus too in his death he gives death, which is normally synonymous with decay, the meaning and value of a metamorphosis, and in his Eucharist—which is a continual Incarnation—he

flesh he assumed is, as such, already universal, as we find in the first
of the celebrated three "visions", "Le Christ dans la Matière": [14] "the
entire universe vibrated"; "Christ was not set within a narrow aura
but radiated into infinity"; "matter in its totality was his garment".
Later on, matter is referred to as "the flesh of Christ".[15] Of course
the entire fullness of him who is hid in God only comes out in the
wake of Resurrection and Eucharist: having undergone bodily Resurrection[16] he assumes dominion over the cosmos,[17] a dominion that was
always his; now he can also take to himself the fullness of the ascending evolution.[18] He has become "coextensive with the world";[19] not
only are the deceased souls, waiting for the final resurrection, gathered
into his corporality,[20] where finally they will form a physical *pleroma*:[21]
all mankind's efforts to build up the world will be found there also;
again and again he emphasizes that it is not only the "merits" of the
human agents but also the "works" themselves that enter the heavenly
Jerusalem.[22] The Risen One is, uniquely, "the bottomless abyss into
which our capacity for achievement can throw itself and there expand
to its full output"; all worldly yearnings have already been sublimated in
him, so that we can take account of them by pursuing Him, their origin
and prototype.[23] "The more our total human endeavor is informed by
the right intention, the more it collaborates in implementing the fullness
of the Incarnation."[24] For Teilhard, however, the Eucharist is central,
as is shown to us, in classical terms, by the second "vision": here we
see how the tiny host expands until it stretches over all things—and
then contracts, embracing everything within it: "The white gleam was
active!"[25] "Transubstantiation is surrounded, as by an aureole, by a real,
albeit diminished, divinization of the whole cosmos."[26] All sacramental
communions together form a single one; indeed, "the communions
of all people of all times . . . in the same way constitute one single,
vastly more comprehensive communion, coextensive with human history. This means that the Eucharist, in its total operation, is only the
expression and revelation of the divine power of unification that has
its effect on every one of the world's spirit-atoms."[27] "Incarnation has

---

incorporates all world reality into himself (92f.).

[14] ET 93–107.   [15] ET 445.

[16] "Résurrection matérielle": X, 190.

[17] ET 53, 352–53.   [18] VII, 404.   [19] IX, 212.   [20] ET 353.

[21] X, 84.

[22] ET 296; IX, 41, etc.

[23] ET 291.   [24] ET 411.   [25] ET 100.   [26] ET 287.

[27] X, 194–95.

never come to an end; it changes all things. There is only one single celebration of Mass on earth, . . . the true, total host is the universe."[28]

Here we must say something about Teilhard's conception of the Cross and Passion. Although he does not wish to deny that "atonement" takes place through "expiation on our behalf", Teilhard pushes it—almost in irritation—into the background,[29] since he wants to see the Cross primarily in the context of evolution. As early as 1916 he writes, "The Cross symbolizes the hard labor of evolution—more than that of expiation."[30] "In his Passion Jesus feels the burden of all human sufferings."[31] Our Christology must adapt itself to the "new world";[32] it should see the Cross as "the symbol and gesture of progress", the "overcoming of resistance to union";[33] the Cross "symbolizes the act whereby Christ lifts up the world with all its burden of inertia";[34] it is "a symbol of progress and of the victory over all deficiencies, disappointments and hard struggles. This is the only Cross that (with a good conscience, with pride and fervor) we can offer the modern world for its veneration."[35] "*Christ-Évoluteur*: it is he who bears the sins, the whole burden of a world that is in a movement of progress."[36] What, formerly, was put forward as a model of "suffering purification and painful letting go" must be changed into a "sign of progress".[37] It is Christ "who carries and supports the burden of the evolving world".[38] Here the Cross is no longer the inner ultimate goal of the Incarnation and the presupposition of the Eucharist. Teilhard is no activist; he knows that all our attempts to further the world's upward movement are fruitless unless renunciation is involved, and ultimately they must give place to purifying and fruitful passivities—when we surrender ourselves into God's hands.[39]

God's foundational act in the work of the evolving world now appears as the complete unity of creation-Incarnation-Redemption (in the above sense). Creation is coextensive with the whole spectrum of evo-

---

[28] X, 90; cf. IX, 93.

[29] X, 170, 191; X, 103: "Il m'a toujours été impossible de m'apitoyer sincèrement sur un Crucifix tant que cette souffrance m'a été présentée comme l'expiation d'une faute que . . . Dieu aurait pu éviter."

[30] ET 61.

[31] ET 56; cf. the essay in VI, 61–66.

[32] X, 95.   [33] X, 104.   [34] X, 157.   [35] X, 192.

[36] X, 211.   [37] X, 258.   [38] X, 191.

[39] ET 33, 46, 57, 130f.; I, 46–47, 117, 345ff.; VI, 107; VII, 256. On the "passivities": IV, 71ff., ET 50, 163, 295, 342f. Cf. also the essay on happiness: XI, 121–40.

lution: "Creation has never stopped",[40] but neither, as we have seen, has the Incarnation, nor the bearing of the world's burden it implies. Accordingly, "the same foundational process can be called creation, Incarnation or Redemption, depending on one's standpoint." These three aspects are "not localized moments that can be defined in terms of time and space but genuine dimensions of the world; they are not objects of perception but conditions of all perception." Of course, there are the "especially expressive historical moments", but they "are only the privileged expression of processes that have cosmic dimensions".[41] The three aspects "appear as three complementary perspectives of a single process: creation, since by its very nature it pursues union, demands that the Creator should immerse himself, in some way, in his work; at the same time, since this necessarily produces evil through the operation of a secondary statistical law of evolution, a certain redemptive compensation is called for."[42] Although Teilhard has not the slightest doubt about the historical reality of Christ's Person, of his Cross and Resurrection, he thus treats the fundamental articulations of his existence and activity as "existential" dimensions of all created being.

The decisive fruit of this view is the idea, which he tenaciously and consistently maintains, that the world is converging toward a Person who (increasingly) is personalizing all evolving reality. It is the integration of human beings into the all-embracing "Body of Christ" that refashions them into "persons" in an eminent sense, within the "super-Person" of the *milieu divin*. From this point of view he assesses all mankind's religious programs, ruthlessly rejecting all depersonalizing atheisms, whether of an Eastern pattern ("l'énorme sophisme oriental") or of neo-humanistic modern provenance.[43] The "mysticism" of which he is an apologist is one of "personalism"; this is the *Sitz-im-Leben* of his axiom, "union differentiates."[44] Properly speaking, this "mysticism" should lead to the trinitarian mystery; in Teilhard it does not do so, or at least not explicitly enough. Teilhard does not get beyond the world principle of the "Christique"[45] as the "religion of tomorrow".

[40] ET 149.

[41] X, 156–57, similarly IX, 240.

[42] X, 229–30, cf. X, 212; XI, 211–13 (cf. the lucid summary in *Comment je vois* [1948], sec. 29). ["My Fundamental Vision" in *Toward the Future* (London, 1975), 163–208].

[43] IX, 137f., passim. Accordingly he shows how the religions "converge" toward Christianity: X, 138–50; XI, 47–64.

[44] ET 351; X, 137, passim. On two contrary kinds of union (downward to what lacks differentiation and upward to what is ever more differentiated): VI, 129.

[45] Teilhard's final sketch: XIII, 93–117.

This will suffice to enable us to look at Teilhard's eschatology. The fact that the world is recapitulated in the God-man means that, more than in any other view of the world, it is possible for the cosmos to be brought home to God—which is the theme of the last part of this volume. Christ has "conquered" the world and, as exalted and eucharistic Lord, can incorporate it into himself: there is no doubt about this; from his perspective the process will "with certainty" have a positive outcome. [46] But what does this fulfillment look like from the standpoint of the individual human being?

TWILIGHT ESCHATOLOGY. Although the noosphere's "reflection" upon itself suggests that love is the only solution ("*amorisation*")—and in the case of the human race, with its reflex consciousness, this is an almost physical requirement—the principle "heightened consciousness implies heightened freedom" forbids us to describe the final process in purely physical terms.[1] From Teilhard's own presuppositions (rather than on the basis of biblical arguments) it follows that humanity must face an ultimate choice and decision for or against Christ. The process must move toward "a final option, a genuinely and fully human act, a Yes and a No to God uttered individually by beings, each of which is endowed with a fully developed consciousness of freedom and human responsibility";[2] it must ultimately create a "schism between those who believe in the world's future and those who do not".[3] Autonomous man will be faced with the temptation experienced by "the Titans, Prometheus and Faust;[4] the higher the level of consciousness, the more destructive is man's potential for disorder, evil.[5] So Teilhard, who is so sceptical about an original sin at the beginning of human history—he regards it as a necessary evil in a contingent and unfolding universe[6]—sees the great sin at the *end* of world development in the form of a decision against Christ.[7] The decision is between righteousness and power.[8] The parousia will take place in connection with this final decision on

---

[46] Le Christ est sûr de s'achever": ET 293. Cf. IX, 163f. "Le Christ guide par le dedans la marche universelle du monde": X, 91.

[1] V, 368–74.   [2] IX, 112.   [3] IX, 144.   [4] V, 238.
[5] ET 56.

[6] In many places, including: X, 49 ff., 61f., 98–102, 157, 174, 219f.; IX, 108f.

[7] "La Parousie n'est-elle pas annoncée comme une aurore qui se lèvera sur une ruée suprême de l'erreur? Au moins, cette infidélité des derniers temps n'aura plus l'approbation apparente, ni les excuses de la vie": ET 83–84. Particularly grave will be "certaines *dernières* révoltes de l'Humanité parvenue à maturité (conscience et responsabilité maxima)": X, 229. Cf. X, 69: "L'humanité, enfin pleinement consciente de ses forces se divisera en deux camps, pour ou contre Dieu."

[8] ET 390.

the part of mankind: "Christ's silent and ever-intensifying presence in things" will reveal itself like lightning. [9] In accord with this final option —and here Teilhard's teaching remains unchanged from beginning to end—mankind has only two possible exits: heaven and hell. Heaven is portrayed as the complete personalization of all the members of Christ in his Mystical Body; only in him do we behold God. [10] Hell is the frightening possibility of evolutionary refuse. [11] In Teilhard's view the latter is connected with the idea (no doubt influenced by Bergson) of a cosmic double movement: matter rises to the realm of spirit, and spirit declines to the level of matter. [12] Of course, hell can only be defined indirectly and negatively, as the opposite of heaven. It is necessary "to have an intense feeling of it, in spite of the fact that one cannot see it directly". It is an abyss "to which one must turn one's back" as one ascends. [13]

When we come to the final stage of the process whereby the human monads, the highest synthesis of evolution, [14] are inserted into Christ, we seem to encounter a certain ambiguity springing from Teilhard's idea of evolution. On the one hand, every higher synthesis (life, spirit) already contains within it what it synthesizes: "the (synthesized) matter is not sublimated (a seductively simple theory, but contrary to dogma) but *dethroned* by the very spirit that, from below, it supports." [15] Since "union produces differentiation", those centers that are united by a higher order center are "not dissolved but, on the contrary, are confirmed and amplified". [16] "Matter permits spirit to exist by constantly providing it with a focus for its activity, by nourishing it. . . . The purity of a being's spiritual apex is proportional to the material fullness of its base." [17] If we apply this structure to eschatology, it would seem that the ultimate (heavenly) synthesis would have to embrace the entire

[9] IV, 196 (and the entire section "L'Attente de la Parousie": IV, 193–203).

[10] X, 83f., passim.

[11] ET 57f., 100, 132, 187, 293, 350, 427–29; X, 192–93.

[12] "The fallen monads, extremely remote from God, constitute a concrete pole of attraction toward dissolution": ET 427. Hell would thus be "une conscience infiniment désunie sur elle-même": X, 192.

[13] X, 193. Teilhard agrees with K. Barth at this point.

[14] This would be the place to discuss Teilhard's axiom that "creation is union" (ET 351, passim), but space forbids. Teilhard sees a problem in the concept of "creation from nothing", since the unifying act always presupposes some matter in the form of a "pure multiplicity", which is thus a "positive nothing". This difficulty does not seem insuperable. Why should not the substratum for every possible union be supplied, as such, by God?

[15] ET 277.   [16] VII, 122.

[17] IX, 78–79; cf. X, 128: "Spirit by no means represents a reality independent of, or contrary to, matter"; XIII, 36.

harvest of the world in all its evolutionary stages, from the material to the life of plants, animals and human beings. Did not Teilhard always insist that not only the *operatio* but also the *opus* itself would be cherished in the kingdom of God?[18]

This is contradicted, however, by a second aspect of evolution. Here matter seems to be a preliminary stage of spirit, spirit in potentiality, something as yet incompletely centered.[19] Thus Teilhard's "centrology"—a transposition of Leibniz's "monadology"[20]—can produce a radical formulation: "Strictly speaking . . . matter does not exist. . . . In the cosmos there is only spirit."[21] Here matter is only a formal concept: it is what is synthesized by spirit in any particular instance.[22] Teilhard's view is that matter's irreversible ascent to spirit renders the latter indissoluble, that is, "immortal", so that, in death, it "separates itself" from bodily matter.[23] What, in such a view, becomes of the "resurrection of the body"? It cannot be a kind of transfiguration of the old cosmos, for this has become superfluous.[24] And yet something corporeal must survive or else come into being in a new way. This, however, is seen only in souls, each of which, "in its spiritual unity, possesses an individual and highly complex structure: it bears the trace (*trace*) of the unifying processes it epitomizes, and this structure alone can enable it to be adopted into a higher 'marriage'"; "it exhibits no superfluous multiplicity and, in its simplicity, bears the mark (*vestige*) of all multiplicities of all times."[25] Thus the soul itself, which is a spirit

[18] ET 296; IX, 41.

[19] ET 425, and the entire hymn-like piece on the ascension of Elijah: the fiery chariot is matter in process of transformation as it ascends: ET 437–46. Materialism as an illusion: X, 125. "La Matière matrice de l'Esprit, état supérieur de la Matière": XIII, 45.

[20] VII, 103–34.

[21] VII, 132.

[22] In "Les Noms de la Matière" (ET 419–32) it is referred to as "matière relative": 423f.

[23] E 247. As seen by the "Grande Monade", therefore, the material cosmos would be left behind as a "corpse" from which the living world of souls had emigrated (ET 237–48). Cf. ET 348: "The more the creation becomes spirit, the less fleshly (*charnel*) becomes the blood that nourishes man's superior part."

[24] "What might the 'resurrected material' consist of? Evidently not in the reconstituted sum of material monads that supported our soul during our lifetime. Initially it is hard to see what purpose would be served, in the transfigured life, by this lower-level multiplicity, whose enriching power has already been exhausted during the earthly phase of the universe": ET 430. In the note he observes that people have a false idea of the indestructibility of lower-level matter.

[25] ET 431–32.

that has existed historically, is in a certain sense the "matter" that is capable of being refashioned in the ultimate Mystical Body. Accordingly "the world must lose its visible form, in each of us and in its totality, if it is to be divinized."[26] "The new earth will be so transparent in its elements that it will seem to consist of nothing but rays of the glory of God, materializing in us."[27] "Only those nuclei with reflex awareness —for they alone can cleave to the Omega—embody the irreversible part of a universe that has become spirit."[28] As for the myriad variety of forms in the animal and organic kingdom, Teilhard regards them as nothing more than diversions and false paths in the vertical course of evolution.[29] Earthly corporality, earthly materiality remains a mere memory.

This one-sided development from matter to spirit prevents one final element of Teilhard's eschatology from reaching maturity, namely, the theme of the duality of the sexes, of the "eternal feminine". To it, during the First World War, he had dedicated an important hymn of praise.[30] Here he understands the feminine as "the magic that is mixed in with the world in order to unite it". Intensifying from stage to stage, it is a power that, through ever greater self-differentiation, results, in the sexes, in ever deeper and more fruitful union. Its magic remains dangerously ambivalent, however, unless it is "redeemed" at the highest level, by Christ; thus, in virginity, it can attain the highest fruitfulness that enables the Logos to be embodied: "I am the Virgin Mary, Mother of all men. . . . I am the Church, the Bride of Jesus." Here the feminine is the real *milieu divin*; "placed between God and the world, like a field of attraction for both sides, I bring them both passionately together."[31] Mary-Church is thus the highest flowering of that movement which ascends from the earth, though we must remember that it is always elicited and purified by the descending movement of grace, which is the movement of the Son, downward, from God. This "bridal" theme is not followed through in his later work. In his commentary on the "Hymn to the Eternal Feminine", de Lubac shows its development, its origins and predecessors (Plato, Dante, Goethe, Soloviev). He shows how the theme recurs in Teilhard, for example,

[26] IX, 91.

[27] IX, 103.

[28] VII, 132.

[29] ET 14f.; VII, 130f.

[30] ET 249–62; together with a commentary by H. de Lubac. Translated into German by H. U. von Balthasar as "Hymne an das Ewig-Weibliche" (Einsiedeln: Johannes Verlag, 1968) and quoted from this edition.

[31] *Ibid.*, 13.

in his marriage homilies,[32] and stresses the importance of the theme of chastity in his whole oeuvre,[33] including the late appendix to his autobiographical work *The Heart of Matter* (1956), which is entitled, "The Feminine, or the Unifying Factor".[34] Here, however, as Teilhard notes, it is not so much an element in itself but rather a light that illuminates the process of convergence. Naturally, the theme of sublimation remains essential: *agape* can only be the higher synthesis of the powers of *eros*.[35] "Purity consists, not in separating oneself off, but in penetrating the universe more profoundly."[36] Devotion to the Mother of the Lord remains a part of Teilhard's prayer to the very end.[37] For him, she is the true Demeter,[38] the natural virtue and grace of the evolutionary current;[39] he hopes that, in its final phase, mankind will transcend the sphere of sexuality and approach a Marian fruitfulness.[40] In the great cosmological essays, however, the theme cannot be pursued.

Teilhard's limitations become visible at those very points that are central in J. Moltmann's system (which was deliberately designed to counter that of Teilhard). The one-sidedly christological emphasis somewhat obscures the trinitarian shape of world redemption; as a result there can be no eschatological *descensus* in Teilhard, and the heaven-hell dualism has the final word (as in Judaism). The one-sidedly incarnational emphasis puts the theology of the Cross—the work of atonement wrought by the Trinity—almost entirely in the shade, with the result that, in spite of the emphasis on freedom, the reality of sin is not brought out in all its New Testament profundity. Furthermore, "becoming" is promoted at the expense of "being" to such an extent that, in Teilhard's syntheses, the differences (including the sexual differences) are in danger of disappearing altogether.

What of Teilhard's concept of hope? In accordance with his phenomenological point of departure he placed neo-humanist hope for the future of the world in opposition to the Christian, vertical hope. In

---

[32] *Ibid.*, 61.

[33] *Ibid.*, 63–80; first and foremost in the treatise *L'Evolution de la Chasteté*: XI, 67–92 ["The Evolution of Chastity", in *Toward the Future*, 60–87], where the highest goal is described as the "suprêmes épousailles": XI, 72.

[34] XIII, 71–74.

[35] H. de Lubac, 112ff.

[36] ET 441.

[37] Quotations in de Lubac, 155f., and also: de Lubac, *La Prière du P. Teilhard de Chardin* (Paris: Fayard, 1964), chap. 9: "La Vierge Marie".

[38] ET 48; X, 76.

[39] ET 163.

[40] VI, 96; XI, 67ff.

fact, his concept is so transformed by the "monistic" theology of the Incarnation that even the "forward" dimension, inseparable from the vertical, acquires theological relevance.

β. *Jürgen Moltmann*

SALVAGING BLOCH. While in Europe the fascinating figure of Ernst Bloch promoted the reintroduction of Jewish themes into Christian eschatology, the liberation theologies of Latin America went back directly to the exhortations and promises of the Prophets in order to substantiate their political programme. They argued that Old Testament prophecy looks forward to a time when a final and definitive peace will reign in the creation as a whole and in the world of men in particular: this peace has not yet been brought about in the Incarnation and Resurrection of Jesus. Moltmann agrees with this view.[1] Associated with it are two topics of great importance. Since the whole Jesus story, including his Resurrection—which only serves as a model for the eschatological implementation of his reign—is not yet complete and has still to assert itself in world history with the help of the Church's proclamation and transforming power, the Old Testament "linear hope" remains in force. Since the trinitarian God has involved himself in world history in the Cross and Resurrection of Christ, he shares a history with the world and can attain self-fulfillment only together with the world. This latter idea brings the "theology of hope" (inspired by Bloch) close to "process theology", which, however, we shall not discuss here. This first theme is the object of the following reflections.

---

[1] "The realism of the promise [points] beyond the New Testament fulfillment": P. Althaus, *Die Letzten Dinge* (Gütersloh, 1957), 309. "But salvation must also be understood as shalom in the Old Testament sense": J. Moltmann, *Theology of Hope* (London: SCM Press, 1967), 329. "If the Christian mission which brings to all men righteousness by faith arises against the background of the Yahwist promise to Abraham and of the prophetic eschatology of Isaiah, by turning these expectations into present activity, then its horizon must embrace not only the establishment of the obedience of faith among the Gentiles, but also that which the Old Testament hopes for in terms of blessing, peace, righteousness and fulness of life": *Theology of Hope*, 329. Israel's messianic hopes are only partially fulfilled by Christianity; therefore the as yet unfulfilled promises of the Old Testament must be acknowledged as persisting in the New Testament context": J. Moltmann, *Kirche in der Kraft des Geistes* (Munich: Kaiser, 1975), 158. "Realized eschatology swallows up history." It is either "platonizing" or "existential". Moltmann, *Die Zukunft der Schöpfung* (Munich: Kaiser, 1977), 26.

As far as Moltmann's theology of hope is concerned, "realized eschatology" is the real enemy; consequently there is no mention of the Gospel of John in his book. In the present work we began by setting forth a nuanced analysis of this "realized eschatology" that is able to comprehend and include the futurist dimension, but Moltmann is unaware of this.

Moltmann's theology attempts to infiltrate Ernst Bloch's atheistic, Messianic philosophy and reintegrate into Christian theology those elements Bloch has taken from the Bible.[2] For Bloch, the real itself is "hope" since it proceeds from the *alpha of nothingness*, through the *self-transcendence of becoming*, which changes utopian visions into reality, on its way to the *omega of being*; here the notion of an absolute God is a utopia that becomes real when this "God" "becomes man": man makes himself absolute and ultimately moves into a "heaven that has become

---

[2] J. Moltmann, *Im Gespräch mit Ernst Bloch* (Munich: Kaiser, 1976); also his "Das Prinzip Hoffnung" and "Theologie der Hoffnung": appendix to 3d German ed. of the *Theologie der Hoffnung* (Munich: Kaiser, 1965) 313–34.

Bloch speaks of the promise "exceeding every immanent fulfillment" (*Gespräch*, 25), and Moltmann feels that this hope—an Old Testament hope—which supports everything, is something he shares with him. But when Bloch himself says, "How could the world attain perfection except, as is proposed by the Christian religion, by exploding and disappearing apocalyptically?" (*ibid.*, 26), Moltmann cannot imagine this explosion taking place "without the resurrection of Jesus Christ and the eschatological horizon of all the reality that it discloses" (*ibid.*, 27). "The hopes that, fundamentally, Bloch has in mind are much larger than the historical materialism with its social movements and goals, to which he wishes to attach them" (*ibid.*, 40). So Bloch's faith is "not so much an atheistic faith as a faith verging on pantheism" (*ibid.*, 69). Accordingly Moltmann takes the risk of suggesting an encounter between them: "On the one hand, there is a militant hope that is in league with the real and the possible, and, on the other hand, there is an all-embracing (Christian) circle of hope in a Creator who created from nothing. It seems to me that the open circle of the former should not close itself to the latter; conversely, theological hope should not isolate itself from the practical hope that wishes to change the world" (*ibid.*, 70). However, things must not stop at the level of reciprocal openness. No: the task of the Christian hope that rests on the fact of the Resurrection of Jesus—which needs only to be believed—and which is subject to "temptations" quite different from those of Bloch, since the latter are "in league with friendly world tendencies", is essentially to overtake them in their susceptibility to disappointment and to strip Bloch's "utopian images of hope" of their magic so that they can be "serviceable to love's imagination; for it belongs to the creativity of love to try to improve things" (*Theologie der Hoffnung*, 333–34). See also "E. Bloch und die Hoffnung ohne Glaube" in *Das Experiment Hoffnung* (Munich: Kaiser, 1974), 48–63. We shall return to this later.

vacant". Bloch's attempt, which is closer to the Exodus atmosphere of the Bible than Marx (and better acquainted with Hegelian logic), is a radically secularized Messianism; he places more emphasis than either Marx or Feuerbach on the New Testament Incarnation of God as an element of the unstoppable "linear" movement, since redemption lies exclusively "in the future".

The "theology of hope" remains within the Christian tradition insofar as it sees Old and New Testament in terms of promise and fulfillment, and—as we have already mentioned—it stresses the fact that the fulfillment cannot have been wholly achieved in the death and Resurrection of Jesus, *even as far as he himself is concerned*, since his kingdom has not established its dominion in a continuing world history: his divine mission is as yet unfulfilled. Moltmann inserts Bloch's model at the point where the dead Jesus is raised by God's power from the "nothingness of death" (which the Lutheran Moltmann takes seriously) and made the principle of what is, in worldly terms, a utopian hope: namely, that sinful and mortal men can escape from death and enter the absolute, the kingdom of the living God, in virtue of the Resurrection of Christ, the "hope of glory" (Col 1:27). What this means can best be seen by comparing it with the "realized" view: the believer and the Church must not turn away from the world and yearn to take refuge in an already fulfilled "above", thus neglecting and betraying their mission to the world; nor should they embrace a crude Old Testament chiliasm and expect fulfillment to come about as a result of the mere prolongation of historical time (for Christ had to go through death in order to be raised); nor should they resign themselves to the condition of the world and put up with personal and social sin and injustice, and with death. Rather, endowed with the "hope of glory" that springs from Christ's Resurrection—and it is Christ himself who has equipped them for this mission—they should work to "liberate" the world from its bonds and to transform men—both individuals and social structures. For this "hope" is a hope for this earthly world, its history and nature, and as for the "glory", it is that transfiguring Resurrection that, from an earthly point of view, remains utopian.

This process, triggered by the Resurrection of the Crucified One, is essentially the Church's mission to continue the mission of Jesus; it is part of the history and "future" of the risen Lord, for "he must reign until he has put all his enemies—including death—under his feet", so that, then, the perfected kingdom can be "delivered to the Father", so that "God may be all in all" (1 Cor 15:24–28). We might ask whether, so far, the "theology of hope" actually goes any farther than Origen's celebrated homily (and the theological line that follows it, via Ambrose and Gerhoh of Reichersberg up to John XXII). According to Origen it is not only Jesus who "waits": together with him, the whole heavenly community of saints "waits" until "I, the last and worst of all sinners", am made perfect and "subject to the Father". When, however, Jesus "has brought to perfection all his work and the full number of his creatures, he too will be subject to the Father in the person of those whom he 'subjected to the Father' and in whom he has 'brought to completion the work that the Father gave him to do', so that 'God may be all in all'." "So it is we who, by neglecting our life, delay his joy." "He mourns as long as we remain in error." Did he not "empty" himself for our sake, seeking, not his own, but our own? How then "could he stop seeking what is ours, how could he who 'wept over Jerusalem' stop weeping over our plight?" In Origen's view all heaven can attain the fullness of joy only "when all the members of the Mystical Body of Christ are together and, together with Christ, can say—for they are his limbs—'All my bones shall say, O Lord, who is like thee?' " [3]

We can trace the parallel even farther. In Origen Jesus "waits for us to follow his example and tread in his footsteps". In Moltmann the time of hope in the wake of Christ's Resurrection stands under the emblem of the Crucified One. "At its hard core, the theology of hope is a theology of the Cross. The Cross of Christ is the actual, present form of the kingdom of God on earth. . . . All else is dreams and fantasies." [4] So if we are summoned to come up with programmes of practical love, as some kind of approximation to the kingdom of God even now, on this side of death, we must not forget that such action is always under the sign of the Cross: it is a "hopeful outgoing into the world". [5] "In the history of which we are a part, freedom and justice" can only come about "through *the representative suffering of Jesus Christ*, and through our discipleship of him, *acting in solidarity* with those who suffer". Thus "the anticipation of Christian hope is vital and effective only when we act on behalf of those who have no future." When believers, "the firstfruits of the new creation, . . . take up their cross, they anticipate the future of redemption". [6] "Thus the eschatology of the future and the theology of the cross are interwoven. It is neither that futuristic eschatology is isolated, as in late Jewish apocalyptic, nor does the cross become the mark of the paradoxical presence of eternity in every mo-

---

[3] *Lev.* hom. 7, 1–2 (Baehrens 6, 370; 380). Cf. Ambrose, *De fide ad Gratianum* I, V, c 13 (PL 16, 682), Gerhoh of Reichersberg, *Liber contra duo haereses* (PL 194, 1178). Cf. Karl Barth, *Church Dogmatics* IV/3, pt. 1 (Edinburgh, 1961) 340ff.

[4] "Einführung in die Theologie der Hoffnung" in *Das Experiment Hoffnung*.

[5] Moltmann, *Theology of Hope*, 163.

[6] Moltmann, *Zukunft der Schöpfung*, 63–64.

ment, as in Kierkegaard."[7] Here it is clear how, in contrast to the liberation theologies, the categorical imperative of Christian action toward a more just world can only produce approximations to the kingdom; it itself is to be expected at the end of time and cannot be constructed. (Nonetheless such approximations, fashioned after the pattern of the Cross, will mediate blessings.) Jesus' "kingdom can then no longer be seen in a historic transformation of the godless state of man and the world. His future does not result from the trends of world history."[8] The kingdom has been initiated, in the Resurrection of Jesus, by a new creation coming down from God, a pledge that all things are to be created anew; this being so, the believer who hopes and works for this new creation cannot be content with anything less. "Because of this universality, the new hope of the kingdom leads us to suffer under the forsakenness and unredeemedness of all things and their subjection to vanity. It leads us to a solidarity with the anxious expectation of the whole creation that waits for the 'liberty of the children of God'."[9] The believer may not simply accept things in resignation: "On the contrary, he is compelled to accept the world in all meekness, subject as it is to death and the powers of annihilation, and to guide all things towards their new being."[10]

This is an imposing project; but we must ask a crucial question of this theology of hope. *For what and for whom does it hope?* Is the object of its hope a risen Christ whose world mission is, however, as yet incomplete? And is its hope that he may succeed in fulfilling his task? Moltmann would not say this, yet he is concerned to salvage the hope of which Bloch speaks, which is "precarious because it must include the possibility of disappointment"[11] because (unlike the Christian hope) it is not erected "on a mythology of fulfillment hypostatized as real".[12] What Bloch here calls mythology is, in Moltmann, the Cross of Christ. Primarily, however, Moltmann understands it not only as an atoning event between God and the world but above all as the eminent, and indeed the only, locus of God's trinitarian revelation in the world. (At last the distinction between the Persons begins to come to light.) Furthermore, since Moltmann holds fast to the identity of the economic Trinity and the immanent Trinity, Christ's Cross is also the locus at

---

[7] Moltmann, *Theology of Hope*, 164.; cf. *Kirche in der Kraft des Geistes*, 219ff.

[8] Moltmann, *Theology of Hope*, 221.

[9] *Ibid.*, 223.

[10] *Ibid.*, 224.

[11] E. Bloch, "Kann Hoffnung enttäuscht werden?" in *Verfremdungen* I (Frankfurt am Main: Suhrkamp, 1962), 214.

[12] E. Bloch, *Das Prinzip Hoffnung* (Frankfurt am Main: Suhrkamp, 1959), 1523.

which the process within the Trinity itself plumbs an ultimate depth. We shall speak of this later. However, we cannot regard the identity of both aspects of the trinitarian life as absolute, otherwise we would fall into pure Hegelianism or a radical process theology; in many formulations Moltmann distances himself from this kind of equation of the process in God and the process between God and the world. All the same the two sides of the process cannot be simply juxtaposed: they do exhibit a reciprocity, and one in which the economic aspect is subordinated to the immanent.[13] According to perspective and emphasis, negativity is regarded as present in the internal history of God or as absent from it. We read, "Out of the pain of the negation of himself", God is experienced "as the God of promise. . . . Only, the god-forsakenness of the cross cannot, as in Hegel, be made into an element belonging to the divine process."[14] This is very close to one of Adrienne von Speyr's formulations: "The 'estrangement' in God must contain the whole turmoil of history."[15] What can "contain" mean here? This is the crucial question. Moltmann's desire to salvage Hegel and Bloch and insert them into Christian theology must cause us to suspect that he would attach no validity to the theology of the Trinity adumbrated at the beginning of this section. There we suggested that the Trinity contains the purely positive archetypes of what, within creation, is reflected in potentialities and in the negativities that result from sin. The origin of Moltmann's doctrine of the Trinity is sought and found, not only gnoseologically but also ontologically, in the *diastasis* of the Cross and in the negativity of estrangement from God that Christ there endures; this obscures the positive archetypes, found within the Trinity, of the *imagines trinitatis* in the world and in salvation history. On the basis of these archetypes, Adrienne von Speyr, commenting on Jesus' address to the Father ("But now I am coming to you", Jn 17:13), says that both the Son's "economic" separation from the Father and their subsequent "economic" reuniting express "a perfect fulfillment of love" in the immanence of God. "When human beings separate and vow love to one another, a love conquering all distance and outlasting everything, they can do so only in God; they are striving to anchor their love in God. Here it is the love of God himself that lays anchor in itself. Sacrifice, forsakenness and darkness are not only indicated

---

[13] Moltmann, *Trinität und Reich Gottes*, 178: eschatologically "the economic Trinity is sublimated in the immanent Trinity." This is only true eschatologically, however: "The doctrine of the *immanent* Trinity is part and parcel of eschatology insofar as it is the very epitome of doxology."

[14] Moltmann, *Theology of Hope*, 171.

[15] Moltmann, *Der gekreuzigte Gott* (Munich: Kaiser, 1974), 233.

and aspired to in the absoluteness of God's love but fulfilled reality; they are anchored in the mutual being of Father and Son—so much so that the communication is almost incidental, because everything is primarily lived, indeed, simply *is*, at the level of essence and being." [16] Even in his cry of forsakenness, the Son, having taken upon himself the negativity of sinful estrangement from God, obeys the Father in a perfectly divine-human way, and this obedience originates in the eternal stance of the Son in the Father's presence. The fact that the Son here embodies the Father's "Other" does not come, as Moltmann thinks, from his humanity—as if God needed first to create a world in order to love "Another" ("like cannot be satisfied with like") [17]—but from the eternal otherness of the Persons in God.

From this position the futurist element, and hence the element of hope (understood in secular terms), is imported into God. The archetype of all temporal process cannot be conceived in terms of an eternal, realized present. [18] Here, hope means not only a hope on man's part but also "God's hope" arising from the secular process. [19] Here again, however, we must ask the question: What does this God hope for? Surely—whether or not we regard the "history of God" as being fused with the world—the process is guaranteed a happy end in any case? In contrast to Bloch, who speaks of hope's precarious nature, Moltmann, sustained by the victory of the crucified and risen Lord, can say that men can have "certainty of hope", "certainty as to the future" and "certainty of fulfillment". [20]

---

[16] 3 Jo 337.

[17] Once more we must point out that Moltmann misinterprets genuine realized eschatology. The only content he will acknowledge in it is either "mystical" (no doubt in Schweitzer's sense), enthusiastic (Paul asserts his theology of the Cross against the Corinthians) or, finally, existential (Bultmann). "Realized eschatology swallows up history" in "a post-Christian message that is in part platonizing and in part existentialist": *Zukunft der Schöpfung*, 26. See also his *Perspektiven der Theologie* (Munich: Kaiser-Grünewald, 1968), 242f. Realized eschatology is coupled with "anthropological eschatology", *ibid.* 244. On Paul's campaign against realized eschatology, in both its Jewish (apocalyptic) and its Hellenistic (epiphanic) form, see *Theology of Hope*, 159–60.

[18] Moltmann, *Experiment Hoffnung*, 65, 79 passim.

[19] Cf. Moltmann, *Zukunft der Schöpfung*, 106 passim.

[20] Moltmann, *Theologie der Hoffnung* 332–34.

Paul's theology is concerned with an "unlimited hope that calls us to go beyond all limits; this hope is open to every godless person, without conditions and preconditions": Moltmann, *Perspektiven*, 178.

Moltmann's "certainty of hope" cannot be disappointed because it is based on the "*extra nos* of God's *promissio*". At the point where sin, constantly intensifying,

Here, somewhat as in Teilhard de Chardin, although on entirely different premises, we find a kind of triumphalism. It lacks the very object of hope on which the theology of the New Testament lays greatest stress, namely, the hope that in virtue of God's mercy we shall survive his judgment. Only in this sense was Bonaventure prepared to say that theological hope could enjoy a "certainty". And only in this sense will Péguy dare to speak of God, of Jesus and of man having "hope".

If, in conclusion, we ask whether Moltmann succeeds in salvaging the horizontal dimension of eschatology and situating it in "realized" eschatology, it is clear that, for him, the question is falsely posed. He builds elements of a realized eschatology into a futurist eschatology, and this alone justifies the use of the word "hope".

INTEGRATING THE HORIZONTAL DIMENSION. Anyone seeking to understand, in theological terms, how Christian hope is related to the world's earthly future will do well to bear in mind the Scholastic distinction between hope understood as a human possibility, as *spes communis* (a *passio animae* that can actually rise to the level of *virtus*) and hope as a theological virtue, which is a pure gift of grace that comes to us from the divine mercy. Augustine himself drew the same distinction between the *spes de terrenis* found in the world and the hope that he describes as "praesumentium de coelestibus, quae promisit non mendax Deus".[1] This second, Christian, hope has God himself for its object.[2] Thomas is of the same opinion, but he discovers nuances in this object: Hope looks forward primarily to the highest good, God himself,[3] our ultimate aim,[4] and secondarily to the acquisition of graces that

---

rules all history and particularly post-Christian history (of which he speaks but little), there stands the Cross. The Cross has from the outset overcome sin, and so has guaranteed salvation "*sub contrario*" (Moltmann, *Theology of Hope*, 223–24). Hell, consequently, has from the outset been swallowed up by the Cross—in diametric opposition to Teilhard de Chardin, where it remains standing like an erratic boulder, since it is not located within the ambience and life of the Trinity.

On this whole topic see H. U. von Balthasar: "Zu einer christlichen Theologie der Hoffnung" in *Münchner Theol. Zft.* 32 (1981), 81–102.

[1] *In Ps.* 51, 6 (PL 36, 603). French draws a distinction between *espoir* and *espérance*.

[2] *In Ps.* 32, 5; cf. 2, 23 (PL 36, 297); cf. *In Ps.* 31, *En.* 2, 6: "Si quod sperandum est, speras: id est vitam aeternam . . ." (PL 36, 262).

[3] *S. Th.* II–II, 19, 9 ad 2.

[4] *S. Th.* II–II, 19, 12 ad 3.

help us attain this final goal.[5] The Psalmist justly finds fault with those who set their hope on a man for salvation; yet, when "subordinated to God", a man *can* "minister to salvation".[6] Bonaventure says the same thing.[7]

A straightforward conclusion follows from this. Christian hope, theological hope, goes beyond this world, but it does not pass it by: rather, it takes the world with it on its way to God, who has graciously prepared a dwelling in himself for us and for the world. This implies that the Christian in the world is meant to awaken hope, particularly among the most hopeless; and this in turn means that he must create such humane conditions as will actually allow the poor and oppressed to have hope. Hope must never be individualistic: it must always be social. It cannot simply hope that others will attain eternal salvation; it must enable them to cherish this hope by creating conditions apt to promote it. Theological hope is not directed toward earthly goods as such; Christians cannot "cash in" the Old Testament hope for worldly well-being. To stay at this level (and here Moltmann is right) would be to part company with the Cross, which is supertemporal and hence ever present to this transitory aeon. As far as the earthly future is concerned, as we saw in *Theo-Drama* III, 452ff., the genuine disciple of Christ is promised chiefly pain and difficulty; he is urged to show courage, trust and confidence in divine help. The whole horizontal thrust of the Old Testament promise of salvation remains a "figure", in Pascal's sense: it is a prefiguring of the eschatological, vertical salvation[8] that will be brought about in Christ. Yet this vertical salvation will have its consequences in the historical drama at the end of time. The con-

---

[5] *S. Th.* I–II, 69, 2 ad 1.

[6] *S. Th.* II–II, 25, 1 ad 3.

[7] In many places the object of theological hope is said to be God alone, understood as man's highest good and bliss. Hence the spiritual goods that come from God and lead to him: III, d 26 dub 1–2. What is crucial is that "even if hope is for earthly goods, the moving cause is not anything created but something infinite, something that pertains to that uncreated good from which hope springs": III, d 26, q 3 ad 3. We can hope in man insofar as he is God's helper, but we do not hope in him as a savior: I, d 1 dub 9.

[8] This is rightly stressed by H. Fries in "Spero, ut intelligam: Bemerkungen zu einer Theologie der Hoffnung" in W.-O. Marsch, ed., *Diskussion über die Theologie der Hoffnung* (Munich, 1967), 81–105.

trary view leads necessarily to some form of chiliasm, whether religious or Marxist and secularized.[9]

It is true that the post-Christian historical arena has something in common with the pre-Christian: it too is a realm of waiting and endurance, of testing and purification; thus patience, *hypomonē*, is set forth as one of the three cardinal virtues of Christians.[10] But such similarity conceals much that is very different. For the Old Testament believer, temptation and even misfortune was primarily a sign that he had become guilty before God; in extreme instances (Job), it represented a baffling evil. For the Christian it is rather a confirmation of his discipleship of the Lord. The Jew cannot give thanks for persecution, whereas the Christian can and must do so.[11] Recognizing his suffering as Christ's, and as a grace, he can enjoy the Christian hope that—in however hidden a manner—this suffering, in union with Christ's, will promote the salvation of the world.

However, the Christian is not in the world only for suffering (and its hidden effects). He is also there to proclaim that reconciliation with God which, in Christ, has come for all; and this proclamation will be witnessed in his Christian life no less than in his words. He has a share in the responsibility for the world that God in Christ has taken upon himself.[12] Such participation arises, not from the hope of doing some Christian work in the world, but quite explicitly from the *mission* of Jesus. When he sends out his disciples he never uses the word "hope".[13] As far as temporal

[9] On this whole topic, cf. my remarks in *The Glory of the Lord* VII (San Francisco: Ignatius Press, 1989) 485–543; *The Word Made Flesh, Explorations in Theology*, 1 (San Francisco: Ignatius Press, 1989), 255–77; "Die drei Gestalten der Hoffnung" in *ThQ* 152 (1972), 101–11. Also cf. Karl Rahner, *Theologie der Zukunft*, ed. K. Füssel (1971); also his "Ewigkeit aus der Zeit" in *Schriften XIV* (1980), 422–32; *Grundkurs des Glaubens* (Herder, 1976) 419–23; *Foundations of Christian Faith* (London, 1978), 436–41.

[10] E. Przywara, *Demut, Geduld, Liebe* (Düsseldorf: Patmos, 1960).

[11] R. Schaeffler, "Der utopische Gedanke und die christliche Heilserwartung" in L. Höde, ed., *Das Heil und die Utopien* (Paderborn, 1977), 65f. R. Schaeffler, *Was dürfen wir hoffen? Die katholische Theologie der Hoffnung zwischen Blochs utopischem Denken und der reformatorischen Rechtfertigungslehre* (Darmstadt, 1979), 230.

[12] Cf. *In Gottes Einsatz leben* (Einsiedeln: Johannes Verlag, 1971).

[13] J. de Guibert, "Sur l'emploi d'ΕΛΠΙΣ et de ses synonymes dans le NT" in *RSR* 4 (1913), 565–69. The author is of the opinion that Jesus deliberately avoided

success is concerned, his own mission is ambivalent: "His own people received him not. But to all who received him" (Jn 1:11–12). His own disciples are sent out with prospects that are just as ambivalent: "If any place will not receive you . . . , shake off the dust that is on your feet" (Mk 6:11). Success is not one of the names of God, or of Christ, or of his Church. The criterion for the mission of the disciples is the mission of Christ: "*As* the Father has sent me, *even so* I send you" (Jn 20:21; emphasis added). So their spiritual equipment is no different from Jesus' spiritual equipment, namely, the Holy Spirit, who gives them both the "theological virtues" and, as well, the "foreboding reminder" of the nature, the challenge and the fate of Jesus: "Do you not remember?" (Mk 8:18). On his journey, the disciple who is sent out is also given hope, along with faith and love; and this hope is the hope for God's help that we find uttered in the Psalms in a hundred different ways—minus the Old Testament hope that looks forward to the satisfaction of ultimately seeing the fall of the godless.

Of course, this hope on the part of Christians who have been entrusted with a mission can be sustained only insofar as they bring their task to completion: "I have fought the good fight, . . . I have kept the faith. Henceforth there is laid up for me the crown of righteousness . . ." (2 Tim 4:7–8). Furthermore, every true mission, however limited it may seem in earthly terms, is universal, like the mission of Christ and the mission of the Catholic Church. It is addressed to the world as a whole; its effects are also universal and Catholic. (Not visibly, but in the grace of God.) This grace justifies the one who is sent in setting to work with divine hope. He is to put his hand to the work of transforming the world in conformity with the spirit of Christ, but this transformation is fundamentally "conversion", *metanoia* (Mk 1:15). Changing structures remains an ambivalent and ineffectual business unless this conversion is undergone by the powers-that-be or those that supplant them.

These few topics comprise the entire repertoire of "political

---

the word *elpis*: "He wanted to avoid all confusion between the better things he was offering and those that were the object of the Jewish hope entertained by his contemporaries" (569).

theology"; it is centered, not on the concept of a hope that hovers between *spes communis* and *theologica*, but on the concept of mission. This mission always looks toward the One-who-sends and envisages the discipleship thus entailed (cf. Jn 21:15–19). Naturally, the person who is sent forth as a Christian is not forbidden to have a human expectation of success. In fact he needs it, just as Christ needed it, having renounced foreknowledge of the "hour". The difference is that, "in that hour" when he is "brought to trial", the Christian must "not be anxious" about what to say, for he must speak out of a deeper confidence that is the gift of the Spirit (Mk 13:11). Such predictions, in that they point to the assistance of the Spirit present in believers, presuppose a human aloneness that underlines, in the strongest possible manner, the fact that vision and possession are "not yet". It is not only the Jews who will not find Jesus once he has gone away; Jesus makes the same prediction to his disciples. Their very lives are drawn into Jesus' hiddenness in God (Col 3:3), but the latter liberates them and empowers them for action. How else should they exercise a mission that springs from the kenosis of Christ?[14]

At all events, mission implies responsibility; and in Christian terms the circle of this responsibility—which is always a limited one—can never be separated from the Church's total responsibility for the world, for the *polis theou* (*civitas Dei*). According to Augustine, what informs this *polis* is the divine *agape*, which in turn cannot exist apart from a living faith and a living hope; it seeks to promote the total offering of the world to God's love (*De Civ. Dei* X, 6). This being so, every theology of hope will have to concentrate on this central point: "We exercise hope by way of anticipation; . . . this is a response to that anticipation whereby God's prevenient love has already anticipated the new

---

[14] To the Jews he says, "You will seek me and you will not find me; where I am you cannot come" (Jn 7:34). To the disciples, "The days are coming when you will desire to see one of the days of the Son of man, and you will not see it" (Lk 17:22). So Jesus urges them to walk in him, in the light, for "if any one walks in the night, he stumbles, because the light is not in him" (Jn 11:10). "Night comes, when no one can work" (Jn 9:4). Paul says that Christians must be a light in the dark universe ("in the midst of a crooked and perverse generation", Phil 2:15). "For you are all sons of light and sons of the day; we are not of the night or of darkness. So then let us not sleep, as others do, but let us keep awake and be sober" (1 Th 5:5).

creation even under the dispensation of the old."[15] This—and
nothing else—is what we mean by saying that hope's horizontal
"forward thrust" is a function of the "realized" action of the
trinitarian love of God in Christ; and it will remain so to the end
of the world.[16]

[15] R. Schaeffler, *Was dürfen wir hoffen?*, 247.

[16] Cf. the chapter "The Hermeneutics of Christian Mission" in J. Moltmann's
Theology of Hope (272–303). "Thus the experiential content of Christian eschatology . . . comprises the experiences that are undergone in the course of the mission
undertaken in world history 'to all peoples'. The Christian consciousness of history . . . is a missionary consciousness in the knowledge of a divine commission,
and is therefore a consciousness of the contradiction inherent in this unredeemed
world, and of the sign of the cross under which the Christian mission and the
Christian hope stand": *ibid.*, 195; cf. 284. On the mission of Christ, cf. Moltmann, *The Trinity and the Kingdom of God* (London: SCM Press, 1981), 65–75. It
is worth pointing out in this context that, as far as the Latin American *liberation
theologies* are concerned, the Christian imperative of active political transformation of social structures is practically never linked with the topic of hope. Rather
it is a response to the appeal for loving solidarity with the poor and oppressed as
practiced and commanded by Christ. This is what we find in the texts compiled by
Claus Bassmann (*Befreiung durch Jesus? Die Christologie der lateinamerikanischen Be-
freiungstheologie* [Munich: Kösel, 1980]); so, for instance, Juan C. Scannone (32);
J. L. Segundo (the same grace elevates man to the supernatural plane and gives
him the means, in love and in the context of history, of envisaging his ultimate
destiny [33]); J. P. Miranda (who, in a Johannine vein, puts brotherly love at the
center [48]); J. Comblin (love as the new revolutionary element in Christianity,
contrasted with the straightforward master/slave relationship [75]); Vidales (love
of the little ones as the quintessence of the gospel [97]); S. Galilea (who lays great
stress on Christ's love of the poor in every sense, [98f.]). Only L. Boff, influenced
by the European theology of hope, understands the Resurrection of Christ as an
anticipation of the kingdom; from it springs hope in the battle against injustice
(143f.). In general, however, these theologies lack the reserve we noted in Moltmann with regard to the effectiveness—on the basis of Christian faith—of the
liberation movement. Typical is the crude tone of Miguez Bonino's manifesto:
"The New Testament is far removed from rejecting worldly hope; it adopts it
into the proclamation of Jesus Christ. Thus he is welcomed by Zechariah and
Mary as the promised Liberator (Lk 1:46–55; 68–79). Jesus himself takes up the
liberation campaign announced by Isaiah (Lk 4:18–19; Mt 11:1–6). In the death
and Resurrection of Jesus Christ, a new world, a new age has begun under the
banner of liberation—from the world, from sin, from death, from the law—
which will be fulfilled in the Lord's parousia" (158).

It is to be hoped that our exposition does justice to the central concern of D.
Wiederkehr in his *Perspektiven der Eschatologie* (Benziger, 1974), 75ff.: "Future
within History and Absolute Future". In fact the object of Christian hope is not
a merely other-worldly "visio beatifica" (79) but the return of the world to God

c. God's Hope

One question remains; but it is one that can only find an answer on a trinitarian basis. At the beginning of this book we endeavored to locate all the genuine dynamisms of creation, but also the positive impulses of faith and hope, in the infinite life of God. Latent in this attempt was the germ of a question: Does not this super-hope in God, which is *immanent* in the Trinity, also manifest an *economic* side? Is there not, right from the start, something we might call "hope" on the part of Father and Spirit, namely, the hope that the Son's mission will succeed? Furthermore, since God has equipped man with such a precarious freedom, cannot we say that God "hopes" that this man will be saved? (Of course it is through the Son's work that he is saved, but he could still reject it.)

Charles Péguy's "mystery" poem, *The Gate to the Mystery of the Second Virtue*, hope,[1] is the bold attempt to find a positive answer to this question in the very heart of the New Testament. To that extent it is a kind of foil to E. Bloch's secularized Jewish "hope principle" (and it must be said that, in spite of all the Christian transpositions and trinitarian perspectives found in J. Moltmann's *Theology of Hope*, the latter ultimately remains dependent on Bloch). Péguy's poem is also a foil to Teilhard de Chardin's attempt, remote from all thought of the Trinity, to find the synthesis of "neo-humanist" hope (which, theologically speaking,

---

—a project in which the Christian has to cooperate responsibly with the grace of God. Belief in the resurrection of the whole human being "must become the exercise of active hope" (88); in this sense one can speak of a "critical integration of the future of the world and the absolute future" (94) within the perspective of Christian hope. Cf. also J. Alfaro, "Die innerweltlichen Hoffnungen und die christliche Hoffnung" in *Concilium* 6 (1970), 626–31. More detail in C. Schütz, *Myst. Sal.* V, 621, n. 272.

[1] *Le Porche du mystère de la deuxième vertu* (1911), in *Oeuvres poétiques complètes* (Paris: Gallimard, 1957), 527–670.

It is not easy to analyze this work since the poet weaves the various themes together. He takes them up again after leaving them aside for a while and repeats topics already presented, but at a higher level and in a new light. The poem has a clear directional flow, yet it can only be understood as a whole after one has integrated all its motifs into each other. A mere juxtaposition of topics will not disclose the total meaning.

is "Jewish") and Christian hope in an overloaded theology of incarnation. Péguy's endeavor, turning its back on an ossified doctrine of a God who merely "foreknows" and "foresees", in all seriousness introduces hope into the very heart of God; in doing so, it relieves us of a one-sidedly Old Testament primacy of the future and commits our hope—which most definitely *is* directed to the future—to an eternal present that is not earthly but overarching and all-embracing. Péguy brings us back to our original (Johannine) manifesto, which is that all "futurist" eschatology has its rightful place within a "realized" eschatology.

The poet begins with the paradoxical assertion in the mouth of God himself that the hope that walks between its two "big sisters", and seems to be pulled along by them, is actually the motive power. Moreover, this hope, compared to the other two virtues that are somehow "self-explanatory", is an incomprehensible miracle implanted in man's existence. "That poor children see how things are, and yet believe that tomorrow will be better—this is astonishing, most definitely the greatest miracle of my grace."[2] To that extent it is "of all the divine virtues perhaps the most pleasing to God".[3] It is concerned with the future: "Faith sees what is / In time and eternity. / Hope sees what will be / For time and eternity. / For the future, as it were, of eternity."[4] Hope acts thus "in my natural and supernatural creation".[5] The fact that hope is the driving force of the natural creation is illustrated in two images. The first is that of the woodcutter in the icy winter forest: as he chops his timber he thinks of his children, of life going on, of his descendants who, when they have come to full estate, will be saluted with his surname; for a while people will think of him too, but then his name will fade away. But "The peasant's life must go on. / And the wine and the wheat. . . . / Like now or not. / Or it may be better. / Christendom, too, must go on, . . . / Just as good as now. / If not better."[6] He is aware of the transitoriness of all things and feels it in his own ageing, but in the midst of "life's relentless decline, loss and collapse"[7] there are always the children—sprung

[2] *Ibid.*, 534.   [3] *Ibid.*, 537.
[4] *Ibid.*, 539.   [5] *Ibid.*, 535.
[6] *Ibid.*, 544.   [7] *Ibid.*, 554.

from the energies of life itself—for whom he toils, and who, unknowing, have this "incomparable confidence, this inimitable security".[8] Toward the end of the book another theme comes to the surface: praise of the farming landscape of France and of the French spirit in general, which not only hopes that "tomorrow morning things will be better, / Tomorrow morning most particularly"[9], but has the astonishing ability to transform and purify the incessant rain of the wretched, hopeless days, when the country sinks into swamp and marsh, and to cultivate gardens of the soil and gardens of the soul.[10] "Something must have taken place, says God", between "all this toil and our little Hope."[11] Péguy's hope—and he would not have had to pass through socialism—is of the kind that fashions and transforms the world, both outside and within. This hope causes "falling souls to rise, / Static souls to flow again. / How can it do this, how succeed? / That, my children, is my secret. / For I am Hope's Father."[12]

In Péguy, however, nothing earthly is self-sufficient. The sequel of the woodcutter story shows this. He remembers that his children had been gravely ill; so much so that he himself thought them beyond help. Then he hit upon the idea of putting them into the arms of the Mother of God. "After all, you have countless others. / What, to you, is one more or one less?"[13] There is not only the "forward thrust" of a Christendom that "must go on": there is also the communion of saints, according to which those who are close to God intercede for the others. This introduces the paean of praise of the "mighty patrons", favorites such as Peter or Geneviève; yet "days will come when patrons and saints will no longer suffice, / For we must rise ever higher and farther, / To the final holiness, the final purity, the final citadel."[14] In his praise of Mary we find the central idea that, in her (in the Immaculate Conception), what is perfectly fleshly is one with what is completely pure; thus Péguy's two great categories, *le temporel* (or *le charnel*) coincide with *le spirituel*. Mary embraces the community of saints because she is the anticipation, and at the same time the created center, of creation's es-

---

[8] *Ibid.*, 553.
[9] *Ibid.*, 629.
[10] *Ibid.*, 632.
[11] *Ibid.*, 638.
[12] *Ibid.*, 640.
[13] *Ibid.*, 558.
[14] *Ibid.*, 566.

chatological hope. At present, in the meantime, "those who are of the flesh lack purity", while "those who are pure," angels, "lack fleshly being".[15] Péguy's hope, which is the mainspring of all world history,[16] is anchored in the heavenly Jerusalem, which not only *is* but from the outset *involves itself* and lends a helping hand. The woodcutter's hope consists essentially in taking a "unique risk", namely, in entrusting to it his children and hence himself.[17]

For its part, however, the heavenly Jerusalem is built up only gradually, out of two "kinds of saints",[18] namely, those who have accepted God's grace and those whom this grace must first convert to itself. Thus two topics are raised that are central to hope. First there is the paradox of cooperation between the "immortal" soul and its "mortal" body (albeit a body destined for resurrection); and it is the soul, common to both, that must work out its salvation, for only together, in perfect mutual penetration, can "spirit" and "matter" build up the kingdom of God.[19] Then there is the complex paradox of penance,[20] the turning away from sin (which is both spiritual and fleshly).[21] This turning away is the substance of the hope—a hope that is in dead earnest—of heaven, of Jesus and of God; yet ultimately such turning away depends on the miracle of grace: "How inexhaustible my grace must be!" says God in amazement.[22]

Mary is called "HOPE": "She who is only faith and love, / Because she is also hope made perfect."[23] This is because she embodied perfect readiness for God's will, the flesh that in no way resists the Spirit, the self-surrender that is uniquely eulogized at the end of the poem. Since she embodies hope in God, she is also the mediational focus for all others who hope in God. Yet hope's innermost content only comes to light in the description of the hope of Jesus the Shepherd, going to look for the sheep that is lost. The ninety-nine righteous who have "remained in faith and love" are left standing; as for the sinner, however,

[15] *Ibid.*, 576.
[16] Cf. the passing of holy water from one generation to another: *ibid.*, 595.
[17] *Ibid.*, 559. [18] *Ibid.*, 617–18.
[19] *Ibid.*, 579–82. [20] *Ibid.*, 606ff.
[21] *Ibid.*, 583. [22] *Ibid.*, 641.
[23] *Ibid.*, 569.

"who almost forfeited himself, / He has unleashed fear and so has caused *hope* itself to well up / In the very heart of God, / In the heart of Jesus. / Trembling and fear and the thrill and horror of hope." For "God was seized by the dread of having to reject someone."[24] "Anxiety" and "hope" arise simultaneously in the heart. The heart of Jesus is by no means concerned about the greater number, for they are safe in the pen, but about the one, the unique one (the individual is always unique) that has got lost:[25] its return will cause greater joy in heaven than the "ninety-nine that did not stray".[26] The poet evinces an insatiable amazement at the the mysterious preeminence of the one over the many and thus comes up against the mystery of the unity of repentance and grace and, at a deeper level, the ineffable fact that God inserts his eternal grace, his eternal Word, into the world of time and flesh—which is always letting him down—in order to bring forth the required, necessary fruit. "Fortune, mystery, danger, wretchedness, divine grace, a unique call, / A terrible responsibility, the misery and nobility of our life, / Ephemeral creatures that we are. . . . / Fragile, it depends on us whether the eternal Voice will resound or lapse into silence."[27] God's eternal Word wishes to be born, nourished and cherished in our hearts of flesh.[28] "Laughable though it is, it is for us to see that the Creator / Is not deprived of his creature." At the outermost limit, within the economy of salvation, we can say that "it is only through the temporal that the eternal is maintained and nourished."[29]

Reciprocal hope is, therefore, ultimate. Hope "promises eternity / A time. To the Spirit / A body. To the Lord / A Church. To God himself / A world."[30] "God has taken the first step. / We must trust God since he has put his trust in us. / We must place our hope in God since he has so placed his in us."[31] "He has put his eternal hope into our weak hands."[32] "The world is topsy-turvy. / All the feelings we ought to have for God /

---

[24] *Ibid.*, 571.
[26] *Ibid.*, 606.
[28] *Ibid.*, 589.
[30] *Ibid.*, 595.
[32] *Ibid.*, 604.

[25] *Ibid.*, 587.
[27] *Ibid.*, 591–92.
[29] *Ibid.*, 594.
[31] *Ibid.*, 603.

He has had for us first."[33] The Lover becomes dependent on the Beloved, and so arises the paradox: "He who is *all* depends on, expects from and hopes of him who is *nothing.* . . . / And who can do nothing (and yet—God forgive us—can do everything)." "The Creator has put himself in the position of needing his creature. . . . / What baneful strength of hope / In us! / What stripping of himself and of his power! / What unwisdom! What failure to foresee, what carelessness! / What improvidence / On the part of God! / . . . We are capable of failing him."[34]

Does this mean that the chances are equally and hopelessly balanced? At this climax the poet inserts two further topics. The first is (again) the communion of saints. It consists of "two kinds", "two regiments", those who are guilty on earth and those who are innocent, for the present constituting a single army advancing against God. They "plot against God / In the presence of God. / So that, inch by inch, justice / Has to give way before mercy. / They subject God to violence. / One cannot imagine all the things they do, all they invent / In order to save threatened souls."[35] The second topic is the "procession of the three parables": the Lost Sheep, the Lost Coin and the Lost ("Prodigal") Son. The third is the crucial one. From earliest times it "has moved countless men to tears. / Even to think of it, who could keep his tears back?" "A man had two sons." The poet never does more than indicate the way it begins. For here it is God himself, the Father, who stands waiting, hoping, for his lost son. It is not portrayed, for no words are adequate beside those of Jesus.

The final scene is separated from the foregoing by the long description of the "people of gardeners" who transform the rainy days into fountains and the swamps into fruitful land, a people whose power to transform the earth comes from the power of divine hope. This hope, in its inexhaustible youthfulness, takes the same old material—in earthly terms—and changes it into something that is ever new.[36] But before passing on to the final scene we must briefly reflect on the mystery that, for Péguy,

[33] *Ibid.,* 611.
[34] *Ibid.,* 614–17.
[35] *Ibid.,* 619.
[36] *Ibid.,* 656ff.

is central. He too, of course, regards hope as a thrust "into the future", but what inspires him is not so much some goal to be reached in the future as the inexhaustible delight of children who, with their energy and tireless legs, happily repeat the same journey over and over again. (Like dogs being taken for a walk, they go back and forth twenty times over the same ground that the weary adult compasses but once.) The poet attributes something of the child's vitality to theological hope, on God's part or on man's; for neither of them, ultimately, loses his way, despite fear, grief, anxiety and mortal danger. The poet tells us that even while the Savior experiences the depth of weakness and distress when his crown of thorns is being plaited, another crown is being woven for him, albeit invisibly. This crown is "entwined with buds and leaves; gentle and fragrant, it refreshes his brow": it is the crown of hope.[37] So it is not God's foreknowledge, not the "overpowering" of his love, but hope's gentle, persuasive self-commendation that enables God to be vindicated (even, so to speak, to his own surprise) after all the dramatic interplay between himself and human weakness and freedom: "We are capable of failing him." But "just as we, in our poor yet glorious churches, ring in the feast of Easter with all our bells flying, / God too rings out an eternal Easter for every soul that is saved, / And says, 'After all, I wasn't mistaken, was I?' "[38] Here the "hope principle" has become Christian: what is at stake is the attainment or the loss of eternal life on the part of man (who is both body and soul), through God's grace and through penance, within and through the communion of saints. Here, in this present reality that is vertically open to God, are the last things, here is the Last Act, and not in some end-time at the close of a horizontal future. Péguy's formulation is very precise: In the horizontal plane as such mankind keeps treading its well-worn and wearisome paths, but theological hope (and it alone) transforms this sameness into something that is ever new. The earthly future is inserted into an ever-new "now" that is a gift of divine grace.

So the conclusion of the poem becomes a praise of self-sur-

[37] *Ibid.*, 598–602.
[38] *Ibid.*, 617.

render (just as the woodcutter had entrusted his children to
Mary), that is, quite simply, of sleep and of the night that is created for sleeping. "It has come to my ears / That there are men
who do not sleep. / I cannot abide people who do not sleep, says
God. / Sleep is, perhaps, the most glorious thing in my creation. /
And I myself rested on the seventh day." Sleep presupposes night,
and if the self-surrender of sleep is, or should be, man's constant,
uninterrupted attitude, night is the all-enveloping ocean that embraces the islands of his days. Men think that the day is what is
important; "They have the courage to work, but they do not
have the virtue of being able to do nothing. / To relax, to rest,
to sleep. / They conduct their affairs very well during the day,
/ But they will not let me look after them at night. / As if I
were not able to take good care of them for one whole night. /
The man who cannot sleep is failing to keep faith with hope."[39]
The theme goes through many variations. Then, at the very end,
God recalls that one particular night which came down like a
linen cloth to cover the body of his dead Son. It shrouded his
sleep in ultimate self-surrender to the Father, and his last hope in
him who had apparently disappeared forever. The poet does not
insist, does not theologize. He simply takes the best God has designed for his children, namely, the renewal of hope in sleep, and
combines it with the darkest reality of trinitarian forsakenness
(the Father having witnessed the execution of his Son) and the
night that has seen the burial of this horror. There is no mention
of the Resurrection; it is latent but unsaid in God's address to his
"most beloved daughter of all", night. For night does for him
what every man has the right to do for himself—to bury his
son. God, however, cannot, for "this adventure means that his
hands are tied."[40] Night does it, here at the end, having taken
the place of a hope that can no longer be named. This is because
self-surrender is ultimate; it is the ultimate in God the Father,
in the Son and in the Spirit, and it is the ultimate in man, too,
when he has reached the end of his crazy path.

[39] *Ibid.*, 658.
[40] *Ibid.*, 669–70.

II. ASPECTS OF THE FINAL ACT

A. THE FINAL ACT AS TRAGEDY

1. The Difficulty: Human Refusal
versus the Trinitarian Embrace

Everything we have said so far in this volume could be felt to be somewhat triumphalist. We have spoken of creation as an image of the divine life, something springing from God and destined to return to him; we have seen the hope of this final event grounded in a proleptic fact, the Resurrection of Jesus, which supersedes both Jewish and pagan notions of salvation. Here, surely, more than ever, we should heed Anselm's warning, "Nondum considerasti quanti ponderis est peccatum"? In other words, should we not restrict, a priori, the extent of created freedom—understood to go as far as plainly rejecting God —and impose limits, accordingly, on the concept of the *causa secunda*?

If, however, we take seriously the mysterious "absoluteness" that characterizes the created will, and its resultant ability to reject God—as the traditional theology generally has done— we cannot fail to be astonished at the cool indifference with which this same theology consigns a part of this creation, supposedly designed for heaven, to eternal perdition. Amazingly, it does not see this as diminishing the glory of God, whose justice is allegedly glorified in this lost portion of mankind just as much as his mercy is glorified in the portion that is to be saved. No doubt this indifference was nothing other than obedience to the New Testament texts that, just like the Jewish and intertestamental writings, assume a twofold outcome of the world's final judgment. So the basic axiom of the theology that is faithful to such texts, and of the teaching that springs from it, is this: "The touchstone of a correct teaching will always be that there must not be any playing with apokatastasis."[1] Today, however, the opposite question must be raised, namely, is there not a playing with hell—not deliberate, perhaps, but ultimately irresponsible?

---

[1] W. Breuning, "Systematische Entfaltung der eschatologischen Aussagen" in *Myst. Sal.* V, 860.

Ivan Karamazov refuses his entrance ticket to heaven so long as innocent children have to suffer in the world. Basically he is relatively unconcerned about the world beyond: what upsets him is the unbearable disorder on earth, for which he makes God responsible. Dostoyevsky implies that Karamazov is thereby entertaining satanic forces; but if we look back at the borderline situations of the world drama, can we really imagine that human beings, living in the impenetrable misery of this world, can be eventually divided into two clear categories—the eternally elect and the eternally damned? How should beings, existing in the contradiction between their attempts at ultimate meaning and the certainty of death, cut their way through the primeval forest toward absolute Good—which proves ever elusive—except by means of compromises (cf. *Theo-Drama* I, 413–24)? If man refuses, in the face of the world's chaotic state, to find meaning (and hence Providence) and turns to the finite as what alone can be attained, should we brand this as "demonic"? Given the ever-increasing rationalization of the planet, which turns people's attention more and more from an overarching meaning and toward the particular, fragmentary and precarious, is not a life decision for good or evil increasingly problematical? And in view of the shifts of consciousness that emerge in different historical periods, can the Church continue, in good conscience, to present the old judgment-eschatology of the New Testament in unchanged form without first submitting it to a thorough critique?

It is not surprising to find, among theologians everywhere today, an open and marked tendency toward the doctrine of apokatastasis; in what follows we shall have to subject it to a serious examination. Some of the attempts to justify this doctrine are superficially optimistic,[2] but there are also deeper ar-

---

[2] E.g., Richard P. McBrien's *Catholicism* (Minneapolis: Winston Press, 1981). McBrien simply contradicts Anselm's warning: "We can have as radical a notion of *sin* as we like so long as our understanding and appreciation of *grace* is even more radical" (1183). Since creaturely freedom is limited, both outwardly and inwardly, since it is only the fundamental option that counts ("no single act by itself is sufficient to merit eternal punishment in hell"), grave sin is so rare that, in the ancient Church, a single opportunity in life for repentance was regarded as sufficient! (955–56).

guments based on hope-inspiring scriptural texts and ultimately on the dogma that Christ died for all men and for all their sins.[3] Moreover, Christ's work was not merely "sufficient" but "superabundant", having made available to mankind an "immeasurable" and hence "inexhaustible treasury" of graces.[4] Christ's merits tower over the sins of mankind not only quantitatively but qualitatively; they not only weigh heavier than these sins, they *undergird* them by the uniqueness of the hypostatic union, since this atoning act is directly rooted in the life of the Trinity. Thus it seems that the Cross of Christ, laden with every sinful refusal of man, must stand at the very last extremity of hell; indeed, it must stand beyond hell, where the Son is forsaken by the Father in a way that only he can know.

But can this kind of a priori consideration disarm all the texts that clearly assume that man in his finite freedom can actually reject this undergirding? Furthermore, if we consider the chronology of the New Testament writings, we find that reflection on these possibilities becomes increasingly serious, and the dramatic thrust of which we spoke in preceding volumes becomes more and more tragic and inevitable. Tragic, not only for man, who can throw away life's meaning and his own salvation, but also for God himself, who is compelled to judge where he wished to heal; in the extreme case he is compelled to judge precisely because he only wished to bring love to man. According to this view, the necessity whereby God has to reject the man who rejects his love appears to signal a defeat for God, who comes to grief in his own saving work. This aspect of

[3] Cf. the condemnation of Jansen's celebrated "fifth proposition" by Innocent X: "Semipelagianum est dicere, Christum pro omnibus omnino hominibus mortuum esse aut sanguinem fudisse" (DS 2005). Cf. the Synod of Quiercy: "Nullus est, fuit vel erit homo, pro quo passus non fuerit" Christus (DS 624), adding that if, in fact, not all reach salvation as a result of Christ's sufferings, this is not due to any insufficiency in the price paid but results from a human deficiency in living faith.

[4] ". . . Innocens immolatus non guttam sanguinis modicam, quae tamen propter unionem ad Verbum pro redemptione totius generis humani suffecisset, sed copiose velut profluvium noscitur effudisse ita, ut 'a planta pedis usque ad verticem capitis nulla sanitas' (cf. Is 1:6) inveniretur in ipso" (DS 1025). This store of grace cannot diminish or fail, because "Christ's merits are infinite", and the more they are used, the more they multiply (DS 1027).

judgment in the New Testament writings needs to be brought
out and given greater prominence, not as a final conclusion,
but as a starting point for subsequent deeper reflection.

2. Judgment in the New Testament

a. Judgment in Paul

At the center of Pauline dogmatics stands the dramatic struggle
between the immense power of sin before Christ, both in pa-
ganism and in Judaism, with which the Epistle to the Romans
begins and the overthrowing of this power by the greater power
of God's justifying work in Jesus Christ, described in Romans
5:15–21 in triumphal terms at the conclusion of a first major
historical confrontation: "For if many died through one man's
trespass, much more have the grace of God and the free gift in
the grace of that one man Jesus Christ abounded for many." And
at the end of a second battle, this time in personal experience,
he repeats the cry of victory: "He who did not spare his own
Son but gave him up for us all, will he not also give us all things
with him? Who shall bring any charge against God's elect? . . .
Who is to condemn? . . . We are more than conquerors (*hyper-
nikōmen*) through him who loved us" (Rom 8:32–37). A third
engagement, seen in terms of a theology of history, begins, like
the first two, with the Judgment. The first battle descended almost like a flood upon a mankind that should have known and
acknowledged God (Jews even more than pagans) but did not;
as a result "every mouth" will be "stopped", and "the whole
world" will be "held accountable to God" (Rom 1–3:20). The
second battle began with the temptation to "continue in sin that
grace may abound"; it proceeds with the awareness of the possibility, or rather necessity, of dying to sin with the dying Christ,
but returns to the old law and the temptation it represents, which
is still alive in the members and brings "death" to them. However, this death is in turn undergirded by the death of Christ,
who died "in the likeness of sinful flesh" so that "in his flesh sin
was condemned"; thus "there is therefore no condemnation for
those who are in Christ Jesus." The third battle begins with the

terrifying picture of a God who is so free that, according to his good pleasure, he can fashion "vessels of wrath" and "vessels of mercy"; he is depicted as a Judge against whom there can be no appeal. The concrete instance of this is Israel's guilt: instead of having faith, it sought its salvation in works (Rom 9:32). Thus it was made a stumbling stone, yet God reprehends it for being "a disobedient and contrary people" (10:21). In chapter 11, however, the whole judgment storm suddenly brightens, revealing itself as a mystery of the end-time: Israel's hardening of heart within the dimension of time was not a "final rejection" (11:1) but a salvific provision for the benefit of the Gentiles; at the outset both Jews and Gentiles were under dire judgment, but now all clouds are swept away: "For God has consigned all men to disobedience, that he may have mercy upon all" (11:32). In each of these three encounters, judgment stands, not at the end, but at the beginning; what triumphs at the end is the fruit of the world's reconciliation through Christ.

First Corinthians concludes in a similarly triumphal way: Christ rules until all his enemies, and finally death, have been made subject to him. "Death is swallowed up in victory" (1 Cor 15:54). Nor is this victory the result of a battle between God and man; it is, rather, the result of a battle between the sinner and the God of love.[5] In God's victory "there is nothing left of defeat: it is sublimated, swallowed up in the victory. Any memory of the enemy, sin, is there only to make the victory more radiant, the joy more joyful."[6] God's victory can also show itself in the sudden extinction of the wicked enemy (2 Th 2:8) and in the overpowering (*katargein*) of all the powers ranged against God.

Here, however, a shift has taken place. The Judgment scene is no longer at the beginning but at the end, after a battle with the "hostile powers", with the "god of this world" (2 Cor 4:4), a battle in which Christians, too, have to join (Eph 6:11–17). This means that, for these combatants, the Judgment is once more a present reality. Under the Old Covenant the eschatological Day of Yahweh was the day when the nations, primarily, were to be judged: for Paul it becomes the day when every individual will

have to stand before the tribunal of God or Christ and give an
account of his works (Rom 2:16; 14:10–13; 1 Cor 4:3–5; 2 Cor
5:9–13).

In the first instance Christians were justified in having the
surest hope of salvation. Indeed, they are saved "in this hope"
(Rom 8:24; Eph 2:5; Titus 3:5), "hid with Christ in God" (Col
3:3) and sealed with the Holy Spirit of God (Eph 4:30; 1:13–14;
2 Cor 1:22). Secondly, however, the greatest demands are laid
upon them: through their following of Christ they, who have
been "saved" (Eph 2:5), must first "be saved" (1 Cor 1:18), lest
they be rejected along with "those who are perishing" (ibid.).
They must go through the fire of judgment along with all the
others (1 Cor 3:12–15); "therefore let any one who thinks that
he stands take heed lest he fall" (1 Cor 10:12). "You stand fast
only through faith. So do not become proud, but stand in awe"
(Rom 11:20).

Paul's doctrine of judgment is and remains bifocal: one line
of thought moves from judgment to the superabundant salvation of Christ open to those who believe in him; the other runs
from the salvation attained in Christ to a judgment that will test
the works performed by those who follow him. The first focus,
with its universal prospect of salvation, seems to tend toward
apokatastasis, whereas the second seems to point to an almost
Old Testament individualism with regard to the Judgment. Must
we say that Paul is inconsistent here? No, if we realize that he
is writing here primarily for the Christians of his community
(for the pagans are by no means condemned root and branch:
Rom 2:5ff.) and that faith can exist only in union with active
love (Gal 5:6), that is, in union with the works that are consonant with it. Grace, for Paul, implies a heightened responsibility
since it is inseparable from mission. This is underscored—in
terms of doctrine, and not merely in terms of exhortation—in
a truly terrifying manner by the Letter to the Hebrews, when
it hammers home the message that the Cross is God's *eschaton*:
anyone for whom the Cross is insufficient, who has "spurned"
and "profaned" it "deliberately after receiving the knowledge of
the truth", can only "fall into the hands of the living God", the
Judge (Heb 10:26–31; cf. 6:4–6). This anticipates something of
what, in John, is the central dramatic theme.

b. Judgment in the Synoptics

To some extent the Synoptic texts, reflecting primarily the pre-Easter Jesus' preaching on the Judgment (after the Baptist's preaching on this theme) use as their "matter" the images of judgment found in the Old Covenant, in Judaism and in apocalyptic. In terms of "form", however, they are transposed in order to point to the figure of Jesus, who is both "present" and "coming". In a different way, therefore, but no less than Paul, the Synoptic texts form a transition to the Johannine conception of judgment.

As found in the tradition, the "Day of Yahweh", the day of his ultimate epiphany as Judge of the world, also signals his total and definitive victory over the world. (A defeat of God would be a contradiction in terms.) It implies a judgment that separates, choosing one party and rejecting the other. So it is in the preaching of the Baptist (Mt 3:7–12) and in Jesus' portrayals of judgment in Matthew 13:49–50 (cf. 7:19, the final separation of mankind: 25:31–46). God's victory judgment in Christ, who will "send his angels" to "gather out of his kingdom all causes of sin and all evildoers, and throw them into the furnace of fire" (Mt 13:41–42), will be a concluding act affecting everyone together and each one personally: all will be brought before his tribunal. Here we see the adoption of a late Old Testament theme, and one that is given a high profile in Paul: the universal Judgment is also portrayed as a particular Judgment.

However, this does not give us an adequate grasp of what is specific to the Synoptics, namely, that the Judge's place is taken by Someone else. Not as if God is dethroned as the highest Lord of Judgment (one only has to recall passages such as Matthew 6:4, 6, 18; 18:35; 20:21–23), but the entire Judgment is handed over to the Son (of Man), as John expressly states (5:22). The Day of Yahweh will be "his day" (Lk 17:24), when he "is to come . . . in the glory of his Father" to "repay every man for what he has done" (Mt 16:27). True, he sometimes portrays himself as a witness or an advocate with the Father (Mt 10:32–33), but this does not alter the fact that he himself will pronounce the final verdict: "On that day many will say. . . . And then I will declare to them, 'I never knew you; depart from me. . . .'" (Mt 7:22–

23). Once the doors have been closed, he will say to those who call from without: "Truly, I say to you, I do not know you" (Mt 25:12).

The One who utters such words stands in the center of history, among men; this very fact shows that the reality of the final Judgment is undiminished, here and now. Thus the Old Testament picture of judgment is decisively outstripped: the future is decided, in detail, by the present. The eschatological separation is carried out by the life of Jesus on earth. "I have come to bring division" (Mt 10:34), and such division is one feature of the "Day of Yahweh".[7] Ultimately there is an identification—in the person of the present and future Jesus—between man's decision regarding him here and now and his final destiny in the Last Judgment: "So every one who acknowledges me before men, I also will acknowledge . . . ; but whoever denies me before men, I also will deny. . . (Mt 10:32–33 parr.). For, both in a realized present and in a future sense, "He who is not with me is against me" (Mt 12:30). This, however, only has meaning if the presence of Jesus itself brings salvation, only if in him the promised kingdom of God has come and/or is in the process of coming. The Synoptic writings show this primarily in the works of grace performed by Jesus, mediating divine healing to soul and body. The signs are so clear that the Israel that will not see them must be blinded, hypocritical (Mt 15:7), its heart far from God (15:8); as a result its house will be "forsaken and desolate" (Mt 23:38). We have already mentioned that this verdict, within the context of internal world history, allows us to see straight through to the Last Judgment (cf. the Synoptic apocalypse). Nonetheless Israel is given one last opportunity for repentance (". . . until you say, 'Blessed is he who comes in the name of the Lord' ", Mt 23:39), whereas the denial of Jesus on the part of the individual leads directly and unconditionally to his own denial in the Judgment. This is the context for the motivation behind election and rejection: "What you have done—or not done—to the least of my brothers": Jesus is encountered in his brothers, not only at his own historical time, but concretely at all times. Henceforth

---

[7] Cf. C. H. Dodd, *The Parables of the Kingdom*, 3d ed. (Collins, 1965), 52ff.

there is a direct link between the historical and the eschatological "now".

It must not be forgotten, however, that Jesus' words on judgment, which sharpen the Old Testament language on the theme by their concrete reference to his presence here and now among men, were all uttered prior to his death on the Cross. This death is the "hour of darkness" (Lk 22:53), itself described in eschatological, apocalyptic colors (Mt 27:45–53) and culminating in Jesus' cry of forsakenness. So, when Jesus' words speak of those who are cast into outer or outermost darkness (*exōteros* as comparative superlative), as in Matthew 8:16; 22:13; 25:30, we must realize that this baffling realm "outside" the sphere of divine salvation is itself outstripped and encompassed by an even more baffling "outside": namely, the Son of God confronted by the salvation-judgment of the divine Father.

Paul's thought is based on this Cross-event, understood as God's final victory; from this vantage point he reflects on the judgment affecting those who refuse to let this salvation take root and grow within them. The Synoptics start from the tradition of the Day of Judgment (which in the Old Testament presupposes the Covenant of grace, and in the New Testament the proclamation of the kingdom); they go on to envisage the ultimate salvation that lies in the Cross and Resurrection, which awaits its acceptance by men (cf. Mk 16:16).

c. Johannine Judgment

Krisis in the sense of "division", "discrimination", is at the heart of the Gospel of John. But here it takes a more paradoxical shape than in the Synoptics, where Jesus comes as a "sword" to "separate" those who seemed to be at one (Mt 10:34; cf. 24:40–41). For now Jesus expressly says both things: he was not sent "to condemn the world, but to save it" (Jn 3:17; 12:47), yet just as firmly he says, "for judgment I came into this world" (9:39). The two assertions are found juxtaposed: "I judge no one. Yet even if I do judge, my judgment is true" (8:15–16). How can we resolve this paradox?

In the imagery of the Prologue, the Word, or Light, which is in the beginning with God and comes into the world to illuminate every man, does not as such intend to judge and separate. If it does take on this role, it does not do so of itself but because the darkness into which it shines fails to receive it. Two attitudes are possible in the face of the Light or Word that comes into the world: a man can "receive" it and so have "eternal life; he does not come into judgment" (5:24); thus such a man fulfills the fundamental purpose of the Light or Word, which is *not to condemn*. He receives by "hearing" (the word is used fifty-eight times in the Gospel): this means "apprehending the meaning of the word" in a "personal event" and involves a decision to affirm the meaning that has been thus understood and accepted.[8] It is possible, however, to reject the Light or Word, with the result that "my word finds no place in you" (*ou chōrei en hymīn*: 8:37). This is the Old Testament "hardening of hearts" or "becoming blind" (12:40 = Is 6:9–10), which is now becoming final and definitive. It makes a man incapable of hearing and receiving the Word: it is a foreign language to him. Jesus expresses this with the greatest precision: "Why do you not understand what I say? It is because you cannot bear to hear my word" (8:43). To "hear", to allow the Word to come in, is the same as to "believe": it is a readiness and an openness for what God's Light and God's Word has to say and to give to man's darkness.

It is the darkness, therefore, that *compels* the light that comes into the world to show itself as judgment. This becomes clear in the saying in which Jesus, identifying himself with the "light of the world" (8:12), distinguishes himself as Person (although he is the Word of the Father) from that word which is not accepted by those who despise it: "If any one hears my sayings and does not keep them, I do not judge him; for I did not come to judge the world. . . . He who . . . does not receive my sayings has a judge; the word that I have spoken will be his judge on the last day" (12:47–48). As in the Synoptics, this decision for or against the Jesus who stands thus in history, is an eschatological one. John gives a precise explanation of the procedure of this Last Judgment: "And this is the judgment, that the light has come

---

[8] J. Blank, *Krisis: Untersuchungen zur johanneischen Christologie und Eschatologie* (Freiburg: Lambertus, 1964), 130.

into the world, and men loved [*ēgapēsan*] darkness rather than light. . . . For every one who does evil hates the light" (3:19–20). It is this hatred that compels the light to become such a man's eschatological judge: so God gives the Son of Man "authority to execute judgment. . . . [All] . . . will . . . come forth, those who have done good, to the resurrection of life, and those who have done evil, to the resurrection of judgment" (5:26–29).

This theology might seem to go no farther than the Synoptic theology or even the Old Testament theology of judgment—where God (or Christ), as Judge, is by definition righteous, and all unrighteousness lies on the side of sinful man, who is thus meet for judgment. In John, however, there is something more, something half-visible, that is rendered wholly visible in other words of Jesus. First of all, of course, the light that penetrates the darkness has the effect of "convincing" the darkness of its self-love (*elenchein* 3:20; cf. 16:8). In exercising this function the Light holds back: it is not its prime concern to execute judgment in every particular (although in fact "I have much to say about you and much to judge" [8:26], in the sense of revealing guilt). But this is by no means a complete description of the effect of light on darkness. It not only uncovers the nature of darkness, it drives it from its hiding place and intensifies it. At this point, as we have already said many times, we stand at the very core of drama and of tragedy.

"If I had not come and spoken to them, they would not have sin"—relatively speaking, at least. "But now they have no excuse for their sin. . . . If I had not done among them the works which no one else did, they would not have sin; but now they have seen and hated both me and my Father. It is to fulfil the word that is written in their law, 'They hated me without a cause'" (15:22–25). Here it is important that they have "heard" the word and "seen" the works, in a kind of hearing and seeing that, in the very act of responding, rejects a positive response. This emerges, for instance, in the catastrophic conclusion of the long dispute on the healing of the man born blind: when Jesus says, "For judgment I came into this world, that those who do not see may see, and that those who see may become blind", the Pharisees ask, "Are we also blind?" Jesus replies, "If you

were blind, you would have no guilt; but now that you say, 'We
see,' your guilt remains" (9:39–41). God's love, which sends the
Light, the Word, into the world, brings hatred to the surface.
"If he loved them less, they would hate him less."[9] For as Jesus
constantly repeats in the Gospel, the Light, the Word, who is
the Son, discloses not only him but also the Father who sends
him and witnesses to him. In the Son, therefore, we have the
disclosure of absolute, causeless love, which, when the darkness
refuses to receive it, causes the darkness to appear as a "causeless" (15:25) abyss. Thus the Old Testament Jew who thinks he
knows the Father is placed in an entirely different situation by
the Son, who, as Light and Word, reveals the Father. "Perhaps
he was quite happy with the Father before, but now, through the
Son, he is shown in a different light; man does not wish to accept
the Son and is alienated from the Father. Although he does not
acknowledge the Son as God, he cannot avoid perceiving the
inner connection between Father and Son, and he is forced to
reject the Father as well."[10]

Here for the first time we have reached the turning point of
the theo-drama. "Hatred implies declaration of war, challenging
God to a duel, and so God himself cannot remain indifferent."[11]
"It is as if the Father's revelatory grace were engaged in a com-
petition with sin. The turning away of man and his reclamation
by God both intensify."[12] "Thus a kind of contest comes about
between man's voice, which gets louder and louder in order to
obscure God's, and God's voice, which maintains its divine volume."[13] We see this contest most clearly in the fact that the darkness of sin *compels* the Light, the Word, to lay down his life (the
ear of corn *must* fall into the earth and die: 12:24), and this on the
advice of Caiaphas and the Sanhedrin (11:49ff.): it causes Jesus
to be "troubled in spirit" (13:21). He parries this "must" with
the assertion that he is no hireling who flees from the wolf, but
the "good shepherd [who] lays down his life for the sheep"; "no
one takes it from me, but I lay it down of my own accord. I have

[9] 2 Jo 299.
[10] 3 Jo 210.
[11] 3 Jo 208.
[12] A 31–32.
[13] M 58.

power to lay it down" (10:11, 18). This freewill self-surrender —which, in concrete terms, means the Cross—will not bring the contest to a close. For "the sinner who receives an invitation from the Cross becomes a more hardened sinner if he rejects the invitation. Through the Cross, more sin comes about."[14] The abyss of divine love that we see in the Father's sending of the Son to save the world (3:16) brings what is implacably hostile to God, what is devilish, out into the open. The devil is mentioned at significant points in the Gospel of John, and we must devote some attention to them.

3. The Devil

We cannot illuminate the *mysterium iniquitatis* in a way that would render its darkness light, even for our understanding, aided as it is by faith. It is part of iniquity's "night", and even our understanding "stumbles because of the lack of light" (cf. Jn 11:10). In a tentative way, however, it can and must be described as that which does not receive the light (cf. Jn 1:5, [1:11]), since it "hates the light, and does not come to the light" (3:19). The concept of hatred, the open, aggressive opposition to that love which characterizes God in his economic and trinitarian self-giving (cf. 1 Jn 4:16), brings us right to the heart of this mystery. This hatred is primarily self-enclosed, but it is the same hatred that spills over into the world of men, who, allowing it entrance and sharing in it, become sucked into the sway of a power that is perhaps more absolute than they are aware of or are prepared to acknowledge. They are "slaves to sin" (Jn 8:34), they are "of your father the devil, and your will is to do your father's desires" (8:44). These desires are the pure contradiction of the divine Light and Word, which is, as such, "the truth" (8:45-46). So the devil, who opposes the Word that is "life" (1:4), "was a murderer from the beginning" (8:44), which is why "any one who hates his brother is a murderer, and you know that no murderer has eternal life abiding in him" (1 Jn 3:15). The devil, hostile to truth (which for John is identical with love and "grace": Jn 1:17), is there-

---

[14] Hj 82.

fore essentially "a liar and the father of lies" (Jn 8:44); the man
who allows the devil's spirit to gain entrance into him is thus
compelled to see as a lie what he—really—sees as the truth (cf.
8:39–41). He is compelled to see the truth as devilish.[15]

So we find that Jesus, who unmasks those who hate him and
accuses them of being possessed by the devil, is himself continually described by them as being possessed: "You have a demon!"
(7:20). "Are we not right in saying that you . . . have a demon?"
(8:48). "Many of them said, 'He has a demon, and he is mad;
why listen to him?'" (10:20). Thus he is constantly persecuted
by a hatred that is "bottomless" and "groundless" (because it
is essentially a lie): "the world . . . hates me" (7:7), "the world
. . . has hated me before it hated you" (15:18), it "hates me
[and] hates my Father" (15:23–24)—and tries to find a way of
killing him. This murder is continually being mentioned. It is
said either that the Jews tried to take his life (7:25; 8:44; 8:59;
11:8; 11:57; cf. 12:10–11) or that he himself wonders why they
want to kill him (7:19; 8:37; 8:40; 10:31–33; cf. 16:2). Thus,
while blasphemy is heaped upon Jesus, he himself is accused of
"blasphemy" (10:33) and so must be stoned. At this level it is a
real life-and-death struggle: it is a question of who can eject and
"cast out" the other.

The idea of "casting out" occurs in a variety of contexts. "The
Jews had already agreed that if any one should confess him to
be Christ, he was to be put out of the synagogue" (9:22). They
try to carry this out in the case of the man born blind (9:34),
and Jesus prophesies that this will happen to his disciples (16:1).
He himself, according to the Letter to the Hebrews, is brought
"outside the camp" of the Covenant-enclosure to be crucified,
and his disciples are challenged to take his disgrace upon themselves and follow him there (Heb 13:12–13). There are many
such cases of literal expulsion in the Acts of the Apostles (7:58;
13:50; 16:37). On the other side, however, there is the expulsion
of the devil as a result of Christ's atoning work for the world:
"Now is the judgment of this world, now shall the ruler of this
world be cast out [exō]" (Jn 12:31), which surely must be seen

---

[15] "He who does not believe God has made him a liar, because he has not believed in the testimony that God has borne to his Son" (1 Jn 5:10).

in the context of the Book of Revelation's description of the casting out of the "great dragon, that ancient serpent, who is called the Devil and Satan, the deceiver of the whole world", who is thrown down from heaven "to the earth" (Rev 12:9). The Jews' "inner" sanctuary is the synagogue, and Jesus and anyone who confesses him must be thrown out. Jesus' "inner" sanctuary is the truth, that is, the trinitarian life that goes on between Father and Son; anyone who comes to it "I will not cast out" (Jn 6:37), whereas the branch that becomes separated from him, the vine, "is cast forth . . . and withers . . . and [is] burned" (15:6). Just as the devil is "cast out", therefore, there is an "outer" region for men who are similarly "cast out": "He who does not obey the Son shall not see life, but the wrath of God rests upon him" (3:36).

At this point we must ask whether or not Karl Barth's attempt to describe the realm of the devil as "nothingness" yields insight into the latter's nature. [16] True, he prefaces his remarks by saying that "we have here an extraordinarily clear demonstration of the necessary brokenness of all theological thought and utterance", which "cannot form a system". [17] Nonetheless he develops a bold ontology of this "nothingness", which is not a mere nothing (as in Leibniz) or only the "absence" [18] of something, nor yet is it "something creaturely" [19] either; even less is it (as in Schelling) something that has its ultimate ground in the nature of God himself, or merely one of the "shadow sides" of the good world —and, according to Augustine, the world is good both on its right side and on its left. Nothingness, however, does lurk behind these "shadow sides" as "chaos", "darkness" and the "element of contradiction". It is a realm of hostility and collapse and to that extent is absolutely "real" [20] and "dreadful". [21] On the one hand Barth attributes to it "a kind of substance and person", but this appearance is "falsehood"; [22] elsewhere he speaks of it as "a receding frontier and a fleeting shadow. . . . It has no substance" [23]. Nothingness is non-creaturely, and this compels us to say that it is real in a "third fashion" [24] (beside God and the creature). We can say only that it is "that to which God says no", [25] the product of

---

[16] Barth's position is to be found in his *Church Dogmatics* III/3, section 50: "God and Nothingness" (289ff.), and section 51, 3: "The Ambassadors of God and Their Opponents" (477ff.).

[17] 293.   [18] 319.   [19] 523.   [20] 523, 524, 525.
[21] 366.   [22] 527.   [23] 361.   [24] 349ff.
[25] 352.

his rejection,[26] which is the "inevitable obverse of divine election and affirmation".[27] Nothingness has being only insofar as God, who can elect, can also *reject* what is contrary to his nature; for he is "Lord both on the right hand *and* on the left. It is only on this basis that nothingness *is*."[28] Nothingness has "being" only insofar as God's *non*-willing is also *potent*,[29] and to that extent God is its "Author"[30]. It is thus directly the "enemy of God" rather than the enemy of the creature, although in the form of evil[31] it can only tempt and overwhelm the creature. The creature, succumbing to nothingness, is powerless to deal with this enemy of God, with its "dynamic . . . with which it cannot cope".[32] Only God has overcome nothingness, and he has overcome it right from the start; indeed, it only exists as something he has rejected and overcome. The overcoming of nothingness is "God's own affair":[33] by becoming man in Jesus Christ, he "casts himself into this conflict"[34] on behalf of man, who cannot and does not have the will to fight. "He might have been a majestic, passive and beatific God on high. But he descends to the depths, and concerns Himself with nothingness, because . . . He does not will to cease to be concerned for His creature."[35] On the Cross of Christ he lets nothingness rage, burning itself out in him.[36] And since this is the goal of all God's ways, we can say that nothingness exists at all only in its relation to redemption.[37] Only in Christ and his Cross do we come to know what evil is.[38] Only in the "concrete event at the core of all Christian reality and truth—the self-giving of the Son of God, His humiliation . . . unto death, even the death of the cross"—do we see to what extent evil is "God's own affair", the "primal antithesis or encounter" with it.[39] The other perspective is equally clear: in the Cross, evil is really vanquished, broken and fundamentally overcome, once for all, so that God's battle is over, he has no eternal adversary.[40] Nothingness is the "ancient non-being" which, in Jesus Christ, is now *past*. "It is no longer legitimate to think . . . as if real deliverance and release from it were still an event of the future."[41] We are free to regard it as "finally destroyed"; this freedom excludes ". . . the pessimism so prevalent in the world".[42]

---

[26] 350.   [27] 361.   [28] 351.   [29] 352.

[30] 330; cf. 351.

[31] 315. Barth regards evil as only one form of nothingness, since there is also "the physical evil concealed behind the shadowy side of the created cosmos".

[32] 310.   [33] 354.   [34] 357.   [35] *Ibid.*

[36] 304f.   [37] Cf. 330ff.

[38] 309. "Biblical demonology is in fact only a negative reflection of biblical Christology and soteriology." 530.

[39] 360.   [40] 361–63.   [41] 364.   [42] *Ibid.*

This means that, for Karl Barth, there can be no equating of "nothingness" with the "oft-repeated doctrine" of the fallen angels. The passages of Scripture that speak of angels having "fallen" are "too uncertain and obscure". [43] Occasionally one finds the beings associated with "the dragon" referred to as "his angels" (Mt 25:41; Rev 12:7), but it would be foolish to see angels and devils as two species of some superordinate neutral genus. However, this assertion can be made only on the basis of a statement in Barth's doctrine of angels, according to which "their creaturely freedom is identical with their obedience", [44] that is, they have "no autonomy" over against God. In contrast to earthly creatures they have no freedom of choice, and thus they "do not belong to themselves", "they have no history or aims or achievements of their own." [45] It is not clear, however, whether this is an advantage or a disadvantage for them. On the one hand, Barth says, "the least of the creatures of earth is thus superior to the highest angel in that, while it belongs to God, it is privileged also to belong to itself." [46] On the other hand, we read, it is "as though the [angels'] freedom . . . were not a real freedom if it were not for them too, or had not been once in some primal epoch, the so-called *liberum arbitrium*". [47] By denying the fact that created freedom necessarily involves a decision in favor of God and of itself, Barth contradicts the basic thesis of de Lubac's *Surnaturel* (1946).

Nonetheless we can agree with Barth's conclusion that there is not, and cannot be, a transparent doctrine of the demonic. "The mysteries of God are much more exposed to us than the mysteries of evil. The abyss in the devil consists both of his will to lie and of his refusal to convert. What this ultimately means remains a mystery that is not accessible to any man, even to the worst sinner. This is also the reason why the destiny of the devil is a mystery to which we have no access whatever. It is the Pandora's box that one is not permitted to touch." [48] But no ontology could entertain the idea that a reality could be a mere appearance and that, furthermore, this kind of pseudo-reality could have a ("third") form of "being" on the basis of mere rejection. The only way of coming to grips, concretely, with the problem of this kind of "being" is to enquire about the ontological quality of a sin that has been performed by a concrete, free human person and yet has been forgiven by God. We must also agree with Barth

[43] 530.   [44] 493.   [45] 480.   [46] *Ibid.*
[47] 531.   [48] 2 Jo 203.

when he says that vanquishing the devil is the concern of God himself, which is why, in the great passage in Ephesians, we read that the devil can be defeated only by "the whole armor of God"; Christians need to be "strong in the Lord and in the strength of his might" (Eph 6:10–11). "It is *God's* own weapons that man may make use of, the same weapons the Lord himself used when he was tempted by the devil." Man "must not turn the weapons gradually into his own, in the opinion that he and his weapons together made up the power capable of resisting the devil. There is in the devil an antidivine power that only God himself can conquer."[49] Accordingly, the wiles of Satan can be recognized for what they are only by those who are near to God.[50] Jesus speaks in a quite matter-of-fact manner of the devil's activity in sowing tares among the crop.[51] He knows that "Satan . . . makes his best catches where true love becomes weak, where it cools off, where it imperceptibly lets itself be falsified into something that still bears the name of love but is the opposite of love— self-seeking enjoyment."[52] The two are often as close together as Jesus and Judas at the Last Supper. Hence the call for constant, sober vigilance, for "there can be no cosy security where the devil is concerned."[53] The pull of the satanic is always active in temptation; "man does not invent sin, in a certain sense he gets it from the devil, acquiring a share in all the prior evil that the devil has effected."[54] Certainly, "a man has his own evil spirit, as if something devilish bursts out from his inner nature"; but "what initially looks quite harmless and neutral soon provides a foothold for the devil."[55]

There is a further point at which we can agree with Barth. The battlefield par excellence between God and the devil is not in God himself (because for God the devil has already been rejected and vanquished) but in the God-man Jesus Christ. "God

---

[49] Ep 254–55. On the temptation of Jesus as combat with the devil, see 3 Jo 239–40.

[50] "The closer we come to God and the deeper the things we perceive of him, the more do we learn of the devil as well and survey his workings" Ep 256–57; cf. Ka I, 178, 194.

[51] Gl 51.

[52] 3 Jo 16.

[53] Ka I, 399.

[54] Ka II, 106.

[55] Ka II, 146.

does not lower himself to fight in person against the devil"; yet, according to the Book of Revelation, the latter's place is "initially in heaven, at the origin of the sending of the Son", and the work of the Cross is carried out by him "in whose sign Satan falls from heaven".[56] Why? Because this work is executed at a deeper level than that to which the devil has access. So when Jesus says, "the ruler of this world is coming" (Jn 14:30), he adds immediately, "he has no power over me." "The devil's work does not touch, inwardly, the work of redemption. The two works occur in parallel: the highest work between Father and Son is accomplished while the devil's highest work is also accomplished. But . . . internally they have no point of contact. . . . But the greater activity of the evil one around the Cross is already a sign that his power is failing."[57] So the dragon of the Apocalypse, thrown down to the earth, has no power over the Marian, immaculate Church.[58]

What is of the devil cannot be apprehended in a single, definite shape. "As serpent, it plays the role of spiritual temptation; as devil, of temptation through the senses. As dragon, it simply inspires fear, intimidating and weakening man, who is forced to yield in the face of its monstrous power." With its "seven heads" —embodying the seven deadly sins that are set against the seven gifts of the Spirit—it ranges its arguments against mankind, "devising all the possible combinations of sins; if one does not succeed, it immediately raises another." The devil "keeps on until he has found a man's weakest point".[59]

Not only is the individual attacked, however: there is also a devilish assault on what Paul terms the "cosmic powers". They are the general "relations",[60] the "structures, and organizations",[61] the "principles of creation", in which evil can incarnate itself in order to "interfere with God's plans".[62] At the level of world process these potencies can be mutually opposed: thus there is

---

[56] Ap 398; 401–2. "Here the devil and the Incarnate One fight at close quarters, where the earth is the point of intersection of heaven and hell, where temptation and fulfillment clash. This battle is so monstrous that only God can bear to watch it": Ap 441.

[57] 3 Jo 157.   [58] Ap 408.

[59] Ap 405–6.   [60] K 31.

[61] Ep 69.   [62] Ep 256.

"the power of death and the contrary power of generation and propagation, . . . the realms of the useful and the useless, of what is deliberately willed and what is suffered, what is chosen and what is imposed, what is planned and what comes as a surprise, what is a building up and what is a tearing down."[63] All these can be invaded by superhuman evil, which incarnates itself in them, but Christ—not in a direct battle with the powers, but through his Cross—has undermined these powers. He has "broken their power", "more and more suppressed their aims"[64] and, through his own "powerlessness", has "disarmed" them. This does not mean "that all principalities and powers were evil before, or that their function has become meaningless in the future. But they are to be seized and made part of a service, which is the Son's service of redemption offered to the Father." The Son can employ these powers "as he wills: he can summon them and also do without them."[65]

As a concluding reflection, nonetheless, we must recall the perspective of the Book of Revelation. Precisely because the dragon has been cast out of eternity into the world of time and is aware of the shortness of his allotted span, his rage is greatly increased in the era A.D., the era of Christ. The "Woe to you, O earth and sea!" of Revelation 12:12 is now highly relevant. Now the paradoxical struggle attains its clearest form: the satanic "great power", whose rage comes from the fact that inwardly it knows it is beaten, fights against the Christian powerlessness of the Cross, which inwardly knows that it is victorious. This is true of Christ, for he has "disarmed" the powers and "triumphed over them" (Col 2:15); but it is not yet true of Christians. The beast from the sea, to whom the dragon gives "his power and his throne and great authority", is "allowed to make war on the saints and to conquer them. And authority was given it over every tribe and people and tongue and nation" (Rev 13:2, 7).[66] Thus Jesus can

---

[63] C 500–501.

[64] C 501.

[65] K 94 (GT).

[66] The "saints" against whom Satan fights can be called "spotless" (Rev 14:5), "which does not mean that they are infallible. . . . It is as if they are in front of a mirror that reflects their image, and at the first real sin they would no longer see their image. . . . Their situation is not without its danger, for such closeness to

raise the question, "Nevertheless, when the Son of man comes, will he find faith on earth?" (Lk 18:8).

Who can estimate how far evil can go in man? A witness beyond suspicion, Ernst Jünger, comes across this sentence on the Brinvilliers: "Les grands crimes, loin de se soupçonner, ne s'imaginent même pas" [Great crimes are not only not suspected: we do not even imagine them]. He comments:

> This is quite correct. The reason is that the crime becomes more grievous the more it rises from the animal level and attains spirit. Similarly, the evidence disappears proportionately. The greatest crimes rest on combinations that, in logical terms, are superior to the law. The crime shifts more and more from the act to the very being of the person, eventually reaching a level where it lives in pure knowledge, as an abstract spirit of evil. Finally even the person's own interest disappears: evil is done for the sake of evil. Evil is celebrated. At this stage the question 'Cui bono?' no longer applies: there is only *one* power in the universe whom it benefits.[67]

Jünger goes on to describe the annihilation camps and speaks of the "hellish masters and apprentices who practice their trade there. This, surely, is the landscape where the nature of Kniébolos (Hitler) manifests itself most clearly, in a way that even Dostoyevsky did not foresee."[68]

What is satanic comes so close to us that we cannot turn our gaze away from its Medusa's head. It has lost all "pagan innocence". It waves its fist in the face of the God of the Old Testament and of the New. So how can we speak of God's Son "triumphing" over death and the devil? Rather, with Paul and John, we must posit a judgment that takes place after the "redemption", a judgment at the end of time that will be more

---

God offers many sides for the evil enemy to attack. Their distance from God is, so to speak, so shortened . . . that they are perhaps no longer sufficiently aware of the danger threatening them. For them, the essence of temptation has changed. If their gaze were not directed exclusively to God, it would take very little for everything to be corrupted into presumption, pride and arrogance. Many have fallen from this state. There are fallen saints. . . . They fell because they extracted a human security out of the divine nearness; somehow they knew what they should not have known: that they possessed more grace, more guarantees" Ap 450–51.

[67] *Strahlungen* II (Munich: Deutscher Taschenbuch Verlag, 1965), 166.

[68] *Ibid.*, 169.

severe than all God's judgments upon Israel ever were. "The wrath of God" rests on the man who will not obey the Son (Jn 3:36). Thus, at least by analogy, we are justified in speaking of an eschatological "tragedy" in the very midst of "God's victory" (and we must remember that God is righteous both in his mercy and in his justice); it is a tragedy insofar as a portion of God's plan for the world has failed, a portion of his creation has turned out to be meaningless.

At this level we encounter what in more recent times has been called the "theology of the pain of God", a concept that, it must be said, tends to obscure certain other perspectives that actually go beyond it. According to its main emphases, it seems to belong to the context of the "final act, seen as tragedy", although some proponents would resist being put in this category. To a considerable extent, no doubt, it arises from a new awareness that in the medieval images of the Judgment, in the tympani above church doors and right up to Michelangelo's *Last Judgment* and Rubens' depictions of hell, we find a view of the world that equates timely exhortation with dogmatics, neutralizes and thus objectivizes what is existentially unavoidable, and in doing so, as Barth has said, makes the victorious God untouchable, sublimely superior to all world process. In what follows we shall set forth these theologies of the pain of God in their various hues and then, in the subsequent section, recapitulate what is true in them on the basis of a more profound view. This will show that many elements found in these theologies have already transcended the level of the "tragic" and are on their way to the one insight that is crucial. The section on the pain of God, therefore, forms a transition to the more detailed analysis that follows it.

4. *The Pain of God*

Today's theologians, while they are aware of the traditional axiom of God's unchangeability, and notwithstanding the danger of falling back into mythology, seem to have no qualms about speaking of the pain of God. This is connected with a phenomenon found not only in Protestantism but also in Anglicanism, Orthodoxy and Catholicism, namely, the abandonment of

a Greek theo-ontology of "absolute Being" and the embracing
of the Johannine definition that God is love. How could a God
of love maintain an unmoved "passionlessness" (*apatheia*) in the
face of sin or (what is more) in the face of the potential damnation of certain of his creatures, to say nothing of his Son's abandonment on the Cross? Let one voice, that of G. Martelet on
the subject of hell, stand for many:

> If God is love, as the New Testament teaches us, hell must be im-
> possible. . . . And yet, if God's love does not remove our freedom
> but is rather the gift that crowns it, this love cannot enjoy auto-
> matic, predictable success in the world. Love that is given always
> requires to be received. . . . In this case hell, the utter rejection of
> love, can only exist for the person who is continually making a
> hell for himself. It is a divine impossibility for God to be involved
> in such an insane project, nor can there be any question of it con-
> tributing to the triumph of his justice and thereby reestablishing
> the glory of his betrayed love, as has too often been maintained.
> So if there is in God a reaction to the existence of hell—and how
> could there fail to be?—it must be one of pain and not of consent;
> it must be one of infinite pain and not of pleasure. We must dare
> to say this: When God's love is rejected, it is as if a red-hot iron
> burns into his flesh, branding it for ever. . . . At this point God's
> pain is as unfathomable as his love; faced with hell, our pain is
> only the echo of his.[1]

At a first glance it might seem that this "susceptibility" on
God's part, even the possibility of him feeling pain, could without difficulty be included among those aspects within the life
of the Trinity that we showed (in part 1 of this volume) to be
archetypes of the creation. Upon deeper reflection, however, this
conclusion by no means follows as a matter of course. After all,
the "suffering" with which the creature is familiar is something
quite different from being "receptive" and "letting things happen". Initially, therefore, we shall have to be extremely careful with this whole theology of divine suffering; any definitive
stance must be deferred for the moment.

Once God is drawn into the total process of being, our speaking of God's suffering provides the context for the further "dark

[1] *L'Au-delà retrouvé. Christologie des fins dernières* (Paris: Desclée, 1974), 181,
188f.

truth of the death of God".[2] Nietzsche will go on to interpret this, no longer in the sense of an ultimate intensification of divine suffering, but as mankind's loss of the experience of God; this second interpretation does not concern us in what follows.[3]

However, God's susceptibility, his pain (which goes to the very limit of his death), cannot be dismissed as contrary to revelation, because the idea of God suffering pain rests on biblical and, in particular, Old Testament statements; as for the notion of the "death of God", it has been current as a christological assertion since the early patristic period and was debated in the fifth and sixth centuries in the context of the formula "One of the Trinity has suffered" (and has died). Accordingly we need to make a brief survey of the antecedents of the modern theology.

a. In the Biblical Realm

α. *The Old Covenant and the Rabbis.* The God of the Old Covenant is susceptible to pain in his relationship with Israel because of the latter's infringements of the Covenant. "The Lord was sorry that he had made man on the earth, and it grieved him to his heart" (Gen 6:6). "They . . . provoked the Holy One of Israel" (Ps 78:41). "But they rebelled and grieved his holy Spirit" (Is 63:10). They "provoke him to anger" (Dt 4:25), they "weary" him (Is 7:13). God's heart seems to be wrung by conflicting emotions: on the one hand, there is painful anger and, on the other hand, love, and the latter must overcome the anger within him (in his "bowels"): Hosea 11:8–9; Jeremiah 31:20.[4] Many passages indirectly point to pain on God's part: the symbolic marriage suggested to Hosea, Yahweh's "bewilderment" (Hos 6:4), his explicit lament (Hos 4:6, and so on), and the fact that he had to abandon and surrender his beloved: "I have forsaken my

---

[2] Eberhard Jüngel, "Das dunkle Wort vom 'Tode Gottes'" in *Ev. Komm.* 2 (1969), 133ff., 198ff. See also his "Vom Tod des lebendigen Gottes" in *ZThK* 65, 93–116.

[3] On "sense and nonsense in speaking of the death of God", cf. E. Jüngel, *Gott als Geheimnis der Welt* (Tübingen: Mohr, 1978), 55–137.

[4] J. Scharbert, *Der Schmerz im Alten Testament* (Bonn, 1955), 215ff. Kitamori (see below) will take Jeremiah 31:20 as the starting point for his theology of the pain of God.

house [that is, the land], I have abandoned my heritage; I have given the beloved of my soul into the hands of her enemies" (Jer 12:7).

In the rabbinic writings this "pain of God" undergoes vigorous development, the details of which are familiar to us today.[5] There are about eighty passages in which God appears weeping, lamenting or making gestures of pain or rituals of grieving, primarily because of the destruction of the first and second Temples. At the burning of the Temple, God says, "I have burned my house, destroyed my city, brought my children into exile among the gentiles; now I sit alone. . . ."[6] God's lament can also be wider in its scope: it may include the banishment of Adam and Eve from paradise, the Flood, the deaths of Aaron and Moses, the necessity of punishing sinful man, the sufferings of the end-time, and so on. As a result of his Covenant, God is bound to Israel in a way that causes him pain: "Woe is me, that I have sworn this oath. And now that I have taken it, who will release me from it?"[7] In these later writings, by contrast with the Old Testament, we have a stronger emphasis not only on the external expressions of God's pain but also on his powerlessness in the face of sinfully hardened hearts and the resultant ill fortune.[8]

β. *The New Covenant.* Bearing these Old Testament texts in mind, when we come to Jesus' weeping over Jerusalem, his anger (in Mark!) or exasperation (Mt 17:17) and, most of all, his words of abandonment by God (Mk 15:34; Mt 27:46), we must not be too quick to restrict such expressions to his "human nature": after all, are they not a revelation of the "heart" of God? This opens up the possibility of considering the "humanity of God":[9]

---

[5] Peter Kuhn, *Gottes Selbsterniedrigung in der Theologie der Rabbinen*, Studien zum Alten und Neuen Testament, ed. V. Hamp, J. Schmid, P. Neuenzeit, vol. 17 (Munich: Kosel-Verlag, 1908), and especially Kuhn's study: *Gottes Trauer und Klage in der rabbinischen Überlieferung* (*Talmud und Midrasch*) (Leiden: Brill, 1978).

[6] P. Kuhn, *Gottes Trauer*, text 35. See text 57 for the same sentiment in the wake of the destruction of the second Temple.

[7] *Ibid.*, text 61 (275).

[8] *Ibid.*, 457–511, esp. 475–89.

[9] Cf. Titus 3:4. K. Barth, *Die Menschlichkeit Gottes*, Theolog. Studien 48 (Zurich,

here, more than in the Old Testament, the whole man with his bodily nature, the language of his emotions, the symbolism of his gestures, his joys, pains, wounds and his dying, becomes the medium in which God "declares himself". Eucharistic mediation of the incarnate Word causes this new language to be a constantly vibrant, intelligible and here-and-now reality for believers.

b. The Fathers

α. *God Is Both Impassible and (in the Son) Passible.* In more recent times there have been many attacks on the patristic idea of a God who is immutable and not subject to suffering (or rather, to passion, *pathos*), the chief objection being that the Fathers took the concept of divine *apatheia* and *ataraxia* from Greek philosophy and imported it into the entirely different realm of biblical thought.[10] We need to approach this whole topic at a much deeper level.

a. The early Christians (no doubt like Plato, Aristotle, the Stoics, and the Middle and Neoplatonists) had to adopt a position vis-à-vis the mythological notions of suffering, changeable gods, and, most of all, they had to counter a mythological interpretation of the Incarnation of God in Christ. If Christ was God, and thus in his human form a *Deus passibilis*, it was necessary to hold fast all the more energetically to the impassibility of the

---

1956). E. Barbotin, *Humanité de Dieu: Approche anthropologique du mystère chrétien,* Théologie 78 (Aubier, 1969).

[10] The range of problems is set forth by I. A. Dorner in his *Über die richtige Fassung des dogmatischen Begriffs der Unveränderlichkeit Gottes, mit besonderer Beziehung auf das gegenseitige Verhältnis zwischen Gottes übergeschichtlichem und geschichtlichem Leben* (1857, reprinted in *Gesammelte Schriften* [Berlin, 1887], 188–377). Subsequently this was developed and achieved greater influence as part of Harnack's program of "dehellenization". Only after Protestant theology had explored the topic did Catholic theologians take it up, opposing the Greek "rigidity" of the Fathers' *apatheia-ataraxia* concept. Here we mention only H. Mühlen, *Veränderlichkeit Gottes als Horizont einer künftigen Christologie: Auf dem Wege zu einer Kreuzestheologie in Auseinandersetzung mit der altkirchlichen Christologie* (Münster, 1970); W. Maas, *Veränderlichkeit Gottes: Zum Verhältnis von griechisch-philosophischer und christlicher Gotteslehre* (Paderborn: Schöningh, 1974).

divine nature. This is the origin of the formulas that speak of "the Impassible One who suffers for us".[11]

b. No doubt individual Fathers defended the *apatheia* of God in a way that shows the influence of Greek philosophy, such as we find, for instance, in the philosophical treatise "On the Unchangeability of God"[12] (Clement of Alexandria, Augustine). But in the Fathers, in general, when such statements are to be taken as expressions of Christian faith, they are balanced by others that speak of the living God, of God's freedom to communicate himself, of his feelings about man.[13] Whether such statements can be explicitly reconciled with God's *apatheia* depends on what the Fathers regard as the opposite of *apatheia* (we shall come to this). But if we are to take seriously passages such as Romans 8:32 and John 3:16, we find that at least pity and mercy are attributed to God—attributes that stand behind the Son's human suffering.[14]

Where the divine nature possesses *apatheia* as an inalienable quality, the sufferings of Christ can be located only in his human nature (the Antiochene position).[15] In this case the divine nature

[11] "Ton apathē, ton di' hēmās pathēton": Ignatius, *Ad Polyc.* 3, 2; "thnēton . . . athánaton": Melito, *On Easter* (SC 123), 3. The topic gains more and more momentum through the patristic period, partly due to modalism and patripassianism, and later as a result of the formula "one of the Trinity has suffered."

[12] "Hoti atrepton to theion", ed. Colson/Whitaker, Loeb Classical Library III.

[13] Tertullian attributes to God all the emotions (even opposing ones) that can be reconciled with his divinely perfect being: *Adv. Marc.* II, 16. For Novatian, feelings are entirely possible in God, since they are in complete harmony with his reason: *De Trin.* 5. Lactantius, who also attributes "apatheia" to God since he is not influenced by anything external, writes his celebrated treatise "De ira Dei" (against the Stoics), in which he says that God feels both love and mercy and righteous anger, since divine life too cannot be without "motion". Here too, however, God's emotions remain under the full control of his reason (chap. 21). "The pagans think that it is unworthy for God . . . to submit to *pathē*, pain and death" (*Div. Inst.* IV, 22, 3; CSEL 19, 369).

[14] Cyril of Alexandria says this explicitly in connection with the divinity of the Logos and of the Father himself: on Heb 4:14 (PG 74, 973A).

[15] Cf. J. Chéné, "Unus ex Trinitate passus est" in *Rech. Sc. Rel.* 53 (1965), 545–88. Theodoret's entire dialogue "Eranistes" is designed to counter Cyril's assertion that God's Word tasted death in the flesh (DS 263). Even Nestorius refused to admit the phrase "God has suffered" (A. Grillmeier, *Christ in Christian Tradition*, vol. 1 [London, 1965], 452).

adopts this suffering (Cyril of Alexandria, the Alexandrines).[16] The preliminary stage of this teaching is that of Clement of Alexandria, who says that Christ suffers in the flesh, whereas in the Spirit he is *apathēs*.[17] This, however, can be correctly understood only when we know how the Fathers viewed the opposite of *apatheia*, that is, what the relation is between *pathos* and the body.

c. First, however, a brief note: by saying that, in Christ, the Godhead had suffered, neither the Monarchians (Noetus, Praxeas, Sabellius) nor the Apollinarians (who regarded the Logos as "in essence" bound to the flesh) nor the Monophysites wanted seriously to subordinate the nature of God to world suffering. What we have here are attempts at formal christological utterance, albeit from quite different viewpoints, in the absence of reflection on their metaphysical (or mythological) implications.

β. *The Opposite of "Apatheia".* Why do the Fathers so strongly emphasize *apatheia*? This becomes clear once we understand what the Greeks mean by *pathos* and why they have to keep their distance both from God and—to a large extent—from the incarnate Son. *Pathos*, however, signifies many things and yields a plurality of aspects.

a. *Pathos* can be understood as some external misfortune, contrary to a person's will. This cannot apply to God at all: when he freely decides to suffer as a man, his suffering (Passion) results from a vigorous "action" by means of which he "undercuts" and destroys both suffering and death. This is the central affirmation in the dialogue "On the Inability and Ability of God

---

[16] "The same both suffers and suffers not", says Athanasius (*Epist. Epict.* 6; PG 26, 1060C), insofar as he is both a man capable of suffering and God incapable of suffering. Cyril uses the same formula (PG 75, 1341A; SC 97, 474). Jesus is able "to suffer in his flesh and not to suffer in his Godhead" (*ibid.*, 1341C; 474–76). J. Galot, in his *Dieu souffre-t-il?* (Lethielleux, 1976), 28–30, shows that, for Cyril, the *communicatio idiomatum* was not a mere external "attribution" of suffering to the Logos but a genuine "adoption" of it.

[17] *Strom.* VII, 2, 5; see also 7, where it is said that Christ "took upon himself the flesh, which by nature is subject to the passions, and educated it to the condition of passionlessness".

to Suffer"[18] attributed to Gregory Thaumaturgus. The detailed questions—Can God suffer if he so wishes? If he cannot, does this not imply a limitation of his will?—anticipate the solution proposed by Karl Barth. If God, says Gregory, wishes to save men by freely choosing suffering, he suffers impassibly; since he suffers freely, he is not subject to suffering but superior to it.

From this clear exposition we can move on to Hilary's less clear one. Hilary is probably animated by a similar intuition, but his idea that Christ's body had no natural needs has a docetic ring. According to Hilary, the Incarnate One feels the pains bodily yet without suffering them; "he is surrendered, according to human nature, to the experience of bodily motions, yet he is not touched by the harm of suffering."[19] This is perhaps the place to mention the (quite different) case of the Monophysite Julian of Halicarnassus, who said that the body of Jesus, which is "per se" incapable of suffering because of its union with the Divinity, experiences suffering only because of the Son's free will.[20]

b. *Pathos* can be seen more sharply as having a necessary connection with sin. In this case the sinner inevitably holds aloof from God and Christ. We find this view, in embryo, in Athanasius, for whom the *pathē* are one with the *phthorā* that invaded nature as a result of Adam's sin and from which we are delivered by Christ's suffering in the flesh.[21] This view is still clearer in Gregory of Nyssa, who does not regard things like being born, growing, the accepting of nourishment (which do not lead to sin) as part of the *pathē*, properly speaking (*kyriōs*); rather, these things belong to the working (*ergon*) of the created nature, which maintains composite beings in harmony by means of manifold vicissitudes. "The real *pathos*, however, is a sickness of the ability to choose." What Christ takes upon himself, without sin or inclination to sin, is the healing of our fallenness from within;

[18] In Pitra, *Anal. Sacra* IV (Paris, 1883), Syrian 103–20, Latin 363–76, German in V. Ryssel, *Gregor Thaumaturgus* (Leipzig, 1880) 71–99. See also H. Crouzel, La Passion de l'Impassible" in *L'Homme devant Dieu*, Théologie 56, Mélanges Henri de Lubac I (Aubier, 1963), 269–79.

[19] *De Trinitate* X, 24.

[20] J. K. Mozley, *The Impassibility of God: A Survey of Christian Thought* (Cambridge: University Press, 1926), 96, with reference to Dorner's interpretation.

[21] *Third Address against the Arians*, chaps. 32–34.

he touches our sickness as a doctor does. Gregory adds that we are meant to see, in this whole *oikonomia* of the Son, the *philanthropia* of the Father.[22]

Maximus the Confessor continues the teaching of Gregory: the natural *pathē* are "not reprehensible", and where they are sullied by evil desire they can be purified and rendered serviceable to the soul.[23] *Philautia*, the fundamental sin, is the root of all evil *pathē*.[24] Thus John Damascene can conclude by defining the *pathē* as a "motion imparted to nature from without"[25]— which is therefore inapplicable to divinity;[26] however, the Incarnate One can suffer the natural, guiltless *pathē* (both because he is man and because his divine will either expressly wishes it so or permits it).[27] This introduces the previous theme of suffering on the basis of a prior "active" will: in Christ, what is genuinely natural is also supernatural, "for we behold nothing constrained in him, but all that he does he does freely."

Finally, when Augustine describes the "*passiones*" mostly as a "movement of the spirit against reason", a "*perturbatio*"[28]— although he admits that anger and grief can serve moral purposes (*in usus justitiae*)—it is clear that God can only be *impassibilis*: in him, regret, mercy, patience are only the expression of his constant attitude, which is the very opposite of insensitivity ("*immanitas in animo, stupor in corpore . . . : quis hunc stuporem non omnibus vitiis judicet esse pejorem?*").[29] The same solution applies to the incarnate Son: "*cuius et infirmitas fuit ex potestate*".[30]

---

[22] *C. Eunomium* VI (PG 45, 721B–725B; Jaeger II, 144–47).

[23] *Ambigua* (PG 91, 1044A); *Quaest. ad Thal.* 55 (PG 90, 541A).

[24] *Cent. Car.* 3, 8 (PG 90, 1020AB); *Ep.* 2 (PG 91, 397). On this whole issue, see my *Kosmische Liturgie*, 2d ed. (Einsiedeln: Johannes Verlag, 1961), 191–203.

[25] *Ekdosis* II, 22 (PG 94, 941A).

[26] *Ibid.*, I, 1 (PG 94, 792A).

[27] *Ibid.*, III, 18 (PG 94, 1074BC).

[28] *De Civ. Dei* VIII, 17 (PL 41, 242). Further references in Mozley, *Impassibility*, 104–9.

[29] *De Civ. Dei* XIV, 9, 3–4 (PL 41, 414–15). "Vicinior est immortalitati sanitas doloris quam stupor non sentientis." *En. in Ps.* 55, 6 (PL 36, 651).

[30] *Ibid.*, 415.

γ. *"Pathos" in the Impassible God.* Having in mind the distinctions
that the Fathers introduce at this point, making it clear how far
they distance themselves from the *apatheia* of Greek philosophy,
we can see that some of the bold expressions used by Origen
are less isolated than it might at first seem. Starting from the
human ability to be moved by others' distress, the Alexandrine
theologian attributes the *passio* of pity to the eternal Son: If he
had not felt pity, in eternity, for our lamentable state, he would
not have become man and would not have allowed himself to
be crucified: "Primum passus est, deinde descendit. Quae est
ista quam pro nobis passus est, passio? Caritatis est passio." If
this is true of the Son, it must be true of the Father: Does not
he, too, the long-suffering and merciful One, "somehow suffer? In his Providence he must suffer on account of men's suffering (*passionem patitur humanam*), just as the Son suffers our
*passiones. Ipse pater non est impassibilis. Si rogetur, miseretur
et condolet, patitur aliquid caritatis et fit in iis, in quibus juxta
magnitudinem naturae suae non potest esse, et propter nos hu-
manas sustinet passiones."*[31] These last words show that Origen
sees very precisely the paradox between God's *apatheia* in himself and his susceptibility in the economy he has established. As
early as *Peri Archon* he rejects the *apatheia* of those philosophers
who say "Deum penitus impassibilem atque his omnibus car-
entem affectibus sentiendum"; when, in order to explain the literal sense, he points to the "*spiritualem intellectum*", he is by no
means using "allegory" as an escape route: as is appropriate to
the analogy in question, he is seeking an affirmation about God
"sicut intelligere de Deo dignum est".[32]

δ. *Conclusion.* Today people who speak of "God's immutability" hasten to distance themselves from the patristic doctrine
of God's *apatheia.*[33] The foregoing has shown, however, how
nuanced is the thinking and teaching of the Fathers, and how,

[31] *In Ez. hom.* 6, 6 (Baehrens VIII, 384f.). Cf. *Comm. in Rom.* VII, 9 (PG 14, 1129A), *Sel. in Ez.* (PG 13, 812A).

[32] II, chap. 4, 4 (Koetschau V, 131–32).

[33] Cf. the treatment of this topic by H. Mühlen, *W. Maas* and—in even cruder form—J. Moltmann, e.g., in his *The Trinity and the Kingdom of God* (London: SCM Press, 1981), 21f.

to a large extent, they converge on a tenable doctrine of God's *pathos*. The following positions are axiomatic and irreducible: There can be no *pathos* in God if by this we mean some involuntary influence from outside. Or, to put it positively, God (and this applies to the Incarnate One also) can only be "passive", subject to *passio*, if this accords with some prior, "active", free decision. Furthermore, such forms of the eternal divine life as mercy, patience, and so on, can be understood on the analogy of human emotions, but this must not involve attributing "mutability" to God. Nor is it correct—and many Catholic theologians have followed Protestant theologians in this—to restrict God's immutability to his attitude of covenant faithfulness within the dispensation he has established: the Bible, in both Old and New Testaments, looks *through* his attitude and discerns beyond it a quality of the Divinity as such.

Theologians in succeeding ages tended to conceive God's impassibility more narrowly than the Fathers. Since a real relationship can exist only from the creature's side toward God, and not from God's side toward the creature,[34] the biblical "reactions" of God to human conduct become mere anthropomorphisms, and any involvement of God in history seems highly questionable. Now God's pity seems to be located only in its effect in the world, whereas he himself cannot be touched by the creature's pitiful state.[35] Deeper reflection on the teaching of the *relatio rationis* between God and the creature could dispel the impression that God is aloof—for, after all, God is in the most concrete sense the Creator of all created reality.[36] The more the scriptural texts were examined, however, the more they seemed—particularly to modern ears—to proclaim something entirely different from the impassibility of the Divine Being. Thus the reaction against it in the nineteenth and twentieth centuries is

[34] Thomas Aquinas, I, d 30, q 1, a 1; *De Pot.* 7, 8–11; Ia, 13, 7.

[35] "Misericors simul et impassibilis quomodo es? . . . Cum tu respicis nos miseros, nos sentimus misericordis effectum, tu non sentis affectum, . . . quia nulla miseriae compassione afficieris": Anselm, *Proslogion* 8 (Schmitt I, 105). "Deus non potest quae posse potentiae passivae sunt": Thomas, *C. Gent.* II, 25.

[36] Cf. Michel Gervais, "Incarnation et immuabilité divine" in *Rev. Sc. Rel.*, 1976, 215–43, esp. 240–41, with ref. to Thomas, *De Pot.* 7, 11 ad 3.

completely understandable, as are the attempts to construct a serious "theology of the pain of God".

c. The Modern Period

α. *Theological Approaches.* The patristic solution on the basis of the *communicatio idiomatum* sufficed for the Middle Ages and the Reformation, so much so that it was possible to speak with Tertullian of the *Deus crucifixus*[1] and to sing, in the words of a hymn, that "God himself lies dead."[2] The situation will be different with the theory of the nineteenth-century German kenoticists (chiefly G. Thomasius, F. H. R. Frank and G. Geß): writing in the wake of Hegel, they introduce a soteriological kenosis into the Godhead and, along with it, also introduce change and suffering,[3] just as did the English theology of the pain of God[4] that began around the end of the century. The German kenoticists

[1] *Adv. Marc.* II, 16: "deum mortuum", II, 27: "deum crucifixum" (CSEL 47, 356, 374).

[2] For details of this hymn, also quoted by Hegel, cf. E. Jüngel, *Gott als Geheimnis der Welt* (Tübingen: Mohr, 1978), 84–85, also footnotes.

[3] Cf. P. Althaus' criticism of the kenoticists, while simultaneously conceding that they were right to question God's immutability and "really" to introduce God "to suffering": *RGG*, 3d ed., III, 1244–46.

[4] J. K. Mozley, *The Impassibility of God: A Survey of Christian Thought* (Cambridge: University Press, 1926), briefly analyzes a whole series of English theologians of "the pain of God": H. Bushnell (1866), Principal Simon (1889), Vincent Tymms (1907), A. M. Fairbairn (1893), G. B. Stevens (1905), Campbell Morgan (1909), S. A. McDowell (1912), Douglas White (1913), Canon Storr (1919), C. E. Rolt (1913), Canon Streeter, William Temple (*Mens Creatrix*, 1919, *Christus Veritas*, 1924), E. L. Strong (2d ed., 1920), Maldwyn Hughes (1924). The list is continued in the appendix to Bertrand R. Brasnett's work *The Suffering of the Impassible God* (London: SPCK, 1928), where there is also a discussion of Dr. Relton and Bishop McConnell's *Is God Limited?* and James Hinton's *The Mystery of Pain*. The most important presentation and discussion remains A. M. Ramsey's *From Gore to Temple, The Development of Anglican Theology between Lux Mundi and the Second World War 1889–1939* (Hale Foundation, 1960). ("Lux Mundi" was a "collection of studies on the religion of the Incarnation", Oxford 1889, published by young professors who were followers of the Tractarians.) Ramsey critically presents the often extremely subtle attempts to reconcile the impassibility and passibility of God (Frank Weston, 1907, P. T. Forsyth, 1909, J. M. Creed, O. G. Quick, etc.).

regard the following as preconditions of the Son's Incarnation: his self-imposed limitations (that is, his renunciation of the attributes of his divinity as they affect the world: Thomasius), the "reduction ('de-potentializing') of his divine consciousness" to the level of a human consciousness (Frank), and the total renunciation of his eternal consciousness of himself (Geß). These all imply something like a "death of God" within God himself. The English theologians insist more strongly on sin's influence on God: he would not be perfect if he did not suffer as a result of sin, either in his essence or in the Person of the Father in particular, who is the first to suffer (that is, before the Son: Bushnell) and at all events continues to suffer along with the suffering Son ("impassibility of God . . . is the greatest heresy that ever smirched Christianity: D. White). Many of them are moving toward the formulation that will be at its clearest, subsequently, in Karl Barth. First, however, we must briefly examine the work of Hegel, which forms the partly patent, partly latent source of these theological attempts.

β. *Hegel's Approach.* Hegel's philosophy, in which he consciously sets out to pick up the treasures of the Christian revelation thrown away by the Enlightenment and integrate them (along with the reasons for the Enlightenment's rejection) into his synthesis, is often described as an all-embracing philosophical Christology. In the celebrated conclusion to *Faith and Knowledge* (1802), Hegel observes that the feeling that "God himself is dead" had introduced an "infinite pain" into the "education" of the human race because of the abstractness of the Enlightenment "religion of reason". Hegel now wants to regain this "infinite pain" and include it as just one "element" in his idea of God; thus he reconstitutes "the absolute suffering or the speculative Good Friday that was formerly (!) something historical, in the whole truth of its harsh godlessness . . . because the untroubled aspect . . . of dogmatic philosophy . . . must disappear", to allow "the highest totality to be resurrected in all its gravity".[5] One sentence from the preface to the *Phenomenology of the Spirit* (1807) may suffice briefly to elucidate this constant ambition of

---

[5] *Werke* I (1832), 157.

Hegel's: "So it is quite possible to regard the life of God and the divine knowledge as love playing with itself; but this idea, deprived of the gravity, the pain, the patience and the agonizing of the negative within it, sinks to the level of tasteless pious sentiment."[6] Even the "painful feeling . . . that God himself is dead" must be integrated into the idea of God.[7] We may wonder whether Hegel really got beyond this starting point (cf. his lectures on "philosophy of religion" of 1824, 1827 and 1831) and moved closer to Christian theology—in which case we could distinguish "three structural forms of Hegelian theology".[8] We should be slow to accept that there was any essential change of Hegel's outline, particularly since, for political reasons, Hegel as an old man had to avoid providing fuel for an atheistic interpretation of his philosophy of religion,[9] although Ludwig Feuerbach, in his dissertation, had already discovered atheism in Hegel as early as 1828.[10]

Essentially, therefore, Hegel's approach, including his talk of the "death of God", is "two-sided, not to say ambiguous".[11] He is trying, on the one hand, to interpret God philosophically as a necessary process and, on the other, to interpret him theologically as "free" self-revelation and self-surrender (in Christ).[12] In

---

[6] *Werke* II (1832). That the "God is dead" idea is a consequence of the Enlightenment is clearly shown by the philosophy of Jacobi and also by Jean Paul's *Rede des toten Christus vom Weltgebäude herab, daß kein Gott sei* (*Werke* [Hanser, 1959], II, 266–71).

[7] *Ibid.*, 590.

[8] See esp. Albert Chapelle, S.J., *Hegel et la religion*, 4 vols. (Paris: Éditions Universitaires, 1963–1967), Emilio Brito, *La Cristologia di Hegel* (Louvain, 1976). The systematic section of the latter is given in French in: *Hegel et la tâche actuelle de la Christologie* (Lethielleux: Culture et Vérité, 1979).

[9] Cf. Jüngel, *Gott als Geheimnis*, 128, n. 192.

[10] According to Feuerbach, Hegel is trying to do the impossible in uniting atheism and Christianity. This contradiction is, however, "concealed from him and obscured because he has made the negation of God, atheism, into an objective development in God: God is a *process*, and atheism is a factor in this process": *Grundsätze der Philosophie der Zukunft* (1843), sec. 21 (*Werke* [1846], II, 277).

[11] Jüngel, *Gott als Geheimnis*, 111.

[12] During his time in Jena, Hegel undertook a definitive reworking of the theological ideas of his early years, refashioning them into philosophical principles. So he can say, "God sacrifices himself, surrenders himself to annihilation. God himself is dead: the ultimate despair of total God-forsakenness": F. Nicolin, *Un-*

other words, he wants to see "absolute religion" as something
that both *abides* and yet, in absolute knowledge, is *overcome*. Or
again, he wants to understand the elements of finitude in the
world—such as pain and death—as both really present in God
and at the same time as elements that have been transcended.
However, the main emphasis is on the idea that any "absolute"
that is unacquainted with suffering and dying is "lifeless and
lonely";[13] to be "divine",[14] to be the living God, he must undergo the experience of death.[15] In Hegel, Resurrection is never
the historical event as told by the Gospels but the living consciousness of the community, the (Holy) Spirit, the Spirit's concrete self-knowledge.

The insurmountable ambivalence of this approach is further
tangible in a concluding observation of the *Philosophy of Religion*.
"A Lutheran hymn says that 'God himself is dead'; this expresses
the consciousness that the human, the finite, the frail, the weak
and the negative are all features of the divine. All this is in God
himself; otherness, finitude, negativity are not outside God . . .
they are an element of the divine nature itself. This insight contains the highest idea of the Spirit."[16] This is of course the idea
of the Trinity, indissolubly bound to the Cross and death of
Christ; yet we can still ask whether Christ is to be regarded, on
the one hand, as the unique historical event or, on the other, as
the necessary, the highest "representation" of the most general
law of being.

---

bekannte Aphorismen Hegels aus der Jenaer Periode, Hegel-Studien 4 (1967), 16.—In
the *Phenomenology* we read, with regard to God's self-surrender in Christ: "This
is *represented* as a *freewill* act; but the *necessity* of his self-emptying lies in the realization that what-exists-in-itself [*das Ansichseiende*] . . . has no genuine, lasting
being"; thus it "empties itself, proceeds to death and so reconciles the Absolute
Being with itself": *Werke* II, 583.

[13] Final sentence of the *Phenomenology, ibid.*, 612.

[14] "It is not this man who dies, but the divine; this is precisely how the divine
becomes man": *Jenaer Realphilosophie*, ed. J. Hoffmeister (1931), 268, n. 3. This
formulation anticipates the modern kenoticists.

[15] For Hegel, the only decisive significance in Jesus' existence is in his death,
the Cross. In this he is followed by theologians like Moltmann.

[16] *Werke* XII (1832), 253.

γ. *Theologies that Speak of Pain and Death in God's Essence.* In Hegel a central role is played by the "death of God" (as the negation of the Absolute's mere "being-in-itself"). The only other writer to take up this theme in a way that is relevant to theology is Gerhard Koch. Otherwise this expression is appropriated by the Hegelians of the left and, as we have seen, by Nietzsche; henceforth they will use it as a slogan for the psychological extinction of the idea of a God who has never existed. This picture does not change essentially in the spectrum of "death-of-God" theologies of the later twentieth century. We shall pass over them here.[17] However, while Hegel speaks less frequently of the pain of God, it is theological discussion on *this* topic (and on the "death" of God as it emerges in *this* context) that now comes to the fore. Considerable differences are evident in this "theology of the pain of God", depending on how and where this pain is located in God's relation to the world. The first group sees God's *essence* coinvolved, in the Hegelian manner, in the world process.

JÜRGEN MOLTMANN'S CRUCIFIED (TRINITARIAN) GOD. Moltmann, to whom we must return at this point, endeavors to reinterpret Hegel by tracing his thought back to the origins of the *Lutheran* Reformation, just as Barth endeavored to reinterpret Schleiermacher on the basis of *Reformed* origins. He develops his doctrine of the Trinity (understood in the Hegelian manner) on the basis of the ultimate *diastasis* between Father and Son on the Cross and in doing so largely adopts Hegel's "ambivalence", that is, without the pain and death of the Cross there can be no Trinity at all.[18]

---

[17] On the "death of God" theology: E. Biser, *"Gott ist tot": Nietzsches Destruktion des christlichen Bewußtseins* (1962). M. Heidegger, "Nietzsches Wort 'Gott is tot'" in *Holzwege*, 4th ed. (1963), 193ff. S. Daecke, *Der Mythos vom Tode Gottes: Ein kritischer Überblick*, Furche-Studenbuch 87 (Hamburg, 1969). H. M. Barth, "Tod-Gottes-Christologie: Der christologische Ansatz der nordamerikanischen Tod-Gottes-Theologie" in *Kerygma und Dogma* 17 (1971), 258–72. W. Hartmann, *Was kommt nach dem "Tod Gottes"? Dialektische Unterhaltung mit einem Trend theologischen Denkens* (Stuttgart, 1969).

[18] On the Moltmann debate: Peter Fumiaki Momose, *Kreuzestheologie: Auseinandersetzung mit J. Moltmann* (Herder, 1978). M. Welker, ed., *Diskussion über Jürgen Moltmanns Buch 'Der gekreuzigte Gott'* (Munich: Kaiser, 1979).

First Moltmann summons witnesses from history who, in part, argue for a "universal theology of pain, which we might describe as panentheistic"; "God and the world are then involved in a common redemptive process",[19] which means that human history is "at the same time the history of God's passion".[20] Then he opts for a connection between world history and the history of God that is neither a necessary process nor dependent purely on God's good pleasure (a view he attributes to Karl Barth): "How is the God who suffers in his love supposed to correspond to a God who exists in untouched glory?"[21] We should rather assume that the world owes its existence to a "free overflowing of his goodness"; "God communicates himself to other beings, not out of compulsion and not out of some arbitrary resolve, but out of the inner pleasure of his eternal love", for "like is not enough for like."[22] God has a "passion for the Other", an "inner thirst and yearning for the Other, who is the object of God's ultimate, boundless love".[23] But since, in the end, this "Other" is the Son who bears the entire sin of the world on the Cross, the trinitarian process (in all its "gravity") and the world process seem to coincide: "This means that the creation of the world and human beings for freedom and fellowship is always bound up with the process of *God's deliverance* from the sufferings of his love."[24] The "immanent" *processio* of the Son (within the Trinity) is identified with his "economic" *missio*.[25] Thus we have arrived at Hegel's view in his *Phenomenology*.

Evidently, however, this is *not* what Moltmann wishes to say: rather, he wants to bring out the other, Christian side of Hegel.

---

[19] J. Moltmann, *The Trinity and the Kingdom of God* (London: SCM Press, 1981), 38–39. Moltmann himself professes this "Christian panentheism" on p. 106.

[20] *Ibid.*, 46.

[21] *Ibid.*, 53–54.

[22] *Ibid.*, 58–59.

[23] J. Moltmann, *Zukunft der Schöpfung* (Munich: Kaiser, 1977) 63–64; "Einführung in die Theologie der Hoffnung" in *Das Experiment Hoffnung* (Munich: Kaiser, 1974), 79. Cf. Moltmann, *Trinity*, 98, 106f.

[24] Moltmann, *Trinity*, 60.

[25] "The sending of the Son therefore finds its foundation in a movement which takes place in the divine life itself: it is not merely a movement outwards." *Ibid.*, 75.

Thus he seems clearly to insist that it is the world, not the Son,[26] that is God's creation; hence "the distinction between the world process and the inner-trinitarian process must be maintained and emphasized";[27] "the trinitarian relationship of the Father, the Son and the Holy Spirit is so wide that the whole creation can find space, time and freedom in it."[28] But the Hegelian ambivalence remains; on several occasions, for instance, he warns the reader not to engage in polemics against the Neoplatonic doctrine of emanations.[29] The pain of Jesus' forsakenness by God on the Cross is because God has forsaken himself: "Why hast thou forsaken *thyself*?"[30] Here we find Hegel agreeing with Luther: "God is only [!] revealed as 'God' in his opposite: godlessness and abandonment by God. In concrete terms, God is revealed in the Cross of Christ who was abandoned by God."[31] If it were possible to restrict the word "revealed" to the meaning "revealed for the world, for the Church"—and Moltmann does not speak of God's being revealed in the Old Testament—it would come close, as an approximation, to the interpretation we shall eventually present as our own. The same applies to the passage we have already quoted: "The 'bifurcation' in God must contain the whole uproar of history within itself. . . . If one describes the life of God within the Trinity as the 'history of God' (Hegel), this history of God contains within itself the whole abyss of god-forsakenness, absolute death and the non-God."[32] This assertion, however, needs some clarification.

GERHARD KOCH'S DYING AND RISING GOD. Koch is aware that his position is an isolated one; on the one hand, it is "dangerously close to the modern affirmation that 'God is dead' ",[33] and, on the other hand, it comes under suspicion of having made "a pact with myth".[34] He energetically resists both views. His begins with a stern rejection of a God who is remote from the world

---

[26] *Ibid.*, 166.　　　　　[27] *Ibid.*, 107.

[28] *Ibid.*, 109.　　　　　[29] *Ibid.*, 54, 113.

[30] J. Moltmann, *The Crucified God* (London: SCM Press, 1974), 151.

[31] *Ibid.*, 27.　　　　　[32] *Ibid.*, 246.

[33] G. Koch, *Die Zukunft des toten Gottes* (Hamburg: Agentur des Rauen Hauses, 1968), 294.

[34] *Ibid.*, 304.

and independent of it, who is seated in majesty and exists for himself—that is, the God of Greek thought, and of Scholasticism, particularly in its late, nominalist phase.[35] But he also rejects the God of Hegel, for whom "the particular" has "no significance" over against the universal, "except insofar as it must perish".[36] He also rejects the transcendent God of Karl Barth.[37] Koch's fundamental axiom is Luther's: "All knowledge of God comes solely from his Word"—from his crucified and risen Christ. So he "opposes all ideas and options that place reason above God. He [Luther] does not recognize natural knowledge; it certainly knows that there is a God, but it does not know who and what he is."[38] As Creator, God is *Deus absconditus*, but he also becomes a hidden God for the Redeemer on the Cross: the two modes of hiddenness demand to be distinguished, but they resolutely resist any attempt to separate them": God wishes to be known, must be known, precisely *in* suffering and death. At this point Koch would like to free Luther from his voluntarism (which regarded the existence of a self-subsistent God as self-evident) and situate him in the present day,[39] since today's completely autonomous man treats the world "as if God no longer exists".[40] No longer can we take refuge in a "timeless God"; Christ is God's only normative Word about himself, and the Crucified One wrestles with the disappearing God. Thus we have seriously to face the Old Testament image of the God who "walks with" his people on their path, is submerged with them in the Exile, and "succumbs along the way"; we must come to see that "God and death belong together."[41] "He himself appears in death, in the powerlessness of his divine power."[42] "Death is immanent in creation, as are its coming to be and its passing away. . . . This creation in motion [is] simultaneously the motion of the Creator. . . . Here we see the real God going to his death in pain

---

[35] *Ibid.*, 177–204.

[36] *Ibid.*, 226. While Koch is aware of the ambivalence of Hegel's concept of God, he says, "nonetheless it cannot be denied that, in itself, the idea constitutes a rule for all world process and has no need to capitulate in the face of reality's elusiveness": 234.

[37] *Ibid.*,139–60.   [38] *Ibid.*, 258.

[39] *Ibid.*, 270.   [40] *Ibid.*, 273.

[41] *Ibid.*, 290.   [42] *Ibid.*, 293.

and utter seriousness. . . . In him the Father can be no longer unscathed, no longer immutable." Therefore the dying Son is united with the Father more intimately than ever. But "does this mean that God perishes just as temporal things perish? . . . Then death would be the real God." No. God's death is a mode of his being in and being with his world, and death as the world knows it is contained within it and—under the sign of Christ's Resurrection—overcome.[43] "In the unfathomable phases of history, in their beginnings and endings, in God's unfathomable dyings in history, trinitarian faith affirms God's resurrection to that destination where the path of transience will be revealed, unveiled, as 'God all in all'."[44]

This "Lutheran Hegelianism" stands on a knife-edge: it deliberately submerges the life of God (including his death) in the world's coming to be and passing away, while wishing to distinguish it, *within* this immanence, from living and dying as the world knows them. Materially this achieves a certain distance from Hegel, but formally his "ambivalence" remains. In short, the model for seeing pain and death *in* God remains pain and death *outside* God in the world, and this cannot avoid the danger of mythology, despite Koch's protestations.

KAZOH KITAMORI'S THEOLOGY OF THE PAIN OF GOD. Whereas Moltmann and Koch cannot envisage a God without the world, Kitamori's thought begins, like the Gospel, with the fact of a world full of sorrow, a world that, because of man, is sinful. He goes back to concepts of the Old Testament (Jer 31:20: "My heart yearns [in pain]" with mercy for the sinner)[1] that are heightened in the Cross of Christ, which finds its purest exposition in Luther but also finds a significant preliminary understanding in the soul of Japan.[2] Like the previous two authors, he criticizes Hegel for not giving appropriate weight (in "absolute knowledge") to the theology of the pain of God.[3] God's

---

[43] *Ibid.*, 294–300.   [44] *Ibid.*, 32.

[1] K. Kitamori, *Theologie des Schmerzes Gottes*, (Japanese 1st ed. 1946; German ed., Göttingen: Vandenhoeck und Ruprecht, 1972) 17: "God's will to love the object of his anger—this is the pain of God." Luther: "Da streyded Got mit Got" ["God wrestles with God"].

[2] *Ibid.*, 131ff.   [3] *Ibid.*, 25ff.

pain is immanent in the pain of the world (he regrets that Greek tragedy had no influence on the Church Fathers!),[4] but since the world's pain is rooted in sin, and God is bent upon dealing with sin, God's pain at the same time transcends the pain of the world, "enwraps it" and "holds it fast".[5]

God's pain has two aspects. The first is grounded in the fact that, since it is hostile to him, God is bound to meet sin with his anger, yet he must cause this anger to be overtaken by his love for the sinner, in faithfulness to the Covenant. The second aspect is "necessarily" implied in the first: in order to make possible this painful transition from anger to love, that is, to justify the sinner and love him, God must do the most painful thing imaginable according to our worldly understanding: he must send his own Son to suffering and death.[6] Like Moltmann, Kitamori takes the Cross as his starting point: "The being of God can be understood only on the basis of the word of the Cross"; this is the primary affirmation, compared with which "the Father's generation of the Son is secondary, necessary . . . only to make the primary affirmation possible."[7] "The God of the Gospel is the Father-God who allows his Son to die; by doing so he suffers pain."[8] Thus the two sides of the pain of God are one: "*In the first place*, God's pain is his will to love the unlovable. *In the second place*, God's pain is his will to allow his own beloved Son to go to his death."[9] "The former testifies to the pain of *God*, the latter to the *pain* of God."[10] Insofar as the sinner comes under God's righteous anger, hell is in God,[11] but the sign that this hell has been vanquished is Christ's descent into hell.[12]

---

[4] *Ibid.*, 130.   [5] *Ibid.*, 103.

[6] "The extreme expression of human pain in this world is when parents have to let their beloved child undergo pain and death": *ibid.*, 45.

[7] *Ibid.*, 44: "The concept of the pain of God contains—as its necessary, constitutive element—the historical existence of Jesus, *although the latter seems to contradict this concept*": 31. Therefore "God's entering into our world already betokens his death": 40. The Son, by being "let go", is already doomed to death, cf. 46. On the over-stressing of the doctrine of the immanent Trinity, in which "something crucial got lost", cf. 128–30.

[8] *Ibid.*, 44. He finds the classical notion of "essence" problematical, but also the concepts *generatio* and *processio*: 45.

[9] *Ibid.*, 90.   [10] *Ibid.*, 80.

[11] *Ibid.*, 60.   [12] *Ibid.*, 60.

Kitamori's view of sin arises from the influence on him of the Buddhist Kyoto School (Nishido, Tausbe, Hatano) and of Luther:[13] sin is love that clings to itself, which both is and produces pain. This love is an essential attribute of man in the world; the Christian who knows of the selfless pain of love that is found in God is meant to cleanse worldly love of its selfishness. He is to do this by putting his own pain into the "service" of God's pain[14] until "our pain becomes a *symbol* of the pain of God".[15] This is a surrender of self (going beyond Buddhist mysticism) that combines mysticism and ethics in a Pauline "*con-dolere*" with God.

Kitamori sees a preparation for this theology—a preparation he regards as indispensable "for the whole world"—in the "*tsurasa*" of the great Japanese tragedies of the Tokugawa period (1600–1868). Here, in the spirit of the Bushido, the ethics of the Samurai, loyalty to the Prince means being prepared to sacrifice one's most beloved possession, for instance, one's own child.[16] However, Kitamori is also aware of the limitations of this preparation: "Even Japanese tragedy is unacquainted with the pain associated with that love which loves someone unworthy of love and even goes as far as loving one's enemy."[17]

It must be said, by way of criticism, that Kitamori very emphatically locates God's pain in his "essence", whereas, he says, "in the orthodox doctrine of the Trinity God's 'essence' has become an essence that has lost its essence."[18] It is hard to see, given this kind of statement, what is meant by expressions such as "the divine decision to implement the redemption" or "God

---

[13] Cf. the illuminating remarks of Bettina Oguro-Opitz, "Analyse und Auseinandersetzung mit der Theologie des Schmerzes Gottes von Kazoh Kitamori", in *Europ. Hochschulschriften*, series 23, vol. 133 (Frankfurt/Berne/Cirencester, U.K.: Peter Lang, 1980), 11ff. On the role of Amida Buddhism: 70f.

[14] Kitamori, *Theologie*, 47ff.

[15] *Ibid.*, 57.

[16] *Ibid.*, 132ff., Oguro-Opitz, "Analyse", 42ff. Kitamori gives a closer analysis of the *tsurasa*. It seems that he is not aware how close the problems involved in Japanese drama are to those of Corneille, for instance. Cf. Reinhold Schneider's study: *Corneille's Ethos in der Ära Ludwigs XIV.* (Leipzig: Insel, 1940).

[17] Kitamori, *Theologie*, 138. He pays great attention to the example of Abraham: 47f.

[18] *Ibid.*, 43.

in his relation to the world".[19] If our reflection proceeds (as in the case of Moltmann) exclusively from the perspective of the Cross, the divine freedom to create the world becomes questionable (just as Moltmann questions it). In Kitamori, furthermore, contrary to Moltmann and Koch, the Resurrection of Jesus has no part to play; the Christian religion ministers exclusively to the pain of God.[20]

If we are to go beyond the inadequacies of these views, we need to do two things. First, we must guarantee God's freedom in his commitment to the created world and particularly to the Covenant. This, furthermore, is insufficient unless—second— we can identify, in the Trinity, the basis for attributing to God things like pain and death. What the following suggestions have in common is that, avoiding a confusion of God and the world process, they attribute to God, impassible in his essence, a passibility that he himself has willed.

δ. *Outlines of Creation and Covenant Theology*

BERTRAND R. BRASNETT: "THE SUFFERING OF THE IMPASSIBLE GOD". In its title, *The Suffering of the Impassible God*, by the Scottish Episcopalian B. R. Brasnett,[1] repeats the patristic formula; but it brings in all the modern problems under this heading. His prime concern is the inner relationship between God, who is absolute and creates in utter freedom, and his creation, which is planned from all eternity and also (in man) operates freely; accordingly, his essay (which includes a treatment of the Incarnation and the

---

[19] *Ibid.*, 42.

[20] Possibly the best way to understand the formula "dolor contra dolorem" (i.e., the more profound pain of love of the heart of God, carrying and enduring everything, as compared to the pain of the world) is to see it in the context of the attempt to overcome Buddhism. Kitamori is unaware that the fundamental intuition is found in Gregory Thaumaturgus, for whom God is not only the death of Death but also the suffering of Suffering (cf. J. K. Mozley, *The Impassibility of God: A Survey of Christian Thought* [Cambridge: University Press, 1926], 64–68).

On these and analogous approaches, cf. the summary of H. G. Link: "Gegenwärtige Probleme einer Kreuzestheologie. Ein Bericht" in *Ev. Theol.* 33 (1973), 337–45.

[1] London: SPCK, 1928.

Holy Spirit) can stand as an example of a study in the "theology of creation". Insofar as God's will for the world remains unshakably constant in the face of all vicissitudes and always envisages the good, God must be called "impassible". This is demanded by every religious sentiment.[2] But since God is profoundly involved in his creation, which sinfully resists him, the latter renders him passible, since he has, as it were, handed himself over to the work of his hands.[3] Against Baron von Hügel he asserts that it is not enough to posit a mere "sympathy without suffering".[4] The Son's Incarnation, and perhaps even more the hidden grieving of the Holy Spirit[5] ("for the Holy Spirit is the Lord of Pain") proves that the entire Trinity is involved in the work of creation. Furthermore, since God always knows in advance what awaits him in his work, he is "dependent upon his creation", not from outside, as it were, but on the basis of his own, free conception of it; and hence it causes him suffering.[6] It is impossible today to return to the idea of a God who is unmoved in the face of his world's suffering (whether or not this suffering has been unleashed by sin)[7]—even if we can speak only by analogy of the mystery of God's feeling pain.[8] For God's suffering as he envisages, beholds and looks back at his world is an integral part of his blessedness. Consequently, if man's ultimate ideal is a sharing in the divine blessedness, we shall have to correct our notion of this "eternal blessedness";[9] and in doing so we shall have to go farther than Origen's celebrated intuition, where he

---

[2] *Ibid.*, 11. On the attempt to get beyond patristic Christology (Christ is impassible as God but passible as man), cf. 34: "We frankly abandon that difficult conception of the early Church." The fundamental concept of his theology of creation emerges when he describes the suffering of Christ, not as his bearing of the world's sin, but primarily as the manifestation, in time, of God's "eternal" suffering: 35f. At the same time Brasnett is anxious not to set up God's "eternity" in contradiction to time: 80–89.

[3] *Ibid.*, 6.   [4] *Ibid.*, 115–40.

[5] *Ibid.*, 24–66.

[6] *Ibid.*, 73, cf. 71: "Whilst yet it was far away the black shadow of its (sin's) coming was grief to an all-knowing God."

[7] *Ibid.*, 71.   [8] *Ibid.*, 16, 167f.

[9] "We are disposed to believe that if suffering be a part of the life of God, a painless bliss can hardly be the heaven of the followers of God": 69.

says that all heaven cannot attain perfect bliss "until I, the least of all sinners, have been converted".[10] Nor can suffering remain as an aspect in blessedness that is negatively-positively "elevated", "let pain be placed as it is . . . in the highest bliss of man."[11]

Brasnett wishes to guarantee full freedom to the Creator; but God "finds more joy in a maculate creation than in an immaculate void",[12] and if freedom is the highest good of the creature, sin will be inevitable.[13] Does this not imply, however, that God is a priori bound to the world in such a way that suffering becomes an inner feature of God's "essence", as in the systems we have already discussed? God would be impassible by transcending the world, but he would remain "cold, dead, static, immobile, passionless"[14] if he were not immanent in his creation, and more deeply immanent in it than it can be to itself.

KARL BARTH: GOD'S TRINITARIAN SUFFERING IN CHRIST. Karl Barth refines the approaches of Brasnett and others through the deliberately christological foundation he lays. Jesus Christ, the center of God's covenant history with Israel and mankind, is not only the subjective point of departure for every genuine knowledge of the living God; he is also, in God's predestination, the objective ground and goal for the very existence of the Covenant, which is in turn the "internal basis" for creation.[1] Here Jesus Christ is to be understood quite concretely as the man whose life story, right from the start, is a the story of a death.[2] His death testifies to God's uttermost faithfulness to the Covenant, for in it God himself takes over the faithlessness of Israel and mankind: in it he adopts their situation of complete lostness.[3]

---

[10] Origen, *Lev. Hom.* 7, 1–2 (Baehrens VI, 370–80).

[11] Brasnett, *Suffering*, 70: "Any pain is good which is in accordance with the mind of God, and which is being borne to aid in the achieving of his will": 18.

[12] *Ibid.*, 71. [13] *Ibid.*, 73.

[14] *Ibid.*, 9.

[1] *Church Dogmatics* (Edinburgh, 1936), sec. 41, III/1, 42–329 (hereafter abbreviated CD). On what follows, see Burghard Krause, *Leiden Gottes—Leiden des Menschen: Eine Untersuchung zur Kirchlichen Dogmatik Karl Barths*, Calwer Theolog. Monographien 6 (Stuttgart: Calwer, 1980).

[2] CD I/1, p. 444.

[3] CD II/2, secs. 32–35, pp. 3–506. As the God of the Covenant and the Cov-

Hence God's abandonment of Jesus is not only the central act of God's reconciliation with the world—which includes the revelation of creation's meaning and of its hope of redemption: the Crucified is the image of the invisible God[4] and hence, too, the image of God's "Passion".[5]

At this point we encounter a first and crucial affirmation: in suffering, God *acts*, since by doing so he is only remaining faithful to his own decision to carry out to the very end the Covenant freely entered by him. In this way judgment, which is executed on the Cross in the person of the one man who stands for all the others, is taken into the service of grace. True, in entering into the reality of sin God goes into a "far country",[6] but even there he "is no stranger to himself"[7] and suffers no loss of himself,[8] no inner contradiction (as Moltmann has formulated it). Nor can we speak of a conflict in God between anger and love, as Kitamori does. Man's freedom to sin does not strike God like an event coming from outside: it is always anticipated and overtaken by God's decision and goal. God remains the one who acts, even when allowing himself to be mistreated.[9] In the Cross he is the "attacker" even before sin attacks him.[10] Accepting suffering and submission, he shows that he is above it. God, in his essence, never becomes dependent on the world.

This brings us to a second fundamental point: How can God's (apparently supralapsarian) commitment to suffering, in Christ, come about without becoming an (apparently infralapsarian) dependent reaction to the contingency of human sin? Or perhaps we should say, "without upstaging human freedom and making it into a mere parenthesis, a trivial interlude"? Barth has been faced with this question from various sides.[11] He refuses,

---

enant Partner, God in Christ endures the conflict *in his own self*; cf. CD II/1, 412–22.

[4] CD II/2, 99.

[5] CD IV/1, 164ff., cf. 187.

[6] CD IV/1, sec. 59, 1. (157ff.)

[7] CD IV/1, 180.

[8] CD IV/1, 186f.

[9] CD IV/1, 254.

[10] Cf. CD II/2, 125. Cf. III/3, 363ff.

[11] For a critique of Barth's Christology, cf. Hans Urs von Balthasar, *The Theology*

however, to allow the "contingency aspect" of his doctrine of predestination to be separated from the aspect of "continuity" within God's consistently maintained primal decision; in general the doctrine of election (*Church Dogmatics* II/2) must not be divorced from Christology (*Church Dogmatics* IV) and its retelling of revelation (which is essentially narrative and not a matter of systematic deduction).[12] According to Barth, it is not a matter of some "eternal suffering within God's trinitarian life that, on the Cross, is simply repeated" and given external representation: in and for himself God does not experience any distress that he needs to avert or from which he needs to turn away.[13] By saying that all sins are swallowed up in the Cross, Barth has left himself open to the charge of teaching apokatastasis,[14] but he has always dismissed this charge with the (perhaps not very convincing) observation that salvation history is not yet concluded and that he is only stressing that God's word must be consistent with itself right to the end.[15]

Nonetheless, the suffering of Christ interprets the whole essence of God, and in particular the heart of the Father who, out of love, gives up his Most Beloved.[16] "In Jesus Christ God himself—the Father with the Son in the unity of the Spirit—has himself suffered what this Man was given to suffer to the bitter end. . . . What are all the sufferings of the world, what are the sufferings of Job beside this suffering of God himself, which is the whole meaning of the event of Gethsemane and Golgotha?"[17] The Father is no mere spectator of the Passion. "No,

---

of *Karl Barth* (San Francisco: Ignatius Press, Communio Books, 1992) 242 and passim. E. Gloege regards him as "indifferent to history": "Die Versöhnungslehre Karl Barths" in *Heilsgeschehen und Welt*, Theol. Traktate I (Göttingen, 1965), 162; in similar vein: E. Bueß, "Zur Prädestinationslehre Karl Barths" in *Theol. Studien* 43 (Zurich, 1955), 47. Otherwise, after all, the history of revelation, with Christ's suffering at its apex, is ultimately imported into God's essence: O. Weber, *Grundlagen der Dogmatik* II (Neukirchen, 1962), 184.

[12] Cf. Krause, *Leiden Gottes*, 101ff., 143.

[13] CD II/1, 322.

[14] E. Brunner, *Dogmatik* (Zurich, 1946), 375–79.

[15] CD II/2, 306ff.   [16] CD IV/2, 751ff.

[17] Cf. CD IV/3, 461ff.

there is a *particula veri* in the teaching of the early Patripassians. This is that primarily it is God the Father who suffers in the offering and sending of His Son, in His abasement." "But He does suffer it [the suffering of the Son] in the humiliation of His Son with a depth with which it never was or will be suffered by any man—apart from the One who is His Son. And He does so in order that, having been borne by Him in the offering and sending of His Son, it should not have to be suffered in this way by man. This fatherly fellow-suffering of God is the mystery, the basis, of the humiliation of His Son; the truth of that which takes place historically in His crucifixion."[18] Barth rejects talk of a "death of God" as a "misuse of *perichoresis*", and he also rejects the idea that, after Christ's temporal sufferings, God continues, as it were, to suffer eternally (rather than proceeding to the victory of the Resurrection): God leaves death "behind him".[19]

The center of Barth's reflection is found in the theology of the Covenant, of which he sees the theology of creation as a part. In the background he often speaks of the "analogy" by which God's life in the Trinity is translated into the terms of salvation history. Because of this, the Son's "form of obedience" within the Godhead becomes the precondition for his acceptance of Incarnation and the Cross.[20] However, Barth's reticence in the field of the divine processions within the Trinity will not allow him to go any farther here.

JEAN GALOT: THE QUESTION OF THE PAIN OF GOD. In his book *Dieu souffre-t-il?*,[1] P. Galot takes up the theme of the pain of God, emphasizing its current relevance.[2] He deliberately and courageously opposes the long tradition of God's *apatheia*, though not

---

[18] CD IV/2, 357. At this point E. Jüngel supports Barth: "Sin is aggression against God. So it led to death and was death's 'sting'. By *enduring* this sting, by *bearing* this negation directed against him, God has deprived death of its power. God is not someone who is above suffering but someone who can suffer *infinitely* and who actually does suffer infinitely for the sake of his love. In this way he is victor over death" (*Tod* [Stuttgart: Kreuzverlag, 1971], 142–43).

[19] Cf. Krause, *Leiden Gottes*, 182–85.

[20] Texts in *ibid.*, 174ff.

[1] Paris: Lethielleux, 1976.

[2] *Ibid.*, 195.

without taking refuge behind J. Maritain's celebrated 1969 essay[3] in which the Thomist adopts a position contrary to Thomas and the aforesaid tradition.

According to Galot, an examination of the Fathers and, even more, of Scholasticism and modern theology (he discusses Déodat de Basly, L. Seiller, but Galtier as well) comes up with nothing particularly useful beyond the already well-known formulae of the "two natures" and the "*communicatio idiomatum*" between the passible, human nature of Christ and his impassible, divine nature. Furthermore, it does not do justice to the Old Testament Scriptures[4] or, in particular, to the implications of the New Covenant: according to this, the whole Trinity accomplishes the Incarnation, which is already a kenosis on the part of the Son; the Son's whole life, and his Passion most of all, is both a work of the Father and a revelation of him; the Father, the perfect Abraham, surrenders his Son (cf. the parable of the Vineyard).[5] Galot points out that there is a certain reversal[6] of perspectives vis-à-vis the received theories of atonement: the one who sacrifices is actually the Father who surrenders his Son;[7] in his love, however, he accepts from himself and from the Church the Son thus surrendered to mankind as a sacrifice for mankind's sin. Thus the Son acts "two roles": he is the "revealer of the Father's suffering"[8] (this does away with the need for any Anselmian "compensation"), and "secondarily" he is the offering of the world, through the Son, to the Father. "Le premier rôle est le plus décisif, mais il comporte l'implication du second."[9]

This raises the question of how far God is affected by sin and pain in the world. Galot discovers several levels. He wants firmly to hold on to the unchangeability of God's essence (and

---

[3] "Quelques réflexions sur le savoir théologique" in *Rev. Thom.* 77 (1969), 5–27, here quoted from reprint in *Approches sans entraves*, ed. E. R. Korn (Fayard, 1973), 292–326.

[4] Galot, *Dieu*, 119–22, 164f.

[5] *Ibid.*, 38–118.

[6] *Ibid.*, 184.

[7] *Ibid.*, 95.

[8] *Ibid.*, 189.

[9] *Ibid.*, 190.

not only his Covenant faithfulness).[10] So he distinguishes between the necessary trinitarian life of God, which cannot be affected by any pain, and the free decision of the Divine Persons to create, out of pure love, a world that can involve these Persons in pain.[11] Secondly, the mysterious[12] suffering of the Divine Persons is more than a "metaphor" (as Maritain calls it): there is a real analogy between world pain and divine pain,[13] but in such a way that the divine pain, as a mode of the highest love in God, should be regarded as pertaining to his perfection;[14] this suffering —N.B., it is *real* suffering—is located within the embrace of the divine joy.[15] Examples from human life show us that great maturity and satisfaction cannot be attained apart from suffering.[16] God, so to speak, is the first innocent Sufferer; thus he provides a measuring rod for all world pain and its meaning, which is ultimately located in the realm of atonement and "satisfaction".[17] Thirdly (though hesitantly and tentatively, since it does not fit in with his basic approach),[18] Galot wonders whether "the bond between love and pain" might after all have its foundation in the inaccessible intimacy of the life of the Trinity.[19] This he finds suggested in the reciprocal "ecstatic love" of the Persons, who "bring forth one another through 'reciprocal surrender of self' ". "The ecstasy is not painful in itself, it is the pure power of love. But the innermost self-renunciation that it implies, and which is part of the ardor of self-surrender, can be regarded as the primal origin of those renunciations that are bound up with

[10] *Ibid.*, 155ff., in opposition to Heribert Mühlen, *Die Veränderlichkeit Gottes als Horizont einer künftigen Christologie: Auf dem Wege zu einer Kreuzestheologie in Auseinandersetzung mit der altkirchlichen Christologie* (Münster, 1970), and J. Kamp, *Souffrance de Dieu, vie du monde* (Tournai, 1971).

[11] Galot, *Dieu*, 166ff. "La possession inaltérable de ce bonheur (éternel, trinitaire) n'a pas empêché les personnes divines de s'exposer la souffrance": 167.

[12] *Ibid.*, 169: "Le mystère est irréductible".

[13] *Ibid.*, 147ff.

[14] *Ibid.*, 150–53, 173.

[15] *Ibid.*, 172f.

[16] *Ibid.*, 181.

[17] "La seule certitude est celle de la finalité rédemptrice de la souffrance": *ibid.*, 201.

[18] Thus he completely rejects Kitamori's thesis: *ibid.*, 175 n.

[19] *Ibid.*, 174.

love for humanity and that, as such, have a painful side."[20] This insight on Galot's part, reflecting much of what we have said in the present work (cf. *Theo-Drama* IV, 313, 322f.) will find its place in our conclusion.

ε. *A Basis in the Immanent Trinity.* If the concept of "foundation" is to attain its full meaning when we speak of the Divine Persons' relation to the world, we should not make such an abrupt distinction as Galot does (in a way that almost recalls Gregory Palamas) between a divine inner life that is completely untouched and the Trinity's relation to the world that *is touched*, at least "affectively", if not "effectively".[21] While Galot widely uses *Maritain's* reflections, he could have profited from them further at this point. Noting that the pain that comes to us in the world "imparts to us an incomparably fruitful and precious nobility"[22] and that it has its origin, by analogy, in God, as attested by Scripture (*viscera misericordiae*), Galot endeavors to identify this essential attribute in God. We have no name for it: in contrast to our suffering and grief, it implies no imperfection; we can perhaps speak of it as "the triumphant seizing, adopting and overcoming" of pain, even of death. "Sin does something to God that reaches his divine depths, not by causing him to suffer something caused by the creature, but by causing the creature in its relationship with God to migrate to the side of that unnamed divine perfection, that eternal prototype in him, which in us is pain."[23] Maritain regards it as part of the incomprehensible paradox of the divine blessedness that "its flames are simultaneously the eternal glory of triumphant possession . . . and the eternal glory of triumphant acceptance", which latter has been made known to us in the suffering and death of the Crucified and also, for instance, in the tears of Mary at La Salette.[24] So

---

[20] *Ibid.*, 175–76.

[21] Galot adopts this distinction from the *Cursus* of the Salmanticenses (vol. 7, [Paris, 1877], 210). The distinction, which is at variance with the tradition, does not get beyond juridical categories (Galot, *Dieu*, 143–47) yet does provide a way of envisaging God being "inwardly offended".

[22] Maritain, "Réflexions", 307.

[23] *Ibid.*, 311.

[24] *Ibid.*, 312.

Maritain can say that "God 'suffers' with us; indeed, he suffers far more than we do"; he "suffers with us", has com-passion, as long as there is suffering in the world.[25]

We need only trace this intuition of the philosopher Maritain back to the life of the Trinity, and we shall see the aforementioned "foundation" concretely set before us. In his book on the pain of God,[26] *François Varillon* is dissatisfied with the results of Brasnett, Barth, Rahner and Galot: "The notion that God is at the same time immutable in himself but mutable in another does not satisfy the mind. . . . We must at least feel that, in God, becoming is a perfection of being, motion a perfection of rest, and change a perfection of immutability. . . . Can we consider life without movement to be life?" Is not God's eternity an "ever-welling spring?"[27] To return to the trinitarian theme, *Martelet* paraphrases the attitude of Teilhard de Chardin thus: "God is unmoved only insofar as he, as Father, is an eternal *transition* to the Son's otherness in the uniqueness of the Holy Spirit."[28] This has nothing to do with Hegel.[29] H. *Schürmann*, who has made a careful examination of Jesus' own understanding of his death, finds himself obliged ultimately to anchor his work in the context of the Trinity: "In Jesus' God-forsakenness it is not only that he drinks the 'loss of God', the 'failure of God' to the last drop. The 'death of God' actually takes place in him in the *kenosis* and *tapeinosis* of the love of God. . . . Jesus' death does not leave God unscathed, for when we say 'love', we must remember that, out of love for his world, God did not spare his own Son. . . . The ontic possibility for God's self-emptying in the Incarnation and death of Jesus lies in God's eternal self-emptying in the mutual self-surrender of the Persons of the Trinity. Ultimately, the death of Jesus can be understood as a saving event only in the

---

[25] *Ibid.*, 316.

[26] *La Souffrance de Dieu* (Paris: Le Centurion, 1975).

[27] *Ibid.*, 60–61. Varillon quotes many authors: Maritain, Bergson, Péguy, and particularly Lachièze-Rey (68f.) and Nédoncelle (51f.). Laberthonnière, however, should have been included.

[28] "Teilhard et le mystère de Dieu" in *Cahier 7 de la Fondation et Association Teilhard de Chardin* (Paris: Seuil, 1971), 77–102.

[29] "Un chrétien doit pouvoir s'interroger sur la souffrance de Dieu sans transposer Hegel" (*ibid.*).

context of events within the Trinity."[30] *Norbert Hoffmann*, with ever-increasing care, has traced the possibility of Jesus' expiatory "pro-existence" back to the "pro" of the Persons within the Godhead: their reciprocal action on behalf of each other.[31]

This principle is at the very heart of the present volume, which aims to understand eschatology, not anthropocentrically, but theocentrically and in trinitarian terms. Accordingly, the question of whether God in his *theologia* can really be influenced by his *oikonomia*—which, as we know, Karl Barth disputed at the very outset—must be tackled with great caution in what follows. *Meister Eckhart's* "divine death", it must be noted, forms no part of the present topic, for it was envisaged as the third stage of a process of dying to oneself: a first farewell to "created being" was followed by a second farewell to archetypal being in the Logos and finally by a third farewell to uncreated being.[32] Here Eckhart is still speaking of man's pathway to God, not of the internal process in God that the fate of Christ enables us to glimpse.

For the moment we must defer the question of God's suffering in connection with the condemnation of individual creatures in the Judgment. It will be treated when we come to the problems associated with judgment and hell. First of all we must consider

---

[30] *Jesu ureigner Tod* (Herder, 1975), 146f.

[31] Initially in: *Sühne. Zur Theologie der Stellvertretung* (Einsiedeln: Johannes Verlag, 1981), and subsequently in: *Kreuz und Trinität. Zur Theologie der Sühne* (Einsiedeln: Johannes Verlag, 1982).

[32] *Meister Eckhart und seine Jünger: Ungedruckte Texte zur Geschichte der christlichen Mystik*, ed. F. Jostes, 2d ed. (Berlin/New York, 1972), no. 82: no doubt he means "the task of *experiencing* God that is so dear to all contemplation-mysticism of the schools of St. Bernard or the Victorines": A. M. Haas, "Christliche Aspekte des 'Gnothi Seauton': Selbsterkenntnis und mystik" in *Zft f. dt. Altertum u. dt. Lit.* CX, vol. 2 (1981), 89–93. This brings out the connections not only between *Meister Eckhart and Fichte* (E. von Bracken [Würzburg, 1943]), but also between Fichte and the God-is-dead theology and Zen Buddhism (G. F. Borne, *Christlicher Atheismus und radikales Christentum: Studien zur Theologie von Thomas Altizer im Zusammenhang von Ketzereien der Kirchengeschichte, der Dichtung von William Blake und der Philosophie von G. F. W. Hegel* [Munich, 1979]). E. Bloch's *Atheismus und Christentum* is of an entirely different hue: it combines an atheistic Jewish Messianism with elements of gnosticism.

the interweaving of Christ's suffering and the suffering of the Trinity. Here it will be crucial to remember the created world's immanence in God (cf. the beginning of this volume), particularly in his triune life, and the resulting *imagines Trinitatis* in the world; nor must we forget that the divine archetypes retain their full transcendence over against their "types" or "copies" as found in the world.

There are no inbuilt securities or guarantees in the absolute self-giving of Father to Son, of Son to Father, and of both to the Spirit. Humanly speaking, it is a total surrender of all possessions, including Godhead. From the giver's point of view, therefore, it could appear to be an absolute "risk" were it not for the *equally eternal* infinite gratitude he experiences for the reciprocal gift he receives—a gratitude that is ready to give the utmost in response to the giver. (Furthermore, as we have seen, it is not only the Son who shows gratitude to the Father for his Sonship, and not only the Spirit who shows gratitude to both: the Father, too, owes his Fatherhood to the Son who allows himself to be generated, and he also owes his power of "spiration"— of "breathing forth" the Spirit—to the Spirit who allows himself to be breathed forth by Father and Son.) Nor is this, as in Hegel, a play of love without any ultimate seriousness; for the distance between the Persons, within the dynamic process of the divine essence, is infinite, to such an extent that everything that unfolds on the plane of finitude can take place only *within* this all-embracing dynamic process. This is because the Father's generation of the Son gives him an equally absolute and equally free divine being; and the Son's grateful response is made, not to a Father who keeps something back for himself, but to a Father who has given everything he has and is. Thus their total reciprocal self-giving is expressed and "breathed forth" in the mutual "We" of the Spirit, who is absolute freedom, love and gift—and selflessly so, since he is only the expression of the Father-Son unity. This is God's "blood circulation", the mutual exchange of blood between the Persons that, as we began by saying, is the basis for there being a "death" in God. He is beyond life and death as known in the world, which is demonstrated biblically in Jesus' Resurrection from the dead (for he takes his "death" with him into his eternal life)[33]; he is the living "lamb as it were slain" of the Book of Revelation. "It is only because pain and death are internal to God, as a fluid form of love, that God can conquer death and pain by his death and Resurrection. . . . Pain and death are superseded, not in virtue of some eternal indifference on the part of God's essence, but because, by his absolute free will, pain and death are eternally the language of his glory (and this applies even to the cry of death, the silence of death, and to *being* dead itself). Of course this must not lead to the view that the Son, in his life in the world, has already —from all eternity—finished and dealt with pain and suffering. On the contrary, both are innermost modes of love, as we see from Jesus' defenselessness, giving himself into the hands of men and learning through obedience what the Son eternally is."[34]

This means, however, that we have in fact overstepped the limits of what we mean by "tragedy"—although the word retains its validity in its own sphere. For in itself, however baffling it may be to the finite mind, the all-embracing reality within which "tragedy" is played out is—eternal blessedness.

---

[33] E. Jüngel, *Tod* (Stuttgart: Kreuzverlag, 1971), chaps. 5 and 6.
[34] Ferdinand Ulrich in a personal letter to the author.

B. THE FINAL ACT:
A TRINITARIAN DRAMA

1. The Descent of the Son

a. Existence in Time as a
Representation of Eternal Life

God the Father has not created the world by "turning outward",
but by turning to the Son within the divine life.[1] This implies
that when the Son definitively embraces the world in his Incarnation and enters the sphere of time, he does not leave eternal
life behind.[2] "God's eternal inward life is so alive that it cannot be passed on in any naturebound form, such as fleshly life."
Thus, "At the birth of eternal life the Holy Spirit always plays
his part. He was there at the birth of the Son into the world,
which, precisely because he took part in it, was an event of eternal life . . . and therefore did not step out of eternal life at all.
But because, all the same, it was a birth in our temporal world,
we receive through this birth a share in eternal life"—which is
thereby opened up to us. Jesus prays, "this is eternal life, that
they know thee the only true God, and Jesus Christ whom thou
hast sent" (Jn 17:3): if this knowledge is informed by faith and
love, eternal life has already begun. This kind of knowledge is
"a true and immediate presentation of eternal life". What is revealed in the Son "is not a human ideal, but divine, eternal life".[3]

So it is that the perfect obedience of the Son, who wants to
do nothing else on earth but the will of the Father who sent
him (Jn 6:38), is both the means and the content of his eternal
relationship with the Father. In the sending of the Son we are
brought closer to the idea of the Father[4] and so, too, to the idea

---

[1] "The Father creates the world with a view to the Son, not by turning (for
once) outward. On the contrary, it is with a view to the Son, to the inner life of
the Godhead, that God creates the world": Cardinal Hermann Volk, *Vollendung
des Lebens—Hoffnung auf Herrlichkeit* (Mainz: Grünewald, 1979), 21.

[2] See the section on Christ's time, pp. 125–28.

[3] 3 Jo 307.

[4] A 51–52.

of the divine attitude of the Son: "The Son has the difficult task on earth of combining a full, unabridged human life with his divine nature, in such a way that his mission remains divine and yet achieves a visibility which is evident to men and women, enabling them to shape their lives according to it."[5] This is possible only if, in full divine freedom, the Son chooses his path to mankind, and chooses it on the basis of his own offer to the Father, with a view to the Father's acceptance of this offer and his command to act upon it.[6] Freedom and obedience coincide in the mission of the Son,[7] not only in the life of the Incarnate One but in the very act of his becoming incarnate.[8] "It is in obedience that God's Son becomes man, and his entire human life remains the expression of his first obedience", which "is embedded in a mystery between the Son and the Father".[9]

So there is a perfect adequacy, perfect correspondence between the word of the man Jesus and the Word of God: "He himself, as the Word of the Father, speaks the language of earth." He becomes a transducer, a transformer of the Word in both directions.[10] He himself is the divine Word in the human word, which means that his whole life becomes an "utterance",[11] and life and action become identical;[12] consequently we can say that the relation between Word and word is actually "super-adequate",[13] just as, on the other hand, "the Body of the Word of God is something concrete that becomes super-concrete through the words of consecration" and "gives us a share in the eternity of

[5] KW 45.

[6] W 153; cf. Ka II, 174–75.

[7] A 74–75.

[8] "The Son's Incarnation and birth is itself an act of divine obedience. . . . His divine obedience deliberately humbles itself, so to speak, by becoming a purely human obedience." Since the twelve year-old boy's parents do not understand his words, "they too are drawn into a more exacting obedience, as is Jesus himself, thus in humility allowing his divine obedience to become a human obedience": Gh 36–38.

[9] Gh 67.

[10] G 91.

[11] Ka II, 22.

[12] Bi 83.

[13] Ps 49.

the infinite God".[14] As man, the Son lives a life that is constantly being "translated" back and forth; this task of "translation" is so demanding that it can only be done in the Holy Spirit: "He was supposed not only, as God, to be man, but also, as man, to be God; he was not only allowed to humble himself, but also had always to elevate himself, and between humbling and elevating there was no fixed mean, but rather a constant movement, for which, to be sure, his divine spirit was strong enough, but for which his flesh would have been inadequate had it not received constantly new invigoration from the Holy Spirit."[15] This constant "translation" had to be *lived*: "The sole reason that he could allow the Word to keep his entire greatness was because it was through his *life* that he undertook the mediation between heaven and earth";[16] even in his smallest acts "he brought heaven down to earth."[17] Indeed, he brings with him the whole of eternity, not only "that which is to come", whither he is bound, but also the eternity "that lies 'behind' him", from which he comes.[18] Initially it may seem that Christ alone possesses this art of representing the eternal in the dimensions of time, but he can communicate it to those who revere and follow him; he can "put the imprint of eternity" on their lives.[19] In his coming he brings the kingdom of God with him, for this kingdom is "his heaven, his eternal life, his will. The whole kingdom is embodied in him", so that when people "seek for the kingdom of God, they find the Son. He, however, does not present them with it as the epitome of his person but as a sober concept, so that they see that all things lead to the Father." He himself "comes from heaven and is going to heaven", but not only as an invidual: for "he has already accomplished his coming from heaven through the mediation of a human being." He "invites us, as it were, to take the path back to the Father along with him. By accompanying

[14] G 92. This "super-adequacy" is simultaneously the result of an effort of obedience: "As man the Son must come to grips with the fullness of the Word that he himself is": M 49.

[15] 4 Jo 103–4.

[16] 3 Jo 321.

[17] C 308.

[18] Ka I, 174.

[19] G 33–42.

him, we show that we are seeking heaven, the kingdom of the
Father. The Father is in eternal life, and the time of his heaven is
eternal time; in seeking this eternal time we are joining the Son
in seeking the kingdom in the super-time of eternal life. From
the moment we begin seeking it, we have already found it in the
Son. So even today, in this world, we are sharers in eternal life."[20]
The presence of the Son is the presence of eternity in time. This
is a factor that transforms the world: "Through him, the relationship of the Father to creatures is altogether changed."[21]

All these reflections on the Christ-event are meant to lead
to this realization: If, in Jesus Christ, eternal life has genuinely
penetrated the world's temporal sphere, this temporal sphere
does not unfold "outside" eternity but within it.[22] We must
not forget, however, that this, just like the Incarnation, remains
a mystery.[23]

b. Death/Life; Sorrow/Joy

The Son's trinitarian mission, which is always carried out in
obedience and which the Son brings with him from heaven to
earth,[1] is at the same time a mission of reconciling the world to
God. Thus it is a mission "in the likeness of sinful flesh and for
sin in order to condemn sin in [this] flesh" (Rom 8:3); it is a
mission unto death, since death has come about through sin.

It is not that death is "evil". "Death too is willed and created
by God", it is "the seal of God's power set over the life of his
creature". It is "not merely the outward limit of life but permeates the whole course of earthly life. Without the ferment

---

[20] B 225–26.

[21] A 59.

[22] See the section above entitled "Time Is from Eternity and to Eternity", pp.
100–102.

[23] "The contemplative cannot strive for the impossible; he cannot intuitively
behold or conceptually define that mysterious point where the Word becomes
flesh and the flesh becomes the bearer of the Word": Bi 105.

[1] G 54; Gh 36–38; 1 Jo 310: "The Son takes his obedience to the Father with
him into this earthly life so completely that he lives on earth solely from the perfect
unity of will between Father and Son. His obedience is the obedience of a God.
And yet, as such, it also is the model of what the perfect obedience of a man to
God *could* be." Cf. 2 Jo 122–23.

of death, finite life would not be life."[2] "But in another sense
both life and death are images of God. Of course, one cannot
say that death, as an end, is in any sense in God, since his eternal
life is unending. But if death is understood to mean the sacrifice
of life, then the original image of that sacrifice is in God as the
gift of life flowing between Father and Son in the Spirit. For the
Father gives his whole life to the Son, the Son gives it back to
the Father, and the Spirit is the outflowing gift of life."[3] "This
'living death' is the absolute opposite of the death of sin", in
which man closes himself to self-surrender and hence to eternal
life, consigning himself with body and soul to isolation from
this life. "For a man like that, who is really dead, God's eternal
life is deadly." The Son's mission was therefore to take "sinful
death" up into his death of self-surrender, which thus meant that
his death would involve abandonment by God. "In the night of
the Cross God himself, through the Son, experienced abandonment and surrender in the form of sinful death. . . . Thus he
received human death into eternal life."[4] "The mysteries of this
unlimited self-surrender and abandonment on the Cross, and of
the night of darkened understanding, are further forms of God's
supreme vitality, the fulfilment of the life of love. . . . In the
world, death is a limitation, a conclusion, an end. In God, death
is always the beginning of new life."[5]

"The lamb without blemish or spot" was chosen for this atoning death even "before the foundation of the world" (1 Pet 1:19–
20). In no sense, however, can we say that the Father willed men
to crucify the Son; this is a mystery "to which we have no access. We only understand "in faith that this hidden mystery of
God must be a mystery of love".[6] When the Baptist says that
the One he calls the Lamb of God *was* before him (Jn 1:30),
this means that "already as Son in the Father he was the Lamb of
God; his whole way existed already in the Father. His mission is
not temporal; it is already perfected before its beginning. Certainly there is a moment in history in which he suffers. But it is

[2] 1 Jo 42.
[3] 1 Jo 42–43.
[4] 1 Jo 43–44.
[5] 1 Jo 44.
[6] C 64–65; cf. also Ka I, 276–80.

preceded by the timelessness in the bosom of God. Everything eternal taking place in time is itself beyond time and before all time. The greater and deeper something is, the more timeless it is. . . . What is timeless is the real; the temporal is only a shadow of it", a "borrowing".[7] Even if the Incarnation (in its concrete form, which ends with the Cross) is surely occasioned by sin,[8] and Jesus therefore comes into the world in order to die,[9] it is more profoundly true that "even his experience of death is ultimately a life experience": "the experience of surrendering his earthly life to heaven"[10] is the translation into temporal terms of his eternal attitude of devotion to the Father. What is contrary to nature in it is sustained by an act of freedom on his part: "I lay down my life . . . of my own accord. I have power to lay it down, and I have power to take it again" (Jn 10:17)—so much so that the Son's active self-surrender unto death already contains its infallible answer, as in God himself: "If the Lord gives his love to a person, truly gives it, then he receives love in return from this person as an answer. . . . And both the gift of self and what one gains in return are basically one and the same thing. The relationship here is not that between a deed and the payment, which can be distinguished from it. Rather, the ray of life generates of itself an answering ray: everything that goes forth returns necessarily to the point of departure," even if it is not "possible to observe this return in the individual case".[11] In this context, Jesus' death, even his most bitter death in abandonment, is the pure expression of his eternal, trinitarian life.

In principle this implies something else, something harder to grasp, namely, that his whole suffering—a suffering that goes to the utter limits—follows from and actually expresses his eternal, triune joy. Many of Paul's words offer us a way of access to this

---

[7] 1 Jo 144.

[8] Ka I, 68; Ka II, 98 ("The whole purpose was to take sin away")–99. "It is because of our sins that the Father has given us eternal life by adapting the life of the Son to our earthly life": Ka II, 217. Cf. C 308.

[9] T 102.

[10] T 100.

[11] 2 Jo 277–78.

paradox. Throughout his entire letter to the Philippians, written in suffering, he expresses pure joy and exhorts his readers to nothing but joy.[12] The beginning of 2 Corinthians speaks explicitly of the consolation God gives in every trial, even when "we share abundantly in Christ's sufferings" (2 Cor 1:4–5). In suffering, just as in death, we must reckon with a basis on the natural level: joy and pain circle around each other in life's turmoil; "neither conceivable without the other, and not merely balancing and neutralizing each other", so that every pain "has its joy within it, or gives birth to joy, and every joy its suffering".[13] Thus the disciples' sorrow at their Lord's departure is inwardly part and parcel of the joy with which the Holy Spirit will fill them when he comes.[14] Even if many suffering believers "no longer experience joy" in their following of Christ, "they too will rejoice in being permitted to suffer." This is a "joy of gratitude" that is anchored so deeply in the Lord "that it does not disappear even when all our power to feel is taken up with suffering."[15] Believers must be brought through the whole spectrum of joy or consolation and suffering or comfortlessness if they are to be given a share in the depths of Christ's love,[16] for "true Christian love is acquainted with both joy and grief."[17] The Passion is therefore the highest act of the Lord's love,[18] just as the birth pangs are for a woman giving birth. "Pain always belongs to woman. But a woman's birth pangs stand between her love for her husband and her love for the child. The Lord, too, causes love to embrace pain. He must include pain, as it were, in order to show his love, in order to satisfy the disciples' expectation—since, at the very moment when his body is stricken with pangs, they desire the fruit of the Eucharist from him." In

---

[12] Ph 10, 90–92. "Every Christian joy (is) embraced in this divine joy and fashioned by it, without limits": 91. Cf. 110, 157: "What now awakens in the hearts of believers is the entire trinitarian joy, . . . for here and now, on earth, it participates in the eternity of heaven." "So Paul can *suffer* in joy as well": K 47.

[13] 1 Jo 22.

[14] 3 Jo 212f.

[15] Ka I, 381; cf. C 530.

[16] W 286–98.

[17] C 145.

[18] 2 Jo 415.

this sense his Passion is womanly, but "it is also manly, because it is his work to suffer on the Cross. . . . And the most manly deed he does on the Cross is, as he dies, to give the Spirit back to the Father. . . . He does not just 'let the Spirit go': he actively hands him back to the Father, thus concluding his mission."[19] It follows quite naturally from this that the Lord thereupon "sends his Church, his Bride, fully conscious into suffering".[20] So too his Eucharist makes present both Cross and Resurrection.[21]

So we must address the difficult task of discerning the fundamental joy that is present even in the Lord's greatest suffering. When he "speaks of his joy . . . in the face of the Cross" (Jn 15:11), he does so because he "rejoices at being allowed to serve God and mankind".[22] "The truer the love is, the more joyful it is in all its suffering. . . . Every love, even the earthly and physical, can be true joy if it does not selfishly close itself, but opens toward God"; even mourning at a graveside can be joy, "for the lover knows that the beloved has gone to God and rejoices in the Lord."[23] "But if God wants the lover to suffer on behalf of a sinner—perhaps extremely—he will tell him himself. He will then be granted permission to suffer in the joy of the Lord."[24] Christian grief, ecclesial grief, is quite proper if it is a sharing in the grief of the Lord who, on the Mount of Olives, utters "a Yes in sorrow, laden with the most extreme burden of suffering"; but beyond this suffering "it is a Yes in the glory of love, in the joy of surrender."[25] It is by no means suggested that, while he bears sin, the Son can actually feel this glory, this joy; but it does not alter the fact that joy is the consistent presupposition for all experience of forsakenness. On the Cross, the lived reality of death, objectively, is life; so extreme suffering, objectively, is joy.

"Death and life form a unity in us, like the faces of Janus. God requires both things from us: dying and living, renunciation and

---

[19] Pa 102–3.
[20] Pa 107.
[21] C 346–47.
[22] 3 Jo 179.
[23] 3 Jo 179–80.
[24] 3 Jo 181.
[25] 3 Jo 229.

acceptance. . . . He makes the unity of death and life visible on the Cross: he adopted a human life in order to die on the Cross, and he dies on the Cross in order to rise again in the Father."[26] The Son "shares fully in whatever the Father possesses, including his joy". When, on the Cross, he redeems the world in order to complete the Father's joy, he does so "in the joy of the Father, but also in his own joy of giving the Father a gift. Yet in the midst of this joy there lies all the suffering of the Cross, which is not thereby lessened. 'If it be possible, let this cup pass from me': these are words of fear that, on the Cross, turn into words expressing his forsakenness. Nonetheless the whole darkness of suffering—even though it is the greatest suffering that ever was —is embraced, as it were, in the encompassing joy." For his part the Father "cannot give any answer, because he desires to give the Son perfect joy, namely, the joy of having died for him in the experience of forsakenness".[27]

It is easy for us to forget that a Divine Person, even in the Incarnation and in the vicissitudes of his human 'I', is nevertheless pure relation and that God's blessedness consists in his *being* self-surrender. Bearing this mind, we can draw the following conclusion: When the Son accepts dying in the agony of God-forsakenness, it is for him (and the other Divine Persons) not only an "external work" undertaken out of absolute love and joy but also the expression of his very own, his very specific life. "He who hates his life in this world will keep it for eternal life" (Jn 12:25): but, right from the outset, the eternal life that the Son brings into this life explodes the self-reference of an egoistic "I"; it *is* perfect self-surrender, manifesting itself ultimately in suffering and death. So it is life, a life that rediscovers itself in the Resurrection to eternal life. "The one who hands over his life and saves it up for eternal life will find his earthly life once again in life beyond death; for the earthly life of the Lord, too, continues to live in his eternal life."[28] Thus "night, ultimately, is always a transition."[29] "Through suffering we are continually being brought back to love; suffering keeps us

---

[26] Ka I, 334–35. Cf. the chapter "Die Objektivität der Freude", in M 84–87.
[27] M 82.
[28] 2 Jo 420 (cf. 416–20).
[29] OM 571.

receptive to love."[30] Those who love bear suffering "joyfully, although the feeling of joy remains hidden".[31] Looking at the Lord, we see that suffering lies at a deep level in love. "The love that God shows us in his Son is so great that it embraces not only the joys of love but also its sufferings." Sufferings, understood and accepted as an expression of love, "lead back to God and increase joy"; they bring us "close to the suffering Son"; "the seriousness of suffering teaches us to know the Son at a new and much deeper level. God himself has fashioned these unfathomable depths. When, from the vantage point of the world, we contemplate heaven and think of its blessedness, and its joy over one sinner who repents, and recall that there is on earth a reflection of this joy (which is not its *cause*, for conversion comes from heaven to earth and leads back to heaven), we can begin to sense why changeable human suffering is necessary for heavenly blessedness. Sometimes this thought can even give rise . . . to the will to suffer completely and without any consolation, because God requires it, and because it and nothing else is to be transformed into heavenly joy."[32] The christological application follows quite naturally. "Life and death reciprocally attest the Lord. In his death he is life, and in life he dies. We human beings remain bound to our development and to the time in which we live. But the Lord, even in his existence in time, lives in the 'now' of eternal life; this is something he teaches us through his death and his life." The Eucharist, in particular, "is a sign of concrete eternity. For here death and life coincide."[33]

c. Separation as a Mode of Union

Anyone who reflects on the uniqueness of the relationship between the Son and the Father will have little difficulty in understanding that the Son, as God-man, went through an experience of forsakenness that took him far beyond Sheol and Gehenna. He who "ascended *above* all the (created) heavens" is the same

[30] OM 93.
[31] OM 562.
[32] OM 23–24.
[33] H 69.

who "descended into the lower parts of the earth" (Eph 4:9), and this "lower", *katōtera* (comparative), could only mean, for him, the "lowest" (*en tois katōtatois tēs gēs*).[1] For "at the name of Jesus every knee should bow, in heaven and on earth and under the earth" (Phil 2:10). Such homage is appropriate only for someone who has not only shared the general lot of mortals but has undergone their fate, including every possible remoteness and alienation from God. Such distance is possible, however, only within the economic Trinity, which transposes the absolute distinction of the Persons in the Godhead from one another into the dimensions of salvation history, involving man's sinful distance from God and its atonement.

We have to show, therefore, that the God-forsakenness of the Son during his Passion was just as much a mode of his profound bond with the Father in the Holy Spirit as his death was a mode of his life and his suffering a mode of his bliss. To understand this, we need to grasp what is meant by saying that the Son's divine power and glory is "*laid up*" with the Father. This concept only summarizes what is described in Philippians 2:6–7 and is grounded in the eternal Son's unerring movement to the Father (*eis ton kolpon tou Patros*, Jn 1:18; cf. 1 Jn 1:2). In the Passion "One is in the darkness of the Son. But, at the same time, one is in the light of the Father, for the darkness of the Son consists in the fact that his light is deposited [i.e., "laid up"] with the Father."[2] When the Father's presence was so veiled that the Son experienced God-forsakenness, "the certainty of being the Heir was laid up within his Sonship, ready to be communicated to men as a gift."[3] The concept is bound to have a metaphorical,

---

[1] The Prayer of Manasseh V, 13, in Kautzsch, *Apokryphen* I (1900), 171.
We have the same expression for Sheol/Gehenna in Ps 63:9; Tob 4:19; 13:2; Sir 51:6. On the meaning of the Ephesians passage, cf. Büchsel, *ThWNT*: κατώτερος The Bible de Jérusalem translates this as "Dans les régions inférieures de la terre", noting that this subterranean region is the realm of the dead. Osty gives the same rendering. Baumont speaks of the "deep places of the earth". The German "Unity Translation" simply drops the crucial ὑπεράνω as well as the κατώτερα.

[2] 2 Jo 328.

[3] SL 51 (GT). Cf. Is. 76. On the passage "Whoever walks in darkness, and has no light shining for him, . . . let him lean on his God" (Is 50:10 JB), we have the commentary: "This does not refer to those who stand afar off but to those who,

anthropomorphic side: "Metaphorically speaking, it is as if the Son had separated himself from the Father at the Incarnation, and in doing so had bequeathed everything to the Father: all his love for the Father, . . . all the divine glory he possesses with the Father and finally the pact they had made with each other. All this remained in the Father, as strong and as living as if the Son were still in him—indeed, almost stronger and more living, because the Father now bears for them both the responsibility for what they have resolved to do."[4] This "economic" reality is only the expression of something "immanent" in the Trinity: "Being in the Father is never an obstacle for the Son, a limitation of his independence. It is rather a necessity for him, on the basis of their reciprocal love. This necessity is so urgent that, even at the moment of separation on the Cross, when the earthly observer sees only a man forsaken, the Son's Godhead is laid up with the Father."[5] So the Son, in his High Priestly prayer, can look ahead, beyond the "economic" separation, and ask for the "glory" he had "before the world was made", which he has always had "with you", with the Father.[6] His loving self-surrender to the Father and the surrender of his life for men "are one and the same thing; for his life itself consists of love. But this gift of life and love is so absolute that it already contains eternity in itself, this eternity of the Son's gift of self radiates back into the eternity of the Father's love, and the Son finds himself again in the Father as the one who has been given." The reciprocal self-surrender of Son and Father appear "as something so strong and so good that everything involving separation and suffering and obligation and obedience that is taken up into this is totally absorbed into love, indeed itself becomes love, as if it had never been anything else."[7] This also solves the riddle of the

---

for God's sake, . . . have been set upon the path of suffering. It is the Son himself who enters the night of the Cross on behalf of men. This is the mystery in which the Son's light is laid up with the Father."

[4] 3 Jo 102.

[5] 3 Jo 128 (GT).

[6] 3 Jo 312. "While the Son hangs on the Cross in suffering, his joy—the joy of glorifying the Father through his suffering—is 'laid up' ": Ka I, 382.

[7] 2 Jo 270.

Son's "economic" not-knowing: his divine knowledge is "laid up" with the Father out of obedience. "Everything can be laid up with the Father except obedience itself."[8] Even as a child, for the sake of obedience, he refuses "to make any use of" the perfect knowledge he could have as the God-man; he resolves to "learn" what, in principle, he already knows.[9] "As man he dispenses with his divine knowledge, because his not-knowing is the important thing, the positive thing now. . . . It is a positive thing in him, as man, to be surprised by events, even to be terrified by them, and to commit himself to what is coming as to a vacant abyss, because he trusts in nothing else but God. Any admixture of divine knowledge would be like an anaesthetic preventing him from experiencing human suffering to the limit."[10] What appears to be purely human in the Son's "not-knowing", having "laid up" his divine knowledge with God, has a mysterious anticipation in God himself:

> It is as if there were this kind of mystery of love in God himself, a place where the left hand does not know what the right hand does. This mystery becomes visible in the Son, who as God and man is both right hand and left; as man he does not wish to know what, as God, he knows, so that he can be fully man and can suffer in total self-surrender. So too, as man, he knows things that, as God, he wishes not to know, for instance his suffering on the Cross. . . . And so it must be if the entire redemption is to be effected. As man, in the dereliction of the Cross, he sinks into a timeless night in which he atones for the infinity of sins, while as God his gaze embraces the whole span of redemption.[11]

What we have said about things being "laid up" in God must not suggest, however, that the "separation" which is begun in the Incarnation and reaches its apogee in the Passion is somehow less than totally serious. In fact the reverse is true, as should be clear from the basis of the separation as found in the Trinity: the infinite distinction of Persons within the one Being. In virtue of this distinction, which entails relations within the Trinity and hence facilitates that "laying up" of which we have spoken,

[8] Hj 130.
[9] MH 88.
[10] Is 91–92.
[11] B 151.

the *Cross* can become the "revelation of the innermost being of God".[12] It reveals both the distinction of the Persons (clearest in the dereliction) and the unity of their Being, which becomes visible in the unity of the plan of redemption. Only a God-man, through his distinction-in-relation vis-à-vis the Father, can expiate and banish that alienation from God that characterizes the world's sin,[13] both in totality for all[14] and in totality for each individual.[15] "Every individual sin is expiated individually on the Cross, each one goes through the totality of his wounds; . . . he takes on every sin with his entire body."[16] The Son, as it were, actively gathers unto himself sins,[17] but also the world's pains,[18] and particularly the sufferings of the Old Covenant, which, far from having no significance for redemption, "attain their fulfillment through the Cross".[19] Thus for the Son, as for us, the Cross grows until it exceeds our grasp.[20] Although it is the overcoming of the chaos of sin,[21] it becomes a "pathless",[22] a "worldless"[23] suffering, unveiling the world itself as chaos.[24] In the Cross the

---

[12] 3 Jo 284. Jesus' promise (Jn 16:25) to tell the disciples openly of the Father is actually fulfilled "on the Cross, at the moment when he is most separated from the Father": 3 Jo 283.

[13] "A mere man could not possibly bear the responsibility for the world's guilt before the Father, even if he were to give up his life in the attempt: What would this human life be in relation to the straying of all, the forlornness of all? For that reason alone, the Son must be God on the Cross": A 80.

[14] 2 Jo 390: "The Lord died not only for good persons, who open themselves to him at once, but also for the wicked, who resist him. . . . For not even the wicked person stands outside the sphere of his power, and the dispersion of the Lord embraces and overtakes even the dispersion of the sinners."

[15] 2 Jo 276: "He offered the total sacrifice for each individual." Nor is there any temporal limitation here: "He disposes of it so freely that he can give it away extravagantly to each individual anew, although he will offer it in sacrifice as a whole once for all on the Cross": 2 Jo 279. Therefore "he has also the power to demand his life again from each individual and from all": 2 Jo 280 (on Jn 10:18).

[16] Ka I, 333.

[17] 4 Jo 35, 72; K 101; Mt 135, 153; Gl 55–56; Ka I, 331; Be 32.

[18] Ka I, 165.

[19] B 122.

[20] 2 Jo 389; Is 96; Ka II, 226–27.

[21] A 38.

[22] 3 Jo 331.

[23] 3 Jo 330.

[24] 3 Jo 261.

whole reality of the world's sin in the sight of God is set forth:
it is the primal confession of sin and can therefore be given to
the Church at Easter as a sacrament.[25]

This sin, laid open before God, is finally concentrated in the
crucified Son; so, on the Cross, God's final *judgment* is pronounced upon this sin, which the Son now embodies (cf. 2 Cor
5:21): it is "the one great judgment that takes place once and for
all, which the Son purchases through his suffering". And though
mankind—Christians, pagans, Jews—puts on a sham trial here,
this "parody of judgment" will nonetheless "stand in the service
of the great judgment between Father and Son, where love is to
win the victory in suffering over the sin of the world": "Now
shall the ruler of this world be cast out" (Jn 12:31), but "now,
at the very moment when he is getting ready to win and . . .
when this becomes totally obvious in human terms", when the
kingdom of the Prince of this world is being finally established
and the Lord's defeat is "so shattering that no one—not even
the believers—will be able to avoid accepting its reality"; at that
very moment "everything is reversed."[26]

This reversal is not the result of a divine decision coming
"from outside"; it is made possible by the fact that the Son's
God-forsakenness is drawn into the love relationship within the
Trinity. The Son "takes the estrangement into himself and creates proximity"[27]: nearness between God and man on the basis
of the union between Father and Son that is held fast through every darkness and forsakenness. The Son experienced separation
when he was bearing the world's sin, but "this separation was
not a remoteness from the Father, for he aligned himself continually to the Father, he looked back to the Father constantly in
order to stand in the exact center of his mission."[28] The Holy
Spirit, who embodies the unity of Father and Son, is "the witness who can always testify to their unity even in separation",[29]
and now he is "forever accepting from the Son's hands the sacrifice of his divinity and laying it in the heavenly Father's lap and

---

[25] 3 Jo 346; KW 15f.; B 87; Be 50–62.
[26] 2 Jo 430–31; cf. Is 243.
[27] Ep 107.
[28] 3 Jo 355.
[29] 3 Jo 329.

consciousness".[30] This takes place finally and definitively when
the dying Son gives back the Spirit of his mission in the "last
act of his love".[31] During the Passion the Spirit maintains the
internal divine diastasis between Father and Son in its economic
form, so that "What seems to us to be the sign of separation of
Father and Son is precisely the sign of greatest unification. . . .
The separation that is perceptible to us is the highest proof of
definitive unity, for if they had not been so certain of their unity,
they would not have been able to go as far as the mystery of
the night of the Cross without producing alienation, misunderstanding or the division of truth." Here we see that "there is
only one single truth: the truth of the Son in the Father and of
the Father in the Son."[32] "The Son's cry of dereliction on the
Cross", which demonstrates God's triune love for the world, is
"the loftiest assertion in the knowledge of God" because, "as
night, it is truth's ultimate confirmation."[33] "Now it genuinely
reveals the Father's infinity" and thus is "revelation in its pure
state".[34] "All is made plain", insofar as Father and Son, in the
Spirit, reciprocally and infinitely "surpass each other in love".[35]
Again, this revelation takes place through the presence of the
Holy Spirit, for "since the Spirit is not separated like the Son
from the Father, he can establish union in the separation of the
Son without abolishing the separation";[36] he can cooperate in
such a way that, in the extremity of suffering, "the deepest mystery of the union of the Lord with the Father" persists and is
revealed to faith.[37] Separation from the Father, which begins in
the Incarnation and is completed on the Cross, is "both the being and the teaching" of the Son, since "precisely in the fact
that he is in the world, visibly separated from the Father, visibly
not received by human persons, lies the proof that he dwells
inseparably in the Father."[38] Whether he feels the Father's nearness or, abandoned and enveloped in darkness, is aware only of
"yawning emptiness", both states testify that the separation is
"accomplished to the full only where it is determined by the

---

[30] Mt 154.   [31] Mt 184.
[32] 3 Jo 358.   [33] M 33-34.
[34] G 63.   [35] Ph 74.
[36] 2 Jo 381-82.   [37] 2 Jo 233.
[38] 2 Jo 100.

commission'', so separation is maintained even within the bond that unites them.[39] Such testimony, however, requires that the separation be experienced not only in the body and senses but also spiritually; otherwise the Passion would be "nothing more than a physical procedure that the Son would allow to pass over him." The Son would merely "let a torture come over him in the manner of a Stoic or fakir".[40] There must be reciprocal personal forsakenness on the part of Father and Son, for only then can the "highest possible summit of revelation" be realized and, hence, perfect faith ("this leap into the open dimension").[41] This "absolute paradox" is necessary to make it credible that the Father "does not leave the Son for a moment, even in the final abandonment". The Son is "at the same time united more and more to the Father in this separation, until he is nothing more on the Cross than the revelation of the will of the Father." "What is Two here can be shown only in unity: what is One here can be shown only in duality."[42] "When the Lord says that the Father has never abandoned him (Jn 8:29), this refers . . . also to the Cross: for he will be with the Father even in the greatest abandonment. . . . This will be true even when he no longer knows it. He knows that, in that abandonment, in which the Father too will be abandoned, he will be in absolute unity with him", the highest union possible in love.[43] "Abandonment by the Father attests his nearness. . . . In his nearness the Father shows that he has forsaken the Son, and by forsaking him he shows that he is near to him",[44] even if this is possible only to God and remains unintelligible to "our limited thinking". Nonetheless the "eternal generation" of the Son from the Father "embraces" particularly "the day of the Son's night on the Cross, just as it embraces every day that has been or is yet to come. It is a matter of secondary importance what relationship the Son has to his own power within this relationship with the Father. He may 'lay it up' with the Father, the Father may show it to him, or the Son may wield it and stand before the Father as a victorious Ruler: at all events everything is embraced by the eternal

---

[39] 2 Jo 120.
[41] 2 Jo 183.
[43] 2 Jo 183–84; cf. 2 Jo 270.

[40] 2 Jo 119 (GT).
[42] 2 Jo 165–66.
[44] Ps 50, 52.

mystery of generation." Thus "in Incarnation and Cross, any alienation of the Son from the Father is impossible. . . . The Father has separated from him, as it were, in order to give him the whole world as his own possession. Yet, through it all, the Son's relationship with the Father who generates him remains intact; in fact, everything serves to reveal this eternal relationship. It is a bond that surpasses all worldly bonds, a nearness that spans all distance, a relationship that has the power of eternity within it and is not interrupted by the Son's coming and going."[45]

Once we have securely grasped and affirmed this, we can inscribe the temporal upon the eternal—paradoxically and in a way that can be misunderstood in a Hegelian direction—and say, "If this separation had never taken place, the mutual act of giving would never have become so perfect."[46] "Only in the sacrifice that lies in separation can love unfold its whole depth"; thus "the Father completes his sacrifice by giving his dearest possession from beyond in sacrifice into this world here below."[47] Or, the more the Son, "during the time of his sojourn on earth", is "missed by the Father . . . the more the Father will appreciate the magnitude of his love for the Son and of the Son's love for him".[48] Formulations such as this simply show how fragmentary all human thinking is about the relationship of the immanent to the economic Trinity; "we can follow [the idea] for a certain distance, then it breaks off." "On the Cross, to all appearances, the Son has become nothing but a finite point. . . . But the Three-Person God has never ceased being One and Infinite."[49] So we cannot speak of a "process" in God, as if he could attain fullness only through the world's sinful alienation from him and through his Son's Cross. The triune love is always there in the perfect form of the Eucharist; "behind the sacrifice of the Son (to the world) stands the consubstantial loving surrender of the Father as the source of the Eucharist",[50] and not only this, but the absolute self-surrender of every Divine Person to every Other—and nothing in the "economic" sphere can intensify this surrender. If God is "light, and in him is no darkness at all" (1 Jn 1:5),

[45] Ps 50, 115. Cf. Is 99–100.   [46] 2 Jo 292.
[47] 1 Jo 287.   [48] 4 Jo 380.
[49] T 73–74.   [50] 4 Jo 381.

this means that there is "no contradiction in him", for the contradiction is "wiped out eternally in his unity". "For the life of
God consists not only of his goodness and greatness and light
but equally of his power over death and darkness, his authority
over small things, his dominion over evil."[51] Darkness in God
is only "an aspect of his eternal light", and this "blinding light"
renders him unapproachable; even the night that God has created is an "image and likeness of a quality of his inaccessible
light".[52] Accordingly, when, in the night of sin, the world opposes the divine mystery of light, nevertheless "our darkness and
his light are not absolute contraries. The darkness of sin is not
beyond the power of God. That is why it is possible for God in
his grace to envelop our sinful darkness in his greater darkness",
wrapping our wretchedness in his grace.[53] Hence it is clear that
God's power and his goodness are equally infinite.[54]

d. A Darkness Reserved to God Himself

If God's inaccessible light is beyond darkness and light as known
to the world, and since both are "expressions of his goodness, of
his essence", it follows that God's darkness is "the aspect of his
light we do not understand". It is "God's preserve, the visible
sign of his power and his eternal authority. He . . . does not give
it to us." This is the meaning of the "You-shall-not" in paradise.
We, however, "cannot bear being deprived of anything"; we fail
to see that eternal love needs its infinite places and its "darkness"
in order "to flow on eternally"; we fail to realize that all love
is "vulnerable and defenseless".[1] When man's sin, the darkness
he has manufactured, violates this reserved area, it arouses what
Scripture calls God's anger: it is God's infinite goodness, "but
now turned against evil". "So we discern attributes of God that
we would never have seen if we had not sinned." This is the
only way to interpret God's "wrathful judgments" in the Old

---

[51] I Jo 18.

[52] I Jo 49–51 (GT); cf. Sc 25.

[53] I Jo 52.

[54] Ps 90–91: "His goodness is not restricted by his power; it does not reach a
certain point before stopping, but stretches into infinity just like his power."

[1] I Jo 50–51.

Testament. It is "a picture of God opposing the contradiction of
our sin. It is, as it were, the Father's 'Cross' that this picture of
him must be unavoidable until, on the Cross, the Son reveals its
ultimate meaning."[2] "God's anger is an expression of his love
of the Son"; both "are identical in their goal: they both aim to
save man. They are also identical in their effect, namely, to bring
man to repentance. Finally, they are identical in their source: they
both spring from love, from the relationship between Father and
Son."[3] Now when the Son becomes man in order to manifest
this love, and the Father, as it were, gives him all his love for his
mission, "it seems for a moment" as though the Father has kept
nothing "for himself but anger".[4] This anger, however, which
"is not one of God's eternal attributes"[5] but "is the counterpart on God's side of the original nature's concealment by sin"[6]
and is therefore "finite", "limited"[7] and "this-worldly",[8] must
contribute to implementing his loving will even against man's
resistance. "God's No is far more forceful than man's No. . . .
He has resolved to go ahead with the great banquet. . . . Even
anger is an expression of this determination."[9] This means that,
initially, even the Son's Cross, which is God's judgment on sin,
will exhibit an aspect of anger. Just as, in the Old Covenant (Is
63:1–6), God appears as the One who treads the winepress in
wrath, his garments stained with the blood of the nations trodden down by him, so in the New Covenant the Son will take
this punishment upon himself. "He will be the trodden grape."
Divine anger is transformed "since the Father's wrath is transferred from the nations to his own Son". No one came to his
help in reestablishing righteousness. "God can count only on
God", and yet he would need "man's help". "The perfect solution is found by the Son becoming man: God reckons with God,
and yet, at the same time, he receives help from man."[10] The
solution is this: On the basis of the Incarnation it is possible to
distinguish between sin and the sinner; on the Cross "the Son
will divert the scourge of eternal wrath on to himself" in order

[2] Is 154–55.   [3] Ap 480.
[4] Ap 481.   [5] Ps 104.
[6] Ep 81.   [7] Ap 483, 499.
[8] Os 211.   [9] Gl 99–100.
[10] Is 194–95.

to spare sinners from it. Thus "the anger of judgment is under the umbrella of God's redemptive will, without rendering his anger unreal or powerless."[11] On the Cross the Son "took all sin upon himself in such a way that God cannot strike the sinner without striking him";[12] so the anger is quieted by the love of the suffering Son.

It is impossible, however, that the Son, experiencing on the Cross the Father's love in the form of his anger, was not also given a glimpse of the results of his suffering. During the Son's earthly life the Father had not shown the Son his own "dark-ness"—the darkness of sin in the form of his anger—but had "kept it in his own power". But when "the Son passes through hell on Holy Saturday, he does so as one to whom the Father shows his secret because he no longer keeps it for himself; he is coming to know what is excluded from the light (because of God's wrath against sin as well as his love for mankind)."[13] This is the "overall view of sin" that "the Lord receives . . . on Holy Saturday on his journey through hell, when the Father shows to him conquered sin".[14] He undertakes this journey in pure "wordlessness"[15] (for, after all, the Incarnate Word of God is dead) and also in "pure obedience", for "the Father is not merely, as was the case on the Cross, veiled and lost to view, but now the Son is forced to enter into that which is the op-posite of the Father", into the pure essence of sin that has been separated from the world, into what has been condemned by God, in which God cannot be found. "It is the most extreme demand that the Father and Son make on one another in love."[16] At this point "the Father allows the Son to experience the most intimate thing that he possesses: his darkness, which was other-wise always concealed by the light, like something about which no one speaks, like the ultimate personal mystery." (Here, of course, we are not speaking of the eternal Son but of the incar-nate Son, who is now dead.) "God *shows* him his mystery; but in showing him his *mystery*, he does not show himself. Often, the greatest nearness and intimacy exists between people, not

[11] OM 314.
[12] Ap 413–14.
[13] 1 Jo 218.
[14] 3 Jo 285.
[15] 4 Jo 211.
[16] 4 Jo 212.

when they speak or associate with each other, but when they
are turned away from each other." The dead Son "therefore accepts the mystery of darkness just as the Father offers it to him:
in the turning away of the Father himself." This disclosed darkness is two things simultaneously: it is the primal mystery of the
Father (the "super-light" of freedom), and it is the sin, permitted
by the Father, of man in rebellion against this mystery. "God has
given two responses to sin: the netherworld and the Son. The
netherworld as the necessary consequence of sin, the Son as the
free willingness to atone for sin. Now, the two encounter each
other." This encounter is two things: "a mystery of communion
between Father and Son. But also a mystery of darkness, since,
in the netherworld, the Son experiences the estrangement of
sin. Yet the darkness of sin remains enclasped in the darkness of
love."[17] "On Holy Saturday, at the end of the mission, before
God turns back once again to the world, he turns away from
the Son in love, in order to allow him to share in his mystery":
no longer a mystery of wrath, but a mystery of love.[18]

Earlier we spoke of death as a mode of (eternal) life, of suffering as a mode of joy, of separation as a mode of union. Now we
have seen dereliction as a mode of eternal communion between
Father and Son in the Spirit, and in conclusion we begin to see
how the "economic" modes of relations between the Divine
Persons are latent in the "immanent" modes, without adding a
foreign element to them as such. The only foreign element is
sin, which is burned up within these relations—which are fire.
God's *fire* is always present;

> The fact that we are there does not add anything to the fire. The
> fact that it is there for us does not change it. It is the fire of love
> and the fire of suffering. As the fire of love, it is an essential feature
> of what . . . each Person in God is for the Other. As the fire of
> suffering, it is the essential feature of the triune God, who puts
> up with nothing, consuming all that is not pure. The Son gives
> himself for love of the Father, so that, bearing all sin and impu-
> rity, he will be burned up by this divine fire. In the cry of derelic-
> tion on the Cross, he allows himself to be consumed by his Father's

[17] 4 Jo 153–54, 157.
[18] 4 Jo 155.

fire because he has finally gathered into himself everything that prevents him from participating in the fire's active burning.[19]

The mystery of Good Friday and Holy Saturday is thus a mystery of the loneliness of love between Father and Son in the Spirit, so much so that the outcome of these events (in their reunion, in the Resurrection), which is a "mystery of eternal life", can take place only in "full loneliness".[20]

2. The Question of Universal Salvation

a. The Problem

The prospect of universal salvation seems to empty God's involvement in the world of every last trace of tragedy. Not only has the everlasting inadequacy between God and his creature been eliminated by Christ: the very trinitarian profundity of the work of reconciliation, by undercutting every refusal the world may make, seems to relativize this same refusal. Now this elimination of the tragic dimension seems to be the same thing as the positing of apokatastasis,[1] or "reconciliation of all things", a theologoumenon that, in its turn, seems to require a reappraisal of the innumerable biblical passages that speak of the twofold result of the Last Judgment and of the eternity of the pains of hell. However, before we draw this apparently inevitable conclusion, we must frankly admit that a great number of passages really do speak in favor of universal salvation; we must give this

---

[19] OM 383.

[20] 4 Jo 155.

[1] On "apokatastasis", cf. the comprehensive bibliography by Gotthold Müller: (1) *Apokatastasis panton. A Bibliography* (Basel: Missionsbuchhandlung, 1969), also in German as an appendix to Müller's work on *D. F. Strauß: Identität und Immanenz* (Zurich: EVZ, 1968). It contains around 240 items but does not claim to be "by any means complete". Supplements until 1974 in (2) "Ungeheuerliche Ontologie: Erwägungen zur christlichen Lehre über Hölle und Allversöhnung" in *Ev. Theol.* 34 (1974), 256–75. Note 35. Also (3) Müller's "Die Idee der Apokatastasis ton panton in der europ. Theologie von Schleiermacher bis Barth" in *Zft. f. Rel. u. Geistesgesch.* 16 (1964), 1ff. Cf. also (4) Müller's "Origines und die Apokatastasis" in *Theol. Zft.*, 1958, 174–90, where he gives a convincing presentation of the biblical and christological basis for Origen's thesis that all will be reconciled.

fact its appropriate place and, as Schleiermacher demands, grant it "at least equal rights"[2] to exist. A whole series of important theologians[3]—by no means all heretics and outsiders—and, in the Middle Ages, many spiritual and mystical writers, compel us to take this demand seriously. Whatever one may think of Karl Barth's great "doctrine of election", it represents the break-through that brought the discussion into being. Even E. Brun-ner, who attacks Barth for his allegedly unguarded doctrine of apokatastasis,[4] allows the theologoumenon to stand, provided the negative possibility is not absolutely excluded.[5] We would do well, therefore, to let both possibilities exist in juxtaposition for the moment and to leave to a subsequent section the possi-bility or impossibility of reconciling them. "A la question: Enfer éternel OU Salut universel? je reponds donc: Enfer éternel ET Salut universel" (Gaston Fessard).[6] "The fact that the Judgment has a twofold result by no means excludes universal salvation" (Wilhelm Michaelis).[7]

First of all, therefore, we shall examine the various elements in themselves in isolation from the total context, before going on to the question of the possibility or impossibility of univer-sal salvation (as it appears to the mind of the theologian who is *docile* to the Word) within a total view. First we must take ac-count of the change that occurs as the aeon of the Old Covenant gives place to the aeon of the New; this is largely neglected in theological reflection on the Judgment. Since the terminology of judgment, and the imagery surrounding it, remains basically the same in Old and New Testaments, we are inclined to overlook the astonishing fact that, in the Old Covenant, it is the God

[2] *The Christian Faith*, 2d ed. (1831), trans. and ed. H. R. Mackintosh and J. S. Stewart (Philadelphia: Fortress Press, 1976), sec. 163, p. 722.

[3] Cf. G. Müller's essays, "Ungeheuerliche Ontologie" and "Idee der Apokatas-tasis", especially on the nineteenth century.

[4] Those for and against Barth, and Barth's own comments, are indicated in Müller's *Bibliography*, 337–38.

[5] "The question is not whether God *can* save all men: what we have to oppose is the idea that this possibility implies the *impossibility* of its opposite": *Dogmatik* I (Zurich: Zwingli, 1946), 365.

[6] "Enfer éternel ou Salut universel?" in E. Castelli, *Archivio di Filosofia* (Rome, 1967), 223–64. This ref., 247.

[7] *Versöhnung des Alls* (Gümligen/Berne: Siloah, 1950), 94, cf. 120.

of covenant justice who rules over the nations and over Israel, whereas, in the New Covenant, judgment is primarily the Cross of the Mediator (Jn 12:31). Here it is the Mediator, the Reconciler and Savior of the world, who conducts the final Judgment himself. Whereas the Old Testament exhibited a certain "symmetry", the New is "asymmetrical", as Paul forcefully asserts in Romans 5:15–21. But there are many precipices to be avoided. We cannot, as many Protestants do, allot "Law" and "condemnation" to the Old Covenant and "gospel" and "salvation" to the New,[8] not least because Paul consistently portrays the final Judgment as "according to works". Rather, following the biblical emphases, we shall note that rejecting the reconciliation of the world wrought by Christ is regarded as much graver than infringing the Law; this is why eternal bliss and eternal damnation are now far more starkly opposed. Here, yet again, we find the dramatic core of the whole theo-drama: the heightened revelation of divine love produces a heightened rejection, a deeper hatred. In the Old Testament the element of the demonic was latent: only in the New Testament does it emerge into the open, only here *can* it so emerge.[9]

It is in this context that man's situation will be assessed in God's Judgment, which, in New Testament terms, has become the Judgment of Jesus Christ (Jn 5:22): How does man, whoever and whatever he is, measure up to the norm of Jesus Christ (who followed and exemplified to the limit the norm of the Old Testament, the *shema*), and what are the existential implications for him? This sheds light on the paradox in which Jesus says that he himself has not come to judge but to save, yet that the one who rejects him and his command *has* a judge, namely, "the word that I have spoken" (Jn 12:47–48).

Only after we have pursued this "dialectic" of grace and judgment into its inner depths can we tentatively approach the final question: whether and how we can envisage a harmony or at least a convergence between the two poles that seem to be mutually exclusive. This is also the place to discuss Karl Barth's

---

[8] As Müller himself tries to do, "Ungeheuerliche Ontologie", 270–72.

[9] It is here, and not in historical influences from Parsee religion, that the deeper answer is to be found to the fashionable attacks on satanic power (H. Haag, *Abschied vom Teufel*, 6th ed. [1978]; *Vor dem Bösen ratlos?* [1978]).

thesis that Jesus Christ, the Chosen One from all eternity, is also the Rejected One on behalf of all others, so that all the rejected can become chosen ones through him. Bearing in mind what we said in *Theo-Drama* IV, 284ff., we must ask whether the notion of mere "substitution" is adequate, or whether this concept, when applied to Christ, does not automatically include an element— a trinitarian element—that lifts it above the mere physical or legal plane. This implies that the Bearer of the world's sin does not simply suffer "hell" in our place: something unique is going on here that cannot be comprehended by the notion of a mere exchange of places.

We shall now devote some time to reflection upon these various aspects.

b. From the Old Aeon to the New

The imagery of judgment in the Old Testament is largely identical to that in the New; taken in isolation it can obscure the qualitative difference between them. The New Covenant is neither the mere completion of something still to be expected, as the pairing of the concepts "promise-fulfillment" might suggest, nor is it a reversal of values, as a one-sided reading of the Pauline opposition between "Law" and "gospel" could lead one to think. It is best illustrated by the opposites of the fleshly, earthly anticipation, or "pre-image" [*Vor-bild*] (1 Cor 10:11), and the pneumatic, eschatological truth. In this view, the anticipation, or "pre-image", has validity insofar as it shares in the truth to which it points. This is demonstrated by the fact that Abraham's faith is given priority over the Law—since the latter was added later in virtue of human sinfulness (Gal 3:17, 19).

Of course God was Judge even before the event of Sinai, because sin already existed (Rom 5:13) in huge proportions, as we can see from the judgment of the Flood and the judgment on the builders of the Tower of Babel, on Sodom and Gomorrah, and on Pharaoh. But the accounts of it are written by men who think in terms of the Sinai Covenant and can use Sinai to assess the gravity of the contradiction offered to that faith which was reckoned to Abraham as righteousness (Gen 15:6). From the perspective of Sinai, "faith" is "faithfulness", and since on

God's side the Covenant cannot be broken, reciprocal faithfulness is implied. Israel's keeping of the "precepts" is nothing other
than the demonstration and touchstone of its faithfulness or its
slipping from faithfulness. Everything that drops out of the ellipse formed by the two foci of God and Israel automatically
exposes itself to God's punitive judgment, whereas everything
that lies within this ellipse is heir to the promise of reward that
is set forth in the Covenant contract. In accord with the inner
meaning of the Covenant, reward has a preponderance over punishment: "For I the Lord your God am a jealous God, visiting
the iniquity of the fathers upon the children to the third and
the fourth generation of those who hate me, but showing steadfast love to thousands of those who love me and keep my commandments" (Ex 20:5–6; Dt 5:9; 7:9–10). The nature of the
earthly partner means, however, that this asymmetry of grace
disappears behind a complete symmetry of promise and threat:
"See, I have set before you this day life and good, death and evil.
If you obey the commandments of the Lord your God . . . , you
shall live. . . . But if your heart turns away, and you will not hear,
. . . I declare to you this day, that you shall perish. . . . I have set
before you life and death, blessing and curse" (Dt 30:15–19).
This is the basis of the parallelism in the long lists announcing
blessing and curse (cf. Lev 26:14–45; Dt 28:15–68). What is set
before the people as a whole applies equally to the individual
once sufficient reflection has taken place: "He has set before
you fire and water; reach out and take which you choose" (Sir
15:16).

The history of Israel with God is an incessant horizontal-
historical back-and-forth between faithfulness and falling away,
and hence between identifiable blessing and equally identifiable
curse. Both blessing and curse manifest the indissoluble presence of the God who is faithful to his Covenant: he remains
One under both forms of manifestation. To that extent Yahweh's eternal faithfulness and (hence) goodness becomes, when
manifested, essentially "righteousness" (*mishpat*), in a sense that
is completely positive theologically and unique to the Hebrew
language.[1] This is why Israel rejoices at the collapse of every-

---

[1] Cf. *The Glory of the Lord* VI: *Theology: The Old Covenant*, 169–73.

thing that stands outside the ellipse of Covenant faithfulness just as much as it rejoices at evidence of blessing within the Covenant: both are theophanies.

Outside, first of all, are the "nations". Not only are they subject to one judgment after another, for instance, at the Red Sea and during Israel's desert wanderings, causing Israel to rejoice with songs of victory; in the Prophets, too, we find a whole series of curses against them (Amos 1; Zeph 2; Is 13–23; Jer 46–51; Ezek 25–32; Joel 3 [RSV]). Increasingly (starting with Amos 2:4ff.) the Prophets insist that Israel, too, can be "outside" the ellipse, not only accidentally but fundamentally, and can thus incur judgment; and when Israel, too, has to experience the symmetry of reward and punishment in its own body, the result is not rejoicing but partly a hardening of heart against God and partly bitter pain. In the fundamental relationship between God and the people, however, nothing has changed: the people must "turn back" and "cry to God" (as a sign of a renewed intention to be faithful) to avert their threatened fate. The Deuteronomist historiography fashions the entire history of Israel according to this principle. It is possible, of course, to conclude from God's Covenant faithfulness that he does not want to punish his people ("Have I any pleasure in the death of the wicked?" Ezek 18:23), so that he can be constantly reminded of his promises. On the other hand, the obverse of his unbreakable faithfulness, his steadfast righteousness, is portrayed concretely in images that are no less extreme: God punishes pitilessly (Hos 5:1–15; 7:12–13; 9:7; Zeph 1:17–18), he enters into judgment against his people, he devours it, he comes as an enraged warrior, in fire, sulphur, hail and blood (Ezek 38:22; Is 29:6; 30:30; Joel 2:30 [RSV] etc.); Jeremiah invents the terrible trio: "sword, famine and pestilence" (14:12; 21:7, 9; 24:10; 27:8, 13; 28:8; 29:17–18; 32:24, 36; 34:17; 38:2; 42:17, 22; this is taken up by Ezekiel: 6:11; 7:15; 12:16). The reckoning that God will mete out to his people knows no pity (Ezek 7:4); it is a case of "a tooth for a tooth": "When you have ceased to destroy, you will be destroyed" (Is 33:1); "Those who despoil you shall become a spoil" (Jer 30:16). So Israel pleads for vengeance upon Babylon: "Requite her according to her deeds, do to her according to all that she has done" (Jer 50:29). It goes on, "For she has proudly defied the Lord": this self-righteousness is the real sin of those peoples living outside the Covenant: Assyria ascribes its power and wisdom to itself (Is 10:13), saying, "I am and there is none else" (Zeph 2:15). Later, Babylon will repeat this boast (Is 47:8, 10), just as Pharaoh claims to have made his Nile (Ezek 29:3, 9), and Tyre prides itself on its perfect, divine beauty (Ezek 27:3; 28:2, 9). At bottom Israel's sin is, however, always the same: opposing its Covenant Lord with its own will, a will that primarily expresses itself in running after foreign gods of its own invention (thus transgressing against the first tablet of the Commandments) or failing to treat his fellow man as prescribed by Yahweh (and thus transgressing against the second tablet).

The ultimate conclusion drawn by Israel from its covenant situation was this: Since it had knowledge of God's righteousness in reward and punishment, it felt empowered to use this knowledge both as a principle for its own action (in obedience to God) and in judging and dealing with others. It felt justified in procuring God's punishment against those who acted contrary to God's commandments, whether outside or inside the Chosen People. Furthermore, since in principle it held fast to the Covenant, it felt able to assert its own righteousness and summoned God to uphold it. These two things, which we find illustrated in various ways in the Psalms and which are based on an ultimately legitimate principle (albeit at an anticipatory [vor-bildlich] level) lead, by a fateful necessity, to the Pharisaic attitude so strongly condemned by Jesus because it has forgotten the real foundation of the Law, namely, *mishpat*, mercy and faithfulness (Mt 23:23). Ultimately it has also forgotten the chief commandment of unlimited love for God (Mt 22:37–38; Mk 12:28–34; Lk 10:27), which underlies the legal fidelity. This commandment of love, formulated with astonishing radicality in the Old Testament (Dt 6:4–9) as man's response to the divine love—a love that showed itself as the radiant source of God's faithfulness for the first time in Hosea—had become so obscured by the "interference" of the Law (Rom 5:20), with its symmetrical justice of reward and punishment, that Jesus' constant reference to this love makes it sound like a new discovery.[2]

[2] One could point to the words of rabbis in Jesus' time and subsequently who

In reality this "new discovery" was something more. It was a complete re-creation of the Covenant itself. For in Jesus we have, not one "party" in a "pact", but someone who, in his Person, has become the unity of God and man. He is the Covenant personified; he is the fully realized truth (*emeth*) and faithfulness (*zedek*) of God, which no longer lie *behind* his righteousness of reward and punishment, but *in* it. This comes fully into view with the emergence of the next two aspects of God's incarnation, which follow from the first aspect: God's whole righteousness (in meting out punishment) attains its expression and its term in the death of Jesus; in breathing forth his Spirit, Jesus creates the conditions necessary so that the divine Spirit may be put into our hearts and we may be incorporated into the "new, eternal and unforgettable Covenant" (Jer 31:31; 32:40; 50:5; Ezek 16:60; 37:26), which in Christ has become a Person. In Christ, therefore, this prophecy has come true: "I will cleanse them from all the guilt of their sin against me, and I will forgive all the guilt of their sin and rebellion against me" (Jer 33:8), as well as the other prophecy that looks toward the abolition of the purely external relationship between the Covenant partners: "I will put my law within them, and I will write it upon their hearts" (Jer 31:33). This means that a member of the new People is no longer related externally to his fellow member, for they are incorporated into the incarnate Covenant, Christ, and so partake of the same Spirit: "And no longer shall each man teach his neighbor and each his brother, saying, 'Know the Lord,' for they shall all know me, from the least of them to the greatest, says the Lord" (Jer 31:34).

We have already seen that, on the basis of this shift, the New Testament sees the Law as removed from its old place. Thus Paul includes references to universal salvation in his theological principles and can say that, for those who walk in Christ, "there is therefore now no condemnation" (Rom 8:1); John, who situates judgment in the Cross (Jn 12:31), says accordingly that he who believes in the Son "does not come into judgment, but has passed from death to life" (5:24). The Synoptic writ-

speak in similar terms (Billerbeck I, 905ff.); the essential difference between them will emerge in what follows.

ers (especially Matthew) portray Jesus' death on the Cross in the colors of the eschatological Judgment; they bring forward the decision about a man's eternal destiny and locate it in his own decision, here and now, for or against Jesus, as well as in the way he treats his neighbor in distress, in whom he is meant to recognize the suffering Lord. If the conclusive Judgment has taken place in the Cross of Jesus, Peter can assure his community that "the end of all things is at hand" (1 Pet 4:7) and that they should not regard the "fiery ordeal which comes upon you" as "something strange" (4:12), since "the time has come for judgment to begin with the household of God" (4:17).[3] This ordeal consists in "sharing the sufferings of Christ" (4:13); it is a time of grace (2:19) and, for Christians, it signifies "glory" (5:10). In Christ's death and Resurrection the bonds of death have been burst and eternity stands before us as our "reward": accordingly, the Old Covenant's this-worldly, symmetrical doctrine of retribution collapses. Now there is a fundamental *asymmetry* insofar as God's judgment has been pronounced once and for all in the Cross and Resurrection of Jesus; whatever follows can only be an effect and consequence of this event, already inherent in it.

To that extent Karl Barth is quite right when he says that we must put out of our minds any "complete balance" between God's elective mercy and his condemnatory righteousness (CD II/2). In fact we can go a step farther than Barth; for he conceives ("double") predestination in such a way that Christ is the One chosen to be solely condemned on behalf of all the condemned. This comprehensive formula is too close, however, to the view that the sufferings of the Cross were punishment, a view rejected in *Theo-Drama* IV, 284–316; the Crucified Son does not simply suffer the hell deserved by sinners; he suffers something below and beyond this, namely, being forsaken by God in the pure obedience of love. Only he, as Son, is capable of this, and it is qualitatively deeper than any possible hell. This signifies an even more radical abandonment of the symmetrical judgment of the Old Testament.

---

[3] This utterance does not have the threatening character it had in the Prophets (Ezek 9:6; Jer 25:29, etc.); it is rather a privilege for Christians to face judgment first (in their following of Christ: v. 13).

The Judgment that takes place within the Trinity can be understood only in terms of the suffering love between Father and Son in the Spirit; henceforth, therefore, all the Old Testament rejoicing at the punishment of the wicked, all eschatological delight at their torment, must fall silent. As M. Nédoncelle says, "I renounce, vehemently and decisively—and this seems to me of the greatest importance—the idea that has poisoned us for centuries, not to say millennia, namely, that God hates sinners and the damned. I regard this as absolutely intolerable, just like the notion that God's love could fail to have an effect on any one of his creatures."[4] In similar vein G. Martelet says, "in speaking of love refused, we do not mean that God refuses his love to anyone, as if beings could be lost forever because God had not loved them sufficiently. Where God is concerned, there can never be those who are in any way deprived of his love, since he is Love itself. . . . The absolute refusal of love (which is hell) exists, therefore, only in the case of him who eternally acknowledges and affirms no one but himself; and it is inconceivable that God could have anything to do with this grotesque possibility."[5] J. Ratzinger says, "Christ allots perdition to no one. . . . He does not pronounce the fatal verdict. It happens where a person has held aloof from him. It comes about where man clings to his isolation."[6] The God of Jesus makes his grace available to the good and the bad: that is the essence of his "perfection".

Ultimately the new "Israel of God" (Gal 6:16) cannot operate with two levels of right conduct, that is, toward friend and toward foe. It is abolished by the new ethics, the ethics of the Cross of Christ, who died for all—while they were yet sinners! (Rom 5:10). The Jewish notion was that the "neighbors" whom we must love were the members of one's own race plus the full proselytes, but not "strangers" who dwelt in the land (Lev 19:34; Dt 10:19) and who did not, within the space of a year, go over entirely to the Jewish people; thus it did not include the Samaritans.[7] Not for nothing, in answering a question characteristic of the teachers of the Law, "Who is my neigh-

---

[4] "Allversöhnung, Problem", 262, n. 4.

[5] *L'Au-delà retrouvé* (Desclée, 1974), 181, 188.

[6] *Eschatologie* (Regensburg: Pustet, 1977), 169.

[7] Cf. Billerbeck's remarks on Mt 5:43 (I, 353–68).

bor?", does Jesus use precisely the Samaritan as an example of the breaking down of all national boundaries. As a result of the Cross of Jesus, the least of all the "prodigal sons" has become Jesus' and God's neighbor, and it follows that he must also be a neighbor to the disciple of Christ. This is not based on some vague Hellenistic philanthropy but because, through the Cross that Christ suffered bodily and his Eucharist that is shared out bodily, this man is a blood relation ("bodily relation") of Jesus Christ; indeed, he has become a limb of his body.

This is the change from one aeon to another. It abolishes all formal continuity between the ideas of judgment in the Old Covenant and those in the New: an abyss now separates them. Before proceeding, we shall give our full attention to this stage of theological reflection.[8]

c. A Comprehensive Redemption

1. First of all we must go through the New Testament texts once more, just as they present themselves to us, and appreciate them in all their deliberate starkness. As a preliminary we observe that all the Lord's words that refer to the possibility of eternal perdition are pre-Easter words, like John 9:39, where Jesus says that he has come into the world in order to judge it. "This is one of those words of the Lord that are spoken before the fact of the redemption on the Cross, at a time when the light has not yet penetrated the whole of the darkness."[1] After Easter the first

---

[8] We should note that even in the Jewish thought of the late apocalyptic writers, a *twofold issue* of the final Judgment is the only conceivable one. Even where, for instance, the Syrian Apocalypse of Baruch presents "a compendium of hope" (Woschitz, *Elpis/Hoffnung* [Vienna: Herder, 1979], 321), it speaks of an eternal time to come that "will not cause those who go immediately into blessedness to undergo corruption, but will have no mercy with those who are destined for punishment" (30, 12). This is also the viewpoint of Daniel 12:2 and Isaiah 66:24. The twofold result of Judgment is an unshakable fact for the entire Fourth Book of Esdras, the spirituality of Qumran (which reckons with the damnation of the "sons of darkness") and the Psalms of Solomon (Ps 13). Speculation about the annihilation of the wicked (P. Volz, *Die Eschatologie der jüdischen Gemeinde im neutestamentlichen Zeitalter* [Tübingen: Mohr, 1934], 309ff.) and the eschatological time of salvation in a world that will have been renewed (Volz, *Eschatologie*, 43–49) is another matter, and one that does not concern us here.

[1] 2 Jo 256.

words we hear are Paul's, full of certainty that, if God be for us, no earthly power can be against us.[2] "The Lord suffers for love of all."[3] "Unless God's demands" on his Son "were divine in character, unless God's acts were unsurpassable, each one surpassing the other, the work of redemption on the Cross could be surpassed by man's negation. But when God makes demands of God he makes sure that God always overtakes man, that grace has more weight than sin, that the redemption is complete."[4] Paul sees that God has set his Son over against Adam, the Second Adam over against the first: "The Son can watch over all, whereas Adam could watch over none. He will be everyone, whereas Adam could be no one."[5] So, according to the Fathers, the Son has "saved Adam and rescued him from hell".[6] This means that the first Adam could only have been envisaged and responsibly brought into being with a view to the Second. "In creating the world, God had already overcome it. Had he not, in divine freedom, overcome the world he created, he would not have been able to endow men with freedom"; but "the giving of freedom is absolutely essential in genuine love."[7] Coming as the Second Adam, the Son was therefore "certain of victory; he possessed victory in himself, victory over everything in the world".[8] For him there is no moment of uncertainty. "The Son's giving is so radical that it looks as though men have taken over what he imparted to them. In his love he represents them to the Father as if they were already lovers."[9]

In John the universality of redemption is stressed with equal emphasis: "Long ago, when the Lord decided to come, he chose us, all of us, in order to redeem us. He took up a work of Redemption that was not designed for individuals only, . . . that was meant for all."[10] "The Lord died not only for good persons, who open themselves to him at once, but also for the wicked, who resist him. He has the time to wait until even these scattered children of God are touched by his light. For not even the wicked person stands outside the sphere of his power, and the dispersion

[2] SL 81f.; 91f.
[3] Gl 79.
[4] T 82.
[5] Is 244.
[6] C 284.
[7] Ka II, 198.
[8] Ka II, 201.
[9] W 255.
[10] 3 Jo 189.

of the Lord embraces and overtakes even the dispersion of the sinners."[11] As the Good Shepherd, he has been commissioned by the Father "to bring back all the sheep, the whole flock, to him",[12] and, when he is lifted up, to "draw all men to himself".[13] And even while he knows of the hatred and indifference of many, "fundamentally [he] is always talking about everyone. Here he speaks of all mankind as those who do not keep the commandment"; for ultimately "none of them is up to this standard of measurement."[14] When, in St. John's Gospel, the Lord refers to the prophecy of Jeremiah (Jer 31:34), "they shall all be taught by God", "the emphasis lies on *all*. God's teaching is made available to all . . . each one who has somehow at some time felt the yearning for God, comes to the Son. There is no longer any possibility of hearing any word of God without thereby coming to the Son. And thus the possibility of the Old Covenant no longer exists: it is transcended into the single possibility of the New Covenant. The rule admits of no exception: each one who hears God comes to the Son."[15] That is why it is forbidden to despair of any sinner.[16] This applies to Judas too.[17] "If you keep my commandments . . .", says the Lord (Jn 15:10). "He does

---

[11] 2 Jo 390.   [12] 2 Jo 260.

[13] 2 Jo 432.   [14] 3 Jo 139 (GT).

[15] 2 Jo 57–58.   [16] 2 Jo 203.

[17] When Jesus prays (Jn 17:12), "none of them is lost but the son of perdition", this means, "except for the one whom he cannot now give back to the Father, because he no longer belongs to the flock . . . because Judas is still going to betray him: if he is to be saved, it can only be through the Cross itself. . . . As long as someone wants to sin, he cannot repent. Once he has committed the sin, there can be an opening for repentance and confession" (3 Jo 335). "By receiving the betrayer, the Lord shows the greatest fidelity to the Father. With full awareness, he accepts the responsibility even for the one whose guilt he sees in advance. . . . He does not only accept those cases that will go well, according to a human evaluation, but also takes on, with the same love and reliability, those who appear from the very beginning to be difficult, indeed, hopeless" (3 Jo 80–81). "The Lord hands the morsel, thus transformed, to Judas. The disciple of love mentions only the Communion of the betrayer. . . . Indeed, the Eucharist itself is the beginning of the Passion, which is suffered precisely for sinners, the evil ones and the betrayers. . . . Judas is merely the most extreme case and is therefore particularly mentioned" (3 Jo 52–53, cf. also 29, 34, 37f., 45). On Judas, see also Mt 101– 7; Pa 61–74, esp. 70–71: "In his confrontation with Judas, Jesus bears everything, including excommunication. . . . That is why hell is nowhere as busy as in the moment of this confrontation: for it is precisely what the suffering Lord cannot

not speak of what would become of his love if they did not keep his commandments, nor does he tell them that he will always love them, even then, in spite of everything."[18] So he prays to the Father: "Thou hast given him power over all flesh, to give eternal life to all whom thou hast given him" (Jn 17:2). "At first this handing over [to the Son] looks like a restriction . . . but this restriction is straight away abolished": eternal life "belongs originally to the Father", but from before all time he has shared it with the Son: "Into this participation the Son leads all those whom the Father has given him, namely all flesh."[19] "His whole mission will be completed only when all will be redeemed from sin and be with the Father."[20] In his Passion he must suffer for all those "who, without him, would have deserved hell".[21] Yet "the darkness of sin remains enclasped in the darkness of love", as the Son suffers it in being forsaken by God.[22]

2. The Cross is the decisive Judgment because here the Son undercuts and undergirds the world's sin, which was deserving of a just condemnation. The Old Testament "judgment of justice was not a mistake and cannot be replaced by another; it remains

---

take upon himself. On the Cross the sin of Judas himself—and of all who have fallen away from the faith—is borne only in a preliminary manner. When, after the Cross, the Lord goes through hell, he experiences it as a new and surprising gift from the Father. Something of it had crept into his Cross by way of anticipation, but how and when no one could say. Judas nails the Lord to the Cross; he approaches him from outside, which means that he cannot be simultaneously in him and borne by him. . . . In the Lord's suffering there are different relationships to sin: some sins are directly taken up and borne, whereas others can only be expiated indirectly, as it were, since, on the one hand, the sinner desires the crucifixion and, on the other hand, does not want to be redeemed by it. To that extent the case of Judas is hidden within the Cross and will be settled only on the far side of the Cross, in hell."

[18] 3 Jo 179.
[19] 3 Jo 305–6.
[20] 3 Jo 82.
[21] 3 Jo 285; cf. 3F 53: "He came to rescue all sinners". G 20: "The Son's self-surrender has broken through the limits of finitude for everyone." SL 22: "In the death of the Son every sin must die."
[22] 4 Jo 157; cf. 248, on the Lord's self-giving to doubting Thomas. By taking this "risk" and showing Thomas his wounds as proof, "he grants him participation in the Cross."

in existence in the law of love, which could unfold only from the foundation of justice. . . . When the Father in judgment looks at the Son with the eyes of justice, he sees nothing that would call for judgment; since everything is right and just in him, there is nothing to be judged. Justice therefore has nothing to look for, and judgment naturally dissolves into love." And since "the Father has given all judgment to the Son" (Jn 5:22) and "the judgment has already become one of love between Father and Son, the Son also cannot pass judgment, which is already dissolved, on men, except as the judgment of love he himself has experienced and received from the Father."[23] "The judgment of the Cross is final, but the Lord waits until the Last Day to reveal its complete result."[24] On the Cross "he has begun to gather up all wickedness, all evildoers on to himself, on to his body of pain", but the weeds of evil keep growing and "seem to prove victorious against him; thus the mission of the Cross points forward to the conclusion of the mission at the end of the world, where what was accomplished on the Cross interiorly, by suffering, must be manifested externally in power".[25]

If all sins are undercut and undergirded by God's infinite love, it suggests that sin, evil, must be *finite* and must come to an end in the love that envelops it. The Church Fathers were familiar with this idea.[26] Christ, we read, has dealt with sin (1 Pet 4:1),

[23] 1 Jo 272. How can God the Father reconcile his love for the Son and his righteous anger toward men? The answer lies in the way in which the sinner is embraced and undergirded by the Son's love, so that now "God's fatherhood enfolds both these infinitely diverse relationships in a single one. . . . When the Father thinks of the darkest sinner there must be room in his thought for the brightest son; he must be able to see sonship and humanity within a single indistinguishable divine righteousness." That is why God "cannot allow even the worst of sinners to fall" A 34. Cf. 2 Jo 443: "The judgment of the Cross is only one single judgment, for every distinction between judgment and love is superseded at the Cross: they coincide."

[24] C 163.

[25] Gl 56: "On the Cross Christ has already made the fundamental separation, the fundamental discrimination. . . . He does not need to go on doing it. (He can leave this work to the angels.) He has already done it. If he were to do it once more at the end of the world, it would obscure the power of the Cross."

[26] According to the Fathers, sin was seen as growing to its full height, and hence to its limit, before redemption came and overcame it. The main texts are in Gregory of Nyssa (collected in J. Daniélou's *L'Être et le temps chez Grégoire de Nysse*

and "so, by suffering, he has put an end to sin. All the sin of the world was included in his suffering, which was an expiation for this sin; thus the end of his suffering, in death, was also the end of our sin."[27] If "the reason the Son of God appeared was to destroy the works of the devil" (1 Jn 3:8), it implies that the devil "has a certain limited power that he cannot overstep", and, "while it can increase toward its zenith, when the work is accomplished it must inevitably reach its limit, nothingness, where all is destroyed", and where God alone can rebuild.[28] This is clear in the Apocalypse, in the case of Babylon: "Sin has done all it can, and now that seduction has become complete, it has no more fuel and accordingly collapses." The devil, "living by seduction, no longer has any possibility of expansion".[29] In other words, men's freedom is not infinite, "they are free within the greater freedom of God."[30] "At the Last Judgment the angels are commissioned to put an end to the evil one: when, at the end of the world, they utter their command—Thus far and no further!—the world will see the end of the evil one."[31] But it is not angels but the Son, through his suffering, who "has set limits to the power of evil over the things of this world".[32] On the Cross "he will wipe out every account by rendering a total self-surrender."[33] "There is nothing partial in Christ's suffering and dying. And since everyone is created with a view to Christ, God applies to them the measuring rod of Christ's unconditional life. He chooses and rejects them according to the measure of Christ. In doing so he does justice to what Christ has done for us; and Christ has suffered unconditionally to bring us the totality of redemption."[34]

[Leiden: Brill, 1970], 186–204) and in his predecessors Irenaeus, Diognetus, Origen (only the ripe abscess can be cured) and Athanasius.

[27] Ka I, 366.

[28] Ka II, 108.

[29] Ap 460.

[30] 2 Jo 121.

[31] Gl 55.

[32] Pf 113.

[33] Gl 69.

[34] Gl 77.

d. The Serious Possibility of Refusal

Is this not too simple? Is not the dissolving of sin through pain, as is alleged to take place on Christ's Cross, an all too physical and mythological idea? After all, it is not simply a question of taking something that has been isolated from the sinner and making it disappear: it is a question of the sinner's own free refusal, which God, if he respects the freedom he has given to man, cannot overrule simply because his absolute freedom is more powerful than created, finite freedom. Nor can we explain it on the basis of an "extrinsecist" pardon on the part of God in view of Christ's "merits"—which are greater than the sinner's misdeeds and weigh heavier in the divine scales. This throws doubt on the whole possibility of someone standing in our place and "representing" us—even in the heightened form whereby the Trinity "undercuts and undergirds" all the world's sin and so goes beyond it.

Here, once again, we come up against the *Mysterium iniquitatis*, and it is impossible simply to avert our eyes from it as Karl Barth suggests we should. This is the central mystery of the theodrama: God's heightened love provokes a heightened hatred that is as bottomless as love itself (Jn 15:25). Jerusalem's blindness and hardness of heart causes the God-man to weep (Lk 19:41) as he sees the earthly failure of his entire saving mission and has to consign the Holy City to its ruin (Lk 19:43–44). As the Letter to the Hebrews puts it in a terrifying passage, this is precisely because it had "once been enlightened" by Jesus' teaching and miracles, had "tasted the goodness of the word of God and the powers of the age to come" and yet had committed "apostasy". In this stage "it is impossible to restore again to repentance those who have once been enlightened, . . . since they crucify the Son of God on their own account and hold him up to contempt" (Heb 6:4–6). Anyone who acts like this is not standing before the Cross but behind it, openly resisting its saving work; even the triune God has no more grace to give behind the Cross. "For if we sin deliberately after receiving the knowledge of the truth, there no longer remains a sacrifice for sins, but a fearful prospect of judgment, and a fury of fire which will consume the adversaries. A man who has violated the law of Moses dies without mercy. . . . How much worse punishment do you think will be deserved by the man who has spurned the Son of God, and profaned the blood of the covenant by which he was sanctified, and outraged the Spirit of grace?" (Heb 10:26-29).[1] Is this mere "exhortation"? Jesus himself speaks no differently in the Gospel when he distinguishes between the sin against the Son of Man, which can be forgiven, and the sin against the Holy Spirit, which can be forgiven neither in this life nor in the life to come (Mt 12:32). He says this in a situation in which he had "cast out demons by the Spirit of God" (Mt 12:28) and was accused of having done so "by the prince of demons" (Mk 3:22). He does not mince his words when, recalling Isaiah 66:24, he speaks of Gehenna, "where their worm does not die, and the fire is not quenched". He prophesies that the hard-hearted towns that do not accept his miracles will go down to hell and (quoting Ezek 16:55f.) that Sodom will find the Judgment more bearable than they (Mt 11:23-24). In the parable of the Last Judgment, following Daniel 12:2, he consigns the "goats", "you cursed, into the eternal fire prepared for the devil and his angels" (Mt 25:41). It is impossible, as some attempt to do,[2] to reinterpret "eternal punishment" (*kolasis aiōnios*, Mt 25:46) as a "temporally limited corrective punishment".[3] There is no suggestion that the fire of "Hades" in which the rich man burns (Lk 16:23-24) lasts only until the Last Judgment. And how can we relativize what is said of Judas: "It would have been better for that man if he

---

[1] Mark 3:28-29 puts it more briefly but no less clearly: "Truly, I say to you, all sins will be forgiven the sons of men, and whatever blasphemies they utter; but whoever blasphemes against the Holy Spirit never has forgiveness, but is guilty of an eternal sin."

[2] E.g., W. Michaelis, *Versöhnung des Alls* (Gümligen/Berne: Siloah, 1950), 53, 57-58.

[3] There are only a few places where the rabbis, after the middle of the first century A.D., conceive Gehenna as a place of temporally limited punishment (P. Volz, *Die Eschatologie der jüdischen Gemeinde im neutestamentlichen Zeitalter* [Tübingen: Mohr, 1934], 315, 326f.). The numerous passages in the apocryphal and rabbinic writings of the time that understand *olām/aiōnios* as "never-ending", "eternal" (*ibid.*, 325ff.) do not permit us to reduce the concept to an indefinite but limited temporal duration. Later we shall come to discuss the relationship of this *aiōnios* of damnation to the *aiōnios* of the kingdom of the Father that has been prepared from before all time (Mt 25:34).

had not been born" (Mk 14:21; cf. Jn 17:12)? Or what of the
passages in John which speak of the wrath of God "resting" on
the disobedient (Jn 3:36), of guilt "remaining" (Jn 9:41), and
of the "sin unto death" (Jn 8:24)? Or what of the references in
the Book of Revelation to the "second death" (2:11; 20:6; 21:8)
of those who are not found in the book of life but are thrown
into the lake of fire (20:14)?

Paul too, who so forcefully put forward his conviction that
the redemption applies to the whole universe, is careful not
to anticipate the result of the judgment exercised by God and
Christ (1 Cor 4:3). He can only hope, for himself and for Christians, that "we may not be condemned along with the world"
(1 Cor 11:32). He distinguishes "those who are being saved"
from "those who are perishing" (1 Cor 1:18). "Do you not
know that the unrighteous will not inherit the kingdom of God?
Do not be deceived; neither the immoral, nor idolaters . . . nor
revilers . . . will inherit the kingdom of God" (1 Cor 6:9–10).
"For if you live according to the flesh you will die" (Rom 8:12),
which means more than physical death (cf. Gal 5:19–21; Eph
5:5–6; Col 3:5–8). Turning to the Jews, he says, "by your hard
and impenitent heart you are storing up wrath for yourself on
the day of wrath when God's righteous judgment will be revealed. For he will render to every man according to his works:
. . . for those who are factious and do not obey the truth, but
obey wickedness, there will be wrath and fury" (Rom 2:5–8).
Christians themselves are not immune to this judgment; particularly if someone approaches the Christians' most holy mystery
without examining himself and distinguishing the Body of the
Lord from ordinary bread, he "eats and drinks judgment upon
himself" (1 Cor 11:29).

The issue here, in a grave case, is the deliberate rejection of that
New Testament grace that was so dearly bought on the Cross;
this is "a negative heightening".[4] Jesus will not "do his work
without the participation of believers; . . . They are not seized
by redemption against their will."[5] "The decision . . . [to be-
lieve] is not only God's gift, it is also their personal act", and one

---

[4] Pa 71.
[5] K 25–26.

that has to be performed anew again and again.[6] It is possible to
"lose [one's] prize" (Col 2:18).[7] "Man is always given the possibility of saying Yes or No to God's offer."[8] "It is possible for
him to become so hardened in his freedom that he must pursue
to the end the path he has chosen in opposition to God."[9] As
James says (2:13), judgment will have no mercy on us if we are
not merciful to others, "because if justice is to have its effect,
it must encounter mercy. . . . In judgment the Lord is looking
for what he put in us, and if he does not find in us the mercy
he gave us, he has no alternative but to let the judgment of the
law—such as we ourselves would demand—take its course in
our case."[10] It may seem "as if the Lord and evil face each other
equipped with equal power, and we always decide the battle in
our favor as a result of our constant inclination to evil."[11] "We
shall not be saved against our own will. We shall be redeemed
as living agents who give lively consent to be rescued. We may
be drowned or asphyxiated; but we will be asked before being
given artificial respiration, for in sin there is no such thing as
complete unconsciousness."[12]

   Christ's work "must not turn into some sort of blurred collective redemption".[13] Such a way of dealing with sinners "would
be unworthy of the human being".[14] "If we refuse to allow
Christ to accept us, we remain in our sin, and the separation
(of us from our sins), which can be performed only in him,
becomes impossible."[15] Man can break off his relationship with
heaven; even "in death he can turn his back on the light of eternal life."[16] Here "negative heightening" plays its part again and
again: "The greater a man's intimacy with the Lord, the greater
the danger that he will become estranged."[17] If a person withdraws from the Son's judgment of love, "the Father has no other
course but to replace love with judgment and sentence."[18] How

[6] K 45.   [7] K 98.
[8] 2 Jo 82.   [9] Is 137.
[10] Ka I, 113.   [11] Ka I, 161.
[12] Ka I, 78.   [13] 4 Jo 15.
[14] Ka II, 100.   [15] Ka II, 218.
[16] C 283.   [17] C 348.
[18] C 351, cf. 1 Jo 274: "There remain those who do not want to be judged by
the Son's judgment of love. . . . These have to be judged by the Father."

we strive for "judgment and recompense" rather than for love! "We prefer to be measured as we ourselves would measure."[19] At the point where we have "one ultimate supernatural link" with God, "through the believing acknowledgment of the Lord and the opening of [our] soul by him", we discover, terrified, that we have "one ultimate natural freedom".[20] "It is possible to abandon oneself to sin in such a way that no fear is able to break the bond thus made", as is shown by the reply of Jesus to Judas' question: Is it I, Master?: "You have said so" (Mt 26:25).[21] This means that "the door of judgment is shut", since one has pronounced oneself an enemy of the Cross.[22] The grace of a vocation (even of that of Judas) "is eternal and irrevocable. . . . This says nothing about whether this grace of the mission is in fact received by the man or not."[23] Such a man would have to see his failure in the light of the Lord; but "if the sinner were to turn to the Lord while still concealing his sin, the Lord would not be able to help him."[24]

Here the Savior, the Good Shepherd, is in a difficulty, for "the sheep are always . . . free to follow or not to follow." They are not content with the Shepherd's life dedication: "they expect their shepherd to save them, although they put up resistance to this salvation. . . . Thus, when the Lord has poured out all his love on the Cross, and men nevertheless continue to sin, they call him to account for the fact that he has not totally redeemed them." And their strictness of account is "quite different from the Father's judgment. Here he is summoned before a judgment seat that is without mercy, and this judgment is conditioned by sin. He himself cannot do anything other than offer his grace to counter this sin, in the awareness that the sin will presume to set itself up as the court of judgment vis-à-vis his grace."[25] So when Jesus says, "He who rejects me and does not receive

---

[19] 1 Jo 287 (GT).

[20] 2 Jo 83.

[21] Mt 23.

[22] Ph 145.

[23] 2 Jo 153.

[24] 2 Jo 154–55 (GT); cf. 158–59: "If the light of love is unable to penetrate the darkness of sin, it rebounds from its darkness."

[25] 2 Jo 261.

my sayings has a judge; the word that I have spoken will be his judge on the last day" (Jn 12:48), it sounds like resignation on his part: in the end we have the judge that we ourselves have chosen, choosing justice rather than love.[26] It is almost as if men sent the Son into hell; in this case hell would be "a divine reality, by no means a mere empty threat. We cannot regard it as something that is already behind us in redemption."[27] Now the situation is that the outcome of the final act seems uncertain on both sides. Sinful man, naturally, cannot be absolutely certain of being saved. "If the righteous man is scarcely saved, where will the impious and sinner appear?" (1 Pet 4:18). "This man may be righteous, but only with difficulty will he be saved. For everywhere we can discern inadequacy and failure, most apparent, perhaps, to those who are most righteous. And since he falls under the Law he cannot possess any certainty of salvation. He may hope to be accepted by grace, but he has no control over the outcome."[28] We cannot bask in even the most insistent promises of eternal life that God gives us; we have to prove worthy of them through responsible action.[29] Sooner or later every earthly human being "recognizes in himself the burden of earth and has some intimation of the vast distance separating him from the heavenly realm. He knows how little he can guarantee his own future."[30] "There is a sin which is mortal" (1 Jn 5:16); "John says this *after* the Lord on the Cross has redeemed the sinner and *after* having instituted the sacrament of penance."[31] But if man's destiny is thus in the balance, what of God's destiny? Can we say, as Péguy did,[32] that there is anxiety and anguish in the heart of God, producing not "certainty of salvation" but something far more, namely, the flower of "hope"?

---

[26] 2 Jo 442–43.
[27] Ap 476.
[28] Ka I, 388.
[29] Ka II, 221.
[30] C 538.
[31] Ka II, 232.
[32] On Péguy, see pp. 183–88.

3. The Judgment of Christ

The question facing us is this: How do justice and love (or grace) constitute a unity in Christ's judgment of man in his failure? "One cannot fail to notice", says Karl Lehmann, "that the New Testament refashions the idea of judgment on the basis of Jesus Christ's redeeming act. Unless God allows grace to take precedence over justice, no one can be saved. Righteousness before God is not something that we can manufacture."[1] But if guilty man is ultimately to be acquitted, does this not imply a humiliation for human freedom? Does it not imply a defeat on the part of God, who has to turn a blind eye to justice and righteousness in order to permit the triumph of a grace that has been "won" by someone other than the guilty party? Kant's objections—which cannot be brushed aside easily—raise their heads at this point.

a. Man Judges Himself

First of all we can leave to one side the question of whether the "particular" and the "general" Judgments are one or twofold: eventually, at all events, the individual human being will be confronted, after his death, with the unveiled truth and demands of God. And this is the frightening part: the greater the love of God offered and demonstrated to man, the more must be expected of man's response. As long as man lives in the carapace of his senses, he can lull himself to sleep with ever-new illusions as to the extent of his guilt; indeed, sin's mendacious nature absolutely requires this kind of self-concealment and constant self-justification. Once he is released, however, from this outer shell, it is no longer possible to deceive himself; man "sees himself: he sees who he was and what he has become. . . . The scales fall from his eyes." Of course "the light that enables us to see all this does not come from ourselves" but from "the decisive encounter with the living God",[2] with the light of truth that streams from him. Origen was the first to describe the Judgment as the radiance of the light of Christ, so that "not only

---

[1] Lehmann/Scheffczyk/Schnackenburg/Volk: *Vollendung des Lebens—Hoffnung auf Herrlichkeit* (Mainz: Grünewald, 1978), 93.

[2] *Ibid.*, 88–89.

no righteous man but no sinner either will be able to mistake the nature of Christ"; even sinners "will recognize their evil deeds in the light of his countenance". For then the light of his divinity will illuminate everything with far more clarity than faith—even the most lively faith—can now perceive it.[3] Basil takes up the theme: The face of the Judge radiates a divine light that illuminates the very depths of hearts, and we shall have no other accuser but our own sins, thus made present to us.[4] Similarly Gregory Nazianzen: Judgment is "the internal burden that weighs upon each man's conscience".[5] Ambrose, as so often, follows Origen: The "opened books" and "judgment seats" are simply images of our own conscience, which, in the presence of Christ, "can no longer hide itself";[6] according to Ambrose, the sentence is nothing other than the confirmation of each person's just deserts.[7] "Thus", says Augustine, "there is a certain divine power whereby everyone is reminded of all that he has done, good or evil. This knowledge, which either accuses or excuses the conscience, is presented to him with such inconceivable rapidity that everyone, every individual, is judged simultaneously. This divine power is called a 'book' in which we read, as it were, what is set forth in it."[8] Peter Lombard takes up the teaching of Augustine,[9] and Thomas follows him insofar as he finds it "more probable" that "the entire judgment, that is, the arguments for and against, the accusation of evil, the acknowledgment of good, and the verdict between them, takes place in the spirit".[10]

"To that extent . . . judgment can be regarded as a kind of *judgment upon oneself*",[11] albeit in the light of the divine truth, which is, as such, the truth of what God has done for mankind in Jesus Christ. It is hard to imagine that any man, faced with

---

[3] *In Mt.* ser. 70 (GCS, Klostermann XI, 165).

[4] *In Ps.* 33, 4 (PG 29, 360); *In Ps.* 48,2 (*ibid.*, 437).

[5] *Poem. mor.* 34, 254f. (PG 37, 964).

[6] *In Ps.* 1, 51–52 (PL 14, 993–94); cf. *In Ps.* 37, 51 (*ibid.*, 1081); *In Ps.* 40, 7 (*ibid.*, 1122).

[7] *In Luc.* 2, 60 (PL 15, 1652).

[8] *De Civ. Dei* 20, 14 (PL 41, 680).

[9] *Sent.* IV, d 47, 1.

[10] *In 4 Sent.* d 47, q 1, a 1 sol 2; Suppl. q 88, 2; cf. "sed contra 2".

[11] J. H. Oswald, *Eschatologie*, 5th ed. (1893), 25.

this standard of action that God puts before him, could so much as mention his supposedly "good works". It is precisely those who have acquired a deeper insight into the absolute nature of the divine act of love on the Cross who are forced to admit that they fall utterly short of the model presented for their imitation. "Our deeds do not conform to what the Father intended from the very first"; we are aware of this even now, on earth, and so "we are bound to fear"[12]—an attitude that Peter actually recommends (1 Pet 1:17). Nothing is more appropriate to the ultimate confrontation between our life and the standard set by Christ than Peter's words to the Lord: "Depart from me, for I am a sinful man" (Lk 5:8). Thoroughly apt is Søren Kierkegaard's approach to this encounter: "In my life I have never got farther, nor will I get farther, than 'fear and trembling', that point at which I am literally quite certain that everyone else will easily attain the bliss of heaven, and only I shall not." "Telling other people . . . 'You are eternally lost' is something I cannot do. As far as I am concerned, the situation is that all the others will, of course, go to heaven; the only doubt is whether I shall get there."[13] It is important to note here that, as yet, there is no question of a kind, forgiving, divine verdict that would supersede this judgment upon oneself: Kierkegaard is giving a precise account of man's experience in this crucial encounter.

This is the context for what Hamann described as "self-knowledge's descent into hell";[14] there are also relevant passages in the *Theologia Germanica*: "Christ's soul had to go to hell before it went to heaven. So it must be with the human soul. . . . When a man knows and beholds himself, and finds himself so evil and unworthy of all the good, all the encouragement God has sent him or communicated to him through creatures, [he sees] only that he is eternally damned and lost—and considers himself unworthy even of that."[15]

Talk of hell and damnation arises from the fact that the ideal of eternal blessedness, which is glimpsed in the illumination ac-

[12] Ka I, 275.

[13] Quoted from E. Geismar, "Das ethische Stadium bei Søren Kierkegaard" in *SSTh* 1 (1923), 260 n. 2.

[14] *Kreuzzüge eines Philologen: Chimärische Einfälle* (Nadler, vol. 2 [1950]), 164.

[15] Chap. 11, ed. Alois M. Haas (Einsiedeln: Johannes Verlag, 1980), 55–56.

companying the Judgment and which constitutes man's sole further possibility, totally surpasses the ideal of pleasurable satisfaction that was the sinner's goal here below; it is alien and actually contrary to it. The "reality principle" (if we may adopt Freudian terminology) is so contrary to the "pleasure principle" that as far as the sinner can see there is no question of accommodating the latter to the former. He is asked to give up his idea of "self-realization" (using his neighbor—and even God, if necessary—as a means to this end) and actually to lose his self; thus he may gain what, in the real and concrete God, is blessedness. And this blessedness is a Hypostasis who is himself precisely by surrendering to the Other. That is what blessedness consists in. Christians may find Mohammed's vision of coarsely sensual paradisal joys simply naïve; but how far removed is its hope of blessedness from that real blessedness of God and of the man Jesus Christ that is presented to Christians in the Judgment![16]

On the stage we encounter a beggar who can only repeat a single word: "unworthy!"[17] There too we meet the king who is told, "You have been quietly eaten up by the hell that is called 'abandoned-by-God'."[18]

b. Approaching the Verdict

The theme of the dead being "weighed", which is depicted in art and on artefacts, the deceased's entire past life being laid in the scales, is older than Christianity. It is found in the Egyptian Judgment of Osiris, who is described as "enthroned in the Hall of Truth together with his son Horus, flanked by forty-two awe-inspiring gods of judgment, each of which is responsible for uncovering a particular sin. Beside the great scales (wielded by Anubis) stands the divine Scribe, Thoth, ready to record the results of the weighing. Nearby is a monster with a crocodile's

---

[16] Clearly, the hypothesis of a final decision proposed by L. Boros (*The Moment of Truth: Mysterium Mortis* [London: Burns and Oates, 1965]) is of no help here. A decision that is taken in retrospect, looking back on life, is not utterly unavoidable, as it will be in the light of Christ, since he alone holds up to us the true standard.

[17] Hofmannsthal, *Der Turm*, 1st version, in *Dramen* IV (Fischer, 1958) 59, 66; 2d version, *ibid.*, 358–63.

[18] *Ibid.*, 1st version, 75.

head, waiting to devour those who are found to be too light."[1] In Christian iconography, too, where the scales are held by an angel, it is clearly a question of weighing a *whole life*; now, however, it is no longer a case of the individual subjectively judging himself (as in the previous section): now his life is judged objectively by the verdict of the divine Judge. This shows that man's verdict on himself in his relation to God cannot be the last act of the Judgment. Human freedom is not self-constituted: it is appointed by God to operate in its limited area; ultimately it depends on *absolute* freedom and must necessarily transcend itself (*Theo-Drama*, II, 207ff.) in that direction. Thus it will be perfected in absolute *freedom*. While infinite freedom will respect the decisions of finite freedom, it will not allow itself to be compelled, or restricted in its own freedom, by the latter. The metaphor of the scales gives rise to several issues.

In applying the scales of judgment, it is clearly not merely a case of quantitatively weighing the good or evil present in a life. Freedom is not exhausted in the momentary choice of finite goods, for, traversing mere finitude, it has an infinite horizon and is able to make a qualitative choice with regard to it. Either it chooses this infinite horizon as its own possession, thus positing itself as absolute autonomy, or it chooses it as its origin and goal and thereby recognizes the existence of a superordinate absolute autonomy (of whatever kind). This fundamental choice, however, which causes the scales to rise or fall, does not take place *in abstracto* but in the succession of individual life situations; it takes place in a series of acts and stances that are all vulnerable to death and thus constantly highlight the finitude of the arena in which this freedom has to exercise its choice.[2] It is difficult to establish the relationship between the fundamental choice that is the primary issue in the objective judgment— and which is not reducible to the individual situations—and the necessary incarnation of this choice in the ever-new decisions

---

[1] N. J. Hein, article "Gericht Gottes" in *RGG*, 3d ed., II, 1415–16.

[2] Some endeavor to escape this finitude by having recourse to the idea of the transmigration of souls. This is no help, however, because every new existence would bring with it the same old dialectic of finite situations in which an "infinite" decision is required.

that such situations require. For, on the one hand, there is the phenomenon of repentance (conversion), central to the biblical message, in which wrong decisions in the past are rejected and annihilated; this gives unqualified justification for the pastoral care of the dying, who are urged to enter the judgment hall affirming their fundamental choice for God. We see the power of finite freedom, as in the case of the crucified thief, in that a man can actually repent of all his wrongdoing and turn toward what he should have done. On the other hand, we must realize that what is placed on the scales is not the mere final state of a life but this life in its totality. Since what is at issue is not a quantitative measuring but the quality of the fundamental decision, and since this fundamental decision is not made in the abstract, prescinding from historical situations, but is actualized in them, we must ask whether a negative fundamental decision, even if it is chronologically the last in a particular life, can have expressed itself in all life situations without exception. What, for example, about early and later childhood? What about those situations that would always require a certain turning toward one's fellow men? From this point of view, a life's tendency can be relativized to a single moment, at least where it is a question of a prevalently negative fundamental decision.[3] Here the Judge will ascertain "whether there is something in the life of the one to be judged that fits into this relationship of love, that *has* been taken up into his living love, or *can* be taken up, or at least could be as a possibility of faith, something at all that is capable of love",[4] a "little seed of love" in response to all the love bestowed upon him by God.[5] [God] "wishes to give him the possibility of receiving at least a part of his grace within the framework created

---

[3] We must remember that it is man's entire life that is destined for God, which is why "resurrection of the body" means "that God will not lose anything of it, . . . that, in God, man will find not only his last moment but also his whole history": W. Breuning, *Myst. Sal.* V, 882.

[4] 1 Jo 291. "In holy Christendom there are more / who pass from earth to heaven / than who go to eternal hell. / Yet righteousness always exercises her power. . . . / But first I will come to the troubled soul as a father, / *if only I have discerned some goodness in it.* / This is the way in which / I am drawn to my child": Mechthild von Magdeburg, *Das Fliessende Licht der Gottheit*, III, 22.

[5] 2 Jo 424.

by his refusal".[6] For "the possibility of the conversion of a sinful man is never so hopeless as the conversion of the devil. If the sinner is baptized, then he has once been touched so much by grace that traces of the earlier workings of grace remain behind in him, traces that make the renewed conversion easier".[7] This is not to imply that a further "conversion" is still possible at the Judgment, after death. Here it is only a question of the Judge's objective evaluation of a life's totality.[8]

This reminds us of the "realized eschatology" of the Johannine corpus. Man's supratemporal fundamental decision is situated in the milieu of the timeless verdict of the eternal Judge, a relationship that is expressed in the word "remain".[9] If a man "remains" in this milieu, the eternal (the very essence of which is to "remain") takes effect in his temporal existence. Thus the Spirit "remains" on Christ (1:32), and the Father "remains" in him (14:10); and the Spirit "remains" in the disciples (14:17). He is the mark of this abiding, mutual indwelling of the temporal and the eternal (1 Jn 3:9). This "remaining", however, is dependent on man's decision. He can move from darkness, where he does not need to "remain" (Jn 12:46), into light. But he can also close his heart to love, so that "God's love does not abide in him" (1 Jn 3:17). So we continually meet with conditional clauses: If anyone does not believe, "the wrath of God rests upon him" (Jn 3:36). "If any man eats my flesh, . . . he abides in me" (6:56); "if anyone abides in me, and I in him, he will bear much fruit. . . . If a man does not abide in me, he

---

[6] 2 Jo 13.

[7] 2 Jo 203.

[8] "We have to accept responsibility for our whole earthly life. 'I tell you, on the Day of Judgment men will render account for every careless word they utter' (Mt 12:36)": Otto Betz, *Die Eschatologie in der Glaubensunterweisung* (Würzburg: Echter, 1965), 210. Matthew 25:31ff. is even clearer: a person's whole attitude to his neighbor is a matter for judgment. Cf. Mt 7:2; on late Judaism, cf. P. Volz, *Die Eschatologie der jüdische Gemeinde im neutestamentlichen Zeitalter* (Tübingen: Mohr, 1934), 293f.

[9] Jürgen Heise, *Bleiben: "Menein" in den johanneischen Schriften* (Tübingen: Mohr, 1967); R. Schnackenburg, *Die Johannesbriefe*, 2d ed. (Herder, 1963); B. Lammers, *Die MENEIN-Formeln der Johannesbriefe* (Rome: Gregoriana, diss. 1954); Raymond E. Brown, *The Epistles of John*, Anchor Bible (1982), 259–61, 339.

is cast forth . . ." (15:5–6).[10] Hence the imperatives: "Abide in
my love" (15:9); "Little children, abide in him" (1 Jn 2:28). It
is crucial to note that it is possible to possess eternal life and
yet not remain in it, which paradoxically proves that such possession was only appearance: it was not real. "You [the Jews]
do not have his word abiding in you, for you do not believe
him whom he has sent" (Jn 5:38). "The slave [the sinner] does
not continue in the house for ever; the son continues for ever"
(8:35). Of the devil it is said that "he did not stand in the truth"
(8:44 Gk); accordingly no "one who hates", who is a murderer,
"has eternal life abiding in him" (1 Jn 3:15). Of the heretics it is
said that "they went out from us, but they were not of us; for if
they had been of us, they would have continued with us" (1 Jn
2:19). So, just as one can move into the milieu of eternity, one
can remove oneself from it; but for John this only goes to show
that the mutual indwelling and "remaining" never really came
about: "No one who sins has either seen him or known him"
(1 Jn 3:6).

Sin here clearly means conscious and complete rejection of the
divine Word and Spirit, "the sin which is mortal" (1 Jn 5:16). It
is a deliberate withdrawal from the milieu in which the mutual
"remaining", "abiding", takes place between God and man. It
is assumed that man can perform such a withdrawal, which thus
makes him a "child" of that same devil who fell from truth (cf.
Jn 8:44). But, given the whole thrust of the Johannine writings
—for many transitional stages between faith and unbelief are
described—it is once again a borderline case, quoted in order to
highlight the absolute seriousness of the commandment of love.
The Johannine "dualism" is not metaphysical but ethical and
hortatory. The Jews call themselves "children of Abraham", but
if they were, they would do the works of their Father. Therefore
they must be children of the devil. Nonetheless, at the end of
the dispute, Jesus can once again say "Your father [!] Abraham
rejoiced . . ." (8:56).

In order to proceed to condemnation, the divine Judge would
have to encounter nothing contrary to a rejection on man's part,
nothing that would relativize it. The Johannine "unless" ("Un-

---

[10] Cf. also 1 Jn 2:17, 24; 3:24.

less he abides in me . . .") would have to have been absolutely verified. Mere external expiation without an inner effect on the guilty person would not suffice for him to be acquitted; it could never make him inwardly blessed. It would be an unresolvable contradiction inside him, a constant humiliation, apt to lead even to rebellion against such external overpowering. "Forgiveness needs to be accepted as well as offered if it is to be complete" (C. S. Lewis).[11]

We can say all this with confidence provided we hold fast to the Christian truth that the One who judges us is also the One who came, not to judge, but to save (Jn 12:47). He will therefore take every available path to bring back the person whose sins he has borne, even if this person rejects him; and, if this proves impossible, he will not positively thrust him from him (the reader will recall the protests of Nédoncelle, Martelet and Ratzinger)[12] but will negatively leave the sinner to his blinded will. This possibility once again raises the idea of a tragedy, not only for man, but also for God himself.

Can we go farther than this? We can say nothing categorical; at best we can proceed by way of hypothesis. This is because the question of hell, as we saw in the case of the sinner "judging himself", can only seriously be entertained as a personal and existential question. "Both the uncritical notion of a bipolar outcome of human history and the strident protest against it contain the same danger. They both want to draw up an eschatology from the point of view of the spectator, not of the man most intimately involved in it. . . . In spite of all the compelling negative evidence I may have, it is beyond my abilities and competence to assess to what extent, ultimately, a man is really persisting in, or can persist in, resistance to Christ."[13]

---

[11] *The Problem of Pain* (London: Centenary Press, 1940), 97.

[12] Cf. K. Rahner, "The model of a vindicatory punishment . . . is not very helpful in explicating the doctrine of hell": article "Hölle", in *Sacram. Mundi* II (1968), 738.

[13] W. Kreck, *Die Zukunft des Gekommenen* (Munich: Kaiser, 1966), 147. "The twofold outcome of the judgment we find in the New Testament cannot be twisted and turned into some kind of 'happy end' theology; on the other hand, it is only correctly understood if, with all its grave warnings, it points us to the God who 'desires all men to be saved' (1 Tim 2:4)": C. Schütz, *Myst. Sal.* V, 665–66. The

If, however, Christianity is the Good News of salvation, and we are told that God desires all men to be saved (1 Tim 2:4), it seems that we must take these steps, expressly hypothetical though they be.

4. Approaching the Reality of Hell

a. The Absolute Good: Freedom

Can man's finite freedom—and for the present we are leaving aside the question of the devil's freedom—so cut itself off from God as to become entirely self-contained in its own decision? Since its very essence is dependent on absolute freedom, it can have no control over its own origin, and it is this origin that governs its goal and its formal object, namely, the good in itself.[1] Only on the basis of this transcendental constitution can it opt for any particular good, even if it decides that it *itself* is

---

element of "turning to the sinner" in Christ's work for us gives rise to "a remarkable confidence in the Christian's eschatological attitude. It is by no means the confidence of a 'knowing', yet expresses a trust that all history has been destined for a positive outcome; nor can it be regarded as a naïve, harmless optimism." For "one of its essential components is the realization that at any time I may falter and fail": W. Breuning, in *Myst. Sal.* V, 849–50. Cf. the chapter on "the conditional nature of our statements on hell", in Betz, *Eschatologie*, 221.

E. Przywara situates the meditation on hell, which is found at the end of the first week of the Spiritual Exercises, in the context of the sinner's preceding three-fold conversation with the Crucified, with Mary, and with the Father. "Having endured the immensity of hell, I find the immensity of this same crucified Lord's mercy and kindness ineffably greater: the Father's love for the Son through hell and beyond hell. So it is not the 'breadth and length and depth' of hell that has the last word, but that whence these attributes are drawn in the first place, namely, the 'breadth and length and height and depth' of that love which 'surpasses' (*tēn hyperballousan agapēn*) because it is the 'fullness of God' (Eph 3:18–19)": *Deus Semper Maior* I, 2d ed. (Vienna: Herold, 1964), 198. Even this absolutely serious meditation on hell remains purely personal and existential.

Louis Lochet, in his passionate book *Jésus descendu aux enfers* (Cerf, 1979), insists that we must hold fast to both poles of our faith. "Christ alone was the God-man, and so he alone can know the terrible grief of the sinner. And only Christ can reveal to man what hell is." Closest to him are the saints who went to hell on behalf of others (e.g., the title of Cesbron's novel *Les saints vont en enfer*). We shall return to this topic.

[1] Thomas, following Plato, lays great stress on this truth (*De Ver.* 21, 4; "om-

the self-sufficient good. God has set his seal on its structure, he has stamped it with his branding iron; positively, insofar as it is privileged to be just that: a freedom that is responsible for itself; and negatively, insofar as it can only *be* itself by being oriented *beyond* itself, to the absolute good. It cannot change the latter, its own formal object, for the absolute good is also absolute freedom, which cannot be controlled by anything else. So we can say that the *causa prima*, which possesses the unique power of giving rise to a *causa secunda* with genuine freedom and control over *itself*, cannot do so except by setting upon this created freedom, in some way, the permanent mark of its origin. If created freedom chooses itself as the absolute good, it involves itself in a contradiction that will devour it: the formal object that informs it—which is in fact absolute, self-positing freedom—is in constant contradiction with finite freedom's pretentious claim to be infinite. This contradiction, if persisted in, is hell.

The fire that burns here is none other than the fire of God himself, as Scheeben rightly saw. "Accordingly the state of punishment visited on the sinner is not merely the negation, but the reverse, of divine glorification, and in its way is as supernatural and mysterious as the latter." It is "the fiery power of the divinity" that "devastates" this nature "without [it] being actually annihilated". This devastation comes more from God than from the creature's self-devastation. Yet it is true that the latter "devastates itself" insofar as its "hate and fury against God" is "proportionate to the supernatural fellowship in love" that God has implanted in the creature's essence, so that this love expresses itself as the "weight and fire of divine wrath, a wrath exactly proportionate in greatness and might to the love which [is] offered to the creature and scorned by him".[2] Hell, in this view,

---

nia naturaliter appetunt Deum implicite": 22, 2) and so contradicts Spinoza, who regards the highest goal of the individual being (which for him is not substantial) as self-preservation (*Ethica* III, 6). For Spinoza, accordingly, the finite creature's love for God is not its own act but "pars infiniti amoris, quo Deus seipsum amat" (V, 36).

[2] *The Mysteries of Christianity* (Herder, 1946), 684–88. Scheeben goes on to speak of a supernatural material fire, but this is not relevant in the present context.

is located in God, but it can equally well be portrayed as being in the condition of the damned person himself.[3]

As we said at the beginning of this volume, however, it is not only a question of the relationship between the absolute (the infinite) and the contingent (the finite). The finite *person* bears the stamp of the *imago trinitatis*, which means that it can only be and become a person by relating to the other persons it encounters on its way through life. It is a relationship between creatures: a man's sexual potential cannot be fruitful unless he goes beyond himself and relates to a woman; so too human freedom cannot find itself except within the context of a freedom shared by other humans. This gives us a shadowy image of the way in which man is called through grace to realize his freedom within the eternal exchange of love that is the life of the Trinity, where the absolute freedom of one Hypostasis is always both *given* to the Others and *received* from them. It shows that, given man's supernatural vocation to trinitarian love, something of the freedom granted him is "laid up" in God, ultimately to be handed over to him, in the exchange of love, as the final gift that will bring his freedom to fulfillment.

If nothing in the world is created without the Word and apart from the Word (Jn 1:3), it follows that the world's "inmost essence" rests

> upon the word and is only intelligible as the word. The creature's relation to God is given to us in the essence of speech: it consists in question, deliberation, and answer. There is God's question, in the word to the creature; there is the creature's deliberation on the word of God received; and there is the creature's answer to God in the word. Such is the creature's nature, and it is not in his power to change it; it does not fall within the sphere of his free choice; on the contrary, prior to the realm of choice and to the sphere of our vacillation and irresolution lies the sphere that does not fall within the orbit of our freedom and which we cannot disturb. That basis is our nature, grounded in God, and it is unaffected by our vacillating utterances. It is only above and beyond this foundation that we enter the sphere of hesitation, the sphere

---

[3] "Hell, of course, is not a place within the cosmos. . . . Suffice it to say that hell is the condemned man himself; where he is, is hell": A. Winklhofer, *Das Kommen des Reiches: Von den Letzten Dingen* (Frankfurt: Knecht, 1959), 105–6.

in which the word of God may be heard or not heard, received or not received, answered or not answered. . . . Though even if man remains silent and refuses to hear the word on this level, that does not alter the fact that the ground of his being, the unalterable character of the creature, whether he wills it or not, is involved in a dialogue with God. Ultimately even silence is a form and an expression, of the word, because the word is in the beginning, and everything is created in the word.[4]

The created person must one day be confronted with this Word that is "laid up" in God and that is fundamental to its creaturely being.[5] Furthermore, since this Word has always been bent on reconciling the world, and since all things are created with a view to the Cross,[6] it is Christ himself who is our essential freedom, laid up in God.[7] "The curve of man's life which begins in God, sweeps away from God and returns to God in death, is enclosed within the curve of the word made man, which runs its pure course in God, from the birth of the Lord to his death. . . . He continued to be the word that was in the beginning and was in God."[8]

In Christ, the life of the Trinity is bent on reconciling the world to God. In this perspective, therefore, if a man tries to

---

[4] 1 Jo 31–32. On the audibility of the word, even in the absence of faith: P 36.

[5] 1 Jo 36; L 93. Hell in this case would be the sinner's persistent opposition to this "word" in God—which the mystics term the "spark" of the soul. Cf. *Eckhart, Die deutschen Werke* I, 334; *Die lateinischen Werke* I, 634 ("neque in damnatis extinguitur synderesis remurmurans malo"). *Tauler* says "The greatest torment of the damned is that they know heaven is present within them, yet they can never reach it" (Hoffmann, 128). "The human spirit, man's ground, has an eternal yearning, a fundamental yearning for its origin. This yearning is not even extinguished in hell. And this is the greatest pain of the damned" (Hoffmann, 412). *Angela of Foligno*: "I say, 'Through thy holy judgments redeem me', because I discern God's goodness in a good and holy man . . . no better than in one of the damned" (Doncoeur, 89). *Ruysbroeck*: "The spirit's essence and being is so noble that even the damned cannot wish their own extinction" (*The Adornment of the Spiritual Marriage* II, 60). *Suso*: "According to my eternal ordinance, the disordered mind is a torment and a heavy punishment to itself" (*A Little Book of Eternal Wisdom*, chap. 12).

[6] Sc 51.

[7] "He has made himself the image of our nature as designed by heaven, and it is in him that we possess this nature": Ka II, 184; "In this sense we are in him before he is in us": Ka II, 237.

[8] 1 Jo 34.

exclude himself from it in order to be his own private hell, he is still embraced by the curve of Christ's being. To that extent he is still determined by its essence and meaning, which aims to communicate to the world the freedom of the absolute good. Only Christ's freedom is powerful enough to break through our restrictions and preoccupations and to integrate their multiplicity into an ordered unity.[9] True, this process of unification ultimately brings us to a "judgment in which all the multiplicity of our living and doing is summed up in a single word, a Word that we have heard, in faith, from the beginning; all our speaking and action have been partial aspects of this Word from the very outset."[10] "What from the outside looks like an earthly attachment to Christ is from the inside our being set free to embrace the eternal. . . . Through our bond with Christ the very concept of 'freedom' is so broadened that all earthly freedoms seem limited and insignificant", leading as they do to ultimate termination. By contrast the space opened up by Christ is the milieu of "the breath of the Spirit, proceeding from Father and Son": it is a trinitarian space.[11] Attachment to Christ, and it alone, leads us into "the perfect law, the law of liberty" (James 1:25), just as Jesus' "being bound to the Cross was at the same time the highest realization of his freedom." To be bound to him, therefore, "means to let freedom rule in us".[12] "It is within obedience that God gives us freedom. . . . The more a person decides for God and binds himself to him, the freer his freedom becomes."[13]

These remarks are designed to shed light on the internal limitations and difficulties involved in the idea that man has absolute power and freedom to turn his back, totally, on God.

[9] Ka I, 110.

[10] Ka I, 109.

[11] OM 25.

[12] Ka I, 83.

[13] Ka I, 318; cf. Ka II, 165–66: Even here on earth the true saints can attain that "true freedom" where they no longer sin; this freedom has become "so vast that it has swallowed up even the freedom to sin". Cf. C 176 for the christological meaning of the Pauline "all things are lawful for me" (1 Cor 6:12): we have been "set free for freedom" in the Lord (C 214); our earthly freedom to choose has been elevated so that it meets a "necessity that comes down from above, from God . . . in heavenly self". It is "a necessity that is an attribute of freedom" (C 260, on 1 Cor 9:16).

b. Analogies of Timelessness

The New Testament uses the same adjective, *aiōnios*, for "eternal" life or salvation and "eternal punishment" (or the "eternal" fire). It is pointless to try to discover some temporal restriction of this where the word is used in a negative context, for example, in Matthew 25:41.[1] The New Testament authors are able to comprehend both forms of "eternity" in a single concept since both represent something final and irreversible, as compared with the changeability that characterizes time. However, this tells us nothing about the specific form of each.

It is well known that, in the early Church, speculation about the nature of immortality (*athanasia*) took place under the influence of two concepts. On the one hand, there is the ontological notion, based on Plato, that emerged from the essence of the immaterial soul; on the other, there is the theological concept that attributed immortality at the level of being to God alone and was only prepared to grant the creature this same immortality provided it acquired an inner participation in the divine *athanasia*. Thus Justin comes to distinguish between a continued existence after death that is common to all men and the specific immortality of the blessed. However, even the former (the continued existence) is a gift, since every created thing differs from God by having a transitory nature; this applies to the soul as well,[2] but God desires it to live. Yet the immortality of the blessed is something higher: it is a participation in the eternal life of God,[3] given to us through Christ. While the details of Tatian's teaching are a matter of dispute, one thing is clear, namely, that he distinguishes two kinds of *pneumata* in man: the higher, which bears God's image and likeness and is immortal, and the lower, which is not. The lower shares the dissolution suffered by the body until the Last Judgment and thereafter undergoes the punishment of eternal death.[4] Ignatius had described the Eu-

---

[1] As W. Michaelis does: *Versöhnung des Alls* (Gümligen/Berne: Siloah, 1950).

[2] *Dial.* 5–6. Justin opposes the Platonic doctrine that the soul is immortal because it is not the result of a coming-to-be.

[3] *Apol.* I, 8, 10, 63; *Dial.* 5, 114.

[4] *Orat.* 7, 12. The sinner's continued existence in wrath corresponds to that of demons: *ibid.*, 14.

charist as a *pharmakon athanasias*[5] to be used in the case of both deaths: it is "everlasting life in Jesus Christ". The first gift of God referred to in the First Epistle of Clement is that of "life in *athanasia*";[6] and the eucharistic prayer quoted in the *Didachē* gives thanks "for the insight and faith and immortality that Thou hast bestowed upon us through Thy servant Jesus".[7] Theophilus holds the first Adam to be neither mortal nor immortal; if he had kept God's command, he would have enjoyed immortality, which probably says nothing against the continued existence of the guilty soul.[8]

Against this background of a participation, through grace, in God's eternity, we can understand Aquinas' assertion that, on the one hand, "many share in eternity by beholding God", and, on the other, "in hell there is no real eternity, but rather, time" (in inferno non est vera aeternitas, sed magis tempus),[9] albeit an "endless" time that is characterized, in the medieval view, by a constant changing of torments.[10] In this context we are only concerned with the different kinds of timeless duration, which can become mutually opposed depending on whether there is a participation in, or a depriving of, divine eternity. The man who, in God, contemplates him is participating in a mode of being "that includes all time within it" (aeternitas includit omne tempus).[11] If he is excluded from the contemplation of God and from a participation in the Divine Being, he is also excluded from this *includit* and so is restricted to the timelessness of his own being, deprived of all contact with God and with his fellow creatures. Such a restricted being is stripped of all those "dimen-

---

[5] *Eph.* 20:2. Cf. Bultmann, article "Athanasia" in *ThW* III, 24.

[6] 35, 2.

[7] 10, 2.

[8] *Autol.* II, 27.

[9] *S. Th.* I, 10, 3 ad 1, ad 2.

[10] On change: I–II, 67, 4 ad 2; Suppl. 97, 1 ad 3; *Quodl.* 8, q 8, a 1. Bonaventure, 2, d 2, p 1, a 1, q 2 (Quar. II, 66b); 4, d 50, p 1, a 2, q 3 (IV, 1034). On "time" in hell, cf. H. C. Puech, *En quête de la Gnose* I (Paris, 1978), 247ff.

[11] *S. Th.* I, 13, 2 ad 3; 10, 2 ad 4; 14, 13c: "aeternitas . . . ambit totum tempus." 14, 9c: "(aeternitas) totum tempus comprehendit . . . praesentialiter." 57, 3c: "Deus toti tempori adest et ipsum concludit." Ricardus de Mediavilla: "Deus . . . superexcelsus quidquid est perfectionis in durationibus omnium motionum". 2, d 2, q 2, a 1.

sions" that characterize the living and that God possesses in an infinite degree: it is thus a dead *nunc stans*. It is the utter removal of the positive durative aspects that are found in time (that is, in the future, and in a past that was alterable, shaped by decisions). In order to express this complete opposition between eternity in heaven and eternity in hell, C. S. Lewis used spatial imagery: Hell is tiny compared to the vastness of heaven.[12]

Thus Franz von Baader can say: "To suffer the torment of eternity is not the same as to suffer eternal torment."[13] In this way he gets beyond the "mistaken view, which is still current, that it is only possible to hold on to the orthodox maxim *ex infernis nulla redemptio* by denying the possibility of all creation being brought back to God, and vice versa."[14] The two statements can be reconciled "if we avoid importing temporality into hell, as the advocates of universal redemption usually do".[15] It is possible, however, for "a creature to pass from *one* mode of being to another in the eternal realm",[16] "provided this eternity is thought of, not as protensive, but as intensive".[17] Evil desire in the creature, once it has taken root, aims to be "entirely self-seeking, self-sufficient", but this way contradicts the creature's innate destiny of union with God; this self-contradiction robs it of peace. In God, however, righteousness (which provides space for finite freedom to operate) is one with love; he can only punish men out of love,[18] and in doing so he can take everything

---

[12] *The Great Divorce* (1946; Glasgow: Collins, 1986), 113–14: "'Do you mean then that Hell—all that infinite empty town—is down in some little crack like this?' 'Yes. All Hell is smaller than one pebble of your earthly world. . . . For a damned soul is nearly nothing: it is shrunk, shut up in itself. . . . Their fists are clenched, their teeth are clenched, their eyes fast shut.'" Hence Lewis can say: "Only the Greatest of all can make Himself small enough to enter Hell."

[13] Letter to Hoffmann, January 10, 1837. *Werke* 15:552; cf. also 561: "We must be careful to distinguish *duratio finita* (time as objectively fixed), *duratio indefinita* and *duratio infinita*": the first refers to purgatory, the second, hell, and the third, heaven.

[14] On the Pauline concept of man being envisaged in the Name of Jesus before the creation of the world, cf. *Sendschreiben* 2, *Werke* 4:361, 999.

[15] *Sendschreiben* 3, *Werke* 4:412.

[16] *Ibid.*, 413.

[17] "Rezension Lamennais", *Werke* 5:187 n.

[18] "Irrtümer und Wahrheit", *Werke* 12, 98. At the end of his *Sendschreiben* (4:420–

from them, timelessly, and return it to them, also timelessly.

For the latter to be true, we must consider a third form of timelessness that coincides neither with the first (the bliss of God and of those in God) nor with the second (hell). We shall deal with this in more detail in the next section; it is the condition of timelessness undergone by the Son on the Cross, for this condition must have sufficient "space" for the (infernal) experience of sinners abandoned by God, in two aspects: the intensity of the Son's forsakenness on the Cross and its worldwide extension. We have already said that it is possible for the Son to take upon himself the sinners' forfeiture of God only on the basis of a communion [*Unterfassung*] that renders the Son's state even more timeless than the timelessness of hell, since he alone, by taking into himself the sinners' God-forsakenness, can fully know what the loss of the Father means. Those Christians who are found worthy to experience something of the dark night of Christ's Cross have a faint idea of what this forsakenness is. Walter Hilton speaks of the experience of the "image of sin" in man being crucified and of the dark night[19] whereby a person is purified with a view to union with Christ. Tauler is more emphatic, saying explicitly that the experience of God-forsakenness on the Cross, to be accepted unconditionally and timelessly, is definitely compatible with the experience of its temporal limitation.[20] Most insistent is John of the Cross, who quotes the psalm, "The pains of hell encompassed me", commenting: "Most vividly does the soul feel the deathly shadows, deathly sighs and the torments of hell. For it feels itself godless, punished and rejected by God, the object of his displeasure and wrath. The soul feels all this, and more: it feels that this state will last for all eternity."[21]

---

22), Baader quotes a whole series of writers in order to show that "the concept of eternal damnation must not be taken to mean endless damnation." Cf. also 8:142.

[19] *The Scale of Perfection* (1494).

[20] *Predigten* [sermons], trans. Georg Hofmann, 2d ed. (Einsiedeln: Johannes Verlag, 1979), Wednesday before Palm Sunday (I, 91); cf. 2d Sermon on 5th Sunday after Trinity (II, 307ff.).

[21] *The Dark Night* II, 8. *Angela of Foligno* speaks of a "terrifying darkness on God's part, from which hope is absent" (ed. Doncoeur, 80); "God is so closed to me and hidden from me on all sides that I cannot in any way direct my thoughts to him or recall thinking of him. I see myself damned" (*ibid.*, 82). *Mechthild von*

This is a participation in the Cross of Christ. To be separated from the Father is, for the Son, "the weight of an eternity. . . .

Magdeburg "plunges among the damned and thinks the conditions there far too good for her" (IV, 12); she has to go "beneath Lucifer's tail" (V, 4), "pressed down into bottomless mire" (VI, 19); "one day is to me as a thousand years if thou wilt hold aloof from me. . . . I would rather go to hell—indeed, I am already in it" (II, 3). *Hadewijch*: "The seventh name of love is hell. . . . There one sees oneself devoured, swallowed up in its abysses, constantly suffering shipwreck amidst burning heat and icy cold, in love's deep and lofty darkness; this is far worse than the torments of hell . . . and so destroys the soul and its senses that it cannot recover" (*Mengeldichte* XVI, in J. B. Poiron, *Hadewijch d'Anvers* [Paris, 1951]), 127f. *Harphius* considers himself damned (*Directorium* 49, 50, 60; *Eden* 13, 17, 26). *Ruysbroeck*: "From time to time God transfers a man from his right side to his left, from heaven to hell" (*Spiritual Marriage* II, 65). Following Christ's instruction that a man should depart from himself, "man goes out and finds himself poor, wretched and abandoned" (*ibid.*, II, 28). *Eckhart* speaks only of the idea of indifference: "If hell were to be God's will for me, this would be my blessedness" (Quint, *German Sermons*, 339, 384); but *Tauler* mentions concrete experiences: abandoned, he feels "hellish pains" (Hofmann 66, 67). He has to work "in thick, heavy darkness, deprived of all comfort", but he would remain thus "if God willed him to stay in this poverty for all eternity" (321). He experiences Christ's forsakenness on the Cross (450). Those who seek God "disappear among blinded sinners, . . . in them there is such an unfathomable depth that they are drawn to the bottom of hell" (489). God can appear to raise his fist to the man who loves him, in which case "such a man regards the very bottom of hell as the only appropriate place for him" (602). Christ, however, was "the most forsaken man", for "he was more bitterly forsaken than any saint ever was" (493). *Suso* gives this account of himself: "The third interior suffering was that he was tempted to believe that his soul would never find succor and was bound to be finally damned, however righteously he acted." He reports that this lasted for ten years until he experienced an apparition of Eckhart that "helped him, and so he was redeemed from hell, where he had been for so long" (*Life*, ed. Lehmann, 52–55; cf. II, 35). Orcibal, in his *Saint Jean de la Croix et les mystiques rhéno-flamands* (1966), 107, adduces a number of (questionable) oriental precursors; but Irénée Hausherr, "Les Orientaux connaissent-ils les nuits de Saint Jean de la Croix?", *Orientalia christ. period.* (1946), 5–46, refutes the parallel. Chapter 11 of the *Theologia Deutsch* is entitled "The Righteous Man Placed in Hell". As for modern authors, we read in Henri Caffarel's memoirs of *Camille C.*: "The abandonment is absolute. Not only does one feel abandoned by God forever; no one can help." She experiences "a forsakenness that is total, complete and eternal" (311). (Camille C., *L'Emprise de Dieu* [Paris: Ed. du Feu Nouveau, 1982], 310.) In *Adrienne von Speyr* we find many experiences of hell: "I feel indifferent as to whether I am in this world or in the other world, in hell. If I am damned, I am damned, wherever I am." "How I would like to have loved God. But now it is too late. Today is eternity." "I will gladly be damned forever, if you believe it to be his will. But I do not believe it

On the Cross he will feel lonesome unto death, unto a limitless, eternal death in which every temporal moment and viewpoint will completely disappear. What will be a short while for mankind [Jn 14:19] will be an eternal while to him."[22] "At every moment we may think that we must die, and yet we do not die, since the death that comes through sin is timeless."[23] Jesus can give us a share in this, just as he gave the Bethany sisters a share "in his coming suffering. We see in this the timelessness of his suffering, the timelessness of the redemption and the timelessness of the imitation of the Lord. This Passion does indeed have a 'where' and a 'when' within the human boundaries of space and time, but it towers above these boundaries on all sides, and one can share in it earlier in time just as easily as a thousand years later."[24] Nonetheless the timelessness of the Cross is not the mere negation of time that characterizes hell, but a "supertime".[25] When Peter says that Christ "died for sins once for all" (1 Pet 3:18), "this 'once for all' expresses both the eternal meaning and eternal content of this event, which loses nothing of its actuality down the ages and communicates its unique character to the Church and to faith."[26] This is within the scope of our understanding insofar as the separation of Father and Son, made possible through the Incarnation, is an "economic" expression of eternal life. When Christ "dies in loneliness, travels to hell, enters into the utmost forsakenness—all of these are sure and infallible expressions of his life. They are not chance experiences,

---

would be to anyone's benefit." She knows that she is damned for eternity. She entreats me to damn her as well, "since the Lord has already done so; it would be easier if we could get rid of this misunderstanding between us" (unpublished notes).

[22] 3 Jo 124.

[23] Pa 132. "At the beginning of the Passion the Son is wrapped in a night that he experiences as timeless. It simply is, it does not unfold. . . . As long as suffering lasts, he suffers now, without hope of its ending. . . . He must endure a duration that cannot be divided up or measured, so that every sin can fill him to the brim. This is the fullness of obedience, that he takes everything into himself, just as the Father intends, . . . whereas no man will ever know what actually took place there" (Gh 47).

[24] 2 Jo 319.

[25] Ka I, 327.

[26] Ka I, 358.

not accidents, not fates but substantial conditions of his life."[27] "He suffered thus in order to bear all sin, . . . because he was God." So "we can never totally grasp any aspect of the Cross, since each one, including the Son's abandonment by God, passes over into the mystery of God. Accordingly, the redemptive sufferings tower immeasurably over all the finitude of sin."[28]

c. Kinds of Forsakenness

These two forms of timelessness—the God-forsakenness of the damned and the God-forsakenness of the Son on the Cross— are not simply unrelated. The latter is because of the former. "The reason the Son of God appeared", John says, "was to destroy the works of the devil" (1 Jn 3:8). "Superficially the proud loneliness of the devil might be compared to the Son's abandonment on the Cross; one could almost say that one balances the other. . . . Yet even here there is no real similarity. For the devil gobbles up sins in his craving for pleasure but does not want to accept their fruits; the Lord takes both sins and their fruits upon himself. The devil draws a limit, taking sins but rejecting their fruits; the Lord sets no limits but takes all."[1] Instead of the devil, we can say the damned, for he too does not want to accept the bitter consequences of sin. He does not want to follow to the end the path that leads him away from God. In his obedience, by contrast, the Son has followed his path to the very end; and this very path has brought him to an encounter with man who is pursuing his path, having turned away from God and "willfully adopted a new standpoint that (he imagines) puts him out of range of God's intervention. But the Son has placed himself in man's way: even if man has turned his back on God, he still finds the Son in front of him and must go toward him. Thus the sinner can move toward God, albeit unawares or reluctantly." The Son "has used his divine attribute of omnipresence in the Incarnation in such a way that, wherever men are pursuing some path, he is there; . . . even those who do not want to will assuredly meet him as they journey, even those who think they

---

[27] 3 Jo 125.
[28] Ka II, 226–27.
[1] Ka II, 108–9.

have finally and completely turned away from him. This is because he has chosen precisely the unexpected, the disowned, the rejected spot as his vantage point."[2]

In other words, anyone who tries to choose complete forsakenness—in order to prove himself absolute vis-à-vis God—finds himself confronted by the figure of someone even "more absolutely" forsaken than himself. We should consider, therefore, "whether it is still not open to God to encounter the sinner who has turned away from him in the impotent form of the crucified brother who has been abandoned by God, and indeed in such a way that it becomes clear to the one who has turned away from God that: this One beside me who has been forsaken by God (like myself) has been abandoned by God for my sake. Now there can be no more talk of doing violence to freedom if God appears in the loneliness of the one who has chosen the total loneliness of living only for himself (or perhaps one should say: who thinks that is how he has chosen) and shows himself to be as the One who is still lonelier than the sinner."[3] "The poor man", says Claudel in one of his poems, "has no friend to rely on except one poorer than himself", and in the last line: "A poor man has at last found someone poorer; thus, in silence, they look at one another."[4] Even if this encounter takes place in each party's timeless zone, it is something very human. Dostoyevsky, for instance, set it in a temporal context, particularly at the end of *The Idiot*, where Myshkin spends the last night (before his insanity takes over once again) in the same narrow berth beside his "brother" Rogozhin, the murderer of Natasha Philipovna, very close to the corpse covered with oilcloth. "The prince reached out his trembling hand and gently touched his head, his hair, stroking them and his cheeks . . . there was nothing more he could do! . . . at length he lay down on the cushions, as though in inner exhaustion or despair, and pressed his face against the pale and motionless face of Rogozhin."[5] It is known that in the

[2] Ph 131–32.

[3] Hans Urs von Balthasar, "Eschatology in Outline", in *Spirit and Institution, Explorations in Theology*, 4 (San Francisco: Ignatius Press, 1995), 456–57. Also quoted by Breuning, *Myst. Sal.* V, 861.

[4] "Mother of Perpetual Help", conclusion of part I of the Corona Poems.

[5] *The Idiot*, trans. A. Myers, The World's Classics (Collins, 1992), 648.

figure of the idiot, Dostoyevsky was trying to create a likeness of the "most beautiful man", Christ. Even more compelling is the end of *Crime and Punishment*. Here Sonya, well aware of the ambition, pride, selfishness and unbelief of her beloved Raskolnikov,[6] eventually succeeds in getting him to confess his murder to the police. At the first attempt, however, after Raskolnikov and the policeman have a fruitless talk and Raskolnikov comes out into the courtyard without having confessed anything, Sonya stands "deadly pale", looking at him "wildly, desperately".[7] He turns around, confesses, and is sentenced to penal servitude in Siberia, whither Sonya follows him. Strangely, "not only was he not interested in her visits, but especially at first he was irritated by her presence and monosyllabic or even rude to her", although he did not want to forgo their meetings.[8] He becomes hardened, is unable to regard himself as guilty, his "conscience could find no particularly terrible guilt in his past"; he is ashamed that he had to "submit to the 'absurdity' of that decree, if he wished to find any degree of peace". He is angry with himself for having failed to put up with his own action and admits "I had no right to permit myself that step" [murder]. Then comes a gentle change: he begins to notice things that concern his fellow prisoners, and "the most surprising thing of all . . . was that terrible unbrigdeable chasm which lay between him and the others." "Why was Sonya so well liked by everybody?" After a nightmare in which he experiences the end of the world—after all, his own world is slipping away—the ice begins to melt in his heart. "He clasped her knees and wept", and "endless springs" of life and love welled up within him. "Life had taken the place of logic." The couple have to spend a further seven years in Siberia, but it is the start of a new existence.[9]

These are remote metaphors for the unimaginable process whereby man, timelessly closed in upon himself, is opened up by the ineluctable presence of Another, who stands beside him, equally timelessly, and calls into question his apparent, pretended inaccessibility. Man's shell is not hard enough, however, for it is

---

[6] *Crime and Punishment*, trans. J. Coulson, The World's Classics (Collins, 1986).
[7] *Ibid.*, 510.
[8] *Ibid.*, 519.
[9] *Ibid.*, 527.

formed of a contradiction. Perhaps the man whose shell can be broken open is not yet really in hell but only—in his rebellious attitude to God—turned toward it. "Therefore it is said," says Paul, "When he ascended on high he led captivity captive" (Eph 4:8, AV); the Lord "takes it back with him and by this means releases men from their captivity to sin",[10] thereby "fashioning this very alienation from God into a way of approach to him".[11] For he has transformed "the path of man's destiny" into the "path of obedience of the eternal Son",[12] and so "he brings comfort to this place of hopelessness, fire to this place of iciness, mercifulness to this place of justice" and "purgatory" to this place of hell.[13] And he paid for this with his own comfortlessness, a comfortlessness beyond compare. This, however, is the very opposite of being closed in upon oneself: it is personality understood as relation to others; God is the prototype of the communion of saints, abolishing the limits of those who limit themselves. "In this milieu a person can pray and sacrifice in place of another; a person can 'stand in' for someone else."[14]

d. The Unusable Residue

In this view (and, as always, we are only trying to get a little closer to our subject), hell would be what is finally condemned by God; what is left in it is sin, which has been separated from the sinner by the work of the Cross. Because of the energy that man has invested in it, sin is a reality, it is not "nothing". Sins "are remitted, separated from us, taken away from us. They are banished to the place where everything God does not want and condemns is hell. That is their place. In the history of the fall and redemption, it is much more necessary that such a place exist than that it not exist, for it is the enduring witness to the remission of sins. In this sense hell is even a gift of divine grace."[1] "The Son presents to the Father, in his own person, the sin of

[10] Ep 163.
[11] C 496.
[12] *Ibid.*
[13] 4 Jo 143.
[14] M 13.
[1] Ep 38. Judaism is also familiar with the idea that "sin will submerge forever

the world that he has taken away", at the same time presenting to him "in his Body, his Bride, the living sinner now stripped of sin".[2] In spite of his forsakenness, his descent to the underworld is objectively "the journey of a victor. Like a triumphant field marshal, he musters the defeated troops and the spoils of victory: the fettered powers of evil and conquered sin . . . , sin of the world as washed away from redeemed men, not actually become more personal but formless and unbounded, whose removal from sinners was the work of his Cross." Now, however, "not in the light of victory does he now want to observe sin, but in the darkness that characterizes it."[3]

Gehenna was the name of the valley outside Jerusalem where, in earlier times, sacrifices to Moloch used to take place and "where, apparently, refuse was constantly being incinerated".[4] But whether refuse was burned here or elsewhere, the process was well known to every inhabitant of Palestine, and so it was often used as a metaphor. Thus the Baptist consigns barren trees and useless chaff "to the unquenchable fire" (Mt 3:10, 12); Jesus commands people to cut off offending members lest they should be thrown entire into "the unquenchable fire" (Mk 9:43 par.). The same thing happens to the barren branches on the vine: they wither and are burned (Jn 15:6). The most eloquent symbol is the destruction of the Great Whore, Babylon, the embodiment of the seduction of the whole world, who will be "burned with fire" (Rev 18:8). People will see "the smoke of her burning; they will stand far off, in fear of her torment, and say, 'Alas! alas! thou great city, thou mighty city, Babylon! In one hour has thy judgment come!'" (18:9). "The smoke from her goes up for ever and ever" (19:3).

---

in the darkness" (Enoch 92:5), and that "wickedness shall be blotted out and deceit destroyed . . . corruption shall be overcome" (2 Esdras 6:27). Thus "all vices are gathered together in hell." For these and similar texts, see P. Volz, *Die Eschatologie der jüdischen Gemeinde im neutestamentlichen Zeitalter* (Tübingen: Mohr, 1934), 333.

[2] Ka II, 37.   [3] 4 Jo 143.

[4] Louis Lochet, *Jésus descendu aux enfers* (Cerf, 1979), 31. On the development of this idea on the basis of Jeremiah 7:32; 19:6 to Isaiah 66:24 (where the Valley of Hinnom is transformed from a historical place of punishment to an eschatological one), cf. J. Nelis, "Gehenna" in *Bibel-Lexikon*, 2d ed. (1968), 529ff.

God once fashioned the world from chaos, but man, through sin, imported a second chaos into it; now, when the Son dies for sinners, it is "as if God had let the world run backward into chaos, in order to refashion it from chaos at a deeper level".[5] Babylon, the chaos produced by sin, is being burned eternally; the devouring pit devours itself eternally. "Now the quality of evil has lost all relationship",[6] in its self-devouring it no longer has any relation to God. And this is because "the Lord also had fellowship with the dead",[7] in the "infinite incomprehensibility of the underworld, which he must pass through before he can arrive at total comprehension in the Resurrection, beyond this night in which he fully tastes God's elusiveness".[8]

e. Can Hope Deceive?

The hope referred to here is the hope that all men will be saved. It presupposes the change from Judaism to the New Testament, since under the former dispensation the twofold result of the Law was not subject to question, or scarcely so. In the New Testament there is a strong tension between expressions that suggest that, since Christ has reconciled the world to God, all may be redeemed and other expressions that either continue the threats of judgment found in the Old Covenant or even— precisely because the atonement wrought on the Cross has taken place—intensify them. The more God's love undertakes for the sake of his sinful world, the more vulnerable this love is and the more unpardonable is any insult offered to it. It is from the New Covenant that we see for the first time the whole scope of what the First Commandment requires of the believer; or rather, now we see that the First Commandment goes beyond everything the believer can aspire to.

For a long stretch of the Church's history, therefore, the tension found in the New Testament documents simply remained open. In fact, after the condemnation of an Origenism that—for the initiates at least—claimed to have a *knowledge* of universal

[5] Mt 190.
[6] Pa 141.
[7] Mt 230.
[8] Ka I, 117.

redemption (DS 411), Augustine's assumption of a twofold issue to the Last Judgment, allegedly justified by a twofold predestination to heaven and hell, was accepted as consonant with sound Christian doctrine. This twofold judgment is part and parcel of Christian iconography: the cathedral's tympanum reminds the Christian of it whenever he enters the sacred building. In Torcello, while gazing ahead to the magnificent Marian sign of redemption, the visitor senses behind him the gigantic fresco of redemption and damnation, even if he has not seen the terrible gesture of Michelangelo's Christ in judgment. High Scholasticism entertains no other eschatology than this, and here the Doctor Seraphicus is even more uncompromising than Aquinas. This is also the period in which Christian princes hold banquets in the halls of their castles and citadels while their enemies languish in lifelong imprisonment in the dungeons below. Somehow Christian reflection seems to have stopped at a preliminary stage— except in certain women, such as Hildegard of Bingen, the two Mechthilds or the Lady Julian of Norwich.

Augustine, as is well known, restricted theological hope to the hoping subject, so that one cannot hope on the part of others and their salvation.[9] Thomas is reluctant to let this view stand; while he too acknowledges that "hope is directed only to one's own good", Christian love can join me so closely to a fellow human being that he means as much to me as I myself: "Thus, where there is this unity of love with another, it is possible to envisage and hope for something on the other person's behalf, just as on one's own behalf."[10] It must be borne in mind, however, that the love referred to here is supernatural *caritas*,[11] and he is speaking only of particular close individuals: for Thomas, on the basis of his eschatology, there can be no question of hoping for the salvation of all. In the East, Origenism flourished right up to the time when it was condemned: Theodore of Mopsuestia's defense of the redemption of all men set the pattern for a Nestorianism that extended as far as China. (There are

---

[9] "Spes non est nisi rerum ad eum pertinentium qui earum spem gerere perhibetur": *Enchiridium* 2, n. 8.

[10] *S. Th.* II–II, 17, 3; also *Quaest. disp. de spe*, art. 4 c.

[11] And not, as a note in the Marietti edition says, an "amor naturalis" or "some other benevolence".

echoes of this as late as the thirteenth century).[12] Gregory of Nyssa[13] and Maximus the Confessor[14] remained untouched by suspicion. In the West, by contrast, apart from Scotus Erigena, there is no question of "achieving a balance" or "leaving the issue open";[15] instead, what we have from the Renaissance, via Pietism, to Enlightenment and Idealism is only a succession of violent swings of the pendulum. In the time between when his sentence was pronounced and when he was burned, John Bradford wrote a treatise "On the Reconstitution of All Things" (1555); even before this, the spiritualist and baptist Hans Denk had taught that the threats contained in Scripture were purely pedagogical in function. In 1699 appeared Jane Lead's book on *The Eternal Gospel of the Universal Reconstitution of All Things*: the ideas contained in it were propagated in Germany by Superintendent S. W. Petersen and his wife (the *Mysterion Apokatastaseos* and the poem "Uranias", which Lessing praised), provoking a highly animated discussion that spawned about three hundred publications for and against. The Württemberg Pietists Bengel, Oetinger and Hahn present this teaching with increasing open-

[12] Cf. the text of the Nestorian Metropolitan Solomon of Basra in E. Staehelin, *Die Verkündigung des Reiches Gottes in der Kirche Jesu Christi* I–VII (Basel, 1951–1965), III, 302. Cf. also Staehelin, *Die Wiederbringung aller Dinge*, Rektoratsrede 1960, Basler Univ. Reden 45 (1960), 9–10.

[13] *De hom. op.*, chap. 17; *De an. et resur.* 69C; 71A; *Great Catechesis* 22–26. On this, cf. J. Daniélou, "Apocatastase", in *L'Être et le temps chez Grégoire de Nysse* (Leiden: Brill, 1970), 205–26.

[14] In my view, some texts by Maximus suggest that he regarded the Origenist doctrine of apokatastasis (which had already been condemned) as an arcane teaching that was not to be preached. Cf. my *Kosmische Liturgie*, 2d ed. (1961), 355–59. This view has been criticized, carefully and in detail, by Brian E. Daley, S.J., "Apocatastasis and 'Honorable Silence' in the Eschatology of Maximus the Confessor" in *Maximus Confessor: Actes du Symposion 1980*, ed. F. Heinzer and C. Schönborn (Éd. Univ. Fribourg, 1982), 309–39. I am not fully convinced by his arguments, however; cf. in particular *Quaest. et Dubia* (PG 90, 796AC; 91, 1061ff.). I still support E. Staehelin's verdict (*Reich Gottes* II, 107): "As far as the end is concerned, he tends (like Origen and Gregory of Nyssa) to hope for the restoration of all things; yet in his exhortations he emphatically teaches that the pains of hell are eternal. He does this in the belief that it is dangerous to speak to the multitude about the restoration of all things."

[15] Apart from John Scotus Erigena, in whose closed system—the world proceeds from God and returns to him—there can be no room for an eternal hell. Cf. *De Div. Nat.* V, 8; V, 29–31.

ness and with the approbation of many listeners. Leibniz's assertion that even the existence of an eternal hell would not disturb
his view of the best of all possible worlds was no doubt largely
diplomatic, but it sparked off a strange dispute in which Lessing
takes up the cudgels with Eberhard[16] on behalf of the eternal
pains of hell,[17] albeit in highly qualified terms that are difficult
to decipher. The "radical evil" that Kant discovered in man,
and which so upset Goethe, has no echo in the philosophy and
theology of Idealism: the "hell" that Schelling believed he had
discovered, based on a divine substratum, cannot be regarded as
such. Following Klopstock, Lavater and Jung-Stilling, Schleiermacher appears as an advocate of the doctrine of apokatastasis:[18]
the bliss of those in heaven would be lessened by the knowledge
that others are excluded from it. This tradition can be traced via
Alexander Schweizer, H. L. Martensen, Troeltsch, Bonhoeffer,[19]
but also via the Catholics J. B. Hirscher and H. Schell, right up
to Karl Barth. It must be said, however, that this whole wave
of reaction against Augustinian, medieval and Reformation rig-
orism is largely the product of a humanistic recalcitrance, an anti-
orthodox feeling, a craving for philosophical system or simply
an optimism in the Enlightenment manner; we hardly ever find
it undergirded by a sufficiently deep, trinitarian theology. Such
undergirding is only present, to some extent, in the Blumhardts
(father and son)[20] and, as we have seen, in Barth.

Given the contradictory assertions of Scripture, however, will
theological speculation ever achieve a result? Perhaps Thérèse
of Lisieux travelled the only possible path; God led her into a
profound inner darkness and gave her to understand that she
should sit at the "table . . . [of] poor sinners"[21] in order, by way

---

[16] *Neue Apologie des Sokrates oder Untersuchung von der Seligkeit der Heiden* (1772, 1778).

[17] *Leibniz von den ewigen Strafen*, ed. H. Göbel (Hanser, 1976) VII, 171–97.

[18] *Über die Lehre von der Erwählung* (1819).

[19] Cf. the quotations in G. Müller, "Ungeheuerliche Ontologie: Erwägungen zur christlichen Lehre über Hölle und Allversöhnung" in *Ev. Theol.* 34 (1974), 269.

[20] Cf. E. Staehelin, *Wiederbringung*, 35–36.

[21] *Story of a Soul*, trans. John Clarke, O.C.D. (Washington, D.C.: Institute of Carmelite Studies, 1976), 212.

of atonement, to be with them and share their lot; she experienced "no inclination" to offer herself as a victim "to God's justice" but, completely taken up with her new and staggering discovery, surrendered herself to his "merciful love" that is so "unknown and rejected".[22] She has "a blind hope in his mercy". And in this blind hope she is permitted to expect everything from him: "Believe in the truth of my words: one can never have too much trust in the good God, for he is so powerful and full of mercy. We receive from him as much as we hope for."[23] She is acquainted with the Lord's words to St. Mechtild: "In all truth I tell you that it gives me great joy when men expect great things of me. However great their faith and boldness, I will give them far more than they deserve. It is actually impossible for man not to receive what he has hoped for from my power and mercy." Thérèse herself does not tire of repeating that "we never expect too much of God, who is so powerful and merciful; we receive from him just as much as we trust him."[24] At the Last Judgment, in Thérèse's *Drama of the Angels*, the Angel of Vengeance summons God's unsatisfied justice, but the Redeemer does not think of it: How could he take vengeance for the Cross that men imposed on him? He waves him away: "Beautiful Angel, put up your sword! . . . The one who will judge the world is I . . . and I am called *Jesus!*" And when "the Angel of the Holy Face" asks forgiveness on behalf of sinners: "I shall listen to your prayer: every soul shall obtain its pardon."[25]

---

[22] *Ibid.*, 180.

[23] Saint Thérèse of Lisieux, *General Correspondence*, trans. John Clarke, O.C.D., (Washington, D.C.: Institute of Carmelite Studies, 1982). 2 vols.

[24] *Histoire d'une âme* (Lisieux, 1923), 246. Cf. my book *Two Sisters in the Spirit* (San Francisco: Ignatius Press, 1992), 330. Cf. also the Lord's words to Gertrud von Helfta: "Whatever a person hopes to receive through you, he will assuredly receive from me. Moreover, whatsoever you promise anyone in my Name, I will most certainly grant him, even if at times, hindered by human weakness, he does not feel the effect" (*Legatus* I, 14).

[25] Von Balthasar, *Two Sisters*, 331–32.

It should also be noted that in 1877, Frederick William Farrar, as Canon in Westminster, published under the title *Eternal Hope* five sermons that he himself had preached, a publication that was a great popular success and in which he pleaded, in correspondence with nothing but his title, for a possible purification of sinners after death.

For the believer, hope remains where all speculative systems have failed: this is a hope that, according to Paul, "does not disappoint" (Rom 5:5). However, it has taken the whole modern movement against the dominance of the Augustinian tradition to liberate this hope with regard to our fellow men, whoever they may be, from the restrictions and reservations that are still latent in Thomas. True, Thérèse obtains this expansion of hope by a daring act of self-consecration to God's mercy; it could not be purchased more cheaply than by this act on behalf of sinners. "Christ demands of man a greater renunciation than he can naturally make, a stronger faith than he can find within himself, a bolder hope than the boldest of which man is capable."[26]

If we look back from this vantage point to the judgment that awaits every sinful human being, the appropriate attitude will be a hope that is not without a certain fear. For if it is true that not only a person's last moment but his entire life is to be the object of judgment, it is impossible that "nothing worthy of damnation" will be found in him. The image of the scales of justice rising or falling is false insofar as this "weighing" is not a quantitative matter: it is something qualitative here that cannot enter into the kingdom of God. Ambrose came up with the daring statement: "Idem homo et salvatur ex parte, et condemnatur ex parte",[27] man is somehow both to the right and to the left of the Judge. Accordingly, his hope can only cling blindly to the miracle that has already taken place in the Cross of Christ; it takes the entire courage of Christian hope for a man to apply this to himself, to trust that, by the power of this miracle, what is damnable in him has been separated from him and thrown out with the unusable residue that is incinerated outside the gates of the Holy City. Thus the "cheap hope" of the common doctrine of apokatastasis becomes a "dearly bought" one, to which the apparently outdated verses of the *Dies Irae* become suddenly relevant: "Quantus tremor est futurus. . . . Quidquid latet apparebit. . . . Qui salvandos salvas gratis. . . . Tantus labor non sit cassus. . . . Mihi quoque spem dedisti. . . ."

---

[26] C 493.
[27] *In Ps.* 118, serm. 20, 58 (PL 15, 1502). "Every sinner will hear both 'Begone into eternal fire' and 'Come ye blessed of my Father'": OM 332–33.

C. MAN IN GOD'S UNDERGIRDING

1. Existence in the Life/Death of Christ

a. Death Underlies Everything

It seems strange that, to date, no theologian has seriously related Heidegger's dictum, "death is existence's *most specific* possibility . . . where what is at stake is the very being of existence",[1] to the christological statement that "because of death, God took it upon himself to be born."[2] Basing himself on Scheler's insight that human life, if it is to be capable of genuine, that is, definitive, moral decisions, must be finite and hence mortal,[3] Heidegger realized that the immanence of death in human existence is precisely what enables it to escape from the void of "everyday facticity" and attain freedom to pursue its "ultimate possibility", namely, "self-surrender".[4] Within this ultimate possibility the acts of existence (which—since they have ethical value— can be evaluated) participate in the quality of this self-surrender. It is a fact, of course, that in Heidegger this "ultimate possibility" is acted out in the face of the unresolved enigma of being (for Heidegger, being is essentially veiled), and so it cannot have any discernible meaning for the totality; accordingly this has a negative effect on the ethical acts initiated in life. It seems that the only way to avoid this effect would be to mask life's radical end by some kind of premature flight into the supratemporal realm, or into the supra-individual realm of the "universal".[5] If

---

[1] *Sein und Zeit* (1927), 263.

[2] Gregory of Nyssa, *Great Catechesis* 32.

[3] "Our life is present to us . . . interiorly at every moment as an *integrated totality*; this is the background to all particular experiences and destinies . . . because it is a necessary and evident constituent in every possible interior experience of the life process." *Tod und Fortleben*, in *Schriften aus dem Nachlass* I, 2d ed. (1977), 23. K. Rahner has expounded this teaching with clarity and enthusiasm. A brief summary can be found in: *Das christliche Sterben* (Myst. Sal. V, 479).

[4] *Ibid.*, 264.

[5] Hegel, in his *Phänomenologie des Geistes*, says, "the dead man, from the long sequence of his scattered existence, has rounded himself into a single, complete form and has lifted himself out of the turmoil of contingent life into the repose of simple universality."

this is to be the goal, the ancient world's evaluation of the body as the spirit's "coffin" seems quite reasonable, as does the image, dear to Enlightenment and Idealist thinkers, of the chrysalis from which the butterfly is liberated. However, this view trivializes the whole tragic paradox of mortality by failing to give due weight to the positive aspect of finitude; right from the outset the precious quality of the transient being and of all its individual moments is underplayed in favor of the eternity that is latent within it (one thinks of *anamnesis* in Plato's *Meno*, but also of the "*Sache selbst*" in Hegel). In the abstract it may sound impressive to say that man is a microcosm of the universe since he is a synthesis of spirit ("immortal" spirit?) and (mortal) nature. However, if we examine what, in concrete terms, this union of the individual person and the species implies for man, we would be more inclined to follow Pascal and call man a "monster" and a "chimera". For man is situated in a temporal plane, incapable of determining its limit, a limit that represents a constant threat to him; freely, and in the knowledge of good and evil, he has to fashion an abiding ethical edifice out of his transitory existence; furthermore he cannot see what he has thus fashioned, nor can he know how it is assessed. This commandment, however, that stands over him and penetrates into his spirit is so imperious that he can be moved to surrender even his physical existence for the sake of the edifice he is fashioning, just as he has already been able to sacrifice his freedom of choice by opting for a lifelong bond that urgently solicits his embrace.

We can say that the individual becomes all the more precious, the more his mortality becomes the dwelling place of a higher and wider consciousness of the Whole. If this is true, it is not merely the individual's transience that makes him precious. Thus, between these two aspects arises the irreducible tragic dimension that the biblical saga of man's origins interprets in terms of punishment: before the Fall, it was possible for there to be a union of personality and the race (with its finitude) that did not involve tragedy; after the Fall, this is no longer possible, and the positive and negative aspects in death cannot be unravelled.

There is one memorable but fleeting moment in the history of mankind—namely, in classical Judaism—when man was able to endure being "eternal" within the bounds of his transitory existence: sharing in a covenant with God, he lived for God to such an extent that he was content to stand in God's light and thus, satiated with this light, to surrender himself to death. He succeeded in maintaining this high level in a few instances, but for the most part it required the support of a notion of reward and retribution in this life, and increasingly, once this notion was shown not to function (as Job and Ecclesiastes showed), man lost his balance and fell from this pinnacle. Nor could this be anything more than a first, anticipatory and ultimately unsustainable demonstration of what genuine liberation from the tragedy of death was supposed to be.

As can be shown in precise detail, this liberation lies in the fact that the human destiny of death is undergirded by the death of Jesus Christ. What does his death tell us? First, that it bears all the essential characteristics of human death, of substantial human death, and not (as in Heidegger) of a death "one merely acknowledges, increasing the temptation to hide from the fact that death is implicit in our most specific being".[6] He who says, "My hour is not yet come" (Jn 2:4), is constantly aware that everything is moving toward his death; only by conscious anticipation of the death he was personally to undergo could he take responsibility for both the radical quality of his words and demands and the eschatological content of his deeds (forgiving sins, healing). Moreover, as Irenaeus says, in demanding that those who follow him should take up their cross daily, he cannot ask of others what he is not willing to do himself.[7] Since his words and deeds are his very own, they anticipate his "very own death".[8] On the one hand, the "format" of his dying— which is the form and rationale of his living—is ever before his eyes, and, on the other hand, he refuses that knowledge of the hour that is reserved to the Father alone. From this perspective we should perhaps attribute the more precise predictions of his Passion to the post-Easter text redactors, whereas the more general allusions to the necessity and the special quality of his death are definitely consistent with his own particular under-

---

[6] *Sein und Zeit*, 253.

[7] *Adv. Haer.* III, 18, 5–6.

[8] H. Schürmann, *Jesu ureigener Tod* (Herder, 1975).

standing of his existence. Throughout his life Jesus is moving toward that project which is "most his own", namely, to seal the New Covenant in his blood and in his forsakenness by God. He is moving toward that act which shows in a definitively incarnational way—in his "self-surrender"—what his whole finite life's path has been. "From this it may be clearly seen that the New Covenant itself is a movement, a dramatic event in which the light enters the darkness, gradually forcing its way into the darkness of death."[9]

In Jesus, however, his life's course toward death and his refusal to know the hour do not come from his "being thrown" from nothingness into existence but from something mysteriously different that takes the place of "thrown-ness": this is his "laying aside" of his divine proportions, which is itself already an act of obedience to the eternal Father (Phil 2:6–7). Here, evidently, the power that "throws" him into his mission is greater than the power of nothingness; this "throw" has as its target an end (*telos*, Jn 13:1) that lies beyond the trajectory of all mere "thrown-ness". The "end" of "thrown-ness" is the cancelling of movement; but the "end" of him who was sent is still an act within his being-sent, the act of self-gift. This is possible because the self-surrender is a perfect response to the act of the One who sends; he is the One who, in all his doings, always gave and gives what is most his own. This twofold self-surrender is the expression of absolute Love.

What is the purpose of this self-surrender on the part of the One who sends and the One who is sent? It is to undergird and embrace the concrete "end" of all those who were unable to understand this end in terms of love but regarded it either as an imposed termination of their finitude or as the welcome surrendering of finitude's burden. The former would have preferred to hold on to their "being-for-themselves"; the latter would have thrown it away as something troublesome. Both approaches contradict the ultimate meaning of dying, as we see from the self-surrender of the Son of God at the absolute end. For he, bearing in himself the darkness of all false deaths and going beyond

---

[9] 1 Jo 55.

them, surrenders himself in this darkness into the hands—which he can now no longer feel—of the Father who sends him, the Father who, in doing so, surrenders himself.

In biblical terms his undergirding death is interpreted in two ways, though both aspects are inseparable from one another. On the one hand, this death takes the place of all sinful deaths; it involves self-surrender to God-forsakenness and powerlessness, thereby undergirding every possible instance of God-forsakenness and powerlessness on the part of sinners. In his surrender to death, he brings the deaths of all sinners with him; he envelops them in his uniquely definitive death and gives them a changed value, thereby changing the value of all life destined for a similar death. This is the first aspect, which made a particular impression on Paul. However, this *deed* on God's part contains the second aspect, namely, the *teaching* that this deed is the proclamation of an absolute love, an absolute love that originates in the triune being of God.

The finitude of this dying in forsakenness is "pure, limitless revelation", because "in ultimate intensification, in this forsakenness", it manifests "the Father's infinity".[10] "The Son's death is the exemplification of the supreme aliveness of triune love"; "to God", it is "a midpoint, which extends right through the center of the Father; for the Son does not cease, even in dying, to be generated by him and to convey his eternal gratitude to him, in a love that expresses its utmost intensity precisely now." So "one can say only that the Son's sonship reaches its supreme temporal exemplification in his redemptive death."[11] Thereby the dying Son "shows, not that he has taken leave of his eternal life, but, on the contrary, that he has thereby proclaimed his eternal life".[12] And of the Father we can say this: "The Father must possess unimaginable power if he can look on, apparently powerless, while his Son moves into suffering",[13] in spite of having the power to keep him from death.

If finite death expresses infinite love (in the two aspects we

[10] G 63.
[11] A 77.
[12] Ka I, 10–11.
[13] Pa 88.

have already indicated: love for sinners and love for the Father),
we can only speak in paradoxes: "Precisely in the fact that he
is in the world, visibly separated from the Father, . . . lies the
proof that he dwells inseparably in the Father."[14] The perfect
fulfillment of his task "is also his teaching".[15] "The unity of life
between the life of the Father and the life of the Son is no longer
visible except in the mission";[16] "The mission of the Father appears as the nourishment of the Son",[17] even when, especially
when, the crucified and thirsting Son seems to be deprived of
all food. This is possible because his life is "laid up" with the
Father, as we have already discussed; this is the precondition for
the Son's being sent to his death, in which "the Son has emptied
himself not only of his being, but also of his meaning."[18] "On
the cross, to all appearances, the Son has become nothing but
a finite point; from the perspective of his visible place in the
world he seems to act as a separate and finite person vis-à-vis
the Father. But the Three-Person God has never ceased being
One and Infinite. Incarnation and cross are a way of looking—
from a finite vantage point—into God's eternal being."[19] "This
inseparability of Father and Son will be made clear to them at
the moment when the separation of the two will apparently be
total. This is the absolute paradox." Accordingly, "precisely here
faith will take its origin, where everything has become totally
incredible and nothing more can be thought out, understood,
felt or touched. Christians will always be closest to faith when
they are abandoned by everything and have nothing more left
than this leap into faith."[20]

[14] 2 Jo 100.

[15] *Ibid.*

[16] 2 Jo 71.

[17] *Ibid.*

[18] "The Father has the Son's being with him; this is how he is able to survive
this hour, whereas the Crucified One is completely abandoned": T 72, cf. 3 Jo
102.

[19] T 74.

[20] 2 Jo 182–83 (GT) "Sacrifice, forsakenness and darkness are not only indicated and aspired to in the absoluteness of God's love but fulfilled reality; they
are anchored in the mutual being of Father and Son": 3 Jo 337. "There has always been a unity between the triune God and his eternal plan of salvation. . . .
The Son is obedient unto death, and he beholds the Father unto the non-vision of

The doctrine of God's triune life, which is an entirely new and purely Christian form of negative theology, remains the doctrine of God's absolute act by which henceforth God will see the world's sin in the light of the undergirding death of his Son. "Since the Son is in our sin as its center, as it were, it is only through the enveloping veil of sin that the Father can have mercy on him."[21] The Father's gaze is "equally fundamental to the Cain who flees before him, to the Son who moves toward him, and even to the Son who feels himself abandoned on the Cross."[22] "The Father can no longer see the sin borne by the Son as isolated sin: now he can only see it in the context of the Son's grace."[23] And not in a merely general sense: "The Father contemplates every individual through the medium of the Son's mission."[24] What he cannot find in the individual he finds in the Son, whose generosity is so exuberant "that the borders and points of transition between the life of the Lord and the life of the person have been wiped out . . . the love bestowed on the man has become so much his own".[25] "This is why the Father loves me", says Jesus (Jn 10:17), "because he recognizes his own outpouring of love in him. For the Father himself has poured out the gift of the Son on the world, so that he may win him back from the world, enriched by the answer of the whole world."[26] Since the Son has dwelt on earth both as man and as God, "the Father recognizes him among us and in us"; not merely as a man among us and as the Spirit in us, but, on the basis of his Eucharist, which is the fruit of his self-surrender unto death, "as Spirit and man in us, by giving us, through his humanity, his divine Spirit". It is this same Spirit who elicited the self-surrender of both Father and Son.[27] The Spirit is the "assurance and guarantee of the unity of love that endured even

---

darkness: this manifests the ultimate lengths to which God's love for man, and man's obedience to God, will go. This is the concrete source of contemplation": Bi 21.

[21] Pa 133. [22] A 58.

[23] Be 24. [24] Ka II, 162.

[25] 2 Jo 269.

[26] 2 Jo 279; cf. G 119; SL 19: "The Father recognizes in us the face of the Son". Ep 106.

[27] Ka I, 190–91.

in separation. He is not only the witness who can always testify to their unity even in separation, but also the ever-present token that, by its exigence, testifies to their unity."[28] "But once he has mankind in him, he becomes transparent to the Father as well: the Father sees us in him."[29]

In itself the Son's death is so much a consummation of the redeeming love of God that it already bears the Resurrection within it, albeit in a hidden manner. What the Father always had with him, namely, the life of the Son, he now takes back in the form of his death, "to dispense it" as life that comes welling "in a new way from his divine source."[30] This does not take place "according to the laws laid down by him for creation, but in a way contrary to them all, inasmuch as he makes life out of death"; the Son's reappearance makes us "involved witnesses" of this, "taken by surprise", and we "must acknowledge the incomprehensible leap, the breaking through that has taken place in death, without being able to explain it".[31] Furthermore, just as Jesus' death comprehended in itself the sinful death of all men, his Resurrection does not take place vertically, with him leaving the world and going to God, but he is "the first fruits of those who have fallen asleep" (1 Cor 15:20): "by his act of vertical obedience to the Father, he opens the door of resurrection horizontally to all deaths."[32] According to Paul, all "who belong to Christ" pass through this door—at all events, those "who have spent their whole lives on earth in living out their faith. . . . From our perspective, however, this category cannot be separated from the other category of those who likewise 'belong to Christ' in the transition from time to eternity. We cannot draw distinctions among these endless multitudes and must leave to the Lord their 'ordering'—to which Paul refers in 1 Corinthians 15:23."[33] For in his Eucharist the Lord "gives away in advance what he accomplishes through Cross and Resurrection, namely, incorruption. . . . Accordingly, his death, too, is included in the vitality of his truth—corruption being clothed with incorruption—and this 'inclusion' signifies the victory of eternal life over

---

[28] 3 Jo 329.   [29] 3 Jo 364.
[30] A 90.   [31] A 86.
[32] C 495.   [33] C 499.

death." In the Eucharist we have "a hidden encounter between eternity and time. But this transforming event is and remains totally God's business."[34]

It follows, finally, that the whole mystery of the Son's annihilation of death must not be understood merely as a mystery of "redemption" (from the annihilation of death that characterizes our existence in the world): it is redemptive only insofar as it manifests the ultimate horizon of meaning, which is God's all-embracing trinitarian love.

This must be asserted against Shizuteru Ueda's ingenious attempt to demonstrate something like a redeeming trinity in Zen Buddhism. As is well known, in Buddhism it is a question of redeeming the (ego-less) self from the "I am I" that is self-inclosed and wants to possess itself. In Buddhism there is a heightened problem of death because man "wants to be 'I' "; in Christianity it is heightened by the problem of sin; the analogy between these two views deserves some serious attention. Instead of a substance philosophy that finds something that is the ground of itself both in the finite and in the (allegedly) infinite "I", Zen Buddhism posits a mode of thinking that dissolves the appearance of substance into relationship. (To that extent it rejects all mysticism, including the union of Atman and Brahman.)[35] The "I am I" constitutes itself out of hatred (for the non-I), out of fundamental blindness about itself (since the "I" is put forward and loved as such) and out of covetousness (since the "I" desires to possess everything). This urge to live is a self-poisoning: it is death. We must die to the "I" that is at the root of our living and dying if we are "to live in the perspective of our death".[36] We must appreciate "the interpenetration of being and nothingness" beyond the illusory opposition of subject and object; we must dissolve the opposition of form and nothingness. In Mahayana Buddhism the discernment of nothingness within the form is called "great knowledge"; "seeing nothingness directly rendered concrete in

[34] C 545–46. This is also why no one saw Christ's Resurrection and why the risen Christ was not recognized. "The uttermost obedience of the Cross and of hell has transformed him. Only faith, now given to the women in a new way, can lift the strangeness and give direction and a receptivity to an obedience that is able to recognize him who has gone to the very limit of obedience": Gh 49.

[35] Shizuteru Ueda, "Der Zen-Buddhismus als Nicht-Mystik" in *Transparente Welt*, ed. G. Schulz (Berne and Stuttgart, 1965).

[36] Shizuteru Ueda, "Der Tod im Zen-Buddhismus" in *Der Mensch und sein Tod*, ed. J. Schwartländer, Kleine Vandenhoeckreihe 1426 (Göttingen, 1976), 162–74, here 165.

the form is called 'great sympathy', great compassion or having mercy on all that exists."[37] The final stage is therefore the ego-less relationship between these two poles. The last three of the ten stages of self-realization in the ancient Chinese Zen text *The Ox and His Oxherd*[38] portray, first, the complete unbecoming of being (and hence of the "I"), then the becoming (resurrection) of this nothingness to a mode of being that is neither objective nor subjective, and finally the encounter of both in the image of an encounter between an old man and a young man, in the "ego-less dynamism of relationship between man and man". "These three should not be spoken of as stages but as aspects. These three aspects form, as it were, the trinity of the true, ego-less self. The self, moreover, is never a 'that', but moves unhindered to and fro between the three aspects, in response to every stimulus and yet spontaneous."[39]

As we shall show, this trinitarian teaching, correctly rejecting an "I am I" notion of substance, gets into difficulties only because it was not able to see the undergirding of the everyday life-and-death world as an identity that has been made manifest in the Cross and Resurrection of Christ, within the absolute trinity of substance and relation. This identity is identical with absolute love.

b. Living in Christ's Death, Christ's Life

Ambrose distinguishes "three kinds of death. The first is the death of sin, as it is written, 'The soul that sins shall die' (Ezek 18:4). The second is the mystical death, when a man dies to sin and lives to God, as the Apostle says, 'we are buried with him by being baptized into his death' (Rom 6:4). The third death comes when we have finished this life's course and work." The first is evil, the second is good, and the third is indifferent, being bitter for the majority who cling to earthly goods and desirable for those who want to be with Christ.[1]

---

[37] Shizuteru Ueda, "Das Nichts und das Selbst im buddhistischen Denken: Zum west-östlichen Vergleich des Selbstverständnisses des Menschen" in *Studia Philosophica: Jahrbuch der Schweiz. Phil. Gesellchaft* 24 (1974), 144–61, esp. 156.

[38] German edition by K. Tsujimura and H. Buchner, 2d ed. (Pfullingen, 1975).

[39] Cf. Ueda, "Das Nichts", 156–57.

[1] *De bono mortis*, ep. 2 (PL 14, 540). Ambrose also speaks of the "dying of the Logos" in a soul that separates itself from him by sin (*De fuga saeculi* II, 13 [PL 14, 576AE]; *Epist.* 32, 2 [PL 16,1066A]). At this point he takes his lead from Origen: *Hom. 2, 2 in Jud.* (Baehrens 7, 473).

However, what is called "mystical death" here—and in the Fathers the word "mystical" always refers to the objective mystery of Christ, in particular in the context of sacramental participation[2]—the believer's sacramental dying with Christ in baptism (and Eucharist), is secondary. It presupposes something primary, namely, the death of Christ, undergirding all human dying. The fact that believers have a special participation in this undergirding death through the Church's sacrament does not nullify Paul's emphatic assertion that all deaths are affected by the one death because of the latter's representative character. Second Corinthians 5:14 puts it in a nutshell: "One has died for all; therefore all have died." The stress in the first part of the sentence is on the "for"; the whole thrust is indicative. What follows is in the imperative mood; it arises from a conclusion drawn by love and which, as far as love is concerned, is final and inescapable: "And he died for all, that those who live might live no longer for themselves but for him who for their sake died and was raised" (v. 15). It is this imperative, objectively applying to all the living, that summons us to be fashioned according to the mind, and ultimately the suffering destiny, of him who died "for" us. This fashioning is "mystical", that is, sacramental, and so—in accord with the nature of a sacrament—it must of course be existential too. As Paul says, however, the One who died for us is also the One who was "raised"; thus the two aspects of his final destiny that are so opposed actually belong together. They are inseparable (as we see most clearly in the Johannine concept of exaltation and glorification).

According to *Paul*, therefore, the lives of those who are animated by the *imperative* inherent in the *indicative*, and who are marked sacramentally and existentially, will be governed explicitly by the unity-in-duality of Christ's death and risen life. Their life will be an eschatological life, bearing the imprint of the most radical dying and the most radical turning to eternal life, not just for a fleeting moment, but constantly. Paul can speak of it as our dying and being buried with Christ (Rom 6:4), as our being crucified with him (Rom 6:6; Gal 6:14), but he also says that God "raised us up with him, and made us sit with him in the

---

[2] Henri de Lubac, *Corpus mysticum* (1949), esp. chaps. 1 and 2.

heavenly places in Christ Jesus" (Eph 2:6); we, therefore, who
"have died" with Christ, must "seek the things that are above,
where Christ is, seated at the right hand of God" (Col 3:1–3).
Being thus dead and risen to new life is not an external attribute
of our self, however: death and resurrection *change* it. It is not
annihilated in a Buddhist sense but *unselved* by being drawn into
the death and life of Christ. It is forced out of its central position so that the essence of Christ may take up residence there: "I
have been crucified with Christ; it is no longer I who live, but
Christ who lives in me; and the life I now live in the flesh I live
by faith in the Son of God, who loved me and gave himself for
me" (Gal 2:20). The same abandonment of self is required of all
who believe in Christ: "None of us lives to himself, and none of
us dies to himself. If we live, we live to the Lord, and if we die,
we die to the Lord; so then, whether we live or whether we die,
we are the Lord's" (Rom 14:7–8; cf. the Lord's abandonment
of self in Rom 6:10–11). Faith's effect of "unselving" us creates
a "vacant space" that is occupied by Christ and his "Spirit",
who "confirms" to us that we, like the Son, are children of the
Father, sharing a relation to the Son through the Spirit, so that
the *imago trinitatis* is fulfilled in us.

Paul immediately warns us, however, to observe the christological order: first the suffering, then the glorification. We shall
be fellow heirs with Christ "provided we suffer with him in
order that we may also be glorified with him" (Rom 8:17).[3] For
the duration of our life, suffering and death come before joy
and resurrection. This is partly because we have still to undergo
our physical death, but more profoundly it is because Christ
attained Resurrection only through his death. There is nothing
to prevent the joy being there at the same time (whether felt or
not); indeed, it can spur us on to desire more suffering. Such
suffering with Christ can be *active*, arising from the trials of the
apostolic life (cf. Paul's "boasting" in 2 Cor 11); but here, too,
there is need for *passive* acceptance of imposed suffering, for example, the "messenger of Satan" who harasses Paul and teaches
him "for the sake of Christ" to be "content with weaknesses,
insults, hardships, persecutions, and calamities" (2 Cor 12:10).

---

[3] Cf. H. Schlier's Romans commentary on this passage.

Not only from time to time, either, but "every day" (1 Cor 15:31)—just as the Lord commanded us to take up our cross "daily" (Lk 9:23)—"every day" (2 Cor 4:16), "all the day long" (Rom 8:36), "always" (2 Cor 4:10–11). Nor is there anything moderate about this suffering; it is brutal: "God has exhibited us apostles as last of all, like men sentenced to death", "the refuse of the world, the off-scouring of all things" (1 Cor 4:9, 13); "we were so utterly, unbearably crushed that we despaired of life itself . . . but that was to make us rely not on ourselves but on God who raises the dead" (2 Cor 1:8–9). These excessive trials can be understood only in a christological context, but they are matched by the "abundant share in comfort" (2 Cor 1:5) and the joy that echoes through all the letters. Indeed Paul positively expects the community to manifest this joy (Phil 3:1; 4:4; 2 Cor 13:11; and so on); its members should even rejoice that Paul, who is himself full of joy, is being sacrificed for the sake of their faith (Phil 2:17–18). The simultaneity of suffering and joy, which are both christological and eschatological, can take the most diverse forms in Christian experience; but the Apostle is interested, not so much in these subjective hues of experience, but in the objective, simultaneous co-inherence itself. This concrete co-inherence is expressed most beautifully in the long "as if" sequence in 2 Corinthians 6:4–10: "We are treated 'as if' impostors, and yet are true; 'as if' unknown, and yet well known; 'as if' dying, and behold we live; 'as if' punished, and yet not killed; 'as if' sorrowful, yet always rejoicing; 'as if' poor, yet making many rich; 'as if' having nothing, and yet possessing everything." Augustine says on this passage that "we can say 'as if' in connection with our sorrowing, but not in connection with our joy, for it is secure in hope." In a dream everything is "as if", but on awaking the "as if" vanishes. "For the Apostle does not say, 'as if rejoicing, but always sorrowful', or 'as if both sorrowful and rejoicing'; rather, he says, 'as if sorrowing, yet always rejoicing'."[4] Nonetheless the "as if" is not a dream but a participation in Christ's dying, which is the immovable precondition of his Resurrection. This is why the Apostle boasts of his weakness, which is the path to his life in Christ and

---

[4] *En. in Ps.* 48, II, 5.

—in apostolic terms—to the community's life in Christ: "For while we live we are always being given up to death for Jesus' sake, so that the life of Jesus may be manifested in our mortal flesh. So death is at work in us, but life in you" (2 Cor 4:11–12). The apostolic power is not Paul's own: it is the power of the Risen One who lives in him; the entire dramatic conclusion of 2 Corinthians rests on this insight (12:9–10; 13:3–4, 7–9).

In *John* the trinitarian dimension is even more prominent. Not only Christ and his Spirit dwell in the believer's heart; the Father himself, explicitly, dwells there. "If a man loves me . . . my Father will love him, and we will come to him and make our home with him" (Jn 14:23). Furthermore it is the Father who tends the Vine, his Son, pruning it of all that is unfruitful and purifying what is fruitful by allowing it a share in his death on the Cross, so that it may bring forth more fruit (15:2). Jesus' act of love for men always flows from the fact that he is loved by the Father (15:9). In the night of death, therefore, the Son's work can be given into the Father's hands (17:11). What believers "know" is, not primarily the love of the Son, but the fact that he has been sent by the Father (17:25); and this knowledge, mediated by him who has been thus sent, is eternal life (17:3). The Spirit of truth introduces believers into this relationship (16:13), which is the absolute truth.[5] Thus, as long as we live, the testimony of the Spirit cannot be separated from the testimony of the water and the blood. (The water and the blood flow from the wound in Jesus' side [19:34], representing the high point of the apostolic testimony [19:35].) For it is only in the context of this triune testimony that it becomes possible to believe "the greater testimony" that God has given by surrendering his Son (1 Jn 5:8–9): it takes the Cross to demonstrate that God is love (1 Jn 4:8, 16). We are marked sacramentally[6] by this trinitarian testimony, which means that we are also marked existentially by it (cf. 1 Jn 3:18: "in deed and in truth").

---

[5] I. de la Potterie, *La Vérité dans S. Jean* I/II (Rome: Biblical Institute Press, 1979).

[6] O. Cullmann, *Urchristentum und Gottesdienst*, 2d ed. (Zurich, 1950).

A life that is marked by the death of Jesus naturally exhibits a longing for what is "far better", that is, "to depart and be with Christ", but Paul also knows that "to remain in the flesh is more necessary on your account" (Phil 1:23–24). On the other side of this choice by which he is "hard pressed" there is his realization that "the life of Christ" will be honored in his body at all events, for it is Christ who is to be glorified, whether by Paul's "life" or by his "death" (Phil 1:20–21). "Christ" and "life" are equivalents whether we live or die, since Christ's death was also the proclamation of his life; this vindicates the Apostle's yearning for death, so that he may "be with Christ". This is a yearning that will echo through the Fathers; most strongly in Ignatius (who is already consecrated to death) when he commands the Christians not to obstruct his martyr's death: he regards it as his true life, whereas his earthly life is a death. "I seek him who died for our sake. I desire him who rose for us. . . . Suffer me, my brethren; hinder me not from living, do not wish me to die . . . for in the midst of life I write to you desiring death . . . there is in me no fire of love for material things; but only water living and speaking in me, and saying to me from within, 'Come to the Father.'"[7] There are similar passages in Tertullian,[8] in Gregory of Nyssa's writing "On the Dead"[9] and particularly in his portrayal of the death of his sister Macrina, who is consumed by the longing to meet Christ: "I too have been crucified with You. . . . Let not the terrible abyss separate me from Your elect. . . . Forgive me, since You have power on earth to forgive sins. . . . May my soul be received into Your hands as incense ascending before Your face."[10]

The problem is that this longing for eternal life, while it expressed something undoubtedly and genuinely Christian, did so in the terms of Stoicism and Neoplatonism. In the Middle Ages this latter world seriously contaminated the Christian language and concepts: the highest stage of Christian love was seen and pursued as a "mystical death", and this *mors mystica* was no longer seen in sacramental terms, as in Ambrose, but in terms of physical experience, in the sense of a self-evident ecstasy of love. Alois M. Haas has collected many examples of this,[11] from Bernard's explanation of the Song of Songs (chap. 52),

[7] Ignatius of Antioch, *Ep. ad Romanos* VI, 1–VII, 2 (Loeb).

[8] *De anima* 53.

[9] PG 46, 497–537.

[10] *De vita S. Macrinae* (PG 46, 984D–985A). Cf. also Gregory's *De anima et resurrectione, ibid.,* 12–160.

[11] "Mors mystica: Thanatologie der Mystik, insbesondere der deutschen Mystik" in *Freiburger Zft. f. Phil. u. Theol.* 23 (1976), 304–92; also in *Sermo mysticus* (Fribourg, Switzerland: Univ. Verlag, 1979), 392–480.

via Thomas Gallus, to Bonaventure (*Coll. in Hexaem.* II, 31), to the mystical writers Ramon Lull (*The Book of the Lover and the Beloved*) and Gerson, who combines Pseudo-Dionysian ecstasy and accounts of cases of physical death in such ecstasies. German mysticism provides many examples, as does Spanish (cf. the celebrated poem by St. Teresa of Avila: "I live without living in myself, / And in such a way I hope, / I die because I do not die. / Since I die of love / Living apart from love").[12] The danger of this approach comes to the fore in Molinos, with disastrous consequences in Madame Guyon. In the Middle Ages, however, it almost always hovers between a yearning to be out of the body—its terminology, at least, is non-Christian, recalling antiquity or a spirituality that is practically Buddhist—and an often somewhat muted theology of the Cross.

It is hard to see why this existential mode of the Christian life, which is expressed so concretely and non-mystically in Paul and the Fathers, should be coupled with a doctrine of psychological ("mystical") stages of experience in such a way that the Pauline counterweight, that greater urgency of carrying out the earthly mission, simply disappears. Ignatius of Loyola energetically restored the balance by saying that, in spite of his yearning for heaven, he would rather do Christ's work on earth until the end of the world, even if it meant remaining unsure of his own final blessedness.

What is the genuinely Christian mark that Christ's dying in God-forsakenness imprints on a human life? It is to be found much less in the direction of the ecstasy of love than in the everyday taking-up of our cross in which "the sufferer does not want to leave the Lord and accepts from his hand whatever is given him, which is above all a grace and a joy, but also at once points to the Cross, to loneliness and death."[13] "Even in the midst of the night of suffering we should not allow ourselves to be separated from the underlying joy of being privileged to suffer. This joy may be laid up with the Father, we may not feel it, yet it must be present, even in the deepest suffering, as the joy of gratitude."[14] Furthermore, "Christian suffering can never remain brooding and enclosed in itself", for the Lord "always gives the sufferer, even within his

---

[12] "Aspirations toward Eternal Life" in *The Collected Works of St. Teresa of Avila* III (Washington, D.C.: Institute of Carmelite Studies, 1985), 375.—TRANS.

[13] SL 54.

[14] Ka I, 381.

suffering, glimpses of and connections with other mysteries".[15]
Far from being a Quietist escape, the imprint of Christ's death
involves those who bear it in the battle with evil in its fight "with
God himself"; once they have embraced God's cause, evil is their
enemy too, though in a "secondary" way. While "only God himself can conquer" the power that strives against him, he nonetheless wants believers to join in the fight, using his weapons.[16] In
this constant battle (cf. 1 Cor 15:31) they die daily, renouncing
the power to "dispose, control and make choices for themselves",
practicing a "renunciation that bears fruit in God". This renunciation implies "a growth on earth of Christ and his kingdom"; the
Christian becomes "to a certain extent the Lord's earthly realm,
there for the Lord's use".[17] Only in this way is he "indifferent"
vis-à-vis the mystery of the unity of life and death in Christ's
Cross and Resurrection, which is always assuming new and different forms in his life.[18]

Bernanos has shown us what a Christian life marked by the
Cross is. He has done this in numerous works and finally, following Gertrud von Le Fort, in his drama of the Carmelites. Contrary to the illusory stereotype that a Carmelite has to die a *mors
mystica* in the ecstasy of love, the old Prioress dies a genuine death
on the Cross, in the most bitter abandonment by God, to the horror and dismay of the entire community. This death, however,
is shown to possess the fruitfulness of the Cross, since it proves
to be a dying on behalf of another's death.[19]

c. Dying into Christ's Life, Christ's Death

Now we come to our physical dying, which all must undergo,
whether they die before or after Christ. From the very beginning it is God who is "life": it is he who breathes something of

---

[15] Ka I, 328.

[16] Ep 255.

[17] C 509.

[18] H 69: "Both life and death testify to the Lord. In his death he is life, and,
living, he dies. . . . Even in his temporal existence he lives in the eternal 'now' of
eternal life, as he shows us in his death and in his life. . . . Holy Mass is the sign
of concrete eternity. For here life and death coincide: they have become one."

[19] G. von Le Fort, *Die Letzte am Schafott* (1931); G. Bernanos, *Dialogues des
Carmélites* (1949) in *Oeuvres Romanesques* (Pléiade, 1961), 1563–1719.

his own life into the nostrils of the first Adam. It may be that, prior to all death that has ever been experienced historically, something like a "neutral" end was appointed for this Adam, but if so, we can discern no trace of it. We can only say in abstract terms that this "end" must have involved the finite life returning and giving itself back to the infinite life whence it came. Man only becomes acquainted with death as punishment (Gen 3:3–19: "Return to the ground!"), a punishment that is the inner consequence of Adam's turning away from God: he dies, brutally parted from life, and sinks into the realm of the dead, *sheol*, where they "no longer see the Lord in the land of the living"; the dead suffer violence, "for Sheol cannot thank thee, death cannot praise thee; those who go down to the pit cannot hope for thy faithfulness" (Is 38:11–18). It is punishment, but grace is latent within it; the man who has turned away from God must die "lest [in this condition] he put forth his hand and take also of the tree of life . . . and live for ever!" (Gen 3:22). Israel knows, right to the very end, that "immortality" (as the Book of Wisdom will call it) belongs to God alone and that it is only by communing with God that man can share in a life that lies beyond his death.[1] Not only will Paul retain this view that death is a punishment, developing it as the counterpart to the new, Christian understanding of death (Rom 5:12–14): he will extend this penal view of death from man to the whole creation that is involved in it with him. Creation is subjected to this servitude against its will and yearns for the manifestation of the new Man who will free it "from its bondage to decay" (Rom 8:19–25).

Man, turned away from God, cannot avoid finding out, when he comes to die, who the Lord of his existence is. Man has come to the end of his excuses, his attempts "to start a dialogue with God from a position of safe concealment, whereas God wants to be close to man. . . . So God restores the clarity of his countenance through the severity of death and punishment. . . . And when, as a result of sin, the harsh contours of finitude stand out and man chafes against them, it is God's providence that finite

[1] Wis 1:15; 2:23; 3:2–4. While the Book of Wisdom is influenced in its language by Greek thought, the Platonic idea that the human soul is by nature immortal is totally foreign to it.

man should thus (in death) come up against God's infinity."[2] "Now death appears to be God's way of forcibly putting man at his disposal, for the dead man cannot do anything for himself."[3] "Where man comes up against his unconditional limits—death —the unconditional power of God takes over."[4]

Now, however, the Son of God has proclaimed God's eternal life in the world by undergirding, in his dying, all the deaths of sinners who die turned away from God; thus, in himself, he gives a totally new value to their dying. In death the sinner is expropriated from himself; objectively we have seen that this puts him at God's disposal in a new way; in turn this expropriation of the sinner is turned toward Christ by the latter's far more radical self-expropriation. Here we see clearly the dissymmetrical relationship—which Paul so emphasizes—between the "all have died" (in the old Adam) and the new dying in Christ (Rom 5:15–21). Adam did not die "for" and "on behalf of" those who died after him, for in Adam's wake everyone dies, falling into non-life, for himself alone. Christ, however, dies essentially "for" (*anti, hyper*) all sinners doomed to death, and so the death of sinners acquires an objective relation to Christ's death, as is so clearly expressed by the use of the dative in the relevant phrases: "If we die, we die *to* the Lord" (Rom 14:8); for "he died for all, that those who live might live no longer *to* themselves (dative) but *to* him who for their sake died and was raised" (2 Cor 5:15). Since Christ's death is "for us", there arises a reciprocity that—in a somewhat different context—is put like this: "The body . . . is for the Lord, and the Lord for the body." This is not, however, a reciprocity between equals; the one belongs to the other: "Your bodies are members of Christ" (1 Cor 6:13, 15). A man may die turned away from God, but it is a dying "unto" God, who, in his undergirding death, manifests his trinitarian life in a totally new and surprising way. In his death he has re-valued all death, since his death was not forced upon him but took place "freely" in accord with the Father's will (Jn 10:18); thus it is an expression of the divine life and

[2] T 27–28.
[3] T 51.
[4] C 181.

already contains the Resurrection in itself. No refusal on man's part can call this reciprocity into question. "When God makes demands of God he makes sure that God always overtakes man, that grace has more weight than sin."[5]

True, "Death will retain its penal aspect until the end of the world", for "the Son did not come to put an end to the Father's work, to the measures he has taken, but to show them to be based on the love of the Trinity."[6] Even for those who are made righteous by Christ's death, it is still true that "your bodies are dead because of sin" (Rom 8:10). "The sting of death is that it is a punishment. But just as our being sinners is transformed by the Son's coming, so death's penal aspect is also transformed." Faced with the Resurrection, we shall realize "that the Father can change even the last enemy, death, into eternal life, punishment into the highest reward, fear into eternal bliss. . . . Now it almost seems as if death has been invented in order to give man ultimate proof of God's superior power."[7] Man's death is already drawn into the death of Christ, so he need not attempt to die it *for himself*: "Renouncing a personal death, a death we have envisaged and manipulated, is only the counterpart of renouncing a life we ourselves have fashioned."[8] Thus, acknowledging that our death has a relationship with Christ's death is simply identical with the act of faith in which we point our entire being —living or dying—away from ourselves and relate it to the life and death of Christ. For the man who wishes to live only in and by Christ, such faith will include his acceptance, now in this (eternal) life, of that death, albeit past and integrated, which yet lies ahead of him.

The Christ of the Book of Revelation appears as absolute Lord over death because he has gone through it: "I am . . . the living one. I died, and behold I am alive for evermore, and I have the keys of Death and Hades" (Rev 1:18). Insofar as the believer's earthly life bears the stamp, in advance, of this life "which was dead", his life can be described as "dead" (Col 3:3, cf. our previous paragraph). This is true in sacramental, mystical terms just

[5] T 82.
[6] T 57.
[7] T 57, 54.
[8] T 63.

as much as in ethical, ascetic terms. On the other hand, those who do not bear this stamp are described simply as "dead" as far as eternal life is concerned (Rom 6:13; Eph 2:1; 1 Jn 5:16; "dead even while they live", 1 Tim 5:6). They do not bear the mark of life—the mark of Christ's death—the seal on the forehead that protects them against annihilation (Rev 7:3). This is why Paul strives to attain an existential "knowledge" of Christ: he wants to "know him and the power of his resurrection", but this must be by "sharing in his sufferings": "becoming like him in his death, that if possible I may attain the resurrection from [*exanastasis* "out of"] the dead" (Phil 3:10–11).

According to Romans, all men since Adam share a common fate: they die through estrangement from God. Even though the law that confronted the sinner, formally describing sin as a turning away from God, had not yet been given, "death reigned from Adam to Moses" (Rom 5:14) because even the pagans, like Adam, offended against their own consciences (which acts as a law in their case: Rom 2:14). Again, however, we have to say that there is no inner solidarity of all mortals in the first Adam: this solidarity only comes about through the unique death of the Second Adam, who is not only a "living being" but a "life-giving spirit", namely, the Spirit of God (1 Cor 15:45), since "by the grace of God he was to taste death *for* every one" (Heb 2:9). So the first Adam shrinks to the level of a kind of prelude to the Second Adam; accordingly "the whole reality of death moves into the past. Death is henceforth only a point of departure set by God so that we may share in his life."[9] By contrast, the love given by Christ and practiced by Christians "is constantly transforming us from death to life".[10]

We can see the "life-giving spirit" of the Second Adam most directly where Jesus raises people from the dead. Here we have no great exertions or wrestling with God as in the miracles of Elijah and Elisha: at the gates of Naim we have the simple meeting of death and life: Jesus touches the bier and commands the dead man to rise; that is sufficient (Lk 7:14). Jesus says that both Jairus' daughter and Lazarus "are sleeping": in this condition they

---

[9] Ka II, 123.
[10] Ka II, 124–25.

are already on their way to him. It is a kind of concession to the disciples' lack of understanding when he goes on to explain that this "sleep" is "death" (Jn 11:14); in the crucial passage he again speaks of physical death "in parenthesis", so to speak: "I am the resurrection and the life; he who believes in me, though he die, yet shall he live" (11:25). Dying, in John, is only the law of a love that shows itself through giving its life: "Greater love has no man than this, that a man lay down his life for his friends" (Jn 15:13)—an utterly free action, but in fulfillment of a charge from the Origin of love, the Father (10:18).

Jesus' touching of the dead prefigures a very different "touching" that the risen Christ, for whom death is past, imparts to those who are living and dying. This "touching" is made concrete in the Church's sacraments, which, in their mystery-objectivity, configure us to the living Lord who died for us. This begins with baptism, which draws us, not only into the death (Rom 6:3) that he has gone through, but also, most explicitly, into a participation in his dying: "You will be baptized with the baptism with which I am baptized" (Mk 10:39). Our baptism is consecrated, by way of anticipation, by his own baptism in the Jordan, but it is carried through in his death, that "baptism", the prospect of which causes him such distress (Lk 12:50). The parallel passage makes it clear that we are to share his death: "The cup that I drink you will drink" (Mk 10:39), the cup of the divine wrath (cf. *Theo-Drama* IV, 338), which, if we drink it, becomes a cup of salvation. Jesus gives his promise to the disciples, but also his own chalice, which will be both sweet and bitter. He gives more: he gives them his own flesh and blood as a sacramental "waybread", but in such a way that they will remember that, in celebrating his Eucharist, they will be proclaiming his death: *mortem annuntiabitis* (1 Cor 11:26). He gives the dying man his eternal resurrection-life, but in the condition that gave it birth: his own death. And, finally, he gives him a share in that anointing which marked him forever as the dying Messiah: "She has anointed my body beforehand for burying" (Mk 14:8).[11] The ancient Church used to speak in this context

---

[11] Today the Anointing of the Sick is not related to death as directly as it was in former times. Nonetheless it is worth remembering that, for the people of

of Jesus' "mystical" gestures by which he configures his own to his death and life, but she was well aware that the sacramental "imitation" of Jesus' sufferings bestows salvation not only metaphorically but really.[12] So Augustine observed that baptism has in view not only a mystical dying but, by way of anticipation, physical death.

Christ's sacramental visitation of the dying takes place, however, in the concrete reality of his Church; in his official representative but also, simultaneously, in the whole communion of saints that is inseparable from him. Just as no sacrament is ever administered by a solitary Christ but only together with his Church (in her objective and subjective holiness), so the Church is present in the ineluctable loneliness that characterizes a man's dying. This comes out most clearly in the heart of the Church, the Mother of the Lord, who "was there when the Son died" and therefore "is always present when anyone is dying; she makes no distinction in her love between the Son of Man and his brethren. . . . Her love's everlasting fruitfulness is felt particularly where a dying person is afraid he will no longer encounter love; where, at the end of his life, he realizes that he has loved too little, believed and hoped too little." At such a time it is precisely the innermost cast of her life, her consent, that can help, "for the dying man can do nothing but let things happen, unquestioningly and in total surrender. So the meaning of death is unveiled through the unveiling of the life of the Mother and the Son." "On the basis of her Son's death [Mary] knows what dying means, and because of her immediate elevation to heaven she knows what the heavenly encounter means"; so she is present "especially in the sacrament of the dying" so that the dying person "need not stare solely at death and judgment" but can look to the grace granted to the Mother and to her media-

---

the Old Testament, sickness and all other life-threatening situations represented a direct foreshadowing, and even a manifest presence, of the world of death in the midst of life. The Psalms show this very clearly. Christoph Barth, *Die Errettung vom Tod in den individuellen Klage- und Dankliedern des Alten Testaments* (Zollikon: Evang. Verlag, 1974). For the modern situation, cf. also G. Greshake, "Letzte Ölung—Krankensalbung—Tauferneuerung angesichts des Todes?", in: *Leiturgia, Koinonia, Diakonia*, Festschr. Kard. König (Vienna: Herder, 1980), 97–126.

[12] T 124.

tion of all graces. The New Adam does not do his work without the New Eve—whether this is Mary or the entire communion of saints joined to her; both together "imbue death with the quality of mercy".[13] This does not mean that the dying man in his loneliness will not taste something of death's quality of judgment; the death that he has to die may be a "dear" one rather than a "cheap" one. What it means is simply that this darkness will be able to be a sharing in the darkness that the Lord had to endure on his Cross (and which his Mother, too, endured as a representative of all the saints). The conclusion of the Hail Mary is of great and ultimate significance for everyone, whether his death is to be hard or easy.

2. The One Judgment

a. Judgment Universal and Personal

The Bible, both Old and New Testaments, knows of only one Judgment, just as there is only one Day of Yahweh or of Christ. This Judgment will assess the weight that the various historical entities have in the sight of God. First to be judged are the nations that are Israel's enemies. For God and his justice are on Israel's side, which means that Israel's enemies are in the wrong. Egypt must be judged because of its arrogance and its enslaving of Israel (Gen 15:14; Ex 3:16; 4:31; 12:12, and so on). Amalek (Ex 17:14), the Amorites (Nb 21:34), Midian (Nb 31:3) and the Canaanites (Josh 8:14; 11:20, and so on) must be judged for having opposed Israel's entry into the Promised Land. Later, in the time of the Prophets, there are all those who threatened Israel: they are all mentioned in oracles of judgment (cf., for example, Amos 1–2; Jer 25:14ff.; 46–51; Ezek 25–32). They are judged as collective persons, often (as in Ezekiel) embodied by their prince: Pharaoh, the King of Tyre, the King of Babylon, and so on.

When we come to Amos, the picture of the "Day of the Lord" changes. Now light is no longer reserved for Israel: the darkness will apply to Israel as well. Thus Yahweh's storm falls upon Is-

---

[13] T 123–25.

rael (Amos 2:4–6:14). Now Israel, treated as a person, as God's first-beloved (Hos 2; Jer 2:2; 11:15), can be compared to other "persons" at the Day of Judgment, for example, "your sister Sodom with her daughters", "your elder sister Samaria": these "have not committed half your sins" (Ezek 16:46–51; cf. Ezek 23 and Mt 11:20–24). The fact that God's people, in its entirety, appears here as a person is ultimately a consequence of the Covenant: the legal covenant is no longer concluded with individuals (like the patriarchs) but with the people as a whole (Ex 15:25), which solemnly promises to keep it (Josh 24). Initially the promises and threats for keeping or infringing the law are addressed to the whole people (Lev 26; Dt 28), just as the fourfold sequence—falling away, punishment, crying to God, salvation—applies (from the Book of Judges onward) to the whole people. Of course, right from the beginning there were individual righteous men and individual transgressors within the nation, attracting individual reward and punishment (Onan: Gen 38:10; Nadab: Lev 10:2, and so on, and later even kings who were punished in their tribe: Eli: 1 Sam 3:13; David: 2 Sam 12:14; Solomon: 1 Kings 11:12; Jeroboam: 14:10–12; Ahab: 21:29, and so on). They serve as admonitory examples to the whole people. In the Prophets the guilty persons coalesce into groups: there are the idolaters, the oppressors of the poor, the false prophets; and their sin is such a burden that it plunges the entire people into calamity. The situation is so disastrous that God's judgment is almost ready to abolish the Covenant (Is 9:8–10:4; Jer 4:5–31); appeals are to no avail: "Though Moses and Samuel stood before me, yet my heart would not turn toward this people. Send them out of my sight, and let them go! And when they ask you, 'Where shall we go?' you shall say to them, 'Thus says the Lord: "Those who are for pestilence, to pestilence, and those who are for the sword, to the sword; those who are for famine, to famine, and those who are for captivity, to captivity"'" (Jer 15:1–2).

After the return from exile, now that Israel knows that God is on its side, although it is weak and surrounded by hostile nations, there is a new outbreak of nationalistic prayer for retribution against its enemies. Anyone against Israel is also against God (Obad 21; Zech 14:9, and so on). There is a call for vengeance

(Is 49:26; Zech 14:12; Malachi 4:1, and so on): God is once more the Warrior of ancient times, fighting for Jerusalem against all the nations (Zech 14:3), and the last slaughter will end with their apocalyptic defeat (Ezek 38–39).

At the same time, however, there occurs a split in Israel, a split that will characterize it so ambivalently in Jesus' time: there are the pious souls who hope to survive the Judgment by meticulously keeping the Law, and there are the others, the "sinners", to whom the later psalms continually refer. The Judgment will separate them from one another (Is 65:11–14, and so on). Even in the Old Testament, therefore, the Judgment of the world—which always involved personal judgment—is more and more individualized; judgment "addresses each person individually."[1] Each person must stand on his own; intercession is useless. Not even the "Son of Man" in Enoch can intercede for sinners, for God chases them away and "delivers them to the angels of punishment, exacting vengeance against them for having ill-treated his children and chosen ones" (*Ethiopic Enoch* 69, 9f.). Each individual act counts and is placed on the scales. It is also possible, however, for a man's entire life's work to be taken into account.[2] With this in mind we can see why in the New Testament—in spite of the entirely new situation brought about by the redemption of the world through Christ—the Gospels and Epistles continue relentlessly to insist that we shall be "judged by our deeds" (cf., for example, Mt 25:14ff.; 25:31ff.; Rom 2:5ff.; 14:10–12; 2 Cor 5:10; Jn 5:27ff.).

This means that, according to the whole Bible, for which there is only one Judgment, the *general* judgment ("Before him will be gathered all the nations" Mt 25:32) will also be an absolutely personal and *particular* judgment. A certain tension may be experienced between these two sides, so that people try to imagine the good and the bad being kept in separate "rooms" and "states" as they wait for the coming judgment; but this cannot alter the fact that there is to be one single Judgment. A theology that follows the biblical revelation cannot speak, therefore,

---

[1] P. Volz, *Die Eschatologie der jüdischen Gemeinde im neutestamentlichen Zeitalter* (Tübingen: Mohr, 1934), 289.

[2] *Ibid.*, 280–84, gives many examples of the various nuances here.

of two different judgments, ultimately putting "all the emphasis on the particular judgment" of each person after his death and regarding the "Last Judgment as merely the public ratification of these particular verdicts before the whole world".[3] Both aspects "are most closely interlinked. They are, so to speak, two stages of a single, all-embracing event."[4] Origen is right, no doubt, when, basing himself on Luke 17:24 ("As the lightning flashes and lights up the sky from one side to the other, so will the Son of man be in his day"), he sees Christ's parousia as "a revelation of his divinity" in such a way that "not only none of the righteous, but no sinner either will fail to recognize Christ's true nature." The location of this revelation, he says, cannot be established. But if it is possible for us to experience, in faith, the beginnings of this enlightenment, how much more perfect will it be when Christ "reveals himself to all, good and bad, believers and unbelievers, not only to faith and those who seek diligently, but by the manifestation of his divinity. When he comes in his glory he will be everywhere: he will stand at every place before the eyes of everyone; all will be everywhere before his face."[5] Other Fathers of the Church up to and including Augustine,[6] as we have already seen, can speak in similar terms.

The most important biblical datum is that the one Judgment of all and each can only take place "at the end". This comes out clearly (after much original vagueness about the time of the "Day of the Lord")[7] toward the conclusion of the Old Testament and, preeminently, in the New. Whether this is the "end" for the individual or for human history in general is not reflected upon.

[3] B. Neunheuser, "Letztes Gericht" in T. Bogler, ed., *Tod und Leben: Von den letzten Dingen* (Maria Laach: Ars liturgica, 1950), 83.

[4] *Ibid.*, 89.

[5] *In Mt. Comm.*, ser. 70 (Klostermann, 164–66). Basil expresses himself similarly: *In Ps.* 33, 4 (PG 29, 360), in proximity to Origen: Pseudo-Basil, *Commentary on Isaiah* (PG 30, 200–201).

[6] "Quaedam igitur vis est intelligenda divina qua fiet ut cuique opera sua, vel bona vel mala, cuncta in memoriam revocentur et mentis intuitu mira celeritate cernantur; . . . atque ita *simul omnes* et *singuli* judicentur": *De Civ. Dei* XX, 14 (PL 41, 680).

[7] *Be'aharit hayyamim* does not have to mean "the end of time" (Hos 3:5; Is 2:4; Micah 4:1; Jer 23:20, etc.), but "in the course of time", "in the long run": R. Pautrel, "Jugement" (AT) in *DBS* IV, 1324.

The primary consideration is, rather, that the whole content of the judgment of the individual (the "particular" or—better— "personal" judgment) is transferred to the general judgment to be processed.[8] The theology of the first Christian centuries held fast to this basic fact, even while reflecting on the so-called "intermediary" state between death and the (Last) Judgment. A welcome means of solving this question was found in the temporary "anterooms" of late Judaism: these were mostly thought to be located in Sheol; in even later times they were imagined to be divided into separate areas for the good and the bad.[9] When

---

[8] E.g., Justin, *Dial.* 5: "The souls of the good rest in a better place, and those of sinners and the evil in a worse, waiting there for the time of judgment." The same in Irenaeus, *Adv. Haer.* V, 31, 1–2 (citing Christ's descent into Sheol): "The disciple is not greater than his Master." Tertullian will coin the expression "refrigerium (interim)"—an expression that will have profound consequences—for the souls of the righteous awaiting judgment. He probably did this to counter a theory of Marcion's, according to whom only the souls of the "psychics" waited there. On this, cf. A. Stuiber, "Refrigerium interim" in *Theophaneia* 11 (Bonn: Hanstein, 1957); H. Finé, "Die Terminologie der Jenseitsvorstellungen bei Tertullian" in *Theophaneia* 12 (Bonn: Hanstein, 1958); H. Finé, "Der Ort der Erquickung" in *Geist und Leben* 33 (1960), 334–48. On Hippolytus, cf. *Adv. Graec.* 1–3 (PG 10, 796–800). Novatian speaks of a pre-judgment (*praejudicium*): *De Trin.* 1 (PL 3,888). Lactantius explicitly rejects the "particular judgment": "Ne quisquam putet animas post mortem protinus judicari", for they are all held in custody together until the Judgment: *Inst. Div.* VII, 26 (PL 6, 813–14). Cyprian follows Tertullian but no longer locates the antechamber in Sheol; the righteous too, not only the martyrs, are with God: *De mortalitate* 20, 26 (PL 4, 596, 601f.). The Greeks avoid the concept of a particular judgment until the very last moment. Augustine often speaks of it in the traditional manner: *De praed. sanct.* 12, 24 (PL 44, 977–78, passim). But he can also distinguish between various kinds of judgment: the Last Judgment is the real one, but lesser judgments take place even during life: *De Civ. Dei* 20, 1, 2 (PL 41, 659); finally (in an isolated passage) he can speak of a judgment after death: "Illud quod rectissime et salubriter credit (Victor) judicari animas cum de corpore exierint, antequam veniant ad illud judicium": *De anima* II, 4, 8 (PL 44, 498–99). Even after Augustine, however, it is usual to reserve this name to the Last Judgment. Cf. *DTC* VIII, 2, 1801f. Thomas speaks only in passing of two judgments (Suppl. 88, 1 ad 1); the Councils of Lyons (1274) and Florence (1438) do not mention them at all, out of consideration for the Greeks.

[9] Jerome is typical: "Diem autem Domini diem intellige judicii, sive diem exitus uniuscujusque de corpore. Quod enim judicii futurum est omnibus, hoc in singulis die mortis impleretur": *In Joel* II, 1 (PL 25, 965). Augustine is similar: "Novissimus dies est cujusque dies mortis. Etenim cum hinc exieris, recipieris pro meritis et resurges ad recipienda quae gessisti": *Sermo* 170, 10 (PL 38, 932).

Origen says that "the soul that departs from this life is treated (*dispensabitur*) according to its deserts",[10] he is not speaking in the context of judgment here. At the Last Judgment all deeds will be examined in the greatest detail.[11] The great Greek Fathers are much inclined to portray the Last Judgment as a strictly personal affair, for example, Gregory Nazianzen[12] and, in particular, Chrysostom: If our deeds condemn us, no one, "neither father, nor son, nor friend, however venerable, will be able to come to your aid".[13] They underline the element of judgment we have already encountered: it is our works, rather than Christ, that condemn us.

b. Resurrection and Exaltation

Jewish eschatology at and before the time of Jesus is extremely varied and contains patent contradictions. However, in its theories about the last things there are two prominent concepts that will be of decisive significance in the development of Christian eschatology, in spite of the fact that they are mutually opposed. First there is the expectation of a partial or general resurrection of the dead at the end of the world, as a prelude to the Judgment; and secondly there is the idea that certain privileged souls—first the martyrs and later the righteous in general—will be elevated (or transported) into the direct presence of God immediately after death. The doctrine of resurrection thinks in horizontal historical terms; the doctrine of elevation thinks vertically, which means that the typically Jewish expectation of the future can fade into the background.

It is pointless, therefore, to engage in polemics against "overemphasis" on the "particular judgment" in the belief that in doing so one is making an ecumenical approach to the Eastern Orthodox (Lambert Beauduin, "Himmel und Auferstehung" in *Das Mysterium des Todes* (Frankfurt: Knecht, 1955), 221-40. All the elements of the particular judgment are contained within the general judgment.

[10] *Peri Archon* I, praef. 5.

[11] *In Rom.* II, 1-2 (PG 14, 870-72).

[12] Or 16, 9 (PG 35, 945).

[13] *In I Cor. hom.* 42, 3 (PG 61, 366-68); *In II Cor. hom.* 9, 4 (PG 61, 465).

1. The Jesus who was dead manifested himself alive and with a physical presence on the third day; insofar as this reappearance of Jesus was understood in the categories of resurrection "from the dead",[14] he was the living proof of the doctrine of "resurrection from the dead";[15] he had in principle initiated the end-time. At the beginning it was possible to draw the most varied conclusions from this. Some said it meant that we ourselves will not die. In the case of the gnostically inclined Corinthians, basing themselves on certain statements made by Paul, for example, that we have already died with Christ in baptism and are somehow risen with him, it could mean that we are already risen. Or, given that some members of the community had already died, it meant that the dead would be the first to rise, going with the living to meet the returning Christ (1 Th 4:13ff.; also 1 Cor 15, where, while mortality is attributed to all the children of the first Adam, some of those who are still living will be "changed" alongside those who rise from the dead: v. 52).

In allowing this somewhat naïve hope of experiencing the end to fade away, it was possible unconsciously to abandon something that was essential in this first hope: namely, that the Resurrection of Jesus has made the future a present reality. John will hold fast to it, as when, in his Gospel, Jesus counters Martha's expectation of future resurrection by drawing attention to the present reality embodied in himself (Jn 11:24–26).[16] This is confirmed from a quite different perspective in Matthew's depiction of an indefinite number of "saints who had fallen asleep"

---

[14] This, and not "from death", is the constant formula. Rom 1:4; 4:24; 6:4; 8:11; 10:7; 1 Cor 15:12, 20; Gal 1:1; Eph 1:20; Col 1:18; 2:12; 1 Th 1:10; 2 Tim 2:8; Heb 13:20; 1 Pet 1:3; 1:21; Rev 1:5; Acts 4:10.

[15] Thus, in the Acts of the Apostles, Peter and John speak to the people of the resurrection from the dead "through" (on the basis of the example of) Jesus (4:2). In Athens Paul proclaims "the gospel of Jesus and of the resurrection" (17:18); in the face of the accusations in 23:6 he defends himself by saying that in his teaching he is putting forward nothing but the "resurrection of the dead" (not "from"). Similar is 24:15, which speaks of a "resurrection of the dead, of both the just and the unjust", and 24:21. In Paul's speech before Agrippa, the Resurrection of Jesus is preeminently an example of God's power of raising the dead (26:8); he is only the first in whom the ancient promise is fulfilled (26:22–23).

[16] The raising of Lazarus, which is realized here and now within time, is a *sēmeion* of the power of eschatological resurrection embodied in Jesus.

and who rise together with Jesus (Mt 27:52–53); the majority of theologians assume that these saints were also received into heaven along with Jesus.[17] Now we have already emphasized elsewhere that Jesus' Resurrection took place in all truth at the end of the world, since he has atoned for those who will come after him in time just as much as for those who were before him and contemporaneous with him (*Theo-Drama* III, 110): accordingly we must say at least the same of those who rose together with him.[18] However, we should also keep in mind the "first resurrection" of those in the Book of Revelation (20:4, 6) who died as martyrs and "live and reign with Christ"; there is no suggestion here that this resurrection is a merely spiritual one.

2. The raising of Christ is also spoken of as an "exaltation" (Phil 2:9; Acts 2:33; there is Johannine double meaning in John 3:14; 8:28; cf. related expressions in Romans 1:4; Ephesians 4:10). This is an Old Testament concept; it is initially applied to God (who, in himself, is the Highest, yet is "exalted" by the praise of the congregation), then to the Suffering Servant (Is 53:10–12) and to the King, who is "exalted" by God, to those whose blood is shed in martyrdom, and finally to the godly in general. When linked with the world of eschatological ideas, it implies that the one thus "exalted" is preserved from Sheol and placed directly in the sphere of God. There is a certain interplay between this and the idea that the godly can be "transported" into God's presence, as is predicated of Enoch and Elijah. It may be that certain passages in the Psalms (49:15; 73:23–28) testify to the dawning of an expectation that the believer will be elevated from death into the eternal sphere of the divine life. In the Diaspora we find the influence of Hellenistic ideas of immortality (Philo). It has also been shown[19] that Palestinian apocryphal writ-

[17] Zeller, "Corpora Sanctorum" in *Zft. f. Kath. Theol.* 71 (1949), 385–465.

[18] 1 Cor 15:23 speaks of a resurrection *tagma*, or "order", this only means a temporal succession when seen in an internal historical perspective. Evidently the envisaged third stage is missing: "First Christ, the first-fruits, then, at his coming, those who belong to him", and finally all others.

[19] On this, cf. Paul Hoffmann, *Die Toten in Christus: Eine religionsgeschichtliche und exegetische Untersuchung zur paulinischen Eschatologie* (Münster: Aschendorff, 1966), esp. 95–133; on the time A.D.: 134–74.

ings, albeit in very different ways, assume that the faithful are set in the divine presence immediately after death. Several passages in the *Ethiopic Enoch* speak of the "dwelling of the righteous in heaven", even if (in chap. 50) this belief cuts across a different idea, namely, that Sheol is the abode of the dead. Generally speaking, the dominant idea in the late period is that the righteous dwell in heaven until the final act;[20] there is clearly a connection here with the figure of Enoch, who was "transported" to God. Belief in a resurrection (from Sheol) occurs sporadically (chap. 51, 1–2), and in chapter 102, 4–103, there is some reflection on the "intermediate state". In the latest writings from the first century A.D. (the pseudo-Philonic book on biblical antiquities, the Fourth Book of Esdras, and—based on the latter—the *Syrian Apocalypse of Baruch*), we find a mixture of resurrection ideas, notions of "waiting rooms" for those in a transitional state, as well as the belief that the souls of the righteous are with God. The Rabbis reflect on the prospect of individual retribution after death; they believe that the righteous will dwell in paradise (*gan eden*), which can be regarded as the first phase of the "coming aeon", subsequently to be spread over the whole world. Sheol is more and more equated with Gehenna, the preliminary place of punishment leading to ultimate damnation.

We have given only a superficial indication of the multiplicity of eschatological ideas current at the time, but it will already be clear how difficult it is to say how far the New Testament (Paul in particular, but also John) uses such categories in order to express an eschatology that is radically changed through the fact of Christ's Resurrection.

Paul's whole interest is concentrated on the hope of a bodily resurrection together with Christ, on the basis of a sharing in his suffering and death (Phil 3:10–11). Here he lays equal stress on two interconnected truths. First, our configuration to Christ ("being made like Christ") excludes an incorporeal state —such as certain Gnostics held; "*soma*" is the central word in 1 Corinthians 15 in his argument with the Corinthians (who were no doubt entertaining some form of early Gnosticism),

---

[20] F. Stier, *Zur Komposition und Literarkritik der Bilderreden im äth. Henoch* (1935), 79, cited in Hoffmann, *Die Toten in Christus*, 113. There are several references in 4 Esdras to souls, separated from their bodies, waiting for resurrection.

whether this *soma* be "psychic" or "pneumatic".[21] Second, this configuration to the Risen One is to take place at his return, which is in the future, whether the Christian has died or is still alive at that point in time (1 Th 4:14–18; 1 Cor 15:51–52). The persistent expectation of Christ's imminent return—despite the fact that deaths continue to occur among believers—brings these two realities so close together that the idea of an "intermediate state" is rendered practically superfluous. There is a different perspective in Philippians 1:21–26, where Paul says that he would prefer to die and be with Christ, but this simply brings out a subsidiary theme in his thought, namely, that those who die are also those *for whom* Christ has died (Rom 14:7–9; 1 Th 5:10; 4:14) and that therefore they are "dead in Christ" (1 Th 4:16; cf. 1 Cor 15:18), and "neither death, nor life, . . . will be able to separate us from the love of God in Christ Jesus" (Rom 8:38–39). Whether they "wake or sleep" they "live with him" (1 Th 5:10).[22]

The perspective becomes more simplified in John, continuing the line we have found in Paul. Everything essential is concentrated in two pronouncements of Jesus: "He who eats my flesh and drinks my blood has eternal life, and I will raise him up at

---

[21] Cf. J. Schniewind, "Die Leugner der Auferstehung in Korinth" in *Nachgelassene Reden und Aufsätze* (Berlin: Töpelmann, 1952), 110–39. "Paul cannot imagine a state of perfection without the body"; "in his thought he is entirely committed to positive statements concerning the new body" (Hoffmann, on 1 Cor 15, *Die Toten in Christus*, 245, 252). Paul's emphasis on our being "clothed" (with the new body) in 2 Cor 5:4 points in the same direction.

"Ita Christus judex secundum unicum simplicissimum atque indistinctum judicium in uno momento (omnes judicat)": Nicolaus Cusanus, *Docta Ignorantia* III, 9 (Petzelt 108).

[22] Thus it is possible to find, in this passage from Thessalonians, "an adumbration" (Hoffmann, *Die Toten in Christus*, 237) of the formulation in Philippians, which must in any case have been written not much later (particularly in part B). Cf. *ibid.*, 327. It cannot be proved that this idea—that the souls of the righteous exist in God after their death—was unknown to Paul before Philippians (after all it was present in the Jewish tradition) or that he is reflecting upon it in 2 Corinthians 5. Instead of interpreting the whole passage with a view to the parousia, as is usual today (following Lietzmann), we might follow Paul's thought as it traverses the preliminary, postmortal state and embraces the longed-for final state. What is quite clear is that Paul does not delay on the preliminary stage. Furthermore, Philippians 1:23 most definitely points forward to Philippians 3:10–11.

the last day" (6:54), and "I am the resurrection and the life; he who believes in me, though he die, yet shall he live, and whoever lives and believes in me shall never die" (11:25–26). Both passages assume that there are those who will die in the intervening world-time, but they are assured that nonetheless they possess eternal life, which means that at the end of world-time they will be raised together with Jesus where he, the exalted Lord, already is. If we follow John's thought, we see Jesus' death and Resurrection, that is, his exaltation, as the inseparable deed and proof of God's eternal love; accordingly, the man who has died in faith already lives in the risen Lord, and whether there will be an "intermediate state" between his death and his resurrection "on the last day" is an open question, and not one of great moment.[23]

For John, physical death is almost an obsolete phenomenon, since the believer already lives in the Lord, who is the resurrection. For Paul it is an event that interposes itself between the believer in his "exalted" state (1 Th 4:17) and the hoped-for union with the Lord. Of course, as death is multiplied among the believers (1 Cor 15:42–50), it turns out to be the "normal" lot of the "psychic" descendants of Adam; but in 1 Corinthians the stress is less on "resurrection" than on the *transformation* of the psychic body into a pneumatic one: "flesh and blood cannot inherit the kingdom of God, nor does the perishable inherit the imperishable . . . this mortal nature must put on immortality" (15:50, 53). This "immortality", however, is conceived in bodily terms (15:35!).

c. Holding Fast to the One Judgment

Theology, by pursuing an ever more systematic elaboration of the doctrine of an "intermediate state", has thought itself into a corner where it finds itself obliged to posit two judgments: man faces a particular judgment immediately after death and a general judgment at the end of the world. Biblically and speculatively,

---

[23] "The question of an intermediate state between death and resurrection . . . does not arise. Jesus *is* the resurrection: consequently faith, which signifies the contact between Jesus and me, means that I have passed over the line of death here and now": J. Ratzinger, *Eschatologie* (Regensburg, 1977), 103.

however, such a twofold judgment—if indeed "judgment" is seriously being proposed here—is unacceptable.

We have already established that in biblical terms the only judgment, in Paul and in the Synoptics, is exclusively an individual judgment. (It should be noted that the New Testament retains a wealth of Old Testament imagery in this regard.) This is in no way affected by the social perspective of judgment (that is, the active love of one's neighbor is the criterion of our love for Christ). The "works" according to which, in Paul's view, "every individual" will be judged are nothing other than the practical consequences of his faith operating as love. This personal judgment, however, can only take place after the individual's death: "Dying, a man steps forth into unveiled reality and truth."[1] Compromise solutions offered by Judaic and early Christian thought ("preliminary" rewards and punishments in the next world) are no longer possible since the Definition[2] given by Benedict XII in 1336, which states that, since Christ's Resurrection, the souls of the departed after their death and the relevant purgation attain to the direct vision of God in heaven "before resuming their bodies and before the general judgment". We shall have to return to the purgation mentioned here, purgatory, and interpret it as one aspect of the personal character of judgment. For the moment it is instructive to note that Paul sees this fire that judges the individual in the context of the one final Judgment: once a man has been judged here, he cannot be judged a second time (1 Cor 3:12–15). So the final Judgment occurs after the death of the individual, which means that, as Karl Rahner puts it so well, it takes place " 'along' the temporal history of the world" and so coincides "with the sum of particular judgments undergone by individuals".[3] Insofar as the individual has to step forth into his particular judgment, which is part of the judgment of the world, acts of faith are required of him, namely, hope and fear. These would not arise in the case of a final judgment that was separate from the particular judgment. If one wanted nonetheless to

---

[1] J. Ratzinger, *Eschatologie* (Regensburg, 1977), 169.

[2] In line with a decision of the University of Paris in 1241. DS 1000 (Neuner-Roos 819).

[3] On the "intermediate state", cf. K. Rahner, *Theological Investigations*, vol. 17 (London: Darton, Longman and Todd).

retain the notion of a final judgment upon world history that
was separate from the sum of personal judgments, it could only
be to show the justice of all God's hidden ways in world history and to locate all the individuals in the ultimate organism of
the perfected kingdom of God. (It would also contradict all Old
Testament and New Testament portrayals of history, which are
always parenetic—hortatory—in tone.) No doubt this "gathering of the whole is also an act performed upon it, and to that
extent it is the final, general disposition [Ge-richt]", but it only
"serves to situate the individual in the whole and give him his
proper place in it".[4] Disposition [Ge-richt] in this sense is not,
however, judgment [Gericht]. Disposition begins essentially with
the Son's exaltation and has the perfection of the Mystical Body
as its goal (Eph 4:8–16).

The foregoing is completely independent of the controversy
about whether and how (in a putative intermediate state) one
can envisage a soul without a body and, if such a state must be
assumed, at what "point in time" the soul is reunited with its
body. We shall not deal with these questions here. In any case
they are ultimately insoluble in a *theologia viatorum*, since the latter cannot imagine the state of those who have died in Christ to
be above time, while the earthly history of the world continues
to perdure. The most we can say is that it is difficult to imagine a
communio sanctorum made up of both embodied and disembodied
souls. We have Christ and those who rose with him at his death,
then Mary and—as many believe—John, the beloved disciple;[5]
but then why not the other apostles? And what of those saints
who have experienced the "first resurrection" and reign with

---

[4] Ratzinger, *Eschatologie*, 157. Of course all things hang together, and there is no
absolute individual in the human race. Thus R. Panikkar can say that the cosmos
has a karma-character ("La Loi du karman et la dimension historique de l'homme"
in Castelli, *Herméneutique et Eschatologie* [Paris: Aubier, 1972], 205–30). The Last
"Judgment" can finally unveil and integrate these interrelationships. Yet such an
act cannot bring the individual before God's tribunal a second time and cause him
to answer for himself again.

[5] Thus Kosmas Vestitor, *Hom. 2 in Assumptionem* (in A. Wenger, "L'Assomption
de la Très Ste. Vierge dans la tradition byzantine du VIe au Xe siècle" in *Archives
de l'Orient Chrétien* 5 [Paris, 1955], 319); Fulbert of Chartres, *Sermo* 5 (PL 141,
325B); Giotto in a famous portrayal in Sancta Croce in Florence, cf. Mechthild
von Magdeburg, *Das fließende Licht der Gottheit* IV, 23, and V, 9.

Christ (Rev 20:4–5)? On the one hand, there would be a great company of those who have risen "in advance", while, on the other hand, there would be all those who have to wait until the "end of the world" to be reunited with their bodies. It is hard to make sense of this. In fact another theme cuts across this idea, namely, that the bodily risen Lord, precisely through his exaltation and as an expression of his glorification, has granted freedom and space for his members who remain on earth to continue their journey toward perfection. (Why should this not apply, by analogy, to other risen saints?) In this way he would be enriching himself in his bodily perfection by the successive perfection of his members. However, our ignorance of heavenly super-time (which does not even need to be internally affected by the end of chronological world-time) prevents us from co-ordinating the two levels satisfactorily.

It must be enough for us to accept Jesus' sovereign answer to the Sadducees, when he bids those who doubt the resurrection to consider the power of the living God, who is "the God of Abraham, Isaac and Jacob, not a God of the dead, but of the living", and who has these living persons with him, both as embodied and "risen from the dead" and as enspirited (for "they are like the angels of God": Mt 22:29–32). Paul will speak of a "spiritual body" (1 Cor 15:44) that will be given by God (v. 38), unfolding out of the death of the corruptible body like a plant that develops from its seed. Some have seen this as a misleading image, as if the "sensual" (*choikos*) first Adam from below were so opposed to the Second, life-giving Adam "from heaven" that the mortal, earthly body could bear no possible relation to the "spiritual body"; but this is refuted by the central Pauline dogma that it was this same heavenly Adam who adopted our mortal flesh, transfiguring it in his Resurrection.

If we are to attempt to answer the question "When does the resurrection take place?" we can again point to Jesus' reply to the Sadducees' question: No temporal hiatus is posited between being with the living God and resurrection. In the perspective of the Old Covenant, the moment of "resurrection" (first a resurrection of the nation as a whole: Ezekiel 38, which later yields the conclusion that the individual will experience resurrection too) coincides with the Messiah's advent to his earthly kingdom.

Where necessary, this Jewish frame is applied by Christians to the time of Christ's return. Are they right to do so? For the Messiah, who calls himself the Resurrection and the Life, has already appeared in history, and in his dying has reached the end of the world. Not only that: the resurrection of the dead, or their glorification in God, has already begun with his Resurrection and the resurrection of those who rose together with him. And if, as we have shown, the one Judgment can and must take place "along" earthly history, it is hard to see why the same cannot be said of the resurrection, particularly if we keep Matthew 27:51–53 in mind.

The Last Judgment can be regarded as the *summa summarum* of all particular judgments, but not in the sense that every individual will stand ashamed in the presence of all the others; for the sinner's profound shame before God is something between him and God alone, as we shall show. The total sum of judgments, therefore, can only be presented to those who have passed through the particular judgment and have jettisoned everything connected with envy, or *schadenfreude*, and now view the world and their own history through the eyes of God.

d. The One Judgment and the Purification

What Catholic theology speaks of as purification beyond the grave must be seen as one aspect of Judgment.[1] This can be granted all the more easily if what we have just said is true, namely, that there can only be one single Judgment including and embracing all individual judgments (which for the individual, however, are always eschatological in character). This said, we can thoroughly agree with J. Gnilka when he interprets the famous passage in Paul concerning God's fire, which tests ev-

---

[1] We have always formulated this in some such manner: "Reducing 'purgatory' from a 'place' to a 'state' would achieve very little unless one were to decide to locate the 'purgative' aspect of this state in the encounter between the as yet unpurified sinner and the Kyrios who appears as his Judge": H. U. von Balthasar, in: Feiner, Trütsch and Böckle, eds., *Fragen der Theologie*, 3d ed. (Benziger, 1960), 411. "It is pointless . . . to distinguish between the 'fire of purification' and the 'eschatological fire' ": H. U. von Balthasar, "Eschatology in Outline", in *Spirit and Institution* (San Francisco: Ignatius Press, 1995) 455.

ery "building"—sparing the well-built edifice, consuming the poorly built, and allowing man to "escape but as by fire" (1 Cor 3:10–15)—in terms of the Lord who is coming to judge, and wants to see in this fire (following Is 66:15–16) a metaphor for the majesty of God as he reveals himself, "the unapproachable nature of the All-holy".[2] Similarly we can agree with J. Ratzinger when he says that "Christ the Judge is the *eschatos*, which means that it is impossible to distinguish between the Judge of the Last Day and him who judges us after our death. Stepping into the realm of his manifest reality, a man steps into his ultimate destiny and so is drawn into the eschatological fire. The transforming 'moment' of this encounter is beyond the earthly calculation of time."[3]

According to Origen, it is God who makes himself a purifying fire;[4] in Jesus Christ he stands in the stream of fire with his flaming sword, "to baptize in this stream all those who are destined for paradise after death yet still need purification".[5] Ambrose follows Origen: "The resurrected who wish to return to paradise must face an ordeal by fire"; they must undergo the baptism of fire announced by John; they must pass the angel's fiery sword at the entrance of paradise. Only sinners, however, will be touched by it.[6] Augustine, in a commentary on this passage in St. Paul, says that the sinner will be "saved as by fire", but "what he has possessed through the seductions of love will now be lost through burning pain."[7]

The doctrine of purgatory has a very complicated history, from its Jewish beginnings (and in the era after Christ "Gehenna" is

---

[2] *Ist 1 Kor 3, 10–15 ein Schriftzeugnis für das Fegfeuer?* (Düsseldorf: Triltsch, 1955), 126.

[3] J. Ratzinger, *Eschatologie* (Regensburg 1977), 187–88.

[4] A. Michel, "Origène et le dogme du Purgatoire" in *Questions ecclésiastiques* (Lille, 1913).

[5] *In Luc. hom.* 24. Cyprian is considered to be one of the founders of the doctrine of purgatory on the basis of his belief (allegedly) that earthly penance is prolonged in the realm beyond. In fact, in the relevant passage (*Ep.* 55, 20) he is only speaking of a continuation of earthly penance: P. Jay, "Saint Cyprien et la doctrine du Purgatoire" in *Rech. théol. anc. et méd.* 27 (1960), 133–36.

[6] *In Ps.* 118, 5, 20 (PL 15, 1487–88).

[7] *De Civ. Dei.* 21, 26 (PL 41, 744). Joseph Ndelika, *Evolution de la doctrine du Purgatoire chez S. Augustin* (1966).

sometimes given a purifying function), via the early Christian intercession for the dead, the numerous late patristic (Gregory the Great) and medieval visions (Bede, St. Patrick) that associate purgatory much too closely with the terrors of hell, up to its definitive form in the late twelfth century. It is not necessary to go into it in detail,[8] but we will indicate a few characteristic features. First there is the temporal prolongation of the Last Judgment, allowing the Pauline fire of testing (as purgatory) to do its work.[9] Then there is the assumption of two fires: one that purifies individuals prior to Judgment, and a fire of judgment that will devour the world and the dross that still remains in the righteous.[10] Then we have an increasing emphasis on the communion of saints, not only between heaven and earth, but also with those who are currently in purgatory.[11] Finally there is the speculation about how far those still being purified, who are of course no longer capable of a free decision, can nonetheless surrender themselves to the painful purification with a "certain limited freedom of the will",[12] since they understand that there is no other means of leading them to God.

Fire is "an essential trait of the triune God, who cannot endure anything impure, but must devour it" (cf. Heb 11:29).[13] Right from the beginning, however, the Son has exposed himself, in love, to this fire: "In his cry of forsakenness on the Cross, he allows himself to be consumed by his Father's fire because he has gathered together in himself everything that hinders him from actively sharing in the burning of this fire. So, in passivity, he becomes fuel for the fire. In purgatory he makes us to be fuel for the fire that consumes him. . . . Unleashing this fire upon us, he is the first to plunge into it", so that "I am drawn into

---

[8] For a theological survey, see *Dict. Apol.* (Bernard) and *DThC* (A. Michel, M. Jugie). Jacques le Goff, *La Naissance du Purgatoire* (Gallimard, 1981) gives a very full compilation, with a particular literary and sociological interest.

[9] E.g., (Pseudo)-Eligius (PL 87, 619), in Hugh of Saint-Victor (O. Lottin, "Questions inédites de Hugo de St. Victor" in *Rech. théol. anc. et méd.*, 1960, 59–60).

[10] *Glossa in libros Sent. IV* (Quar. 1957), 370.

[11] Cf. Le Goff, *Naissance*, 334ff.

[12] Quotations from Alexander, Albert, Bonaventure and Thomas in A. Michel, "Purgatoire" in *DThC* 1240.

[13] OM 383.

his fire, which is a fire of love."[14] Properly speaking, therefore, purgatory comes into existence on Holy Saturday, when the Son walks through "hell", introducing the element of mercy into the condition of those who are justly lost.[15] Purgatory "has its origin in the Cross. The Father makes use of the fruit of the Cross in order to temper divine justice, which held the sinners captive, with new mercifulness. From the Cross, hope is brought down to the netherworld; from the Cross, a fire is unleashed in which justice and mercifulness are intermixed. Through the Lord's arrival there, the powers of the netherworld, of death and of evil are driven, as it were, into the backmost recesses of hell, and the devil's chain is made shorter. Purgatory arises as if under the Lord's striding feet; he brings comfort to this place of hopelessness, fire to this place of iciness."[16] It is this fire, according to Paul, that tests a man's life's work to see if it is built on the foundation of Christ; thus the fire of testing is one with the foundation.[17] The severe righteousness of this testing is a work of love;[18] it is so objective that the process of transformation may begin with fear[19] and resistance.[20]

"The Day of the Lord will disclose it" (1 Cor 3:13); "not the day when, in death, *we* go to the Lord, but the day on which the Lord will come. It is his day because he has died for us, because his fire is the fruit of his Holy Saturday, because he planned to begin with us once we had come to the end of ourselves."[21] Hence the testing is something that takes place between himself alone and the individual; all human works are now concentrated on the Lord: "Whatever you did—or did not do—to

[14] OM 383–84.

[15] Cf. also OM 333.

[16] 4 Jo 143.

[17] C 101.

[18] "Purgatory, for example, which we see as an act of justice, is seen in this light as nothing but an act of love of the Son, who wants to purify us so that this substitution that makes us sons of the Father can come about": 1 Jo 273. "We would fear Purgatory if we did not see that it is a mystery of love. And so we submit willingly . . . we understand that justice must be satisfied within love": 3 Jo 321–22.

[19] OM 338.

[20] OM 339.

[21] OM 321.

one of these, you did it—or did not do it—to me" (Mt 25:40, 45). Purgatory is "experienced in total isolation";[22] the soul is "essentially isolated in a kind of 'solitary confinement', entirely taken up with God's relationship with it";[23] "one's fellow men play no part whatsoever in this whole process; they do not exist, and so there is no need of communication, no desire to know how they are faring in this condition."[24] The soul is "totally preoccupied, not susceptible to any distraction".[25] "For a moment the communion of saints is suspended. When the time of testing has come, it is impossible to have recourse to what others have done, to be carried by them. Everyone stands there in isolation. . . . Though this does not mean that prayers for the dead in purgatory are ineffectual."[26] "The soul sees itself only in [the Lord's] mirror. . . . The one being purified does not see his neighbor and his faults at all. He is wholly occupied with God and with himself. He sees his brother only after he is so cleansed by the Lord's love that he can regard him with the Lord's eyes."[27] "For the moment my neighbor is exclusively the Lord, I have no other. Only at the very end, before entering heaven, is one given back one's fellow man by the Lord himself, for now I can encounter him as the Lord does and as God loves him."[28] For the present "the only necessity is to be face to face with the Lord and respond to him."[29] It is clear that this descent from the impersonal "one" into personal being is the genuine point of departure for a new, authentic and definitive community.

Man stands before God objectified in his life's work. This is the "test material"; "in the work that is exposed to view, naked, one's confession is already made; it speaks for itself. Any light the person himself might want to shed on it, any commentary he might want to give, is too late. His confession is already objectified in his deeds."[30] "Man's love for the Lord has now taken the form of his work, and the Lord's love for man has taken the form of fire."[31] A man's work embodies "the thoughts and intentions of the heart" (Heb 4:12), "not only those at the hour of his

---

[22] OM 363.   [23] OM 340.
[24] OM 347.   [25] OM 348.
[26] C 102–3.   [27] 3 Jo 81.
[28] OM 386.   [29] Ka I, 373.
[30] OM 327.   [31] OM 322.

death, but those of his whole life".[32] "All sins" of this life "are intimately connected with one another."[33] Thus it is possible "to evaluate the difference between what was and what might have been".[34] In this experience man is helpless and stripped: he stands "for the first time naked before the Lord" and realizes that the Lord "has always seen him naked".[35] This gaze is now the only thing that matters. What is important is not how I love the Lord but "how he wishes to be loved".[36]

This great change or conversion governs the whole process. "Our average view of sin on earth is anthropocentric." "I am accustomed to fashioning and arranging my actions according to my own views. Now this has to stop."[37] My sin is no longer simply "contrary" to God, it is now "absolutely contradictory; sin is what is radically and utterly excluded from God's presence."[38] "All at once I am in the presence of an absolute authority, at the mercy of the sole ruling power. It is not obedience (which would be something within my own capability): I simply fall prostrate under the influence of this power."[39] "Self-knowledge becomes unreliable, since all assessment has passed to God."[40] In the face of God's radiant evidence, man says Yes, but "this is not the Yes of insight; it is the surrender of my sight to the way God sees things."[41] God's view of things is immutable, and so is the process that is to be carried out in me. While I know that he is "immutable", my "knowledge itself is not in me but in the Lord."[42] This insight "creates an—as it were—artificial preparedness, which must eventually become spontaneous".[43]

A change of polarity has to take place: "I am not to be put to shame within my own sinful state: rather, I am to experience

---

[32] OM 326.

[33] OM 373. "It is less a question of the chronologically last moment than of the entire period of one's life": OM 390.

[34] OM 380. Man "understands what God would have wished and expected from him. God puts him in a state in which, given this realization, he could start afresh": C 104.

[35] OM 349.   [36] OM 362.
[37] OM 335.   [38] OM 336.
[39] OM 339.   [40] OM 343.
[41] OM 345.   [42] OM 360.
[43] OM 361.

my impurity within the purity of God."[44] "Purgatory has, as it were, a great stratagem . . . : the 'I' is so disintegrated that the 'Thou' gradually acquires contours"; what comes into being is "a hope" (which "resides totally in the Lord") "which is the end of my knowing better and the beginning of my surrender".[45] "I have to be extracted from 'being with myself' so that my 'I' can be 'situated' in God."[46] "Insofar as the 'I' is the possessor of this material", it is what "has to be burned. My 'I', destroyed in purgatory, will be returned to me by God: it will be a new 'I', an 'I' in God."[47] This is the "holocaust" that, in the Old Covenant, was an intimation of "God's fire" and now, as the 'I', is consumed on the altar.[48] The Word of God, having accommodated himself to us in our life, now accommodates us to himself in death;[49] the Word of God "cuts, divides, distinguishes, inerrantly, implacably, to the division of soul and spirit, joints and marrow (Heb 4:12). Until now man thought that, in his innermost spiritual life, he was a self-possessed unity, constantly choosing and distinguishing, accepting and rejecting, according to a system of discrimination involving responsible statements on his part. Now, however, he sees that God's Word penetrates at this very point, dividing and revealing deep fissures, just where he thought his innermost structure was sound and solid. . . . The real boundaries run in quite a different direction. Part of what he was maintaining as truth turns out to be a lie, and part of what he had rejected contains the central issue."[50] Finally he arrives at "a kind of collapse in which, once and for all, he bids farewell to himself".[51] "Not only can I no longer carry my own sin: I cannot carry my own self. I have only one wish left: to be liberated from myself. I am ready to pay *any* price."[52]

This process, however, is not something I can control. I cannot register any "progress",[53] cannot assess how much longer it will take;[54] I seem to be endlessly "working away" at the same point without getting any farther.[55] Objectively speaking, it is a "tem-

---

[44] OM 354.
[45] OM 350.
[46] OM 369.
[47] OM 371.
[48] OM 319.
[49] OM 318.
[50] OM 325.
[51] OM 384.
[52] OM 378.
[53] OM 359.
[54] OM 338.
[55] OM 342.

poral suffering" (like that of the debtor servant who is handed over to the torturers until he has paid the last penny: Mt 18:34),[56] but the duration of purgatory—which can vary greatly[57]—is a hidden matter reserved to the Lord. It does contain an element of punishment, manifested in shame and stripping:[58] "The fire is actually the ever greater awareness of shame."[59] It means that one "has to do without all apparatus";[60] there is no place for concessions of any kind. "Now I see that my entire system is going to be exploded. No one is interested in examining it, and I am given no time to get acclimatized. I am treated peremptorily, and the first task thrust into my hands is the most distressing one of all."[61] What is going on here is not a process of education, for that would require some cooperation on my part.[62] All the same there is a certain "initial freedom"—as the great Scholastics were right to insist—and it is possible "to acquiesce in being put through God's recuperative procedure". It is like someone who gives his consent to undergo an operation: "Once the operation has begun and the surgeon is at his work, no one takes any account of any protest I may make."[63]

Since all assessment belongs to the Lord, the aim of the whole procedure is that I grasp and acknowledge his absolute prerogative, which is the prerogative of his love. The pains involved point directly to his Cross, and from them I read off his sufferings. "Videbunt in quem transfixerunt" (Jn 19:37; Rev 1:7): "What he must have suffered, if he can apportion such punishment!" My punishment teaches me to recognize the sin "for which he accepted the ultimate suffering".[64] In this whole process, "paradoxically, I walk with the Lord toward the Cross and join him in bearing sin: but this sin is my own, utterly personal and personally experienced sin. Characteristic of purgatory is this view of the Cross: from the experience of one's own sin one acquires eyes to see what the Lord has done on the Cross: *he* has borne *my* sin."[65] "So I feel my way toward the point where love

---

[56] Gl 79.
[58] OM 356.
[60] OM 355.
[62] OM 345.
[64] OM 364.

[57] OM 374.
[59] OM 382.
[61] OM 353.
[63] OM 340.
[65] OM 368.

and punishment form a single unity";[66] but this unity resides not in me: its origin lies in the trinitarian relationship between Father and Son. Moses had to stand still before the Burning Bush: "Not until after the Son's Holy Saturday did it become possible for someone to entrust himself to God's fire and plunge into God. This is a trinitarian mystery",[67] whereby the Father gives permission to the Son so that he may allow himself to be consumed in the divine fire for mankind's sin. The Son "is the very fire he has come to cast upon the earth, but between heaven and earth this fire has undergone the transformation into suffering." "Because he himself is entirely pure and there is nothing in him to be consumed, he takes the world into himself as his fuel and consumes it in himself . . . suffering on account of each one of us."[68]

Purgatory ends at the precise point where man, looking at the Cross, begins to realize the extent of the world's sin, which somewhere or other contains his own sin. He would have deserved far more punishment. "At the moment when I cry out for this 'more', the end of purgatory is near."[69] "When prayer acquires depth, our understanding of punishment grows too; this in turn gives rise to the desire that punishment may proceed to its full extent."[70] Furthermore, since it is the Lord who is suffering, my desire is for punishment not only for my particular sin but also for all sin. The end is reached when "the patient, overflowing with gratitude, requests to stay under the knife for as long as the surgeon wishes", because the operation "has given him that unconditional love that is ready to suffer on behalf of others".[71] "Finally all merit is dissolved in the Lord's grace, and at this point the reflection upon himself that is characteristic of man subject to original sin is itself dissolved in the original, paradisal relationship between God and the human spirit."[72]

Here too the *eschaton* is not man but the triune God, who, in Christ's Cross, descent into hell, and Resurrection, undergirds all human activity—whether it be sin or love. "I can escape from my condition only if the Lord has mercy on me and

---

[66] OM 371.
[67] OM 317.
[68] OM 330.
[69] OM 351.
[70] OM 367.
[71] OM 341.
[72] OM 364.

leads me whither I do not wish to go, making his leadership stronger than my will. The transition point here is the Lord's suffering. The sinner's fear of surrendering himself is *undergirded* by the Lord's anguish in the face of sin and for sin."[73] I too am near hell, which is "visible and tangible"; "my purgatory is my knowledge of hell; it is even my decision to embrace hell insofar as I am bound to recognize that, in all justice, I belong in its fire. The life I have lived utterly convinces me of this."[74] Purgatory, however, "contains God's fire, burning off everything in me that belongs to hell and is destined to be thrown into the fire of the serpent".[75] Thus man is drawn into the final discipleship of Christ. "In the process of purification, through a slow and hidden time of contemplation, he will be brought to a complete insight into the Cross and an ever closer discipleship. Then he will walk together with the Lord, from the Cross, along the path that leads to the Father. This, for the individual, is the Lord's final and definitive appearance in him."[76]

[73] OM 361.
[74] OM 332.
[75] OM 384.
[76] Ka I, 279.

III. THE WORLD IN GOD

A. EMBEDDED IN GOD

A *theologia viatorum* may not attempt to give a complete account of the *theologia comprehensorum*. For the most part, if it attempts to do so, it gets stuck in unproductive abstractions or in empty, embarrassing enthusiasms. Modern theological thought[1] has largely abandoned the attempt to document this final phase of all theology. There is one sole vantage point, however, from which we can enjoy a glimpse of the otherwise invisible "absolute future" of man and mankind. We find this vantage point in the Resurrection of the Crucified One. For through his trinitarian existence he has made it possible for us to believe that this finite, historical world can be enfolded in the life of the infinite, eternal God; in his "forty days" and his sending of the Spirit, he has given us a kind of foretaste of what man's ultimate salvation will be. The Risen One communicates a feeling of a unique freedom, encouraging his disciples to touch him while at the same time, since he cannot be "grasped", continually withdrawing and disappearing. His vista is staggering in its breadth: "In my Father's house are many mansions" (Jn 14:2). His command of his bodily presence is baffling: while it is his in a much deeper way than his once-tortured body was, it extends far beyond his separate, individual corporeality; alive in God in a new way, he shares himself out eucharistically (Lk 24:30; Jn 21:9–10, 13) and hence feels himself touched, bodily, in the "least of these my brethren" (Mt 25:40, 45; Acts 9:4). "If the Resurrection of Jesus does not mean the reconstitution of the separate reality of an individual corporeality, separated off from others, this will apply to the resurrection of believers as well. . . . This does not need to obliterate all individual difference, since the risen Christ is not only one with the Church that is his body but, while enjoying union with her, is distinct from her. This interpenetration of unity and distinctness is bound to remind us of the distinction of Persons in the

---

[1] The most comprehensive treatment is in M. Schmaus: *Von den Letzten Dingen* (Regensburg, Münster, 1948); cf. also his *Dogma*, vol. 6: *Justification and the Last Things* (Westminster, Md.: Christian Classics, 1984).

Trinity who yet enjoy the unity of the divine life."[2] Origen had
already spoken of an analogy of the Eucharist in Christ and those
who believe in him.[3] Over and above all individual aspects, the
Risen One's behavior seems to spread a heavenly fragrance upon
the earth, making it clear, with the greatest possible insistence,
that, of all that is so familiar to us on earth, nothing will be lost
in God or excluded from him. (*He* is as close to them as ever,
indeed more than ever: it is *they* who are far from him.) Once
it has been transfigured, all that has been will remain present;
now, for the first time, its full meaning will become clear. In
the forty days we glimpse more fully than ever before that, in
Jesus, the kingdom of God has come near and heaven has started
to arrive on earth.[4] But just as heaven becomes visible through
these forty days, they are also the fruit of the Son's earthly life
and death—his wounds are taken up to heaven, too, as signs of
all that he has undergone—so that, when his life reaches its end
in death, it is as if a husk bursts and the ripe fruit comes out.
"The beginning lies in the end. Behind us lies that succession
of stages that had the power in itself to lead to resurrection, to
ripen the seed for something that is no longer bound to the law
of succession. . . . Incorruptibility follows from corruptibility,
resurrection follows from being sowed in death."[5] But the way
the end becomes the beginning is something purely christological; it is a mystery that "can be explained neither on the basis
of nature, to which the dead body of Christ no longer belongs,
nor on the basis of the supernatural, spiritual, heavenly world, to
which (since he is dead) he does not yet belong. Between these
two there is no neutral third realm that would embrace them:
there is only the change from one to the other."[6] Jesus alone
is the way, the resurrection and the life. He affirms the whole
finitude of creation right up to death; he also affirms creation's

---

[2] W. Pannenberg, "Die Auferstehung Jesu und die Zukunft des Menschen" in
Kerygma und Dogma 24 (1978), 115-16.

[3] *Hom. in Lev.* 7, 5 (Baehrens 7, 96).

[4] On the theology of the forty days, cf. my *A Theology of History* (San Francisco:
Ignatius Press, 1994), 83-93. "Through his forty days on earth . . . our belief in
eternal life is to become a genuine, irrefutable human experience": A 88.

[5] C 524.

[6] C 528.

longing gaze beyond itself, a longing to embrace a continuance of life that it cannot grasp; but it is he who is prior to and the ultimate ground of all this longing, he is the transition from the end to the beginning: "The resurrection is in no way a natural process; the fact that it is a final goal does not make it natural. Of course, if by 'nature' one means that natural being that man is, it can be said that man exists for the sake of resurrection; but this 'for the sake of' refers to the final purpose of the creation of man, not of nature. The ground of creation is not, in fact, nature; hence the final goal of creation is not actually the final goal of nature."[7] The firstfruits of resurrection, however, making resurrection possible for all, is Christ. His Resurrection "is not an individual act but the center on which the entirety of Christian doctrine rests."[8]

1. He Ascends to Prepare a Place for Us

At the commencement of this study we described at some length the way our earthly life transcends itself in the direction of eternal life; we also spoke of the way in which heaven is "open" to the earth and of how eternal life begins right here in the midst of earthly time. All this must be borne in mind if we are to understand what follows. Heaven and earth are there for one another; their original distance and abiding distinctness from one another has been established *in order that* they can approach one another (*Theo-Drama* II, 173–88; III, 43–56).[9] The fact that God has given the earthly realm its own autonomy, so that it can freely turn and move toward him,[10] shows that there is room for it in God.[11]

However, the perfect expression of this "leaving" of God and "returning" to God is found uniquely in Christ. He is eternal,

[7] Albert, *De Resurrectione*, tr 1, q 3 sol (vol. XXVI [1958], 244b).

[8] C 490.

[9] Ap 409.

[10] 3 Jo 17; C 181, 410; Ka I 422.

[11] "Earth belongs to heaven. And mankind is created for heaven. The heaven of the triune God, with every infinity at its disposal, has enough space to accommodate earth and its inhabitants": Pf 127; Bi 17.

yet he lives an earthly life, filling it with eternal content[12] so
that, returning to the Father in heaven, he may find a place in
eternity for the life he has lived on earth.[13] He is the concrete
"exchange";[14] and he alone:[15] in the movement from earth to
heaven it is his death (in which his Resurrection is hiddenly
present) that holds earth and heaven together *and* holds them
apart.[16] That is why eternal life can never be understood as a
continuation of earthly life.[17] Only if eternal life is lived in utterly temporal terms (which includes death) can temporal life
(including death) attain maturity and so be ready for eternal life.
So Jesus promises that, once he has returned to his Father, he
will prepare a place for those who are his among his Father's
many mansions (Jn 14:2): this place becomes "available" only
when, in the Person of him who is the firstfruits of the Resurrection, what is earthly attains heaven. "Jesus' 'going to his Father'
can be understood as the creation of heaven, that is, of a new
dimension of God's creation, made to receive man and the old
creation as they begin to come to God. Essentially, this 'being
with God' means being with Jesus Christ, being in communication with the God who has become incarnate; it means that
men are gathered together as the definitive Body of Christ. . . .
Heaven is a reality that is growing."[18]

Before the coming of Christ, people can have had only shad-

[12] Ka II, 213.

[13] A 126–27.

[14] Is 30; 4 Jo 54, 82, 289; K 34, 97. "The Son of God" has "perfected the unity
of heaven and earth in his own Person": Ph 45; Ep 47, 50; KW 45; Gl 71; B
110, 118, 172f., 280, 284, 309. "Where the two meet, where the Lord appears as
eternal life and we as what we would be if he had not come, namely, utterly transitory, the Old and New Covenants meet. . . . Thus the transition (from Old to
New) is the meeting point of heaven and earth; the Incarnation intersects them
both. But it is also a moving point coming from heaven to earth, causing the
boundaries between heaven and earth to fade away as transitoriness is taken up
. . . into heaven": Ka I, 53.

[15] C 528.

[16] C 523.

[17] 4 Jo 345.

[18] H. Vorgrimler, *Hoffnung auf Vollendung. Aufriß der Eschatologie*, QD 90 (1980),
166–67. In his *Theological Investigations*, vol. 2, K. Rahner speaks of heaven's "becoming"; for him, Christ's "return" takes place "as the world is perfected, acquiring the perfected reality he already possesses".

owy intimations—nothing more than metaphors—of a heaven accessible to earthly beings. Jacob sees a ladder reaching from earth to heaven, with angels going up and down it; Christ will take over this image and fulfill its truth (Jn 1:51). We read of Isaiah's and Ezekiel's visions of the glory of God, of Elijah being carried away in a fiery chariot, and of the yearnings of the psalmists and the wisdom writers for a permanent dwelling with God. They all "did not receive what was promised", for they were not to "be made perfect" (Heb 11:39–40) before the Firstborn of the dead. He, however, opens the new life to us: those who arose from their graves "after his Resurrection" and showed themselves in the "Holy City" will also have ascended into heaven with him.[19] His Mother followed him in her entire humanity. The same was assumed of John the Evangelist, as we have already mentioned.[20] And what of the "first resurrection" in Revelation 20:5? Could this not refer to the resurrection of the "saints and blessed ones" who, together with Christ, "rule"[21] world history during the time of the Church on the basis of their special missions? We simply do not know how resurrection is implemented along (and across) chronological world-time.

Where does resurrection lead us? To the dwelling places that Christ has opened to us. They certainly cannot be localized in the old cosmos. Poets like Dante spoke of paradise in physical terms: it was superfluous for theologians like Thomas to do the same.[22] He would have done better to follow his teacher Albert, who spoke of the Son returning to the "heaven of the Trinity": "The Apostle says that Christ ascended far above all the heavens (Eph 4:10); but there is no place beyond all the heavens, unless we speak metaphorically of the heaven of the Trinity as a 'place'. For the Trinity is not contained in any created or physi-

---

[19] Zeller, "Corpora Sanctorum: Eine Studie zu Mt 27, 52–53" in *ZkTh* 71 (1959), 384–465. "We are not told (Mt 27:52f.) which of the saints rose again, nor whether all who rose were seen in the Holy City, nor how many. The word 'many' is not a limitation, although it does not mean 'all': it leaves it open. The primary message is that now the final resurrection of the dead can begin": Mt 194.

[20] For references cf. p. 358, n. 5.

[21] Cf. Ap 655–62.

[22] *S. Th.* III, 57, 1.

cal place. So the heaven of the Trinity will not be anything created or physical, but the Trinity itself."[23] Dietrich von Freiberg
has the same view of those who experience resurrection,[24] and
Nicholaus Cusanus says that Christ ascends to a place above "all
influences of the heavens": "It is true that we speak of a place
of eternal bliss and eternal peace above all the heavens; but this
'place' can be neither conceived, nor described, nor defined. It
is both the center and the circumference of spiritual nature, and,
since the Spirit embraces everything, it is above everything. . . .
So when we read that Christ has ascended 'above all the heavens,
that he might fill all things', we understand it to mean that he
ascended above all places and all times to a dwelling that will
not pass away."[25] John Scotus Erigena was the most passionate and thorough advocate of the view that in Jesus' Ascension
the whole of mankind—including the whole of creation—had
begun its return to its divine source. Thus he says that a man
must be "mad" (amens) to think that "Christ's body, after his
Resurrection, is contained within a physical heaven".[26] Rather
"there can be no doubt that Christ's body can be contained by
no place and changed by no time; in fact it surpasses all places,
times and limitations."[27] Only in this way can it "become the
path, the perfection and the fullness of his body, the Church.[28]
It is *he* who is the only, the most spacious house: in him everything is contained and ordered as in a state (*res publica*); in him
the universe is established by God and in God, in innumerable
and manifold dwellings. . . . Christ is this house; Christ, who
enfolds everything by his power . . . , adorns it with grace, fills
it with wisdom and perfects it with divinization."[29] "For what
he brings to completion in himself, he will do in all those who
are made perfect. I do not say merely in all men, but in all phys-

[23] *De Resurrectione*, tr 2, q 9, a 3 (vol. 26 [1958], 286). For other passages, cf.
ibid., n. 29.

[24] E. Krebs, "Dietrich von Freiberg" in *BGPhM* V, 5–6 (1906), 109*.

[25] *Docta Ignorantia* III, 8 (Petzelt, Nicolaus von Kues, *Philosophische Schriften* I
[Kohlhammer, 1949]), 107.

[26] *De Divis. Naturae* V, 6 (PL 122, 872A).

[27] *Ibid.*, 38 (993B).

[28] *Ibid.*, (992C), cf. V, 19 (894BC).

[29] *Ibid.*, 38 (994C).

ical creation too; for when God's Word took human nature to
himself, he excluded no created substance that he would not
have taken up with him in that nature."[30] That is why Erigena
says that Augustine's realistic descriptions of the resurrected bodies are "horrible";[31] he can explain them only by assuming that
"such highly intelligent men" wrote these things for the simple,
in the hope of gradually bringing them to more spiritual things.

In the case of these authors it is possible that certain ideas
from Platonism and ancient astronomy played a part in their
rejection of a heaven "within the cosmos" as a place for the
eschatological transformation of a world subject to death. But
the issue is not one of a mere change from one cosmic sphere
to another, from the sublunary to the nontransient, planetary:
rather it is a case of transforming the mortal world, precisely
through the radicality of death, into a world that will not pass
away. Here the Christ-event leads ahead (*archēgos*, Acts 3:15; Heb
2:10; 12:2), not only as a personal event, but also as something
archetypal and cosmological. Furthermore it does so in an essentially trinitarian manner: the transformation proceeds from the
dying Son (whose death contains the germ of the new world),
from the Father (who awakens him to life) and from the Spirit,
who is the "glory" that "comes from the Lord who is the Spirit"
(2 Cor 3:18) and characterizes the newly formed world. Christ
the Victor receives his "due reward" in the form of an utterly
unexpected "grace".

Now, by analogy with the fundamental christological pattern,
we can anticipate something of the mystery of the "place" reserved for us in Christ: "When I go and prepare a place for you,
I will come again and will take you to myself, that where I am
you may be also" (Jn 14:3). Is this speaking only of a completion
of the Father's "old" creation through the triune work of the
Son, who completes the world of creation by using those very
aspects (pain, futility and death) that seemed most remote from

---

[30] *Ibid.*, 36 (984B). Following Erigena, Honorius of Autun sees heaven as a
"locus spiritualis . . . ubi ipsa Divinitas qualis est . . . contuetur": *Elucidarium*,
LIII, 1 (PL 172, 1157A). "Domus Patris . . . est visio omnipotentis Dei" (*ibid.*,
III, 8; 1162B). On the other hand, we find in III, 15–16, 18, the description of a
new physicality.

[31] "Stupefactus haesito maximoque horrore concussus titubo", *ibid.*, 7 (986B).

eternal life? Again we come up against the paradox that the Son is "rewarded" and "glorified" by the Father for something that seems to have removed him farthest from the Father's fading presence. If the Father is to "honor" (Jn 12:26) the men whom the Son will bring to his "place", it presupposes two things simultaneously: on the one hand, what is offered is a pure gift of grace beyond anything that could be expected; and, on the other hand, so as not to shame the recipient, this gift is linked to something he brings with him, something that (as the Bible says) he has "earned". The recipient of grace must belong, in some particular way, to the ranks of the "victors" as described in the Book of Revelation if he is to share in the wondrous things God wishes to give him. For he is to be given "power", the "morning star" and the "white robe"; his name is to be written "in the book of life"; he is to "sit on my throne" and "eat from the tree of life"; he is to be a "pillar in the house of my God", to enjoy the "hidden manna" and to receive a "new name which no one knows except him who receives it" (Rev 2–3). All these unmerited goods would remain external, alien and strange to the recipient if he could not discern some link—however surprising—with an earthly destiny that he had affirmed or at least endured; his earthly destiny must in some way have resembled that of Christ, whether he was aware of it or not, even if only in the stripping that precedes death. The "new heaven and the new earth" (Is 65:17; 66:22; Rev 21:1) are not a "different" world replacing the first: as the Old Testament passages show, they are the result of a transformation effected by God and with God as its goal. A child can innocently accept a present he has not expected, but it will not delight him unless it at least corresponds to some expectation he already has; in this case the present will fulfill a kind of anticipated image in the child, otherwise he will abandon it and turn back to some familiar, favorite toy; the adult can accept an excessively generous gift without embarrassment only if this gift expresses a sentiment of love that he actively receives and reciprocates. Thus the Son, on behalf of himself and those who are his, is always doing nothing but his Father's work of creation; his Father cooperates in this fulfillment by giving gifts and "rewards": both, however, together with those who are the recipients of these gifts, allow themselves to be filled with the overflowing bounty of the Holy Spirit.

In saying that the world of Christ's Resurrection must be at the same time the transformed world of his Incarnation and Cross—"Behold my hands and feet: touch and see that it is I" (Lk 24:39)—we have in mind that identity of the transfigured body and the earthly body which is so heavily underlined in the Church's documents.[32] Clearly, this identity cannot refer to the materiality that is constantly changing, but to that mysterious medium in which the individual human being expresses himself in freedom and which is at the same time a medium he inhabits in common with all others, since otherwise it could not sustain reciprocal communication. On earth there remains a manifold alienation between this inner freedom and the organism that expresses it; the organism is prone to atavisms, sickness, and physiological processes that are not under the control of inner freedom, and accordingly it responds to the requirements of this freedom in a very inadequate way. The organism has demands of its own, shown in tiredness, sleep, hunger, motion, to which—whether it wills to or not—the spirit must accede. We see the expressive organism responding fully to the direction of self-expressing freedom in the Lord's Resurrection body: the risen Lord makes himself known as and when he wishes. This does not imply some kind of Protean, utterly arbitrary self-expression on the part of those who have risen from the dead: each one's freedom is always that of his own unique, unmistakable personality. This personality will manifest itself in ever new ways that spring from its inexhaustible depths, yet specifically and unambivalently within the medium of the world of communication shared by all.

In coming to be, the new world dimension that is shown in symbol when Jesus is received up into the cloud has the quality of his crucified and risen body, which is also a eucharistically shared body. The space of this new dimension is essentially the space opened up through this endless sharing and proliferation of his body, in whatever state of transformation the matter em-

---

[32] J. Ratzinger, "Auferstehung des Fleisches" and "Auferstehungsleib" in *LThK* I, 1050, 1052.

ployed may be. We cannot imagine the state of this ensouled corporality: it has both the particular, human shape and form of the Risen One as well as the eucharistic ubiquity that guarantees room for mankind and the cosmos. (The cosmos thus returns to him who is its determining origin.) Nor can we imagine that explosion of the constrictions of earthly consciousness that enables the eucharistic Lord henceforth to address himself quite personally to every human being on earth or in heaven. (Thus, for instance, he can minister to each one of the countless dying, waiting for judgment and purification, as if he were the only person of importance.)

It would be wrong to regard the eucharistic state of Christ's body as "figurative"—that is, confined to his sacramental mode of presence on earth and only valid in this mode—as compared with his "real" or intrinsic body in heaven. Christ's body has become finally and definitively eucharistic, both since he suffered for all human sin and since the mode of being of this body has been assimilated to the trinitarian mode of being of the ascended Son: its being is not for itself but for the other. Clearly, from the Resurrection onward, the Body that breathed the Holy Spirit upon the disciples at Easter has a share in the trinitarian process: breathing forth the Spirit, he pours himself forth.

However, since the eucharistic reality opens up these new places (and times) of the transfigured world, those who enter these new dimensions can do no other than take part, analogously, in this poured-forth existence. We are ourselves by simultaneously making ourselves a dwelling place for others. We have already mentioned that Origen discovered this analogy; he refers it even to the Church on earth:

> Our Lord and Savior says, "If you do not eat my flesh and drink my blood, you will not have life in you. For my flesh is food indeed and my blood is drink indeed." Thus, since Jesus is utterly pure in all respects, all his flesh is "food" and all his blood is "drink". For all his works are holy and all his words are true. That is why his flesh is "food indeed", *true* food, and his blood is "drink indeed", *true* drink. For with the flesh and blood of his word he feeds and refreshes the whole human race, as with pure food and pure drink. In second place, after his flesh is the "pure food" of Peter and Paul and all the apostles, and, in third place, their disciples. In the same

way everyone can be "pure food" for his neighbor according to the quantity of his merits or the purity of his mind. . . . Every man has a certain food in him; if it is good, and someone takes some of it and it brings forth good "from the good treasure" of his heart, he is offering his neighbor "pure food".[33]

For Origen this gift of oneself is at the center of Christian truth: it is a straightforward, natural response to God's gift of himself to me in and through "whatever is in the world": "Do we think that man does something great in offering himself to God? No, God was the first to offer himself."[34] He is obeying the command of Christ, who said that the only way to gain one's soul is to lose it: "There must be a certain wholesome shipwreck of the soul for Christ's sake, as the prelude to a blessed rescue."[35] Accordingly, when we believe that we can call on the saints at any time and in any place (for example, the final petition of the Hail Mary), we are presupposing that the saints have this same eucharistic openness toward us.

This eucharistic "permeability" of all subjects to one another, even now in our mortal existence, is the very basis of the *communio sanctorum*. It is axiomatic that it does not interfere with the mysterious freedom of every person. As we shall show, everyone shares in the divine, trinitarian freedom in such a way that totally new and serendipitous things can come about. There is nothing inert and deterministic about this "permeability".[36]

[33] Origen, *Hom. in Lev.* 7, 5 (Baehrens 6, 386–87).

[34] *Hom. in Num.* 24, 2 (Baehrens 7, 229–30).

[35] *Mt. Comm.* 12, 26 (Klostermann 10, 128).

[36] Scholasticism was well aware of the necessity of some element that would go beyond finitude, that would "de-finitize" the knowledge that the blessed have of God (and also of the world). It tried to answer the question by speaking of a "divinizing" *medium deducens* or *disponens*, a "*medium confortans videntem*" (Albert) that is given in the manner of a dowry (*dos*) to the finite spirit so that it can share in the infinity of God's knowledge of himself (in the "light of glory"). This disarms the objection of the adage "infiniti ad finitum nulla est proportio". Alexander of Hales "identifies . . . a certain infinitude in the intellect, which it acquires through an irradiatio Dei". N. Wicki, *Die Lehre von der himmlischen Seligkeit in der mittelalterlichen Scholastik von P. Lombardus bis Thomas von Aquin*, Stud. Friburgensia NF, 9 (Fribourg, Switzerland: Universitätsverlag, 1954), 147–61: "Die Ausrüstung des Verstandes zur seligen Gottesschau". All that is missing in this speculation is the christological mediation that we have outlined in the foregoing, and which

In our discussion of the process of purification it became clear
that the latter consists essentially in exploding the encapsulated
"I" and that this is only possible in the recollection of genuine
isolation; this process achieves its goal where the eucharistic
prodigality of the Cross elicits a response from man that shows
that he is willing to atone, not only for his personal sin, but for
every sin, whoever may have committed it. This "confession" in
the fire of purification is the only possible, direct apprenticeship
for the eucharistic form of existence in heaven.

By the same token we can begin to see that beholding and
inwardly participating in the Son in his eucharistic self-giving
becomes a beholding and a participating in the life of the Trinity.
For when the Son allows himself to be poured out, he directly
reveals the love of the Father, who manifests himself in his Son's
eucharistia. We do not behold him as a "subject" distinct from
the Son but as the unfathomable primal spring of love, revealing himself as such in generating the Son and giving him away
for us. Now that the veils of earthly faith have fallen away, we
begin to appreciate the ultimate meaning of Jesus' saying, "He
who has seen me has seen the Father" (Jn 14:9). This "seeing",
as we shall show, must participate in the uncaused freedom—
which is therefore beyond our intellectual grasp—of the Son's
generation; it is therefore far beyond the mere contemplation
of objects. The Spirit too, however, becomes directly evident
in this same *eucharistia* of the incarnate Logos as he pours himself forth in the "mystical" body of the world; just as he (the
Spirit) implemented the Son's Incarnation, he now remains the
executive of the Son's prodigal self-giving, not only on earth
but in heaven too. Not for nothing does the apocalyptic Son of
Man hold the seven stars in his hand and walk in the midst of
seven torches of fire "which are the seven spirits of God" (Rev
4:5); the seven horns and seven eyes of the Lamb "are the seven
spirits of God sent out into all the earth" (5:6), while the entire mystery of Father and Son is set in a seven-hued "rainbow"

---

is intended as a continuation, in concrete terms, of the exposition begun by K.
Rahner in his much-quoted essay on the eternal significance of the humanity of
Jesus for our relationship with God ("Die ewige Bedeutung der Menschheit Jesu
für unser Gottesverhältnis" in *Schriften* III [1956], 47–60).

(4:3). All these images are presented to the earthly beholder to translate for him the incomprehensible atmosphere of trinitarian love, radiating and actively working through everything; in this love he beholds and experiences what, proceeding from the divine converse of Father and Son, draws into this converse all those abiding[37] in heaven.

2. Recourse to the Idea

Might it not be, however, that these theological solutions are premature so long as the fundamental philosophical question is not clarified, namely: How are we to conceive finite being—time-space being—located in the embrace of the absolute? And in doing this we must avoid, on the one hand, a pantheistic absorption of the one by the other and, on the other hand, a mere juxtaposition of the two. We find the first attempt at an answer in Platonism's dualism of the (divine) Idea and the thing that comes from it. (Here we shall not go into the pre-Christian attempts made to substantiate and overcome this dualism.) The Fathers, in particular Augustine and Maximus the Confessor,[1] take up this doctrine of the divine Ideas, seeing in them the archetypes of things that can be, are being, and have been created, as they exist in the Spirit of the Creator. Scholasticism, accordingly, inquires into the relationship of these two. Its answer exhibits a remarkable alternation between the (Platonic) preference for the Idea of a thing, since the Idea is essentially in God and hence is divine —"creatura in Deo est creatrix essentia"[2]—and the (Christian)

---

[37] The author uses the verb *weilen*, which means to "dwell for a while" or "tarry". —TRANS.

[1] Augustine, *83 Quaestiones*, q 46, n 2. Maximus the Confessor is clearer when (in *Ambig.* 7, PG 91, 1081C), explaining Gregory of Nazianzen's easily misunderstood assertion that we are "parts of God": "We are, and may rightly be called, a part of God insofar as the Ideas of our being are preexistent in God." Every existing human being is fashioned according to these Ideas (*ibid.*, 1084), without thereby being dissolved in God. This passage, translated by Scotus Erigena, was doubtless the starting point of his own ("dynamic") interpretation—and of all those who followed him.

[2] Thomas, *Evang. Joh.* lect. 2, III (Marietti, no. 91). On the various ways of punctuating verses 3–4 of the Prologue, cf. Paul Lamarche, "Le Prologue de Jean" in *RSR* 52 (1964), 497–537, esp. 514–23.

positivity with regard to created reality, which is by no means something that has fallen to earth out of the heaven of Ideas. This holds even if we take the punctuation of the Prologue of St. John customary in former times: "What was created was life in him" (Jn 1:4–5), for everything in God, including his ideas, is eternal life, even if such ideas are of mortal things or even of lifeless things. Thomas draws a precise distinction on the basis of this alternation: when asking about the mode of being of the *thing*, he says that its real, existent mode of being is truer (*verius*) than the merely ideal; whereas, when he asks about the mode of being *as such*, he replies that the being of the idea—since it is divine being—is "truer and more noble" than the being of the thing.[3] We should notice, however, that in *De Veritate* the first approach, giving priority to the truth of created reality, is again substantiated in Platonic terms, for "according to Dionysius what is caused, in imitating its causes, does not attain the level of the causes; they are superior to it. Because there is a gap between the cause and the caused, it is possible to say something true about the effect that cannot be said of the cause: pleasures do not enjoy, though they are the cause of our enjoyment; the reason for this is simply that the mode of being (*modus*) of the cause is higher than that of the effects."[4] This Platonist notion is brought into the Christian environment by Bonaventure. Where God is concerned, according to Bonaventure, the likeness between thing and idea does not come from an "impression upon the mind from outside" as it does with us. "In the case of God it is the other way round, for the ground of knowledge is truth itself; what is known is a likeness to truth, namely, the creature itself." In God, truth expresses itself from within, which is why "the ground of knowledge in God has the greatest expressive power (*est summe expressiva*)". At this stage the Platonic argument can be put forward in terms of the Christian *analogia entis*: similitudo imitationis est modica, quia in modico potest finitum imitari infinitum, unde semper maior est dissimilitudo quam similitudo. Similitudo vero expressionis est summa, quia causatur ab intentione veritatis . . . quae est ipsa expressio; ideo

[3] *Sent.* I, d 36, q 1, a 3 ad 2; *De Ver.* q 4, a 6; *S. Th.* I, q 18, a 4 ad 3.
[4] *De Ver.* q 4, a 6 (body of article).

Deus summe omnia cognoscit."[5] So the likeness of what God expresses in himself is greater than what created reality expresses through itself.[6]

This raises a question: Must it remain impossible to bridge the discrepancy between the divine fullness of the Idea of some creaturely thing and the self-realization of this creature? Should we say, as Staudenmaier did in his great work on the "Idea", that "the realized Idea of the world"—by which he means the concrete world, a "unity of the ideal and the real", of concept and reality[7]—corresponds entirely to the eternal, divine Idea of it and that this is what is meant by "the world's original perfection" prior to the Fall?[8] Or should we say that the assertion in Genesis that the world is "very good" can only be made by looking ahead to a supernaturally adequate representation of God in finitude by the incarnate Son, who *does not abolish* the distinction between Creator and creation at the level of being, but *unites* it in his person?[9] Such an adequate representation would mysteriously transcend the *maior dissimilitudo*. In the latter case the solution to the perplexing problem of the gap between God's idea of creation and creaturely existence itself would lie in the realm of the Trinity. We shall return to this.

The creature is not unaware of this gap between idea and reality, and this in turn implies that he should do something about it. The creature's very nature challenges him to realize and "catch up" with this Idea. Moreover, if the Idea is nothing other than a concrete thought on the part of God, who wishes the creature to collaborate in making it a reality, why should the latter not be able to "catch up" with the Idea, given the assistance of God's elevating grace? Scholastic thought did not really address this question: the *maior dissimilitudo* or the ontic *superexcellentia causae* seemed to be the last word. In the German Middle Ages,

---

[5] Bonaventure, *Sent.* I, d 35, a unicus q 1 ad 2 (Quarenghi I, 601b).

[6] "Similitudo, quae est ipsa veritas expressiva . . . melius exprimit rem, quam ipsa res seipsam exprimit": *ibid.*, ad 3.

[7] *Die Lehre von der Idee in Verbindung mit einer Entwicklungsgeschichte der Ideenlehre und der Lehre vom göttlichen Logos* (Gießen, 1840), 821.

[8] *Ibid.*, 914.

[9] Cf. our earlier remarks on the adequacy and "super-adequacy" of Christ's being and work.

however, Platonist mysticism does not insist on a correspondence between every individual detail of the creature[10] but sees in the Ideas more what is common to the species—ultimately it sees the Logos himself.[11] Here there is a tendency to transcend the static, archetypal image that confronts it and penetrate to a "ground" in which every *dissimilitudo* is surpassed.

It is surely only in John Scotus Erigena that there is a bridge between the rigid opposition of Idea and creaturely reality, on the one hand, and the mystical dissolution of all opposition, on the other. In him we find that the Ideas (which in Erigena are both the "primordialia exempla" or "praedefinitiones", or "divinae voluntates" or "ideae, id est species vel formae")[12] move toward an individual and creaturely reality that proceeds from them;[13] at the same time what has come forth from the matrix of ideas experiences a mysterious attraction, a movement backward into that matrix,[14] enabling individual, creaturely reality to have contact with the absoluteness of God, who is understood to be "no longer creating".[15] Thus all individual reality is identical with its Idea and exists henceforth in eternity.[16] Erigena, too, however, discovers a trinitarian basis for the whole process, and, as we have seen, the risen Christ is the Firstborn of creatures in their return to the Idea and hence to God.[17] All the same, this process-in-motion remains ambivalent insofar as we do not know how far the Ideas, as creative principles, are part of God's essence, and how far they are to be attributed, at least in an inchoate sense, to the created world.[18]

We must get beyond this ambivalence, but in doing so we need to keep hold of the reciprocal movement of Idea and real

---

[10] "Idea in Deo . . . est ratio expressiva cognoscendi non tantum universale, sed etiam singulare, quamvis ipsa non sit universalis nec singularis, sicut nec Deus": Bonaventure, *Sent.* I, d 35, q 4. Meister Eckhart will be of a different opinion.

[11] On the Fathers' view that Christ took to himself the entirety of human nature, cf. *Theo-Drama* III, 217, 235f., and the texts cited in E. Mersch, *Le Corps Mystique* I, chap. 8, sec. 5. Scotus Erigena understands this unity of the adopted nature in a Platonic manner (*Hom. in Prolog. Joh.*, PL 122, 290A: *De Div. Nat.* V, 25, 910ff.; V, 27, 921ff.). There are constant references to this in Eckhart.

[12] *Div. Nat.* II, 2 (PL 122, 529AC). [13] *Ibid.*, 16 (549AB).

[14] *Ibid.*, 15 (547C). [15] *Ibid.*, 2 (528CD).

[16] *Ibid.*, 11 (539D–540A). [17] *Ibid.*, 14 (543D–544A; 545AB).

[18] *Ibid.*, V, 16 (887D–888A).

individuality that Erigena discerned: for, though on earth we are always more or less reluctant and fail to come up to the mark, it is God's will that we should finally be conformed to the idea he has of us. Not by some mystical submersion in a trackless, divine "un-ground" in which both the triune God and the personal creature lose all definition, but on the basis of a definition that is appropriate to both God and the creature.

The foundation for this is provided by the doctrine we have set forth above: Everything that, in the created world, appears shot through with *potentiality* is found *positively* in God. We shall come back to this doctrine again later; for the moment it must be taken as read. In the course of our investigations, however, we kept coming up against the notion that God does not "expel" or "expose" his creature (pp. 99–100), and so cannot give man his finite freedom in such a way that it would be cut loose from its profoundest origin: its rootedness in the divine freedom. Finite freedom, to fulfill itself, must be ordered to divine freedom. Our freedom is "laid up" in God's Word (p. 132); thus, so is our true "I" (pp. 145, 283, 300–303). If our ultimate freedom is laid up in our Idea, there are necessarily two sides to it: one side concerns the Idea in God, who waits for us to be fully realized in him. The other side concerns the structure of the created spirit: Thomas terms this the *syneidesis* or *synteresis*, which infallibly cleaves to the Good, however much we may fall away in sin; it alone, in fact, makes it possible for us consciously to turn away from the Good.[19] Man is held fast, unconditionally, by the principle of the Good: Thomas also speaks of this as the *scintilla*, the tiny spark found in man that comes from the fiery core of the Good.[20] The mystics will speak of the "spark of the soul" and will concentrate on this *supremum mentis* that unites both what is given to man in the Idea and what is withheld from him, for the present, in his creatureliness.

---

[19] *S. Th.* I, 89, 12c; *ibid.*, le ad 3; I–II, 94, 1 ad 2; *De Ver.*, 16, 1 c + ad 12; *ibid.*, 2c.

[20] "Sicut scintilla est id quod purius est de igne et quod supervolat toti igni, ita synderesis est id, quod supremum in conscientiae iudicio reperitur, et secundum hanc metaphoram synderesis scintilla conscientiae dicitur": *De Ver.* 17, 2 ad 3; cf. *2 Sent.* 39, 3, 1c.

It was surely Ruysbroeck who gave the most impressive portrayal of the encounter with one's own uncreated Idea, an encounter that can take place only at the point where the Father eternally generates both the Son and, simultaneously, that Idea of the world which is to be implemented in the Son. Concretely this generation always takes place where God implants grace into a created soul that is open to him, but the highest degree of divine favor and the greatest purity of soul are required if the soul is to discern this divine process, since it is beyond the soul's spiritual and intellectual faculties (which spring from the very ground of the soul). From the womb of the divine fruitfulness,

the Son, the Eternal Word of the Father, came forth as the second Person in the Godhead. And, through the Eternal Birth, all creatures have come forth in eternity, before they were created in time. So God has seen and known them in Himself, according to distinction, in living ideas, and in an otherness from Himself; but not as something other in all ways, for all that is in God is God. This eternal going out and this eternal life, which we have and are in God eternally, without ourselves, is the cause of our created being in time. And our created being abides in the Eternal Essence, and is one with it in its essential existence. And this eternal life and being, which we have and are in the eternal Wisdom of God, is like unto God. For it has an eternal immanence in the Divine Essence, without distinction; and through the birth of the Son it has an eternal outflowing in a distinction and otherness, according to the Eternal Idea. And through these two points it is so like unto God that He knows and reflects Himself in this likeness without cessation, according to the Essence and according to the Persons. For, though even here there are distinction and otherness according to intellectual perception, yet this likeness is one with that same Image of the Holy Trinity, which is the wisdom of God and in which God beholds himself and all things in an eternal *Now, without before and after.* In a single seeing He beholds Himself and all things. And this is the Image and the Likeness of God, and our Image and our Likeness; for in it God reflects Himself and all things. In this Divine Image all creatures have an eternal life, outside themselves, as in their eternal Archetype; and after this eternal Image, and in this Likeness, we have been made by the Holy Trinity. And therefore God wills that we shall go forth from ourselves in this Divine Light, and shall reunite ourselves in a supernatural way with *this Image, which is our proper life, and shall possess it with Him, in action and in fruition, in eternal bliss.*[21]

What Ruysbroeck goes on to say about the trinitarian birth of the Son in the soul, and the fact that Ideas will ultimately disappear in the unity of the triune life, belongs to a later stage of our discussion.

If, however, we inquire as to the Idea's content in God, the central issue is not so much that it coincides with the divine nature (since its being is in God), but: How is the creature's *ideal* envisaged? Two factors present themselves, the second dependent on the first. The first is this: Since the world is designed and created in Christ, our Idea is also "in Christ": "He has taken on the task of showing us our nature as heaven planned it; we have our nature *in him*."[22] In thus showing us what our nature is meant to be, he causes our Idea in him to move (in Erigena's sense) toward us, in a sense that is both universal or Catholic (as in the case of the Platonic Idea), but equally in an individual and personal sense that cannot be overtaken by any *reditus* to God. When the Logos-made-man addresses the individual—and this takes place through the words and the whole being of Christ—I am granted an insight into and access to that Idea God has of me. On earth the individual can strive for this Idea; but if we reflect upon the purification that takes place after death, it emerges that the definitive recasting of the I is carried out in the divine fire.

---

[21] John of Ruysbroeck, *The Adornment of the Spiritual Marriage*, trans. C. A. Wynschenk (London: Dent, 1916), bk. 3, chap. 3 (pp. 172–73). On the ideas as "life in God" according to John 1:4–5, see "Le Miroir du Salut éternel" in *Oeuvres de Ruysbroeck*, 3d ed. (Brussels: Vromant, 1922), vol. 1, 87. Between our idea and our existence there is an unmediated continuity (*ibid.*, 88). "For the essence and life that we possess in God, i.e., in our eternal Source, and which we have within us according to our essential being, is reciprocal, not separated by any wall": F. M. Huebner in the German edition of Ruysbroeck (Leipzig: Insel Verlag, 1924), 338. Cf. Tauler's *Sermon* 53: "The spark of the soul . . . does not rest until it returns to the divine Ground whence it came and where it was in its uncreated state" (Hofmann II, 407). Suso, in his defense of Eckhart (*Büchlein der Wahrheit*), points to the trinitarian "distinction" as the abiding foundation for all creaturely distinctions: "At the very least this Nothing (i.e., God in his all-surpassing Being) already has distinction in itself, and from this distinction, insofar as it is fruitful, come all proper distinctions in things" (chap. 6, Bihlmeyer, 353).

[22] Ka II, 184; "In this sense we are in him before he is in us": Ka II, 237.

The pattern for this is the total self-surrender of Christ: those who are waiting to enter heaven contemplate this self-surrender and are transformed into it. "We forget that when they come out of purgatory, purified, they will experience a new birth in the Holy Spirit through the Son's sacrifice; this will refashion them according to the Father's original intention in creating them." We shall all "be the realization of a unique idea on God's part, we shall share in the 'ever-greater' life of the Son and in the mystery of the Holy Spirit. Everyone will be a personality, able both to reveal himself and to be open to all others; they too will express a unique idea on the part of God, who wishes to glorify himself in them."[23] And since this Idea has its foundation in the nature of Christ, who is both God and man, "in God we shall see how man was intended to be, and in man we shall see how God reveals himself to him. In heaven the mystery of Christ . . . that accompanies us on our earthly path of faith will continue to be the center that illuminates everything."[24] When Paul says, "We are his workmanship, created in Christ Jesus for good works, which God prepared beforehand, that we should walk in them" (Eph 2:10), "Paul gives this second creation complete preponderance over the first. We are no longer creatures of the first creation but creatures of the redemption. Just as God sent his Son as the second Adam, so too he recognizes in us now the children of the second covenant. . . . He wants to behold us as creatures who exist within his generated Son."[25]

The second factor in the Idea should now be clear. After all we said in *Theo-Drama* (III, 149–259) about the unity of *processio* and *missio* in Christ, the second factor has to be the Idea of our mission (or our charisma) within the economy of Christ's universal redemptive Body.[26] For if, according to the Areopagite, the Ideas are essentially the "divine acts of will" (*theia thelēmata*),[27] how could God's idea of the individual be anything other than the particular contours of what, in Christ, he is to be and to do? Ultimately there is only one single mission: that of the Son;

---

[23] OM 564.
[24] OM 565.
[25] Ep 92.
[26] *Theo-Drama* III, 263–71.
[27] *De Div. Nom.* V, 8 (PG 3, 824C).

"every secondary mission, in its origin and in its acceptance by the one who is called, draws its life from the first." "The Son grants to each who follows him participation in the same substance, in the same directedness and limitlessness of his eternal mission. . . . But even when God has the intention of achieving something specific and finite through a certain mission, he nevertheless bestows, in each case, the *whole* mission, the mission of the movement, of discipleship, and only within this larger gift the specific purpose. What is to be achieved remains, as it were, one point within the whole mission."[28] Christ calls man to a mission "at the point where he has accepted his own from the Father. It is like a flowing fountain of missions: a constantly new gushing forth from the central source. And because the Son desires that every mission should serve the glorification of the Father, he does not have the missions link up with his in a peripheral way but, rather, lets them arise centrally, out of his own center."[29] The mission embraces life, for it comes from eternity: the certainty with which Paul speaks of his attaining salvation

> can only be explained on the basis of his mission. It is more certain than he is himself, for it comes directly from God, and it fills him with such an unshakable firmness that he can think of nothing that could oppose it. . . . It embraces all temporal duration: his own lifetime, but also his eternal "time" that is yet to come, because his mission originates in God's eternal plan; his mission is only "lent" to him, so to speak, for the duration of his earthly life, but with a view to the "always" of eternity. Not as if now he is creating something that will retain its value for eternity: no, it is that he has received from eternity, and from the values of eternity, something that is so powerful that transitory time and human accident cannot touch it. He is safe and secure in this mission.[30]

"The mission draws its time from eternity. . . . The mission's means are not sanctified retrospectively; rather, everything that corresponds to the mission is already holy. Nor can we speak of 'aims', for the mission is greater than any aim a man can envisage."[31] If the mission is the real core of the personality, it opens

[28] 4 Jo 216 (GT).
[29] 4 Jo 398.
[30] Ph 33-34.
[31] Ka II, 322.

up the latter—because it comes from eternity and is destined for eternity—far beyond the dimensions of which it is conscious in the world or which others allot to it. This is why a mission that is begun on earth, if it really originates in Christ's mission, does not cease with death but comes to perfection in eternal life. Little Thérèse had this certainty and showed it to be justified.

Of course, after this christological explanation of the Idea, and of man's return to it, open questions remain. They will be dealt with in what follows—insofar as solutions can be attempted here. One question remains unanswered: How far can the task that, on earth, is never fully completed, or only superficially so (and sometimes not at all), be regarded as being fulfilled in heaven? We shall reflect on this question in connection with the relationship between heaven and earth. Another unsolved question is this: How can we imagine "mission" at all in the context of eternity? We shall have to address this question when we come to discuss the way in which the world of becoming is embedded in the eternal trinitarian event.

3. The Creature in God

How is it possible for creatures to be embedded in God in such a way that they attain perfection without losing their creaturely nature? We have prepared for this question by setting forth three ideas. First, we described the fullness of life within the Godhead: as such it contains—in a supra-essential way—all the elements that, in the creaturely sphere, are permeated by potentiality (which is inapplicable to God) yet still retain an undeniably positive aspect (cf. pp. 66ff. above). Second, we set forth a theology of the world in its pilgrim condition, a theology that pointed the world beyond this condition in every respect, indicating an ultimate, though unimaginable, state "with" God. This state is reached via a transformatory death that both concentrates its temporal duration into a summary unity and hands it over, in its totality, to its origin—which has now become its goal (cf. pp. 99–118 above). Third and finally, there was the idea permeating everything that the world, *in spite of and because of* its being genuinely created, and created in freedom, cannot be "outside"

God; there cannot be such an "outside"; on the contrary, the world must have its locus within the trinitarian relations. This locus, in its finitude, must be always embraced and surpassed by the infinite distinction between the Divine Persons—which provided the basis for our attempt to interpret the redemption of even a world that is sinfully alienated from God (cf. pp. 247–321 above). There can be no question, therefore, of the world moving from a position "outside God" to a position "inside God": instead there must be a change in the condition of the world while it remains equally close to, and immanent in, God. This is why Anselm, in the first chapter of his *Proslogion*, "reflects upon this question in prayer": "Domine, si hic non es, ubi te quaeram absentem? Si autem ubique es, cur non video praesentem?"[1] We cannot go into the question in all its breadth; it must suffice to point out that, if God has given a creature freedom, he must—for the sake of that very freedom to choose and to act —allow it to choose the good that it itself *is not* (although this good is indelibly inscribed in its being, however alienated it may become through sin). Further, since man is a creature existing in time, unlike angels, this freedom is only possible through a process that is spread over distinct moments of time, the sum content of which is manifested in death, judgment and fire. It is self-contradictory to think even of an angel (who is essentially timeless) being created in a *state* of supernatural vision of God, which implies freedom.[2] This is a further confirmation of the statement that there is no distance between heaven and earth, only between earth and heaven—if by earth we mean freedom in its pilgrim state and by heaven we mean freedom's ultimate state, the ratification of its positive fundamental choice by the One it has chosen, namely, God, who can now openly entrust himself to this freedom.

Thus the infinite Being, who is also infinite Freedom, entrusts himself to us. The only way we can imagine this is as the opening-up of endless rooms: describing God's entrusting of himself to us as *visio Dei* is always an inadequate and one-

[1] Cf. the profound study by Ferdinand Ulrich: "Cur non video praesentem? Zur Implikation der 'griechischen' und 'lateinischen' Denkform bei Anselm und Scotus Eriugena" in *Freiburger Zft. f. Phil. u. Theol.* 22 (1975), 70–170.

[2] H. de Lubac, *Surnaturel* (Aubier, 1946), pt. 2: "Esprit et liberté", 187–321.

sided portrayal of this open encounter, since God can never be
an object totally available to our sight. If we wish to keep the
metaphor of "vision", we must speak in dialectical terms of the
highest presence of something that is beyond all that we can
grasp.[3] Thus we shall come to see that, although God will offer
himself to the creature (through his own power and on the basis
of his own self-beholding) by the "lumen gloriae" as a "medium
deducens",[4] even in heaven he cannot be beheld "plene et secundum totum",[5] not *comprehensive*.[6] The Greeks were fond of
emphasizing God's incomprehensibility even in heaven,[7] and the
teaching of Scotus Erigena that God can only be beheld through
theophanies was unwelcome to a Scholasticism that, following
Augustine, assumed that a direct and full vision of God was possible. Albert produced a "reinterpretation of genius" by synthe-
sizing East and West: he explained that the Greek "theophany"
was what the West meant by the "light of faith", a "medium
confortans videntem".[8]

This is to speak of the encounter with God in the terms of
vision, but we cannot stop there. God's infinite life is a freedom
that cannot be plumbed; its rooms cannot be "beheld": we are
to hurry through them as in a "race" that will never end. Thus
Scotus Erigena gives a twofold derivation of the word *theos*: "Ei-

---

[3] "Videtur autem quod ubi praesentissima est divina essentia seu veritas non
esset necessaria umbra vel imago nec medium aliud. . . . [Thus for instance the
soul is directly given its joy or sorrow. But can God be given in this way?] In
hoc autem dicimus quod licet divina essentia essentialiter praesentissima sit an-
imabus nostris ac proxima, sua tamen supereminentia et incomprehensibilitate
remotissima est ac distantissima ab illis, vel quod congruentius est, illae ab ipsa":
William of Auvergne, *De retributionibus sanctorum*, in *Opera omnia* (Paris, 1674) I,
517v (reprint Frankfurt, 1963).

[4] Bonaventure, *2 Sent.* d 23, a 2, q 3 ad 7 (Quarenghi II, 546).

[5] Cf. Gregory the Great: "In futuro reperietur omnipotens per speciem, sed
non ad perfectum, quia ejus essentia a nullo plene videbitur", *Moralia* 10 (PL 75,
928C).

[6] For a collection of texts, some printed for the first time, cf. H.-F. Dondaine,
"L'Objet et le 'medium' de la vision béatifique chez les théologiens du 13 siècle"
in *Rech. théol. anc. et méd.* 19 (1952), 60–130.

[7] Chrysostom, *Hom. in Joh.* 10,1; Cyril of Jerusalem, *Catech.* 6, 6.

[8] On this whole issue, cf. N. Wicki, *Die Lehre von der himmlischen Seligkeit in der
mittelalterlichen Scholastik von P. Lombardus bis Thomas von Aquin*, Stud. Friburgensia
NF 9, (Fribourg, Switzerland: Universitätsverlag, 1954), 154ff.

ther it comes from the verb *theorō*, which means 'I see', or from
the verb *theo*, 'I run'; or more probably, since both verbs contain
a similar meaning, from both. For God sees in himself everything that is, . . . since there is nothing outside him . . . , but he
also runs through everything, never standing still, fulfilling all
things in his course, although he does not move in any sense.
For of God it is most true to say that he is motion at rest and
rest in motion."[9] The knowledge of God, accordingly, is simultaneously a beholding and a "running".

Gregory of Nyssa had dwelt on this simultaneity in celebrated
texts. God says to Moses, "Since your longing impels you toward what is beyond you, and since no satiety hinders your
course, . . . understand that there is in me so much space that
the one hastening through it will never be able to halt his flight.
Nonetheless this headlong motion, seen from a different angle,
is also rest. . . . Of course, that rest and motion can be the same
thing is a great paradox."[10] Gregory uses the image of the spring
to explain this: anyone who observes a spring

> is amazed (*thaumasei*) at its welling-up endlessly (*apeiron*), its rising
> and flowing forth, but he will never suggest that he has seen all
> the water. . . . Even were he to stand for a long time beside this
> wellspring, he would still be at the very start of observing the
> water. . . . So it is with the one who contemplates the divine and
> eternal beauty: since what he discovers at every moment is newer
> and more paradoxical than what he has already grasped, he can only
> be astonished at what presents itself to him in ever new ways (*to
> aei prophainomenon*), but his desire to contemplate never slackens
> and the revelations he awaits will be more and more wondrous
> and divine than what he has already glimpsed.[11]

This astonished beholding is not, however, as the image of the
spring might suggest, something static and quantitative, for the
divine wellspring is always a free self-giving that renders the recipient more and more able to receive more: "The two things
grow simultaneously: the ability is increased, nourished by the
bounty of good fare, and the supply of nourishing goods in-

---

[9] *De Div. Nat.* I, 11 (PL 122, 452C).
[10] *De Vita Moysis* (PG 44, 465AC).
[11] *In Cant. hom.* 11 (PG 44, 1000AB).

creases as a result of the heightened receptivity to them."[12] The one receiving these goods is bound to become more and more like his Lord, so that, according to the Lord's words, he who drinks from the well becomes in turn a wellspring, and he who receives the divine word becomes a word himself.[13] Or the flowing spring is compared to a mouth or a wound, and then the recipient himself becomes a welling wound, a wound of love that "goes as deep as the innermost heart, that is, as deep as participation in divinity; for love, we read, is God."[14] In the Song of Songs the Bride says that she is wounded by love, struck by the Bowman who has taken accurate aim at her. Yet

> hardly does the Bride feel herself struck by love's arrow, when her wound changes into nuptial joy. It is well known how the bowman's hands manipulate the bow: the left hand grasps the bow, the right stretches the bowstring, pulling the arrow into the notch that the left hand aims at the target. And the soul, which a moment ago was the missile's target, suddenly sees itself as the arrow between the Bowman's hands. . . . "His left hand", says the Bride, "rests under my head, and his right will embrace me", so that the word of Scripture is describing the path to God in a double metaphor: it shows us that our Bridegroom and the Bowman are the same Person and that the soul is both his bride and his arrow; he directs the soul as an arrow to its target, and he lifts up the soul as a bride to the intimacy of an unspotted eternity. . . . That is why she says "His left hand rests under my head" (for it is the left hand that aims the arrow at the target), whereas "his right hand" attracts and draws me toward him, giving me great lightness for my upward flight. But though I am shot forth toward the target, I am not separated from the Bowman; at one and the same time I fly up at great speed and yet repose in the hands of the Lord.[15]

The wealth of diverse and complementary images used by Gregory provides a splendid illustration of the twofold derivation of the name of God and hence of the "vision" of God in the work of Scotus Erigena to which we have already referred. For him rest and motion (and hence a kind of spatial fullness),

---

[12] *De anima et resurrectione* (PG 46, 105C).

[13] *In Cant. hom.* 9 (PG 44, 977D); cf. *De virginitate* 7 (PG 46, 352AC).

[14] *In Cant. hom.* 2 (PG 44, 801B); *hom.* 13 (PG 44, 1044CD).

[15] *In Cant. hom.* 4 (PG 44, 852A–853A).

being and overflowing life, remaining the same and yet heightening (so a kind of temporal fullness), coinhere in an effortless manner. We cannot imagine these coinherences; we can only say at the abstract level that the positivities implicit in the potentiality of earthly, creaturely existence are not swallowed up by the supposedly absolute positivity of a "pure act". Rather, we are invited to realize that the "act" in its fullness, which is to say, understood in a trinitarian context, by its own nature already has these creaturely positivities within it: consequently it can send them forth and re-incorporate or re-"embed" them into itself without harming them. This "embedding" means that the way they are contained in God provides us with a measure for their creaturely form; it is given to the latter purely by grace as an ontological space in which to exist. "What is promised us is a bliss that surpasses our longing, a gift that exceeds our hope, a grace that overflows our nature."[16] This is clearest, as we have shown, where it is a question of the positivity of otherness: the positive otherness of the Son, eternally begotten from the Father, makes possible the positive otherness of creatures.

Again it was Ruysbroeck, in contrast to the German mystics (who thought in terms of the sole positivity of a Unity conceived along Neoplatonic lines), who best realized this. Thus in his *Book of Supreme Truth* he describes the trinitarian "mutual relations of the Persons in the Godhead", in their "embrace", which does not destroy their mutual otherness, as the "home and the beginning of all life and of all becoming" of "all creatures with their proper being".[17] "Therefore the creature [even] in its inward contemplation feels a distinction and an otherness between itself and God"; and the unity of "superessence" into which God, through grace, draws us into his trinitarian unity has its prototype in the unity for which Christ prays on earth. "And this was prayed for by Christ when He besought His Father in heaven that all His beloved might be made perfect in one, even as He is one with the Father through the Holy Ghost."[18] "But the relations which make the personal attributes [in God] remain in

---

[16] *Beatitud. or.* 7 (PG 44, 1277C).

[17] John of Ruysbroeck, *The Book of Supreme Truth* in *The Adornment of the Spiritual Marriage*, trans. C. A. Wynschenk (London: Dent, 1916), 241.

[18] Ruysbroeck, *Book of Supreme Truth*, 244, 246.

eternal distinction."[19] This distinction both eternally justifies the distinction beween God and the creature and eternally surpasses it in that love which is the gift of grace and which comes from the unity of the divine essence. "And though we live wholly in God and wholly in ourselves, yet it is but one life; but it is twofold and opposite according to our feeling, . . . for we cannot wholly become God. . . . Did we, however, remain wholly in ourselves, sundered from God, we should be miserable and unblest. And therefore we should feel ourselves living wholly in God and wholly in ourselves; and between these two feelings we should find nothing else but the grace of God and the exercise of our love." The latter comes down upon us from "the brightness of God" and draws us up into itself.[20] Thus Ruysbroeck speaks much of "meeting" with God, which is "without intermediary" and as such is "highest blessedness".[21] The spirit, possessing its "eternal blessedness", "flows forth again, through the eternal birth of the Son, together with all the other creatures, and is set in its created being by the free will of the Holy Trinity", where it "incessantly receives the impress of its Eternal Archetype"; but "This essential union of our spirit with God does not exist in itself, but it dwells in God, and it flows forth from God, and it depends upon God, and it returns to God as to its Eternal Origin."[22]

We cannot imagine how our earthly existence is embedded in God. This is because the mode of this embedding is given to us from above, on the basis of its trinitarian original. This does not destroy our creaturely modes (which are copies and likenesses) but causes them to transcend themselves. Thus they attain their real destination (gratia non destruit, elevat, perficit naturam). Since in God there is eternal life and hence "eternal surprise", we too shall experience this surprise.[23] Since within the divine fruitfulness there is a kind of eternal "ever-more", "everything that lives in heaven seems to be growing"; but this takes place "beyond

[19] Ruysbroeck, Adornment, 99.

[20] Ruysbroeck, The Sparkling Stone, in Adornment, 205–6.

[21] Ruysbroeck, Adornment, 77, 129. In chap. 56 (pp. 124–25) he describes this "meeting" as something taking place from different and opposite points.

[22] Ibid., 126–7.

[23] OM 75.

time and space" in the mode of being of eternal Love.[24] And since God's freedom and love require something like "super-times" and "super-space" so that his love can expand infinitely, we too shall experience, beyond our transitory nature, a kind of "elasticity" of duration in which there will be a coincidence of the "eternal here" and the "eternal now". "Everything bursts the bounds of finitude, not like a river bursting its banks, but by life transcending the tiny form it has in us and being taken up into the immeasurable form that God gives."[25] This also applies to *prayer*, which, as we have seen, has its original shape in the life of the Trinity: in heaven "we do not pray our own prayers: we are taken up into prayer. This is a gift coming directly from God. . . . What the Church presents to us on earth as a task and an obligation" is, in heaven,

> our insertion into the will of God. . . . It is God who shows us hidden things and initiates us into them, but we do this in concert with the whole of heaven. What might seem to be an obstacle is only the weight of beauty. . . . The joy of discovery is joy unalloyed, without toil or hardship. Our discoveries will take us from one degree of astonishment to another. . . . There is adoration, the soul's complete openness before God, and in love we allow God to fill and fulfill us. There is also intercessory prayer, but this too is utterly new, since it comes to us from the hand of God at every moment. Thus sacrifice becomes rejoicing, intercession becomes gratitude.

Every prayer is "carried and borne aloft by such a plenitude" by the trinitarian event that is marked by the Son's death on the Cross, that it "acquires its ultimate meaning and brings to the person at prayer experiences that, though eternal, are utterly unique. . . . There is nothing superfluous in the heavenly super-fluity."[26]

---

[24] OM 73.
[25] OM 74.
[26] OM 75–77.

4. Freedom, Vision and Creation

The foregoing gives us an opportunity to reflect on that human freedom which is also brought to perfection in this process and on the implications of this perfecting. Ever since Augustine it has been regarded as established that the crowning of creaturely freedom, having succeeded in the process of affirming itself—and hence God—lies beyond the ability to choose between good and evil: this freedom is entirely and resolutely devoted to the good: "The *arbitrium* that can no longer fall victim to sin is all the more free."[1] "The first freedom was concerned with the ability to avoid sin; the last freedom will be far greater: not to sin at all . . . , not to be able to forsake the good."[2] Anselm agrees: "The will that cannot turn aside from the rectitude of not sinning is more free than the will that can."[3] Thomas, too, accepts this view and points out that this inability to sin presupposes both the vision of the absolute good and the grace that proceeds from it, since the creature's will, created as it is from nothing, could not cleave to the good by its own power.[4]

But as to what the blessed can do with this perfect freedom, we learn little either from Augustine's theology, with its ideal of "rest", or from the Scholastic theology, with its ideal of "vision". We only begin to discern the activity of this perfect freedom through a theology of the absolute: here we find the basis for both the infinite freedom of self-revelation and the resultant idea of eternal newness; this in turn is reflected in the creature and its own creaturely freedom.

Let us begin with the creature. The earthly experience it has on the basis of its freedom teaches it that what is most precious is not so much its decision in favor of the good (even if this may have been immensely difficult and meritorious) as its creative activity. (And by creative activity we do not mean merely making some form out of matter but also presenting and surrendering oneself to another free person.) Even the concept "eternal life"

---

[1] *Enchiridion* 105 (PL 40, 281).

[2] *De corr. et gratia* XII, 33 (PL 44, 936).

[3] *De libertate arbitrii* c 1 (Schmitt I, 206, 26f.).

[4] *De ver.* q 24, a 8. Fundamentally this also applies to angels insofar as they have to choose God as their supernatural goal. Ia, q 63, a 1 ad 3.

implies an indispensable creative element; it cannot be reduced to a spectacle in which we enjoy endlessly the vision of the Divinity. It is pointless to speculate on the way in which this ability and responsibility to be creative—which is at the very heart of the gift of freedom that is ours—will unfold in eternal life; yet we can understand Goethe, the old pagan, when he says, for instance, "the conviction that I shall continue to exist comes to me from the concept of activity; for if I engage in activity ceaselessly until the end of my present life, nature is obliged to open up for me another form of existence when the present existence can no longer endure my spirit."[5] Or even, "I must admit that I would not know what to do with eternal bliss if it did not provide me with new tasks and difficulties to surmount. But no doubt there are plenty of them."[6] Of course such sentiments lack the contemplative element, but the ideals of *visio* in the ancient world and in Judaism, of enjoyment (*frui*), of Sabbath rest (from the priestly code right up to Hebrews), are surely too much under the sway of an unconscious epicurism. Paul's repeated assertion that we shall know God as we are known by him, and even that our being known by God will enfold and surpass our knowledge of him (1 Cor 8:3; 13:12; Gal 4:9; 2 Cor 5:11; Phil 3:12), does not mean a reciprocally fixed gaze or a reciprocal exploration, but primarily God's prior, free election of my creaturely freedom to move and unfold in God's infinite space.[7] The fact that finite freedom is always embedded in and surpassed by infinite freedom, unequivocally expressed here, does not put the former at a disadvantage: on the contrary, it speaks of God's prevenient care in preparing the necessary breadth and scope for the creature's freedom (cf. Eph 2:10).

This also implies something fundamental to our argument,

---

[5] To Eckermann, February 4, 1829.

[6] To V. Müller, September 23, 1827. "Let us go on working until we are summoned back to the ether by the world-spirit, whether you or I go first! Then may the eternally living One not refuse us new tasks analogous to those in which we have already proved ourselves! And if in his fatherly kindness he were also to grant us a memory and a sense of the right and the good we here desired and actually did, we would surely get to work all the more energetically with the world's machinery": To Zelter, March 19, 1827.

[7] H. Schlier, *Galaterbrief* 202, n. 5; ref. to Bultmann, *ThWB* I, 709f.

namely, that creaturely freedom is a mystery inseparable from the dignity of the person; it must be preserved in eternal life. That most precious gift that is brought forth from the depths of my self-disclosure and offered to others, and is actually produced by me and out of me, cannot be known in advance, cannot be totally grasped by anyone. The "know-it-all" is the most dreadful spoiler of all real, exciting fun. It is just not right to look at other people's cards; and as for "truth drugs" and machines, they constitute a direct attack on the dignity of the person by violating our precarious earthly freedom. However we try to portray the unimaginable eternal life in the communion of saints, one element of it is constant: we shall be filled with astonished joy, constantly being given new and unexpected gifts through the creative freedom of others; and we for our part shall delight to invent other, new gifts and bestow them in return. And, on the other hand, the fact that I cannot penetrate another person's freedom from outside or from above does not mean that I cannot know or trust him. On earth, of course, there are limits and disappointments in this area because the other person's freedom can always turn aside to the path of deceit; but in eternal life this is not possible: here we can trust limitlessly, without this beautiful trait being corrupted by a superior knowledge. For the word "trust" leaves the field open for "faith" and "hope": in the interpersonal sphere these two are most at home where two people know each other so well that they can take the risk—without fear—of depending on the other.

This obliges us finally to face the daunting problem of how we should understand "seeing" God. Scripture itself poses a strange paradox. We find it even under the Old Covenant, when, on the one hand, it is asserted that no one can see or even hear God and live (Ex 19:21; 33:20; Lev 16:2; Nb 4:20; on hearing: Ex 20:19; Dt 5:24–26), and yet individuals testify in amazement that they actually saw God and are still living (Jacob: Gen 32:30; Moses: Dt 5:24; Gideon: Jg 6:23; Isaiah: Isa 6:5). In the New Covenant it is emphatically insisted that no one has seen God at any time apart from the incarnate Son (Jn 1:18; 6:46; cf. 1 Jn 4:12), that "[God] dwells in unapproachable light, whom no man has ever seen or can see" (1 Tim 6:16)—and yet that we "shall see him as he is" (1 Jn 3:2), "face to face", "then I shall know [him] as fully as I am known" (1 Cor 13:12; cf. Mt 5:8).

In the history of theology we find this paradox reflected, as it were, in the two opposing theorems of Gregory Palamas and Pope Benedict XII. Palamas endeavors to draw a distinction between the divine essence (*ousia*), which is unknowable in itself, and its uncreated energies (*energeiai*): "Illumination and divine, divinizing grace are not God's essence, but his energy."[8] "God is called light, not according to his essence, but according to his energy."[9] Palamas is here basing himself on a long prehistory, beginning with the vehement rejection, by the Cappadocians[10] and John Chrysostom,[11] of the crass rationalism of Eunomius, who said that we know God just as well as he knows himself,[12] a rejection that is continued in the negative theology of Diadochus, Dionysius and Maximus the Confessor.[13] On the other side, at the end of a long tradition (from Origen, via Bernard, to John XXII) that denied that it was possible to see God prior to the resurrection of the flesh at the end of the world, we have the definition of Benedict XII (DS 1000), which asserts that after Christ's ascent to heaven the souls of the righteous (having undergone the necessary purification) "see the divine essence intuitively and face to face so that as far as the object seen is concerned no creature acts as a medium of vision, but the divine essence shows itself to them plainly, clearly and openly" (Neuner-Roos 818–19).

---

[8] *Theophanes* (PG 150, 941C).   [9] *Operum Argumenta* (PG 150, 823).

[10] Cf. especially Basil and Gregory of Nyssa in their writings against Eunomius.

[11] In his sermons on God's incomprehensibility. Five sermons were given in Antioch, 386–387 (crit. edition by Malingrey, Flacilière and Daniélou: *Sur l'Incompréhensibilité de Dieu*, SC 28bis 1970), and there was another series in Constantinople in 386.

[12] "God knows no more of his being than we do; it is no clearer to him than it is to us. All we know of him, he knows equally; all he knows of himself, we can find easily and without any difference in ourselves": Eunomius in: Socrates, *Hist. Eccl.* IV, 7 (PG 67, 474B).

[13] Summary in Vladimir Lossky, *Schau Gottes* (Zurich: EVZ, 1964). The work also shows, however, how full of lacunae is the Greek tradition prior to Gregory Palamas. On the Greek Fathers who deny the *visio facialis*: V. de Broglie, *De fine ultimo humanae vitae* I (Paris: Beauchesne, 1948), 122f.

Since, as we have explained, intimate knowledge can be reconciled with the granting of freedom, it should be fundamentally possible to envisage a reconciliation of views in this matter too. Palamas strongly resists the assertion that he is dividing divinity into two parts; for him the vision of God in his uncreated light (such as the disciples saw on Tabor) is real vision, yet a vision that leaves room for the divine mystery, which can never become an "object". With respect to the teaching of Benedict XII, it cannot (nor does it intend to) conflict with the maxim common to all Scholasticism, namely, that God can never be seen in entirety, even in *visio*. Thomas puts this very clearly: "Anyone who beholds God's essence sees in him that he is infinite and infinitely knowable; but this way of being infinite does not apply to him (the beholder). Thus someone can know with certainty that a proposition can be proved without being able to master the proof himself."[14] If *comprehensio* is taken in a strict sense, "God is comprehended by no one . . . , for since he is infinite, he cannot be enclosed in anything finite in such a way that a finite being would comprehend him to be infinite in the way he himself actually is infinite."[15]

This becomes even more evident once we emerge from abstract reflection on essences and once more address the aspect of freedom. God is the ground [*Ungrund*: "groundless ground"] of all freedom, but while he can be known as such by some other knower (as Thomas says in the first passage above), his proportions can never be grasped, for that same reason. Thomas himself puts it like this: "The will of the willing person cannot be known on the basis of a knowledge of his essence."[16] He must make it known by putting it into speech. It is probably true to say that the theology of "vision" neglected to explain that the *visio* does not obviate the *auditio*. The active, exploratory eye does not rob the passive, receptive ear of its function, particularly as the Son of God remains for all eternity the Word of the Father.[17]

---

[14] S. *Th*. I, 12, 7 ad 3.

[15] S. *Th*. I, 12, 7 ad 1.

[16] C. *Gentes* III, 56, Amplius.

[17] "Therefore in eternal life we shall be more blessed in virtue of hearing than of seeing. For the act of hearing the Eternal Word is in me; the act of seeing goes out from me": Eckhart, sermon 58. Quint, *Deutsche Predigten*, 430–31.

In eternity, therefore, however intimate our loving knowledge of God may be, we shall always be dependent on the Word of God whom we shall receive, ever new, in the Holy Spirit from the Father: in every instance we shall thus come to know something of God's Word that is new and heretofore unknown.

Nor is this all. A man may see God, but he does not thereby grasp God's infinite possibilities. But what of the incomprehensible trinitarian event in virtue of which God is God? Surely he grasps this even less? Is it possible for us to understand the generation of the Word—to understand the Father—if there is no cause beyond the act of generation that would give a "reason" for it? As Eckhart tirelessly repeats, this act has no "why": it is the abyss of a love that cannot be circumscribed by any logic; by comparison, the "Logos" is that-which-is-generated. The origin of the Logos is plain to see: "He who sees me, sees the Father", he sees him in me, for in me he has uttered and revealed himself completely.[18] So we cannot say with Palamas that God's essence remains hidden and inaccessible "behind" his revelations. At least we cannot interpret his words in that sense. Rather, we must hold fast to the paradox that God, precisely in the trinitarian event that he always *is*, manifesting himself and communicating himself totally in the Son and the Spirit, remains ever more mysterious; the trinitarian event that he *is* remains beyond freedom and necessity; it has no "why".[19] In the abstract contemplation of essence (essential energies, *visio essentiae*) this interplay of vision and nonvision does not emerge with due clarity; only when God's trinitarian reality is revealed as event do

---

[18] "In that day you will ask nothing of me" (Jn 16:23). "For they will perceive him clearly. But this perception is the effect of the Holy Spirit. . . . Men will continue to question the Father, on the other hand, because the Father remains veiled in the mystery of his invisibility and only becomes evident to them in the fullness of gifts that he gives in the name of the Son. They do not see the Father himself; it is not as if they could deduce and work out his essence bit by bit, on the basis of his gift. His mystery remains undivided. . . . And yet the revelation of the Father in enduring mystery is also a work of the Holy Spirit": 3 Jo 275–276. Irenaeus's celebrated dictum is appropriate here: "What is invisible in the Son is the Father, and what is visible in the Father is the Son": *Adv. Haer.* IV, 6, 6.

[19] On this whole range of problems, see the author's philosophical work *Wahrheit. Ein Versuch. Erstes Buch: Wahrheit der Welt* (Zurich: Benziger, 1947); the theological continuation is found in his *Theologik*.

we see that the two aspects can be reconciled. So we must allow that both Benedict XII and Gregory Palamas saw an aspect of the truth, albeit at a level beyond the level of their thinking and formulating.[20]

In asking how perfected freedom is exercised in eternal life, we must remember that the three theological virtues remain, albeit transformed, in eternal life. Given God's "event"-character, the freedom of the blessed needs infinite spaces and times in God in order to be forever plumbing his depths. If Gregory of Nyssa is right to understand eternal life as the unity of rest and motion, of having arrived and aspiring farther, we must also say that Irenaeus is right when he assures us that "even in the kingdom that is to come, God will always have something to teach, and man will always have something to learn of him."[21] This view, as has been conclusively demonstrated,[22] can be firmly based on Paul and on a correct reading of 1 Corinthians 13:13: In contrast to all the good things that perish with earthly life —prophecy, speaking in tongues, special insights (*gnosis*)—Paul lists those that remain, introducing them with the adversative *nyni de*, "but now . . .": "But now abide faith, hope and love;

---

[20] Jean Meyendorff has attempted to interpret the theology of Gregory Palamas as an "existential personalism": "His thinking is expressed really clearly when he speaks of God as an acting subject; at such a time he feels closer to the reality than when trying, with greater or less success, to conceptualize his thoughts in philosophical terms" (Meyendorff, "St. Grégoire Palamas et la mystique orthodoxe" in *Maîtres spirituels* [Paris: Seuil, 1959], 131). Palamas writes, "God, with regard to all things, is transcendent, incomprehensible and ineffable; yet out of an overflowing kindness he deigns to make us participators. Invisible, he renders himself visible in his superessential and inalienable might" (*Triades* I, 3, sec. 10, ed. J. Meyendorff [Louvain: Spicileg. Sacr. Lovaniense, 1959], 128).—It remains a mystery how the creature can "see God", and the explanatory theories produced can only stammer as they circle around it. The "uncreated energies" of the Greeks represent only an apparent solution since they belong to God, whereas Thomas' "lumen gloriae creatum . . . non infinitum" (*S. Th.* I, 12, 7c), since it is created, seems not very helpful. The notion was constructed by analogy with the unavoidable *gratia creata* (a concept that remains problematical), facilitating and guaranteeing the presence of *gratia increata* in the soul. Cf. K. Rahner, "Zur scholastischen Begrifflichkeit der ungeschaffenen Gnade" in *Schriften* I, 347–57.

[21] *Adv. Haer.* II, 28,3.

[22] Dom Marc-François Lacan: "Les Trois qui demeurent, 1 Cor 13,13" in *RSR* 46 (1958), 321–43.

and the greatest of these is love." A later theology regarded faith and hope as essentially virtues of the pilgrim state, which would not continue to exist in that form in eternal life (or would exist, at most, reduced to their central core);[23] but to understand Paul we must adopt the horizon of his thought. In Scholasticism it was part of the soul's "dowry" (*dotes*) that hope would vanish in *comprehensio* and faith in *visio*, whereas love would become *fruitio*.[24] Paul, however, thinks in biblical terms. Here everything rests on the Old Testament faith of Abraham, which remains a model for Christians and signifies the total surrender to God; this trust is the ultimate reponse to the love of the Covenant God, which in the New Covenant is the self-giving love of Christ. (The best example here is Galatians 2:20.) The Old Covenant is summed up in Yahweh's fundamental assurance: "I will betroth you to me in faithfulness; and you shall know the Lord" (Hos 2:20). In Old Testament terms, that hope which Paul here, as elsewhere, inserts between faith and love means trusting in, taking refuge in, finding security in God.[25] We hardly need to mention that the third, love, is the essential aspect of both the Old Testament and the Christian attitude to God and Christ; what is central is that the three concepts, on the basis of their biblical origin, are interpenetrating traits of a single basic attitude of the man who has been drawn into the Covenant with God;[26] each trait implies the others.

Of course Paul is acquainted with those modalities of faith and hope that are determined by our pilgrim existence on earth.

---

[23] Hugo a S. Caro, *In 1 Cor.* 13, 10 (Opp. VII, 110d); Albert, *3 Sent.* d. 31, a 7 (Borgnet 28, 586); Bonaventure, *3 Sent.* d 31, a 2, a 1 (Quar. III, 680sq); Thomas, *3 Sent.* de 31, q 1, a 1 qlae 1 + 3; *S. Th.* I–II, q 67, a 3 + 3.—Guillaume of Auxerre sees faith substantially as *illuminatio*; what drops away in heaven is simply its enigmatic side: *Summa Aurea* 3, tr 20 q 1–2 (Regnault, fol. 230d, cf. fol. 253a).

[24] *S. Th.*, Suppl. q 95, a 1 + 2 + 5; *S. Th.* I, 12, 7 ad 1.

[25] Van der Ploeg, "L'Espérance dans l'Ancien Testament" in *Revue biblique*, 1954, 481–507.

[26] This gives the basis (and also indicates the limits) of an attempt such as that of F. Kerstiens: *Die Hoffnungsstruktur des Glaubens* (Mainz, 1969). He says, "Hope does not vanish in the fulfillment. Rather, we become aware of its fundamental structure for the first time: it is an astonished and trusting surrender to God who is ever greater, and to the freedom of his love" (732). Cf. E. Brunner, "Der Glaube als Hoffnung" in *Dogmatik* III (Zurich: Zwingli, 1960), 379–87.

For the present, faith relates to a proclamation that does not yet permit the object of faith to be seen (*dia pistēos*—*dia eidous*; 2 Cor 5:6–8), and hope, too, must above all have patience (*hypomonē*) in this sightless state, which will eventually be transformed into vision (Rom 8:24). At the root of this patience, however, there is the fundamental attitude of unshakable persistence. Scholasticism was right to say that those things that are bound up with the earthly condition will disappear; Benedict XII's definition settled the matter. But there are "three" that "abide" after what is earthly has departed: these are simply aspects of the "one", love, which is the greatest of them since it is the bond of perfect harmony (Col 3:14, cf. Dt 6:4f.).

All this goes to show that existence in God—who will remain for all eternity the "mystery laid bare in holiness" (Goethe)—will be no less full of tension and drama than earthly existence with its obscurities and its freedom of choice. Augustine concludes his *City of God* with four concepts that are meant to epitomize the bliss of heaven: *vacare, videre, amare, laudare*: these concepts must be filled, at the very least, with all the vitality of spontaneous, free, inventive living. Human freedom, which lives and operates entirely within the inspiration pouring forth from the God, who is always eternally free, is not in any way a puppet play, the deterministic result of string-pulling; this is evident from the Christology that speaks of two wills in the incarnate Son. In inspiring us, God gives us freedom, launching us into far-expanded possibilities. Eternal bliss is not like the ceremonial of some oriental court; the scenery in Revelation 4 may seem reminiscent of the latter, but we should note the breathtaking abruptness with which the images of heaven in this book keep changing: we are even presented with battles fought in heaven itself, songs of victory, marriages, cities filled with life day and night, rivers and fruitful trees. It can be objected, of course, that what is portrayed here is a heaven that is very much related to earthly events; indeed, this relationship between heaven and earth (or the world beyond and this world) raises a whole series of questions, and we must now turn to deal with the most important of them.

B. RECIPROCITY

1. Heaven to Earth

In the present work (II, 173ff.; IV, 15ff.; V, I B) we have constantly returned to the topic of the relationship between earth (man's "place") and heaven (God's "place"). This *diastasis* goes right through Scripture, first of all in cosmological guise and then in more and more varied forms through Old and New Testaments. When we come to the last book of the Bible, the *diastasis* is by no means superseded: rather, it is brought to a conclusion, albeit in an interweaving that goes beyond logic. Our analysis of the Book of Revelation (*Theo-Drama* IV, 15–67) showed such reciprocity and interaction that many scenes that seemed to be enacted on earth were also taking place in heaven, while the heavenly events were concerned with earth and exercised influence on it. Mortal men, living in tribulation, at the same time were "present" in heaven in a way of which they were unaware—or perhaps even partly aware (7:1–8, 9–17; 14:1–5); something that produces great lamentation on earth (18:9–19, 21–24) results *without any sense of hiatus* in exultant Alleluias in heaven (18:20; 19:1–4, 6–8), so much so that earth is invited to join in the exultation (19:5). After the great Judgment executed by the Invisible One on his throne, "before whose face heaven and earth fled away, and no place was found for them" (20:11), the Seer beholds "a new heaven and a new earth" (21:1). Again we have the same *diastasis* as at first, but now paradoxically "the holy city, new Jerusalem" does not ascend from earth to a definitive existence in heaven: on the contrary, it comes "down out of heaven from God", thus fulfilling what was foreshadowed in the Pentateuch on Sinai: "Behold, the dwelling of God is with men. He will dwell with them, and they shall be his people, and God himself will be with them" (21:3). Similarly "the Bride, the wife of the Lamb" comes "down out of heaven from God, having the glory of God" (21:9–11). It emerges that this Bride is the city on whose gates the names of the twelve tribes of Israel are inscribed and on whose foundation stones are written "the names of the twelve apostles of the Lamb" (21:12, 14). In

attempting to explain this "descent" it is not sufficient to point
to apocryphal writings that speak of the preexistence, in God,
of realities that are to take place at the end of time: it is clear
that something of this "descending" reality—Bride or city—is
fashioned by what is earthly and historical; and the earthly and
historical are *simultaneously* in heaven. Heaven is clearly the origin of the fundamental missions of salvation history: the tribes of
Israel and the apostles of Jesus; when Jesus chooses his disciples,
he does so—as with everything he does—in the name of the
Father and as commissioned by him (cf. Jn 17:11–12; Lk 10:20).[1]
The final tableau of the Book of Revelation shows heaven and
earth totally interpenetrating, so much so that "God's tabernacle
with men" of 21:3 has given place to the immediate presence of
God: "And I saw no temple in the city, for its temple is the Lord
God the Almighty and the Lamb. And the city has no need of
sun or moon to shine upon it, for the glory of God is its light,
and its lamp is the Lamb" (21:22–23). Since the Lamb at the
center of the Book is both God and man, he definitively embraces heaven and earth and causes them reciprocally to enrich
each other. This he does in virtue of his own union with the
glory of the triune God but also in virtue of his union with the
redeemed world, which is expressed in the images of the city,
the stream of living water, the fruitful trees, the "nations" and
"kings of the earth", and the worshipping "servants of God"
(21:22–22:5).

Thus we see that the reciprocity of heaven and earth, like the
interaction between them set forth in the image of marriage,
begins much earlier than the original *diastasis* would lead us to
expect; it also leads to a much closer interpenetration—without
abolishing the distance between them—than this distance would
seem to permit. The final key to this relationship of interaction
is to be found in Christology as it was summed up by Chalcedon in the terms "unconfused and unseparated" (DS 302). In
all things, of course, God (and that includes his "place") has the
primacy, just as in Christology the Person of the Son has the
primacy over his human "nature".

---

[1] Jesus "renounces . . . having his own disciples in the sense of his own fatherhood. . . . He wants to let every mission issue from his having been sent by the
Father": 4 Jo 398–99.

It follows from this that the world has a teleology, a destination in God; mankind and its history is moving toward that great "harvest" which, in the image of the grain harvest, the catch of fish, or the winepress, is a constant theme in Scripture (Joel 3:13 [RSV]; Is 17:5; 63:1–6; Mt 13:39; 13:47–48; Rev 14:15–16). This indicates that earthly history is unfolding toward a final "day" when the time for free decisions will have run out and the harvest will be brought into the "eternal barns". Such an end, however, taking place within the dimensions of the world, raises a difficult problem: Is there anything corresponding to it in the life of heaven? What is certain is that our earthly existence, though refined and transformed in God's fire, will enter into heaven; the new world will remain *our* world.[2] In heaven, the life we have led on earth will be not only a memory but something like an abiding presence. How is this possible? We must again return to the reciprocity of heaven and earth: everything that is lived in a fragmentary and incomplete way on earth has always had its ultimate ground in heaven. No earthly moment can be fully exhausted (this is the problem in Goethe's *Faust*); whatever eternal content it contains—and our temporal existence cannot bring it forth out of the depths—is "laid up" for us in heaven: in heaven we shall live the full and eternal content of what on earth was present only as a transcendent, unsatisfiable longing. This is at least *one* aspect of heavenly life. In heaven, therefore, our earthly existence—and we have only *one* existence—will be present in an unimaginable and unimaginably true manner.

There is a further, correlative aspect. Our earthly mission—in the ultimately christological sense, under grace—comes from heaven and, insofar as it constitutes our very core as theological persons (*Theo-Drama* III, 203), will not disappear when our earthly life collapses. "The mark that the Spirit stamps into a person is ineradicable. It is unthinkable that a human person, for instance Joan of Arc or little Thérèse, who exercised a certain function in this world . . . , no longer possesses this mission in

[2] H. G. Pöhlmann, *Abriß der Dogmatik* (Gütersloh, 1973): "The new world that God will bring into being is not a super-world that will explode into this world from above, but *this our world* (cf. 2 Pet 3:13), which he will renew and which he once created. God's second work does not annul his first work" (267f.).

heaven. A person's mission and singularity can be expanded but not abolished: the function remains."[3] When Paul says, "it is my eager expectation and hope that I shall not be at all ashamed" (Phil 1:20), his certainty "can only be explained on the basis of his mission. This is more certain than he is, because it comes directly from God. He possesses this certainty now, but he possesses it forever. He is secure in this mission, at home in it, and in it he possesses every Christian certainty."[4]

The problem that arises can be put like this: Can there be something like a "Last Day" for those in heaven, even if it is only a kind of "incident" within their "eternal time"? The answer given is usually Yes, for two reasons. First, when we consider eternity as it accompanies the temporal plane, we unconsciously import a certain temporality into it. Perhaps we do this in order to give the blessed at the "Last Judgment" a moment in which they can become aware of the historical effects of their deeds and omissions. We have already seen, however, that it is inadmissible to speak of a twofold judgment of the same person, even in this reduced sense. The second reason is more serious: Heaven seems to be somehow not yet complete prior to "the death of the last just man". As several Church Fathers say, Christ is not really complete in his Mystical Body until "even the last sinner" (as Origen says of himself) has entered salvation.[5] It may be, however, that there is something anthropomorphic in this, as in the first idea. For "entry" into eternity does not take place at a particular "point in time"; moreover, when the risen Lord opens up fields of action for new missions, which he creates out of the fullness of his own mission, he does so out of his plenary power and not, as certain "theologies of hope" seem to think, out of a sense of incompleteness and in the hope of fulfilling himself in his Mystical Body.

We must try to understand that, even when all history in this

---

[3] 3 Jo 117.

[4] Ph 33-34.

[5] Origen, *Hom. 7 on Leviticus* (Baehrens 374-80); similarly Chrysostom: "Plenitudo Christi Ecclesia. . . . Caput impletur a Corpore. . . . Tunc impletur corpus quando omnes simul fuerimus conjuncti et conglutinati" (*Hom. 3 in Eph.*, PG 62, 26). The idea is already present in Irenaeus' doctrine of recapitulation (*Adv. Haer.* V, 23, 2). Quotations in C. Schütz, *Myst. Sal.* V, 583.

temporal plane has come to an end and passed away, everyone who has lived on earth will possess his earthly existence not only as a memory of what is past but as something that is proper to him, albeit something that has undergone the renunciation of death and the purifying transformation of the fire of God's judgment. Here the failings of his earthly existence will be as evident to himself as to others; they will be "confessed" just as will his virtues. He will be as little ashamed of the former as he will be proud of the latter, for it is by God's grace that he has been redeemed, and the life he leads before God and in the communion of saints is in every respect "to the praise of his glorious grace" (Eph 1:6). So the question that occupied Thérèse of Lisieux, whether the pardoned sinner (the "red rose") or the one who has not sinned (the "white rose") loves God more,[6] remains insoluble, because the grace of Christ's redemption, in its fullness, is visible in both of them. There is no envy in heaven, only gratitude for every greater grace, whoever may have received it.

This means, of course, that the "great" figures whose mission, openly or hiddenly, helped to shape the Church's history will keep their "format" in heaven; after all, it is from heaven that they received their mission in the first place. We need not think it foolish to interpret the "first resurrection" of the "blessed and the saints" in Revelation 20:6 as referring to these "qualitatively superlative" apostles who, as "priests of God and of Christ", help to shape the earthly destiny of the kingdom of God. We can see a kind of proof of this in the unique way in which the Lord of the Church causes his Mother—she who is the most humble and hidden—so frequently and effectively to appear and exer-

---

[6] The author here refers to texts in his book *Two Sisters in the Spirit* (San Francisco: Ignatius Press, 1992), 344ff. The solution Thérèse finds is "that Jesus has forgiven me more than St. Mary Magdalene since He forgave me in advance by preventing me from falling" (*Story of a Soul: The Autobiography of St. Thérèse of Lisieux*, trans. J. Clarke [Washington, D.C.: Institute of Carmelite Studies, 1976], 83). While the white rose possesses "innocence", the red rose has "humility". Furthermore Thérèse is aware that she herself would have been capable of every sin if she had not been preserved by grace. "If I had not been accepted into Carmel, I would have gone into a house of refuge to live unknown and despised among the poor penitents. I would have thought it a great blessing to be regarded as such in the eyes of everyone."

cise her influence on earth. In these appearances (for example, by recommending the Rosary) she directs attention to her own earthly existence, her work, her contemplation, her endurance of suffering and her glorification, in all this showing us the ideal Christian life. The fact that she can point to herself as a work of pure grace (as the model of the Church), allows us to glimpse much of the interior life of heaven.

It is the Eucharist, however, that must reveal the most profound truth about heaven's presence to earth. We would do well to pay attention to Jean Corbon's unusual thesis that the full, eucharistic liturgy (which of course presupposes the Cross of Jesus) begins when Jesus ascends and goes to meet the Father, who has given his all, and when the Spirit is subsequently poured out upon the Church;[7] thus, in *synergy*[8] with the latter —analogously to the Spirit's synergy with Mary in the Incarnation—the Spirit will draw into himself the heavenly perfection of the sacrifice of Jesus. On earth, prior to this fulfilled liturgy, there was only "cult". The Son's return to the Father with his transfigured earthly body, which also pours forth and radiates eucharistically, causes his human nature to acquire trinitarian dimensions. In him "the whole fullness dwells bodily" (Col 1:19; 2:9), in him is manifested all the compassion, the "torn love" of the Father (to whom, through the Son, the liturgy is directed); in him the Spirit goes out into the world in union with the Church, in order to make present the sacrifice of the "Lamb as it were slain" and thus to enable the Church to share—anew each time—in the Pasch of Christ, now that the Lamb's sacrifice has become heavenly and eternal. In this liturgy heaven continues to have its effect on earth, but on the basis that what has been taken up into heaven has realized itself in time, that is, what has been taken up into heaven has been "consummated" (Jn 19:30). Once again we see, this time illustrated by the archetype

---

[7] *Liturgie de source* (Paris: Cerf, 1980), quoted from the German edition: *Liturgie aus dem Urquell* (Einsiedeln: Johannes Verlag, 1981).

[8] "Synergy" expresses an inseparable yet unconfused interaction. Thus it is primarily christological in the sense of Chalcedon; but this first synergy yields a second, which is both its effect and its response, namely, that between the Spirit and the Church. Corbon calls the interpenetration of these two "liturgy": 13f.; 79f.

of all missions, that earthly missions are continued and brought to perfection in heaven; it also shows that the earthly mission always originates in heaven (as the Fourth Gospel most strongly emphasizes in the case of the Son) and, even on earth, has an effect that transcends the earth and reaches up into heaven. Only when the grain of wheat dies can it bring forth much fruit, and it is impossible to say whether it has greater effect in heaven or on earth. Now, at the center of this whole fruitfulness, stands the Body; every spirituality and mysticism that wants to escape from the body will prove to be deeply unchristian. For this is the Body through which the life of the Trinity comes down from heaven and penetrates the earth; this is the Body that, gathering the world into itself through the Holy Spirit, brings this same world to the Father. This is the place for Augustine's great vision of the perfected cosmic "sacrifice" to God of the whole Christ.[9]

2. Earth to Heaven

The reciprocity of earth and heaven is so close that we have already covered this ground in the previous section. The image of the ripening grain and the harvest that is such a constant theme in the parables of Jesus says both things: it says that everything earthly grows toward heaven; and it also says that in this process heaven is not only the future but always the perfecting factor and the present. The more the heavenly dimension governs and penetrates an earthly life in terms of mind, action and self-surrender, the riper this life is for heaven and the less God's refining fire will have to burn away (1 Cor 3:14).

The harvest is always both individual and universal. It is individual, as we saw in the section on judgment and purgatory; and it is universal, since God's will to save embraces the whole of humanity (1 Tim 2:4) and the cosmos: Christ is to reign "until he has put all his enemies under his feet" and subjected the whole kingdom to the Father "so that God may be everything to every one" (1 Cor 15:25, 27-28).

---

[9] *De Civ. Dei* X, 6-7, 20; XVI, 22; XIX, 23; XX, 25-26. On the crucial significance of Jesus' corporeality, cf. the commentary on the Transfiguration on Mt. Tabor: Ka I, 430-46.

This means, first of all, that world history, in its developmental character, is to acquire a place in eternal life. Just as it is futile to speculate on what people's age will be when they are raised—for the answer can only be, "all ages"—it is equally futile to assume that history will go into eternity only in the form it will have at its final (and possibly most grim) stage. Whatever positive elements the world has known, at any of its stages of development, will be worthy to participate in God's eternally new event. Then we shall see that what seemed primitive and undeveloped could have greater latency and potency than what was highly developed; for the latter, by its nature, can spin relatively little out of itself. Jesus' praise of the little child, who is more receptive and docile than the adult, is relevant here. What applies to world history in general can be applied in more concrete form to the history of the Church. "Ranke made the celebrated observation that every period in world history is equally immediate to God; in an even more definite and more tangible sense Church history is immediate, in all its periods, to Christ; all churches acknowledge that their only legitimate meaning and content is to witness to him and make him present."[10] Both world history and Church history are characterized by tensions and battles of ideas ceaselessly springing up again and again, and very often the latter are more than mere power struggles; with regard to such antagonistic points of view, which may well be justified, we can confidently assume that they will be "sublimated" and "eliminated" (in Hegel's twofold sense of the word *aufheben*) in eternal life: they will not be swallowed up in some synthesis that shows them to be obsolete but kept intact in their justified difference and divergence. This refers back to what we said about the "positivity of the other", both in God himself and in all the substances and missions that come from him.

In parabolic language the Book of Revelation expresses the fact that what we regard as a preliminary stage has not, in fact, been superseded. Thus the same heaven in which the Lamb reigns and is adored is filled with Old Testament cultic objects: the Temple of the Lord opens, revealing the "ark of his covenant"

---

[10] H. von Campenhausen, "Weltgeschichte und Gottesgericht" in *Lebendige Wissenschaft* I (1947), 2.

(11:19); the angels are continually coming out of it (14:15, 17; 15:6); as in Isaiah's vision, the Temple is filled with the smoke of God's glory (15:8); it can also be described, however, as the "tent of witness" (15:5). There is also the altar (for example, 6:9), the censer, the trumpets, the winepress of wrath, and so on; and, most important of all, the twelve representatives of the Old Covenant are joined to twelve representatives of the New Covenant in a single, undifferentiated company of the "twenty-four elders"; and, standing on the crystal sea, those (without distinction) who vanquished the Beast sing "the song of Moses, the servant of God, and the song of the Lamb" (15:3). Indeed, as a broad generalization one could say that the whole Book of Revelation portrays the New Covenant in images of the Old, in order to give the latter full fellowship, as it were, in the final consummation.

It is true to say that the New Testament does not see it as its task to make predictions about "the future of the cosmos"[11] because the theological heaven/earth dimension is utterly untouched by all scientific consideration of the world. Nonetheless a change has come about with the bodily Resurrection of Christ, and Christians look toward this change being made effective on a universal scale; indeed, the "whole creation" yearns for it. Thus it is a process of central concern to the gospel. Paul speaks of the "new creation" in purely "realized" terms (Gal 6:15; 2 Cor 5:17);[12] in the magnificent passage about "the eager longing" with which "the creation waits . . . for the revealing of the sons of God" (Rom 8:19, cf. 8:18–25), it is the final glorification of these children of God that is at the center of interest, and not the condition of creation "set free from futility", a futility or transitoriness (*mataiotēs*) to which it was subjected

---

[11] Cf. A. Vögtle, *Das Neue Testament und die Zukunft des Kosmos* (Düsseldorf: Patmos, 1970). Vögtle's book is directed in particular against the "cosmological Christ" of Teilhard de Chardin, and to that extent, in spite of its exegetical scrupulosity, it is somewhat polemical and one-sided, as E. Schweizer noted in a review (in *NZZ*) despite his general approval: the promises of salvation at the end of the world cannot be divorced from the doctrine of creation, since man and his environment are reciprocally interdependent; most importantly, however, "since we cannot speak of God's ultimate lordship without including the worldwide overcoming of pain, hunger, sickness and death".

[12] *Ibid.*, 178.

"not of its own will". All this is entirely natural, considering the whole thrust of Romans. But it does not change the fact that, as a result of its violated condition, the whole created world (at least) has been drawn into the destiny of redeemed man. Most commentators read *ktisis* (in v. 19) as "the whole visible creation outside man, including everything both living and nonliving". The "eager longing" (*apokaradokia*) it experiences is "a tense and anxious waiting" that, since we are talking about the subhuman world, can only be unconscious.[13] This world is "in the pangs of childbirth", doubtlessly a reference to the Jewish idea of the "birth pangs" that precede the advent of the Messiah, with all "the implications for the extra-human creation (the universe, the world of plants and animals) suggested by apocalyptic and rabbinic theology".[14] In verse 22 Paul underscores the universality of the expectation by using the phrase "*pāsa ktisis*", the whole creation, which no doubt includes, as well as the subhuman creation, the whole of extra-biblical humanity; the epistle stresses the solidarity of this yearning by a repeated *syn*: there is both a "groaning with" and a "being in travail with". It is true, of course, that the thrust of the argument is toward the theological center of this universal yearning: "But we too, who have the first fruits of the Spirit, groan . . .", and more profoundly: the Holy Spirit himself groans in our hearts "with inexpressible groanings" (vv. 23, 26); nonetheless one cannot fail to see that the cosmic basis, so powerfully portrayed, is within the ambit of this theological center. All the more, since in the background we have the Jewish concepts of a reconciliation, a pacifying and a liberation that will include a "world that has been subjected, against its will, to futility".

In this perspective, incidentally, the eschatological picture of the world put forward by medieval speculation is a chimera. According to Thomas it is only human bodies and the mineral world that enter the resurrection world, while the world of plants and animals simply falls into oblivion; this is because the latter is subject to the *motus caeli* that has now been brought to a stop—

[13] *Ibid.*, 186.
[14] *Ibid.*, 194.

it was in any case incapable of the vision of God.[15] This cruel
verdict contradicts the Old Testament sense of the solidarity between the living, subhuman cosmos and the world of men (Ps
8; Ps 104; Gen 1, and so on), the prophetic and Jewish ideas of
divine salvation in images of peace among the animals (Is 11:6–
9; 65:25),[16] and it also goes against a deep Christian sense that
Joseph Bernhart has vividly expressed in his work *Heilige und
Tiere* (Saints and animals);[17] finally one can refer (with Wolfram
von den Steinen) to the role of the animals in the biblical heaven
—the lamb, the dove, the living creatures with animal faces before the throne of God—and to their indispensable employment
in Christian art.[18] The Book of Revelation is particularly telling

---

[15] *S. Th.*, Suppl. 91, 5 = 4 *Sent.* d 48, 2, 5; *De pot.* 5, 9; *Comp. Theol.* 170, C.
Gentes IV, 97.

[16] Cf. also the texts in Billerbeck III, 247–55. There are references to God's
pact not only with Noah but with all "birds, cattle and wild animals" (Gen 9:10),
to Yahweh's "covenant with the beasts of the field, the birds of the air and the
creeping things of the ground" (Hos 2:18). There is also the remarkable idea that
at the Last Day the souls of the animals will accuse men for all they have done to
them (*Slavonic Enoch* 58:6), while Ezra bitterly complains to God that he treats the
animals more kindly than man (*Gesicht des Esdras* 62 [cf. 2 Esdras 7], Rießler 354).
On the theme of peace among the animals (cf. Virgil's 4th Eclogue): Wildberger,
"Jesaja 1–12" in *Bibl. Komm.* X/1 (1972) 437. On this theme in Philo and the
Sibyls: P. Volz, *Die Eschatologie der jüdischen Gemeinde im neutestamentlichen Zeitalter*
(Tübingen: Mohr, 1934), 383.

[17] Munich: Jos. Müller-Verlag, 1937; cf. esp. those passages in the introduction
where he describes animals seeking refuge with innocent people and gives illustra-
tions. "Why should we be surprised", says the *Vita Cuthberti*, taking up a cardinal
notion of Augustine and anticipating Francis of Assisi, "that a human being who
is faithful and obedient to the Creator of all beings should find animals obedient
to his own commands and wishes? We forfeit dominion over the creation because
we ourselves no longer take our service of the Creator seriously" (in Bernhart,
25).

[18] *Homo caelestis* I (Berne-Munich: Francke, 1965), chap. 5: "Animantia, Tier
und Mensch", 181–99.—In the Psalms and the Book of Job we find the animals,
too, praising God. In the text to which we have referred, *Docta Ignorantia* III, 8
(Petzelt, Nicolaus von Kues, *Philosophische Schriften* I [Kohlhammer, 1949]), Cusanus argued that all creatures of sense would be drawn into the consummation.
Mechthild von Hackeborn sees Christ in an ornate fur cloak, which means "that
all the hair of men, animals and plants are gleaming in the Most Holy Trinity
through the humanity of Christ" (*Revelationes* IV, 3). Elsewhere she says, "we
should not doubt that irrational creatures stand before God as living persons, . . .

here: not only does it draw the historical "prehistory" of the Christian community into its world of imagery—going so far as to equate the two—it also provides the basis on which man's cosmic prehistory can attain salvation together with him in God's world, which will ultimately achieve wholeness: God's creation, in all its multiplicity, is one.[19]

We can agree with A. Vögtle that we cannot and need not try to imagine what the earth will look like in its final form, when the "earth" comes under the law of heaven. However, the hymn in the Letter to the Colossians (1:15–20), however hard it may be to interpret, tells us that this final form will bear a christological stamp. The question is asked: How can a world that is said to be created *in* Christ as the image of the invisible God, through him and for him, still need to be "reconciled"? "Nowhere is anything said about a discrepancy between the two." "Does not reconciliation necessarily demand the deliberate response of that which allows itself to be reconciled?"—which can hardly be said of the universe as such.[20] But if this Hymn with its ancient way of thought—Christ as the Head of the universe—is given concrete soteriological form by the Church's redactional activity (the "Body" is no longer simply the universe but "the Church", and reconciliation takes effect "through the blood of his Cross"), this is to insert into an originally static, "eternal" world view a dynamic, this-worldly view marked by Cross, Resurrection and the Church. This explains how the cosmic powers ("thrones, dominations, powers, authorities"), which are fundamentally created through and for Christ, are subjected to him through this historical process, thus reconciling "what is in heaven" with "what is on earth". Once a static, cosmic pic-

---

for no creature is invisible to him" (*ibid.*, III, 7). It is said of Gertrude von Helfta ("the Great") that "she had compassion on all creatures, birds and beasts; she regarded them as the work of the Lord's hands and felt pity for them, offering up to the Lord all the suffering of the irrational creation, because of the dignity in which every creature, according to its kind, has been perfected and ennobled in him" (*Legatus* I, 8).

[19] Strangely enough, considering his Platonism, Scotus Erigena argues in favor of animal souls being included in the final salvation: *Div. Nat.* III, 39. Cf. Johannes Huber, *Johannes Scotus Eriugena* (Hildesheim: Olms, 1861), 307–8.

[20] E. Schweizer, *The Letter to the Colossians* (SPCK, 1982), 84.

ture is overlaid by a dynamic, soteriological one, inconsistencies may result in matters of detail. But from the Pauline horizon, in particular, there can be no objection to the universalistic (and hence cosmic) meaning of this decidedly "particular" historical Christ-event. In general the twofold vision of the Colossians hymn corresponds to that of the present book: the trinitarian *diastasis* between God (the Father) and "the image of the invisible God" (Col 1:15, the Son) forms the all-embracing frame: at its center is the historical drama of Cross-Resurrection-Church that is acted out within history, in such a way that "becoming" is already lodged safely in "being"; accordingly no opposition can be set up between the process of "being reconciled" and the state of "always having been reconciled".

C. IN THE TRIUNE LIFE

1. Participation

a. Born of God and Endowed with the Spirit

We have already stressed that, for spiritual creatures, eternal life in God cannot consist merely in "beholding" God. In the first place, God is not an object but a Life that is going on eternally and yet ever new. Secondly, the creature is meant ultimately to live, not over against God, but in him. Finally, Scripture promises us even in this life a participation—albeit hidden under the veil of faith—in the internal life of God: we are to be born in and of God, and we are to possess his Holy Spirit. The Church, too, challenges us to get to know the mysteries of faith better, particularly with regard to their ultimate form,[1] and Leo XIII takes up this admonition of Vatican I when he speaks of the "wondrous union" of the Holy Spirit with the justified soul, saying that the latter differs only "condicione tantum seu statu ab ea . . . qua coelites Deus beando complectitur" (DS 3331). Pius XII refers explicitly to this, expanding it considerably and stressing that, in eternal life, we shall not only see the Divine Persons "with eyes strengthened by supernatural light" but shall be "eternally most intimately associated (*proxime adsistere*) with the processions of the Divine Persons, and so share in the bliss of the Most Holy and Undivided Trinity" (*Mystici Corporis*, DS 3815).

This participation in the internal divine life is an absolute mystery; Paul "proclaims" it: it is "hidden wisdom" that "none of the rulers of this world have known". Moreover it is "what eye has not seen, nor ear heard, nor has it entered into the heart of man", but has been prepared "by God for those who love him": this is the gift of that Spirit "who searches all things, even the depths of God", since he "comes from God". As for Paul's preaching, it is "inspired by the Spirit; thus we express spiritual things in spiritual words". This possession and transmission of the Spirit of God is possible because "we have the

---

[1] "Aliquam Deo dante mysteriorum intelligentiam . . . e mysteriorum ipsorum nexu . . . cum fine hominis ultimo": DS 3016.

Spirit (*nous*)[2] of Christ" (1 Cor 2:7–16). It is important to note, in Paul, that possession of the Spirit always requires man's active collaboration: the Spirit whom the Father has sent into the hearts of believers as the Spirit of his Son does not cry "Abba, Father" without these hearts (Gal 4:6; Rom 8:15); rather, he "bears witness with our spirit [*symmartyrei*] that we are children of God" (Rom 8:16). The astonishing thing is that the Spirit sent to us and implanted in us utters the cry of the Son, thereby showing that we are fellow sons of the eternal Son: "*Since* you are sons, God sent the Spirit of his Son." Our fellow-sonship is asserted to have been planned even before the creation of the world (Eph 1:4–5; Rom 8:29–30; 1 Cor 2:7), and it is effected through the Son's surrender on the Cross; on the basis of this it is actually the Son who lives the life of God in the believer (Gal 2:20; Rom 8:10; Eph 3:14, 17). There could be no stronger insistence on the indwelling of the Son and hence the communication to believers of his filial character. In Paul there is also an unmistakable ecclesial and social element: the Son's indwelling makes believers members of Christ only because the Church, in her totality, is the Body of Christ (Rom 12:5, and so on); the Spirit's indwelling makes them spiritual people only because the community as a whole is God's temple (1 Cor 3:16, and so on).

In John there is a new element: we are explicitly described as being begotten or born of God. This follows from the fact that the Son, in becoming incarnate, was begotten "not of blood nor of the will of the flesh nor of the will of man, but of God" (Jn 1:13; the original singular in this verse should be retained once and for all).[3] In thus referring to the Virgin Birth as constituent of the Son's birth from the Father, the Prologue of St. John is

---

[2] "*Nous* here has the same meaning as *pneuma*": Conzelmann, *1 Kor.* (1969), 87.

[3] J. Galot, "Etre né de Dieu. Jean 1,13" in *Analecta Biblica* 37 (Rome: Biblical Institute, 1967). Particularly important is the indirect witness of the earliest tradition: Ignatius, Justin, the *Epistula Apostolorum*, Irenaeus, Tertullian (11–49, 72f., 77f.); the reasons for the change to the plural (50f., 87–89, Schnackenburg's objection is refuted: n. 250); the connection between verses 13 and 14 (104f.); and, most important of all, the whole context of Johannine theology. If it is to be genuine Christian faith, "la foi . . . doit entrer dans le mystère de la relation qui unit le Christ au Père, afin de permettre de participer à ce mystère. Ce doit donc être une foi en 'celui qui fut engendré de Dieu' " (110).

proclaiming not only the Son's eternal (1:1) and temporal (1:13)
archē but also his *archē* or role as archetype of all subsequent "divine birth" on the part of Christians. This is discussed thoroughly
in the debate with Nicodemus (as "birth from above" *anōthen*,
3:3–8); the Farewell Discourses circle around the indwelling
of Son and Father in the believer (14:23) but also speak of the
indwelling of the Spirit who, from within, will lead believers
"into all truth" (16:13); Jesus' breathing upon the disciples on
Easter evening makes clear this inner transfer and transmission
(20:22). The First Letter of John puts forward the teaching of
divine birth and the immanence of the Divine Persons in the
believer and develops it in many directions. To be begotten (or
born) of God (2:29; 3:9; 4:7; 5:1–4, 18) is the mark of true, that
is, living, faith, which shows itself to be love of God and love of
neighbor. This mark is the preliminary, earthly stage of an ineffable union that is to come: "See what love the Father has given
us"—our divine birth is from the Father, who is the origin of
the entire economy of love—"that we should be called children
of God; and so we are. . . . Beloved, we are God's children now;
it does not yet appear what we shall be" (3:1–2). But what is
to come will in no way replace the grace of being begotten of
God and of being his children; it can only be illuminated by the
truth of this relationship: "But we know that when he appears
we shall be like [*homoios*][4] him" (3:2)—which must refer, not to
God's essence, but to his personal exchange of love. This "being
like" is not only the result of a personal dialogue between God
and man:[5] it is faith and is based on our acceptance of God's
Only-Begotten (Jn 1:12), who in turn is the One given up for
us all by the Father (3:16) and who through his blood (1 Jn 5:6,
8) reconciles us sinners with God (2:2). Those of us who are
believers can only grasp the Son's *processio* from God in his *missio*,
which goes to the utter "end" of love (Jn 13:1). That is why we
too, if we are begotten of God, are called to give our lives for
the brethren (1 Jn 3:16) and to avoid sin (3:9): "We know that
everyone who is begotten of God does not sin but holds fast to

---

[4] Bauer, *WzNT*, 1122; Zurich Bible.

[5] Cf. J. Auer, "Gnade" in *Handbuch theol. Grundbegriffe* I (Munich: Kösel, 1962),
559.

his divine begetting" (5:18).[6] As in Paul, this "holding fast" is
made possible by the indwelling of the Spirit in the one who
believes and loves. His witness is the completion of the trilogy of
the revelation of the Son: the water (Incarnation and baptism),
the blood (Cross and Eucharist) and the Spirit (the Easter gift),
who is the ecclesial Spirit since he is the Spirit of love of the
brethren (as in Paul). "Every one who believes that Jesus is the
Christ [the Crucified] is a child of God, and every one who loves
the parent loves the child" (5:1)—which can refer both to the
Son and to the "children of God" mentioned in the following
verse. This faith that shows itself to be genuine through love
is, as the Spirit testifies (5:11), "eternal life" (5:13), which again
demonstrates the substantial equivalence between the earthly life
of faith and the life in God in the world beyond, where we shall
participate openly and manifestly in the trinitarian relations.

It is insufficient, therefore, to portray the life of grace in terms
of a special "presence" and "indwelling" of the Persons of the
Son and the Spirit (sent by the Father) in the souls of the recipients of grace;[7] the *purpose* of this indwelling is to enable men
to participate in the relations between the Divine Persons; and
relations are precisely what these Persons are, wholly and entirely.

This participation, which is at the core of eternal blessedness,
has been explored in more detail at particular points in the history of theology. Here we concentrate on three of them, going
backward in time. John of the Cross described this participation
as the greatest nearness to God that can be attained on earth,
separated from eternal blessedness by only a "thin veil". Meister Eckhart and those of his school (Tauler, Suso, Ruysbroeck)
put the believer's divine birth, and his trinitarian relationships
that follow from it, at the center of Christian dogmatics. In the
Church Fathers, however (whose texts have been collected and
set in order with great clarity by Hugo Rahner), this theologoumenon has a theological wealth that one finds lacking in
later writers. This wealth is indispensable if we are to set forth
the Christian's participation in the trinitarian relations and in

[6] Fr. Von Balthasar's translation. RSV has: "We know that any one born of
God does not sin, but He who was born of God keeps him."—TRANS.

[7] Cf. (one example among many): Paul Galtier, *De SS. Trinitate in se et in nobis*,
2d ed. (Rome: Gregoriana, 1953), 293–350.

eternal life, unfolding it without any narrowing of focus in the whole breadth of the *communio sanctorum*.

b. Breathing with the Spirit: John of the Cross

John of the Cross seeks, not heaven, not blessedness, but God alone; at all costs he must annihilate the distance between his worthlessness and God's infinite worth. Hence the passionate prayer:

> Ruler, God, my Beloved! If You will continue to remember my sins and so not grant what I implore of You, may Your will be done in this matter also, for I look for nothing higher than Your will. Let it therefore express Your mercy and kindness, for in them You will reveal Yourself. If it be that You are waiting for works on my part, so that on their account You can hear my prayer, then do You give them to me and perfect them Yourself along with the pains You willed to accept. Let it be so! But if You are not waiting for my works, what are You waiting for, most kind Lord? Why do You delay? For if grace and pity—for which I implore You in Your Son—must eventually show themselves, take my penny (*cornadillo*, the smallest coin at that time) since You desire it, and give me this good since it too is what You desire![1]

Only a thin "web" (*tela*, a threefold web) hinders the sweet encounter (*este dulce encuentro*): first, all that is creaturely; next, all natural doing and desiring; and finally the soul's attachment to the body and the senses. The first two webs are already torn apart in the "dark night" and all the renunciations involved in the "ascent of Mount Carmel": "All these obstacles were destroyed . . . by the searing blast of the divine fire . . . so that only one web remains." Since there is only this one obstacle standing in the way of the ultimate encounter, "the soul imagines that it is nearer to that moment when the web of (earthly) existence will be dissolved."[2] In this encounter, however, there is a kind of death that is anticipated in the "whirlwind of love"; the soul

---

[1] *Vida y Obras de San Juan de la Cruz* 2d ed. (Madrid: Bibl. de Autores Cristianos, 1950), 1281 [*The Collected Works of St. John of the Cross*, trans. Kieran Kavanaugh, O.C.D., and Otilio Rodriguez, O.C.D. (Washington, D.C.: Institute of Carmelite Studies, 1979)].

[2] *Llama* I, 29–30.

"feels the power of eternal life", and from this vantage point everything earthly seems as fragile as a spider's web,[3] "so that the soul wishes the web of its life to tear asunder in a trice . . . in the whirlwind of a supernatural encounter of love".[4] But how can we describe an encounter between two parties when ultimately it is a question of union? An attempt is made by using the images of "touching" (*toque*, which comes from the tradition of German mysticism), of branding with a branding iron (*cauterio*), of the wound (*llaga*) that, unlike a bodily wound, can be healed only by being deepened "until the soul at last is one single wound of love . . . and so is healed in love",[5] as one sees in the stigmata of St. Francis.[6] In this experience of love, love is felt to be an "endless ocean", and its "beginning and middle seems to lie in the soul itself". At the same time it is a trinitarian experience: "You granted it to me through the caresses with which You caressed me, that is, through the 'effulgence of Your glory and the image of Your essence', Your only Son. With him, merciful hand of the Father, You have wounded and deeply branded me."[7] The soul that has become wayless[8] can, like something negative, take into itself the positive: the triune life. This is "a kind of foretaste of eternal life, though in this life we do not attain full enjoyment of it, as we shall in glory".[9] In order to portray this experience of transition, the poet-mystic produces a final, most pregnant image: the divine torches or conflagrations (*lampares de fuego*) so inflame the soul that it is simultaneously "*within* their fire", seeming to combust together with the Holy Spirit—and yet, on the other hand, it is the shadow cast by the divine light (but a shadow that is entirely irradiated by this brilliance): "The shadow created on the soul by the torch of God's beauty is itself beauty, corresponding (*al talle y propriedad*) to the primal, divine beauty."[10] Insofar as it is a shadow, the soul is other than God,

---

[3] *Ibid.*, 32, cf. 27.   [4] *Ibid.*, 33–34.

[5] *Llama* II, 7.   [6] *Ibid.*, 9, 13.

[7] *Ibid.*, 16.

[8] "Ajeno to todo modo y manera y libre de todo tomo, de forma y figura y accidentes" (in connection with the Logos, but applicable also to the purified soul): *Ibid.*, 20.

[9] *Ibid.*, 21.   [10] *Llama* III, 14.

God's "other"; but insofar as it is the shadow cast by the light and filled with that light, it is not only a creature made by God but a creature divinized throughout by him. So John can affirm with great daring that "All that is good in us is lent (*prestada*) to us, and God regards it as his own work; God and his work is God."[11] The irradiation of the created powers of the soul by the divine torches, however, which takes place on the very threshold of the transition to eternal life, is a revelation of the triune life, albeit still in shadow: what is present in the soul is "the same wisdom, the same beauty and the same power of God, (but) in shadow, because the soul on earth cannot completely grasp it. Yet this shadow is created according to God's form and nature, thus according to God himself, and so the soul is well able to recognize God's sublimity (*excelencia*), . . . tasting the glory of God in the glory-shadow."[12] As the soul tastes this, God "grants it to live and dwell in the Father, in the Son and in the Holy Spirit".[13]

If the soul acts purely as the loving recipient, it can retain all it receives just as it received it.[14] Its

knowing, which prior to this union grasped things in a natural manner, by the power of its natural light and nourished by its senses, is henceforth in motion and is steered by something higher, by the primal power of the divine and supernatural light. Now, elevated above the senses, it has become divine . . . , and its will, which loved heretofore in a base and mortal way with its natural feelings, is now transformed into the life of divine love, animated by the mighty breath of the Holy Spirit, in whom it already lives the life of love. . . . As a true daughter of God, the soul will move at the prompting of God's Spirit in all things. This is also Paul's teaching: All who are led by the Spirit of God are sons of God (Rom 8:14). . . . Of course, the substance of the soul is not God's substance, and it cannot change itself into him; but since it is enveloped in God, it is God by participation in him."[15]

[11] "Dios y su obra es Dios": "Puntos de Amor" 29 (*Obras*, 1291), the "flame of love", 192.
[12] *Llama* III, 14–15.
[13] *Llama* prol. 2; cf. I, 6, 15; III, 2.
[14] *Llama* III, 34.
[15] *Llama* II, 34.

With all its being, the soul strives so that its answering love will not be left behind by the love of God that addresses it. This becomes possible by the indwelling of the Spirit: "It can only attain this likeness by a total transformation of its will into the will of God. . . . This does not destroy the soul's will: it becomes God's will. Thus it loves God with the will of God, which is its own will; now it loves as much as it is loved, for it loves with the divine will, that is, through the Holy Spirit."[16] So the breathing of the Holy Spirit by Father and Son also becomes a breathing on the part of the soul.

> The Spirit forms and equips the soul so that, in God, it can carry out the same breathing of love that the Father fulfills in the Son and the Son in the Father. This breathing of love is the same Holy Spirit whom they breathe forth to one another in this transformation. For the transformation would not be genuine if the soul were not unveiledly and patently refashioned into the three Persons of the Most Holy Trinity. . . . The soul breathes God in God, and this breathing is the breathing of God himself. . . . It must not be thought impossible for the soul to desire something so sublime, for if God gives it grace to become God-like and united to the Most Holy Trinity, and so become God by participation, why should we not believe that it attains its insight, its knowledge and its love within the Trinity and in participation in the Trinity, just as the latter does itself . . . [albeit through] participation, since God is at work in it?

Passages from John are quoted in order to heighten the credibility of this miracle: Christ has merited for us "the power to become children of God" (Jn 1:12-13); then Jesus prays to the Father, asking him to set us where he, the Son, is (Jn 17:24), "working in us by participation the same work that I (the Son) work by nature, namely, breathing forth the Spirit"; finally there is the Son's prayer that we may be one as he and the Father are one (Jn 17:20-23). Peter says that believers become "partakers of the divine nature" (2 Pet 1:2-4); "for souls this means that they participate in God and collaborate with him in the work of the Holy Trinity."[17]

---

[16] *Cantico* (version A), stanza 37.

[17] *Ibid.*, stanza 39, 3-6.

John of the Cross puts this forward explicitly on the basis of a frontier situation that he has experienced and that is accessible to those who are thoroughly purified; in this frontier situation the condition of eternal blessedness is already discernible. In this his approach is different from those to which we shall now turn. He also shows his independence of them in that his access to active participation in trinitarian process is not fatherly generation nor filial being-generated, but quite straightforwardly the *spiratio* of the Holy Spirit by Father and Son.

c. "The Birth of the Son": Rhenish-Flemish Mysticism

In John of the Cross, the participation of the saints in the breathing of the Spirit had a solid basis in Scripture: the Spirit is given to Christians, not for themselves, as a static, private possession, but for the benefit of the community. The medieval spirituality of the Rhenish-Flemish school, taking as its central spiritual reality the theologoumenon of the birth of the Son from the Father, was no less securely founded on Scripture: to be endowed with grace essentially means being accepted as sons in the eternal Son (Rom 8:15–17). Thus John speaks of our being "born anew from above" from the womb of the Father (Jn 3:3–6); it is through this door that we are enabled to participate in the triune life of God. *Das fließende Licht der Gottheit* [The flowing light of divinity] of Mechthild von Magdeburg[1] provides us with a prelude to this clearly defined spirituality, which is experienced and for-

---

[1] Both God and the soul are portrayed in a dynamic exchange in Mechthild von Magdeburg's *The Flowing Light of Divinity* (Zurich: Benziger, 1956)—the title of this book was given to her by Christ himself, as she says in I Proem. God is an ever-flowing spring (I, 4), a "God who pours forth in his gift" (I, 17). There is a constant interchange of the images of light and water: "The radiance of divinity penetrates it with an incomprehensible light . . . , the Holy Spirit touches it with his torrent" (II, 3). Just as the soul, by its very nature, has "flowed" from God's heart (V, 6), it is rendered so fluid by the constant inflowing of grace from the triune God (II, 26; IV, 12; V, 1; V, 11; VI, 22) that it is incessantly flowing back to God (VI, 16) and "dispersing" itself in God (VI, 1); it "flows and plays" in the Trinity "and drowns like the fish in the sea" (V, 25). The blessed can no longer sin: "They are so saturated with God" (IV, 16), and their drowning is a drinking (IV, 12); for Mechthild this means in practice that "the more insignificant the soul becomes, the more flows into it" (I, 22). The images of "flowing" merge with those of Christ's wounds (thus divinity flows from the dead body when it

mulated in a wholly trinitarian manner. The constantly repeated "flowing" refers not only to the animated, circling unity of life within the Godhead but equally to the overflowing of this life into the world, drawing all who believe and love into this torrent of trinitarian life. Apart, however, from one place where there is mention of the "birth of the Holy Spirit" in the soul, there is as yet no sign of the topic that, soon afterward, in Eckhart, will dominate the entire field with its magnificent monotone— though in Eckhart himself it will remain strangely nuanced. His followers will speak in simpler but paler terms.

Eckhart. It is essential, lest we get lost in Eckhart's paradoxes, to start with a brief discussion of his extreme Neoplatonic ontology, in which he chose to express a genuinely Christian idea.[2]

---

is pierced: V, 24; II, 3) and of the flowing breasts of the Mother of the Lord (I, 22). The result is a "reciprocal irradiation" and "inflowing" on the part of the God and the soul: V, 1; V, 35; "This is the playing of the torrent of love that flows secretly from God into the soul and back to him": VI, 22. This can also be expressed in the image of breathing ("Lord, heavenly Father, between Thee and me there is a ceaseless and incomprehensible breathing": II, 24, cf. IV, 13). This exchange always takes place with the love of the whole Trinity: "From what, O Soul, have you been created, that you should rise so high above all creatures and consort with the Holy Trinity, while yet remaining entirely in yourself?" (I, 22).

Corresponding passages can be found in Gertrude, e.g., when God commands her to be receptive to "the outflowings" of his divinity "just as the air receives the rays of sunlight; thus you will be inwardly penetrated by this ray of union and rendered capable of union with Me" (*Legatus* II, 6). We find the same in Mechthild von Hackeborn: she sees "the Most Blessed Trinity in the form of a flowing wellspring, pouring forth without beginning and containing all things in itself, yet, while flowing out in infinite beauty, remaining in itself . . . watering the universe and causing it to bear fruit" (*Rev.* I, 24). Cf. also her vision of the flowing lamp (II, 21). In the *communio sanctorum* Mary "pours out" her full grace, and even her virginal motherhood, into all the blessed (I, 11); so too the angels pour the "stream of mercy" over the whole world, over purgatory and heaven (II, 26–29).

In all these instances we are being shown, in a single image, that there is an inner participation in the triune life of God that is communicated to the world. As yet there is no mention of us being "born of God".

[2] Our being "born of God" is the subject of an initial discussion in Eckhart's German writings. We cite these mostly according to Quint's small edition (= Q): Meister Eckhart, *Deutsche Predigten und Traktate* (Munich: Hanser, 1955). Where we quote from the larger, Kohlhammer edition, La refers to the Latin works and D to the German.

God is "all being", and "outside God there is nothing but nothingness";[3] "insofar as the creature has being", God can be said to be "super-being".[4] Everything that departs from the absolute indivisibility of being,[5] such as space and time and number,[6] is a "declension from God's unity",[7] the celebrated *regio dissimilitudinis*[8] that has come down to us from Plato and Plotinus. For Eckhart, even before Cusanus, God is the *Non aliud*.[9]

This gives rise to two difficulties. One concerns the inner life of the Trinity: Can a (supernumerical) multiplicity in God be ultimate? Eckhart emphasizes the equality of essence between the Father, his Son and Image, and the Breath of the Spirit "blossoming" from both,[10] but at the same time he strongly stresses the difference between "God" (the triune Creator vis-à-vis his creatures) and "divinity" beneath or above all that is relation in God and all that is anything outside God.[11] The absolute unity of the divine essence can only be imagined as the trinitarian process "flowing back" into the "darkness",[12] "desert"[13] and "stillness" of the "pure, clean Oneness".[14] "The light shineth in darkness, and the darkness comprehended it not": Eckhart is not afraid to apply this verse to the relation between the triune God who is Light and the unilluminable Ground of divinity.[15]

---

[3] Q 251.

[4] Q 195. "Being is his outer court": 197; the "super-divine God": Q 421; La V, 44f.

[5] D III, 531, 517.

[6] D III, 533; Q 325; D III, 545.

[7] La I, 160; "all division is an evil, all multiplicity is an obstacle on the path to God": D I, 476, 529; Q 193, 274, 383, 389.

[8] Cf. V. Lossky, *Théologie négative et connaissance de Dieu chez Maître Eckhart* (Paris: Vrin, 1960), 175ff.

[9] D V, 67 n. 15; La IV, 98.

[10] Q 202, 297, 390.

[11] La I, 439; D I, 464; Q 198, 272: "God and divinity are as remote from one another as heaven and earth."

[12] See n. 15 below.

[13] Q 206, 213; D III, 434, 508, etc.

[14] Q 355.

[15] "It is the hidden darkness of eternal divinity and is, was, and will be always unknown. There God remains unknown in himself, and the light of the eternal Father has shone eternally into this darkness, but the darkness does not comprehend the light": Q 261. Similarly Q 266; this goes beyond the negative theology

For Eckhart, however, in spite of this difference, the trinitarian "welling forth" (*bullitio*),[16] the procession of Son and Spirit from the Father, remains something that comes from the groundless, "reason-less" Love, in which unity and difference are necessarily but incomprehensibly one.

The second difficulty is greater and concerns the created world. The world's entire being comes from God and *is* God; hence creatures, in themselves, are nothing.[17] They exist only insofar as they are constantly receiving themselves from God. Here Eckhart strongly commends Augustine's *adhaerere Deo*, "to cling to God",[18] but since, on the other hand, he is always asserting that the Augustinian (trinitarian) structure of the soul (*memoria-intellectus-voluntas*) unites itself in the "ground of the soul" (also an Augustinian feature) and is dissolved in it,[19] it is impossible for any active *causa secunda* to come into being (and for Thomas this *causa secunda* is the most sublime of God's works). The act of the creature is merely to accept the divine gift of being (this is the *pati Deum*)[20]—not to accept God would be to kill him[21]—and, in the very act of accepting God, to give its entire being back to God: "You are to be from him and for him, not from yourself and for yourself."[22] For Eckhart, therefore, "analogy" does not mean *analogia entis* but the purely creative (?) effulgence of Being, which *as such* endows the creature—which is itself nothing

---

of the tradition of Palamas (cf. the statement that "love . . . wisdom, truth, power and ardor belong to the perimeter of Being, which hovers above them, entirely devoid of nature": Q 377). So Eckhart demands that we "leave God for God's sake" (Q 214) and that we "become free of God" (Q 305) in order to arrive at that place where the Persons "are extruded [intrude] into Being", where "the Persons are grasped in Being's abiding-in-itself": D V, 529.

[16] La II, 21; "The One remains forever, welling up in itself": Q 302.

[17] Q 171, 205 ("all creatures are nothing *in themselves*"), 248 ("they are all a nothing compared with God").

[18] D I, 444; D III, 522–23; 531, 546.

[19] Q 315: "As regards the powers of the soul in Being, they are all one."

[20] Q 307, 416, 430; logically, therefore, Eckhart denies the possibility of a natural knowledge of God: Q 373. It is the Being of God that inheres in the creature and "semper docet continue, monet, movet, inclinat, suggerit, ostendit et suadet quid faciendum": La I, 550–51.

[21] Q 172.

[22] Q 226.

—with a being that is "borrowed" (*ze borge*),[23] not entrusted to it as its own. Thus man's true philosophical and theological act consists in constantly giving back to God what has flowed forth from him.[24] Thus the individual person is relativized: "In God there is neither Henry nor Conrad";[25] the abstract, the universal, has more being and so is nearer to God than the concrete;[26] in truth, therefore, God alone can say "I".[27] The creature's true "I" is in God, in the Idea;[28] but in the Idea, insofar as it is God, all beings are one.[29] This is why Eckhart holds fast to the notion that Christ took upon him, not an individual human nature, but human nature in general.[30]

This determines everything that will follow in the theology of divine birth. Most importantly we have here the doctrine of the image [*Bild*], which is the effulgence of Being: in God, the Son is the image of the Father, and he can have his substantial Being in the identity of the divine essence; by contrast, in the creature —which is the image of God—its being-as-image [*Bildsein*] lies "directly in God" who is both Original [*Urbild*] and Being in the same way that what is mirrored in the mirror belongs to it "directly" on the basis of what thus mirrors itself.[31] Hence the

---

[23] D V, 36.

[24] On this subject, cf. the very illuminating article by J. Koch: "Zur Analogielehre Meister Eckharts", printed in K. Ruh, ed., *Altdeutsche und altniederländische Mystik: Wege der Forschung* XXIII (Darmstadt, 1964) 275–308. Eckhart develops his doctrine of analogy (particularly in *Eccli.* n. 52f.; La II, 280ff.) in a quite deliberate fashion: "Analogata nihil in se habent positive radicatum formae secundum quam analogantur. . . . Omne ens creatum habet a Deo et in Deo, non in se ipso ente creato, esse, vivere, sapere positive et radicaliter" (*ibid.*, n. 53, p. 282). "Edunt (Deum) quia sunt, esuriunt, quia ab alio sunt" (*ibid.*).

[25] D III, 523.

[26] "Humanity in itself is dearer to me than the human being I carry about with me": Q 339.

[27] Q 350.

[28] "When man (still) existed in God's eternal Being, what lived in him was not something other: what lived in him was he himself": Q 305.

[29] "In God the blessed behold only *one* image, and in this image they know all things": Q 429.

[30] D I, 420 (gives parallel references).

[31] Set forth in detail in Q 224–26. "An image takes its being directly and exclusively from the one whose image it is, and it has *one and the same* being as him; it is the same being." Hence the application to the Christian life: "You are to be

necessity for the doctrine of the uncreated "spark" in created man, for only in this innermost realm of the human spirit does the image [*Bild*] of God reside.[32] Initially the Original [*Urbild*] can be nothing other than the Son in God: "We shall know God as we are known (1 Cor 13:12), . . . just as he knows himself in that Copy [*Abbild*] that alone is the image of God and of divinity, . . . insofar as (the latter) is the Father. We shall know him correctly insofar as we resemble *this* image (the Son as Image of the Father), in whom all images have their origin, and . . . are inscribed in the image of the Father."[33] On the other hand, the Son is both "the image itself" and "imageless" or an "image beyond image", since he is God by essence.[34] To that extent, the primal images [*Urbilder*] of creation are more absolute, more noble in God than in creatures: the latter are in God more than they are in themselves.[35]

All these weighty presuppositions lead Eckhart to propose his doctrine of divine birth in a much more radical form than did his patristic models. In order to survey this doctrine we must divide it into five assertions.

1. In a single act God the Father generates his eternal Son and creation; this creation, as we have seen, has its reality more in the Son than in itself. Thus Eckhart comments on Psalm 62:11 [RSV] ("Once God has spoken; twice have I heard this . . ."): "God always spoke only one thing. . . . The prophet, however, says 'I heard two', that is, I heard God and the creature."[36] But

---

from him (God) and for him, not from yourself and for yourself": 226.

[32] "The 'image' of the soul is transferred . . . to this 'spark'": Q 318. Like Thomas, but in the context of his own ontology, Eckhart equates this *scintilla* with the *synderesis*: Q 243; D I, 334; La I, 634 (where n. 2 has refs. to further passages). Since the "spark" clings to the absolute Good, it cannot be extinguished even in the sinner, even in hell. This is why the damned burn in their own self-contradiction. Cf. above, pp. 300–321.

[33] D III, 542.

[34] D III, 537–38, 549.

[35] "My body and my soul are in God more than they are in themselves": Q 201; "Consider a fly in God: it is nobler in God than the highest angel in himself. All things are equal in God, and all are God himself": Q 215. "Res ex primo et in primo modo habent veritatem et sunt vere id quod sunt. . . . Extra vero non habent esse plenum, indivisum et impermixtum": La I, 521; cf. La I, 238.

[36] Q 357.

since the eternal "spark" in the creature has its specific reality in God and is the true image of God, it does not matter whether one says that the Father generates us in his Son—which can be understood in the usual Scholastic way, which is to say, that the Ideas that constitute the world are present in the Logos—or that God generates his Son in us. For "there is no distinction between the only begotten Son and the soul."[37] Moreover, God generates and creates from all eternity and out of time. Time (terminative) only exists within the created world.[38] Eckhart, however, differentiates between the realm of nature and the realm of grace,[39] for it is in the latter that the divine birth effectively asserts itself. Since the world is brought forth along with the generation of the Son, this act, for the Father, has a divine, trinitarian necessity; the Father exhausts himself, consumes himself in this giving birth.[40]

2. This means that the eternal trinitarian process, in which the Son proceeds from the Father in an eternal Now, becomes in man a temporal process in which man is fashioned in and according to the eternal Son. "God performs all his works so that we may be the only begotten Son."[41] "The Father drives and hounds us, so that we will be born in the Son and become the same as what the Son is." This comes about "when all the powers of our soul, which previously were bound and imprisoned, are set free . . . : then the Father causes his Son to be born in us."[42] "The Father gives birth to the Son as the righteous man, and to the righteous

---

[37] Q 205.

[38] Text in G. Théry, "Edition critique des pièces relatives au procès d'Eckhart" in *Archives d'histoire doctrinale et littéraire du MA* I (1926), 194. Cf. Q 206: "God creates the world and all things in a present Now." La I, 190.

[39] Q 226: There is "a natural image of God, which God has impressed in all souls naturally"; but this is only a starting point for our receiving of the image [*Bild*] and being fashioned [*Einbilden*] in the primal Image [*Urbild*] through grace: Q 310–11, 426–27: this birth cannot fully take place in the sinner for "it cannot coexist with the darkness of sin, although it does not take place in the powers (of the soul) but in the being and ground of the soul."

[40] Q 269; "The Father can do nothing but generate, and the Son can do nothing but be born": Q 293; "In this birth all things have flowed forth, and (God) so delights in this birth that he squanders all his power in it": Q 396–97.

[41] Q 213.

[42] Q 269.

man as his Son."[43] If the righteous man is completely in harmony with the will of God, "the Father of heaven gives birth to his only begotten Son in himself (and simultaneously) in me. Why in himself (and simultaneously) in me? Because I am one with him: he *cannot* exclude me."[44] In the whole of creation this kind of birth is only possible within the spiritual soul, for only the soul, "naturally created in the image of God", is capable of being assimilated to the Son: "This image must be adorned and perfected by this birth."[45] As we have said, however, the image is impressed only in the soul's innermost ground (the "spark"): the powers of the soul must (through contemplation) gather in this unity and operate henceforth solely from it.[46]

3. What we have said about the temporal process of the Son's birth in the soul leads on to a third aspect. The Father also gives birth to the Son *through* the soul. Here we recognize themes treated in the patristic period, for example, that Mary and every righteous soul bring God and Christ to birth. If the soul had become entirely purified, "the Father of heaven would give birth to his only begotten Son in my spirit so purely that the latter would give birth to him again."[47] "God thinks it more worthy to be born spiritually in any . . . good soul than to have been born bodily by Mary."[48] "A righteous man is one who is fashioned and refashioned in righteousness. . . . God is born in the righteous man, and the righteous man is born in God; so God is born through every virtue of the righteous man."[49] As often as "the soul is reborn in God in a present Now, . . . so often does it give birth to the only begotten Son".[50]

[43] Q 268.

[44] Q 337.

[45] Q 425.

[46] Q 415–16. "There [in the 'spark'] the birth takes place; there the Son is born": Q 393. The powers gather in the ground of the soul and operate from that center: Eckhart sees in this the superiority of "Martha" over the "Mary" who merely receives: Q 280ff.; he can also praise Elizabeth of Thuringia, who saw the world as a school preparing her for the vision of God: Q 295.

[47] Q 341.

[48] Q 256.

[49] Q 267.

[50] Q 204.

4. If we reapply this third aspect to the second, we find that a fourth emerges: the soul that gives birth to the Son out of itself gives birth to itself in the Son. To illustrate this, we can recall what Paul says: "I must go through the pain of giving birth to you . . . until Christ is formed in you" (Gal 4:19 JB). The "Child" to which the soul is to give birth is the Son, and thereby the soul itself "is made God's Son"; true discipleship, says Eckhart, achieves this: "Thus the Child is born."[51] The third and fourth aspects imply each other: Insofar as we are "refashioned in the Son," the Son "is born in us to that same extent, and we are born in the Son and become *one* Son."[52] This means, in turn, that the Father gives birth to himself in the Son, and this becomes a rebirth of God in God: "God gives birth out of himself and gives birth again into himself."[53] "Out of itself the soul gives birth to God from God and into God; it gives birth to him properly *out of itself*. It does so in order to give birth to God at the point where it is godlike, where it is an image of God (in the 'spark')."[54]

5. The final step is now unavoidable, for Eckhart always pushes affirmations to their extremes. This step, which can be regarded as mere hyperbole, is in fact meant seriously on account of two deficiencies in its foundations. In the first place, it is not based on a genuine *analogia entis*. There is no creaturely *potentia receptionis*, grounded in a genuinely constituted *causa secunda*, which would be active in ("passive") reception. In short, what is missing is the Marian principle. Then there is no genuine distance between, on the one hand, the divine generation or giving birth and, on the other, the possibility that is granted to the creature, by God's grace, to fashion the Son by and in itself and in God. As a result, man's giving birth to the Son by grace is identified with the generation of the Son within the Godhead: the creature thus usurps the place of the Father himself; it becomes the generating primal Ground, *causa sui*. "In my first origin I had no God and was the origin of myself. . . . Then I wanted

---

[51] Q 321.
[52] Q 373.
[53] Q 397.
[54] Q 399.

myself and nothing else; what I wanted was I, and what I was was what I wanted. . . . But when, through a free decision of the will, I went forth and received my created being, then I had a God." "Unborn I have been eternally, am so now and will be eternally. . . . In my birth all things were born, and I was the origin of myself and of all things; had I so wished, neither I nor all things would have been."[55] (Notice the way he plays with the different meanings of "I" and the way he slides from "being God" to "having God".) The grace of "giving new birth to Jesus in God's fatherly heart" becomes, for those thus giving birth, the power to "cooperate in fruitfully giving birth out of the same ground whence the Father gives birth to his eternal Word".[56] "Together with the Father the (created) spirit gives birth to the same only begotten Son and to itself as the same Son; it *is* the same Son."[57] "The Father gives birth to his Son without ceasing, and I say more: He gives birth to me as his Son and as the same Son. And I say more: Not only does he give birth to me as his Son, he gives birth to me *as himself*, and he gives birth to himself as to me, and he gives birth to me as his own being and nature."[58] Here he even jumps over the trinitarian difference between Father and Son, and the grace of creaturely fruitfulness is, without further ado, equated with absolute, divine fruitfulness.[59]

Given this attempt to penetrate the most primal act of generation, it is not surprising that, in the end, the "Ideas" are transplanted into the Father, since the Son and the world have moved so close together.[60] Nor is it surprising that, having explained the trinitarian process,[61] Eckhart looks for some deeper primal

[55] Q 304–5, 308.

[56] Q 160–61.

[57] Q 163.

[58] Q 185.

[59] Only on the basis of the divine unity of natures can one say: "Id ipsum dicenti est dicere active quod est verbo dici passive, id ipsum generatio activa et passiva, pater proles, paternitas filiatio": La I, 519. This cannot be applied to the creaturely world; but Eckhart actually takes the truth specific to the creaturely world and imports it into the world of Ideas within the Godhead.

[60] "In the Father are the prototypes of all creatures": Q 256.

[61] While Eckhart often refers to the Holy Spirit, he does not work out a clear locus for him in his speculation. The Spirit is mostly compared to a "blossoming"

Ground where the multiplicity (albeit a numberless multiplicity) and activity of this process is transcended or undercut. Certainly, there are many places where the Father himself appears as this primal Ground, whither all the outflowings of the Son, of the Spirit and of the world return,[62] as the Father who—it has an almost Arian ring to it—retires back to his primal Ground "in enjoyment of himself, the Father as Father himself in the unity of the One".[63] He is termed the "root of Godhead",[64] as the *fontalitas*.[65] It would be possible on this basis to construct a doctrine of the Trinity in which the divine birth would be given its true value. Unfortunately, however, the whole trinitarian process is clearly undermined in favor of a (Neoplatonic) trend toward absolute unicity,[66] with the result that every multiplicity is regarded as "wretchedness",[67] every "likeness" must be transcended because it is not identity,[68] just as every "encounter" must be transcended because it is a relationship between elements of a duality.[69] In Eckhart's thought, accordingly, it must be feared that the Trinity, though interpreted as Love (as it often is in Eckhart), cannot be the Ground of all things.

What fascinates Eckhart is the transcendent Ground, whereas everything categorial and concrete is a matter of indifference to him, which is to say, leads him to the practice of indifference. This applies even to Christ's Cross, just as it applies to

---

of the Godhead (Q 181, 225, 313), held to be God's love for himself (Q 370–71) and for the creature (Q 344), God's first gift, which includes all the others (Q 392). Eckhart adopts varying views vis-à-vis Peter Lombard's thesis that the *caritas* with which we love God is the Holy Spirit: in Q 204 he does not contradict it, whereas in D III, 521, he rejects it, and in Q 387 he affirms it. His undervaluing of creaturely spontaneity pushes him toward this thesis. There is no reflection on the role that Jesus ascribes to the Spirit in man's birth or rebirth (Jn 3). Cf. on this issue: Yves Congar, "Aimer Dieu et les hommes par l'amour dont Dieu aime?" in *Rev. des Études Augustiniennes* 28 (1982), 86–99.

[62] Q 234: "Being is the Father . . ."; Q 253.

[63] Q 264.   [64] Q 348; 390; D III, 539.

[65] La II, 359.

[66] "There can be no doubt that Meister Eckhart's mysticism is ultimately unitarian, not trinitarian": L. Cognet, *Gottes Geburt in der Seele. Einführung in die deutsche Mystik* (Herder, 1980), 88.

[67] Q 295.   [68] D III, 54; Q 220–21.

[69] D III, 519.

all suffering and pain. "Christ says: 'If anyone will follow me, let him deny himself and take up his cross and follow me.' The meaning of this is: Cast out all your heart's pain so that there is nothing in your heart but constant joy. Then the Child will be born."[70] "The more a man gives up, the easier he finds it to give up things. . . . This is how it was with the apostles: the heavier their pain, the easier they suffered it."[71] Thus God himself has the virtue of indifference when the Son is suffering on the Cross: "When the Son in the Godhead willed to become man, and actually became man, enduring suffering, it affected God's unmoved seclusion as little as if he had never become man."[72] The angels, too, "cannot experience sadness for the sins of men".[73] Naturally there are isolated passages that sound more Christian: "God died so that I should die to the whole world and all created things."[74] Christ "endured his suffering out of love",[75] "God is with me suffering in his pain"; but such statements are provisional, for Eckhart goes on: "If my suffering is in God and God suffers with me, how can such suffering be pain to me? For the suffering loses its pain; my pain is in God, and my pain is God."[76] We must turn to Eckhart's followers, who thought in a more Christian way, for reflection on the link between the Christian's redemption through the Cross and his divine birth.

Tauler. Eckhart, the "amiable" and "noble Master",[1] spoke from the perspective of eternity.[2] Tauler, who owes a great deal to

---

[70] Q 321.   [71] Q 359.
[72] D V, 542.   [73] Q 394.
[74] Q 292.   [75] Q 260.

[76] Q 133. These words are found in the *Book of Divine Consolation,* which was written for Queen Agnes of Hungary, who had to endure great suffering. Josef Sudbrack, in his book *Wege der Gottesmystik* (Einsiedeln: Johannes Verlag, 1980), clearly and unflinchingly shows that Eckhart "dissolves" pain and, indeed, all love between human beings: 116ff.

[1] Tauler is quoted according to the modern German translation and edition of Georg Hofmann: *J. Taulers Predigten,* 2d ed. (Einsiedeln: Johannes Verlag, 1979) (hereafter JT). Hofmann corrects many uncertain passages in the Middle High German edition of F. Vetter (Berlin, 1910). The Eckhart quotations are on pp. 103–4.

[2] JT 103.

him, particularly in his teaching on the Trinity and his anthropology, brings him down to earth and into Christian soteriology. So much so that Tauler himself becomes a "true witness of our Lord", who "came down from heaven and ascended back into heaven and above all the heavens,[3] and so mediates between heaven and earth. Insofar as Tauler is such a witness, this "between" is his proper sphere, namely, "between" the highest union with God and the lowest abandonment by God. According to Aquinas, man is "set between two limits: time and eternity", and Tauler will echo this,[4] but his personal experience is more acute: "Poor man feels as if he hangs *between* two walls, and neither here nor there does he have sufficient room";[5] "thus man hangs in the middle between heaven and earth: with his higher powers he is elevated above himself and all things and dwells in God; while with his lower powers he is humiliated beneath all things in the very ground of humility."[6] This penetrates to Tauler's innermost experience: along his "exceedingly narrow path there are two points *between* which a man must squeeze; one is called 'knowledge' and the other 'ignorance'. He must not tarry at either but pass *between* them in simple faith. Two further points are certainty and uncertainty, and man must proceed *between* them full of sacred hope. There are two more . . . : the peace of the Spirit and the restlessness of nature. A proper calmness should bring man *between* them."[7] Finally he stands *between* two contradictory things: image and the absence of image.[8] This pure "hanging" in faith leads to an ultimate surrender: "We are as little able to say what truth is as what God is. God is truth."[9] Those who are striving toward God "go patiently along the paths where the Lord leads them. . . . They do not say that they have found peace, but nor do they live without peace, for they are pursuing the narrow path *between* peace and restlessness, *between* (arrogant) hope and exaggerated fear, *between* certainty and doubt." On this narrow path, "above all else, they must make sure to keep firmly and resolutely in the footsteps of our dear Lord Jesus Christ."[10]

[3] JT 148.
[4] JT 417.
[5] JT 286.
[6] JT 148.
[7] JT 472f.
[8] JT 474.
[9] JT 594.
[10] JT 603.

It is discipleship of Christ that marks the profound abyss between Tauler and Eckhart. While Tauler can use the same Neoplatonic and Areopagite language of "becoming nothing", of "nothingness" and of "sinking into the Ground", the "desert" and the "emptiness" of God,[11] he speaks from a concrete experience of discipleship in Christ's Passion and of utter humiliation. When someone, in amazement, asks him whether he has not yet got beyond Christ's humanity, he answers, "No. No one can get beyond the example of our Lord Jesus Christ."[12] Even when looking into his own "ground", he does not lose sight of "the image of our Lord's sufferings": with the help of grace, "the suffering and life of our Lord looks inside you, in complete love and simplicity, with one single glance, as if *everything* stood before you."[13] So he warns against empty speculation[14] and points to an entirely different openness: the openness of love in the wounds of Christ.[15] The "life" of Jesus is not forgotten in favor of his "suffering",[16] but it is in the suffering that the whole trinitarian dimensions of the God-man are made manifest; here we see him giving everything back to the Father,[17] here we also see "what great disgrace and manifold pains God, our eternal Father and Lord, has suffered";[18] here, most of all, whither only the Holy Spirit can conduct us,[19] the praying soul must linger. Here he can grasp the full implications of the interplay *between* God and man: we "go forth from the humanity into the divinity and back again".[20]

So it is that, in this ascent and descent, the central paradox in Tauler's spirituality takes place: his participation in incarnate

---

[11] Several times he quotes Proclus and Plato: 201, 338, 407, 414, 459, and often Dionysius. He also refers to Neoplatonic teachers such as Richard, Albert, Dietrich von Freiberg.

[12] JT 106, and also (against free spirits) 401.

[13] JT 327.

[14] JT 112, 175, 200, 230.

[15] "Enter his glorious wounds": 372; "soar up into his holy wounds": 515; 615–16; 122.

[16] JT 309.

[17] JT 94.

[18] JT 75.

[19] JT 501–2.

[20] JT 269.

and suffering love is both "experience" and "non-experience".
On the one hand, this penetrating into the reality of love is a
"prodigious, increasing, inner discernment of God",[21] a "becoming aware",[22] a "feeling in oneself",[23] a "savoring",[24] in which
one "experiences and tastes it as it wells up from the source like
a spring".[25] Ultimately one attains to a "genuine foretaste of
eternal life",[26] has "a glimpse of eternity",[27] a "foretaste of the
hidden nuptial delight",[28] and, together with the Lord ascending
to heaven, experiences that "our commonwealth is in heaven."[29]
On the other hand, the experience of the Son who descends from
heaven consists precisely in *non*-experience, so that our sharing
in the eternal feast is "necessarily" a sharing in an "unfelt feast"[30]
that, while it is "hiddenly and secretly present",[31] is nonetheless
beyond "sense and illumination"[32] since it is a resting in the unknowable and ineffable God. Hence his stern, almost sarcastic
remarks on all desire for experience: "Our sisters . . . would so
like to feel and taste"; but "we do not follow God by experiencing a sense of well-being but by taking up our Cross."[33] If
we cling to "pleasant feelings like the bear to his honey, . . . we
shall not attain spiritual poverty".[34]

For Tauler, the crucial experience is that of *non*-experience, of
desolatio, forsakenness, in which he approaches Jesus' experience
of being abandoned on the Cross. There *is* "consolation",[35] but
we should "use" it (*uti*), and "not enjoy it" (*frui*).[36] We can almost say that it is given to us so that, subsequently, we shall feel
our loss even more deeply: "Great coldness in all grace", "ex-
tinguishing", "night", "dryness", "darkness", "abandonment",[37]
"an unbearable oppression, dried up through grief".[38] God no

---

[21] JT 39. [22] JT 172, 179.
[23] JT 14. [24] JT 227.
[25] JT 90.
[26] JT 82, cf. 83: A "feast of eternal bliss", a "true feast of eternal life".
[27] JT 325. [28] JT 601.
[29] JT 138. [30] JT 84.
[31] JT 88. [32] JT 419.
[33] JT 455. [34] JT 572.
[35] Depicted in 90, 135, 163 (the building of the three tabernacles on Tabor), JT 170 (God's stream overflows).
[36] JT 165. [37] JT 91, 321.
[38] JT 285.

longer listens;[39] "Jesus has gone away."[40] This is necessary; it is a "testing" of man's faithfulness[41] whereby he acquires practice[42] in the highest art, namely, "to be without God, to feel the lack of him: this surpasses all."[43] It is also what is most fruitful.[44] In many cases this absence of God can last a lifetime.[45] In such a case, love burns in its own privation.[46] So we become acquainted with the lowest place, which is also, however, the most useful one: "Nowhere does heaven have such a fruitful effect as in the lowlands. So God's work, too, is never more fruitful and divine than in man at his lowest." God's "lightning" can shine into man's ground in such a way "that all pain seems too little to him".[47] Now, therefore, an entirely new meaning is given to the *pati Deum* that we encountered in the Areopagite and in Eckhart: If we "inwardly suffer through God", we are shown "what an unutterable good is hidden in suffering".[48] Tauler understands this descent into suffering in christological terms, which means that it is an approach to the divine mind of Christ. Thus he can say, "the more one descends, the more one ascends";[49] the "exaltation comes from the humiliation."[50] It is from the Cross that the "darkness of God" (his "superabundant brightness"), which we find in the Pseudo-Dionysius and also in Tauler,[51] acquires its concrete truth.[52]

It is perhaps true that, in Tauler, Eckhart's theses are not

[39] JT 64, 331.

[40] What we find in the Farewell Discourses ("It is good for you that I go away"), which Eckhart likes to quote in support of clearing out sense images from the soul's ground, is given an entirely different meaning in Tauler: JT 108, 166, 286, 465.

[41] JT 481.

[42] "You must let God search for you; you must make yourself small and annihilate yourself in order to learn humility in all situations of life. Thus you will be much thrown about and battered in suffering, so learning meekness": JT 267.

[43] JT 184.   [44] JT 194.
[45] JT 246, cf. 369.   [46] JT 273.
[47] JT 403, 405.   [48] JT 552.
[49] JT 421.   [50] JT 509.
[51] JT 623. God as "Nothing": JT 419, 500 passim.

[52] On the Cross Jesus is "completely forsaken. . . . No mind can grasp what lies hidden in this real and true forsakenness": JT 183. "God sends the most terrible darkness and the most profound misery of utter forsakenness to those who have the greatest thirst for suffering": JT 437.

completely at one with his Christ-centered spirituality. He, too, speaks of clearing out all images and forms,[53] aiming at that "emptying" the "I" that clings to itself,[54] that total poverty of spirit[55] that is like a shipwreck.[56] For him, too, the *imago Trinitatis* resides not so much in the higher powers of the soul (as in Augustine) as in the *mens*, in "what Augustine calls *abditum mentis*",[57] in the "ground";[58] "the precious image of the Holy Trinity lies in a delightful dell".[59] Man consists of "three men, the sensual man, the man of the higher powers, and the ground";[60] and as for this "ground", its entrance is largely "overgrown"[61] and needs to be opened up by a "dying" on the part of the outward man;[62] if this is to take place, even the higher powers of the spirit must transcend themselves, "submerging" into the wayless, unknowable unity of the Godhead.[63] On the other hand, there is no talk of a divine unity lying beyond the Trinity. As for the "ground" or "spark",[64] Tauler, like Eckhart, sees it (and the powers of the soul gathered into it) destined to "flow back"[65] into the primal Ground of God, where it will find its true fruitfulness, more than through activity in the world: "just like the water which flows from its source and returns again thither, and like the sea which flows forth and yet is always hastening back to its origin"[66]. As in Eckhart, the "spark" in man finds its way back to God's idea of it. The only difference is that Tauler does not say that the spark is "uncreated": it is uncreated only insofar as it is

---

[53] JT 41, 101, 274, 513, 528, 601, 608.

[54] JT 171, 178.

[55] JT 303.

[56] JT 314–15, 320.

[57] JT 538.

[58] JT 458.

[59] "It is for this reason that St. Augustine says that the soul has within it a hidden abyss": JT 167, 155. Cf. M. Schmaus, *Die psycholog. Trinitätslehre des hl. Augustinus* (Münster, 1927), 309.

[60] JT 28, 80, 409, 457, 486.

[61] JT 388, 618.

[62] JT 142, 229.

[63] JT 51, 80–81, 101, 147f., 171, 197, 228, 277, 309, 402, 436, 472.

[64] JT 252, 264, 407, 411.

[65] JT 15–16, 547, 551; 137.

[66] JT 47.

an "idea" in God: "This spark does not rest until it once again reaches the (divine) Ground from whence it came and where it was in its uncreated state."[67] The spark "recognizes itself as God in God, and nonetheless it is created".[68] Uncreatedness belongs only to the "idea" in God.[69]

We see that Tauler's language is largely that of Eckhart, but since the center of gravity is shifted to Christology, his vocabulary acquires a changed meaning. This becomes very clear if we examine more closely the terms associated with "divine birth". Eckhart's identification of the generation of the Son with the creation of the world has disappeared, as has all talk of an unmediated giving birth to the Son *together with* the Father, apart —significantly—from those few places where he is speaking of the Mother of God. Like the Fathers, Tauler is acquainted with a threefold birth of the Son (as in the three Masses of Christmas): there is an eternal birth in God, a temporal birth of Mary, and a spiritual birth in the Christian.[70] "God's birth in us" should be blessed by the Son's birth of Mary and "saturated" with her graces.[71] She is urged to take us under her guardianship and "give birth to us again [so that we may return] to our Origin".[72] For the "birth performed by the heavenly Father is also hers: *she* too, has born this birth." We, however, allow ourselves to be prevented by worldly trivialities—"by alien births"—from reproducing in us this birth "through which God wished to be (and should have been) produced in you".[73] In saying that we can be born again (back) into our Origin, Tauler shows that he really means to speak of a reciprocal birth: "They [purified human beings] are born in God and he in them."[74] It is clear, however, that the picture has faded somewhat, for here this reciprocity is based no longer (as in Eckhart) on an identification of God's birth and the birth of the soul, but arises from the Son's trinitarian disposition: "The Father's power summons man to himself through his only begotten Son, and just as the Son is born of the Father and flows back (!) to the Father, so man is born in the Son by the Father and flows back, together with

[67] JT 407.
[69] JT 458, 481–82, 486, 525, 539.
[71] JT 445.
[73] JT 424–25.

[68] JT 411, cf. 337.
[70] JT 13f.
[72] JT 429.
[74] JT 241.

the Son, to the Father."[75] This toned-down language (which no longer aims exactly at the birth of the eternal Son in the soul) permits a broader use of the image: on the one hand, one can say in general terms that God is born in man,[76] or that the Trinity is born in the soul's "ground",[77] or that grace is born there.[78] On the other hand, the birth is seen in a christological context: if man is to attain his perfection, "the Lord must be born, must die and rise again in him."[79] More precisely, this means that descending and dying with Christ—which Tauler portrays with such insistence—is the precondition if Christ is genuinely to be born (and if God is to be born in him): "Through the Cross we are to be renewed in the sublime dignity we possessed in eternity; through the love of this Cross, we shall be born again into eternity."[80] The conclusion of this sermon bids us so to cling to the dear Cross that is Christ "that he is continually being born anew in us".[81] When God sends us trouble, "he does so to bring about a new birth in us." The person who "endures this darkness and tribulation to the end" will take "the shortest path to real divine birth".[82] Tauler says that a genuine mortal fear, which is both fear of dying and fear of its pangs, precedes this birth. Man goes through "an unbearable anguish. . . . You are loth to die." But Paul says, "You are to proclaim the Lord's death until he comes. This proclamation does not take place by words or thoughts, but by dying, . . . in the power of his death. . . . You must know that the true birth will not take place in you unless it is preceded by this anguish."[83] "The measure of self-emptying is the measure of divinization."[84] Christ's Cross is to be "in you and outside you, before and behind you"; the whole burden of the Old Covenant must weigh down upon you so that "Christ can truly be born in you in the New Covenant." You should entrust yourself to God in all sufferings, and then "God will surely come, he will be born. When? That you must leave to him."[85]

[75] JT 202.
[77] JT 200.
[79] JT 220.
[81] JT 451.
[83] JT 221–22.
[85] JT 384–85.

[76] JT 330, 425, 445.
[78] JT 327.
[80] JT 446.
[82] JT 310–11.
[84] JT 220.

The center of gravity in Tauler is our sharing in the humiliation of Christ. This facilitates two experiences: we experience the "ineffable difference" between God and man, but this "inner experience of incongruity" causes their "congruity to appear all the more apt and inward".[86] The distance of humility is the true way of coming close to God. Having discovered this law, Tauler is the master of "the discernment of spirits".[87] But the same law leads him one further step lower. As man, through humility, is led into the highest union with God, he is given a certain understanding of the Trinity. He is given "a fairer, a more delicate discernment than others" and has an intimation of "how Father, Son and Holy Spirit are *one* God. . . . No one better grasps the true distinction than those who attain the unity."[88]

Suso. Now we come to the astonishing writings of Heinrich Suso.[1] Again, we are only considering them from the aspect of "divine birth", and here there is a clear hiatus in his work. In the *Little Book of Truth* (c. 1326), his skillful apologia for his beloved teacher Eckhart, he takes up the topics proposed by Eckhart and cautiously corrects them; whereas in his personal work, the *Little Book of Eternal Wisdom*, which appeared shortly afterward, the idea of the "birth" disappears almost completely,[2] giving place to the theme of discipleship of Christ in his Passion—since Christ is the eternal Wisdom.[3]

[86] JT 197.

[87] JT 365.

[88] JT 80.

[1] Suso's German works are quoted according to the edition by Karl Bihlmeyer (1907, repr. 1961) = KB; *Horologium Sapientiae*, crit. edition by Pius Künzle (Fribourg, Switzerland: Universitätsverlag, 1977) = Ho.

[2] At the end of the autobiographical part, there are eight chapters on the Trinity in which Eckhart's basic concepts return, carefully refined. These chapters cannot be precisely dated since Elsbeth Stagel is evidently responsible for the arrangement of material.

[3] In spite of the fact that, in the *Horologium*, Suso follows the Vulgate and accordingly quotes Wisdom (Sir 24:26): "Transite ad me, omnes qui concupiscitis me, et a generationibus meis implemini" (Ho 419, 3), which he renders [in German] literally as: "Come to me, all you who desire me, and you will be filled with my births" (KB 223, 6). Similarly Jeremiah 53:8: "Generationem ejus quis enarrabit?"—to which he connects Sir 24:5: "Ego ex ore Altissimi prodivi . . ." (H 421, 12), rendering it thus: "I am high-born, of noble family, I am the bodily

Suso had to protect Eckhart against the free spirits who wanted to take him over.[4] He adopts his vocabulary and topics but avoids dangerously overstepping the limits. He takes the risk of drawing the distinction between "God" and "Godhead/divinity", but for him Godhead, the wayless Essence into which "the threeness of Persons sinks", is always "the divine nature of the Father, which at that very moment is pregnant with the fruitfulness" of the divine processions.[5] He can say that God's "unfathomable Being"[6] is "nameless" and that, compared with all existing things, it is "non-being" and "nothing",[7] but (with Eckhart) he emphasizes that from this primal Ground comes everything that is preexistent in it in the form of an idea ("exemplar").[8] As to the question of whether created things are nobler in the idea or nobler in themselves, Suso answers in the same terms as Thomas Aquinas.[9] He seldom speaks of the generation of the Son and the creation of the world as a single act.[10] On the contrary, the notion that man is "born of God" sticks close to John 1:13a, just as the concept of his "rebirth" (of Spirit and water) is closely related to John 3:3–5.[11] Here Suso regards the activity of man, thus renewed, as the one essential work, corresponding to the unique and eternal birth of the Son from the Father.

Eckhart's extreme doctrine of analogy is quietly dropped; Christology is crucial here, for (since Maximus the Confessor) it takes serious account of two wills, the "two *contraria*".[12] "The soul always remains a creature."[13] What happens, then, to Eckhart's "breakthrough", his "submerging"[14] into union with

---

Word from the Father's heart" (KB 224, 11f.). In neither case, however, is the theme developed.

[4] KB 158f.

[5] KB 330, 21; 180, 10.

[6] God as pure Being, unmixed with otherness: KB 176–77.

[7] KB 328–29; 342, 7.

[8] KB 329–31.

[9] KB 331–32.

[10] KB 179, 27–28.

[11] KB 340, 348.

[12] KB 341, 2, 10.

[13] KB 345, 20.

[14] KB 332, 26; 94, 11.

God[15] in "self-dissolution"? The answer proceeds via Christology: while Eckhart had spoken of the Son's *assumptio* of universal human nature, Suso interprets this in the sense of the Church Fathers. Thus the Incarnation of God has ennobled all those who share human nature; this in itself surpasses that "union with God which is attained in the hearts of the blessed",[16] and so man's return to God must take place through union with Christ, the "Head of Christendom". We must therefore become sons "in Christ" (Rom 8:29) "in all patience and self-abnegation",[17] which now simply means following Christ. If we are to follow the Son, who partakes of two natures, we must therefore "hover between heaven and earth" on the Cross, in accordance with the "way in which the Son took human nature".[18] This discipleship presupposes a genuine human subject.[19] As to the insistent and oft-repeated question about man's personally distinct being, even when enjoying the highest union with God, it is answered in the affirmative.[20] Similarly a clear distinction is maintained between Christ, the natural Son and image of the Father, and us, who are only "fashioned *after* the image of the Trinity".[21] Here we have reached the final question. Suso agrees with Eckhart about the ecstatic union with the Divine Unity, a union in which all distinction is forgotten and superseded.[22] This ecstasy does not last, however, and once the soul reflects upon its condition, it becomes aware in a new way of its distinctness from God: "In knowing and grasping that it knows, beholds and grasps Nothing

[15] KB 349–50.

[16] KB 334, 4–5.

[17] KB 334, 20–21.

[18] KB 338, 19f.; 139, 5.

[19] Cf. the observations on the five kinds of "self" (= being a subject): the first four are generic; the fifth "belongs specifically to him as a personal human being, both according to his essential personal dignity and according to his accidental qualities": KB 335, 2–3.

[20] KB 350, 21ff.

[21] KB 355, 7–12.

[22] When the soul beholds God purely, it takes all its being and essence and draws all that it is—insofar as it is blessed—"from the Ground of this Nothing (i.e., God), and after this beholding it can speak neither of knowledge nor of love, nor of anything at all. Be completely calm and alone in the Nothing and know nothing of essences, or of whether God is or is not" KB 346, 9–14.

(that is, God), it slips out of this highest state and, according to natural order, falls back upon itself."²³ Is this a "sinking" into the *regio dissimilitudinis*, the evil bi-polarity, of which Eckhart speaks? No. Suso takes a different path. In response to the question, "How can man be both a creature and not a creature?" he replies, "God is both threefold and one."²⁴ Thus the question, "Is there then no otherness?" is seen to be obsolete: man can be both a creature and united with God at the same time.²⁵ So the disciple can give the decisive answer to the pantheistic "free spirit": God's eternal super-essence "is itself *already characterized by distinction*, and from this fruitful distinction comes all proper distinction between things." Again, in response to the question of whether the creaturely distinction is not dissolved through union with the Ground, he replies, "No. . . . For it is not only in the Ground; in itself it is something creaturely apart from this Ground. It remains what it is, and it must be grasped as such."²⁶ Ruysbroeck will give the final clarification here.

Suso's development, like that of Tauler, is marked by his embrace of Christology: what Eckhart speaks of as the "flowing back" into God is only possible through a concrete following of the Cross of Christ. The interplay of question and answer at the beginning of part 2 of the *Little Book of Wisdom* sounds almost humorous. The soul says, "Lord, I rejoiced to hear of the union of naked reason with the Holy Trinity, and how, in the genuine reflection of the generation of the Word and the rebirth of its own spirit, it was stripped of its self and of all that might hinder it." The Eternal Wisdom replies, "The man who is as yet on the lowest rung in life should not enquire about the highest matters of doctrine. I will teach you what is necessary for you", namely, to die, to live accordingly, to receive Jesus (in the sacrament), and to praise God.²⁷ According to Suso, this "lowest" teaching, given by Eternal Wisdom, is in reality the only way in which the "highest" things for which the soul is striving can come to pass. The real, bodily and intellectual death is the concrete path of the

²³ KB 346, 14–16.
²⁴ KB 345, 11.
²⁵ KB 344, 29–345, 2.
²⁶ KB 353, 25–27; 353, 34–354, 1.
²⁷ KB 279, 4–16.

Eckhartian "unbecoming"; the real Christian life will consist in discipleship of the Lord who suffers for us.[28] The primary, exemplary union with God on earth is union with the Lord's eucharistic Body, with his incomprehensible humiliation. As the servant exclaims, "How can I follow the highest if I cannot grasp the lowest?"[29] In sum, the proper, calm resignation that is the aim of all Rhenish mysticism is not an end in itself; it is for the praise of God. Even the desire for suffering must be subordinate to, and integrated in, the wish to praise God: "Lord, I desire no suffering from you, . . . I submit myself completely, according to the yearning of my heart, to your eternal praise, since, left to myself, I could never properly yield to you."[30]

These four doctrinal points form the core teaching concerning God and man according to Eckhart and Suso. Since the soul is "a copy of the Trinity and an image of eternity", of God who is without end and without becoming, "you too", says God to the soul, "are unfathomable in your yearning."[31] This unfathomable yearning is like an open wound that cannot be healed by anything worldly; the healing that comes to the soul on earth does not come simply through a divine presence—"there is, in time, no real foretaste of the heavenly indwelling" apart from the praise of God[32]—but in the open wound of the divine love.[33] Whereas for Eckhart the most profound image of the union of God and man is the "divine birth", for Suso the central picture is the "spiritual marriage with Eternal Wisdom" in the wounds of the Cross: one heart open to another. In a great prayer Suso praises God in "the pains of all wounds, the groans of all the sick, the sighing of all who mourn, the tears of all who weep, the insults borne by all the oppressed"; this is possible because God the Son is "the sole Sufferer": thus all who suffer should form a circle around him, thirstily drinking from him who is the "overflowing wellspring of grace".[34]

---

[28] Cf. pt. 3 of the *Little Book of Wisdom*.
[29] KB 294, 2–3.
[30] KB 307, 1–4.
[31] KB 237, 8–10.
[32] KB 313, 7–8.
[33] KB 320, 16–26.
[34] KB 90–92.

Ruysbroeck.[1] The most important material foci of Ruysbroeck's thought are these: the Augustinian *imago trinitatis*, located in the highest part of the soul;[2] the "spark" of the soul (natural and supernatural);[3] the eternal procession of the "ideas" of creatures in the Son;[4] the not infrequent distinction between "God" (as trinitarian fecundity) and "Godhead" (as divine ground of the absolute unity),[5] parallel to the distinction between a psychologico-mystical "encounter" of man with God and a union of love with God that is above knowledge. Outwardly there is no substantial difference between Ruysbroeck and the Rhineland mystics in this material, but these common themes cannot obscure the fundamental difference of his thought and experience. First of all, there is a total change of perspective that is very significant for our current topic: Ruysbroeck starts with the mystery of the Trinity; it is on this basis that he sets forth his consideration of the creature, following it through in a whole host of subtle detail that, unfortunately, we cannot go into here.[6]

This, it seems to us, is the core of Ruysbroeck's thought: God the Father, the fecund ground of divinity, utters a single Word in which he expresses himself and all things.[7] He generates this Word out of himself; in the One thus generated he sees and contemplates the Son's personal Otherness, and *in him* he sees and

---

[1] The author quotes according to the German editions of Huebner (Insel, 1924) = Hu, and Verkade, 4 vols., (Mainz: Grünewald, no date) = V, and the French complete edition, 6 vols., (Brussels and Paris: Vromant, 1920–1930) = Fr. He also refers to the German edition of *The Sparkling Stone: Vom blinkenden Stein*, ed. E. Schacht, (Graz: Styria, 1937), and a *Selection*, ed. Kuckhoff (Munich: Kösel, 1938). [For English translations, see John of Ruysbroeck: *The Adornment of the Spiritual Marriage*; *The Sparkling Stone*; *The Book of Supreme Truth*, trans. C. A. Wynschenk (London: Dent, 1916) = Dt; also *The Seven Steps of the Ladder of Spiritual Love*, trans. F. S. Taylor (London: Dacre Press, 1944) = Ta.]

[2] Hu 136, Fr I, 89.

[3] Hu 63, 217, 339; Fr I, 89.

[4] Hu 387.

[5] Hu 143; Fr I, 12.

[6] The celebrated Plotinus scholar Paul Henry has done this in some detail in his articles: "La Mystique trinitaire du bienheureux Jean Ruusbroec" (in part continuing the research of Albert Ampe): *RSR* (1951/52) 335–68; (1953) 51–75. B. Fraling, *Der Mensch vor dem Geheimnis Gottes: Jan van Roosbroec* (Würzburg: Echter, 1967), 44–58.

[7] Hu 383.

contemplates the creaturely otherness of the world of creation. Thus he contemplates otherness primarily within the identity of his own Godhead; or rather, he contemplates the non-identity of the created world within the Son who, as God, is identical with him. Thanks to the "eternal birth (of the Son) all creatures came forth eternally prior to being created in time. God saw them in their distinctness in himself and recognized them as living causes existing in otherness from himself. Yet they are not other in every respect, for everything that is in God is God." On the one hand, our created being depends on the idea of us that is in God; "according to its essential being it is one with this idea, and so God wishes us to go forth out of ourselves in the supernatural light (of grace); we should strive in a supernatural way to attain this image which is our real life and, together with him, possess it; our destiny is both to work (within the trinitarian fecundity) and to enjoy (within the oneness of the Persons in the Ground of Godhead) in eternal blessedness." On the other hand, "thanks to the Son and according to an eternal decision, there is an eternal outflowing and an otherness that manifests distinction", whereby God recognizes and reflects his likeness in his eternal image; this image is "the Wisdom of God, in which God beholds himself and all things in a single Now, without before and after."[8]

It is characteristic of Ruysbroeck that the distinction he draws between "God" and "Godhead" is purely conceptual. In practice this means that he understands the Father as the primal Ground of the divine unity,[9] a Ground "beyond which" we cannot get. Equally he regards the Holy Spirit—the love between Father and Son[10]—as the perfection of this same unity. Thus there cannot and must not be any distinction between unity (of essence) and union (of Persons). The Father, the unilluminable primal Ground, can be referred to as "dark and formless", yet at the same time this Ground is utterly light, manifest to itself, in the reciprocal love that is effulgent in the Son.[11] This represents the definitive overcoming of those gradations, found in Eck-

[8] Hu 387–88; V 191–92.
[9] Hu 141, 357, 388.
[10] Cf. Henry, "Mystique trinitaire", 357–58, 362.
[11] Hu 388.

hart, between the trinitarian process and the "dark", "desolate", "silent" primal Ground. The Son and the Spirit "flow back" into the Father: this is both the self-transcendence of the Persons into the simple identity of essence and the highest bliss of love of the Persons, who are perfected as such in this very self-transcendence. Thus God remains eternal event, yet without temporal becoming.[12]

If the creature is to be able to participate in this event, it can only be through the grace of God and through discipleship of the Son. Ruysbroeck is scornful of the attempts of free spirits to reach this participation in the divine by sitting still and practicing self-absorption.[13] The creature never becomes God substantially,[14] but in the Son's Incarnation,[15] in his *pro nobis*,[16] in his Cross and dereliction,[17] in his Eucharist,[18] the Incarnate One enfolds in his embrace, by the Holy Spirit, everything that is striving toward the Father; he is the "pattern that was and is and will remain for eternity".[19]

Ruysbroeck seldom speaks of God being "born". He repeats the traditional scheme of the three births of the Son, in eternity, of Mary in time, and in us,[20] but speaks in more concrete and biblical terms of our "rebirth", when "we are born anew of the Holy Spirit as chosen sons of God."[21] It would be a mistake to

[12] "There is a reciprocal intercourse of Persons in the Godhead that continually renews their mutual delight; each new outpouring of love results in a new embrace full of unity. This is outside time; it has neither before nor after but takes place in an eternal Now": Hu 82, V 27.

[13] Hu 70–71, 204, 368f., 374; Fr I, 180. [Dt 154–55; 229; Ta 45–46.]

[14] Hu 177–78; Fr I, 88. [Ta 51].

[15] Hu 221.

[16] Hu 321.

[17] Hu 159, 187, 213, 225, 227, 305; Fr I, 63, 86.

[18] Fr I, 68ff.; Hu 323.

[19] Hu 320.

[20] Hu 338–39.

[21] Hu 146; cf. also Eckhart's early work *The Kingdom of the Beloved*, chap. 25. There is a "divine moving or touching of man's spirit that comes from the Father's eternal begetting, whereby he gives birth to his Son in the upper part of the mind (that is, in the reason), in the soul's essence" (V 70). Ruysbroeck often speaks of this "touching" (Hu 58, 60, 80, 189, 217, 270, 330, 359). In this he is probably following Tauler, who often uses the term (JT 36, 50, 57, 140, 223, 363, 381). Perhaps these instances of "touching" represent an earlier stage of what John of

take this theologoumenon in isolation from his whole anthropology: God begets his Son in the apex of the soul (often identified with the Augustinian *memoria*), but from its unity flow
the three powers of the soul that contain the traditional image
of the Trinity, namely, mind, reason and will (love). For their
part, the powers of the soul, insofar as they are abilities, strive
for active realization; this they cannot do without employing
the "lower" powers of sense and body that are involved with
the world. For Ruysbroeck, this threefold layering in man—an
essential unity corresponding to the superessential unity in God,
and the trinity of spiritual powers that are exercised in a soul oriented to the world—forms an indissoluble unity. It corresponds
to a primal "structure" in God himself, who, too, is unity of
essence, trinitarian fecundity and the effectual revelation of his
own nature; so much so that man is perfected, not, for instance,
through a mere reduction to the "wayless" unity (of Eckhart),
but by integrating the three aspects of his being. Ruysbroeck
speaks here of the "common", "comprehensive" life (*dat ghemeyne leven*) in the sense of a simultaneity of active, intellectual
and mystical life.[22] This ideal, which demands more than a mere
contemplativus in actione, seems practically unrealizable if one considers the ecstatic character of the highest union (which goes
beyond the three powers).

However, Ruysbroeck does not mean, either, a synchronous
realization of all levels. Man can sense the most profound touch
of God and yet feel himself unable to ascend any higher with
his reason, "for the radiance that hovers over it, occasioned by
the divine touch, causes blindness in every earthly eye because it
is unfathomable."[23] For Ruysbroeck in particular, therefore, the
mystic continues to strive; he thirsts and pursues; he longs for
the highest union that, essentially, is reserved to heaven. The
spirit "eagerly strives for love, for it sees its repose"; it is "a
pilgrim who sees his homeland, a warrior who, beholding his
crown, fights for love's victory".[24] "God, in his radiant glory,

---

the Cross describes, in greater intensity, as the *toques* (cf. Fra Luis de San José,
Concordancias . . . de las Obras. S. Juan de la Cruz, [Burgos, 1948], 1061–64).

[22] *Marriage*, II, 37–38 (Hu 308–313), *Kingdom*, chap. 35 (V 108–13).

[23] Hu 331.   [24] Hu 366.

hovers above all spirits"; the man who receives his touch here on
earth must "remain outside the gate", but the Spirit continues
to drive him "nonetheless to penetrate farther".[25] The Spirit
who, in God, is the unity of love of Father and Son, draws
("breathes/sucks") them both into the unity of the Godhead;
he exercises the same power on man.[26] On the other hand, the
"effect" of the powers of the soul is strongly stressed: it can
be a "bodily" effect (which the author sees in entirely positive
terms),[27] but there are other, spiritual modes of effective "outflowing": "to God and all saints", "to sinners and apostates",
to souls "in purgatory", and finally "to all good men".[28] Thus
Ruysbroeck completes what Eckhart had started in his notorious
sermon on Martha and Mary, in which Martha was held to be
superior to her sister because of her ability to contemplate in
the midst of an active life, whereas Mary was only learning.[29]
Tauler had taken up this theme with far more discretion.[30]

Thus we discern and respond to Ruysbroeck's rhythm, which
he incessantly emphasizes. It is a pulsating life between being
"breathed into" God and being sent out by him into the world:
systole and diastole. "The Spirit of God breathes us forth to
cultivate love and good works, but he also draws us into himself so that we may surrender to rest and enjoyment: and this
is eternal life. Just as when we breathe out the air that is in us
and take in fresh breath: that is our mortal life." Nor is it any
different in the supernatural realm: we go in and out "while all
the time remaining united in God's Spirit".[31] Ruysbroeck even

[25] Hu 332.
[26] Hu 88, 90, 142.
[27] Hu 356.
[28] Hu 314.
[29] Q 159, 164.
[30] Tauler returns to the customary interpretation that Martha is being repri-
manded (JT 362–63) and that Mary has chosen the better part (JT 390). But
he insists on the union of the contemplative and the active life (364, 541). On
this issue see Dietmar Mieth, *Die Einheit von vita activa und vita contemplativa in den
deutschen Predigten und Traktaten Meister Eckharts und bei Johannes Tauler* (Regensburg: Pustet, 1969); B. Fraling, *Mystik und Geschichte: Das "ghemeyne leven" in der
Lehre des Jan von Roosbroec* (Regensburg, 1974).
[31] Hu 145; also 174–75; 186: "As we are being drawn in, we must be entirely
(God's); here we learn to die and to behold. But as we are flowing forth, he wishes

inscribes this twofold motion into the Trinity; in the creature it belongs to the triune image: the unity of having and being,[32] of doing and suffering ("enjoyment"),[33] of always being there and always arriving anew,[34] of striving and fulfillment.[35] We should not be too hasty to speak of anthropomorphisms here; these are unavoidable ways of conceiving the fullness of life within the Godhead, as we described them at the beginning of this book.

With this rhythm of his, Ruysbroeck completes the picture of the authentically "Catholic", universal man that Tauler[36] had already put forward. Since he is entirely devoted to God, he can be sent out into the world in the greatest possible degree of exposure. "The man whom God sends into the world from such a height is full of truth; . . . he has a rich and gentle ground that is grounded on the richness of God. At all times, therefore, he must flow out toward those who need his help and love. For the living fountain of the Holy Spirit is his wealth; it never dries up. So his life is an all-embracing life, for he is equally apt to contemplate and to do."[37]

d. The Birth of the Logos and Mary (or the Church)

The mystical tradition we have just described is in continuity with the great patristic tradition from Irenaeus to Cyril of Alexandria, Ambrose and Augustine and their many heirs in the Early and High Middle Ages, right up to the Victorines. Such a wealth of texts has already been collected, set in order and eluci-

---

to be entirely ours: thus he teaches us to live in the fullness of virtue." 189: "When we flow forth, God's touch makes us alive in the Spirit, . . . whereas when he draws us in, God's touch requires us to be one with God." 315: "The flood that carries us into God always carries us out again, for God is an ocean that flows and ebbs, ceaselessly flowing out into all his faithful ones according to the needs and worthiness of each . . . and drawing them back into him together with all their possessions and capabilities." See also 329, 380.

[32] Hu 188.

[33] Hu 77, 367, 390–91.

[34] Hu 338.

[35] Hu 354.

[36] JT 313, 332, 380.

[37] *The Sparkling Stone*, chap. 14 (Schacht, 60–61); cf. Hu 314, 317–18, 357.

dated[1] that we do not need to examine them in detail here. But since we are discussing the participation of creatures in the internal process of the Trinity, we must refer to this patristic tradition, since its teaching is drawn from a theme that simply dropped out of the medieval and Spanish mysticism we have been describing, namely, the Church and her model, Mary. Whereas in medieval times the spiritual commentaries on the Song of Songs gave a threefold interpretation of the "Bride" as the Church, Mary, and the individual faithful soul,[2] in the wake of Origen and Methodius the soul had been considered to be "Bride" only in the sense that it had attained soulhood within the Church and had become an ecclesial soul (*anima ecclesiastica*).[3] We cannot do without this mediation, which is both creaturely and supernatural (insofar as Mary is a virgin and is overshadowed by the Spirit of God). Mediation through a feminine principle that conceives and gives birth guards against Eckhart's intolerable conclusion, which is that the human being, as an Idea in God, has created himself by his own will because the generation of the Son and the creation of the world (of Ideas) are one and the same act. Not only is this mediation important for the economy of salvation in this life: in the image of the eschatological marriage (to which we shall come), it points ahead to eternal life.

Furthermore, the ultimate dignity and relevance of the feminine principle in the constitution of our eternal blessedness is demonstrated and confirmed in our theology of the sexes (*Theo-Drama* II, 365–82; III, 292–360) and in the equal importance we have attributed to the "active", generating love and the "passive" love that conceives and gives birth, both in God[4] and in

---

[1] The following texts are drawn from Hugo Rahner's classic treatise to which we have already referred: "Die Gottgeburt: Die Lehre der Kirchenväter von der Geburt Christi aus dem Herzen der Kirche und der Gläubigen" in *Symbole der Kirche* (Salzburg: O. Müller, 1964), 11–87.

[2] H. Riedlinger, "Die Makellosigkeit der Kirche in den lateinischen Hoheliedkommentaren des Mittelalters" in *BGPhThMA* 38/3 (1958), chap. 4: "Die mariologisch orientierten Kommentare: Daselbst Literatur über die Parallele Maria/Kirche in Patristik und Mittelalter".

[3] Origen, *Hom. I on the Song of Songs* (Baehrens VIII, 41, 13).

[4] Cf. our own article on the dignity of woman, "Die Würde der Frau" in *Internat. Kath. Zeitschrift Communio* 11 (1982) 346–52.

its reflection in the creature (see above, pp. 85–91). It is obvious that there can be only *one* such universal principle of mediation; even if it displays different aspects in Mary and in the Church, they are inseparable. This is shown by Irenaeus' dictum —previously contentious, but by now finally clarified: "How should men overcome their birth that leads to death except by being born again by faith (that is, by baptism) in a new birth, which God has given us against all expectation as a sign of salvation, and such as took place in the womb of the Virgin?"[5] Though not without antecedents, Irenaeus' words here can be regarded as the starting point for the theology of the birth of the Logos from Mary/Ecclesia. Their unity is expressed even more closely where he says that the Prophets "preached the Emmanuel who comes from the Virgin, thereby indicating the union of the divine Logos with his Image, namely, that the Logos should become flesh, the Son of God should become Son of Man, and that he himself, the Pure One, should in purity open the pure womb that he created pure and that gives rebirth to men unto God."[6] Both aspects of the mediating Virgin-Mother are simultaneously visible and invisible: in Mary the Spirit's overshadowing and her preparation are invisible, but the birth is visible; in the Church the sacrament of rebirth is visible, but the rebirth itself is invisible.

Now there begins the almost dizzying series of variations and permutations of the aspects contained in this twofold mystery. While Mary gives birth to the Church's Head, the Church (in the font) gives birth to the Head's members who, incorporated in him, are "mystically" the Logos himself. These members, however, together form the Church—and the more perfect the individual members are, the more perfectly they realize the Church's nature—and they themselves, for their part, give birth to Christ. It was primarily Hippolytus, no doubt inspired by Irenaeus, who dared to ponder the interaction of these aspects. "The Church

---

[5] *Adv. Haer.* IV, 33, 4. God's sign, the virgin with child, is the sign given to Ahaz. In the understanding of the tradition it points unequivocally to Mary. Rebirth through faith points with equal clarity to baptism, whereby the Church becomes virginal. Cf. the "note justificative" in the *Sources chrétiennes* edition 100, I (1965), 269f.

[6] *Adv. Haer.* IV, 33, 11.

never ceases to give birth, from her heart, to the Logos,[7] although in this world she is persecuted by unbelievers (a reference to the persecuted Woman of Revelation 12). . . . By continually giving birth to the Logos, the Church teaches all nations."[8] Yet the children born to the Woman are themselves members, and so they are Church. Thus Hippolytus can add that the Word that issues from the Father's mouth is born a second time "from the saints: the Word constantly gives birth to the saints and is constantly being given birth by them."[9]

Every believer is "born again of water and the Spirit" in the font, which means that the Church's "giving birth" acquires a certain priority. The oldest commentaries on the Book of Revelation reject the interpretation that says that the Woman in her birth pangs is Mary; all the same this shows that this interpretation was current at a very early stage.[10] The metaphor persists, through Origen and Methodius, and comes to dominate especially in Augustine: "The Church as the fruitful, virginal Mother of believers is one of Augustine's favorite themes",[11] though Augustine thinks primarily of the sacramental event, not the subsequent process whereby "the Church shapes and gives birth to the mystical Christ in the hearts of believers." Mary too, for Augustine, remains first and foremost the "bodily pattern", not the archetype of the Church in salvation history. Yet this archetype, with its momentous historical significance, can never be forgotten in the life of the Church, for Mary gives birth to

---

[7] H. Rahner points out that in the ancient world the "heart" is the "*hegemonikon*", the "*principale intellectus*" (Origen), the spiritual center from which the *logoi*, the thoughts and wishes, are born. This idea is crucially important for the theology of the Trinity in its initial stages. The eternal Father gives birth to the Logos from his heart ("Gottgeburt", 14–17). The Church is part of this process since she receives and carries the Logos.

[8] *Antichr.* 61.

[9] *Commentary on Daniel*, I, 10, 8. The conclusion of the Epistle to Diognetus, which is dependent on Hippolytus, supports this view: The Logos, who proceeds from the Father, "seemed to be new and yet was found to be old, is constantly being born anew in the hearts of the saints": II, 2.

[10] Texts in H. Rahner, "Gottgeburt", 69. In a homily on the Book of Revelation (later attributed to Augustine) Gennadius says: "Semper enim in cruciatibus parit Ecclesia Christum per membra" (PL 35, 2434).

[11] H. Rahner, "Gottgeburt", 60.

the world's Savior and so remains the elevated midpoint between the Old and New Covenants. Ambrose sees this most clearly. Mary is the believing, virginal pattern for every soul that desires to imitate her fruitfulness. "Fac voluntatem Patris, ut Christi mater sis."[12] Ambrose's commentary on St. Luke continues to have an influence in the Middle Ages: "Mary as the type of the Virgin-Mother, the Church; Mary as the pattern of the virginal soul; the mystery of Christmas as the beginning of the spiritual life: these are the main ideas from now on."[13]

It is not simply a question, however, of the act of giving birth, whether in Bethlehem or in the baptismal font. There is always the matter of schooling and "fashioning" the Logos or, rather, of shaping the particular member of the Church in the Spirit of the Logos. This aspect takes up a vast area in the tradition, and in two directions. The first is ethical and pedagogical (and here, after Clement, Origen is the chief voice): every day the Logos is to increase in us; every day we are to be born eternally of the Father. Origen is followed by Methodius, who says that those trained by the Church must themselves take on the ecclesial task of training those who are as yet imperfect in the life of the Logos.[14] Ambrose will hand on this approach to the Church of the Middle Ages as an ascetic tradition. The other direction is the mystical path laid down by Gregory of Nyssa, which reserves the actual "birth" of the Logos in the soul for the highest stage of the soul's fashioning into its ecclesial form. Gregory's intuition is brought to fullness in Maximus the Confessor's basic principle: To the extent that man is divinized, God becomes man and the Incarnation of the Logos is perfected.[15] This mystical strand is carried over into the Middle Ages (Honorius, Hugh and Richard of Saint-Victor) by Maximus' translator, Scotus Erigena. It will eventually reach Eckhart.[16]

This whole chapter, however, is concerned with our participation in the divine processions—beginning hiddenly on earth

---

[12] *Commentary on Luke* X, 14, 25.

[13] H. Rahner, "Gottgeburt", 69.

[14] Esp. in the eighth speech of the *Symposion*.

[15] Texts in H. Rahner, "Gottgeburt", 48–56.

[16] *Ibid.*, 65–87. It is important that Scotus' homily on the Prologue of St. John was considered to be by Origen. Thomas Aquinas shared this view.

and reaching fullness, openly, in heaven—and so, finally, the dogmatics of Cyril of Alexandria must occupy center stage. For he focuses not only on the Logos, his birth and growth, but on the whole Trinity: "It is the Holy Spirit who perfects in us the divine work of gracious pardon, just as once he overshadowed the Holy Virgin and fashioned the body of the incarnate Logos."[17] "Thus, therefore, Christ is formed in us, because *the Holy Spirit causes us to share in a divine process of formation*. . . . Thus the stamp (*charaktēr*) of God the Father's nature (Heb 1:3, that is, the Son) is impressed in our souls, the Holy Spirit sanctifying and conforming us to Christ."[18] In speaking of this "principle of formation" (*morphōsis*), Cyril does not, of course, forget the Church's baptism; but its grace needs to be sustained and nourished by a life of faith. "For Cyril too, the pattern of this divine birth in the heart of the believer, a birth that is continually being repeated, is the unique Incarnation of the Logos from the Holy Virgin. Thus men's sanctification is a continual copying, in Christ's Mystical Body, of Christ's birth from Mary."[19]

This concludes our survey of the Church's mystical tradition with regard to the creature's participation in the internal "processions" of the Trinity. We enter on this participation, of course, through the *oikonomia*, the birth of the Logos in human nature; but this birth remains abstract and unintelligible unless we take account of the two factors that make it possible, namely, the Father's sending of the overshadowing Holy Spirit and mankind's consent in the womb of the Holy Virgin. The latter's theological relevance had almost entirely disappeared from view in medieval mysticism, even though in Tauler (and still more in Suso) it had remained an object of personal devotion. The ultimate reason for this is that even in the Fathers—apart from the few exceptions such as Irenaeus—it was seen too exclusively as the physical (or ethical) model for the Church's mysteriological activity. Only in more recent times was it realized that Mary is a mediatrix of the graces of the Trinity: she mediates in and with the Church (since she is Mother of God) and together with her Son and as

---

[17] *Ibid.*, 44.

[18] Cyril of Alexandria, *Commentary on Isaiah* IV, or. 2 (PG 70, 936BC).

[19] H. Rahner, "Gottgeburt", 46, and the refs. to Cyril in nn. 19 and 20.

the Model of the Church. We need to reflect further, however, on the mediatorial character of Mary/Ecclesia even in eternal life: there, as we have shown, the earthly missions are not suspended but, rather, brought to perfection. Elsewhere we have shown that the scope of a believer's mission extends far beyond his psychological subjectivity; thus it is possible for Mary's mission to extend to the whole Church, and, indeed, to the whole of mankind.[20] If even the missions of the twelve tribes of Israel and the twelve apostles of the Lamb are to remain forever in the heavenly Jerusalem (Rev 21:12, 14), how much more will the mission of Mary remain in this Jerusalem, since she is the holy Bride and Spouse of the Lamb, and the one who, through her consent, gave the world its Savior.

This is given symbolic expression in a vision from the wonderful book of visions of Mechthild von Hackeborn. Here Mary and the Church appear in inseparable unity. Mechthild glimpses a kind of transfigured celebration of Mass in heaven; as Communion approaches, "a table was set down and the Lord sat at it, and his Mother sat down beside him. The whole community approached the table, and every one knelt down and, from under the arm of the Blessed Virgin, received the Body of the Lord from the Lord's hand. The Blessed Virgin held out a golden chalice containing the stream of gold that came from the Lord's side, and all drank from it that wondrous drink which flowed from the Lord's breast."[21]

Our question concerned the participation of the creature, through grace, in the Father's trinitarian generative power. The patristic explanation directs our attention to the Church's feminine fruitfulness, which includes and embraces the fruitfulness of the Petrine office. In terms of *oikonomia*, this participation is intelligible only through the mediations exercised by the Son and the Spirit, insofar as the Father communicates to them all that is his—except the act of giving, which he cannot give away—and through the mediations of the Church/Mary/Soul, who is

---

[20] "Who Is the Church?" in *Spouse of the Word, Explorations in Theology* II (San Francisco: Ignatius Press, 1991), 143–191.

[21] *Revelationes Gertrudianae ac Mechtildianae* II (Solesmes-Paris, 1887), I, 27, 95–97.

granted participation in the Father's primal fruitfulness in a fundamentally creaturely, receptive and feminine way. Apart from
this participation, Jesus forbids anyone to claim the title of "father" in the Church (Mt 23:9), since the first effect of the graces
that come from Jesus and through the Church is to make "brothers" of everyone, including those exercising oversight over communities. This does not prevent the comprehensive fruitfulness
of the Church of Jesus from expressing itself in a masculine
way as well, in a generative, spiritual fatherhood such as Paul
attributes to himself (1 Cor 4:15); but, characteristically, such
fatherhood does not exclude the feminine images of painful birth
(Gal 4:19), of the nurture and care of children (1 Th 2:7). A holy
woman founding a religious order needs to be no less creatively
fruitful, for the sake of her future family, than a male founder.
As for the masculine ecclesial authority, it cannot be traced back
as such directly to the Father: its *exousia* is entrusted to it from
Jesus (Mk 3:15), who has received it from the Father: "All that
is mine is thine" (Jn 17:10).

What was the purpose, in this discussion of heaven, of these
lengthy historical detours, from John of the Cross, via Eckhart,
back to the Fathers? They were not explicitly concerned with
the situation of the end, but with a process that begins with baptism (thus the Fathers) and unfolds in the Christian's progress
in perfection here and now (thus the mystics). But they are all
intent on describing something so ultimate, so divine, that its
inchoate state on earth quite obviously points ahead to the ultimate, blessed destiny that awaits the human being filled with
grace. This is quite explicit in John of the Cross: only a thin veil
separates what he portrays from heaven; once the veil is rent,
the mutual breathing of the Spirit by Father and Son will be the
most intimate bliss. Ruysbroeck has been suspected of failing
to preserve a sufficient distinction between mystical experience
and heavenly vision; he takes note of the objection, but perhaps
more formally than in terms of content. In Irenaeus both sides
are clear: he knows about the eschatological transformation, but
he is equally certain that there is no further possibility beyond
the indwelling in us of the Logos who reveals the Father. Eckhart is quite clear that he is making affirmations about ultimate

validity: the structure of divine birth, in all its five aspects, cannot be surpassed.

In this chapter we have been exploring the depths of what
theology, all too abruptly, calls *"visio beatifica"*. It is a participation in the life of God himself, but as such it is a completion
and perfection of something that began in the Incarnation of the
Logos.

2. Meal and Marriage

a. The Dialectic of Images

There are many images for the mystery of eternal life. In the
prophetic passages of the apocalyptic epistles, for instance, they
circle around something that is unimaginable, for the most part
employing symbols drawn from biblical tradition. There is "the
paradise of God" with the "tree of life", whose fruit is now
given to the victor by the Lord himself (Rev 2:7); there is the
imperial authority of the Messiah—following Psalm 2:8—who
gives the steadfast his "iron scepter" with which he breaks the
nations in pieces like "earthen pots" (Rev 2:26–27). There is
the "temple of my God", in which the victor will be a pillar
and the "city of my God", the "heavenly Jerusalem" (Rev 3:12),
both of which have a long prehistory in the Old and New Testaments. Stretching from Isaiah to the Book of Revelation there
is the vision and portrayal of the heavenly liturgy, in which the
creature's eternal blessedness dissolves in praise, reverence and
service to the divine Majesty.

There are two images, however, that occupy a special place.
While the images themselves arise from fundamental human
gestures and needs, they are elevated "apophatically" in order
to portray heaven fulfilling (and overfulfilling) the dimension
of human intimacy through an entirely different intimacy with
God: these are the images of "meal" and "marriage".

We are familiar with the use of these images, supported by Old
Testament texts. The "meal" is characterized by the solemn assurance (overshadowed by the Passion and his farewell to his disciples) that Jesus gives when offering the chalice that contains
the "blood of the Covenant": "Truly, I say to you, I shall not

drink again of the fruit of the vine until that day when I drink it new in the kingdom of God" (Mk 14:25; Mt 26:29 adds "with you" and calls the kingdom of God "my Father's kingdom"). Very important are the meals that the risen Lord prepares for his disciples (Lk 24:30–31; Jn 21:9–13; "who were chosen by God as witnesses, who ate and drank with him after he rose from the dead": Acts 10:41). There is also a direct line running from the great banquets and marriage feasts in Jesus' parables to the "marriage feast of the Lamb", an invitation to which means blessedness (Rev 19:9). Here, already, we discern the inner connection between meal and marriage; even in earthly life they are situations of self-surrender, reciprocal nurturing, fruitfulness and joy. In the New Testament, reciprocal intimacy often appears as an element of the meal, since Jesus not only is present as Master of the feast but also gives himself as food; he clearly appears as Master of the feast when he requires the disciples to make their contribution to the common meal (Jn 21:10) or when he makes this promise to the community in Laodicea: "Behold, I stand at the door and knock; if any one hears my voice and opens the door, I will come in to him and eat with him, and he with me" (Rev 3:20). He is both Master of the feast *and* food when he promises that "the bread which I shall give for the life of the world is my flesh" (Jn 6:51). Finally he is food: in the metaphor of the physical the truth of the nuptial "one flesh" and "one spirit" takes place: "He who eats my flesh and drinks my blood abides in me, and I in him." "He who eats this bread will live for ever" (Jn 6:56, 58). We must include those passages in Paul in which the mystery of the eucharistic meal (1 Cor 10:16; 11:23ff.) transforms itself, in its essence, into a nuptial union: in contrast to the transitory relationship of body and food ("God will destroy both one and the other": 1 Cor 6:13), the relationship of Christ's Body and the believer's body is a mystery that is both somatic and pneumatic: "The body is . . . for the Lord, and the Lord for the body. . . . He who is united to the Lord becomes one *pneuma* with him." The unity of both bodies, thus effected, promises eternity: "God raised the Lord and will also raise us up by his power" (1 Cor 6:13, 17, 14).

Thus the mystery of the meal clearly shows that what we have in these two related images is not merely a "comparison" between an earthly, transitory process and a heavenly one: rather, there is "vertical" communication between both planes, a communication that is expressly a nuptial mystery. Just as the post-Easter meals and the Church's Eucharist are a feast in which heaven and earth are united, the Epistle to the Ephesians finds the archetype of marriage in the mystery of conjugal love between Christ and the Church that takes place between heaven and earth. The marriage relationship between man and woman, which is acted out in transitory terms, must adhere to this archetype, for the mystery of marriage is great only "because of the relationship to Christ and the church" (Eph 5:32). The mystery of the marriage between heaven and earth that is celebrated in the Eucharist is both *now* and *in eternity* a mystery of body and spirit: the nuptial union depends both on the unitive power of Christ's flesh and blood, given up for us, and on the internalizing power of the Holy Spirit. If the conjugal union makes man and woman "one flesh" (Gen 2:24), we can interpret this in two ways. On the one hand, it can be applied to the unity of Christ and the Church, since the Church becomes in reality the Body of Christ, and in her he "loves his own flesh" (Eph 5:29–30); alternatively, applied to the purely sexual union, it can be seen as the opposite of that movement whereby the Body of Christ and the body of the believer are united in "one *pneuma*" (1 Cor 6:16–17).

In sublimating the purely earthly content of both images, we must be careful not to destroy the analogy made possible through Christ's bodily Resurrection. Thus all chiliastic ideas of a Messianic meal at the end of time, such as Judaism projected into the future,[1] are obsolete; here below, it is true, we can "drink and eat to the glory of God" (1 Cor 10:31), but "the kingdom of God does not mean food and drink but righteousness and peace and joy in the Holy Spirit" (Rom 14:17). God will abolish the body's need for nourishment (1 Cor 6:13), and death, suffering and mourning will be obsolete (Rev 21:4). Even more forcibly, Jesus himself says that the use of sexual functions will cease in eternal life: "You are wrong," he replies to the Sadducees' casuistic question, "because you know neither the scriptures nor the

---

[1] Paul Volz, *Die Eschatologie der jüdischen Gemeinde im neutestamentlichen Zeitalter* (Tübingen: Mohr, 1934), 367f.

power of God. For in the resurrection they neither marry nor are given in marriage, but are like angels in heaven" (Mt 22:29f.; cf. Rev 14:1–5). Both these statements are categorical, for the human body will no longer be subject to natural urges, which serve partly to maintain life and partly to ensure procreation in the context of mortality. Nonetheless there is in both bodily functions an element that transcends their immediate aim and causes them to participate in the *imago trinitatis* in man. There is an ascending analogy, designed with a view to that descending analogy that extends downward from the triune God, through the Son's humanity, to the earthly human being in his mortal, provisional nature.

Transcendence is most clearly seen in the sexual area. God created the human being as man and woman, and thus "in the human being, loneliness is overcome." "(In paradise) the man, situated in freedom between God and the woman, is entrusted by God with leadership and must take account of the woman. The woman, in turn, must acknowledge the man's leadership; she is to show him that he has received it from God and must be guided by God." "Each is to the other a means of reaching God." So their self-transcendence is not merely toward another immanent person, the child, but toward a transcendent Person, God. "Without God the reciprocal love of man and woman would be meaningless; it would run itself into the ground. On the other hand, without this interpersonal community the human being's relation to God would be impossible; every attempt to enter a relationship with the triune Love would be bound to fail and drive man to despair; he would be stifled by God." Since God does not initially reveal himself as triune Love, but as One, man is taught a lesson: "Being occupied with the interpersonal Thou and recognizing in it a mystery of distance and nearness, difference and interdependence, he understands that this relationship points to an absolute Love and can only be fulfilled in it." Moreover, this Love is triune: "If God were only Father and Son over against the human being who is man and woman, there could not develop a living relationship between God and the human being." It is the Holy Spirit, in whose love Father and Son transcend themselves, who enables man and woman to transcend themselves, not only in the child, but toward God;

in such a way, furthermore, that each finite person can have a
direct personal relation to God as well as participate in an indispensable common relation to him.[2] The command "Be fruitful" (Gen 1:28b) does not apply only to the sexual field; man
is to be fruitful in his totality, that is, primarily in the spiritual-
intellectual dimension. This is both a gift and a command to be
carried out in obedience to God. "Human fruitfulness differs
from that of animals in that, in all its phases, it is rooted in the
knowledge of God."[3]

The meal too, however, has its own transcendence. At the
purely natural level it is a necessity; but it has a spiritual dimension too: learning, acquiring experience, allowing God to give us
the nourishment that is essential to us in our need and accepting
it gratefully: all this is part of what it means to be a human being.[4]
Thus, as a creature, he is ennobled by God while at the same
time he is shown his dependence. "[God] humbled you", says
Deuteronomy, "and let you hunger and fed you with manna . . .
that he might make you know that man does not live by bread
alone, but that man lives by everything that proceeds out of the
mouth of the Lord" (Dt 8:3). Jesus applies this as an argument
against the Tempter, who was offering him merely earthly nourishment (Mt 4:4). Elsewhere he lifts the ascending analogy to its
highest level: "My food is to do the will of him who sent me, and
to accomplish his work" (Jn 4:34). What follows, pointing to
the coming spiritual harvest among the Samaritans, which Jesus
the Sower has prepared for the reaping disciples, shows how the
obedient fulfillment of God's will nourishes the one who lives
by it: the meal becomes fruitful through the toilsome (*kopiān*)
mission: "The fields are already white for harvest" (Jn 4:35, 38).
And since the One speaking these words is not just any man, but
the Son of God, they have a trinitarian depth to them: the word
that comes forth from Yahweh's mouth, this instruction from
the Father that is the Son's nourishment, is ultimately the Son
himself. For he is continually receiving himself from the Father:

[2] Sc 53–56.
[3] Sc 72–75.
[4] We cannot enter into the philosophical and theological issues involved here.
Cf. Franz von Baader, "Alle Menschen sind im seelischen, guten oder schlimmen
Sinn unter sich: Anthropophagen", *Works* IV (1853), 223–42.

his "being nourished" coincides with his "being". Thus he can boldly reduce human anxiety about tomorrow's food and drink to pure trust in the Father's provision (Mt 6:31–32); we are to ask him directly for the "bread sufficient for the day" (Mt 6:11).

The One who sets forth this ascending transcendence of the law of nourishment and requires the believer consciously to act in accordance with it is the same Person who, in the descending analogy from the triune God, is offered to the world both as the "seed of life" (*sperma*, "God's seed" 1 Jn 3:9 JB) and the "bread of life" (Jn 6:35, 48). To give due weight to this aspect, we must first reflect on the role of the body.

b. The Body and Self-Surrender

A distinction is rightly drawn [in the German language] between *Körper* ("body") and *Leib* ("body")[1]. The former, though informed by the soul, is subject to the powers of the external world; the latter, which according to a "natural eschatology" (as the only surviving form of connection with matter) is a pure "expression" of the spiritual person, *can* incarnate itself in the *corporal* world but does not *have to*. (Thus the risen Christ *can* eat but does not *need* to.) Now this transitory *Körper*, embedded in the cosmic powers, is an instrument not only of action but also of that suffering which is an essential expression of authentic human self-surrender, whether this surrender is to other persons or to a cause sufficiently worthy. In genuine sexual love, the man's part, which seems to be pure "action", is really self-surrender only if the loss of its own substance is seen as a gain and a possibility of further development in the other (the woman).

> The man opens the woman from outside; he penetrates inward in order to initiate the woman's movement (in giving birth) from inside outward. The two belong together; each is both an end and a beginning. We see here a dialectic of unilateral and bilateral roles: the man addresses the woman's ability to conceive and bring to

[1] H. E. Hengstenberg, *Der Leib und die Letzten Dinge* (Regensburg: Pustet, 1954). Gabriel Marcel, Journal métaphysique (Paris: Gallimard, 1927). [The distinction between *Körper* and *Leib* is elusive in English. *Körper* recalls "corpse, corporal"—the body as subject to disintegration—whereas *Leib* is of course the English "life"—the body as a vital unity.—TRANS.]

birth in order to act generatively in her; by exercising his male
role in the conjugal act, he shows the woman her power, while the
woman, in conceiving and giving birth, shows the man his power.
In the conjugal act the man is active, the woman contemplative,
whereas in giving birth the situations are reversed.[2]

The man is hardly aware of the extent of his self-surrender; it
becomes clear to him only through the woman's pregnancy, the
birth of the child and his own responsibility for bringing up the
child.

In the Christian dispensation, the connection between bodily (corporal) self-surrender, sacrifice and fruitfulness is revealed
in the renunciation of marriage "for the sake of the kingdom"
(Christ and Mary are paradigmatic here) and in everything involving corporal penance (cf. 1 Cor 9:27: *castigare—castum agere*)
and "mortification" (*mortificare*—to impart the form of death:
Rom 8:13, 36; Col 3:5) for the sake of greater fruitfulness. There
are many ways in which even that death which is appointed for
the body, although it is a physical event, can be assimilated in
advance to that spiritual event that it is meant to be (and shall be,
whether or not one wishes it to be), namely, the handing over
of corporality to the Giver who fashioned the dust of the earth
into a human instrument (Gen 2:7). The Christian's attitude to
the body will be governed by this final sacrifice, which he is
to perform as a conscious act; even in health and active life he
will make the coming final surrender of corporality the inner
meaning of all his action. He will be inspired to do this as he
contemplates the surrender unto death of Jesus' virginal flesh,
making possible God's gift of the Eucharist, which is "seed" and
"blood" for eternal life.

In his experience of death on the Cross, Jesus seals his total
spiritual-intellectual surrender to the (vanished) Father with the
surrender of his utterly expropriated body (*Körper*); but he takes
this experience with him into his Resurrection body (*Leib*). As
his permanent scars show, this body (*Leib*) is henceforth governed completely by his spirit; thus it expresses nothing other
than his constant purpose of self-surrender. His body no longer

[2] Ps 113-14.

needs to suffer,[3] but it is marked by a unique experience of death that is both spiritual and bodily, and this experience has returned him to the Father's hands as a perfect sacrifice, to be "exploited" in any way the Father wishes; by the operation of the Holy Spirit he has become a eucharistically fruitful Body for the reconciled world. At this point the descending analogy of "meal" and "marriage", coming down to the world from God, shows a clear profile. The wounds in Christ's body remain open: this body is for all eternity (and not merely "until the Last Judgment") the "pierced" body (Zech 12:10; Jn 19:37; Rev 1:7) from which the "new fountain" (Zech 13:1; Jn 19:34; 7:38–39) flows. When Scripture says that "without the shedding of blood there is no forgiveness" (Heb 9:22), it is not merely a historical reference to the sacrifice of the Old Covenant; it is pointing to a much more profound and universal law, namely, that no salvation can be expected without spiritual wounds that attain some physical expression. Many mystics have said that a Christian wound can only be healed through a deeper wounding.[4] Devotion to the Blood of Christ, which enlivens the Church and the world—such as Catherine of Siena practiced—and to the Five Wounds of the crucified and risen Lord are not narrowly "late Gothic": they belong, without sentimentality, at the heart of dogmatics.

As we have just observed, the Eucharist, a descending gift from God to the world, is a trinitarian gift: it is the Father who gives his Son's Body for the world through the unitive mediation of the Spirit; this Body is given up through divine love more than through the world's hatred. The image of the trinitarian "mercy seat" gives human expression to these processes. On God's side the innermost law of triune love is revealed here: in virtue of this

[3] "The higher, divine life which [God] has promised us for eternity will no longer need the infrastructure of the present natural order. The framework of nature, man's connection with a body that is full of natural needs, is a training and a preparation for supernature": C 178.

[4] Cf. the aforementioned commentary of John of the Cross on the phrase "O glorious wound" in stanza 2 of the "Living Flame of Love": "Wounds produced by a material burning can only be healed by medicines; the wound produced (by God's burning love) can only be cured by that same fire, healing the wound by deepening it. . . . The wound is all the more glorious, the more the wounding of love penetrates to the innermost substance of the soul" (*Llama* II, 7–8).

love every Hypostasis, in its own "decline", causes the Other to "arise". This is the prototype of what we described earlier as the sexual interaction of man and woman. The divine Father, Eckhart says, exhausts himself in generating the Son.[5] He shows the world this "self-consuming" in the Son's "consumed" Body, which the fire of the Holy Spirit makes present in us "so that I am burnt up and totally fused with him and become entirely love".[6] Without the Cross and the Blood of the Cross, and without the permanent wounds in the risen Lord, we would never have guessed the depth of the mystery of the Trinity.

Now, however, this divine gift is offered to the world as meal and as marriage, mediating the life of the Trinity but also as a concrete, prototypical realization of earthly existence. What is essential is that the Lord's Body, both as eucharistic meal and as a pledge of the eternal marriage, is offered not only *to* the transitory sphere, but really *in it*. It is mortal men who receive the eucharistic food as *pharmakon athanasias*, and it is a visible, earthly Church that Christ the Bridegroom purifies through Cross and baptism and presents to himself as his Bride. Neither image would have any meaning if the gift failed to achieve genuine reciprocity, not only beyond history, in heaven, but here and now through the operation of the Spirit. For the Spirit, by giving us this gift to be our very own, achieves a freewill acceptance of it (*voluntaria susceptio*) and hence an appropriate response.[7]

This eucharistic and spousal relationship between Christ and the Church (in which we are all members) is not, however, some Idealist process hovering above the abyss of this world and its resistance to God. It takes place in world-time, and so it must be seen in the deadly realism of world-time. The world, both inside and outside the Church, is always resisting being transformed into the Body of Christ; this means that crucifixion and the piercing of the heart are always going on, and God is ceaselessly wooing man in the Person of the Crucified who, for his part, can do nothing but take "all who receive him" with him

[5] "In him consuming all his nature", *German Works* II, 263. For parallels see n. 2.

[6] Eckhart, *German Works* II, 264.

[7] DS 1528 (Trent, *de justificatione* c 7). Cf. the remarks of W. Breuning in: *Communio Christi* (Düsseldorf: Patmos, 1980), 122–33.

into his Cross. From the perspective of heaven, it is a victory won through death on the Cross; from the perspective of the world, it is a desperate refusal, a resignation, a dying that—in the teeth of all contradiction—must yield to the superior strength of love. No one has followed this whole drama more tenaciously, from all sides, than Erich Przywara,[8] nor has anyone else tried so to express it. Here are a few fragments:

> Is this Your secret will undreamed-of, that
> with gentle force
> howe'er the heart resists,
> we, receiving You, become our own,
> bread in Your Bread and wine in Wine?

But this takes place—

> In night unutterable, the cold void
> 'tween earth and heaven, expelled—
> In night unutterable—from eternities
> You
> eternally near, to pardon and
> to kill me,
> Night unutterable.

* * *

> And are we sword drawn
> against drawn sword:
> O how loneliness bleeds
> O how anger weeps
> O how banishment begs
> O how tender is the curse!
> Is it darkness plunges eye to eye?
> Does the sword-thrust clasp heart to heart?

* * *

> You drained the cup to Your end—
> now we drink of it as Your consoling.
> You gave Yourself over to forsakenness
> 'tween heaven and earth—

[8] Throughout his entire oeuvre, but most clearly in his poetry. The following lines are taken from his "Homo" (Munich: Kösel/Pustet, 1933) and "Hymnus" (Paderborn: Schöningh, 1936).

Now this forsakenness is
You.

        * * *

Curse, that seeks You out
to batten on You!
Curse, that You seek out
to be the womb of blessing.

        * * *

Praise to You in forsakenness
that yawns and flows!
For You are high
out of the abyss,
And Your light is blinding
out of the darkness,
And Your fullness is beyond measure
out of forsakenness.

        * * *

Why do You waken the dry branches
into new buds—
that new mildew multiply
in the fall?
Because newer far, through spring,
Through fall—
Marriage in heaven,
Love eternal
beats Your heart.

        * * *

You open an abyss before our feet
where One Deep yawns to bury us.
You cleave our heart to One Sword
that One Wound should burn and consume us,
You strew One Night upon our eyes
That One Death's sweetness swallow us:
One Body, One Blood, One Life, One Love.

        * * *

God became the fear of him,
Alleluia.

Here the mystery of the One Body is grasped eucharistically and nuptially in its whole trinitarian breadth. Here there is room for all the world's horror to expand to its full extent, but there is also a depth that is "deeper than the abyss of hell" and a theo-dramatic scope that knows no boundary. Przywara, who said of himself that he had "become frozen to the Gaurisankar[9] of the Eckhardian point", sees God's destiny in his Cross and the destiny of the world in its opposition to God in a single unity—not a pantheistic or mythological unity, but a eucharistic and nuptial unity. What we said earlier, echoing John of the Cross, applies here with all its force: the deeper the wound, the greater the healing. The poet endeavors to traverse the abyss in the child-likeness of a Thérèse of Lisieux.

The drama of the abyss that Przywara lives and portrays is aiming for something beyond itself: its destination is a heav-enly Eucharist and marriage in which the terrifying chasms be-tween time and eternity will be—not closed, but illuminated by God's triune life, and in which the sea that swallowed Jonah will become a "sea of glass mingled with fire" (Rev 15:2). On this sea the victors will stand, singing their hymn: "Who would not fear you, O Lord, and praise your name?" There will be a Eucharist; it will no longer nourish our mortal bodies (*Körper*) but those vital bodies (*Leiber*) which will simply be the "ex-pression" of our freedom and essentiality, what Hengstenberg calls "bodying-forth" (*Darleibung*); and for this very reason they will not be able to do without God's eternal nourishment. Eu-charist, as an event of love, will remain something reciprocal. Thus Ruysbroeck often spoke of God being devoured by the avid spirit and of the spirit being devoured by God.[10] Novalis echoes him in his "Hymn":

> Who has discerned the earthly Body's lofty meaning?
> Who can say he comprehends the Blood?

[9] A Himalayan mountain.—TRANS.

[10] "The avid spirit thinks it is eating and devouring God, but in coming into contact with God it is itself devoured" (Huebner, 336). "I know not whether Thou eatest me or I eat Thee, for in my heart I think on both": *The Seven Steps of the Ladder of Spiritual Love* (London: Dacre Press, 1944), 39.

Only in "heaven's unfathomable deeps" is the mystery made known: there

> never-ending is the sweet repast,
> Love is never sated there.
> The Beloved's ne'er enough to her,
> Cannot be enough love's own. . . .
> Had the sober and staid e'er tasted the gift
> They would have left all and sat down with us
> At the board, ever-laden, the table of longing.
> They would have known love's infinite fullness
> And blessed the banquet of flesh and of blood.

It was Baader who provided the philosophical infrastructure for such poetry.[11]

Much that we have already set forth comes together here: the interpretation of heavenly time as the opposite of a *nunc stans* —rather, as the opening-up of a boundless reality; the unity of rest and motion described by Irenaeus and Gregory of Nyssa; the Son's humanity as a mediation between the Trinity and us —but only as a gift directly communicated and enjoyed; and, finally, the definitive nature of the nuptial relationship between man and woman, Christ and the (Marian) Church, which is far above sexuality, since the two images ("one Mystical Body" and the "oneness of husband and wife") have become inseparably intertwined.

c. *Communio Sanctorum*

The last concept to be dealt with here must be the *communio sanctorum*. We have already discussed its earthly shape in *Theo-Drama* IV, 406–23. Even there we became aware of a great number of heavenly aspects: in connection with the unity of the theological person and the mission, the transferring of Christ's merits (Cajetan/Nazarius) to the members of the Mystical Body; and the power that believers have, in faith and love, to "stand in" for each other, even to the extent of dying on another's behalf. Now, however, we must focus on the final form of this *communio*, which can be illuminated by the creature's participation in

[11] See p. 474, n. 4.

the trinitarian processions as we have described. The archetype is the *circumincessio* of the divine Hypostases and their total "being for one another", but this is always mediated by what, on earth, was the sacrament of *communio*, the surrender of the Son's Body by the Father in the Holy Spirit, which now steps forth out of sacramental latency into patent truth. This surrender, too, remains an eternal archetype, the economic side of inner-trinitarian relationships.

In sacramental *communio*, even on earth, the recipients are necessarily drawn into the Son's attitude of self-surrender, his "sacrifice". In its final form, therefore, this will be all the more the case—although, naturally, there will be no smoothing out of the difference in level between the originating Archetype and its effect in the participants. It is the same ineradicable difference as between the *communio* of the immanent Trinity (where the total self-surrender of each Hypostasis to each Other—beginning with the Father's self-surrender—grounds eternal life) and that of the economic Trinity (where the Son's self-surrender through the Father in the Spirit remains the abiding icon of the mystery of God's essence). When Augustine shows us the eschatological, total sacrifice, Christ's self-surrender as High Priest of creation, including every creature that is dedicated to God,[1] we must not forget that this universal homage is first addressed to the Father, whose sacrifice is prior. "The Father is not only the One who accepts all these sacrifices. He it is who sacrificed and delivered up his Son for us all, and continues to do so through all time. Sacrifice now embraces everything: . . . the sacrifice of the Church with all her members, the sacrifice of Christ, the sacrifice of the Father."[2] "Here, too, the mystery of the Eucharist begins as it proceeds from the Trinity . . . ; behind the sacrifice of the Son stands the consubstantial loving surrender of the Father as the source of the Eucharist. The Son takes men up into this mystery." In order to illustrate this connection, the Father "lends, so to speak, transtemporal, divine forms of being to the Son's worldly existence in the Eucharist. He now generates his

[1] *De Civ. Dei* X, 6–7, 20; XVI, 22; XIX, 23.
[2] H 82.

Son continually under this eucharistic form."[3] And just as the
Son's whole attitude on the Cross is initially preserved sacramentally in the Eucharist as a *commemoratio passionis*,[4] henceforth the
sacramental Eucharist will be kept safe in "the Son's one, eternal, heavenly purpose of sacrifice and self-surrender, inseparable
from the love of the triune God. Only in God is the meaning of
the Cross whole and entire; the Son's eternal self-surrender, his
sacrificial death in time and the Church's Eucharist are all integrating elements, essential to its full meaning."[5] What is hidden
and sacramental in the Eucharist "is something designed only for
our time", but its substantial content will remain the same "in its
resurrection form".[6] The latter has come into being, however,
only through that death which summed up the Son's ultimate
self-surrender on the Cross: this was both "the beginning of his
eucharistic incarnation" but also the moment when his temporal
existence was given "participation in eternity". This, in turn,
shows "just how much the Eucharist is a gift to us from the
Father".[7] By accepting the Son's total surrender, he opens up
for him the path of the Eucharist, through which he can integrate the Church and the world into his sacrificial spirit and so
assimilate them to the mode of existence of the Trinity.[8]

As we showed earlier, man's dying within the paradigm of
Christ's death, his purification in the fire of Christ's love that is
set forth on the Cross, causes man's self-centered "I" to explode
and take on a eucharistic and trinitarian form. "The 'I', in particular, must be brought into the sacrifice."[9] Here the harvest
of Cross and Eucharist is reaped, here the grain of wheat that
dies on the Cross is seen to rise again in the ear, here the sower
and reaper rejoice together (cf. Jn 4:37), here the Son reveals
that he has power to lay his life down and take it again, "he has

[3] 4 Jo 381 (GT).
[4] C 345–46.
[5] C 345.
[6] C 540.
[7] 4 Jo 436.
[8] Christ, in taking us into his sacrifice, causes us to be sacrificed with him; but
thereby he also challenges us to offer sacrifice with him: 4 Jo 338; Ep 203–4; B
86, 88–90; H 79, 81.
[9] B 119.

also the power to demand his life again from each individual and from all."[10] The Holy Spirit's role is crucial here: just as, in the sending of the Son to become man, the Spirit took on the role of the Father, so he does "in the ever-new making-present of the Son in the Eucharist".[11] He is no less active in communicating the Son's sacrificial mind and heart to those who receive him, so that they can make sacrifice, together with the Son, to the Father.

The final, heavenly shape of the *communio* as the reciprocal openness of the redeemed is so much a part of the mystery of the Trinity that there are hardly words and concepts to describe it. Most importantly, we must refer back to the one freedom of the divine Essence that is possessed by each Hypostasis in its own specific way; this means that the unity of the divine will is *also* the result of an integration of the intentions of the Hypostases.[12] It is true that the creature's freedom is entrusted to it as an irrevocable gift on the part of divine freedom, yet this freedom that is given to all the redeemed is bound—precisely because it is oriented to the Prototype and Origin of all freedom—to assimilate itself to whatever decisions are uttered by the triune God. This is the first truth that the willful creature needs to be taught; it is the severe lesson which Doña Proëza is given, before her death, by her guardian angel.[13] What is difficult to grasp is that the triune divine freedom, which allows scope within its unity for each Hypostasis to exercise its own mode of seeing and deciding, similarly does not absorb all creaturely freedom into itself but *freely and generously* gives itself to all. In the harmony of all freedoms, the freedom of each individual retains its own timbre. The divine freedom is so all-encompassing that it makes room, within its single Truth, for countless aspects; thus it does not override or infringe the area of mystery of each individual's creaturely spontaneity.

In the community that comes into being through the Son's eternal *communio*, everyone is utterly open and available to each other, but this openness is not like the total perspicuity of states

[10] 2 Jo 280.
[11] Ap 496 (and this whole context).
[12] Cf. p. 88 above.
[13] Claudel, *Le Soulier de Satin*, day 3, scene 8.

or situations: instead we have free persons freely available to each other on the basis of the unfathomable distinctness of each. What is offered to the other is thus always an unexpected and surprising gift. Again we see that the perfection of the creature corresponds to the element of surprise in the eternal life of God himself, which we discussed earlier.[14] Every personal act in which, within the all-encompassing light of the divine will, the individual person purposes to do something contains a creative element; the coincidence of this element with the equally creative freedom of the other corresponds, not to an analytic unity, but to a synthetic unity, and this resultant coincidence is doubtless an aspect of eternal blessedness itself. God's will, embracing the entire, infinitely diversified heaven, is so generous that it draws into itself all the fullness of redeemed human freedoms, pride of place being given to that of the incarnate Son; and even though it is the originating will, providing the (analytic) norm for all freedom, it nonetheless desires to be simultaneously the (synthetic) will that is the resultant of all the others.

Otherwise it would be impossible to maintain the postulate formulated earlier,[15] which says that eternal blessedness can by no means consist of a mere *visio*, but must involve genuine, creative activity. It seems, however, that we cannot envisage genuine creativity except as the overcoming of a resistance, a "contrary state" (*Wider-Stand*) Is this not the deepest reason for the project of the Hegelian dialectic? Where "the seriousness, the pain, the patience and the toil of the negative is lacking, . . . the life of God may well seem to be love at play within itself", but it sinks "to the level of pious edification and even of insipidity" where there is no "overcoming of alienation".[16] This alienation has taken place, and been overcome through an extreme of alienation, in the Cross and death of the Son. Had there been no meaningful result from this overcoming, the dialectic would have been nailed to its cross for all eternity, and we would have found ourselves marooned in the world of Nietzsche, in an aimless, chaotic and self-devouring nightmare.

[14] Cf. p. 89 above.
[15] Cf. above pp. 402ff. and 425ff.
[16] Hegel, preface to his *Phenomenology of the Spirit* (1832).

In eternal life, creativity will always be the offspring of personal freedom, but it will no longer take place in the loneliness of the genius. Now creativity will emerge in the medium of a *communio sanctorum* that both affirms it and celebrates other aspects of truth; the resultant syntheses, however, will be beyond all prediction.

D. "IF YOU COMPREHEND IT,
IT IS NOT GOD"

1. A Faceless Drama?

Of course we needed to have recourse to mere images and symbols, just as Revelation itself does, in order to describe the world's fulfillment in God. Looking back, however, over the path we have traced in the volumes of this *Theo-Drama*, does not our presentation seem far too simple in the face of the world's labyrinthine complexity and the abyss of God's incomprehensibility that yawns beyond it? We portrayed it as a drama—albeit a drama in which God was supposed to have taken a role, the role of protagonist—but is the simplicity of this whole idea not an insult in the face of the riddle of existence? We gave an overall survey of the Christian "world stage" (*Theo-Drama* I, 135–257), built up, in an apparently logical way, out of interlocking statements of Christian faith; but is this not the kind of thing that many of our contemporaries find narrow and obsolete, the kind of thing that prevents mankind from putting out for new shores?

In order to set the play's central scene in motion, it was necessary to expound the essential mystery of the world's divine Ground in the three aspects that correspond to the Hypostases of the Trinity in Christian dogma. Only one of these becomes comprehensible in earthly terms, namely, the figure of the man Jesus of Nazareth, who speaks of his special relation to his Origin, whom he calls Father, and of the divine Spirit whom he desires to send forth. If his words are reduced to an abstract system, how can we avoid an intolerable rationalization of the mystery of Being? In spite of the precautions taken (*Theo-Drama* I, 54ff.; 578ff.), does this not lead necessarily to an absolute Idealism in which man is the creative subject?[1]

Christian dogma, by comparison, seems trite, almost mythological. God, originally giving men commands (and prohibi-

---

[1] In *Das Schicksal der Metaphysik von Thomas zu Heidegger* (Einsiedeln: Johannes Verlag, 1959), G. Sieworth shows the ways in which this transformation has taken place.

tions), is offended by his subjects' disobedience; he sends his eternal Son from heaven to earth, and, while the latter impresses his contemporaries through his wisdom, in the end he is rejected by them because of his inordinate demands. The sufferings of his death, allegedly, have the power to reconcile God with the world, and, although the new message of this reconciliation provokes sinners to resist and become even more obstinate, God wins the game on the basis of the Passion of his Son and of his followers.

Surely a question mark can be put after every item in this simplistic scheme? Sin, for instance. Of course the world is full of guilt and blame, but in view of the condition of the world in which we have to live, how dare we give the name of "Love" to its Originator, to someone who is so over sensitive to the conduct of human beings that he is "offended" by it and then "reconciled" again by a single historical event? Is our guilt not inextricably matted with the whole sickness of being, and hence irremediable? Can we locate the alleged turning point of the tragedy of world history in the one accident of Golgotha, as if a huge pyramid with its base in heaven were balanced on its point on the earth? In any case we do not know for certain how this convicted man saw his own death or what measures were taken, in the post-Easter period, to justify the catastrophe of his death. May it not well be that "late" Christologies, like the Pauline and Johannine, so inflated what had taken place that it came to be regarded as a turning point in world history and so—in the councils of the first centuries—provided a pretext for the doctrine of one God in three Persons, which only Christians could find acceptable?

And what of this supposedly central event in which the world is reconciled with God: Does it make sense in terms of history? "All things have continued as they were from the beginning of creation" (2 Pet 3:4). Have hatred, envy, murder diminished among nations and individuals? Have Christians themselves not contradicted their gospel with their wars, with the consequences of their dogmatic intolerance? So much so that one would need to be an archaeologist to dig out the traces of healthy Christian origins from the mountain of debris. Is mankind still interested in this kind of archaeology? True, some people try to undergird dogma's "castles in the air" with a supporting basis of "fundamental theology", but what serious scientific discipline is concerned about such substructures and superstructures? There are attempts, contrary to the warnings of Jesus and Paul, to make accommodations to the concrete way of the world. Jesus and his disciples extolled poverty, but even as this message was echoing from the walls of Assisi, the realists were translating it—since it was so remote from the world—into an ethics of social action: "solidarity with the poor against poverty".[2] Cluny had become a quarry in its time, so why shouldn't the ancient spiritual cathedrals of Church dogma yield a few stones for today's building programs of puritanical world transformation?

The more Christianity acts in a triumphalist and absolutist manner in the world of today and tomorrow, the more it is felt to be a ghost. So again, at the end of this theodramatic enterprise, the question can be asked: Haven't we been building a castle in the air, remote from the real world, out of our own eccentric mind, which will be completely ignored by the thousands of millions—and this includes the majority of Christians—who see the world quite differently? Such people are often satisfied, as we know, with a vague reference to the Man who preached about God's goodness and who, for his pains, came to a sad end. Wasn't this Man ultimately faceless? Wasn't this, too, central to his "cause", if we compare it with the sharp profiles of worldly reality? This facelessness is a distressing phenomenon, when we consider the thousands of attempts—in spite of everything—to fit a face (or perhaps a mask?) to him.

What, after all, was Jesus' "cause"? People say it was *he himself*. But what was he? He is called "the image of the Invisible" (Col 1:15). But is this not a contradiction in terms? In our work *The Glory of the Lord*, we insisted on his "form" (*Gestalt*); but in that case he would be the form of the Formless, which (or who), in essence, could not enter into any form. It is possible to cling to the figure of Jesus as it appears in the Gospels and try to show how its distinct aspects, seen together, call for and complement each other; but the only result is that the very core

---

[2] E.g., in the manifestos that, in the wake of the Council, more than one great religious order proclaimed officially as the course to be followed.

of this figure eludes our grasp and slips away. "My teaching",
he says, literally, "is not mine, but his who sent me" (Jn 7:16).
What then? Has he a teaching of his own ("my teaching"), or
hasn't he ("is not mine")? Nor is it only a matter of teaching,
but of who he is: "He who has seen me has seen the Father" (Jn
14:9). So do we see, not him, but someone else? Is his face only
a mask? Must we look through the mask to see some other face?
But whose? Is his "I" only a prism through which we are to
discern another "I"? Yet he is a human being of flesh and blood,
not some Indian avatar that can dissolve into mist. Or *is* he? "It
is good for you that I go away"—or vanish (a favorite text of
the German mystics), otherwise the Spirit could not come and
"explain all things to you". What things? That, while he was
there, he could not be known,[3] that he had to be absent in order
to be really present?

The point of these tormenting questions is simply to indicate
one thing: Unless we say that Jesus of Nazareth is a deranged idiot or that he never uttered these words, we must admit that we
are in the presence of an impenetrable mystery, which is none
other than the mystery of the Trinity. "My teaching", which
really is his, "is not mine", because it really is from the Other
"who sent me". This might be still tolerable and explainable
if the one sent had received the Sender's teaching as *someone
else's* teaching and had subsequently made it his own. But this
strained interpretation is rendered impossible by the words, "He
who has seen me has seen (not me, but) the Father." Here we
have one "I" within another: the Invisible, apparently, is "seen"
in the visible. Similarly, in the Spirit who has come, the Absent
One is beheld as present; while the understanding of him-who-
is-present is absent! Leaving aside all Jansenist pessimism, we can
agree with Pascal when he says that the darkness of revelation
is dazzling enough for us to realize—if we are privileged to and
willing to believe—that we live and move within the mystery
of God. The only way to grasp the "figure" of Jesus, the central
actor of the theo-drama, is by *not grasping* it and by allowing it
to take its place in the "ungraspable" context of the mystery of

---

[3] F. Guimet, *Existenz und Ewigkeit* (Einsiedeln: Johannes Verlag, 1973).

the Trinity.[4] This grasping by "letting go" is what we mean by
faith, and it probably requires more letting go than it is prepared
for; fortunately, however, what it tries to hold on to will ultimately be wrested from it anyway. Mystery does not begin at
the point where reason, having taken many rational steps, does
not know how to proceed: mystery begins right in the middle
of the Prologue.

Jesus slips through the clutches of psychology and withdraws
into mystery—although he is a true human being and not an
element of *maya*. That is what is irritating about him. But this
"withdrawal" is continued in those who can be described as
his fellow actors in the drama, genuine Christians. How can we
understand Paul's paradoxical (and hardly translatable), "it is no
longer I who live, but Christ who lives in me; and the life I
now live in the flesh I live by faith in the Son of God, who
loved me and gave himself for me" (Gal 2:20)? Again, just as we
saw above, we have a trans-psychological reciprocal indwelling,
although here it is different from the reciprocal indwelling of
Jesus, Father and Spirit: the "I" that is "no longer I" is *faith*,
which surrenders itself to him who surrendered himself for this
"I". This is a new form of reciprocal indwelling, but it is based
on the first form.[5] The picture, however, is the same: we have an
apparently well-defined personality whose mystery—and what
great personality is not mysterious?—seems to lie in his self-
surrender to an "Idea": and yet it is the "Idea" that comes first
in self-surrender; if we fail to see this, we have no hope of understanding such a personality from within. This mystery continues the presence, in the world, of the trinitarian mystery that
permeates everything: Jesus lives in Paul, but this is only a model
instance of what Paul describes as the very nature of the Church:
the Church is the Mystical Body of the one Christ in his members, which he loves as "his flesh" (Eph 5:29) and which at the
same time, in the Church, form his "Bride" and "Spouse".

At its edges, this Church, which is also, however, a tangible
institution, merges with the rest of mankind. In Christian belief

---

[4] "Sich halten—an den Unfaßbaren" in *Geist und Leben* 52 (1979), 246–58.

[5] N. Hoffmann, "Das trinitarische 'Für' als Urgrund des staurologischen 'Für'"
in *Kreuz und Trinität: Zur Theologie der Sühne* (Einsiedeln: Johannes Verlag, 1982),
56ff.

Jesus died for this mankind no less than for the Church; on the basis of the Cross he enfolds it in himself, sinful, unbelieving and hostile though it is. Here, more than anywhere else, we must allow the mystery to stand; we must not attempt to soften men's alienation from and hostility toward God (for instance, by devaluing sin and regarding it as a merely negative factor in the dialectic), nor must we exaggerate the sovereign power of grace (won by Christ on man's behalf) in such a way that the sinner's justification does not need his conversion and consent. Who could possibly penetrate to this hidden, dramatic wrestling of God and the sinner?

One might be tempted to think that the complicated, dialectical God of the Old Covenant (of whom one never knew whether he was smouldering in anger or melting in "bowels of compassion", whether he had forsaken his faithless wife or—against all expectation—was standing by her) has given himself a new, "Enlightenment" image; that now he has become an unequivocally loving, fatherly God. The "Veiled Image of Sais"[6] has revealed its face—or so one might think. But what of the earthly collapse of Jesus' mission, not only then, but down through the ages: Is the image of God not once more obscured by the most impenetrable veil in the cry of abandonment with which Jesus sinks into the dark night? Is it not the case, once again—and even more terrifyingly than in the Old Testament—that the "loving Father" proclaimed by Jesus turns out to be a pitiless, even cruel and demonic God? In his meditation on the Cross, Luther comes close to this frontier. In order to circumvent this whole issue, the Gnostics split God into two halves: the lightness above the Cross and the darkness that is responsible for the demonic in the world. Anyone who cannot take this path must face the Lutheran dialectic; and if he wants to get beyond Luther, he must at least take seriously the fact that God is incomprehensible even in his highest revelation, profoundly veiled even when he unveils himself.

"If any one imagines that he knows something, he does not yet know as he ought to know" (1 Cor 8:2). "Anyone who thinks

---

[6] Reference to a poem by Goethe with that title.—Trans.

he can come to a satisfying conclusion on the basis of knowledge simply shows that he does not know the kind of knowledge that faith consists of." He imagines that "God becomes less mysterious, the more he surrenders his mysteries to man; and that man can accumulate and store the knowledge thus received. This only goes to show that such a person does not know in the way he should."[7] "God's ways and thoughts do not hide themselves from men's gaze, but precisely what they *do* reveal shows that all human concepts are inadequate."[8] "What is revealed is the *mystery* that does not cease to be a mystery on account of being dispensed." Paul emphasizes that what was "previously . . . *hidden*" is now "brought to light": "one understands in the clear light of God that it is a mystery. It is, for example, clear that Mary conceived the Son of the Father by the working of the Holy Spirit, but this fact does not cease to be infinitely mysterious. It even becomes all the more sublime, many-sided, and mysterious, the more the believer penetrates into it, the more he understands of it."[9] The closer the mystery draws and the more it reveals itself, the more mysterious it becomes: we are overwhelmed by God's nearness, and "what creates the distance between us and God is in fact his incomprehensible and overpowering nearness."[10] Finally, at this point, the mystery of the creature's origin and goal, hitherto vague and lacking in nuance, suddenly crystallizes and becomes evident as the mystery of the Trinity. "The more a person loves the Lord and the greater the mission given to him, the more trust the Lord demands of him, which ultimately means *the more invisible and unfathomable the Father becomes in him*. The more clearly-focused the knowledge that the Lord gives, the greater is our 'not-seeing', because we realize more and more how much remains hidden behind each revealed mystery."[11] In the Old Covenant the Father could not be approached; in the New Covenant he addresses the world through the voice of the Son, and this results in a paradox: "He

[7] C 238.
[8] Is 118.
[9] Ep 131–32.
[10] Ka II, 96.
[11] Ka II, 169.

is concealed, as it were, behind the Son, but this concealment reveals him more than all previous revelation did", albeit the concealment remains:[12] in the ultimate concealment on the Cross,
when he abandons the Son, he is most revealed in his love for
the world. And the Son, whose naked body on the Cross "holds
no mystery for the world", has himself entered into the paradox of the greatest unveiling together with the greatest concealment. "The mystery is exposed through the *wound* that opens
his side and affords a view into the mystery of the Lord's human
body. . . . Not even his dead body belongs to him any more;
he exposes it. This, too, belongs to the mystery of fruitfulness
—that he himself wishes to hold no more mystery for us. Too
much is asked of him in exposing the mystery, yet he allows it,
and precisely this leads from one mystery to another, indeed, is
itself the greatest mystery. Every mystery that he communicates
gives birth to a new one: that is his fruitfulness; but all these
mysteries are ones of love and therefore of self-surrender."[13] This
is true of every item of Christian faith-knowledge: "As clarity
increases, the mystery grows." When Mary receives the angel's
announcement that the Spirit will overshadow her and she will
bear a child, "her experience inundates her knowledge, with the
result that she receives more insight, and at the same time everything becomes more mysterious than she thought. The mystery grows in her: it becomes brighter and yet accumulates into a
store of knowledge that is undisclosed, a treasure from which all
generations of the Church will draw sustenance in order to penetrate into her mystery. They will never come to an end. Every
believer who senses that he has a mission to illuminate aspects
of divine revelation needs to possess both a deeper knowledge
and a deeper awareness of the mystery."[14]

If all these formulations are to have an abiding meaning, and if
the paradoxes they contain are insurmountable, this meaning can
only be found in the trinitarian character of truth itself. To the
man who will not accept this, Christian truth will always seem

[12] Ka II, 78.
[13] 4 Jo 140–41 (GT).
[14] OM 26–27.

to be flat and one-dimensional, such as it is in liberal theology and in the liberal mind. But the man who can believe that "the Logos was in the beginning with God, and was God", that this Logos is begotten from the Father before all time and that from the Father and from him proceeds the Spirit of Love most free —such a man must admit the following: Everything concerning the Logos is neither a subsequent development on the basis of a prior divine Ground (this would be Gnosticism and Arianism, for the Father begets the Son from all eternity); nor does the Logos and everything connected with him claim to be the Father of all truth, for the Son eternally refers "back" to the generative "bosom of the Father" (Jn 1:18). Equally, on the other hand, the Logos and his sphere cannot be made into a closed, absolute, (logic-al) system; for he goes beyond himself and, together with the Father, breathes forth the free Spirit of Love. This Spirit by no means relativizes the Logos; rather, the Spirit guides men "into all the truth" of the Logos (Jn 16:13). But the latter can only *be* the Logos by *revealing* the Father's "causeless" begetting and its unfathomably profound meaning and by causing himself to be interpreted by the Spirit of absolute Love.

Thus it becomes obvious that anyone who refuses to approach this "holy and manifest mystery" is bound to hover uncertainly, not knowing in what direction he is to look for the absolute Good, the goal of man's dramatic existence (cf. *Theo-Drama* I, 413ff.: "The Good Slips Away"). Then the situation changes: the "characters" on the human stage (the stage of life or of the theater), taking up some good cause that they feel obliged to posit as absolute, ultimately become faceless in the all-embracing context of the mystery of the Good; whereas the One who is apparently incomprehensible, because he wishes to be only the exegesis of Another, the Father (leaving his own mystery to be interpreted by yet Another, the Spirit), remains the adequate "expression" (*charaktēr*, Heb 1:3) of the essence of truth.

2. *"This Slight Momentary Affliction"?*

Georg Büchner:

On his deathbed, "in a calm, loud, solemn voice", he said: "It is not that we have too much pain: we have too little, for it is through pain that we go to God."

Caroline Schulz's diary on Büchner's last days.
February 1837.

Sigismund:

"Man is one single glory, and it is not that he has too much suffering and pain: he has too little. That is what I want to say to you."

H. von Hofmannsthal, *Der Turm* [The tower],
1st version, II, 2.

To someone who is really suffering, Paul's words on the relationship between earthly suffering and heavenly joy are hardly to be endured: "This slight momentary affliction is preparing for us an eternal weight of glory beyond all comparison" (2 Cor 4:17). He says these words when describing the tribulations that sweep over him from all sides, rendering him a bearer of the sufferings of Jesus. Nor is this enough: elsewhere he takes all the suffering of the world, of "creation groaning under bondage to decay", and puts it on the scales, where it seems too light compared with the weight of glory to which he is looking forward: "I consider that the sufferings of this present time are not worth comparing with the glory that is to be revealed to us" (Rom 8:18).

It really is a case of comparing two weights (*baros*), and the entire weight of world suffering (the first passage even includes the suffering of the Cross) cannot hold the balance against the hoped-for "glory"; it cannot even hold the balance against the "new aeon". In the second passage every comparison is abandoned, while in the first, however, a kind of causal connection *is* drawn between the "slight" earthly suffering and the "eternal weight of glory": the former actually "prepares" for the latter. On the one hand, there is no connection; on the other, there *is* a connection. The weight of glory would not be ours without the present slight tribulation.

This presents us with the ultimately insoluble question of the relationship between temporal life and eternal life. Our notions of time are deceptive: eternal life is not a continuation of transitory life; it does not begin "after death" but is perpendicular to it; it is the manifest face of a totality that, for the present, is accessible only in veiled form. So while this veiled form is essentially transient, it nonetheless prepares us for what is not yet manifest. The passage from Romans sees the pain of transitoriness, which governs everything else, precisely in its subject fate: in creation's groaning for what is at present unattainable, a groaning that is unconscious, somewhere outside the realm of revelation. This groaning is deeper and more conscious in Christians who, in virtue of their hope—but a hope that does not see—live with their eyes set on redemption, most deeply perhaps in the "sighs too deep for words" (Rom 8:19–26) that come from an anguished heart. Suffering is not seen here as a fate that closes the earthly world in on itself, robbing it, above all else, of every transcendence, since "all prospect of a beyond has evaporated"—and challenging us to embrace the prime task of improving intolerable conditions in the world; no: suffering is a phenomenon laid upon us by the beyond; in all its utterances it speaks to us of the beyond.

Might it not be, in the end, that this baffling weight of suffering in the world is a feature of transcendence (of which we are largely unconscious), a way of training us for the great act of self-surrender that concludes our temporal life? Might this be true even where the sufferer has been drained of all inner resources and struggles with all the fibers of his being against a process that seems to him pitiless and pointless? Might it not be that all the blood spilled in vain has something to do, after all, with that "precious Blood" with which we have been "bought" and "washed"? Can the many tears that human beings shed, unfruitfully, on their own behalf or because of a friend's sufferings, be transformed into something that is fruitful for eternity? Mechthild von Hackeborn is instructed by the Lord to give a message to an acquaintance of hers: "Tell her in my name to ask me, of my goodness, to change her former, useless tears and

make it as if she had wept them out of love for me and in devotion and repentance for her sins. She must only believe in my
goodness, and in the measure that she believes, I will make the
transformation in her."[15]

If this degree of transcendence and this kind of transformation are possible, should we not read the Lord's "Beatitudes"
in this light? The first beatitude, in Matthew, gives no indication of time: "Blessed are the poor in spirit, for the kingdom of
God is theirs"; the others locate the promised blessedness in the
future: "Blessed are those who mourn, for they shall be comforted. . . ." But the absence of the future in the first beatitude
clearly suggests a blessedness that is supratemporal, that is always
here-and-now: insofar as the poor in spirit—all who, whether
they wish it or not, are made poor by the Spirit—endure being
plundered, they become real citizens of the kingdom of God,
which henceforth can reign in them. As for this kingdom, it is
not located in an other-worldly and purely future beyond: it is
meant to come and assert its authority, on earth as in heaven. Of
course, those who have been plundered do not experience this
through their senses, otherwise they would not be poor. That
is why the following beatitudes are in the future: those who
mourn will one day learn that they had always been comforted
in eternal life, even while they were mourning in the life that
is transitory. The pure of heart, too, will one day learn that,
while they were feeling after God in the darkness of faith, they
were already beholding him. It is both correct and important,
theologically, that Matthew should record beatitudes both for
the suffering and for those who are active—the merciful, the
powerless, the peacemakers—for such activity presupposes the
same renunciation and impoverishment in their inner life as is
asked of the suffering. In life, for the most part, the two categories merge into one another: the attitude of the meek and
the peacemakers presupposes a wisdom that is the fruit of their
experience of the evil inherent in violence and war.

It is not a question of glorifying earthly suffering (often the result of worldly injustice [Mt 5:6], persecution [5:10] and abuse
[5:11], which could be morally doubtful) but of whether we

---

[15] *Revelationes* IV, 38.

are open or closed to the fundamental values of the kingdom of God. Such openness can prove itself through action, even through militancy, just as much as through endurance. There are enough places in the New Testament that summon us to God's call-to-arms and challenge us to seize the "sword" brought by Jesus; there seems to be nothing against a just defense, even the armed protection, of earthly goods that we hold to be willed and given by God. It is surely right, while eschewing avarice and egoism, to take action to preserve earthly goods that, while they are transitory, nonetheless have a rightful place in the will and rule of God.

This perspective sheds new light on what we tried to say earlier[16] about our earthly life, in heaven, being not a mere memory but a real present. The Book of Revelation takes up a phrase from Isaiah (Is 25:8) and says that in the new world God will wipe away all tears (Rev 21:4). This undoubted truth does not exclude the fact that the blessing hidden in earthly tears will remain simultaneously, as it were, "bodily" present. This blessing can be so final and all-embracing that it really constitutes a "weight of glory beyond all comparison" with the suffering experienced, as Paul says. And if it is true that the suffering of the Crucified One can transform even worldly pain, unintelligible to itself, into a co-redemptive suffering, then the most unbelievable, most cruel tortures, prisons, concentration camps and whatever other horrors there may be can be seen in close proximity to the Cross, to that utter night, interrupted only by the unfathomable cry of "Why?"

John brings Cross and Resurrection together in the one word "exaltation": this means that the anguish of being forsaken by God—and all suffering associated with it down the centuries—does not need to be excluded from some upper spiritual faculty of the suffering Christ (as Scholastic theology thought, assuming that the latter constantly dwells in the light of eternal blessedness). It is true, nonetheless, that what the Son experiences on the Cross as total night is in God's sight the Son's ultimate obedience and hence his highest glory. In the Crucified, this glory is reflected solely in his letting-be, that is, in the fulfillment of

[16] Cf. above, "Heaven to Earth", pp. 402–10; cf. also *Theo-Drama* IV, 15ff.

his mission, since he is the Lamb led silent to slaughter (Jer 11:19; Is 53:7).[17] In his discipleship, the Christian tries to combine genuine forsakenness [*Verlassenheit*] with genuine resignation [*Gelassenheit*].[18] Only man is given the ability to maintain this tension; so we can understand why man's unique dignity is seen in his endurance of suffering, a glory that is specific to him and his path to God. If for the moment we prescind from all the pain caused by human freedom and wickedness, what we see here is a last trinitarian mystery, one that is profoundly hidden. The Son is eternally begotten by the Father: within the infinite divine nature, in other words, one Person is "let be" in absolute Otherness; what deep abysses are here! God has *always* plumbed them, but once a finite world of creatures has been opened up, these depths must be traversed stepwise as forms of alienation. Nonetheless these steps can only be taken as part of a journey already (and always) accomplished in the infinite Trinity. And when the particular mystery of the Son's Incarnation takes place, he traverses—as man and together with all sufferers and on their behalf—the realms of forsakenness that, as God, he has already (and has always) traversed.

Once more it is clear from this that we cannot establish any comprehensively evident relationship between the creature's transitory and eternal life. It is not to be denied that in eternal life all tears are wiped away and the sea of tears has ceased to be (Rev 21:1), but nor can it be denied that, in the wisdom of God, the depths of pain have helped to prepare the realm in which the soul can be the recipient of eternal joy.

Behind the riddle of suffering—physical and spiritual—in the world, there lies another, equally distressing: the riddle of evil, which arises in the free refusal to accept God's will and command. This *cannot* be said to be an element that is present as a possibility in the Son's relationship with the Father. Accord-

---

[17] Cf. the interpretation of temporality and esp. of the Cross in Jean Mouroux, *Le Mystère du Temps*, Théologie 56 (Paris: Aubier, 1962), 110ff., 126ff.

[18] "The more severe your external suffering is and the more composed you are internally, the more you resemble Me," Suso, *Little Book of Eternal Wisdom*, chap. 18. "If suffering were not painful, it would not be suffering. . . . Suffering is a short pain and a long pleasure": chap. 13.

ingly, we cannot find any traces of it in the eternal realm; as the Book of Revelation shows, this Babylonian principle of temptation has already "fallen" (Rev 14:8; 16:19; even before Babylon is shown and interpreted), just as the blaspheming beasts have already been unmasked in their nothingness and deceit and are ultimately consigned to be burned in the lake of fire (20:9, 14; 21:8). Now, however, the dramatic dialogue between this ever-intensifying No and God's Yes undergoes a further change: the nothingness of evil—of even the most deliberate evil—with all its satanic raging in world history, is shown in the fact that nothing remains of it except what it has achieved in terms of fruitful suffering. This alone, even in the darkest of earthly nights, has an objective, correlative joy in eternal life.[19] Evil, in spite of the baffling freedom it has, has only enough power to manifest the far more baffling mercy of God, which causes the fountain of salvation to spring forth from the very wounds that evil has inflicted. However terrifying the "deep things of Satan" (Rev 2:24) may be, his skill in seducing innocence, in spiritual torture, in inventing sophistries against God—Dostoyevsky and Bernanos have endeavored to plumb the depths of the demonic—it is also frightening to discover how false this pseudo-profundity is, how restricted its scope, and how quickly fascination with it turns into pure boredom.

We might be afraid that, if there is no contrast between light and darkness in the kingdom of God and everything is bathed in ceaseless brightness ("there shall be no night there": Rev 21:25), some new form of boredom could emerge, that "surfeit" which Origen feared, leading him to predict a new "fall" of souls from the light into the enticing darkness. Led astray by Platonic arguments, even great Christian thinkers have regarded this Rembrandtesque interplay of contrasts as indispensable for the beauty of the cosmos and of history. But those who see the richness and multiplicity of the created universe as belonging to the complete picture of the divine fullness, as Thomas Aquinas did, yet import into this kaleidoscopic fullness the opposition between good and evil, have failed to think this idea through. It is not evil that makes the world more interesting but the multiplicity

---

[19] Cf. above, the section entitled "Death/Life; Sorrow/Joy", pp. 250–56.

of the good, freely brought into being; as we have shown, this finds its highest development in the kingdom of God. Here there will not only be eternal day but also an ultimate form of night. In the unfathomable depths of this night we shall both rest—as a lover rests in the freedom of the beloved—and be drawn on to ever-new discoveries. For then even created freedom will share, through grace, in the depth and inexhaustibility of the divine freedom.

A word should be added here about the glittering intermediate realm of *eros* which is found in Plato's *Symposium* and throughout all human history. Anders Nygren entertained a deep mistrust of the *eros* that seeks to arise from the creature to God; he held that it could not be harmonized with the *agape* that comes down from God. There is some truth in this insofar as everything that links human longing to the realm of sex, genealogy, the clan and sensual fellow feeling belongs to finitude and cannot pass the gates of death—to say nothing of the fire of divine love. "I tell you this, brethren: flesh and blood cannot inherit the kingdom of God" (1 Cor 15:50). It is naïve of Christians to ignore these words and imagine a continuation of earthly conditions and a "reunion" in the "beyond" with those they have loved; for though *eros* can be a great deceiver on earth, promising things "forever" and immediately breaking his vows, once we have passed beyond death he will have no power to perform things that belong to earthly life. How quickly *eros* erases the memory of those who have died! Scripture evinces an almost cynical realism in this regard:

> Weep bitterly, wail most fervently;
> observe the mourning the dead man deserves,
> one day, or two, to avoid comment,
> and then be comforted in your sorrow; . . .
>
> Do not abandon your heart to grief,
> drive it away, bear your own end in mind. . . .
>
> Once the dead man is laid to rest, let his memory rest too,
> do not fret for him, once his spirit departs.

(Sir 38:17–23 JB).

Can this be dismissed as merely Old Testament wisdom? Paul too can say: "We would not have you ignorant, brethren, concerning those who are asleep, that you may not grieve as others do who have no hope" (1 Th 4:13). The only part of earthly love to survive will be the heavenly love that has become incarnate in it. That may be a great deal; there may have been an almost complete transformation and refashioning of *eros* by *agape*. What is covertly egoistic and only seeks the advantage of the species can experience the "resurrection of the body" in a love that has become selfless and that loves solely in God; it can experience the miracle of metamorphosis from chrysalis to butterfly.

The possibility of *eros* being transformed into something beyond itself once it has sloughed off everything earthbound becomes clear in the apparently paradoxical fact that manhood and womanhood cross the frontier of death, whereas sexuality—now superfluous—does not. "For in the resurrection they neither marry nor are given in marriage, but are like angels in heaven" (Mt 22:30). Nonetheless Christ remains a man, Mary a woman.[20] Doubtless there remains a form of interpersonal fruitfulness that shares in divine fruitfulness but that, since death has ceased to exist, no longer expresses itself in begetting and giving birth. The preliminary, earthly forms of this heavenly fruitfulness are more than mere metaphorical pointers, they are a first installment of something final, albeit always under the sign of the Cross. (Examples of these preliminary forms are the Eucharist, which is an exchange of love between Christ the Bridegroom and the Church/Bride, and the life of virginity, which is a sharing in this suprasexual bridal life such as we see in Catherine of Siena's "betrothal" and "marriage".) This is where the *dotes sponsae* belong, the soul's adornment for the divine wedding; in High Scholasticism, which speaks much of this, the wedding present coincides with that *lumen gloriae* that is preparatory to union and actually facilitates it.[21] This doctrine, which had in

---

[20] "It is part of human nature to be man or woman. High Scholasticism regarded it as self-evident that the physical constitution of the human being would not suffer any alteration in this regard": H. J. Weber, *Die Lehre von der Auferstehung der Toten in den Haupttraktaten der scholastischen Theologie von Alexander von Hales zu Duns Scotus*, Freib. Theol. Studien 91 (Herder, 1973), 256f.

[21] *S. Th.* 95, 1–5. N. Wicki, "Die Lehre von den dotes animae" in *Die Lehre von*

mind primarily the individual's direct relationship with God, can be transferred to the *communio sanctorum*, which takes something of earthly marriage beyond itself, perfecting it in a final state that is free of all sexual cause and effect.

The relationship between the first Adam, earthly, of the earth, a man of the senses, and the Second Adam, the Life-giver who comes from heaven (1 Cor 15:45–47) cannot be dissolved on the one side or the other: for the Second, eternally superior to the first, has taken the latter's form into himself in order, not to destroy it, but to transfigure it through incorporation into his own heavenly form. "This mortal reality" must not be annihilated but "clothed with immortality" (1 Cor 15:53). If this were not so, the order of redemption would not be the originally intended perfecting of the order of creation but would hover above it, unrelated, in a gnostic manner. For this reason all genuine, positive aspects of the order of creation must be embedded in "immortality". In this context we again see the relevance of what was said at the beginning about the richness of the *analogia trinitatis*. The more trinitarian (which is to say, the richer) our picture of God is, the more we are able to have a positive attitude to the eternal perfecting of the world created and redeemed in God.

3. What Does God Gain from the World?

In this volume we have tried to set forth a trinitarian and christological eschatology. Thus, for instance, the problem of eternal damnation was put not so much from the anthropological perspective ("What does man lose in losing God?") as from God's perspective: "What does God lose in losing man?" Of course there are problems in formulating the question in this way; but to do so obviously presupposes that God actually can lose something, and accordingly that he "gains" something if his

---

der himmlischen Seligkeit, Stud. Friburgensia, New Series 9 (Fribourg, Switzerland, 1954) 202–37. "The *dotes* constitute the soul's supernatural equipment; they alone render *visio, dilectio* and *comprehensio* possible. The *dos* of *visio* corresponds to what would later be called *lumen gloriae*": 229.

will "for all men to be saved" (1 Tim 2:4) is achieved in such a way that, at the end of his work of creation, "God is all in all" (1 Cor 15:28). So we cannot avoid the final question: What does the entire work of creation and redemption mean to God? The question seems unanswerable. We cannot say that God only attains his ultimate fullness by involving himself with the world, that he needs the world, or that God's goodness radiates forth of its very essence, so that it *has to* communicate itself. On the other hand, it will not do to locate the reason for the creation of the world in God's will to procure his own ("accidental") glorification (primary goal) by leading rational creatures to share his blessedness (secondary goal). While we must hold on firmly to God's freedom in the work of creation in order to avoid all pantheism,[1] the final goal of creation, the *gloria Dei* (*formalis*), can only be properly reached from the trinitarian perspective. On the one hand, it is based on the ultimately gratuitous character of the essential divine "processions" within the Trinity—for without this gratuitous character it would be unthinkable that these processions "proceed" in love—and, on the other hand, it follows from the fact that the creature is drawn into the reciprocal acts of love within the Godhead, so that the collaboration of each Divine Person in the work of creation is intended to magnify the "glory" of the Others. In two ways this avoids giving the impression that the creation is basically a superfluous work since God gains nothing from it toward his own perfection and blessedness: creation's gratuitousness (which also implies that it is *not* necessary) is grounded in the more fundamental gratuitousness of the divine life of the Trinity; all suspicion of divine solipsism is removed from the *gloria Dei* in creation, since the inner participation of creatures in the life of the Trinity becomes an internal gift from each Divine Person to the Other: this overcomes every appearance of a merely external "glorification".

On the basis of this perspective, we were obliged to raise the question of a possible failure of this purpose of creation, which would result in a partial rejection of created beings, since they

[1] L. Scheffczyk, *Die Welt als Schöpfung* (Aschaffenburg: Pattloch, 1968), 68f.: "The freer the act of creation, the greater the interest in it and its result. Only absolute freedom can show a 'quasi-absolute' interest. Furthermore, it is only this freedom that safeguards the divine character of the act of creation."

were unsuitable for the work of inner glorification. This in turn induced us to speak of the "tragic aspect" or "tragedy" of God. As long as the *gloria Dei* remains intact—whether bringing bliss or damnation—the problem does not become acute. But where the purpose of creation is most closely bound up with the life of the Trinity, the question will not go away. We have to be aware of the limits of human speculation here—we have already said that the widest attainable horizon is the "hope that all will be redeemed"—but at the same time it would be wrong timidly to lag behind the boldness of this hope, while bearing in mind that the question of the fate of demons is insoluble in a *theologia viatorum* and must therefore be excluded.

The standpoint of "gratuitousness", involving the combination of two different modes of being (inner-divine process and the creation) must also allow us to get beyond the apparent contradiction that either God is all Being and the world cannot therefore add anything to him (which leads of necessity to a form of *maya* doctrine) or that the world has a genuine being, in which case God cannot be the fullness of Being (which leads logically to the view that the world is necessary to God). This quantitative way of looking at things—"Is God plus the world more than God on his own?"—is erroneous, because it leaves out of consideration the absolute freedom of Divine Being, a freedom that, even in God, has no "why". Both in the trinitarian self-communication and again in the decision to create the world, it is *its own necessity*. The decision to create is purely gratuitous, and we cannot get "behind" or "above" it to find some external necessity. The whole thrust of this book has been to show that the infinite possibilities of divine freedom all lie *within* the trinitarian distinctions and are thus free possibilities within the eternal life of love in God that *has always been realized*. This eternally realized love in God, therefore, does not require the positing—in a Hegelian manner—of these free possibilities so that it may realize itself. It is not a question of moving from the "play" to the "seriousness" of Love. The eternal Son, as such, has always chosen the perfect Yes of thanks to the Father, and to that extent the possibility of the *deliberatio* (gnōmē) of a *liberum arbitrium* is already "behind him". This *liberum arbitrium*, however, remains possible as a gift of divine gratuitousness, which, if it becomes reality, would entail the possibility (or rather, the freely willed "necessity") of the Cross and of forsakenness by God. The divine Father gives the Son absolute, independent existence as God, and in doing so he makes the "idea" of creation —up to and including the Cross—realizable; at the same time, however, this "idea" has already been overtaken and surpassed by the divine life and as such is incorporated into the absolute gratuitousness of trinitarian freedom and vitality.

The effect of this is that the conduct of *theologia* and *oikonomia* leaves room for a diversity in ways of speaking. Insofar as, in *oikonomia*, things with a high degree of reality are taking place, what corresponds to this reality in God initially seems to be a "mere" possibility (the "idea" of it); this is not incorrect provided we remember that what is realized in "economic" terms is rooted in an all-embracing divine freedom that for all eternity has been actually performing these "possible" things: this is far removed from "mere" possibility in a negative sense. We must also bear in mind that infinite richness is rich in freedom and can enrich others (and hence itself) in ways that are ever new; all the more so, since absolute richness lies precisely in the gratuitousness of giving, which presupposes a will to be "poor", both so that it may receive and so that it may expropriate itself. If this is true of relations within the Trinity, surely it should and must be true of the *oikonomia* that is rooted in the *theologia*. In conclusion, therefore, we shall try to illuminate the theodramatic interplay in its various aspects.

1. From all eternity the divine "conversation" envisages the possibility of involving a non-divine world in the Trinity's love. This conversation has always included the preliminary stages that will be necessary: the creation of a finite freedom in its twofold relation (to God and to other free creatures), which, however, "cannot perfectly fulfill love". If finite freedom is to be drawn into divine freedom, what is needed is, first, the Incarnation of the Son, which in turn draws the Church and, through her, the world "into the multiplicity of the Son's relationships with the Father and the Spirit", and then, secondly, the Cross, which opens a path whereby men can get beyond their refusal and allow themselves to be drawn into God. "Now the Father need

no longer regard his world as something *extra muros*, since it is
embedded in the relationship of love between Son and Spirit and
shares in the triune love." For the Cross is not only an "anti-
dote against individual sins" but overcomes "the totality of sin
(including original sin) and roots the world deeper in God than
sin could alienate it from him".[2] This means that the creature's
alienation was always considered as a possibility in the divine
conversation, as was the overcoming of this alienation through
the Son's blood on the Cross, in anticipation of all other means
of salvation.[3] "The Son has been offering his sacrifice to the
Father from the very beginning."[4] There is a certain quality of
"renunciation" in the eternal trinitarian life: it is seen in the very
fact that "the Father, renouncing his uniqueness, generates the
Son out of his own substance", which can be designated a "pre-
sacrifice". Once sin emerges, this "pre-sacrifice" turns into "actual renunciation", "just as, on the basis of the 'pre-sacrifice' of
the Son's eternal generation, God will unfold the Son's redemptive experience of forsakenness on the Cross."[5] The Cross, and
the Incarnation that envisages it, remain present reality within
time "because they themselves are not the first thing: they are
grounded in an eternal, heavenly will on the part of the Son to
surrender and sacrifice himself, inseparably linked to the love of
the triune God. The meaning of the Cross is only complete in
God; it is in God that the Son's eternal self-surrender, which inte-
grates his sacrificial death in time and the Church's Eucharist, attains its full meaning." It is true that, in the parousia, everything
temporal enters into eternal meaning, "but the Cross cannot be
superseded, because in eternity the Son's will to give himself
goes to these extreme lengths, nor does it retreat from that position after the fulfillment of the Cross; on the contrary, it keeps
this fulfillment alive until the end of time and for all eternity."[6]
Thus there is nothing hypothetical about the "pre-sacrifice" of
the Son (and hence of the Trinity): it is something utterly real,
which includes the absolute and total exhaustion of the Cross.

[2] OM 90–92.
[3] Ka II, 24.
[4] Ap 428.
[5] C 345.
[6] C 345.

"All this is implicit from all eternity in the Son's decision, even if it is only completed historically on the Cross." "To avoid giving the impression that, after the Cross, everything is behind us, . . . the Eucharist was instituted as a commemoration of his Passion", so that no one should regard the Lord's sacrifice and sufferings as past.[7] "In the Christian context, sacrifice, suffering, the Cross and death are only the reflection of tremendous realities in the Father, in heaven, in eternal life"; indeed, "they are nothing other than manifestations of what heaven is, namely, the love of God that goes to the ultimate. If the Father gives us these things, he does so because the Son has brought them to us; the Son, however, has mediated them to us so that we can receive them directly from the Father. . . . The Son's entire human life has only one meaning: to make us familiar with heaven, to show and give us heavenly things in a human way so that we can understand them."[8]

2. Eternal life, as the word itself says, is not a complete state of rest, but a constant vitality, implying that everything is always new. "We must not imagine the unchangability of God as something static: it is the movement of all movements, a streaming of eternity out into endlessness."[9] "Eternal life is not a state of rest," so, as we have already said,[10] the incarnate Son is a "truth" that is "always growing" since he is "the way".[11] Thus, according to Irenaeus, the Son has brought everything new with him and "given the Father's name a new stamp and a new meaning in the world; it is no longer the name of a "law or ordinance to which one is subject"—people were already acquainted with

---

[7] C 346.

[8] B 229. "It has pleased the Father to smite the Son with suffering. . . . Now it suddenly looks as though both tribulations and judgment have an entirely subordinate role, as though things are being decided at a much higher level, namely, in the unique love between Father and Son. In the Father this love is an infinite delight in the Son's love, and in the Son it is an infinite willingness to perform the Father's loving will to the very end": Is 99.

[9] A 112.

[10] Cf. above pp. 77f.

[11] 3 Jo 93. There is order, of course, on the Lord's way; "but this order exists only to cause everything to flow; it is what makes the inner richness of life possible": 3 Jo 102.

this—but the name of "a living Father, living even as a concept because he is understandable as Jesus' own Father", and, in him, the living Father of all.[12] Of course God does not "become" in the sense that creatures "become". "In God, becoming is a confirmation of his own Being. And since God is immutable, the vitality of his 'becoming' can never be anything other than his Being. . . . We are to 'become' what God 'is'. But between the two, preventing their confusion, is the 'ever-more' of the Divine Being."[13] Nonetheless it is precisely this quality of eternal life that enables temporal becoming to be a kind of copy of it. "God, the Eternal One, is Creator and does not cease to work in his creation, causing new things to come into being. And the mystery of this unceasing becoming is rooted in the mystery of his unceasing Being." For example, the absolute novelty of the Son's Resurrection lies "ultimately in the Father, who begets the Son and, after the pattern of this eternal event, has created human beings and endowed them with grace, calling them to share in the triune life together with the world in which they live and their particular bodies".[14] Since eternity is life, God created time "without in any way affecting the substance of eternity. He did not cut time out of eternity. On the one hand, there is transitory time; on the other, there is an intact eternity." But they are involved in "a living relationship between heaven and earth".[15] This is how the incarnate Son could be "eternity open to the world, eternity that has come into time. The time between the Incarnation and the Ascension cannot be separated from eternity. Thus by carrying out the will of God (on earth) we share in eternity, which consists in accompanying the Son."[16] The goal of eternal duration is constantly being reached, "the glorification of the triune God. In reaching it we are only reaching something that has already been reached; becoming coincides with being." But the goal of all earthly becoming is eternal life, which God implants, by anticipation, in the life of the true believer, and "then it is as if the stages of maturity in a man's life come closer

[12] 3 Jo 314.
[13] OM 105.
[14] C 318-19.
[15] T 34-35.
[16] Ka II, 66.

and closer together, a sign that eternal time is coming near to him, that he is becoming more ready for God."[17]

Primarily, what we have said about heaven is meant to show that neither creation nor Incarnation necessitates a change in God and his eternal life. In fact, the concept of eternal life "cuts off all possibility of positing a change in God".[18] "The love of God, too, like his other attributes, is subject to no change."[19] "The Incarnation never caused any interruption in the triune converse."[20] The Son on earth "was not deprived of his divinity in any way".[21] "In exchanging the strength of heaven for the weakness of earth", he nonetheless "lost nothing of his divinity, his omniscience and his bond with the Father; even at the point where he went down into the ultimate weakness of the Cross and felt abandoned by the Father and separated from heaven. In this way he completely relativized human distinctions and values."[22] The concept of *kenosis*, which theologians regard as indispensable in expressing the Son's descent, has an entirely anthropomorphic side. "As the one descending from heaven to earth, from the earth to the Cross, from the Cross to hell, he was always the same person he has been from eternity in heaven. He does not need to expropriate himself of his essence and character in order to live for a while in time. As man, [Christ] is not a modified God, and, as God, he is no altered man. He is fullness in person: God and man, and both in a perfect, immutable manner"[23]. For he simply expresses in the *oikonomia* what he has always expressed anew in the eternal, triune life: his complete readiness to carry out every one of the Father's wishes. "God is not in the least restricted by the incarnation; it neither hinders nor weakens him; it does not put him in a state of unconsciousness; nothing is lacking to him of his divinity, his eternal life and omniscience. But nothing is lacking to Christ the man as a result of his being God; he does not run up against his divinity

---

[17] C 501–2. In more detail: Ka II, 213–16.
[18] Ps 43.
[19] Ps 142.
[20] Is 246.
[21] Ka II, 183.
[22] C 383.
[23] Ep 165–66.

as though encountering an obstacle to his genuine, full humanity."[24] Earlier we spoke of Christ's divinity being "laid up" in
God, which is the precondition for the Incarnation; this does
not change the relationship between Father and Son. For the
Son's giving of himself back to the Father is an eternal element
in trinitarian existence. That is why the Son's life in heaven is
absolutely compatible with his life on earth (even including his
abandonment on the Cross): "The Son lived on earth a life that
was simultaneously an earthly life and a heavenly life"; nor was
it only the life of an individual: he "invites everyone to let their
earthly lives be embraced by his eternal life. . . . The Son has
eternal life in him because he is God. When he comes to us as a
man, he carries within him all the mysteries that link him with
the Father and the Spirit; for the most part we do not see this;
we only sense it. He brings about the perfect unity between
unabridged eternal life and unimpaired human life. This does
not render him unreceptive to creation and its values . . . and
yet he wears all that is earthly in such a way that it is never in
opposition to the eternal. He unites both in perfect harmony."[25]

We must think of this in such a way that the work of the
oikonomia, which is "not nothing" either for the world or for
God, actually does "enrich" God in a particular respect, without adding anything that is lacking to his eternal life. For the Father does thank the Son for bringing creation back to him, and
there is "an enrichment of heaven, an adornment of the Father's
realm", which is glorified by the Son's deed.[26] "The fact that
the Son returns to the Father richer than when he departed, the
fact that the Trinity is more perfected in love after the Incarnation than before, has its meaning and its foundation in God
himself, who is not a rigid unity but a unity that comes together
ever anew in love, an eternal intensification in eternal rest."[27]

---

[24] K 77–78.

[25] Ka II, 213–14. "In becoming man, the Son will even take upon him our time
and our development, without there being any hiatus in eternal duration. The
presence of eternity, which is expressed in the form of his subjection to time, is
not thereby reduced to the categories of time or divided into days and years":
Is 32.

[26] 4 Jo 135.

[27] 2 Jo 292.

Time is intensified as it ascends to God, and this movement becomes part of the eternal intensification of the internal life of the Trinity; this "eternal unity is sealed and confirmed in a new manner. . . . Again and again, the Father and the Son are more in their mutual relationship than they themselves would have supposed. We men, too, know this overwhelming of faith by love: this is the experience, in its perfect form, of God himself. But the one who is the author of this eternal inundation of love is the Holy Spirit." In him "the Father and the Son are always and eternally one, and yet this unity is never a finished fact but always the miracle that fulfills itself and enriches itself beyond all expectation."[28] The changes in the Son's life in time are, as such, the expression of his changeless eternal life: "His life, then, is limited by its beginning and ending in God, but these limits are not really limits, because beginning and end are one and God is *in* him: its having no limits is even the chief characteristic of his life. It is so little limited that it has its origin in eternal life and flows into eternal life, and yet it is eternal change, change in the Father's love as well as in love for the Father and for us. His love is so rich that it can eternally change, without growing less or being altered. In every circumstance it is entirely itself and proves its vitality in this eternal capacity for transformation."[29]

We need not be shocked at the suggestion that there can be "economic" events in God's eternal life. When the Father hands over all judgment to the Son, "something happens in God." When the risen Son returns to the Father, "a new joy arises after the renunciation involved in the separation. This new joy . . . perfects the Trinity in the sense that the grace that is to be bestowed becomes ever richer, both in the world into which it pours forth and in God himself, who is willing to bestow it."[30] Through the Incarnation "it is as if a new movement, a new current, is brought into the divine love, so that our love may be drawn into it. It is as if an incision is made in the divine love, to make room in it for the creature's love."[31] As a result of the *oikonomia*, something in the internal life of God has become

[28] *Ibid*.
[29] 3 Jo 92.
[30] 2 Jo 211–12.
[31] Ka II, 164.

different: "The new and changed dimension consists above all in the fact that judgment has now been absorbed into love. It has been superseded by the Cross. . . . But now love emerges precisely out of justice, out of the law, out of the judgment. Life emerges out of death."[32]

3. Thus all apparently negative things in the *oikonomia* can be traced back to, and explained by, positive things in the *theologia*.

"It is truth's paradox that the Son separates himself from the Father in order to show him the extent of his great love. Thus he renounces his divine form, . . . allows his divine Word to enter the murky realm of human words, sayings and parables. But this paradox is the truth, and this whole movement has only one meaning: that there be more love."[33] And this "more love" was always rooted in God and is always in him in a new way. In becoming man, the Son acquires something that Father and Spirit do not have, but for the Son this "possession of something that is his own represents a limitation, which sheds light on the nature of his poverty and of all poverty. On the basis of his divine poverty, which consists in his having nothing of his own and sharing everything with the Father, the Son accepts a limitation. . . . He must do this so that he can possess something, so that he can have something to give away."[34] His "having" a human nature, which is given away without reserve in the Eucharist, is therefore nothing other than the earthly representation of the trinitarian poverty, in which everything is always already given away. This poverty is God's infinite wealth, which is perfectly manifested in Christ's eucharistic love; this means that "in the end it is of no great importance to distinguish between wealth and poverty, for both are attributes of his one mediatorship."[35] The same poverty can be seen in the Father, who "deprives himself of his Son in heaven for love of us", but this love that accepts renunciation for our sake "cannot be separated from his love for the Son", since the Father, in sending the Son, "fulfills the latter's will" to bring the world back to the Father.

[32] 2 Jo 161.
[33] Ka II, 324–25.
[34] Ka II, 25.
[35] Ka II, 184.

"Thus the same love gives rise both to his sending of the Son and to his granting his will."[36] What looks like renunciation is nothing other than a modality of the Father's love for the Son. We see the Son "letting things happen" and are inclined to think of it as passivity—for instance, he allows himself to be carried by the Holy Spirit into the womb of the Virgin[37]—but this is only the "economic" expression of the fact that, in God, he, the "Eternally Begotten", ceaselessly allows himself to be begotten;[38] in his perfect, divine freedom he regards the execution of the Father's will as the best expression of his filial love.[39] What, in God, is his "allowing things to happen", becomes, in human terms (intelligible to the creature), that obedience which is the hallmark of Jesus' life. "Through the obedience of the Word-made-flesh the Father causes divine things to be understood in a human way. In God the divine attributes remain what they always were, but in the flesh of Christ they become accessible to us, and we can imitate them. . . . In the folly and weakness of the Cross, God causes the divine attributes to become visible in a *positive* manner."[40] Again, this is one of the most important themes of this volume: What we see in Christ's forsakenness on the Cross, in ultimate creaturely negativity, is the revelation of the highest positivity of trinitarian love. Here "the Son transfers the image-world of creation above and beyond itself into a nonimage. And yet the fatherhood of the Father was never more distinct, never more earnest, than at this hour of the Cross": the Son does the Father's whole will, and the Father grants the Son his whole will. "The divine unity of essence is not for one moment shattered; the Son's equal standing with the Father is fully evidenced and not for one moment called into question; while the distinction of the Persons has never been more clearly revealed than in the relationship between the Son who is abandoned and the Father who abandons him."[41] The continuity of "[The Son's] divinity and eternity . . . suffers no break even

[36] Ka II, 160–61.
[37] W 45.
[38] W 48.
[39] W 59.
[40] C 53.
[41] A 84.

through his death'', and the Father brings him back from death
because his life was a living-out of a "love that is so living as to
embrace all that it encounters, all men, the entire world".[42] It is,
precisely, eternal love, that love in which the Father begets the
Son and in which the Son allows himself to be begotten. "This
act also embraces the day when the Son will be enveloped by
the night of the Cross, just as it embraces all past and future
days. . . . To what extent the Son will be able to exercise his
own power within his relationship with the Father appears to be
a secondary issue; whether his power will be laid up with the
Father, whether the Father will show it to him, or whether the
Son will wield it and stand before the Father as a victorious ruler
—this is all part of the eternal mystery of the divine begetting.
In virtue of the Word (which the Father eternally speaks to the
Son), it will be impossible for the Son to be alienated from the
Father through Incarnation and Cross; their unity is eternally
immutable, and this applies equally to the temporal dimension
in which God, through the mediation of his Holy Spirit, has begotten the Son from the womb of the Mother. The Son belongs
to his Mother, subsequently he belongs to the apostles, and finally, on the Cross, he belongs to all sinners; it is as if the Father
has separated from him in order to give him the whole world as
his own. Through all this, however, the Son's relationship with
the Father who begets him remains intact; in fact, everything else
simply serves to manifest this eternal relationship. The bond between them is far above all worldly bonds; it is a closeness that
bridges all distance, a relationship that is not interrupted by the
Son's coming and going."[43]

Now the purpose of the Son's "going" was to bring the world
back into this unbreakable unity; hence his return to the Father
has no other meaning but to complete the world's incorporation
into the triune life. "Nothing in revelation was terminated with
the Ascension of the Son: the Father and the Spirit remain what
they are, and the Son remains the Savior of the world in his
surrender to the Father, and so the openness of heaven to earth
which was brought about through the Incarnation remains too.

[42] A 128.
[43] Ps 115.

The Son returns to heaven, but it does not close after him."[44]
Nor is this all:

> The Father does not simply deposit us in the world after this
> Resurrection but rather receives us into heaven together with his
> Son. Here, too, he does not separate us from the Son. In an in-
> frangible unity with him, we enter the place reserved for him in
> the heavens. We are, in other words, copartakers of eternal life
> thanks to our coresurrection. We are no longer shut up in a limited
> earthly existence but are received together with him into heaven,
> and even now our soul is allowed a part in the joys of eternal
> life. We obtain a share in them in a union with the Lord, whose
> love for the Church and in the Church lives on earth as it does in
> heaven, so that heaven and earth are bestowed upon us anew in
> him and the Christian can affirm from now on that in faith—that
> means, *in Christ Jesus*—he lives as much in heaven as on earth.
> The boundaries between the two have tumbled away; they have
> been removed by the Father in the Son; but because we were in
> union with the Son, this removal affected us as well. And whatever
> can concern us in any way from now on does so in this double
> relation of life on earth and in heaven. In his Incarnation, the Son
> lived this double existence as our perfect archetype. Not only that,
> but as something that was not conclueded with his Ascension but
> through all ages comes to be ever anew in him and in us.[45]

"On earth he drew the Old Covenant into the New, to present
it to himself fresh and new; similarly at his Ascension he will
take his earthly life into his heavenly life, to present it to himself
fresh and new. Thus the earthly will be fulfilled piece by piece
in the heavenly."[46] True, he announces his return on the clouds
of heaven; but this means, most of all, that "his abiding with
the Father will be, simultaneously and eternally, a coming. His
visibility will be that of a movement of coming, approaching,
taking place. His first coming was in prophecy, his second in the
Incarnation, and now he will be 'from henceforth' the Coming
One, in ever new ways. . . . It is not simply a case of the Last
Judgment. His coming to the earth has not come to an end; it
has become a constant movement. That is why we cannot have

---

[44] Pf 49; cf. 116f., 137.
[45] Ep 84–85, cf. 17.
[46] B 65.

an exhaustive grasp of divine prophecy: all that is fulfilled will continually be fulfilled in a new and greater way."[47] " 'Behold, I am with you until the close of the age.' After the Ascension this abiding with men will be hidden as by a cloud. They will no longer see him with their eyes. But his abiding will unfold all the more openly and unrestrictedly."[48] Believers will be drawn into this abiding, which is a vibrant coming and going. "The Son is always coming from the Father and returning to him; we cannot ascertain the portions of his journeying, just as, in the eternal begetting of the Son, we cannot distinguish particular elements in the Father's act. And now we believers find ourselves on a similar path. We have been given the knowledge that enables us to set out, but we are continually receiving new knowledge, and we have never arrived."[49] Far from meaning that we are left behind without hope, it means that we are already sharing in the "ever-more" of incarnational life: "The Son who once was born a man through Mary never ceases to become man through the Father and the Spirit."[50]

For the dimension of time, eventually, the moment comes when its movement is taken up into God's eternal super-movement.

There comes the moment of the Son's full victory when nothing more opposes his will, when all beings are animated by his breath. The word "all" here does not mean only all men but also all the things that were created for man, and hence also for the Son. The entire creation bears the sign of the Son; all things strain toward him and all things are held together by him in his kingdom, . . . freely surrendering themselves, inwardly, in an obedience that comes from the Son's obedience. Men and things are differentiated from the Son only by the distance that God has put into his creation; and the ultimate form of this distance is that between the Head and the Body, whereas the distance occasioned by sin is abolished. "Then the Son himself will be subject in his turn to the One who subjected all things to him, so that God may be all in all" (1 Cor 15:28 JB).

[47] Mt 86.
[48] Mt 160–61.
[49] Ph 137.
[50] Ka II, 203.

The Son brings his mission to a close at the point where everything enters into the triune life; "he subjects himself once again, in a new way, to the law of the triune life. Every act of obedience that distinguished the Son during his mission is now translated by the Father into that eternal form of subjection that will now enfold all the world's beings. It is as if the Son's final subjection is also the last condition for the world's eternal subjection to God. Thus, through the Son's subjection, which is a form of the Eucharist for all eternity, all things are marked with the sign of God."[51]

What does God gain from the world? An additional gift, given to the Son by the Father, but equally a gift made by the Son to the Father, and by the Spirit to both. It is a gift because, through the distinct operations of each of the three Persons, the world acquires an inward share in the divine exchange of life; as a result the world is able to take the divine things it has received from God, together with the gift of being created, and return them to God as a divine gift.

[51] C 506.

INDEX OF PERSONS